The Law Relating to Schools

by Neville Harris LLM, Ph.D, Barrister,
Reader in Law, University of Liverpool

Tolley Publishing Company Limited
A UNITED NEWSPAPERS PUBLICATION

0 85459 765-4

First published 1990
Second edition 1995

Published by
Tolley Publishing Company Limited
Tolley House
2 Addiscombe Road
Croydon
Surrey
CR9 5AF
0181-686 9141

Typeset in Great Britain by
Kerrypress Ltd, Luton, Bedfordshire

Printed in Great Britain by
Mackays of Chatham plc, Chatham, Kent

Preface

This book aims, like its previous edition, to offer a comprehensive account of the law relating to schools in England and Wales. Just as the volume and scope of education legislation and case law have grown dramatically over the past four and a half years, so the range of issues covered by the book has had to be broadened. The book's overall size has also increased considerably. Over the past few years we have seen the longest ever education statute enacted by Parliament, the Education Act 1993, with its 308 sections and 21 Schedules. This has replaced the provisions of the Education Reform Act 1988 (ERA 1988) on grant-maintained schools (introducing new funding arrangements, extending opportunities for schools to opt out and enabling new schools to be established as grant-maintained schools) and most of the Education Act 1981, which covered special educational needs. Among the important changes made in the area of special educational needs (some of which have been made by regulations) are parents' new appeal rights and time limits in assessment and statementing procedures. The 1993 Act has also made far-reaching changes in respect of local administration of education, rationalisation of school places, powers over 'failing' schools, the school curriculum (including sex education), school government and many other areas. The Act also established a new School Curriculum and Assessment Authority.

The 1990s have also so far witnessed the Teachers' Pay and Conditions Act 1991, with its changes on the arrangements for determining teachers' conditions of employment and rates of pay and allowances, and the Further and Higher Education Act 1992, which in effect took sixth-form colleges and further-education colleges out of the local education authority sector. Another major education statute is the Education (Schools) Act 1992, which reformed the school inspection system, put the Office of the Chief of Her Majesty's Inspectorate on a firm statutory footing and made provision for the publication of 'school performance information', including comparative tables of examination results. This Act also led to the establishment of the Office for Standards in Education. Most recently, the Education Act 1994 has made changes to the legal framework governing teacher-training arrangements.

In addition to the enactment of these statutes, there has been no let-up (indeed there has been a substantial increase) in the issuing of statutory instruments (over 70 relevant to schools between January and October 1994) and in education litigation. Indeed, so far as the latter is concerned,

Preface

1994 saw the launch of the first dedicated *Education Law Reports*, following on from the establishment of the Education Law Association in 1991. Government circulars and other forms of guidance continue to be issued in great profusion.

This edition of the book contains a few additional chapters: an introductory chapter, explaining who does what, and a chapter on school inspections and 'special measures'. The growth of almost all areas of the law relating to schools has also necessitated discrete chapters on finance, school admissions, publication of information, discipline and school attendance. I have also attempted to deal more fully with particular areas, such as collective worship and special educational needs. Coverage of the Children Act 1989 has been extended, and there is discussion of child protection.

I repeat my comments in the preface to the first edition. Many areas of the law relating to schools are complex and the language used in the legislation and by judges is frequently highly technical. (I have added the word 'highly' here!) I have attempted to state the law as clearly as its substance allows. I continue to hope that the end-product is comprehensible and will, in particular, serve the needs of all those with a professional, academic or 'consumer' interest in the education system and its now extremely intricate legal structure.

Legal and policy developments up to 1 December 1994 are covered. The revised Code of Practice on Procedure in respect of Admissions, Exclusions and Reinstatements (County, Voluntary and Maintained Special School Appeals) referred to in the text at various points, was published in December 1994 (by the ACC and AMA). The Department for Education has also published revised guidance in respect of appeals in grant-maintained schools. In January 1995 the Health and Safety Commission published new guidance on safety in schools and colleges. Finally, there are signs (see *Times Educational Supplement*, 20 January 1995) that the Government has now accepted the need (see pp 342–343) for compulsory registration of outdoor activity centres and may back a private members' bill on the subject.

Special thanks are due to Irene Kaplan at Tolley for her enthusiasm and support and to Simon Howard, also of Tolley, for coping so well with the plethora of amendments to the text, necessitated by the pace of legal change in this field.

This book is dedicated to Marie, Amy and Rosanne.

Neville Harris
Faculty of Law
University of Liverpool
January 1995

Contents

Table of Statutes

Table of Statutory Instruments

Table of Cases

Abbreviations

ASB	'aggregated schools budget'
AT	attainment target
CA	Court of Appeal
Choice and Diversity	White Paper Cm 2021 (1992)
DES	Department of Education and Science
DFE	Department for Education
DoH	Department of Health
CI	Chief Inspector of Schools
EA	Education Act
E(No 2)A	Education (No 2) Act
ERA	Education Reform Act
ESA	Education (Schools) Act
ESG	education support grant
ESO	education supervision order
EU	European Union
EWO	education welfare officer
FA	funding agency
FAS	Funding Agency for Schools
FE	further education
FEFC	Further Education Funding Council
FHEA	Further and Higher Education Act
GEST	grants for education support and training
GM	grant-maintained
GSB	'general schools budget'
HL	House of Lords
HMI	Her Majesty's Inspectorate/Inspector
HSC	Health and Safety Commission
HSE	Health and Safety Executive
ILEA	Inner London Education Authority
LEA	Local education authority
LEATGS	Local Education Authority Training Grants Scheme
LMS	'local management of schools'
NCC	National Curriculum Council
OFSTED	Office for Standards in Education
PS	programme(s) of study
PSB	'potential schools budget'

QBD	Queen's Bench Division
RE	religious education
RI	registered inspector (of schools)
RRA	Race Relations Act
SACRE	standing advisory council on religious education
SAO	School Attendance Order
SATs	Standard Assessment Tasks
SCAA	School Curriculum and Assessment Authority
SDA	Sex Discrimination Act
SGR	Education (School Government) Regulations
SEAC	School Examinations and Assessment Council
SENT	Special Educational Needs Tribunal
SFCW	Schools Funding Council for Wales
SSA	'standard spending assessment'
TES	*Times Educational Supplement*

Chapter 1

Responsibility for the schools system of England and Wales

1. Introduction

Recent legislation giving effect to the Government's stated aim of introducing greater diversity into the education system (see *Choice and Diversity* White Paper Cmn 2021 (1992) Chapter 1) and redefining the role of LEAs has effected a radical restructuring of the education system of England and Wales. Whilst the familiar structure which resulted from RA Butler's landmark Education Act enacted exactly 50 years ago is still very much in evidence, superimposed on it is the system of quasi-independent grant-maintained schools (which the Education Act 1993 (EA 1993) aims to expand), city technology colleges and Further Education Funding Council (FEFC) sector sixth-form colleges.

What also marks a significant departure from Butler's concept of 'partnership' between central and local government in the management and administration of education has been the increasing centralisation of control over key aspects of the system, particularly those linked most directly to the allocation of resources. Much of the recent legislation has not only devolved power downwards to schools (most particularly through financial delegation under Local Management of Schools – LMS), it has also concentrated greater power in the hands of the Secretary of State. In many cases this power is exercised through government-appointed agencies, which are entrusted with the task of allocating resources to education providers and in most cases are required to exercise quality control over them. The two major agencies are the FEFCs, created by the Further and Higher Education Act 1992 (FHEA 1992), and the funding authorities (Funding Agency for Schools and Schools Funding Council for Wales), established by the EA 1993. The FAs may, if certain conditions are met, be given responsibility for ensuring the provision of sufficient schools in an area – LEAs' traditional role.

Centralisation has been most evident in the area of the curriculum, with the creation under the Education Reform Act 1988 (ERA 1988) of the National Curriculum and the advisory bodies (the National Curriculum Council and School Examinations and Assessment Council) – recently replaced (under the EA 1993) by the School Curriculum and Assessment Authority – charged with oversight and development of it, whose members are appointed by the Secretary of State.

Another important development has been the privatisation of key aspects of the state education system. The law has played an important role here. The assisted places scheme introduced under section 17 of the Education Act 1980 has in recent years enabled the fees and certain other expenses in relation to over 30,000 children a year attending independent schools to be met wholly or in part out of the public purse. The requirement that certain services provided to schools be put out to tender (e.g. under the Local Government Act 1988) has meant in some cases that services end up being bought in from the private sector. A further example of partial privatisation (under the ERA 1988) is the provision of state funds to support the introduction and management of quasi-independent city technology colleges, via agreements between the promoters and the Secretary of State, complementing (and generally far outstripping) sponsorship by the private sector. Partial privatisation has also occurred in the area of quality assurance, in particular with the schools inspection system under the Education (Schools) Act 1992, which involves not only the pared-down HMI but, more significantly, the contracted-out inspections by private registered inspectors. Perhaps the only exception to this general trend towards privatisation is the opportunity provided by the EA 1993 for independent schools to 'opt in' to the state system by being established as Grant Maintained (GM) schools (see the discussion of EA 1993, s 49, below and in the next chapter).

Another important element in the reformed education system of recent years warrants particular mention here. The Education Act 1944 said very little about parental rights and provided very little scope for parental involvement in decision-making. However, as the White Paper suggests, 'since 1980, the Government has been intent on widening parental choice, and entrenching parental influence and control' (*Choice and Diversity*, para 1.17). As the chapters on, for example, school government and school admissions in this book demonstrate, this is clearly the case, although it is important to recognise the limitations to parental choice and involvement. Whilst the law has provided parents with many new rights over their children's education and important avenues through which to call schools and LEAs to account, the scope for parental choice tends to be far more limited in practice than the ideal suggested by the concept of a *Parent's Charter* may suggest. In any event, it is worth commenting here that the emphasis on *parents'* rights under education law is out of line with the general recognition of the *independent* rights of *children* in the social welfare context (see A Bainham, *Children: Modern Law* (1993) Chapter X), as reflected in particular in the Children Act 1989 (in fact parts of that Act also deal with education matters). The author has commented elsewhere that in relation to matters such as choice of school, complaints about schooling, appeal rights and discipline, the autonomy interests of children are recognised only indirectly, through the rights given to parents (see N Harris, *Law and Education* (1993) Modern Legal Studies, Sweet and Maxwell, pp 19–22).

The education system today operates within a tight regulatory framework. This has been seen as a necessity in order to subject increasingly autonomous institutions to necessary control, providing not only for greater accountability of education providers to parents and central government and its agencies (which allocate funding), but also greater powers of direction by central government in matters of policy. The latter has been particularly true of the curriculum: the National Curriculum has been the subject of scores of statutory instruments since its inception. As noted elsewhere (N Harris, *Law and Education*, *op cit*), regulation has been used to foster competition, which the Government consistently argues will provide a spur to the improvement of schools, by forcing schools to play the 'market game'. In particular, the detailed legal requirements on the publication of information (including information about examination results and National Curriculum assessments) by schools, and its compilation, are intended to facilitate the exercise of parental choice, thereby engendering greater competition, and to enhance schools' public accountability.

The extent to which school government (discussed in Chapter 4) is now regulated is a reflection both of the degree of autonomy and the extent of the responsibilities now resting with school governing bodies. Recent years have witnessed a move towards a corporate model of school government, with boards acting like businesses (marketing their 'product', balancing their budgets, hiring and firing staff etc). Under the EA 1993 governing bodies of all county and voluntary schools have acquired corporate status, previously enjoyed only by GM schools and FE and sixth-form colleges (under the ERA 1988 and FHEA 1992). At the same time, it has been important to recognise the need for public-sector accountability. Standardised procedures have been introduced for the conduct of school government, as have rules on qualification for membership of school governing bodies and on what constitutes a direct or indirect personal interest which should bar participation in decision-making by governors.

Increasing regulation has also provided some important safeguards for parents and children in the area of special educational needs. The law, now found in Part III of the 1993 Act (and discussed in Chapter 9 of this book), gives parents various appeal rights and a guarantee of participation in various aspects of the procedures for the assessment of their child's needs and the issuing of a statement of needs and provision by the LEA. The 1993 Act has extended these appeal rights and has created new independent Special Educational Needs Tribunals. It has also made provision for speedier processes of assessment and statementing (in particular, through a new statutory Code of Practice – to which all those involved in special educational provision must have regard).

Today, therefore, we have an education system which is considerably more complex in its legal and institutional structure than the system established by the Education Act 1944. Moreover, within this system there are many more *active* players: parents (and children), governors, LEAs, head teachers, teachers, funding and other agencies, central government and private-sector providers. The growing volume of litigation in the field of education is in part the product of the interaction between the various factions and the provision, to consumers, of a growing 'voice' and wider avenues of redress.

2. Responsibility for the schools system today

The schools system of today is mapped out in detail in the ensuing chapters of this book. In this chapter the aim is to sketch out the institutional framework of the public sector of education in order to provide a broad overview which sets the later discussion of the law in context and enables the reader to appreciate the principal changes to the system wrought by recent legislation – in particular by the Education Act 1993.

(a) Central government: the DFE and the Secretary of State for Education/Secretary of State for Wales

The Department for Education (DFE) was formed from the Department of Education and Science in 1992. It carries out central administration and monitoring of the education system. Its civil servants advise ministers and draft policy documents, circulars and administrative memoranda. The Welsh Office carries out most of these functions in relation to schools in Wales.

Given the wide range of powers resting with the Secretary of State under the legislation, the DFE has a more dominant role in the administration of the education system than ever before. The Government has argued that it is partly because of the even greater burden placed on the Department resulting from the growth of the GM schools sector (since in this sector there is very little LEA involvement and schools are centrally administered) that the establishment of the new funding authorities under the EA 1993 is justified (*Choice and Diversity*, para 3.5).

It is said that the Secretary of State acquired over 200 separate powers under the ERA 1988. The EA 1993 has added several dozen more. In response to the criticism that it has been intent on centralisation, the Government has sought to highlight the considerable devolution of power to schools themselves. Nevertheless, the Secretary of State is now able to exert considerably greater authority over the system than ever before, and many of the greater powers and increased responsibilities which now rest with schools were in effect presented to them at the expense of LEAs.

The Secretary of State's main powers and duties are set out at greater length in other chapters; what follows below is a brief outline of them. He has a general duty to promote education (see s 1 of the EA 1993). Grants may be paid to LEAs, funding authorities and schools – including grants for voluntary schools (see EA 1991, s 281) and GM schools, 'grants for education support and training' (formerly education support grants and LEA training grants) (see EA 1993, s 278), grants for the education of travellers and displaced persons (ERA 1988, s 210) and (via the Home Secretary) for the education of immigrants (Local Government Act 1966, s 11). He has a wide range of legislative powers: regulations and orders cover the content of the National Curriculum, the publication of information, the conduct of school government and the financing of GM schools. He also has a power to make a statutory Code of Practice on special educational needs (see EA 1993, s 156). The Secretary of State also appoints the members of various bodies which exercise important and quite powerful roles within the system, including the School Curriculum and Assessment Authority, the Education Assets Board, the Funding Agency for Schools, the Schools Funding Council for Wales and Education Associations (set up to take responsibility for the conduct of a school found to require 'special measures' because it is failing to provide pupils with an acceptable standard of education: EA 1993, ss 204 and 218–223). He can also appoint additional governors to schools in certain situations (see e.g. EA 1993, s 66).

Greater powers have now also been given to the Secretary of State over the organisation of local schools. As in the past, his approval may be needed for a significant change in the character of, or closure of, a school (see EA 1980, ss 12 and 13, and EA 1993, ss 96–99), but he now also has a power to direct rationalisation of provision and, in default, to publish proposals for school changes himself (EA 1993, s 234). The Secretary of State's approval is also needed for an LEA's Local Management of Schools (LMS) scheme and for any significant variation of an existing scheme (see ERA 1988 ss 34 and 35, as amended by EA 1993, s 274).

Surviving from the EA 1944 are the Secretary of State's important, although little-used, general default powers which may be exercised 'on complaint or otherwise'. They enable the Secretary of State to issue directions to an LEA or a governing body in certain situations. The first of these powers, in section 68 of the 1944 Act, may be exercised where the Secretary of State is satisfied that an LEA or a governing body have acted or are proposing to act 'unreasonably' (interpreted by the House of Lords as meaning acting in a way that no reasonable LEA would act) with regard to the exercise of any power or the performance of their duty (see further *Secretary of State for Education and Science* v *Tameside Metropolitan Borough Council* [1976] 3 All ER 665). The other default power, in section 99 of the 1944 Act, may be exercised where the Secretary of State is satisfied that there has been a failure to carry out a statutory duty (see *Watt* v *Kesteven County Council* [1955] 1 All ER 473; *Bradbury* v *Enfield LBC* [1967] 3 All ER 434; *Meade* v *Haringey LBC* [1979] 2 All ER 1016; *R* v *Secretary of State for Education and Science ex p Chance* (1982) (unreported); *R* v *ILEA ex p Ali and Murshid* [1990] The Times, 21 February; and *R* v *Secretary of State for Education ex p Prior* [1994] ELR 231, where there was a successful challenge to the Secretary of State's failure to use his power in s 99 (see pp 135–136 below). The Secretary of State's power under the EA 1944 (s 67) to determine disputes between governing bodies and LEAs also survives. There is now also a power to resolve disputes between funding authorities (FAs) and LEAs over their remit in particular circumstances (EA 1993, s 20) and to investigate complaints about FAs' activities (EA 1993, s 9(4)).

Finally, the Secretary of State is able to exert considerable control over entry to the teaching profession, not only by determining numbers of teacher-training places at colleges and universities but more fundamentally by laying down the requirements for qualified teacher status (see the Education (Teachers) Regulations 1993); and power may, if anything, increase as the new legislation on teacher training, the EA 1994, comes into effect. In recent years the introduction of the 'licensed teacher' scheme and proposals for experienced adults to enter primary school teaching and train on the job have been promoted. The Secretary of State must, of course, take account of European Union Law in laying down these requirements (see for example, EC Council Directive 89/48) – EU Law is discussed in (i) below. Control over teachers also extends to the determination of their pay and conditions (laid down in the *School Teachers' Pay and Conditions Document*) under the machinery provided by the Teachers' Pay and Conditions Act 1991.

(b) Her Majesty's Inspectorate of Schools

HMIs are appointed by Her Majesty by Order in Council under section 1(2) of the E(S)A 1992 (see, for example, the Education (Inspectors of Schools in England) Order 1992). The Government planned a reduction in the size of HMI from 480 to 175 following changes to its role following the E(S)A 1992 (see below). However in 1992, 298 HMIs were appointed, yet the Government still plans to achieve its target figure.

The balance between HMI's inspection of schools work and its general overview and monitoring of provision has shifted more towards the latter since the passage of the Education (Schools) Act 1992; moreover, many members of HMI are now involved in monitoring school inspections carried out by registered inspectors under section 9 of the E(S)A 1992. Her Majesty's Inspectors may be required to inspect in place of registered inspectors where it is not reasonably practicable to secure that the inspection is carried out by a registered inspector (see EA 1993, s 205). The Chief Inspector can also order an inspection of a school by HMI under sections 3 or 7 of the E(S)A 1992.

The office of Chief Inspector of Schools has been made statutory, under sections 1 and 5 of the E(S)A 1992. The Chief Inspectors (one for England and one for Wales) must keep the Secretary of State informed about, *inter alia*, the quality of provision in schools, educational standards being achieved, whether resources for schools are being managed efficiently and the spiritual, moral, mental, physical and cultural development of pupils (E(S)A 1992, ss 2(1) and 6(1)). Other functions include maintaining the register of inspectors under section 9 and keeping the schools inspection system under review (ss 2(3) and 6(3)).

Under the control of the Chief Inspector for England is the *Office for Standards in Education* (OFSTED), which was established following the Education (Schools) Act 1992 to administer the new school inspections system operating under section 9 of that Act and to monitor and report on standards being achieved in the schools in England and Wales, in a way that was formerly the preserve of Her Majesty's Inspectorate of Schools. The head of OFSTED is the Chief Inspector of Schools in England. HMI was largely independent of government, and this was seen as one of its major strengths in that it was able to comment uninhibitedly on the state of schooling in the nation's schools. There were fears that, whilst HMI was being retained (see below) despite the partial privatisation of the schools inspection system under the 1992 Act, some of its independence would be lost. Nevertheless, the initial work of OFSTED and the Office of HM Chief Inspector of Schools (OHMCI) suggests that forthright and constructive criticism of aspects of the education system will continue to be offered. Indeed the Government expects the 'new and powerful' OHMCI to play a 'central role' in ensuring that schools offer quality provision by 'commenting not just on academic performance but [also] on the ethos of schools' (*Choice and Diversity*, paras 1.14 and 1.28).

(c) Local education authorities (LEAs)

The LEAs in England and Wales (there are 116 in all) are the county councils, district councils in former metropolitan counties, and the outer and inner London boroughs (EA 1944, s 6, as amended; ERA 1988, ss 162 and 163). The Inner London Education Authority (ILEA) was abolished in 1990. Provision for the transfer of staff and property was made under the 1988 Act (see ss 172–175, 178 and 179) and a series of Orders (for example, the Education (Inner London Education Authority) (Property Transfer) Order 1990 (SI 1990 No 124, as amended)). Schools formerly within the ILEA were designated to particular LEAs (Education (Inner London Education Authority) Schools Designation Order 1989 (SI 1989 No 1280, as amended)).

The requirement that LEAs have an education committee has been removed by the EA 1993 (the Government argued that LEAs needed more flexibility in the light of their changed/reduced role) (EA 1993, s 296). It is expected that education will be just another function to be handled within the local authority committee structure operating under the Local Government Act 1972 (as well as being subject to the requirements of Part I of the Local Government and Housing Act 1989 on the political activities of officers etc). In relation to committees with sole or joint responsibility for education, and joint committees of two or more local authorities with such responsibility (as permitted under s 102(1) of the Local Government Act 1972), the Secretary of State may direct that any such committee includes representation of those who appoint foundation governors for voluntary schools in the area (EA 1993, s 297(1)–(4)). Such representation will also be required where the functions in question are delegated to a subcommittee of the relevant committee (s 297(5)).

The EA 1993 could have a profound impact on the position of LEAs in the education system. At present over 90 per cent of state schools remain within the LEA-maintained sector. But there are a growing number of grant-maintained (GM) schools, although their spread has been patchy, with very few in Wales and the North-East and many in Kent and some of the outer London boroughs. Once at least 10 per cent of children attending state schools in an area are pupils at GM schools the Secretary of State can direct that the government-appointed funding authority assumes (on its own, or jointly with LEAs) certain powers and responsibilities which would otherwise rest exclusively with LEAs (see EA 1993, s 12, discussed in Chapter 2). The most important of these responsibilities is the duty to ensure the provision of 'sufficient schools' in the area (under s 8 of the EA 1944; this is discussed in detail in Chapter 2). But LEAs will retain an exclusive overall responsibility for special educational needs, the enforcement of school attendance (under Pts III and IV of the EA 1993) and alternative provision for those excluded from or otherwise unable to attend school (EA 1993, s 298). They will also retain responsibility for ensuring that education is organised into 'three progressive stages' – 'primary education, secondary education and further education' – and, so far as their powers allow, 'contribute towards the spiritual, moral, mental and physical development of the community by securing that efficient education throughout those stages shall be available to meet the needs of the population of their area' (EA 1944, s 7).

Among the various other responsibilities resting with LEAs (described more fully in later chapters) are: the administration of LMS schemes (with all that that entails, including the arrangements for publishing various financial statements); school admissions in respect of county schools; maintenance of schools (but note the division of responsibility discussed in Chapter 4); publication of various types of information, including that relating to school performance and admissions arrangements; the making of instruments and articles of government for county, voluntary and maintained special schools; governor training (see E(No 2)A 1986, s 57); the duty to ensure that schools offer a basic curriculum, and the National Curriculum, in accordance with the provisions of the ERA 1988; duties in connection with the acquisition of GM status by a school, including compliance with restrictions on the disposals of land and other property and on staff changes; the maintenance of a complaints procedure under section 23 of the ERA 1988 (complaints concerning the carrying out of statutory responsibilities regarding the curriculum and the provision of information); making instruments and articles of government for county, voluntary and maintained special schools; and establishing a standing advisory council on religious education for the area.

LEAs also have various powers, including powers to: propose changes to schools (including changes of sites, closures etc); appoint a limited number of governors to schools maintained by them; order the reinstatement of excluded pupils; enter and inspect schools for certain purposes; provide assistance to voluntary schools and to pupils; provide boarding accommodation or meet its cost in appropriate cases; provide milk and meals to pupils; and establish nursery schools. However, once a funding authority is in operation in their area, they will lose the general power to publish proposals for the establishment of a school unless the new school is to provide education for pupils in place of one of the schools maintained by them which is now closing (EA 1993, Sch 2, para 7; see (d) below).

(d) Funding authorities

The EA 1993 (ss 3 and 4) makes provision for two funding authorities (FAs) – the Funding Agency for Schools (FAS, which will operate in England) and the Schools Funding Council for Wales (SFCW). Their members (10–15 for the FAS and 8–12 for the SFCW) are appointed by the Secretary of State. Each FA is to have a chairman. In appointing members of the FAs the Secretary of State must 'have regard to the desirability of including' persons with experience and capacity in:

- (i) the field of primary or secondary education;
- (ii) industrial, commercial or financial matters or the practice of any profession;
- (iii) provision for pupils with special educational needs; and
- (iv) (in relation to the FAS only) provision of education in voluntary schools, or in GM schools having foundation governors.

The Government's intention is that FA members will be 'drawn from various backgrounds to reflect a broad mix of educational and other experience' (*Choice and Diversity*, para 3.8). Provision as to members' tenure, delegation of functions, the keeping of accounts etc is made in Sch 1 to the Act. Each FA is to have a 'chief officer' (Sch 1, para 7); the first appointment will be made by the Secretary of State, thereafter by the FA.

As indicated above, funding authorities acquire joint or sole responsibility for ensuring the provision of sufficient school places in an area, under section 8 of the EA 1944, once an order is made by the Secretary of State under section 12 of the EA 1993. When an order is made funding authorities also acquire several important powers and duties to add to their duties to administer grants to GM schools (under Chapter VI of Part II of the EA 1993) and carry out value-for-money studies of these schools (EA 1993, s 8). They can also be given specific, and mostly relatively minor, functions by order of the Secretary of State under EA 1993, ss 17–19, such as the payment of grants to immigrants and approval of changes to GM schools' instruments and articles of government. Powers under the 1993 Act triggered by a section 12 order include their power to establish new GM schools and GM special schools (ss 48 and 183), the power to propose a significant change of character or enlargement of the premises of an existing GM school and the right to make statutory objections to proposals by the LEA under section 12 of the EA 1980 for the closure, alteration, etc of county schools (ss 97 and 231(3)). Funding authorities can also be required to publish proposals to remove or reduce a surplus of available schools places (s 232(2)).

But the most important consequence of an order under section 12 concerns the role of ensuring that there are sufficient school places in the area. As noted above, section 8(1) of the 1944 Act (discussed more fully in Chapter 2) requires LEAs to ensure, *inter alia*, that there are in their area 'sufficient' schools for primary and secondary education. Under section 12(1) of the 1993 Act the Secretary of State may make an order giving a funding authority sole responsibility or joint responsibility with the LEA for ensuring that there are sufficient school places in the area. Such an order may relate to primary education, secondary education or both, depending on whether the appropriate threshold figure has been reached in the sector(s) in question.

There are two thresholds. The first, described in Chapter 4 of the White Paper (*Choice and Diversity* (1992)) as the 'entry point', is reached when at least 10 per cent of the aggregate number of pupils attending county, voluntary and GM schools in the area are pupils at GM schools (s 12(4)(a)). If that threshold is reached, the Secretary of State may make an order under section 12(1)(a) for joint responsibility or, if the LEA requests it (which seems unlikely to happen in practice), an order under section 12(1)(b) giving sole responsibility to the FA. The second threshold, described in the White Paper as the 'exit point', is reached when the aforementioned proportion of pupils reaches 75 per cent. At or beyond this point the only order that can be made is a section 12(1)(b) sole responsibility order (the LEA's consent not being required). The sector(s) of education (primary or secondary education or both) covered by an order under section 12(1) is/are defined as 'relevant education' (s 12(7)).

When an order is made under section 12(1)(a) for shared responsibility between the FA and LEA, then, in relation to 'relevant education', the LEA will retain its responsibility under section 8 of the 1944 Act, but, in addition, 'a separate duty will be placed on the funding authority so that wherever schools which are available for an area providing relevant education are not sufficient, the funding authority will be under a duty to publish proposals for securing the availability of sufficient school places' (*per* Baroness Blatch, Minister of State, *Hansard*, HL, Vol 544, col 1503, 20 April 1993). For this purpose, the FA's duty to publish proposals for additional places only extends to the GM sector (EA 1993, Sch 2, para 3(5)). However, if an order under section 12(1)(b) is made (giving sole responsibility to the FA), 'the duty under section 8(1) of the Education Act 1944 shall be discharged by the funding authority instead of the local education authority' (EA 1993, Sch 2 para 5(1)). As noted above, LEAs will lose their general power to establish schools (with the exception of nursery schools, special schools and schools in either the primary or secondary sector, if outside the scope of 'relevant education' for the purposes of the section 12(1) order). As also noted earlier, they may, however, establish a school if it is to replace one maintained by them which is closing (Sch 2 para 7).

(e) School governing bodies

The Government's policy of devolving power from LEAs to schools resulted in a transformation of school government during the 1980s. Governing bodies' role changed from relatively distant oversight of the conduct of a school to active management of the institution. The change was precipitated by the conferment of numerous new legal responsibilities on them at a time of increasing regulation of educational provision in general. At the same time, there was restructuring of governing bodies themselves, involving increased parental representation, co-option of business community representatives and a reduction in the numbers of LEA appointees. Also, the conduct of school government was more closely regulated (under the Education (School Governing Bodies) Regulations of 1981 and the Education (School Government) Regulations of 1989). School government and the constitution of governing bodies are dealt with fully in Chapter 4.

Governing bodies are responsible for, *inter alia*: the general conduct of the school (subject to the instruments and articles of government: E(No 2)A 1986, s 16(1); EA 1993 s 55); management of their school's budget (under LMS or as a result of the school having GM status); the employment of staff; and the fulfilment of statutory requirements on the curriculum (see Chapter 8) and special educational needs (see Chapter 9). They also have overall responsibility for matters such as discipline and provision of information to parents and others. In relation to several of these matters the responsibility is shared with head teachers. In voluntary schools and GM schools the governing body also has responsibility for school admissions and is the 'responsible body' for the purposes of the Sex Discrimination Act 1975 and Race Relations Act 1976.

Among governing bodies' many powers are those relating to the determination of the school's starting and finishing times, control over the use of school premises (most of the time), proposals for making significant changes to the size of a school or to its character and most staffing matters (including the award of allowances and disciplinary matters). In LEA-maintained schools, the governing body has the power to initiate the procedure for the acquisition of GM status by the school. In consequence of their being incorporated (by virtue of section 238 of the EA 1993), governing bodies of county, voluntary and maintained special schools (defined in Chapter 2) are empowered 'to do anything which appears to them to be necessary or expedient for the purpose of or in connection with the exercise of any of the functions conferred on them under or in pursuance of any enactment' (EA 1993, s 239(1)). The 1993 Act prescribes (in section 239(2)) the following specific powers, which have effect subject to the instrument and articles of government of the school and the provisions of the LEA's LMS scheme:

- to acquire and dispose of land or other property;
- to enter into contracts, other than contracts of employment;
- to invest any sums not immediately required for the purposes of carrying on any activities they have a power to carry on;
- to accept gifts of money, land and other property and apply it, or hold and administer it on trust, for any of those purposes; and
- to do anything incidental to the conduct of the school.

The same powers as are listed above are also enjoyed by the governing bodies of GM schools (EA 1993, s 68(5)).

In some cases the Secretary of State may order that a school which is providing an unacceptable standard of education be managed by an

Education Association (a small group of individuals (generally five or six) appointed by the Secretary of State), which will act in place of the governing body (see EA 1993, ss 218–223, discussed in Chapter 10).

(f) Head teachers

A maintained school must have a head teacher (Education (Teachers) Regulations 1993 (SI 1993 No 543), reg 6(2)(a)). Head teachers generally serve as members of school governing bodies *ex officio* (although this is not obligatory in LEA-maintained schools). Nevertheless, they have independent powers and duties, some of which are statutory and the remainder of which are contractual, although set out partly in the *School Teachers' Pay and Conditions Document* (see Appendix 3 to this book). Most of their specific statutory duties and powers relate to the curriculum and discipline. For example, they share with the governing body (and in some cases the LEA) duties under the ERA 1988, Part I, Chapter I concerning the implementation of the National Curriculum, religious education and collective worship and the requirement (in section 1(2) of that Act) that the curriculum must be 'balanced and broadly based'. The head teacher has a power to except a pupil temporarily from all or part of the National Curriculum relevant to him/her (ERA 1988, s 19). In the area of discipline, it is the head teacher's duty to ensure that measures are taken with a view to securing acceptable behaviour among pupils (E(No 2)A 1986, s 22(a)). The power to exclude a pupil from school rests with the head teacher alone (E(No 2)A 1986, s 22(f)).

With the exception of the matters prescribed for this purpose by the Education (School Government) Regulations 1989, the governing body may delegate functions to the head teacher.

(g) Teachers

The duty to ensure the provision of 'sufficient' schools in section 8 of the EA 1944 includes a duty to ensure that there are sufficient teachers (see *R* v *Liverpool City Council ex p Ferguson and others* [1985] The Times, 20 November), although the duty in section 8 is not an absolute one, as shall be shown in Chapter 2. The Education (Teachers) Regulations 1993 state that 'At any school . . . there shall be employed a staff of teachers suitable and sufficient in numbers for the purpose of securing the provision of education appropriate to the ages, abilities, aptitudes and needs of pupils . . .' (reg 6(1)). However, as shown in Chapter 5, there have been teacher shortages in some parts of the country and in certain specialist subjects, although recruitment has improved markedly over the past couple of years.

Teachers have the same general statutory duties as other employees (for example, under health and safety legislation). Otherwise their duties are contractual (set out partly in the *Teachers' Pay and Conditions Document*: see Appendix 3 to this book). The important decision in *Wandsworth LBC* v *National Association of Schoolmasters/Union of Women Teachers* [1994]

ELR 170 (CA), discussed more fully in Chapter 5, confirmed that unlike head teachers and governing bodies, teachers have no statutory duty to carry out formal assessments of pupils under the National Curriculum (the qualifications required for teaching in schools are discussed in Chapter 5).

(h) Other bodies with responsibility for education and education-related matters

The other bodies with responsibilities which give them a role in the education system fall into two main categories: public sector and private/religious.

First there are public-sector bodies such as health authorities or trusts and local authority social services departments. As later chapters will show, health authorities/trusts have a role in identification and assessment of pupils with special educational needs and non-educational provision for such pupils specified in statements under Part III of the 1993 Act. They also carry out, under arrangements made by LEAs and governing bodies of GM schools, medical and dental inspections, and in some cases treatment, of pupils under section 48 of the EA 1944 (as amended). Social services departments may also play an important role in connection with assessment of pupils with special educational needs in addition to carrying out their responsibilities under the Children Act 1989, which include registration and inspection of independent schools that are children's homes and day-care provision for pre-school children who are in need (with a power to make such provision for other children) (CA 1989, s 18 and Pt VIII and Sch 6).

Secondly, there are the private-sector individuals and organisations which operate in fields of school inspection and contracted-out services (such as meals and cleaning) and the charitable organisations (governed, *inter alia*, by the Charities Act 1993) and religious bodies which establish and/or support schools (through endowments, trusteeship of property used for educational purposes, appointment of foundation governors and contributions to maintenance costs of voluntary aided schools, as applicable). Charitable organisations are particularly active in the independent sector, including substantial involvement in independent special schools. School sites are often provided to schools under the terms of a trust; the Schools Sites Act 1841 and the Reverter of Sites Act 1987 will govern the legal position where the school ceases to be used for educational purposes (see, for example, *Marchant* v *Onslow* [1994] 2 All ER 707 (Ch D)). Many voluntary schools, and GM schools which were formerly voluntary schools, must be run in accordance with the terms of their trust deed, which may limit the scope for changing the character of the school. In addition to any application of general charity law (see, for example, *Gunning and Others* v *Buckfast Abbey Trustees Registered and Another* [1994] The Times, 9 June (Ch D)), there are specific provisions governing religious educational trusts for the benefit of voluntary aided and GM schools (see the Endowed Schools Acts 1869–1948, EA 1944, s 86(1), EA 1973, s 2 and EA 1993, ss 287 and 288 and Sch 17).

The Diocesan Boards of Education Measure 1991, passed by the Synod of the Church of England, requires each diocese to establish a Diocesan Board of Education (constituted in accordance with Schedule 1 to the measure). The functions of a Board include the promotion, within the diocese, of both 'education which is consistent with the faith and practice of the Church of England' and religious education and worship in schools. It is also required to provide guidance to governors of schools and trustees of church educational endowments. It must be consulted over various matters including an application for GM status and the appointment of a representative of the Church of England on a standing advisory council for religious education. It has a power to give directions to the governing body of a Church of England voluntary school where, *inter alia*, it is not discharging, or discharging in a way that is contrary to the interests of the school or church schools generally, any of its functions relating to the status, continuance, size or character of the school.

As noted above, privatisation has occurred in several areas of provision, such as school inspections, which may be carried out under section 9 of the ESA 1992 by private inspectors registered with the Office of the Chief Inspector (see Chapter 10).

(i) The role of the European Union

Although the European Union (as the European Community has become after the Maastricht Treaty) is concerned with social affairs, its influence in the area of education has been largely confined to *post*-school education and training, which are more closely linked to its major fields of activity in trade, agriculture and economic matters (see J Shaw, 'Education and the European Community' (1991) 3:1 *Education and the Law* 1 and C Barnard, 'The Maastricht agreement and education: one step forward, two steps back?' (1992) 4:3 *Education and the Law* 123). It has supported a number of programmes aimed at promoting student mobility and exchange (the best known of these being ERASMUS), initial and continuing training of language teachers and the promotion of foreign languages in education and in the workplace (e.g. the LINGUA programme). It has also supported the training of young people (the PETRA programme, established under art 128 of the Treaty of Rome). The European Union's regulation of aspects of employment and professional activities has become relevant to the employment of teachers (see Chapter 5), particularly in relation to the conditions for recognition of teacher-training qualifications (as noted in (a) above). But it is to the law of the Council of Europe (the European Convention on Human Rights (1950) and the European Social Charter (1961)) and United Nations (such as the UN Convention on the Rights of the Child (1989)), rather than to European Union law, that one would generally turn for sources of international obligations on education matters. Reference is made to such obligations at appropriate places in the text.

Nevertheless, the Maastricht Treaty has given considerable additional impetus to the involvement of the new European Union in matters of education. Two articles of the Treaty, articles 126 and 127, form the legal basis for further EU action in the field of education and training and give the EU new competence in the area of school education. Article 126 aims to ensure the EU's contribution to the development of quality education by encouraging and supporting co-operation between Member States, including co-operation between educational establishments, youth exchanges and 'developing the European dimension in education, particularly through the teaching and dissemination of the languages of the Member States'. Article 127 aims to make improvements to vocational training, including the stimulation of co-operation between educational and training establishments and firms.

The European Commission has been developing an integrated programme to give effect to the aims set out in these provisions of the Maastricht Treaty. At the time of writing the proposed programme is known as SOCRATES. Its significance for schools is that Chapter II is concerned with 'school education'. The programme proposal document states that Union involvement in relation to school education is necessary because:

> 'School has now become the centre around which various partners (teaching staff, administrative staff, pupils, parents, local communities) are grouped; there is dynamic interaction between this centre and its social and cultural environment. This new situation requires more adaptability from school education, the introduction of a European Dimension at this level and co-operation between schools at Community level' (Commission of the European Communities, *Proposal for a European Parliament and Council Decision Establishing the Community Action Programme 'SOCRATES'*, COM(93) 708 final, 1994, para 36; see also the Commission's *Green Paper on the European Dimension of Education*, COM(93) 457 final, 1993).

Three areas of action are proposed:

(*a*) co-operation between nursery, primary and secondary schools and the establishment of networks; this includes support for European Education Projects designed to promote children's understanding of various aspects of the EU, such as its cultural heritage and environmental protection, the mobility of school children, the joint development of teaching materials and the development of innovatory teaching methods;

(*b*) promotion of and assistance for the schooling of children of 'migrant workers and gypsies'; and

(*c*) updating of skills of educational staff in charge of teaching, guidance and 'psycho-pedagogical' care of school children and their families.

If, as seems highly likely, SOCRATES is adopted, it will run initially for the period 1 January 1995 to 31 December 1999.

3. Parents and children

Writers have contrasted the position of parents under children law in general and under education law. Children law has established the primacy or paramountcy of the children's interests over those of the parents, and has consequently rendered largely inapplicable the concept of parental rights. In this regard to the paramountcy principle in section 1 of the Children Act 1989 is of particular significance. Education law, on the other hand, has put great emphasis on parental rights, in a way that has probably hindered the development of independent education rights for children (although children's education rights are recognised in international law, especially under the UN Convention on the Rights of the Child 1989) (see N Harris, *Law and Education: Regulation, Consumerism and the Education System* (1993), pp 19–22). As later chapters show, parental rights (increasingly seen now as forming a key element in the growth of education consumerism and promoted most recently through the updated *Parent's Charter – Our Children's Education* (DFE, June 1994)) are evident in relation to many areas of education decision-making and activity, including school admissions, access to information, the 'opting out' process and school government. Parents also have important obligations, for example in respect of the attendance of their children at school and assessment of a child's special educational needs. In many areas of education decision-making, the law fails to recognise children's independent interests, instead treating the parent as the 'consumer' with rights. For example, even though education law defines a 'child' as someone who is of compulsory school age (EA 1944, s 114(1)), a young person aged 16 or 17 may not serve as a governor at his or her school and has no independent appeal rights (for example, over his or her permanent exclusion from school – even though the parent's legal duty to ensure he or she attends school no longer applies). School pupils of any age have no independent rights to withdraw themselves from religious education or sex education (only a parent may do this) (this general issue is discussed at length in N Harris, *op cit*). The *Code of Practice on the Identification and Assessment of Special Educational Needs* (1994) (see Chapter 9), however recommends that schools should 'make every effort to identify the ascertainable wishes and views of the child about his or her current and future education' (para 2:36).

While education law and child care law may differ in relation to the place of parental rights, there is a degree of consistency in relation to the persons who are recognised as having 'parental responsibility'. The definition of 'parent' under the Education Acts has been broadened to include not only actual parents but also persons (who must be individuals) who are not the parents of a child but who have 'parental responsibility' for or 'care of' him or her (EA 1944, s 114(1D)–(1F), added by the Children Act 1989). The following have parental responsibility for a child, under the Children Act 1989: parents of the child who were married to each other at the time of the child's birth (s 2(1)); unmarried mothers (s 2(2)(a)); unmarried fathers, but only where they have acquired parental responsibility via a parental responsibility agreement or have had it conferred on them by a court via a parental responsibility order (s 4(1)); a guardian appointed by order of the court (s 5(6)); a person in whose favour a residence order is made under the Act, by virtue of which he or she has parental responsibility conferred on him or her automatically (see s 12; note that in some cases leave of the court is required before a residence order may be applied for – s 10). There are now, therefore, a wide range of people who could qualify as parents for the purposes of the Education Acts. One problem for schools and LEAs is that there could well be people who, because they have parental responsibility under the Children Act (and note that parental responsibility cannot be surrendered by such a person – CA 1989, s 2(1)), have parental rights under education legislation even though they may, perhaps as a result of divorce from the parent with whom the child lives, have little contact with the child and an inadequate perception of what is best for the child concerned. This may be an inevitable consequence of the Children Act's policy of continuing (joint) parental responsibility for children after divorce. In any event, there are inconsistencies in the meaning of 'parent' offered by the wide range of official guidance on various aspects of education, for example access to school records, special educational needs and entitlement to vote in a ballot on GM status (see C Piper, 'Parental Responsibility and the Education Acts' [1994] 24 *Family Law* 146), which need to be addressed.

Among the points to be borne in mind by teachers and education authorities is the fact that those who have parental responsibility generally hold it independently of anyone else who also holds it (Children Act 1989, s 2(7)). This could result in conflicts between, for example, divorced parents, which may be difficult for schools to reconcile and which may ultimately have to be resolved in the courts (for example, via a specific issue order under section 8 of the 1989 Act). Those with parental responsibility cannot act in a way that is contrary to a court order (s 2(8)). Schools will have to make sure that where, for example, they are made aware that contact with the child by one parent has been restricted by a court, they impose the required limitation on that parent's access in the school context. Another point to be borne in mind is that parental responsibility may be delegated by the holder (s 2(9)), for example to a person who collects children from school, in the sense that the person with parental responsibility is able to arrange for another person to exercise it on his or her behalf. Such an arrangement involving delegation could also be made with a teacher, although it should be noted that a person who does not have parental responsibility for a child but who has care of him or her 'may (subject to the provisions of this Act) do what is reasonable in all the circumstances of the case for the purpose of safeguarding the child's welfare' (s 3(5)).

'Parental responsibility' is defined in the 1989 Act as including 'all the rights, duties, powers, responsibilities and authority which by law a parent has in relation to the child and his property' (s 3(1)). In the context of education, issues relating to discipline, safety and welfare, access to information and the content of educational provision will be of particular relevance. These are covered in later chapters. There is further specific discussion of the concept of 'parental responsibility' in Chapter 13, Part 4(c).

Chapter 2

Schools

1. Introduction

The categories of school in the public sector of education in England and Wales are still broadly those established by the Education Act 1944 (EA 1944), although, in pursuance of the Government's policy of introducing greater diversity into the education system, there are now also grant-maintained schools, city technology colleges and city colleges for the technology of the arts. The Education Act 1993 (EA 1993), as well as giving pupil referral units a proper legal identity, has introduced a further category: grant-maintained special schools. Sixth-form colleges have ceased to be schools as a result of the Further and Higher Education Act 1992 (FHEA).

Although there is a flourishing private sector of education, the public sector is by far the more important, at least in numerical terms. According to DFE statistics, the 24,000 maintained schools provide education to some nine million pupils. By contrast there are some 2,300 private and independent fee-charging schools.

Schools in the public sector are generally referred to in current legislation as 'maintained' (see EA 1993, s 305(1)). For the most part this means wholly or partly maintained by local education authorities (LEAs; see the definition of LEA in Chapter 1, at page 7). Grant-maintained schools and grant-maintained special schools are maintained by the Secretary of State via government-appointed funding agencies (which are non-departmental public bodies; see Chapter 1, page 9) rather than by LEAs. City technology colleges and city colleges for the technology of the arts (ERA 1988, s 105 – see below at 4(e)) are not classed as 'maintained' for the purposes of the Education Acts.

Public education in England and Wales must be organised into 'three progressive stages': 'primary education, secondary education and further education' (EA 1944, s 7) (as to the definition of 'further education', see below at 2(e)). LEAs must, so far as their powers allow:

> 'contribute towards the spiritual, moral, mental and physical development of the community by securing that efficient education throughout those stages shall be available to meet the needs of the population of their area' (EA 1944, s 7).

'Efficient' in this context has not been defined, but would seem to include, for example, making adequate curricular provision, although the need to provide a 'basic curriculum' and to follow the 'National Curriculum', under the ERA 1988 and certain regulations, are independent requirements (see Chapter 8).

In any event, the vagueness of much of section 7 of the EA 1944 suggests that it is extremely unlikely that the section could be enforced in the courts. Moreover, a parent has generally to request the Secretary of State to use his or her powers to give directions to LEAs and governors under section 68 or 99 of the same Act before the court will entertain an application for judicial review (*R* v *Northamptonshire County Council ex p Gray* [1986] The Times, 13 March (DC); see further 2(b) below). In any event, there are more specific duties in section 8 of the 1944 Act.

Note that the duty imposed by section 7 does not extend to matters within the remit of higher education funding councils or further education funding councils (FHEA 1992, Sch 8, para 2). This means that, for example, education in sixth-form colleges and colleges of further education will generally lie outside the scope of the section 7 duty, following the FHEA.

2. Duty to ensure that sufficient primary and secondary schools are provided

LEAs must ensure that there are available in their area 'sufficient' schools for *primary* and *secondary* education (EA 1944, s 8(1)). However, as noted in Chapter 1, if an order has been made by the Secretary of State under section 12(1)(a) of the EA 1993, this responsibility will be shared with the funding authority (Funding Agency for Schools or, when it comes into operation, the Schools Funding Council for Wales). If, on the other hand, an order is made under section 12(1)(b) of the 1993 Act, the 'sufficient' schools duty will rest exclusively with the funding authority. The circumstances in which an order may be made under section 12(1) were described in Chapter 1, at page 10. The order may relate to primary or secondary education or both, and this means that in certain circumstances the LEA could, for example, have exclusive sufficient schools responsibility for the primary sector, and the funding authority for the secondary sector.

(a) 'Schools' and 'pupils'

(i) Schools

The definition of 'school' for the purposes of the Education Acts 1944–1993 is laid down in section 14(5) of the FHEA 1992 (EA 1944, s 114(1), as amended by the FHEA 1992, Sch 8, para 13(2)(e)). A 'school' is defined as 'an educational institution not being within the further education sector or higher education sector, being an institution for providing one or more of the following':

(i) primary education;

(ii) education which is secondary education by virtue of section 14(2)(a) (full-time education for pupils of compulsory school age); and

(iii) education which is secondary education because it is full-time education for persons aged under 19 provided at a school where full-time education for persons of compulsory school age is also provided (see FHEA 1992, s 14(1) and (2)(b)).

Schools are empowered to provide further education (defined below) and part-time education for the under-fives (EA 1993, s 68(8) – but note the restriction in s 128 of that Act – E(No 2)A 1986, s 16A and EA 1944, s 8(1A)). Schools which are divided into two or more separate departments may be divided into two or more separate schools by order of the Secretary of State (EA 1946, s 2(1)).

The different types of school – primary, secondary, special, etc – are defined below.

(ii) Pupils

The definition of 'pupil' for the purposes of the Education Acts 1944–1993 is laid down in section 14(6) of the FHEA 1992 (EA 1944, s 114(1), as amended by the FHEA 1992, Sch 8, para 13(2)(d)). A pupil is any person 'for whom education is being provided at a school' *other than*:

(i) a person aged 19 or over for whom further education (see below) is being provided; or

(ii) a person for whom part-time education suitable to the requirements of persons of any age over compulsory school age is being provided.

Note also the definition of 'junior pupil' and 'senior pupil' for the purposes of primary and secondary education (below).

Neither full-time nor 'part-time' education is defined in the Education Acts. It can be assumed that a mode of attendance which is not full-time should be construed as 'part-time' education. ('Full-time' education is, however, defined in relation to nursery schools or classes, in the Further and Higher Education Regulations 1981, reg 10.) At the time of writing, it has been announced that the Government is considering whether to introduce universal mandatory hours for different categories of school after OFSTED reported wide disparities between the number of hours of teaching provided by different schools. If this step is taken there would in effect be a definition of full-time education (albeit probably within a range, with minima and maxima).

(b) 'Sufficient' schools

(i) The scope of the 'sufficient' schools duty

The 1944 Act states that the schools for an area must be sufficient in:

'number character and equipment to afford for all pupils opportunities for education offering such variety of instruction and training as may be desirable in view of their different ages, abilities, and aptitudes, and of the different periods for which they may be expected to remain at school, including practical instruction and training appropriate to their respective needs' (s 8(1)).

In fulfilling this duty LEAs must, *inter alia*, ensure that special educational provision is made for those with special educational needs (s 8(2)(c)).

The duty in section 8(1) is deliberately couched in broad and general terms to allow the LEA to have regard for a wide range of considerations which might affect its performance (e.g. financial constraints, which led to an LEA dropping music tuition from the school curriculum: *R* v *Hereford and Worcester LEA ex p Jones* [1981] 1 WLR 768). In *Meade* v *Haringey LBC* [1979] 2 All ER 1016, the Court of Appeal considered that an LEA might not be in breach of section 8 by taking a decision to close its schools during a caretakers' strike, if the authority was seeking to minimise the longer term disruption to pupils' education which could result from a deterioration in industrial relations. But there would, in the words of Eveleigh LJ (at p 1028), have to be a 'just and reasonable excuse' for any such emergency closure.

Although the argument that this part of section 8 reveals an 'absence of a clear-cut definition of any essential minimum standard and content of the education which must be provided in schools' (P Meredith 'Individual Challenge to Expenditure Cuts in the Provision of Schools' [1982] JSWL 344) is still valid, the curriculum requirements of Chapter I of the Education Reform Act 1988 (see Chapter 8) have made the scope of the duty more clear. Nevertheless, so far as the organisation of education is concerned, the fact remains that the general duty in section 8 to provide 'sufficient schools' is regarded by the courts as no more than a target duty, which leaves LEAs a 'broad discretion to choose what in their judgment are the means best suited to their area for providing . . . instruction' (*Secretary of State for Education and Science* v *Tameside Metropolitan Borough* [1976] 3 All ER 665 (HL), *per* Lord Diplock at 695b). So, in *Cumings* v *Birkenhead Corporation* [1972] Ch 12, an LEA's policy of automatically allocating places at Roman Catholic secondary schools to pupils who had attended RC primary schools did not put the authority in breach of section 8 (nor of section 76 of the same Act, which lays down a general condition that pupils are to be educated in accordance with the wishes of their parents). Moreover, this broad discretion means that a LEA can fulfil its duty to provide schools 'sufficient in . . . character' by, for example, providing comprehensive or selective schools or both (*Smith* v *Inner London Education Authority* [1978] 1 All ER 411 (CA); *Equal Opportunities Commission* v *Birmingham City Council* [1989] 1 All ER 769 (HL) *per* Lord Goff at p 775c).

Although it is clear that the section 8(1) duty extends not only to the provision of buildings and equipment, but also teachers and other essential personnel (*Meade* v *Haringey LBC* (1979); *R* v *Liverpool City Council ex p Ferguson and Others; Same* v *Same, ex p Grantham and Others* [1985] The

Times, 20 November), it has to be understood that the duty is not considered absolute. In one case the Divisional Court (*per* Woolf LJ) held that a temporary failure to comply fully with the standard set by section 8, arising out of a situation beyond the control of the authority (in this case a shortage of teachers due to difficulties in recruitment in inner London), did not put the LEA in breach of its duty (*R* v *ILEA ex p Ali and Murshid* [1990] The Times, 21 February).

What *would* put an LEA in breach of its duty to provide 'sufficient schools' (enabling intervention by a court or by the Secretary of State under the 1944 Act) would be a decision which was unreasonable in the sense that no reasonable authority would have taken it (*Secretary of State for Education and Science* v *Tameside Metropolitan Borough* (*op cit*) *per* Viscount Dilhorne at p 687d; *Associated Provincial Picture Houses Ltd* v *Wednesbury Corporation* [1948] 1 KB 223). Judicial intervention via judicial review would also be possible if a decision was *ultra vires* in other ways – for example where relevant considerations were not taken into account or irrelevant ones were. The Court of Appeal in *Meade* v *Haringey LBC* (*op cit*) made it clear that if it was established that the LEA's decision to close schools had been taken for purely political reasons, it would have been unlawful. It would also be unlawful if the LEA 'flies in the face of the statute, by doing something which the statute expressly enjoins, or otherwise conducts itself, by omission or commission, as to frustrate or hinder the policy or objects of the Act' (*per* Denning MR, at p 1024), or where it acts 'in total disregard of its responsibilities as an Education Authority' (*per* Watkins LJ in *R* v *Liverpool City Council ex p Ferguson*, *op cit*).

It is probable that the Secretary of State alone could be the judge, under section 99 of the 1944 Act (which enables the Secretary of State to issue directions if there is a failure to carry out a duty), of an alleged *simple* failure in respect of the section 8 duty. The remedy offered by that section (directions to the LEA/governors, enforceable via *mandamus*) would be regarded as exclusive (see *Watt* v *Kesteven County Council* [1955] 1 All ER 473 (CA); *Bradbury* v *Enfield LBC* [1967] 3 All ER 434). The court would not be able to intervene, because Parliament did not intend that the section 8 duty should be owed to individuals personally (see HWR Wade, *Administrative Law*, 6th ed (1988), p 749). In *R* v *ILEA ex p Ali* (*op cit*), Woolf LJ emphasised that section 8(1) was 'intended to enure for the public in general and not intended to give the individual litigant a cause of action' (this was fatal to Mr Ali's claim for damages in respect of the LEA's failure to provide his son with a school place).

(ii) 'Sufficient' schools and sex discrimination

LEAs must also comply with section 23 of the Sex Discrimination Act 1975, which requires them to carry out their various functions under the Education Acts, including those under EA 1944 s 8, without practising sex discrimination (*R* v *Secretary of State for Education and Science ex p Keating* (1985) 84 LGR 469; *R* v *Secretary of State for Education and*

Science ex p Malik [1992] COD 31; but see *R* v *Northamptonshire County Council and the Secretary of State for Education ex p K* [1994] ELR 397, (CA)). Funding authorities have parallel duties, under section 23C (added by EA 1993, Sch 19 para 57). Note that in a case of alleged sex discrimination under section 23, it is not necessary to show that the LEA is in breach of section 8 of the 1944 Act (*Equal Opportunities Commission* v *Birmingham City Council, op cit*, at p 776). In other words, the LEA may be providing 'sufficient' schools for the purposes of section 8 of the 1944 Act, but if there is inequality of opportunity as between boys and girls in relation to, for example, single-sex schooling, there would clearly be breach of the Sex Discrimination Act 1975.

In *R* v *Secretary of State for Education and Science and Another ex p Keating* (1985) (*op cit*), Taylor J found unlawful an LEA's decision to close the only single-sex boys' school in their area while continuing to maintain single-sex girls' schools. In *Equal Opportunities Commission* v *Birmingham City Council* (1989) (*op cit*), more places were available to boys (540) than to girls (360) in the LEA's voluntary aided single-sex grammar schools, there being 5 such schools for boys and 3 for girls. One result of this was that as selection for admission to these schools was based on ability, on average a girl would have to achieve higher examination marks than a boy to gain a place. The LEA had a definite equal opportunities policy, but could do nothing about the inequality here because the governors of the schools insisted on selection by ability. The High Court, Court of Appeal (Woolf LJ dissenting) and the House of Lords in turn held that there was discrimination. In the House of Lords, Lord Goff said that discrimination resulted not from any supposed disadvantage resulting from the denial of selective education to a higher proportion of girls than boys – on the basis that education under a selective system might be better than under a non-selective system – but rather, it flowed from the denial of choice. However, in *ex p K (op cit)* the High Court and the Court of Appeal were prepared to accept that in some cases sex discrimination that results from closures of single-sex schools which are the inevitable consequence of falling school rolls is not unlawful. In the High Court Hutchinson J concluded that the Secretary of State (who generally has the final say on school closures) is entitled to weigh the LEA's non-discrimination duty against the need to save unnecessary public expenditure by closing schools with rapidly falling rolls and removing surplus capacity. The Court of Appeal held that because the numbers on the school roll had fallen so low that the school's budget could not adequately support the curriculum, the school had ceased to be educationally or economically viable. The LEA could not, therefore, fulfil its duty under section 8 of the EA 1944 so far as the school was concerned. Although the closure of the only maintained single-sex school for boys in Kettering meant that there was potentially a breach of the Sex Discrimination Act 1975, as a girls' grant-maintained school remained open, it did 'not mean that [the LEA] may not, in appropriate circumstances, close a particular school . . . If the standard of education prescribed by the 1944 Act cannot be maintained by the school remaining open, then [the LEA] has the duty to transfer the pupils to a school where they can be properly educated' (*per* Farquharson LJ at p 402).

LEAs' general non-discrimination duty in section 25 of the 1975 Act may also be relevant (see *Equal Opportunities Commission* v *Birmingham City Council, op cit*). There are also parallel duties in relation to race discrimination under the Race Relations Act 1976 (ss 18 and 19). The duty in section 25 of the 1975 Act rests on LEAs and on any other bodies which are responsible bodies under the Act 'to secure that facilities for education provided by [them], and any ancillary benefits or services, are provided without sex discrimination'. There is clearly some overlap between the section 25 duty and that in section 23. Indeed a specific instance of discrimination may fall foul of both sections, although unlike with section 23, the Secretary of State alone may enforce section 25. In *Equal Opportunities Commission* v *Birmingham City Council* (1989) (*op cit*) Lord Goff explained the relationship between on the one hand sections 22 (covering discrimination in admissions, exclusions etc) and 23 (above) and, on the other, section 25. His Lordship could see 'no reason why these two sections should not, in the field of education, embrace all cases of unlawful discrimination as such by [LEAs]' (at p 775). So what is the purpose of section 25? His Lordship felt its purpose was rather different to that of the other two sections. It was intended:

> 'not to outlaw acts of discrimination as such, but to place on ["responsible"] bodies a positive role in relation to the elimination of sex discrimination. The idea appears to have been that such bodies are, so to speak, put on their toes to ensure that sex discrimination does not occur in areas within their responsibility' (at p 776).

Guidance issued by the Equal Opportunities Commission (*Formal Investigation Report: West Glamorgan Schools* (1988) Appendix B) states that in order to assess whether there has been a breach of the section 25 duty it is necessary to consider:

(*a*) whether educational provision has been planned on the principle of equality of opportunity for pupils of both sexes;

(*b*) whether the actual provision made is in accordance with the equality principle;

(*c*) whether the actual provision made results or is likely to result in any act of unlawful sex discrimination.

Note that the duty in section 25 does not apply to the admission of pupils to single-sex schools. Single-sex schools are popular with some parents, often on cultural or religious grounds (see SM Poulter, *English Law and Ethnic Minority Customs* (1986), pp 191–5 for discussion of the legal and policy issues). It is not unlawful to discriminate in relation to admission to a single-sex school (Sex Discrimination Act 1975, s 26(1)). A single-sex school which admits members of the opposite sex in comparatively small numbers to particular courses of instruction or teaching class groups (e.g. a single-sex school which has mixed sixth form) is regarded as a single-sex school for this purpose. There are also special provisions permitting discrimination where selection of one sex or the other is necessary because the school is changing from a single-sex to a co-educational school (s 27, and the Education (Schools and Further Education) Regulations 1981, as amended). But where an LEA provides single-sex education it has to do so in such a way that its policy does not result in one sex being treated more favourably, as noted above.

Although LEAs are not responsible for grant-maintained schools, educational provision at them is relevant for the purposes of LEAs' duties under section 8 of the 1944 Act. In other words, if the LEA is responsible for ensuring that there are 'sufficient' schools in their area, it should take into account for this purpose not only the schools which it maintains, but also the places provided by grant-maintained schools. This means that for the purposes of the duty in section 23 of the Sex Discrimination Act 1975, as it relates to the performance of the duty in section 8 of the 1944 Act, the ratio of boy to girl single-sex places across *all* maintained schools (LEA-maintained and grant-maintained) must be looked at by the LEA (see *R* v *Birmingham City Council ex p Equal Opportunities Commission (No 2)* [1994] ELR 282 (CA)). As LEAs cannot do anything about the grant-maintained sector, any imbalance can only be rectified by them via changes to the schools for which they are responsible.

Equal opportunities provisions also appear in both EC law (Directive 76/207, providing for equality between men and women in the provision of access to vocational training) and in the European Convention on Human Rights 1950. Article 14 of the Convention forbids discrimination on the grounds of, *inter alia*, sex, race or colour in relation to the various rights guaranteed by the Convention, including, under Article 2 of the 1st Protocol, the right to education. Council of Europe Recommendation R(85)2, Principle II.3, calls for equality of access to education between men and women.

(c) Primary education

LEAs must ensure that there are sufficient schools for primary education available in their area, as stated above. Primary education is defined as:

> 'full-time education suitable to the requirements of junior pupils who have not attained the age of ten years and six months, and full-time education suitable to the requirements of junior pupils who have attained that age and whom it is expedient to educate together with junior pupils who have not attained that age' (EA 1944, s 8(1)(a)).

Junior pupils are pupils aged under twelve years (EA 1944, s 114(1)). Education provided to pupils aged between two to five years is nursery education, which LEAs may provide, but are under no duty to do so (see below, at 5). It may be noted that the division of the primary stage into two segments, 'infants' and 'juniors', has become common practice but is not, in itself, a statutory requirement.

(d) Secondary education

LEAs must also ensure that there are sufficient schools for secondary education. Secondary education is defined as:

> 'full-time education suitable to the requirements of pupils of compulsory school age, being either senior pupils or junior pupils who have attained the age of ten years and six months and whom it is expedient to educate together with senior pupils' (EA 1944, s 8(1)(b), substituted by FHEA 1992, s 10(1)).

A 'senior pupil' is one who is aged twelve to eighteen (EA 1944, s 114(1)).

Full-time education provided to persons aged over compulsory school age (defined in EA 1993, s 277; see Chapter 11 Part 3(a)) and under nineteen years of age is secondary education, and not further education, if it is provided at a school where education falling within section 8(1)(b) (above) is also provided (FHEA 1992, s 14(1) and (2)(b)). If a person aged nineteen is receiving education at a school, but he or she is continuing a course which he or she began before attaining the age of eighteen and which was secondary education, he or she is to be treated as continuing to receive secondary education (FHEA 1992, s 14(3)).

(e) Further education

Secondary education provided to those aged sixteen or over must be distinguished from further education. Persons aged above compulsory school age attending a full-time education course (or a part-time one if they are aged nineteen or over) are in receipt of 'further education' (FHEA 1992, s 14(1) and (3)), unless deemed to be receiving secondary education (see above).

The introduction of further education funding councils (FEFCs) under the Further and Higher Education Act 1992 has meant that LEAs have only a residual responsibility for further education. Further education lies outside the scope of this book, but a brief account of the law is incorporated here.

The FEFCs (whose members are appointed by the Secretary of State under section 1 of the FHEA 1992) are bodies corporate. Their principal duty is to ensure that there are 'sufficient facilities' for full-time education for sixteen to eighteen year-olds (FHEA 1992, s 2(1)) and 'adequate facilities' for part-time education for this age group and for full-time education for those aged nineteen or over (FHEA 1992, s 3(1)). In carrying out these duties FEFCs must have regard to the requirements of those with learning difficulties (*ibid*, s 4(2)) and must make arrangements for alternative provision for any sixteen to twenty-five year-old for whom further or higher education institutions do not offer adequate facilities, provided they consider that it is in his 'best interests' for them to do so (s 4(3)). They may also make such provision for others aged sixteen or over who have learning difficulties and for whom existing facilities are inadequate (s 4(5)(a)). Boarding accommodation may also be provided for those over compulsory school age who have learning difficulties (s 4(5)(b)). 'Learning difficulty' is defined in the same way as it is in respect of LEAs' duties (below) (see s 4(6)).

LEAs' responsibilities vis-à-vis provision of further education are laid down in the EA 1944, s 41, as substituted by section 11 of the FHEA 1992. For the most part these responsibilities now relate merely to adult education and organised leisure activities.

LEAs must make sure that there are 'adequate facilities for further education' in their area (EA 1944, s 41(1)). 'Further education' is defined, for this purpose as (a) full- and part-time education for persons over compulsory school age ('including vocational, social, physical and recreational training'); and (b) 'organised leisure-time occupation (defined in s 41(5)) provided in connection with the provision of such education' (EA 1944, s 41(3)). LEAs may not provide any further education which is the responsibility of the FEFCs under sections 2 and 3 of the FHEA 1992 (above) (EA 1944, s 41(2)). Nevertheless, subject to this, LEAs may secure the provision for their area of part-time education for those aged sixteen or over and full-time education for those aged nineteen or over as appropriate to meet the needs of the local population (EA 1944, s 41(2)). LEAs may also secure the provision of further education (of a kind that is within their remit) for persons living outside their area (*ibid* s 41(6)).

In exercising their functions with regard to further education, LEAs must consider the requirements of those above compulsory school age who have learning difficulties (EA 1944, s 41(8)). A person has a learning difficulty for this purpose if he or she has:

> '(*a*) . . . a significantly greater difficulty in learning than the majority of persons of his age; or
>
> (*b*) . . . a disability which either prevents or hinders him from making use of facilities of a kind generally provided by the local education authority concerned in pursuance of their duty [to secure that adequate facilities for FE are provided]'.
>
> (EA 1944, s 41(9)).

(Note: a person does not have a learning difficulty solely because the language or form of language in which he is taught differs from that which has at any time been spoken in his home: s 41(10).)

3. Primary, secondary, middle and special schools

Having considered the legal definition of primary and secondary education (and distinguished the latter from further education) we can consider the schools in which such provision is to be made. *Primary* schools are those providing primary education, although when the school is for two to five year-olds it is a nursery school (see page 44). *Secondary* schools are those providing secondary education, whether or not they also provide primary or further education (EA 1944, s 114(1)). In fulfilling their duty to provide 'sufficient schools' in their area, LEAs must have regard, *inter alia*, to the need for securing that primary and secondary education are provided in separate schools (s 8(2)(a)). However, 'middle schools', providing education to pupils of primary and secondary school age, may be created, on the approval of the Secretary of State (EA 1964, s 1; Education (Middle Schools) Regulations, SI 1980 No 918, as amended). Such schools will officially be designated as primary or secondary schools, depending on whether the majority of their pupils are to be of primary or secondary school age.

A *special school* is one which is 'specially organised to make special educational provision for pupils with special educational needs and for the time being is approved by the Secretary of State' (EA 1993, s 182(1)). Approval will be in accordance with section 188 and the Education (Special Schools) Regulations 1994. There are two types of special school that may be approved under section 188 (see s 182(2) and (3)):

(i) A special school maintained by an LEA – 'a maintained special school'; and

(ii) A 'grant-maintained special school', which can either be established by a funding authority or be a maintained special school which has received approval to become a GM special school by the Secretary of State.

Special schools are specifically excepted by EA 1944, s 8(2), from the requirement that primary and secondary education should be provided in separate schools (above), although approval may, in individual cases, be subject to the school offering only one or the other stage of education. In the case of special schools for pupils with emotional and behavioural difficulties (EBD schools), the DFE considers that, wherever possible, separate 'primary'-stage and 'secondary'-stage schools should be available (DFE Circular 9/94 and DoH Circular DH LAC (94)9, *The Education of Children with Emotional and Behavioural Difficulties*, para 67). A survey by HMI (Report 62/89) resulted in the conclusion that all-age schools for EBD pupils are less successful.

The provision of special schools may be one way in which an LEA complies with its duty to secure that there are sufficient schools for providing special educational provision for pupils who have special educational needs (EA 1944, s 8(2)(c)) (see further, Chapter 9). In fact, provision may be also arranged in, for example, a non-'maintained' special school; under EA 1944 s 8(1) LEAs only have to ensure that sufficient schools are *available*. But an LEA may not arrange for provision to be made at an independent school for a child in respect of whom it maintains a statement as to his special educational needs (under EA 1993, s 168), unless:

(i) the school is approved (under EA 1993, s 189, and in accordance with the Education (Special Educational Needs) (Approval of Independent Schools) Regulations 1994 (SI 1994 No 651) made thereunder) by the Secretary of State as suitable for the admission of such children; or

(ii) the Secretary of State consents to the child being educated at the school in question.

(EA 1993, s 189(5)).

4. The main categories of school

(a) Introduction

One of the reasons that parts of education law dealing with schools are so complex is that there are so many types of what are referred to as maintained schools. In particular, there are county schools, voluntary aided and controlled schools and special agreement schools, which categories were established by the 1944 Act (ss 9(2) and 15(1)). These schools, together with maintained special schools (above), are collectively defined (in EA 1993, s 305(1)) as 'maintained schools'. In addition there are grant-maintained schools (and GM special schools – see above). Independent schools are not classed as 'maintained'.

As it has been the intention that the various categories of school should enjoy differing levels of self-government and autonomy from their LEAs (the governors of voluntary aided schools, for example, have traditionally had more control over staff appointments and the use of premises than governors of county or controlled schools (see below)), separate legal provisions covering each category appear at various places in the legislation. Nevertheless, it may be observed that 'for the most part LEAs and voluntary schools form a harmonious and indivisible entity and see themselves very clearly as working under the same umbrella within the maintained sector' (D Nice, *Education and the Law* (1986), CLEA p 61).

It is unlikely that a similar degree of harmony is achievable between LEA-maintained and GM schools. Nevertheless, they are expected to co-operate with each other over such matters as school admissions, although the fact that co-ordinated admission arrangements can be imposed on them acknowledges the potential for disharmony, especially when rivalry is exacerbated by unequal distribution of resources between these sectors.

Governing bodies of GM schools have enjoyed incorporated status under the ERA 1988, and subsequently under the EA 1993 (see below). The EA 1993 now provides also for the incorporation of governing bodies of county, voluntary and maintained special schools (see ss 238 and 239 and Sch 13). One of the effects of incorporation is that land, property and the rights and liabilities of the governing body will vest in the incorporated governing body. This should be borne in mind in the ensuing discussion. The protection from personal liability for individual governors is discussed in Chapter 4 (Part 11 pp 108–109).

(b) County schools

County schools are the major educational providers in England and Wales: approximately 75 per cent of pupils in the maintained sector attend them. The majority of secondary schools in this sector are comprehensives, although there is no legal duty to establish such schools. A legal duty to establish comprehensives was introduced by the Labour Government under the Education Act 1976, but was subsequently removed under the incoming Conservative administration's Education Act 1979 (s 1). The impetus for the wholesale introduction of these schools had come partly from DES circular No 10 of 1965 (10/65), which had urged reorganisation along comprehensive lines (see further N Harris, *Law and Education: Regulation, Consumerism and the Education System* (1993) Sweet and Maxwell, pp 43–46).

County schools (see EA 1944, s 9(2)) are maintained wholly by LEAs, who own their buildings, and usually their sites, and employ staff to work in them. The upkeep of the school premises and the cost of alterations or improvements have traditionally been the responsibility of the LEA, although significant alterations are generally financed by the DFE. The LEA also controls the use of premises during school hours – defined as 'any school session or during a break between sessions on the same day' (E(No 2)A 1986, s 42(a)). At all other times use of the school premises is to be under the control of the governing body. Such control by the governors must be exercised 'subject to any direction given to them by the [LEA]' and with due regard being given to making the premises available to the community served by the school (*ibid* s 42(b)).

County schools have, of course, gained a considerable degree of autonomy under the arrangements for financial delegation (see Chapter 3).

(c) Voluntary schools

Over 20 per cent of pupils in the LEA-maintained sector attend voluntary schools, of which approximately two-thirds are Church of England and most of the remaining third Roman Catholic. There are also a small number of schools with a Jewish foundation. Voluntary schools fall into three categories: controlled, aided or special agreement (EA 1944, ss 9(2) and 15). In this section of the book we shall be concerned solely with distinguishing between these categories, with reference to their chief characteristics, as with county schools above. More specific legal provisions relevant to them – such as those dealing with governing bodies and the appointment and dismissal of teachers – are discussed elsewhere in the book.

As shown below, the classification of a particular voluntary school will depend, *inter alia*, on whether certain maintenance expenses may be borne by the governors (with a contribution from the Secretary of State) (EA 1944, s 15). If the Secretary of State is satisfied that the expenses can be so borne, the school will be aided or special agreement; if not, the school will be controlled.

Among the powers of LEAs to assist voluntary schools (discussed more fully below) is a general power to assist promoters who establish them (see EA 1993, s 283). LEAs also have a duty to provide a site for a voluntary school (EA 1946, First Sch, para 1).

(i) Voluntary controlled schools

There are well over 3,000 voluntary controlled schools in England and Wales. A voluntary school will be classed as controlled if the Secretary of

State is not satisfied that the governors are able and willing to meet (with the help of a contribution from the Secretary of State) certain maintenance costs (set out in s 15(3) – see *(ii) Voluntary aided schools* below) (EA 1944, s 15(2)). The 1944 Act, with the creation of the controlled category, has enabled voluntary bodies to exert a certain amount of influence over a school without the burden of paying for its maintenance and running costs – which must be borne by the LEA (see s 15(3)). The foundation (basically the body which established the school) will own the building(s) – although the LEA has legal rights if the property is sold or if the school is discontinued (see EA 1944, s 14, as amended by EA 1946). This is because the LEA must provide a site for the school and buildings (EA 1946, First Sch, para 1, above). The LEA retains ownership of playing fields.

Significant enlargement (as defined in EA 1944, s 114(1)) of school premises will require the Secretary of State's approval (EA 1980, ss 13 and 14) (see below).

Generally speaking, the governors have control over the use of school premises (EA 1944, s 22(3)) – although, subject to certain exceptions, LEAs may give directions as to their use (EA 1944, s 22(1), as amended by EA 1980, Sch 1). As in the case of county schools, it is now possible for the governing body to enter into a 'transfer of control agreement' (EA 1944, s 22(3A)–(3E), added by EA 1993, Sch 13, para 4), enabling a third party to put the premises to use for the benefit of the local community. If the agreement will involve a transfer of control during school hours, the LEA's consent is needed (EA 1944, s 22(3B)).

As will be seen below, governing bodies of controlled schools enjoy the same powers over staff appointments and dismissals as governors of county schools. Controlled schools with up to and including 599 pupils are required to have an equal number of LEA and foundation governors on the governing body – a gain for foundations as compared with the pre-1986 legislation. In larger schools the LEA has one more governor than the foundation (see Chapter 4).

(ii) Voluntary aided schools

There are approaching 5,000 voluntary aided schools. These schools have always enjoyed considerable independence from their LEA, with the voluntary body exerting overall control. Aided status is particularly favoured by certain religious denominations because the school is controlled almost exclusively by the governing body, on which the foundation governors must be in the majority (E(No 2)A 1986, s 4) (see Chapter 4). The school must be conducted in accordance with the terms of its trust deed (as modified by the Secretary of State because of any inconsistency between those terms and the school's instrument or articles of government: s 17(4)).

The chief advantage of aided status is that the school enjoys its independence at the cost of only a relatively small contribution towards the cost of alterations and repairs for which the governors are responsible, *viz*:

> 'such alterations to the school buildings as may be required by the local education authority for the purpose of securing that the school premises should conform to the prescribed standards, and . . . repairs to the school buildings . . . [other than those to] the interior of the school buildings, or for repairs to those buildings necessary in consequence of the use of the school premises, in pursuance of any direction or requirement of the authority, for purposes other than those of the school'.
>
> (EA 1944, s 15(3)).

This means, *inter alia*, that the LEA is responsible for the interior of the school buildings and for the playground and playing fields. The LEA is also responsible for payment of teachers' and other staff salaries. The governors are responsible for most repairs to the actual buildings, although they are entitled to a contribution towards the cost (EA 1993, s 281) (below). Note that section 15(3) of the EA 1944 also makes the governors responsible for meeting liabilities incurred by them, or by former governors or trustees, in connection with the provision of premises or equipment for the purposes of the school. The governors are also responsible for meeting the cost of a significant enlargement of premises and of new premises where a school moves to a new site or when a new school is established (but the LEA is responsible for the site, grounds, playing field etc). In such cases the governors can claim a contribution from the Secretary of State (see below).

The rate of contribution required from the governors (with the Secretary of State paying the rest) was originally set at 50 per cent. But the 1944 Act was subsequently amended so that the governors' contribution became 15 per cent, at which rate it still stands (see EA 1993, s 281, which replaces EA 1944, ss 102 and 103). However, it should be noted that in some cases the Secretary of State must pay an 85 per cent contribution, whilst in other cases the contribution is to be *up to and not exceeding* 85 per cent. The full 85 per cent contribution is always payable only in the case of maintenance and repair of buildings and alterations to buildings to bring them up to required standards (EA 1993, s 281(5)). LEAs are empowered by section 282 of the EA 1993 to assist schools in meeting their 15 per cent maintenance contribution and in complying with their duty to defray expenses of providing school buildings on a site to which a school is transferred (see EA 1946, First Sch, para 2).

LEAs' rights concerning the use of voluntary aided schools' premises are limited. Provided that an LEA requires the use of the premises for any purpose in connection with education or the welfare of the young and is satisfied that there is no other suitable accommodation for the purpose in the area, it may require the governors to allow it to use the premises free of charge on any week day (up to a maximum of three in any week) at times when they are not required for school purposes (EA 1944, s 22(2)). The provisions relating to 'transfer of control agreements' described above in relation to voluntary controlled schools apply also to voluntary aided schools.

(iii) Special agreement schools

This category in effect dates back to the Education Act 1936. It currently numbers around 100 schools, all of which are in the secondary sector. Special agreement schools are so called because of the special agreement under which the LEA will pay a contribution of between 50 and 75 per cent of the cost of building a voluntary school or enlarging an existing one. Such schools are hardly ever created today because aided status is more advantageous. Note that on repayment of the grant the governors may apply to the Secretary of State for voluntary aided status (see EA 1944, s 15(5)).

For the purposes of sections 15 (maintenance, repairs etc) and 22 (use of premises) of the EA 1944, and sections 281 and 282 of the EA 1993 (85 per cent DFE contribution in respect of certain costs and LEA powers to provide assistance), special agreement schools are bracketed together with aided schools (see above).

(d) Grant-maintained schools

(i) Introduction

Grant-maintained (GM) schools were first introduced under the Education Reform Act 1988. Although local financial management (discussed in Chapter 3) has given schools a significant degree of independence from LEAs, a school that has grant-maintained (GM) status is outside the LEA sector altogether. The possibility of a school becoming grant-maintained is stated to provide 'an additional route to autonomy' and lend 'a new and powerful dimension to the ability of parents to exercise choice within the publicly provided sector of education' (DES, *Grant-maintained schools: Consultation Paper* July 1987). More recently it has been claimed that the existence of these schools will 'prove to be a stimulus for higher standards at all schools' (DES Circular 10/88, para 2), although there have been claims that such schools will be perceived as 'better resourced and elitist' and that their existence will promote 'greater divisiveness' in the education system (P Meredith, 'Educational Reform' (1989) 52 *MLR* 215, 228). OFSTED reported in 1993 that in general the first 143 schools to acquire GM status had gained a significant financial advantage in doing so (see OFSTED, *Grant-maintained Schools 1989–92, A report from the Office of Her Majesty's Chief Inspector of Schools* (1993)). This was not simply due to higher funding levels (particularly through special purpose grants (see below)), but also through being able to obtain better terms from suppliers and contractors because payment is direct (*ibid*, paras 21–25).

Whatever the arguments, the GM sector is now well established and the Government is committed to its further expansion. By the end of 1993 there were barely 1,000 GM schools; the Government predicts that by 1996 most secondary schools and a 'significant proportion' of primary schools will have GM status (*Choice and Diversity*, para 3.2), which now seems unlikely. The opportunities for schools to acquire GM status, which results in their leaving the LEA sector and being funded by central government, have been enhanced significantly by the EA 1993. Schools can now apply for GM status in groups (see Pt II, Ch IX, of the 1993 Act), as well as singly. Furthermore, new schools can be established as GM schools. It is possible, via this route, for schools to cease to be independent schools and join the state sector as GM (although this will be permitted rarely, if at all, in practice). Also, the procedure for the acquisition of GM status has been streamlined, with the removal of the need for a second governors' resolution on a decision to publish proposals and a reduction in the length of the opting-out timetable.

Although the discussion below concentrates on the law governing *GM schools*, currently in Part II of the EA 1993, it should be borne in mind that under the provisions of the EA 1993 applicable to *GM special schools*, regulations have been introduced applying many of the requirements of Part II to these schools as well (see the Education (Grant-Maintained Special Schools) Regulations 1994 (SI 1994 No 653) and the Education (Maintained Special Schools becoming Grant-Maintained Schools) (Ballot Information) Regulations 1994 (SI 1994 No 1232)).

(ii) Definition of 'grant-maintained school'

A grant-maintained school is a school conducted by a governing body which was incorporated under the ERA 1988 or which has been incorporated under the EA 1993, Pt II (EA 1993, s 22(1)). A governing body could only be incorporated under the 1988 Act following the approval by the Secretary of State of proposals by the governing body which were published following a ballot of parents in favour of GM status. Under the EA 1993, s 22(2), a governing body of a GM school may be incorporated either:

- (*a*) as a result of approval by the Secretary of State of proposals by the governing body of a maintained county or voluntary school after completion of the required procedure (ballot of parents etc) – i.e. 'opting out'; or
- (*b*) in pursuance of proposals by a funding authority or promoters for the establishment of a *new* GM school (see ss 48 and 49 of the EA 1993); or
- (*c*) following approval of proposals for grouped GM status by two or more schools, under the procedure in Chapter IX of the 1993 Act.

The EA 1993 requires a GM school to be either a secondary school or a primary school (s 22(3)).

(iii) Eligibility for grant-maintained status

Any county or voluntary school is eligible to be considered for GM status (EA 1993, s 23(1)), *with the exception of*:

- (*a*) county or voluntary schools which have received permission from the Secretary of State to close, on application of the LEA under section 12(1) of the EA 1980, or which do not require approval for closure but the LEA has informed the Secretary of State of its decision to close the school concerned (EA 1993, s 23(2)); or

(*b*) voluntary schools in respect of which the governors have given notice of intention to discontinue the school, or have been given permission by the Secretary of State to do so (*ibid*, s 23(3)).

(iv) Acquisition of GM status or establishment of GM schools

The law governing the procedure for the acquisition of GM status by a county or voluntary school is set out in *Appendix 1*. The rules governing the acquisition of GM status as a *group* will be contained in regulations made under section 127 of the EA 1993, which also deals with the situation where an LEA-maintained school is to join a GM group. The regulations are also to contain similar procedural requirements concerning a governors' resolution, parental ballot, publication of proposals, and so on. The procedures for the establishment of *new* GM schools, under proposals made under sections 48 or 49 of the EA 1993, are outlined in Part 7 of this Chapter (Establishment of schools).

(v) Property

The general rule is that when a school acquires GM status, property rights (and liabilities) are transferred from the LEA to the governing body (but generally not in respect of property held on trust) (ERA 1993, s 38). The governing body and LEA may, however, enter into an agreement, prior to the date of implementation of the proposals for GM status, under which property, rights and liabilities can be excluded from transfer – provided the Secretary of State agrees (EA 1993, s 38(5)–(7)). Loan obligations incurred by the LEA and premature retirement payments to former staff remain the LEA's responsibility (*ibid*). Transferred property is held by the governing body for the lifetime of the school; any transfer of the school to a new site will be treated as continuation of the school for this purpose. The governors are only able to dispose of premises with the consent of the Secretary of State (EA 1993, s 68(5)(c) and (7)).

Property not used for school purposes is not transferred. Property with joint community/school use will, so far as possible, be divided (ERA 1988, Sch 10, para 1, as amended).

Responsibility for ensuring that property is transferred to the governors by the required date rests with the Education Assets Board (ERA 1988, s 198(3)). Appointments to the Board are made by the Secretary of State, and selection must be made from among persons with experience in property management, local government or education (ERA 1988, s 197(3)). The Board must act in accordance with the powers and procedures laid down in Schedule 8 to the 1988 Act (see EA 1993, ss 104–108).

LEAs are restricted from disposing of property liable to be transferred on a school becoming grant-maintained and incorporated as such (EA 1993, s 41(1)). The restriction applies as soon as, and for so long as, the procedure for GM status is pending. The procedure is 'pending' when either the governing body have given the LEA notice of their resolution to ballot parents on GM status or where they have received a request from parents (under s 26(1) of the EA 1993) for such a ballot (EA 1993, s 40). Note that any disposal under a contract entered into before opting out procedure was initiated is not covered by the restriction in section 41(1).

The effect of the restriction is that the consent of the Secretary of State and existing governing body is needed for disposals (and contracts relating to them), save that in the case of a disposal (or contract) *after approval for GM status has been granted*, a disposal of land with a value of not more than £6,000 requires the consent only of the new governing body, but all other disposals or contracts require the consent of the Secretary of State and the new governing body (EA 1993, s 41(2)–(5)). The Secretary of State has the power to vary the specified sum (£6,000) by order (s 41(10)).

If a contract for the sale of land is made by the LEA in contravention of section 41(1) of the Act after approval of the proposals for the acquisition of GM status, it can be repudiated by the Education Assets Board (EA 1993, s 42(2)–(4)). If the contravention of section 41(1) consists of a wrongful disposal of land, the Board has the power to acquire the land compulsorily and must thereafter convey its interest in it to the governing body (EA 1993, s 42(5)–(8)).

There is also a general restriction, under section 43 of the EA 1993 (subject to exceptions in subs (7)), on entry into contracts by the LEA which, if GM status for the school were implemented, would or might bind the governing body on its incorporation. Such contracts may be repudiated by the Education Assets Board (EA 1993, s 44). There are also restrictions, which apply when the procedure for the acquisition of GM status is pending, on any change of purpose for which property is used or held. Such a change may not take place without the required consent (i.e. the consent of the new governing body, or, if approval of GM status for the school has not yet been granted, the consent of the existing governing body and the Secretary of State (see EA 1993, s 45)).

(vi) Staff

The position concerning staff, which is governed by section 39 of the EA 1993, can conveniently be dealt with here. As from the date of implementation of GM status for the school, all staff employed to work wholly at the school, including staff preparing meals for consumption on the premises, will be transferred to the governing body's employ (unless their employment terminates or they are assigned to another school by the LEA as from that date) (see, for example, *Pickwell and Another* v *Lincolnshire County Council* (1992) The Times, 13 October (EAT)). The 1993 Act states that:

> 'The contract of employment between a person to whom this section applies and the former employer shall have effect from the date of

> implementation of the proposals as if originally made between him and the governing body of the grant-maintained school' (EA 1993, s 39).

All the previous employer's rights, duties, powers and liabilities under the contract of employment with the employee shall vest in the governing body of the GM school on the implementation date (s 39(7)). The employee cannot treat the change of employer as a 'substantial change . . . to his detriment in his working conditions' such as would be sufficient to give him or her a right to terminate his or her contract of employment (s 39(8)). A teacher's pay and conditions will not be adversely affected merely by the transfer and will continue to be governed by the *School Teachers' Pay and Conditions Document* which is in force at the time.

The appointment, dismissal and withdrawal of staff by the LEA will be restricted once the application for GM status is pending. (The definition of 'pending' for this purpose is in EA 1993, s 40 – see above under *(v) Property*.) Parallel provisions to those governing transfer of property, outlined above, will apply (EA 1993, s 46).

(vii) Funding

The funding authorities (the Funding Agency for Schools and, when operational the Schools Funding Council for Wales – see Chapter 1, Part 2(d)) are under a legal duty to maintain grant-maintained schools (EA 1993, s 81(1)). The payments are to take the form of annual 'maintenance grants', paid to the governing body. Despite this, central block grants to LEAs reflect a notional need to spend on the provision of education for *all* pupils who are resident in their area and who are attending maintained schools, including GM schools. The maintenance grant paid by the Secretary of State to the governors of GM schools has been recouped from LEAs, either through direct payments to the Secretary of State (and into the Consolidated Fund) or by deduction from revenue support grant or other grant(s) (EA 1993, ss 93 and 94; see also *R* v *Secretary of State for Wales ex p Gwent County Council* (1994) The Times, 16 March (CA)).

The amount of the maintenance grant is to be determined under regulations: presently the Education (Grant-maintained Schools) (Finance) Regulations 1994 (SI 1994 No 938) (SI 1994 No 2111 in the case of GM special schools), which apply for the financial year 1994–1995.

The Government's stated intention on the funding of GM schools has been that:

> 'the acquisition by a school of grant-maintained status should not change the financial position either of the school or of local ratepayers in the LEA which previously maintained the school' (DES Circular 10/88, para 53).

This financially neutral effect flows from the fact that, on the one hand, GM schools will not receive support services from the LEA (other than those bought in), and so will actually be entitled to a larger grant than that paid to LEA-funded schools under financial delegation arrangements, and on the other, the fact that administrative costs and the cost of support services will have to be borne by the school. Nevertheless, as noted above (at (*i*)), a survey by OFSTED of some of the first schools to acquire GM status has revealed that many received higher overall levels of funding than under their previous status (OFSTED, *Grant-maintained Schools 1989–92*).

In the White Paper (*Choice and Diversity*) proposals were announced for the introduction of a common funding formula for GM schools. GM schools would receive a share of the Government's Standard Spending Assessment for the LEA concerned. (See further, House of Commons Select Committee, Second Report, Session 1992–93, *Some Aspects of the Funding of Schools.*) A common funding formula is prescribed by the 1994 Regulations (*op cit*) in respect of GM secondary schools in five LEAs – Calderdale, Essex, Gloucestershire, London Borough of Bromley and London Borough of Hillingdon (Regs, pt 3). In respect of all primary schools, and secondary schools in areas other than the five above, the maintenance grant is based on the sum of the following:

(i) the amount that a comparable school would receive under the LMS budget share allocation formula (subject to adjustment depending on the date the school became GM);

(ii) a percentage addition (different percentages are prescribed for each LEA, with separate percentages for primary and secondary sectors), intended to reflect the cost of services provided to LEA-maintained schools but which have to be bought in by the GM schools;

(iii) an amount in respect of school meals, contingencies, nursery education and administration of section 11 'grants in respect of the local ethnic minority population' (see Chapter 3, Part 5); and

(iv) (where applicable) the amount of any unspent sums (provided in a previous year's budget share) (Regs, pt 2).

If the school's incorporation date does not coincide exactly with the start of the funding year, apportionment is to be made. Provision is made for certain other adjustments, where necessary. Requirements which may be attached to the payment of the maintenance grant are spelled out in the Regulations.

The 1993 Act states that provision may also be made, via regulations, for 'special purpose grants' (s 82), 'capital grants' (s 83) and 'loans' (s 92). Parallel provision for Wales is made in ss 87–92.

Special purpose grants

These may cover, *inter alia*, expenditure in connection with a prescribed educational purpose, or in respect of special educational needs (see EA 1993, s 82 and the Education (Grant-maintained Schools) (Finance) Regulations 1994, reg 31 and Sch 9) expenditure for the purposes for which grants for education support and training (under section 1 of the Education (Grants and Awards) Act 1984, as amended by EA 1993, s 278, see below) and grants for the education of travellers and displaced persons (ERA 1988, s 210) are recoverable by and payable to LEA-maintained schools. Section 11 funding, i.e. grants made under section 11 of the Local Government Act 1966 for the education of pupils of New Commonwealth origin, will also be available to GM schools: ERA 1988, s 211. Special purpose grants may also cover expenses, of a class or description specified in the regulations, which 'it appears to the Secretary of State the governing bodies of [GM] schools cannot reasonably be expected to meet from maintenance grant' (EA 1993, s 82(1)(c)). Requirements may be attached to the provision of these grants (EA 1993, s 84).

Capital grants

Capital grants of 100 per cent of the costs they are intended to cover may be made in respect of prescribed categories of expenditure of a capital nature (EA 1993, s 83 and the Education (GM Schools) (Finance) Regs 1994, *op cit*, reg 38 and Sch 8). The Secretary of State will 'consider each application for capital grant on its merits and in the light of the total resources available nationally for building projects and other capital expenditure at all maintained schools' (Circular 10/88, para 60).

Various requirements, with which governing bodies will be under a duty to comply, may be attached to special purpose and capital grants, including a requirement to repay all or part of them (EA 1993, s 84; 1994 Regs, reg 32). In fact, a repayment of excess maintenance grant received can also be ordered if an overpayment (defined in EA 1993, s 85(5) as the amount paid in grants less the amount payable in accordance with the regulations) is made to the governing body in any financial year (s 85(3)). Repayments of either of these types may take the form of deductions from further grants (s 85(4)).

It is for the funding authority to decide when, and at what intervals, maintenance, special purpose and capital grants shall be paid (s 85(1)).

Loans

The funding authorities also have a power to make loans to governing bodies of GM schools (EA 1993, s 92; Education (Grant-maintained Schools) (Loans) Regulations 1993, SI 1993 No 3073). (In Wales, where the SFCW is not yet in operation, the Secretary of State may make such loans: *ibid.*) Such loans are recoverable from the grant paid to the schools concerned by the funding authority (*ibid*).

(viii) LEAs' continuing responsibilities

After a school has acquired GM status an LEA will remain responsible for, *inter alia*, the availability of 'sufficient schools' (but see p 9), the enforcement of school attendance, provision of free transport, and provision in respect of pupils with special educational needs.

LEAs will be under a duty (EA 1993, s 129(1)) to ensure that pupils in GM schools receive no less favourable treatment than pupils in schools they maintain in respect of the exercise of any of their powers and duties to provide benefits and services for pupils at both LEA-maintained and GM schools. A similar duty is owed in respect of persons receiving further education at a GM school (under the power in EA 1993, s 128) (s 129(2)). LEAs will continue to have a duty to provide a careers service (Employment and Training Act 1973, s 8) – which must be made available to pupils in GM schools.

GM schools will receive no allowance in their annual maintenance grant for certain LEA central services like careers. But many other such services do not have to be provided by LEAs to GM schools. Services which the LEA will not be obliged to provide include school meals and milk and the advisory services. The governors of GM schools will have legal responsibility for the provision of free school meals to eligible pupils. The maintenance grant provided to the governors will contain an allowance for such provision. Governors may contract with outside bodies for the provision of such services (ERA 1993, s 68(5)). However, new rules apply in respect of the provision of services to GM schools by LEAs. Under section 295 of the EA 1993, the Secretary of State may make an order specifying the goods and services which an LEA may provide to GM and GM special schools which lie inside its boundaries or those of neighbouring authorities. The LEA must charge the full cost of providing the goods and services. Once the order is made, it may only authorise the supply of goods and services to GM schools for a period of two years. It is important to bear in mind, however, that LEAs may continue to provide services to GM schools under the Local Authorities (Goods and Services) Act 1970 indefinitely, provided they trade within the margin of capacity (that is, to the extent that they do not need to employ extra staff or acquire extra equipment for this purpose). Services like museums, libraries and payroll services would seem to be within the margin of capacity. In the case of certain services (for example, cleaning), competitive tendering will be necessary (Local Government Act 1988, Pt I).

(e) City technology colleges and city colleges for the technology of the arts

The Government originally intended that about 20 of these 'centres of excellence' would be established (at present there are 15), with the help of considerable injections of private capital. Public money, which it now seems is required in greater amounts than had previously been thought necessary, may also be provided, under a funding agreement between the promoter/proprietor of the college and the Secretary of State (ERA 1988, s 105(1) and (4)). This public element means that city colleges' decisions may be amenable to judicial review: *R* v *Governors of Haberdashers' Aske's Hatcham College Trust ex p Tyrell* [1994] The Independent 12 October.

City colleges must be located in an 'urban area' (the first was set up in Solihull). They must cater for pupils aged between 11 and 18 who have 'different abilities' and who are wholly or mainly drawn from that area

(ERA 1988, s 105(2)(a) and (b)). There must be a 'broad curriculum', but with an emphasis on science and technology (in the case of city technology colleges) or on technology in its application to the performing and creative arts (city colleges for the technology of the arts) (s 105(2)(c)). The requirements of the ERA 1988 relating to the National Curriculum, religious education and collective worship do not apply to these colleges because they are not 'maintained schools' for the purposes of Chapter I of Part I of the Act (in ERA 1988, s 105(1), they are referred to as 'independent schools'; see also s 305(1) of the EA 1993). Nevertheless, under the funding agreement the promoter/proprietor of the college will have given an undertaking to make the kind of provision required by the ERA 1988 relating to the curriculum. Corporal punishment may not be administered (SI 1987 No 1183 as amended).

(f) Pupil referral units and other alternative arrangements

A pupil referral unit is a school, not being a county or special school, which is established and maintained by an LEA and which is specially organised to provide full-time or part-time education for pupils of compulsory school age who, by reason of illness, exclusion from school or otherwise, may not receive suitable education unless arrangements are made for them (EA 1993, s 298(2)). Pupil referral units have been put on a firm legal footing by the 1993 Act. Schedule 18 and the Education (Pupil Referral Unit) (Application of Enactments) Regulations 1994 applies to PRUs (with or without modification), or excludes from PRUs, various provisions applicable to schools in general governing the curriculum, discipline and other matters. See further DFE Circular 11/94, which also deals with individual and home tuition, and Circular 12/94 (also DoH Circular LAC (94) 10) on *The Education of Sick Children*, which also deals with hospital schools. Alternative provision for sick or excluded pupils is a legal requirement in respect of pupils of compulsory school age (EA 1993, s 298(1)). LEAs have a discretion to make such provision for older children (s 298(4)).

(g) Independent schools

(i) Definition

An independent school is defined in law as:

> 'any school at which full-time education is provided for five or more pupils of compulsory school age (whether or not such education is also provided for pupils under or over that age), not being a school maintained by a local education authority, a grant-maintained school or a special school not maintained by a local education authority'.
>
> (EA 1944, s 114(1), as amended).

(ii) Registration

For the operation of an independent school to be lawful, the school must be entered on the register kept (under EA 1944, s 70(1)) by the Registrar of Independent Schools. In most cases, where a person operates an independent school which is neither registered nor provisionally registered (under EA 1944, s 70(1)(b)) that person may be liable on summary conviction to a fine and, in the case of any further offence, up to three months' imprisonment (s 70(3) and (3A)).

(iii) Controls

Independent schools enjoy a considerable degree of autonomy, especially in relation to financial matters. They are frequently registered as charities, but may also be run as businesses with a view to profit. They are free from the requirements concerning the National Curriculum (see Chapter 8). There are, however, certain controls which may be exercised by the Secretary of State, and a school may be inspected by Her Majesty's Inspectorate of Schools.

The proprietors must submit to the Registrar (above) annual particulars concerning such matters as pupils enrolled and examinations for which pupils are being prepared (Education (Particulars of Independent Schools) Regulations 1982, as amended). Regulations may require that information needed by the local authority in order to determine whether the school is a children's home for the purposes of the Children Act 1989 (see below) must be included (EA 1944, s 70(4A), added by EA 1993, s 292(2)). The Registrar must also be notified of changes in the management personnel and in the name and location of the school. If these requirements are not met, the Secretary of State may, after giving two months' notice of the specific shortcomings, order that the school be removed from the Register of Independent Schools (1982 regulations, *op cit*). Moreover, the Secretary of State is under a duty to serve on the proprietor of a registered or provisionally registered school a notice of complaint if he is satisfied that the school is 'objectionable' on certain grounds. These grounds (the apposite one(s) of which should be specified by the Secretary of State in his notice) refer to the unsuitability of the school premises or parts thereof, the inadequacy or unsuitability of the accommodation, any lack of efficient and suitable instruction, and the unsuitability of a teacher or proprietor for their position (EA 1944, s 71(1)). Any teacher considered unsuitable is entitled to receive a copy of the notice (s 71(2)). According to one case, where a school caters for the special traditions and characteristics of a particular sect, it is 'suitable' if it primarily equips children for a place in the community in which they live, rather than in the wider community, so long as it leaves the children with the option of adopting some other way of life in the future if they so choose: *R* v *Secretary of State for Education and Science ex p Talmud Torah Machzikei Hadass School Trust* [1985] The Times, 12 April.

The controls over independent schools have been widened by the EA 1993. First, the unsuitability of employees other than teachers can now render a school objectionable under section 71 (see above, and EA 1993, s 290(2)). Secondly, a school may now be refused registration or struck off the Register (see below) if a person whose employment is restricted under section 218(6) of the ERA 1988 is employed there or is the proprietor of the school (EA 1944, s 71(4) and (5), added by EA 1993, s 290(1)).

In every case the notice of objection must specify a time, of not less than one month, in which the complaint may be referred to the Independent Schools Tribunal (EA 1944, s 71(3)). The Tribunal, which is to be constituted in accordance with EA 1944, Sch 6, has various powers when determining the appeal – including annulment of the complaint, ordering that the school be struck off the Register or struck off unless certain problems are rectified, and disqualification of a teacher or other employee or proprietor from holding that particular position (EA 1944, s 72(2), as amended). (In the last case, it is an offence for the person concerned to continue in that position after being disqualified: s 73(2) and (3).) It is possible subsequently to have the disqualification removed by the Secretary of State or, on appeal from his refusal, the Independent Schools Tribunal (s 74)).

In some cases independent schools may be approved to admit pupils with statements of special educational needs (EA 1993, s 189 and the Education (Special Educational Needs) (Approval of Independent Schools) Regulations 1994 (SI 1994 No 651), under which conditions of approval will be imposed).

(iv) Independent schools that are children's homes

In some cases an independent school will be a children's home for the purposes of Part VIII of, and Schedule 6 to, the Children Act 1989. The consequence of this is that the school will be subject to requirements as to registration, standards of care and inspection under that Act. The definition of 'children's home' for this purpose has been amended by section 292 of the EA 1993, although, as before, a school approved as suitable for the admission of pupils with statements of special educational needs is outside the definition. The change of real substance lies in the removal of the minimum number of children for whom accommodation is provided. Previously, if 50 or fewer children were provided with accommodation by the school it was a children's home (subject to the exception in the case of special schools). Now, an independent school providing accommodation for pupils will be a children's home if for each of the previous two years 4 or more children were provided with accommodation for more than 295 days in the year or if it is intended to accommodate such number for more than 295 days in the year (see further Chapter 13, Part 4(b)(i)).

(v) The Assisted Places scheme

The Assisted Places scheme was introduced under the Education Act 1980, with effect from 1 October 1980. (For a critical review, see T Edwards et al, *The State and Private Education: An Evaluation of the Assisted Places Scheme* (1989).) It aims to enable pupils 'who might otherwise not be able to do so to benefit from education at independent schools' (EA 1980, s 17). The scheme provides for:

(*a*) the remission of school fees by 'participating schools' (i.e. independent schools with which the Secretary of State has entered into individual 'participation agreements') (EA 1980, s 17(2)); and

(*b*) the reimbursement of the school concerned by the Secretary of State (*ibid*, s 17(1)).

The average cost of day fees at independent schools is around £3,500 a year, and the average assisted place contribution from the Government is approximately £2,700. The fees covered by the scheme are tuition and other fees which are required in order to be able to attend the school, but excluding boarding fees and any others excluded by the participation agreement (s 17(3)(a)). Also covered are entrance fees for public examinations paid for by the school (s 17(3)(b)). Certain incidental expenses, relating to such things as school uniform and transport, are also covered (Education (Assisted Places) (Incidental Expenses) Regulations 1989, as amended).

Schedule 4 to the 1980 Act makes provision for the termination of participation agreements by either party if certain conditions are met. Three years' notice is needed, unless the Secretary of State is terminating the agreement because educational standards are not being maintained at the school or because a condition under the agreement or relevant regulations (see below) is not being met.

Eligibility for assistance under the scheme is governed by regulations (currently the Education (Assisted Places) Regulations 1989, as amended), which must be reviewed, following consultation, every two years (EA 1980, s 17(9)). Conditions of eligibility refer to such matters as residence in the British Isles, age, and parental income. Income scales are periodically amended. The extent of any remission of fees hinges on the level of income as determined under the regulations.

Around 30,000 assisted places are financed by the Government at present. That figure might be higher, but for the less than complete take-up of the scheme.

5. Nursery schools and pre-school education

The benefits of nursery education to a child's social and intellectual development are well documented. Yet in provision of education for the under-fives, Britain lags behind much of the rest of Europe (see K Sylva and P Moss, *Learning Before School*, National Commission on Education Briefing No 8 (November 1992); see also OECD survey reported in *The Independent*, 9 December 1993). In 1994 the Government announced an interest in seeing an extension of nursery education, but there is no legislation on the subject in immediate prospect. An Opposition amendment to the Education Bill in 1993, which would have had that effect, was not carried.

(a) Nursery education

There was always uncertainty about whether the Education Act 1944 had imposed a duty on LEAs to provide nursery education. Under that Act, a primary school could be a nursery school if it was mainly concerned with the provision of education to two, three and four year-olds (EA 1944, s 9(4)). Moreover, LEAs were required (*ibid*, s 8(1)(a)) to ensure that there were sufficient schools offering primary education – full-time education suitable to the requirements of *junior pupils*, defined in section 114(1) as pupils below the age of twelve. But the Education Act 1980 (s 24(2)) states that LEAs' duty under section 8(1)(a) of the 1944 Act does not apply in respect of pupils below the age of five years. The *power* of LEAs to maintain or assist schools providing nursery education is stated to be preserved (EA 1944, s 9(2); EA 1980 s 24(2)), and LEAs are empowered to establish nursery schools, to maintain such schools whether established by them or not, and to assist any such school not established by them (EA 1980, s 24(1)). The prohibition against charging parents for the admission of their child to a maintained school, or in respect of provision made (subject to exceptions – see Chapter 8, Part 12), seems to apply to nursery schools.

The requirements of Part I of the ERA 1988 covering the National Curriculum apply neither to a nursery school nor to 'a nursery class in a primary school' (ERA 1988, s 25(2)). Moreover, there is no duty to provide the National Curriculum to *any* child below the age of five (ERA 1988, s 2(1)(b)), even one in a reception class in an infants' school. The first 'key stage' in relation to an individual pupil runs from the date he or she reaches compulsory school age (ERA 1988, s 3(3)(a)) (see Chapter 8, Part 6(a), Chart 3). In practice, of course, an under-five-year-old would almost certainly be taught the National Curriculum if others in the class who were aged five were.

A nursery school will be neither a county nor voluntary school (EA 1944, s 9(2)). Most nursery schools are maintained, and funded in the same way (although obviously not on the same basis) as county schools and are covered by the same procedure on the proposed cessation of LEA maintenance of the school (EA 1980, s 12(1)). Some nursery schools are independent; the Secretary of State has a power to pay a grant direct to such schools, in accordance with regulations (EA 1944, s 100, as amended; Direct Grant Schools Regulations (SI 1959 No 1832)). Nursery schools are not within the categories of school specified in the EA 1993, s 23(1) which can become grant-maintained, nor are they entitled to delegated budgets. Furthermore, a new nursery school cannot be established as a GM school, and an existing GM school cannot be changed into a nursery school (EA 1993, s 231(1)). However, new GM schools can be established to include, in the provision made, provision for children aged under five;

similarly, existing GM schools can be altered for this purpose (EA 1993, s 231(2)).

(b) Day care and pre-school provision

Although this book is concerned with the law relating to schools, it is appropriate to consider day care and pre-school provision because such provision is sometimes made on school premises and because LEAs have certain responsibilities in this area, especially in the case of children with special educational needs. In fact, it is local authorities rather than LEAs that have the principal responsibilities.

The Children Act 1989 (to which all references in this paragraph relate) requires day-care provision to be made for children 'in need' in their area who are aged five or under and who are not yet attending school. The day care provided must be such as the local authority considers appropriate (s 18(1)). There is also a power to provide day care for pre-school children who are *not* in need (s 18(2)). 'Day care' is defined as 'any form of supervised activity provided for children during the day (whether or not it is provided on a regular basis)' (s 18(4)). A child is in need in any one of three circumstances. The first is where the child is unlikely to achieve or maintain, or have the opportunity of achieving or maintaining, a reasonable standard of health or development without the provision of any such services (s 17(10)(a)). 'Development' is defined for this purpose as 'physical, intellectual, emotional, social or behavioural development' (s 17(11)). 'Health' covers physical or mental health. The second circumstance in which a child is in need is where his or her health or development is likely to be significantly impaired, or further impaired, without the provision to him or her of such services (s 17(10)(b)). Finally, a child is in need if he or she is disabled (s 17(10)(c)). 'Disabled' is defined for this purpose as being 'blind, deaf or dumb or suffering from a mental disorder or being substantially and permanently handicapped by illness, injury or congenital deformity (or such other disability as may be prescribed)' (s 17(11)). Some, indeed many, of these children will have special educational needs for the purposes of Part III of the EA 1993 (see Chapter 9).

Local authorities are required to keep a register of persons who provide day care (other than on domestic premises) in their area and of persons who act as childminders (see generally CA 1989, s 71, Sch 9 and SIs 1991 Nos 1689, 2076 and 2094). The regime for registration and inspection is outside the scope of this book. Note, however, that any day-care provision made in a school, including a grant-maintained or independent school, is exempt from the requirements concerning registration under the 1989 Act (Sch 9 para 3(1)). However, this exemption only applies where the day-care provision is made by the school as part of its activities or by a person employed to work at the school and authorised to make the provision as part of the school's activities (*ibid,* para 3(2)). It might therefore be thought that where school premises are used for pre- or post-school day care, as is becoming increasingly demanded, with so many families having both parents in full-time employment, the exemption would not apply to a service run by groups of parents themselves. Indeed, the Government expressed a clear intention in the White Paper in 1987 to remove from the list of exemptions provided for under the previous legislation (the Nurseries and Childminders Regulation Act 1948) 'private day care facilities run on school . . . premises' (Secretary of State for Social Services, *The Law on Child Care and Family Services*, Cm 62, HMSO, para 73). However, for the purposes of registration under the 1989 Act, day care is only provided where the period, or total periods, for which the children are looked after exceed(s) two hours in any day. Where day-care provision is occasional, i.e. for less than six days in any year, registration is not required provided notice has been given to the local authority before the first such occasion (CA 1989, Sch 9, para 5).

6. Changes to educational provision

The circumstances in which changes to educational provision may occur have widened as a result of measures included in the EA 1993. In particular, there is now provision for funding authorities and the Secretary of State to take steps for the elimination of surplus capacity in schools, through, *inter alia*, school closures. Before considering the new provisions, and the continuing provisions laid down in the EA 1944 and 1980, in detail, reference must be made to the special provisions introduced under the Education Reform Act 1988, and now contained in sections 272 and 273 of the EA 1993, which are concerned with ensuring that before certain changes to a school are made, via procedures in EA 1980, ss 12 and 13, the governors are given an opportunity to apply for grant-maintained (GM) status. The rules may be summarised thus:

(*a*) Before formulating any proposals for ceasing to maintain, or to make significant changes to the character or significantly to enlarge, a school which might be eligible for GM status, the LEA must consult the governing body of the school (EA 1993, s 273(1)). There is also a new statutory duty on an LEA to consult with 'appropriate persons' before publishing proposals under section 12 of the EA 1980 for the establishment of, or significant changes to, a county school.

Consultation is a prerequisite to many changes in education administration and organisation. Failure to consult, where such consultation is a mandatory requirement, will amount to procedural *ultra vires*, i.e. the decision will have been taken unlawfully and may be quashed by the courts (see *Bradbury* v *Enfield LBC* [1967] 3 All ER 434; *Lee* v *DES* (1968) 66 LGR 211; and *Milne* v *Wandsworth LBC* (1992) 90 LGR 515, *per* Stuart-Smith LJ at p 522). In fact, even where there is no statutory requirement to consult there may still be a public law duty to do so. In *R* v *Brent LBC ex p Gunning* (1985) 84 LGR 211 the LEA had decided, on 12 July 1984, to make proposals for the amalgamation and closure of secondary schools. The decision was held to be *ultra vires* because the authority had failed to consider a report from its education committee. A similar failure had occurred in respect of the LEA's decision on 10 May 1984 to consult with interested parties on the draft proposals. The authority had not consulted with parents. Although the court did not infer a duty *per se* to consult parents, Hodgson J felt that parents had a legitimate expectation to be consulted and, accordingly, 'they had the same legal right to consultation as if such a right had been expressly conferred on them by statute' (at p 187). This concept of 'legitimate expectation' is of growing importance in public law and affects decision-making by LEAs and other public bodies. In one of the leading cases, Lord Fraser explained that 'Legitimate, or reasonable, expectation may arise either from an express promise given on behalf of a public authority or from the existence of a regular practice which the claimant can reasonably expect to continue' (*Council of Civil Service Unions* v *Minister for the Civil Service* [1985] AC 374 at p 401). Nevertheless, in *R* v *Secretary of State for Education and Science ex p Yusuf Islam* [1994] ELR 111, QBD Macpherson J said that the doctrine of legitimate expectation was 'much overworked'. In that case the proprietor of an independent Muslim school had applied for voluntary aided status for the school, partly on the basis that there were insufficient school places in the area. By the time that the matter came to decision by the Secretary of State there was no longer a shortage of places, but the proprietor had not been shown the new figures or given an opportunity to comment on them. This failure of consultation constituted a manifest unfairness, according to Macpherson J.

It may be noted that successive circulars since 1980 dealing with school changes have emphasised the importance of consulting parents. Successful challenges against a failure to consult over school closure have been made in a number of unreported cases (*R* v *Secretary of State for Wales ex p Hawkins*, 28 May 1982 (unreported) (CA); *R* v *Secretary of State for Education and Science ex p Collins*, 20 June 1983 (unreported) (QBD); *R* v *Secretary of State for Wales ex p Russell*, 28 June 1983 (unreported) (QBD); all cited in P Meredith, 'Falling Rolls and the Re-organisation of Schools' (1984) JSWL 208, 218 n 69; see also P Meredith, *Government, Schools and the Law* (1992) Routledge, Chapter 5).

Once an adequate consultation period has expired, there is normally no obligation on the LEA to consult further (*R* v *Hertfordshire County Council ex p George* [1988] Lexis Co/856/87 (QBD)). If there is inadequate consultation by the LEA, proper consultation by the Secretary of State at a later stage in the decision-making process might rectify the deficiency (*R* v *Gwent County Council ex p Bryant* [1988] The Independent, 19 April; *R* v *Northamptonshire County Council ex p Tebbutt* (1986)).

Proper consultation for the purposes of school closures (etc) would probably involve:

(i) consulting when the proposals are still at a formative stage;

(ii) giving those affected sufficient reasons for any proposal to enable them to consider and respond intelligently;

(iii) providing adequate time for consideration and response; and

(iv) taking representations, etc, into account in coming to a final decision (see *ex p Gunning, op cit*).

The statutory requirement in section 273(1) of the EA 1993 (formerly in section 73 of the ERA 1988) to consult the governing body of the school is mandatory. There is a specific purpose to the requirement, as DES Circular 10/88 (para 33) made clear:

> 'This provision will allow the governing body time to consider whether the LEA's plans are such that the parents' views should be sought on the advisability of preparing an application for grant-maintained status'.

In effect, therefore, it aims to encourage schools to consider opting out of LEA control.

(*b*) No proposals concerning the establishment, significant alteration or closure of a county school (under EA 1980, s 12) or establishment or alteration of a voluntary school (*ibid*, s 13) may be published in respect of a school which has been given approval to become grant maintained (EA 1993, s 273(2)).

(*c*) Where the procedure for GM status is pending (see EA 1993, s 40(1)) no notice for the discontinuance of a voluntary school may be served by the governing body under section 14 of the EA 1944.

(*d*) The next set of rules, in section 273(3)–(7) of the 1993 Act, is one of the most complex applicable to school changes. The rules apply in two situations:

(i) the governing body has applied for GM status and proposals under EA 1980, s 12 or 13 for a significant change of character, closure, etc, to/of the school are published while the application is still pending; or

(ii) proposals have been published under EA 1980, s 12 or 13 and have not been determined or withdrawn and the governing body apply for GM status for the school.

Particular legal consequences arise out of (i) or (ii).

First, all proposals for school changes (etc), under section 12 or 13 of the EA 1980 require the approval of the Secretary of State. In other situations, such proposals do not always require approval.

Secondly, the proposals for GM status and for a change to or closure of a school must be considered together. But the change (etc) proposals cannot be determined by the Secretary of State until after he has made his determination on the application for GM status.

Thirdly, if the application for GM status is approved, the consequences depend, *inter alia*, on whether the school is *county* or *voluntary*:

(i) If the school is a *county* school, and the proposals are made by the LEA under section 12(1)(d) of the EA 1980 for a significant change in the character (etc) (see below), those proposals may only be approved if the governing body approves them. If the governing body does not approve them, the proposals must be rejected (EA 1993, s 273(5)(a)).

(ii) If the school is a *county* school, and the proposals are made under section 272 of the 1993 Act, the Secretary of State may approve them. Proposals under section 272 are proposals for a significant change in the character/alteration of a county school made when an application for GM status is still pending. If the GM application is rejected, the section 272 proposals must also fail.

(iii) If the school is a *voluntary* school, the Secretary of State may only approve proposals made by the governing body, under EA 1980, s 13, where the proposals were made 'to ensure consistency in the provision made in the area of the [LEA] if the proposals by the authority are implemented'. Otherwise the Secretary of State must reject the proposals.

Litigation has helped to clarify the duties of the Secretary of State when in receipt of both GM status and school change proposals – which has proved to be a common scenario up and down the country. It is clear that the Secretary of State must, when weighing up these proposals, consider the possible impact of each (*R* v *Secretary of State for Education and Science ex p Avon County Council* (1990) 88 LGR 716). Nevertheless, the Secretary of State is entitled not only to have, but also to apply, a policy preference in making determinations (*R* v *Secretary of State for Education and Science ex p Avon County Council (No 2)* (1990) 88 LGR 737). In any event, a process of 'judgment and evaluation' must be followed, taking account of past experience and an assessment of likely future events and 'of the prospects for the success of (his) policy in achieving (the desired) objects' (*ibid per* Ralph Gibson LJ at p 740). The case of *R* v *Secretary of State for Education and Science ex p Newham LBC* [1991] The Times, 11 January confirmed the extent of the Secretary of State's discretion in weighing up policy considerations (see N Harris, *Law and Education: Regulation, Consumerism and the Education System* (1993) Sweet and Maxwell, pp 56–57; and P Meredith, 'Opting-out litigation: the Newham experience' (1992) 4 *Education and the Law* 69).

7. Establishment of schools

(a) County schools

LEAs must act within the strict framework laid down in section 12 of the

EA 1980 (as amended) if they wish to establish a county school or to maintain as a county school any school which is not such a school. Note that LEAs' power to establish schools is severely circumscribed once an EA 1993, s 12, transfer order (see Chapter 1, at pp 9–10) has been made in favour of a funding authority (see below).

The first stage is consultation with 'appropriate persons' (EA 1980, s 12(1A), added by section 229 of the EA 1993). The Secretary of State may issue guidance on such consultation (EA 1980, s 12(1B)). Once formulated, proposals must be published in a local newspaper and must be posted in at least one conspicuous place in the area and, in the case of an existing school, at or near the main entrance of the school to which they relate (Education (Publication of School Proposals and Notices) Regulations 1993). Non-compliance with this requirement may not necessarily invalidate the procedure as a whole; in *Coney* v *Choyce* [1975] 4 WLR 422 the court held that non-compliance with such a requirement (then contained in the 1968 regulations) did not affect the legality of the authority's subsequent action, because no person had suffered any substantial prejudice and the requirement could only be said to be 'directory' rather than 'mandatory'. The published proposals must also be sent to the Secretary of State (EA 1980, s 12(1)). Adequate and accurate details of what is proposed must be stated (*Legg* v *ILEA* [1972] 3 All ER 177). Particulars of the admissions total for the school and the time or times at which it is intended to implement the proposals are to be stated (s 12(2), as amended by ERA 1988, Sch 13 Pt I). The published proposals must also explain rights concerning objection to the proposals (*ibid*).

If, at any time within two months after publication of the proposals, ten or more local government electors for the area submit an objection to the LEA, the LEA must transmit it to the Secretary of State within one month of receipt (EA 1980, s 12(3)). In *Milne* v *Wandsworth LBC* (1992) 90 LGR 515 the court considered whether two separate sets of objections, involving, in aggregate, fourteen objectors, amounted to an objection by ten or more persons for the purposes of section 12. The court held that the objections must come from one source or make explicit reference to each other. They did not in this case. Beldam LJ also observed (at p 524) that there is no express requirement for objectors to state the reason(s) for their objections. Thus, merely registering objection would seem to be sufficient. Note that an application for GM status is treated as a statutory objection (above).

Once a funding authority has been given joint or sole responsibility for ensuring the provision of sufficient school places in an area (following a transfer order under section 12 of the EA 1993; see pp 9–10 above), it may make objections for the purposes of section 12 of the EA 1980 (EA 1993, s 229(3)). At the same time, if the transfer order is for sole responsibility to be held by the funding authority, the LEA may only publish proposals for the establishment of a county school if the school is to replace a maintained school that is closing (EA 1993, Sch 2 para 7). Note that the transfer order, and thus the restriction on the LEA's power to establish a school, may relate to primary education, secondary education or both (see EA 1993, s 12(1)).

The next stage is approval or otherwise by the Secretary of State (see DES Circular 3/87), save that approval is not necessary if either: (i) the Secretary of State gives notice to that effect to the LEA within two months of receipt by him of the proposals; or (ii) if objections have been made under section 12(3) (EA 1980, s 12(5)). Secretary of State approval for the maintenance as a county school of a school which is currently a voluntary school is always required (EA 1980, s 12(4)). The main reason that the 1980 Act was drafted in such a way as to allow LEAs to proceed with certain changes (more especially closures) without seeking Secretary of State approval, was to cut down on delays resulting from administrative pressures on DES (now DFE) staff. Even in cases where approval may not be necessary the LEA will still have to 'determine whether the proposals should be implemented' – within four months of submission of the proposals to the Secretary of State (EA 1980, s 12(7)). Such determination must be notified to the Secretary of State (EA 1980, s 12(8)).

If the proposals *do* require the approval of the Secretary of State he may reject them, approve them without modification, or, after consultation with the LEA, approve them with such modification as he thinks desirable (EA 1980, s 12(6)). On the formalities of giving approval (etc) under section 12(6) for the establishment, significant alteration or closure of a school, see *R* v *Secretary of State for Education and Science ex p Hardy* [1988] The Times, 28 July. The LEA must implement the proposals as approved under section 12(6) or, where approval was not necessary, as determined by the LEA under section 12(7) (above) (EA 1980, s 12(9)).

(b) Voluntary schools

Proposals for the establishment of a voluntary school, which is to be maintained as such by an LEA, must be published (EA 1980, s 13(1) and the Education (Publication of School Proposals etc) Regulations 1993) by the persons wishing to establish the school. Before publishing their proposals, those persons must consult with the LEA and 'such other persons as appear to them to be appropriate' (EA 1980, s 13(1B), added by EA 1993, s 230(1)). Any guidance on consultation for this purpose by the Secretary of State must be taken into account by the person(s) concerned (*ibid*). A copy of the published proposals must be sent to the Secretary of State (*ibid*). Similar provision to that in section 12 (above) is made for objection to the proposals by local government electors (EA 1980, s 13(2) and (3)). An application for GM status counts as a statutory objection, as in the case of county schools. Such differences as there are in the procedures flow mainly from the fact that there is an extra party involved when a voluntary school is proposed. Thus, for example, when the Secretary of State decides to approve proposals with modification, both the LEA *and* the proposers must be consulted (EA 1980, s 13(4)).

All proposals for the establishment of a voluntary school require the approval of the Secretary of State; he may approve or reject them outright or approve them with modification (*ibid*). The LEA and proposers must implement approved proposals (EA 1980, s 13(5)). The LEA has a separate duty to provide any playing fields or buildings (other than school buildings) required by virtue of the approved proposals (s 13(6)). Subsequent modification by the Secretary of State of proposals to be implemented is possible (s 13(7)).

(c) Grant-maintained schools

The provisions governing the establishment of a GM school, and in particular the arrangements for a ballot of parents, are set out in *Appendix 1*. In addition to the route to GM status for existing maintained schools (see above), it is now possible for new schools to be established as GM schools. Proposals may be published either by a funding authority or by promoters.

(i) Proposals by a funding authority (EA 1993, s 48)

A funding authority may publish proposals for the establishment of a new GM school only if it has been given joint or sole responsibility for ensuring the provision of sufficient schools in an area (EA 1993, s 48). As this responsibility will relate to 'relevant education' - primary education, secondary education or both (the transfer order under section 12 of the EA 1993 will state which) – only a school offering 'relevant education' may be established. The proposals must be published in the 'prescribed manner' (EA 1993, s 48(3)(a) - Sch 3 and the Education (Publication of School Proposals and Notices) Regulations 1993, SI 1993 No 3113 make further provision) and sent to the Secretary of State. The funding authority must consult with 'appropriate' persons (the Minister said that this should include the LEA: *Hansard*, HL, Vol 544, col 1829), having regard to any guidance issued by the Secretary of State (EA 1993, s 48(4)).

The content of the proposals must include, *inter alia*, details of the proposed initial governors, the date of implementation of the proposals and arrangements for admission to the school (EA 1993, Sch 3, para 7; 1993 Regs, *op cit*). A statement must be annexed to the proposals, briefly describing the character of the proposed school (*ibid*, para 8). Objections may be made to the funding authority by the Further Education Funding Council (if further education provision is to be made at the school – see EA 1993, s 50(5)), by any ten or more local government electors for the area (see *Milne* v *Wandsworth LBC* (1992) (*op cit*) – discussed above, in (a)), by the governing body of any school affected by the proposals, and by the LEA concerned (EA 1993, Sch 3, para 10).

The Secretary of State's approval of the proposals is needed if he gives notice to that effect (within two months of the submission to him of the proposals), or if objections have been made (as above) and have not been withdrawn, or if the proposals name a sponsor of the school (EA 1993, s 51(1)). The Secretary of State has the same powers as in the case of proposals for the establishment of other types of school (s 51(3); see (a) above).

(ii) Proposals by promoters (EA 1993, s 49)

Promoters may publish proposals for a new GM school (EA 1993, s 49). This does not apply to LEAs (s 49(3)), but the Minister has explained that it includes voluntary bodies and proprietors of independent schools (see *Hansard*, HL, Vol 546, col 1158). The funding authority and other 'appropriate' persons must be consulted before the proposals are published (s 49(2)). The requirements as to publication applicable to proposals by funding authorities under section 48 (above) apply also to proposals under section 49 (see EA 1993, Sch 3, Pt II). But note that in the case of schools established under section 49 which have a particular religious character, the statement annexed to the proposals must state this character and the religious denomination in accordance with whose tenets religious education will be provided (EA 1993, Sch 3, para 8). Also, as the school may be housed on the land and in the buildings used, immediately before its establishment, for an independent school under a trust, the proposals must state any arrangements for the land (etc) to be held for the purposes of the new GM school (EA 1993, s 50(3)).

The same persons who may object to section 48 proposals (see above) may object to section 49 proposals, with the addition of the funding authority (EA 1993, Sch 3, para 11). Proposals under section 49 *always* require the approval of the Secretary of State (EA 1993, s 51(2)). The premises require the approval of the funding authority (s 51(6)).

(d) Approval of school premises: county and voluntary schools

Where proposals are made for the establishment of a county or voluntary school, the persons making the proposals must submit to the Secretary of State for approval particulars relating to the premises or proposed premises. Such particulars must be given at such time and in such form and manner as the Secretary of State may direct (EA 1980, s 14(1)). If a voluntary school is being proposed, the proposers must consult with the LEA before submitting particulars of premises to the Secretary of State (s 14(2)). Once approved, the particulars must be implemented (s 14(3)).

When the plans are submitted to him, the Secretary of State is empowered to grant exemption from certain legal requirements concerning the erection of buildings required for the purposes of a school (EA 1944, s 63(2)). Such buildings are not subject to building regulations under Part II of the Building Act 1984.

8. Alteration of schools and transfer of site

(a) Significant changes to county or voluntary schools

The procedures in sections 12 and 13 of the EA 1980 concerning establishment of a school, which were discussed earlier, also apply to a 'significant change in the character, or significant enlargement of the premises of', or 'transfer to a new site' of, a school which is a county or voluntary school (ss 12(1)(d) and 13(1)(b) respectively) (EA 1993, Pt II, Ch VI deals with such changes when they are to be made to a GM school).

(i) Change of character

A change of character shall:

> 'include, in particular, changes in character resulting from education beginning or ceasing to be provided for pupils above or below a particular age, for boys as well as girls or for girls as well as boys, or from the making or alteration of arrangements for the admission of pupils by reference to ability or aptitude.'
>
> (EA 1980, s 16(2)).

The EA 1993, s 103(1) uses exactly the same definition for the purposes of significant changes to GM schools under Ch VII of Pt II of that Act; see also s 103(2) of the 1993 Act.

(ii) Significant

A change is significant, in relation to the character of a school or the school's premises, if there is 'a substantial change in the function or size of the school' (EA 1944, s 114(1)). In *Vaughan* v *Solihull Metropolitan Borough* [1982] The Times, 25 May, Lawton LJ referred to a 'long-standing administrative practice which regarded a change of 20 per cent in unit totals as a guide to what constituted a reorganized school'; but this was in the context of the Burnham rules for determining head teachers' pay with reference to the size of a school. The 20 per cent figure has, in the past, been relevant in the case of reductions in school places. However, the procedure in the Education Act 1980 (s 15) governing reductions in school places at county or voluntary schools has gone (repealed by ERA 1988, Sch 13, Pt II). Reductions in admissions limits are now governed by ERA 1988, s 28, and SI 1988 No 1515. This is discussed in Chapter 7, Part 3(d).

The Government has said that schools will be able to specialise by selecting up to 10 per cent of their intake on the basis of prospective pupils' particular aptitude for, for example, technology, music, etc, and that this would not amount to a significant change in character for which approval would be needed. In addition, the Government has said that it wants to encourage schools to specialise by obtaining approval for a significant change of character so that, for example, 'technology schools' could be created (*Choice and Diversity*, paras 1.48 and 10.1).

The question of whether a change is 'significant' in this context is one for the Secretary of State to decide (EA 1944, s 67(4), as amended).

(iii) Transfer of site

If it is proposed that a county or voluntary school should be moved to a new site, Secretary of State approval will be required (see EA 1944, s 16, as amended). It will be necessary to show that the premises will meet required standards. Conditions relating to the transfer may be imposed (see, further, DES Circular 3/87, Annex 3).

(b) Significant changes to GM schools and transfers of GM schools to new site

Proposals for a significant change in the character, or a significant enlargement in the premises of, a GM school, or for a transfer of a GM school to a new site, must be published by the governors under requirements very similar to those for county and voluntary schools (EA 1993, s 96). The proposals will require the approval of the Secretary of State (s 98(1)). The governors' decision to publish proposals will be invalid unless affirmed at a further meeting held not less than 28 days after the first (s 96(8)). When publishing their proposals, the governors must state the time or times of their proposed implementation and the number of pupils to be admitted to the school following the changes (s 96(4)). They must also publish a statement 'describing any effect the implementation would have on provision at the school for pupils who have special educational needs' (s 96(5)(a)). Any changes affecting the religious character of the school require the consent in writing of the trustees of the school (if any) (s 96(2)).

The proposals must be posted at or near the main entrance to the school and in at least one conspicuous place in the area (or if there is more than one entrance, both or all of them). As soon as possible thereafter, details must be published in a local newspaper circulating in the area served by the school (Education (Publication of School Proposals and Notices) Regulations 1993, reg 4 (SI 1993 No 3113)).

As with proposed significant changes to county and voluntary schools, provision is made for objections to be made (direct to the Secretary of State) within two months of publication of the proposals (EA 1993, s 96(6) and (7)). The right to lodge objections has to be stated in the published proposals (s 96(5)(b)). Objections may be made by any ten or more local-government electors, the governing body of any school 'affected by the proposals' (i.e. other schools in the district), *any* LEA concerned (i.e. not just the one in whose area the school is situated) and the FEFC (if the proposals affect further education provision) (s 96(6)). If the school is moving to a new site in a different local authority area, the local government electors for that area may also object to the proposals (s 96(7)).

Proposals for a significant change of character, a significant enlargement of premises and the transfer of a school to a new site may, in the case of GM schools, also be proposed by a funding authority under section 97 of the 1993 Act. These proposals will not require the approval of the Secretary of State unless objections are made to them and are not withdrawn or the Secretary of State gives notice to the funding authority (within two months after the proposals have been submitted to him) that his approval is required (EA 1993, s 98(2)).

The Secretary of State's powers to approve, approve with modifications or reject the proposals, and the governors' duty to implement the proposals if approved, are identical to those applicable on the establishment of new GM schools (see page 53 above) (EA 1993, s 98(3)).

(c) Approval of school premises on significant changes to school

Where proposals are submitted to the Secretary of State under sections 12 or 13 of the EA 1980 for the making of a significant change in the character of a county or voluntary school, or a significant enlargement of its premises, approval for the premises or proposed premises must also be sought, under EA 1980, s 14, in the same way as when a school is established (see page 54 above). When such changes are proposed for a grant-maintained school, the Secretary of State's approval must be sought in like manner (EA 1993, s 99).

9. Rationalisation

(a) Introduction

Throughout the 1980s the Government pursued a policy of encouraging the removal of surplus capacity from schools, which had resulted from falling rolls in some areas. In Liverpool, for example, the number of primary-school pupils fell by around 30 per cent in the 1980s. Many LEAs embarked on a programme of rationalisation. After the ERA 1988, this practice in fact ran into difficulty as a result of some schools' application for GM status to avoid closure (see below).

Rationalisation was encouraged because '. . . there are limits to what the country can afford to spend on education. What we spend must be spent constructively and not wasted on keeping open empty classrooms and buildings' (*per* R Dunn MP, *Hansard*, HC, Vol 51, col 267, 20 December 1983). But despite the Government's exhortations (see, e.g., DES Circular 3/87, *Providing for Quality: The Pattern of Organisation to Age 19*) there were, by 1992, still some 1.5 million surplus places in schools in England and Wales (see *Choice and Diversity*, para 4.2). The Government acknowledged in the White Paper that many LEAs had closed and/or amalgamated schools in line with government policy. But new powers were promised, to hasten rationalisation in cases where LEAs were procrastinating.

(b) Compelling rationalisation: new powers under the EA 1993

The EA 1993 now provides that the Secretary of State can order a governing body of a voluntary school to put forward proposals for alteration of its school where there is an 'excessive' number of school places in an area (s 232(1)(b)). A power for LEAs to propose a significant change in the character of a voluntary school was in the Education Bill as originally drafted but was subsequently dropped. LEAs can, however, be ordered to publish proposals for the establishment, alteration or discontinuance of a school – again if local provision is 'excessive' in scale (EA 1993, s 232(1)(a)). There is also provision for the Secretary of State to put forward rationalisation proposals of his own if the LEA or governing body do not comply with his order (EA 1993, s 234). If there are sufficient statutory objections, the proposals must be referred to a public inquiry (see EA 1993, ss 235 and 236). Where a funding authority has been given joint or sole responsibility for ensuring that there are sufficient school places in an area (see Chapter 1, pp 9–10), it can also be ordered to publish proposals for establishment, alteration or closure of GM schools (EA 1993, s 232(2)). No order can require a change to be made to the religious character of a voluntary school (EA 1993, s 237(1)).

(c) School closures: procedures

We now turn to the procedures for closures (note that those set out below do not apply to proposals published by the Secretary of State under section 234 of the EA 1993 (referred to in (b) above)).

(i) County, voluntary and nursery schools

The provisions, referred to earlier, governing proposals for the establishment of county schools, including those relating to Secretary of State approval and the right of objection within two months of publication of the proposals, apply also to decisions to 'cease to maintain' any county, voluntary or nursery school (EA 1980, s 12(1)(c) and (e)). Note that where a closure is concerned, section 12 of the EA 1980 also applies to voluntary schools and the governors have a right to object (EA 1980, s 12(3)). These provisions were described in some detail (see pp 50–52). The governors may resolve to discontinue a voluntary school, and must serve on the LEA and Secretary of State two years' notice of their intention to do so (EA 1944, s 14(1)). But when expenditure on the school has been incurred by central government or the LEA, the Secretary of State's leave for discontinuance is required and he may attach such conditions for repayment of sums expended as he considers just. In *R* v *Secretary of State for Education and Science ex p ILEA and Another* [1990] The Times, 3 March the Secretary of State had granted leave for discontinuance of the Haberdashers' Aske's Schools at Hatcham, which were to be replaced by a city technology college. The Inner London Education Authority challenged the Secretary of State's refusal, on giving his permission for the discontinuance, to attach conditions requiring repayment of sums spent by the Authority in improving the schools. The application for judicial review was unsuccessful. The court held that while the purpose of the leave requirement (with conditions) is to protect the public interest where an educational asset has been created partly out of public funds, the Secretary of State has been granted a wide discretion by Parliament and is entitled to take into account various factors when deciding what requirements, if any, are just. In this case he was entitled to have regard to the fact that, first, the college would cater for pupils drawn from the same catchment area as before, and secondly, that the LEA would not have to make replacement provision if the school became a city technology college.

County or voluntary schools may be closed by order of the Secretary of

State after being managed by an Education Association under Part V of the EA 1993. This is discussed in Chapter 10.

(ii) Grant-maintained schools

Similar provisions to those above apply in the case of a decision by the governors to discontinue a GM school (discontinuance of GM schools is covered by EA 1993, ss 104–116, and the Education (Publication of School Proposals and Notices) Regulations 1993, SI 1993 No 3113). However, the procedure is more drawn out, presumably in order to minimise the chances of such schools deciding to discontinue. Since the introduction of GM schools, the Secretary of State has expected the discontinuance of such a school to be 'exceptional' (DES Circular 10/88, para 69). He actually has the power to cease maintaining such a school (EA 1993, s 109). This could be exercised if he considered a GM school to be 'unsuitable to continue as a grant-maintained school' because:

(i) 'the number of registered pupils at the school has become too small for sufficient and suitable instruction to be provided for them at reasonable cost'; and/or

(ii) 'the governing body have been guilty of substantial or persistent failure to comply or secure compliance with any other requirement imposed by or under this Act or any other enactment'.

(EA 1993, s 109(1)).

Notice must be given to the governing body stating the specific deficiencies and, if the deficiencies are considered irremediable, that the Secretary of State will cease to maintain the school on a stipulated date (EA 1993, s 109(3)). If the Secretary of State feels that the deficiencies can be remedied, he may specify in the notice the measures which should be taken (within six months or longer) by the governing body, and can later extend the deadline if he feels that they are making progress (*ibid*, s 109(4) and (5)). The notice may, in fact, subsequently be withdrawn or its terms varied (EA 1993, s 110).

The governors may themselves decide to publish proposals to discontinue a GM school, although the Secretary of State would not expect this to happen within ten years of the school acquiring its GM status (DES Circular 10/88, para 70). A governors' resolution to publish proposals relating to discontinuance must be confirmed at a subsequent meeting held not less than 28 days after that at which the resolution was passed, otherwise it will be of no effect (EA 1993, s 104(1)). After giving notice to the LEA as soon as may be practicable (s 104(3)), the governors have six months in which to publish their proposals in the prescribed manner (s 104(4) and the Education (Publication of School Proposals and Notices) Regulations 1993, SI 1993 No 3113). Objections may be made to the Secretary of State within two months of such publication, by the same groups who have such right on a proposed significant change (see page 56 above) – namely, any ten or more local government electors, the governing body of any school affected by the proposals, any LEA concerned and, in some cases, the FEFC (s 104(7)). The proposals require the approval of the Secretary of State (EA 1993, s 106(1)). Funding authorities may also publish proposals for the discontinuance of particular GM schools (EA 1993, s 105). If there are objections to a funding authority's proposals, or if the Secretary of State gives notice to the funding authority, these proposals will also require the Secretary of State's approval (EA 1993, s 106(2)).

On provision for disposal of property (etc) on the discontinuance of a GM school, see sections 111–116 of the EA 1993.

(d) Legal challenges to closures

In the face of falling rolls and the financial pressures on LEAs there has been rationalisation of provision which many parents and governors have in effect been unable to resist. This process is likely to continue; indeed, as we have seen, the 1993 Act has introduced a number of provisions which are designed to make it possible for LEAs to be placed under an obligation to close schools – if necessary, by order of the Secretary of State. Mounting a successful legal challenge to any decision to close a school has always been difficult and is certain to remain so. As in the past, reliance will mostly have to be placed on procedural grounds, such as failure to consult (as in *R* v *Brent ex p Gunning* (1985) 84 LGR 211), or departure from the statutorily-required procedure (see, for example, *Lee* v *DES* [1968] 66 LGR 211) – of which consultation in fact now forms part. The effect of the *Gunning* ruling was merely a delay for the authority, although with local elections due in the near future the parents hoped for a more permanent victory (see *Education*, 3 May 1985, p 390). This was one of several successful challenges on the ground of failure to consult (as noted above, at 6(a)). As pointed out earlier (*ibid*), and as the *Gunning* case illustrates, even in the absence of a statutory requirement to consult interested parties it has been possible to argue that on procedural grounds such consultation is necessary. Now, of course, there are statutory consultation duties, including a requirement on LEAs to consult the governing body (on which parents are represented) before formulating their proposals to close a county school.

Challenges on other procedural grounds have included one case where it was successfully argued that details of closure proposals, such as the date of closure, must be fixed by the education committee and not by its chairman alone (*R* v *Secretary of State for Education and Science ex p Birmingham City Council* (1985) 83 LGR 79). A further case concerned an LEA's decision to proceed with a school closure without having considered a report on the matter. It merely acted on a bare recommendation for closure from the education committee, which was held not to be a 'report' – consideration of which was required, by EA 1944 Sch 1, Pt II, para 7, before exercising certain functions in relation to education (*R* v *Kirklees Metropolitan Borough ex p Molloy* [1988] 86 LGR

115 - applied, but distinguished on the facts, in *Nichol* v *Gateshead Metropolitan Borough* (1989) 87 LGR 435).

Closures have also been challenged (without success) on the ground of denial of parental wishes contrary to section 76 of the EA 1944 (which requires LEAs to have regard to such wishes when exercising their powers and duties, so far as is compatible with the provision of efficient instruction and training and the avoidance of unreasonable expenditure: see *Wood* v *Ealing LBC* [1967] Ch 346). In relation to the equivalent provision in Scotland – the Education (Scotland) Act 1980, s 28(1) – see *Harvey* v *Strathclyde Regional Council* [1989] Public Law 160. The courts have held that parental wishes in general are only one of a number of factors falling to be considered by an LEA in exercising its functions under the Education Acts, and that the principle has to be weighed against these other factors (see, for example, *Watt* v *Kesteven County Council* (1955), and see also *R* v *Lambeth LBC ex p G* [1994] ELR 206). As noted earlier, generally any school closures which result in unequal provision in a locality, as between male and female pupils, such as in the case of the availability of more places at single-sex schools for boys than girls (as happened in *R* v *Secretary of State for Education and Science ex p Keating* (1985) 84 LGR 469; but see *R* v *Northamptonshire County Council ex p K* [1994] ELR 397 (CA), discussed on page 23 above), would result in unlawful sex discrimination in the performance of the duty to ensure that sufficient schools are available.

Chapter 3

Finance: local management of schools and other aspects of funding

1. Introduction

Various aspects of the funding of schools are discussed throughout this book. Funding plays a crucial role in shaping all areas of local schools provision and, not surprisingly, is often a central issue in policy debates. As most schools are still LEA-maintained, the amount available depends on local authority Standard Spending Assessments (SSAs). Indeed, as we saw in the previous chapter, even the level of funding of grant-maintained schools has in part depended on the LEA's funding allocation for schools, giving the GM school broadly the amount which would have been allocated to it had it remained LEA-maintained, although the introduction of a common funding formula will change the basis of funding.

In Chapter 2 the Assisted Places scheme in independent schools and financial support for voluntary schools were also examined. Like the funding of GM schools, they were included in the earlier chapter because they were inextricably linked to the other issues under discussion. This chapter is devoted, therefore, to discussion of the remaining, and most important and complex of all areas of financial provision affecting schools, Local Management of Schools ('LMS'). There is also discussion of 'grants for education support and training' (formerly known as education support grants) and 'section 11 funding'.

2. Local management of schools

(a) Introduction

LMS represents a spectacular reduction in LEA control. Within the overall parameters set by the approved formula for calculating a school's budget share, and apart from the retention by the LEA of a small percentage to cover central services, the governing body has the entire budget delegated to it to spend as it thinks fit. Governing bodies, the argument goes, are in a far better position to judge the real needs of the school than the LEA, and can respond to them more directly and efficiently. Spending decisions can be made more effectively by those who, because of their close involvement with the school, know what the chief priority is at any point in time – whether it be maintenance of the buildings, more teaching hours, new equipment, and so on. Decisions on such matters can be implemented quickly, as they will no longer have to compete for the attention of the various tiers of the LEA bureaucracy. A recent Audit Commission report has confirmed that these advantages are actually being enjoyed by schools (*Adding up the Sums: Schools' Management of their Finances* (1993), HMSO).

There has at no point been any suggestion that LMS necessarily results in reduced overall costs. This point was made clear in the Coopers and Lybrand report (*Local Management of Schools* (1988)), on which the key elements of the policy of LMS were based. The report was said to represent 'not a statement of Government policy, but . . . valuable advice for LEAs and schools on the principles of local management and the practical steps necessary for its effective implementation' (DES Circular 7/88, *Education Reform Act: Local Management of Schools*, para 26). The report stressed that 'LMS should not be seen as a means of cost reduction', but rather as a means of producing 'a more effective and responsive school system'.

The Government has emphasised that a key aim of LMS is to increase the education system's responsiveness to its 'clients – parents, pupils the local community and employers' (DES Circular 7/88, para 9). This in turn means greater accountability. Thus the governing bodies and head teachers who are making these decisions on expenditure must realise that, as Maclure has put it, 'more power at the school level means more power to make mistakes and fail' (*Education Re-formed* (1988), Hodder and Stoughton, p 54). As we shall see, the ERA 1988 provides protection for governors who act in good faith. In practice many decisions will be taken by, or at the behest of, the head teacher, to whom delegation of some of the governors' spending powers may be made (ERA 1988, s 36(5)(b)). (See Chapter 4 for discussion of delegation by governing bodies to head teachers.) In the past, most governing bodies have adopted what has been termed 'the "Woolwich" approach . . . where governors have automatically entrusted their responsibilities to headteachers in whose hands the investment feels "safe"' (Blanchard et al, *Managing Finance in Schools* (1989), Cassell, p 95). Now, however, governors are required to play a more direct role and will have to meet more frequently (as a whole board or in subcommittees), although some may not wish to increase their level of involvement. In June 1992 a governor recruitment campaign was launched by the Government because of the continuing difficulties of recruiting sufficient extra parent governors to fulfil the requirements of the Education (No 2) Act 1986 on the composition of governing bodies. All governors, including those representing local commerce and industry, may lack the time, expertise and experience to perform their new role in financial management. This lack of capacity has been described as one of the 'most uncertain and worrying' aspects of the Education Reform Act changes (Blanchard et al *op cit*, p 96).

A further major problem is the small amount of choice the governors have when it comes to spending their budget allocation. Some are left with little room to manoeuvre because of the way that schools' budget shares are determined (see *Adding up the Sums, op cit*, para 38). Moreover, some schools have become worse off than before LMS. Schools are, in effect, being charged the *actual* cost of their teachers, while receiving an allowance in their budget based on *average* teacher costs across all the LEA's schools. Total teachers' salaries costs typically amount to around 70% of a school's costs. The practice of averaging staff costs out in this way, thus ignoring the differences between schools in terms of their proportion of experienced teachers (whose salaries are relatively expensive), and basing the allocation largely around pupil numbers at the school, creates inequalities between schools. In a survey of over 1,500 schools by the National Association of Schoolmasters and Union of Women Teachers prior to the implementation of LMS, 58 per cent of the schools were expected to lose money, and 38 per cent to lose more than £25,000. Schools in each of the five worst off authorities – Liverpool, Manchester, Derbyshire, Salford and Rochdale – were expected to lose a combined total of over £100,000 (*The Times*, 2 October 1989). Many LEAs, including some which are Conservative controlled, decided to ignore the Government's initial guidelines on financial delegation schemes because they saw them as threatening some children's education (*The Observer*, 30 July 1989; *Times Educational Supplement*, 8 December 1989). In fact, the Government has since built better safeguards into LMS. In the revised guidance in 1991 the Government acknowledged the problems resulting from the way that LMS deals with teaching costs. A flexible element was introduced, allowing LEAs to compensate schools for extra inherited salary costs (DES Circular 7/91, *Local Management of Schools: Further Guidance*, para 44). However, the Audit Commission concluded in 1993 that devising LMS schemes which enable salary costs to be taken into account in full would be extremely problematic, indeed probably unworkable (*Adding up the Sums*, *op cit,* paras 12–16). (See, further House of Commons Education Committee, Second report, Session 1992–93, *Some Aspects of the Funding of Schools*, HC 419 (March 1993), paras 1–14.)

Having considered the background, we shall now examine the legal provisions. It should be borne in mind that while there is a uniform legal framework to LMS, there is variation between local schemes.

(b) The delegation scheme

By a date to be determined by the Secretary of State (fixed, under the power in ERA 1988, s 34(1), as 30 September 1989) each LEA in England and Wales was required to submit a financial delegation scheme for approval (ERA 1988, s 33(1)). Only county and voluntary schools maintained by the authority have to be covered by a scheme (*ibid*). In primary schools, the delegation scheme originally had to apply if a school had 200 or more pupils on a qualifying date in the previous financial year or was forecast to have such a number on a qualifying date in the year to which the budget related (ERA 1988, s 39(2) and (3)). It *could* apply to smaller primary schools, if the scheme so provided. The Secretary of State has had the power to amend section 39(3) to substitute a lower number than 200 (ERA 1988, s 41(1)(a)), and this power was exercised in 1991, when the Education (Financial Delegation for Primary Schools)

Regulations 1991 (SI 1991 No 1890, subsequently amended by SI 1992 No 110) were made. The regulations amended section 39, removing the 200-pupil threshold from primary schools. So the position now is that all county and voluntary schools in England and Wales are covered by LMS.

Such special schools as the Secretary of State directs are to be delegated a budget share. In any event, delegation to special schools in any English LEA *may* be included in a scheme, in relation to either or both the financial years 1994–95 and 1995–96, and, in any Welsh LEA, may be included in a scheme in any financial year. Furthermore, delegation to all special schools in England *must* be included in a scheme from 1996 (SI 1993 No 3104, reg 3).

All children at a school, including those aged under five years, whether in a reception or nursery class, are to be included in the calculation; but note that financial delegation does not apply to nursery schools.

Before preparing a scheme, the LEA must consult governing bodies of all schools it maintains, along with those of GM schools and GM special schools (ERA 1988, s 34(4), substituted by EA 1993, s 274(1)). The scheme will not come into force until it has been approved by the Secretary of State or until such date as the Secretary of State, on giving approval for the scheme, specifies (ERA 1988, s 34(5)). Once the scheme comes into force, delegation must take place within three years (ERA 1988, s 40(1) and (2)), or immediately, in the case of special schools (ERA 1988, s 43(2), substituted by s 276 of the EA 1993). The actual date will be provided for in the scheme (ERA 1988, s 40(2) and (3)), or by order of the Secretary of State (s 40(4)).

The schools initially covered by LMS under the ERA 1988 have enjoyed maximum delegation from 1 April 1993, although schools in inner London will not experience maximum delegation until 1 April 1995. Small primary schools will achieve maximum delegation over the next few years. The funding of special schools was brought within the scope of delegation schemes by the Education (Application of Financing Schemes to Special Schools) Regulations 1993 (SI 1993 No 3104), made under section 43 of the ERA 1988, as substituted by section 276 of the EA 1993. The run-in period of three years applicable to other schools covered by LMS will not apply to special schools.

An approved scheme must be published on its coming into force and on any other prescribed occasions (s 42(1) and the Education (Publication of Schemes for Financing Schools) Regulations 1989). A statement of financial provision for schools must be published by an LEA prior to the start of each financial year; it must contain various detailed particulars (see (g) below).

Such is the extent of the Secretary of State's powers that he can modify a scheme and/or attach such conditions to it as he considers desirable (ERA 1988, s 34(5)). Moreover, if an LEA fails to submit a scheme, or, in the Secretary of State's opinion, unreasonably departs from his guidance on the preparation of schemes (which LEAs are required to take into account: s 34(2)), the Secretary of State can impose a scheme of his own (s 34(6)). Before doing so, the Secretary of State must consult the LEA and 'such other persons as he thinks fit' (*ibid*). In such a case, the scheme is to be treated as if made by the LEA (s 34(7)).

(c) A school's budget share

The scheme must provide for the annual determination of each school's 'budget share' and for its delegation to the governing body as required or permitted under the scheme (s 33(2)). The Secretary of State expects school budgets to be given as cash limits. Any in-year cost increases may be covered by contingency provision in an LEA's school-specific reserve (SSR) built into their general schools budget (defined below), or, if the cost cannot be met from within the SSR, then the service-wide reserve may be tapped (DFE Circular 2/94, *Local Management of Schools* (1994), paras 70–74).

A key element in the determination is the size of the LEA's *general schools budget* for the year in question. The general schools budget (GSB) is defined as – 'the amount appropriated by the authority for meeting expenditure in that [financial] year in respect of all schools required to be covered in that year by any [delegation] scheme' (s 33(4)(a)) – i.e. direct costs such as salaries and repairs and maintenance plus indirect costs such as school transport, central administration, advisory services, and so on. Contingency provision at the start of the year for unpredictable costs arising out of an emergency (for example, gale damage) and which is not school-specific will not be included (DFE Circular 2/94, para 73). School-specific contingency provision, to cover, for example, unpredictable changes in pupil numbers, *is* to be included (*ibid*, paras 70–72). Coverage of special schools by LMS schemes means that expenditure by LEAs on such schools must also be included in the GSB. This means that there should be included in the GSB, for example, the cost of maintaining residential special schools and special schools established in a hospital and the cost of providing education for pupils with special educational needs in special units (see DFE Circular 2/94, *op cit*, paras 46–51).

From the general schools budget certain excepted items must be deducted. The residue is known as the *aggregated schools budget*, representing the amount available for allocation to schools. The aggregated schools budget (ASB) is defined as 'the part of the general schools budget of any . . . authority for any financial year which is available for allocation to individual schools under a (delegation) scheme . . . (being) the amount remaining after deduction from the amount of the general schools budget . . . excepted heads or items of expenditure . . . and . . . any other amounts which fall in accordance with the scheme to be deducted' (ERA 1988, s 33(4)(b)).

The excepted heads or items of expenditure – which are to be left out of account in determining the LEA's aggregated schools budget for the year in question – are comprised in the mandatory and discretionary exceptions. The *mandatory exceptions* (ERA 1988, s 38(4)) are:

(i) all expenditure of a capital nature;

(ii) repayments on loans to cover capital expenditure;

(iii) expenditure falling to be taken into account in determining central government grants of a prescribed description;*

(iv) such other items as may be prescribed.*

*The expenditure to be left out of account under these categories is defined presently in the Education (Financial Delegation to Schools) (Mandatory Exceptions) Regulations 1994 (SI 1994 No 277).

These mandatory exceptions under (iii) and (iv) comprise (in 1993–94 and 1994–95):

(*a*) expenditure falling to be taken into account in determining central government grants of the following types:

- Grants for the support of education and training, paid under Education (Grants and Awards) Act 1984, s 1, as amended;
- Grants paid under Local Government Act 1966, s 11;
- Grants for the education of travellers and displaced persons, paid under ERA 1988, s 210;
- TVEI grants paid under Employment and Training Act 1973, s 2, as amended;
- Urban Programme grants paid under the Local Government Grants (Social Need) Act 1969, s 1;
- (LEAs in Wales only) Bilingual Education Grant paid under EA 1980, s 21.

(*b*) expenditure falling to be taken into account in determining specific grants from the EC (EU) which support school activities.

Note that the LEA contribution towards these grants is also excluded under the regulations, although LEAs may devolve expenditure which is supported by specific grants outside their delegated budgets, 'i.e. earmarking funds for the specific purpose' (DFE Circular 2/94, para 59). The Government has consistently said that the scope of items excepted by regulations will be reviewed in the light of experience (DES Circular 7/88, para 62; DFE Circular 2/94, para 60).

Discretionary exceptions are the items which the LEA wishes to except from the GSB in addition to the mandatory exceptions. They are defined as 'other amounts which fall in accordance with the scheme to be deducted in determining the authority's aggregated budget for (the year in question)' (ERA 1988, s 33(4)(b)(ii)). LMS is based on the principle of maximum delegation, and when it was first introduced LEAs were advised that 'provision should be delegated unless there is a clearly identified need for the LEA to retain control' (DES Circular 7/88, para 63). Thus the expectation has been that the extent of any discretionary exceptions should be limited. Indeed, initially (for the first three years) most of the categories of discretionary exception could not exceed, in aggregate, more than 10 per cent of the general schools budget. The items covered by this limit included structural repairs and maintenance (a complex area, because of the need to distinguish between the LEA's and the governing body's area of responsibility for repairs under the LMS scheme), premises and equipment insurance (generally the LEA to remain responsible), educational psychologists, education welfare officers, peripatetic and advisory teachers, pupil support (uniforms, clothing, education maintenance allowances, etc), library and museum services, and other approved items. LEAs were expected to review the scope of excepted items within three years of their scheme's introduction and to reduce progressively the total cost of discretionary excepted items to 7 per cent of the general schools budget. However, this target has been replaced following the introduction of the *potential schools budget* (PSB) concept, under which the allocation requirement is presently 85 per cent of the PSB (see below).

The main category to be covered by the initial 10 per cent limit has been structural repairs and maintenance, which has proved a difficult area in practice. The Circular (7/88, *op cit*) recommended that a typical 'landlord-tenant' division should apply to responsibility for repairs. This means that the cost of day-to-day internal maintenance should be provided for in a school's delegated budget share. LEAs would be responsible for the structure and exterior of the buildings, playgrounds, car parks and perimeter walls. It was felt desirable, however, to allow schools to carry out minor emergency repairs to items which would otherwise fall within the LEA's responsibility, such as a leaking roof or a protruding paving stone (*ibid*, para 68). Because of statutory and common-law requirements concerning health and safety, however, schools have needed advice from their LEA. It has been suggested that schools should lean towards contractors vetted and approved by the LEA (see Blanchard et al, *Managing Finance in Schools*, *op cit* pp 55–57). Maintenance work must, in any event, be put out to competitive tender (the requirements concerning competitive tendering, and the interaction with LMS, are considered below). In aided and special agreement schools, *all* the costs of maintenance met by the LEA must be delegated to the governors, in the light of their 'greater experience . . . in dealing with maintenance matters' (DES Circular 7/88, para 71; see now DFE Circular 2/94, paras 85 and 86). DES Circular 7/88 offered a possible division of responsibilities, in a detailed breakdown in Annex A. This has been reproduced as Annex G to DFE Circular 2/94 and is set out as *Appendix 2* to this book.

Certain items were discretionary items although not subject to the initial 10 per cent limit, including premature retirement compensation and dismissal costs (which will, in fact, become mandatory exceptions from 1995–96), transitional excepted items and school meals. School meals is an expensive area, and one where provision must meet health and nutritional standards and the requirements of social security legislation as regards free provision to some pupils; here there could be no delegation until the expiry of any agreement entered into voluntarily by the LEA or under the competitive tendering requirements of the Local Government Act 1988. An LEA may bid to provide the meals service itself via its Direct Service Organisation.

Turning to the '*potential schools budget*' (PSB), this is a concept that arose out of the Government's review of LMS, and was incorporated into its revised guidance which was published in 1991. The aim was (and remains) to provide for 'a minimum requirement for the allocation of resources through the formula' (DES Circular 7/91, para 27). This minimum requirement is based on a prescribed percentage of the PSB. The PSB consists of the GSB less expenditure on the mandatory exceptions and prescribed discretionary exceptions. For the financial years 1993–94 and 1994–95 the only discretionary items falling into this category (i.e. lying outside the PSB) are home-to-school transport and school meals (discussed above), although the scope for delegation is described as 'tightly constrained' (see DFE Circular 2/94, paras 62–65). If delegation does occur the costs are included in the PSB. Four additional areas of expenditure will be classed as discretionary exceptions from 1995–96 (pupil support, governors' insurance, LEA initiatives (for example in the areas of curriculum or management development) and school-specific contingencies (see DFE Circular 2/94, paras 66–74)).

The reason that transport and meals are excluded is that these items show considerable variation across LEAs and are determined partly by statutory obligations and partly by circumstances. Funding for school transport, for example, 'does not easily lend itself to allocation by formula at the outset of the financial year, since it relates very largely to statutory obligations which can only be costed, at the level of the individual school, once all its pupils' addresses are known' (DFE Circular 2/94, para 64).

Most LEAs must delegate 85 per cent of the PSB – a figure which replaced the target of 7 per cent of GSB for discretionary exceptions, referred to earlier, from April 1993 (but, in the case of inner London LEAs, not until April 1995). When the list of discretionary items lying outside the PSB increases in 1995–96, the percentage of the PSB which must be delegated will increase to 90 per cent – apart from in inner London LEAs, where the percentage will not rise to 90 per cent until 1996–97 (see further DFE Circular 2/94, Annex F).

Of the excepted items counting towards the permitted percentage 'holdback' by the LEA, one of the most problematic has, as indicated above, been structural repairs and maintenance. Whilst not seeking to be overly prescriptive, and whilst accepting that there is scope for delegation of responsibility for structural maintenance to schools, the Government has expressed concern that schools which have taken on a greater share of such responsibility may find that their budgets could be forced into deficit by substantial bills resulting from unpredictable repair needs (DFE Circular 2/94, para 83). Accordingly, if this kind of additional delegation occurs, schemes need to make provision to deal with such eventualities, such as by leaving the LEA with a central fund to distribute funds to individual schools facing large bills. Other items in respect of which funds should be held back include certain elements of supply-staff costs and salary safeguarding (most of these are expected to be delegated via the ASB), LEA support teams for pupils with special educational needs (see DFE Circular 2/94, paras 90–93), residual transitional excepted items (see para 94), and support for schools requiring special measures. Certain funds which are outside the scope of delegation under LMS (for example, funds supplied by central government for expenditure in schools for specific purposes) may nevertheless be earmarked for 'devolved' funding, and schools will have to account separately for this (*ibid*, paras 96–98).

(d) The budget share formula

Provision in a delegation scheme must be made for the determination, in each financial year, of each school's budget share. Such determination is to be in accordance with 'a formula laid down by the scheme for the purpose of dividing among all such schools the aggregated budget for that year of the local education authority concerned' (ERA 1988, s 38(1)). 'Formula' is, for this purpose, defined as 'methods, principles and rules of any description, however expressed' (s 38(2)). The formula need not be in algebraic form, 'but it must apply a consistent set of criteria for distributing resources' (DFE Circular 2/94, para 101).

The Government expects that the formula should provide for objective needs. It is hoped that through the opportunity afforded to take a fresh look at the way schools in an area are funded, a more 'equitable' basis for allocation of resources than applied before LMS will operate. Nevertheless, there are innumerable variables which affect the amount needed to operate a particular school efficiently. In many cases, these include historic costs of sufficient magnitude to warrant allowance being made in the allocation formula for them. For example, some school buildings, because of the design or specification favoured at the time they were built, may be more expensive to heat or clean.

The Government chose as the key determinant of the resource allocation the numbers and ages of pupils at the school. The law states that the delegation scheme *must* take into account these indicators (ERA 1988, s 38(3)(a)) and *may* take into account 'any other factors affecting the needs of individual schools which are subject to variation from school to school' (s 38(3)(b)) (see below). Note that in special schools there is to be less emphasis on pupil-numbers-led funding (see below). In sections (i) and (ii) below, the discussion concerns county and voluntary schools only. Section (iii) is concerned exclusively with special schools.

(i) Numbers, ages and any special educational needs of pupils

Since the introduction of LMS, the number of pupils in each school, weighted for differences in their ages, has been the central determinant of the school's objective needs (see DES Circular 7/88, para 104). The aim of the pupil-led basis of funding is said to be not only to help to ensure that schools' particular needs are met, but also to give schools a clear incentive to attract and retain pupils (DES Circular 7/88, para 105; DFE Circular 2/94, para 104). Until the reforms introduced under DES Circular 7/91, the total amount allocated on this basis had to account for at least 75 per cent of the aggregated schools budget. The 1991 Circular announced that the Secretary of State would require this proportion to be raised to 80 per cent from 1 April 1993 (1 April 1995 in the 12 inner London boroughs) and would permit a broader range of factors to be taken into account in weightings in certain cases (see below).

There is no prescribed, uniform, method of working out the actual weightings; the Secretary of State merely requires that they should be applied by the LEA consistently across all county and voluntary schools covered by the delegation scheme. They might, however, be expected to take into account assumptions about teaching costs at various ages, given that teaching costs are the principal costs of providing education. Although no examples are given, a typical model might be: up to age 7 – weighting of 1.5; ages 7–10 – weighting of 1.0; ages 11–16 – weighting of 1.85; ages 16–18 – weighting of 2.35.

Consistent weighting will also be needed in respect of nursery classes and pupils with special educational needs (see ERA 1988, s 38(3)(b)). The requirements vis-à-vis special educational needs were altered by Circular 7/91 (by 1 April 1993) so that the pupil-led element of the formula could, if the LEA wished it, include not only the age factor but also weightings for pupils with special educational needs (but, in respect of statemented pupils, this can only apply where provision for such pupils is delegated). In the case of pupils without statements, the total amount allocated on this basis may not exceed 5 per cent of the actual schools budget (DFE Circular 2/94, para 105). On the position of pupils educated in special units in mainstream schools and pupils with statements of special educational needs who are placed individually or in small groups, see DFE Circular 2/94, paras 107–111.

Where pupils are excluded in the course of a financial year, there will be an adjustment to the budget of the excluding and receiving schools (EA 1993, s 262; DFE Circulars 2/94, paras 123–127, and 17/94).

The effect of basing the budget share largely around age-weighted pupil numbers was discussed earlier (at p 64). Because the allocation will reflect average teaching costs across the LEA's schools, some schools, whose costs are higher, might lose out. Particularly hard hit would be those schools carrying large numbers of experienced, and thus higher paid, teachers, and those with a lower than average staff-pupil ratio. Whilst adjustment may be possible, it will take some time. Moreover, small schools will attract fewer resources, enabling them to pay for fewer teachers (at a time when the statutory provision now demands a wider expertise) and less equipment. Consequently formulae may make provision for the additional costs in small schools (i.e. schools with up to 10 teachers, excluding the head or deputy, or 330 pupils) (see DFE Circular 2/94, paras 129–131). This provision must be accommodated within the 20 per cent of the ASB which is to be allocated on other than a pupil-numbers (etc) basis.

(ii) Other factors affecting the needs of individual schools

Further factors which might call for adjustment in budget allocations include the extent of social deprivation in the area, the location in which the premises are situated (which might, for example, make the school prone to vandalism), the type of premises (e.g. design – perhaps it has a flat roof: such roofs are prone to leak; or perhaps it is difficult to heat), the condition of the premises, and whether there are any special facilities such as a swimming pool (see DFE Circular 2/94, paras 134–138).

(iii) Special schools

The Government's decision to extend LMS to special schools was informed by a specially commissioned report by management consultants Touche Ross (*Extending Local Management to Special Schools* (1990)). To make LMS feasible for special schools, funding had to be based mainly on the places provided, rather than on pupil numbers. DES Circular 7/91 advised that LEAs must determine the balance between place and pupil elements, although the pupil element would be expected to be set at a 'low level' (para 86 – see now DFE Circular 2/94, para 117, below). The Circular also stated that other factors, such as premises-related costs and costs related to exceptional needs, would also be taken into account under approved formulae (para 80). The relevant guidance is presently in DFE Circular 2/94, paras 113–121.

So far as the *place element* is concerned, the costs of teaching and non-teaching staff and specialist equipment needed by children likely to occupy a place will be taken into account in assigning value to each place. Relative weightings are to be attached to each of the place factors (para 116). The number of places to be used in the formula should be 'set at a level which will permit' a stable resource base to be maintained, whilst also allowing for the admission of pupils whose needs are identified during the year' (para 114).

The *pupil element*, which, as in other LEA-maintained schools, will be based around weightings for ages (etc), will reflect the cost of 'consumable items such as books, stationery and inexpensive equipment, which are related to actual pupil numbers, and, for some older pupils, examination fees' (para 117).

Further factors, such as the costs resulting from outreach work (see paras 118–121), premises costs, contingency provision, and small schools' higher unit costs (see (i) and (ii) above), would all need to be taken into account.

(e) Transitional arrangements

Inherited costs may make certain schools' particular requirements extraordinarily great. The delegation scheme may provide for a period of phased adjustment where necessary. A transitional period of up to four years has been allowed. The transitional period, in respect of county and voluntary schools outside inner London, ended on 1 April 1994. It ends for the inner London boroughs, and for all special schools, on 1 April 1996. After this period, variations in a school's total budget between years may be limited by LEAs (if their scheme so provides) to 5 per cent in constant prices (DFE Circular 2/94, para 141).

The Government has stated that it will look sympathetically at transitional arrangements designed to ease the difficulties faced by schools with above-average staff costs (DES Press Release 253/89, 3 August 1989). DES Circular 7/91 made provision for 'selective extension to the 4-year transition period' when needed because of high inherited staff costs, where, *inter alia*, a school faced annual reductions of 1 per cent or more in its total budget for each year over the 4-year period (para 115), and this is also provided for in DFE Circular 2/94 (para 140).

(f) Conditions attached to delegation

Delegation of the school's budget share to the governing body may be subject to conditions under the scheme (ERA 1988, s 39(11)). These conditions 'may in particular relate to' the following (s 39(12)):

- (i) the arrangements for management of expenditure from the delegated sum and transactions (and in particular for authorising such expenditure or transactions);
- (ii) the keeping and audit of accounts and records relating to expenditure;
- (iii) the provision to the LEA of information, in the form of copies of accounts and records, and other documentation and information as required.

The Circular (2/94, *op cit*) contemplates that LEAs should monitor carefully financial management by individual schools (see also (k) below), whilst allowing governing bodies a certain amount of freedom. For example, schools will be expected to purchase goods and services on a value for money basis, and LEAs are told that they should consider advising the governors on the best arrangements for securing that they receive value for money. At the same time, schools must be able to purchase from whichever source they think most appropriate taking into account not only price but also quality and convenience (para 160). Schools (especially secondary schools) will need to open external bank accounts (para 161).

The Government's view is that there is scope for LEAs to relax some of the detailed conditions and requirements placed on schools; DFE Circular 2/94 states that 'such conditions should be no more restrictive than is reasonably necessary to enable the LEA satisfactorily to discharge its own statutory responsibilities' (para 143).

(g) Publication of schemes and financial statements

Section 42 of the ERA 1988 provides for publication of LMS schemes. Such publication is to be made in the prescribed manner (under the Education (Publication of Schemes for Financing Schools) Regulations 1993) on the coming into force of a scheme and on other occasions (ERA 1988, s 42(1)), such as when a scheme is varied. The LEA must make copies of the scheme available to governing bodies and head teachers of schools covered by it and to governing bodies of GM schools in the area, and must ensure that copies are available at public libraries and the authority's offices.

LEAs are also required, *before the start of each financial year*, to prepare a statement of intended financial provision in respect of county and voluntary schools (ERA 1988, s 42(3)). This statement is known as a 'budget statement' (Education (School Financial Statements) (Prescribed Particulars etc) Regulations 1994 (SI 1994 No 323), reg 1(3)). This statement must contain various particulars relating to the financial year in question, such as:

- the general schools budget;
- the aggregated budget;
- amounts deducted in arriving at the aggregated schools budget (the regulations break these down into over 30 separate items);
- the allocation formula used in the scheme;
- planned expenditure per pupil arising from the division of the school's budget share.

(s 42(4) and (5), as amended by EA 1993, s 275(1)).

The regulations (*op cit*) require budget statements which contain a detailed breakdown of expenditure to be prepared in four parts (reg 2). They must be set out in the form specified by Schedules 1–4 to the regulations. Budget statements must be published 'before the beginning' of the financial year to which they relate (reg 7(1)).

At the end of the financial year an 'outturn statement' must be prepared (Education (School Financial Statements) (Prescribed Particulars etc) Regulations 1994, *op cit*, reg 1(3)), giving information concerning actual expenditure incurred on all schools covered by the scheme, and the expenditure incurred, or treated as incurred, per school (ERA 1988, s 42(6); see further reg 5 of the regulations *op cit*). The form of such a statement and the manner and timing of its publication are prescribed in the regulations (*op cit*). The regulations require the statement to be in two parts, one relating to expenditure on all schools, the second on expenditure on each school (reg 4). The statement must be published before 1 November next following the financial year to which it relates (reg 7(2)).

The LEA must furnish governing bodies of schools covered by LMS and governing bodies of GM and GM special schools in the area with a copy of the above statements; for their part, the governors must make such statements available for inspection (without charge) at the school at all reasonable times (ERA 1988, s 42(8) (as substituted by EA 1993, s 275(1)(d)) and s 42(9)). The Secretary of State may direct an LEA or any class or description of LEAs, or LEAs generally, to require the Audit Commission to certify any statement prepared by an authority under section 42 (ERA 1988, s 42A, inserted by EA 1993, s 275(2)).

Note that a statement containing similar categories of information on expenditure to those required by section 42 has also had to be prepared in respect of schools *not* covered by delegation schemes (see ERA 1988, s 50, and the Education (Pre-Scheme Financial Statements) Regulations 1989, as amended). Such schools have enjoyed only limited control of their own budgets – over expenditure on books, equipment, stationery and other prescribed heads (ERA 1988, s 49). All LEA schools are now covered by LMS schemes, unless the right to a delegated budget has been suspended (see below).

(h) Actual delegation

A sum equal to the school's budget share is to be 'put at the disposal of' the governing body of the school at such times and in such manner as provided for in the delegation scheme (ERA 1988, s 36(1)-(3)). The governors may, subject to any stipulations in the scheme, spend the school's budget share in such a way 'as they think fit for the purposes of the school' (ERA 1988, s 36(5)(a)). This appears, on the face of it, to be a far-reaching provision which concentrates much control in the hands of governors but also the responsibility of making hard choices about how the budget might best be allocated. Governors will have to work in close harmony with senior staff at the school and, in particular, the head teacher, who will be expected to make recommendations to the governors in addition to drawing up school development plans. The link between the budget and the school's objectives, as outlined in the school development plan, should be made clearer by schools, according to the Audit Commission (*Adding Up the Sums: Schools' Management of their Finances* (1993), para 59). The governors will be able to delegate to the head teacher powers of expenditure over any part of the delegated budget – to such extent as is permitted by the scheme (s 36(5)(b)). But research suggests that governing bodies have, in fact, been too liberal in their delegation of powers of expenditure to head teachers, leaving governors with insufficient control over actual expenditure (Audit Commission, *Adding Up the Sums* (*op cit*)) and placing head teachers under undue strain (M Arnott et al, *The Impact of Local Management on Schools* (1992)).

(i) Competitive tendering

Local authorities are required by legislation (the Local Government Act 1988 and Local Government, Planning and Land Act 1980) to put certain activities out to competitive tender. Compulsory competitive tendering is set to be extended into a number of white-collar activities over the next year or so, including finance, information technology, property management and legal services (see DFE Circular 2/94, Annex H). LMS schools may be affected by compulsory competitive tendering, in that resources for certain services, such as school cleaning or grounds maintenance, will be delegated to them. Schools which choose to obtain the service from their LEA will find that the service will either be provided by a private contractor who is under contract with the LEA or by the LEA's direct labour organisation. Alternatively, the school may wish to hire a contractor direct. The provisions on compulsory competitive tendering will not apply in this situation, although the school must engage the contractor in accordance with the LEA's standing orders on tendering and contracting and in accordance with the terms of the LMS scheme. EU procurement directives may also be relevant in respect of contracts involving relatively large sums (see DFE Circular 2/94, paras 212–216).

If, however, the school wishes to employ staff to work in a school-based direct service organisation, it will be required to subject the required service to the competitive tendering process (the Local Government (Direct Service Organisations) (Competition) Regulations 1993 will apply – see DoEnv Circular 10/93, *Competition in the Provision of Local Authority Services*). Generally, the rules will not apply to voluntary aided schools (but see DFE Circular 2/94, para 222). Services likely to be covered by compulsory competitive tendering (CCT) are, according to DFE Circular 2/94, building and maintenance work, building cleaning, grounds maintenance, school catering, repair and maintenance of vehicles and sports and leisure management (para 194). The requirements as to CCT include advertising the tender and drawing up a detailed specification of the work (with a maximum and minimum period for which the contract would run – for example, three years and four years, respectively, in the case of building cleaning and grounds maintenance) (see further DFE Circular 2/94, paras 197 and 219–221).

(j) Governors' liability

Governors are protected by section 36(6) of the ERA 1988 against personal liability in respect of losses incurred by doing anything in good faith in their management of the school budget. This is in addition to the protection now afforded by incorporation of governing bodies (see p 108 below). Insurance cover in respect of any losses caused as a result of negligence by governors is expected to be arranged by the LEA, is a discretionary exception deductible from the general schools budget in calculating the aggregated budget (see above), and will fall outside the PSB from 1 April 1995 (or 1996 in inner London boroughs). Governors are advised to make sure that the LEA has made appropriate insurance arrangements (DFE Circular 2/94, para 68). Governors' liability is discussed more fully in Chapters 4 (at Part 11) and 13.

(k) Evaluation and accountability

LEAs will have to monitor carefully the management of schools' delegated budgets, not only in view of LEAs' duties concerning implementation and provision of the National Curriculum and their wider duties under the Education Acts, but also because of the need for provision to be effective and efficient. LEAs are required to incorporate into their schemes procedures for monitoring (see above).

DFE Circular 2/94 spells out how the Government believes LEAs should approach the task of monitoring schemes effectively. LEAs will be expected to develop:

'(1) effective financial monitoring arrangements; (2) appropriate management information systems in schools and centrally; and (3) performance indicators for the financial and wider management functions of the governing bodies of schools with delegated budgets: these should be based on and take into account the indicators used by schools themselves'.

(DFE Circular 2/94, para 166).

An aim of effective monitoring is to identify potential problems so that they can be tackled before they become serious. In some cases LEAs may make use of various sanctions. They have a power (under ERA 1988, s 37(1) and (2)) to *suspend financial delegation* on giving one month's notice to the governors (and a copy to the head teacher). The reason(s) for suspension should be specified in the notice. This power may be exercised if the governing body:

'(*a*) have been guilty of a substantial or persistent failure to comply with any requirements applicable under the scheme; or

(*b*) are not managing the appropriation or expenditure of the sum put at their disposal for the purposes of the school in a satisfactory manner'.

(ERA 1988, s 37(1)).

What amounts to a failure to deal with the money in a 'satisfactory manner' will be for the LEA to determine; clearly disputes are possible in view of the imprecision of the wording.

In certain cases the LEA will be able to suspend the right to a delegated budget before the date specified in the notice. They may do so if it appears necessary because of the 'gross incompetence or mismanagement on the part of the governing body or other emergency' (ERA 1988, s 37(3)). In such a case the governors must immediately inform the Secretary of State of their action and the reason(s) for it (*ibid*).

LEAs may also suspend a school's right to a delegated budget if, for the purposes of Part V of the EA 1993, the school is failing to provide pupils with an acceptable standard of education (EA 1993, s 215). Any such suspension will have effect as if made under section 37 of the ERA 1988, so the requirements described in the following paragraph will be applicable to suspensions under the 1993 Act as well, save that the right of appeal under section 37(8)(a) of the ERA 1988 is disapplied (by EA 1993, s 215(4)).

Any suspension must be *reviewed* by the LEA before the beginning of every financial year that it remains in force (ERA 1988, s 37(5)(a)). The LEA's decision thereon must be communicated in writing to the governing body and head teacher (ERA 1988, s 37(6)). The LEA must give the governors and head teacher an opportunity to make representations before it makes its decision (ERA 1988, s 37(5)(b); DFE Circular 2/94, para 245). Suspensions should be revoked when the LEA considers it appropriate (ERA 1988, s 37(5)(c)), such revocation to take effect at the start of the next financial year (s 37(7)). The governors have a right of *appeal* to the Secretary of State over the suspension or the continuation of it (s 37(8)) and he may allow or reject the appeal (s 37(9)(a)). The Secretary of State must have regard, when making his or her decision, to 'the gravity of the default on the part of the governing body and the likelihood of its continuance or recurrence' (s 37(9)(b)).

When delegation is suspended, the LEA's duty (in ERA 1988, s 36(2)) to put a school's budget share at the disposal of the governors will not apply in relation to the particular school's governing body (ERA 1988, s 37(4)). However, the school will still be funded at the level of its budget share – but the governors will not have power over the way that this share is spent. Moreover, their powers concerning staffing (see ERA 1988, ss 44–46) will also be suspended (DFE Circular 2/94, para 244).

(l) Variation of schemes

Under section 35 of the ERA 1988, as substituted by section 274 of the EA 1993, LEAs may vary LMS schemes. Variations may be 'significant' or 'minor'. The Secretary of State may specify, by order, what descriptions of variation shall be regarded as 'significant' (ERA 1988, s 35(4)). Under the previous version of section 35, the Secretary of State made the Education (Significant Variation of Schemes for Financing Schools) Order 1990, and any new order is likely to make similar provision (see further DFE Circular 2/94, paras 16–26).

If the LEA proposes to make a minor variation, it must give the Secretary of State brief particulars of the nature of the proposed revision (ERA 1988, s 35(5)). The LEA may be required to send the Secretary of State a copy of the proposed scheme within two months (ERA 1988, s 35(6)). There is no statutory duty to consult with governing bodies over a minor variation. Where, however, a significant variation is proposed, the LEA must consult with the governing body and head teacher of all schools maintained by the LEA plus the governing bodies of GM and GM special schools in the area (ERA 1988, s 35(3)). The proposals for a significant variation must be sent to the Secretary of State, whose approval will be necessary (*ibid*). The Secretary of State may approve the significant variations with or without modification and subject to any conditions he sees fit to impose (*ibid* and ERA 1988, s 34(5)).

(m) New schools

New schools (see ERA 1988, s 48(2)) of a type to which a delegation scheme applies will be subject to LMS from the date their temporary governing body is constituted. A school which the LEA proposes to maintain where it did not before is regarded as a new school for this purpose. Generally speaking, new schools will be treated in the same way as other schools falling within the scope of a financial delegation scheme (ERA 1988, Sch 4). There may be modifications in the scheme, for example to make allowance for the fact that significant teaching salary costs will not arise prior to opening, or to permit delegation to be phased in (DFE Circular 2/94, Annex D).

3. Grants for the support of education and training

The Government has recognised that a considerable amount of support and in-service training is necessary for schools striving to cope with the challenges imposed by the National Curriculum, LMS and other changes. Consolidation of the two schemes under which funds for curriculum and management support etc, plus in-service training, are provided to LEAs – the Education Support Grants (ESG) scheme and LEA Training Grants Scheme (LEATGS) – will be effected by the EA 1993. There has been increasing co-ordination of these schemes, resulting in the GEST (Grants for Education Support and Training) programme, although the schemes have remained distinct. Under section 278 of the EA 1993, the LEA Training Grants Scheme will formally disappear, although grants for the same purposes will still be available to 'persons other than local education authorities'. LEAs will receive support henceforth via 'grants for the support of education and training' under the amended Education (Grants and Awards) Act 1984 (see below).

Pupils and parents have become familiar with the setting aside of five days in the year ('Baker days') for staff training covering preparation for the National Curriculum, records of achievement, and other aspects of the 'new' curriculum. These have in fact been able to be supported via LEATGS and/or ESGs. Areas supported specifically by LEATGs in 1993–94 included training for school management (£3m), head teacher mentoring (£1.4m), designated courses for enhancing primary teachers' subject knowledge (£25m), training for special educational needs (£10m), training for educational psychologists (£3.5m), training for the development of vocational qualifications in schools (£5.5m) and training of articled teachers (£10m).

Under the Education Support Grants scheme, the Secretary of State has provided an annual grant to LEAs to meet part of the cost of certain (prescribed) heads of expenditure (Education (Grants and Awards) Act 1984 and annual Education Support Grants Regulations). Up to 60 per cent of the cost of expenditure has generally been met under the scheme (it was 70 per cent prior to 1 April 1990). Under the 1989–90 Education Support Grant allocation, for example, the Government agreed to provide support in respect of up to £4.9m for governor training and £25m for local financial management – to cover the introduction of management information systems into schools, the establishment of central LEA teams for LMS preparation and implementation, and the training of school administrative staff. For 1993–94, allocations included 60 per cent grants towards, *inter alia*, up to £29m of expenditure on general support for school management, £16.5m for LMS and £85m in general support for the basic curriculum (see DFE Circular 10/92, *op cit*). LEAs have had to bid for available funds. Generally provision has been made for all LEAs to receive grants, subject to making satisfactory bids.

Under the arrangements provided for by the EA 1993, education support grants are known as 'grants for the support of education and training' (amendment of Education (Grants and Awards) Act 1984 by s 278 of the EA 1993). The ceiling of 60 per cent on the prescribed proportion of expenditure which may be met by grants will be removed, but so far only a small number of areas of expenditure attract 100 per cent grants; 60 per cent is the prescribed maximum for others (see Education (Grants for the Support of Education and Training) Regulations 1994 (SI 1994 No 612)). It is possible for conditions attached to grants made to the LEA to require certain spending decisions to be delegated to prescribed persons (s 1(4A) of the 1984 Act, inserted by s 278 of the 1993 Act; see the 1994 regs, *op cit*). The DFE had already taken steps to devolve grants to schools: in 1993/94 conditions attached to two broad grants, General Support for School Management and General Support for the Basic Curriculum and Assessment, required such devolution. The Secretary of State 'believes that schools should have a greater role in deciding the precise deployment of GEST funds' (DFE Circular 10/92, *op cit*, para 30). This has continued under the arrangements for GEST support in 1995/6 (see DFE Circular 18/94). In particular 80 per cent of the new block grant on 'School Effectiveness' will have to be devolved to schools. The GEST programme for 1995/1996 also includes new grants on, *inter alia*, child protection and drugs prevention. Some grants will now be allocated to LEAs on a formula basis which means that allocations are related to pupil or school numbers etc. For others, bids will still be required (see DFE Circular 18/94, *Grants for Education Support and Training 1995–1996*).

4. Grants for the education of travellers and displaced persons

Section 210 of the ERA 1988 enables the DFE to pay grants to LEAs in respect of provision of education for travellers or displaced persons. Travellers are persons 'of no fixed abode' and those who leave their main abodes to live elsewhere for much of the year (ERA 1988, s 210(2)(a)). The relevant DFE circular defines travellers as:

> 'Gypsy and other Travellers whether living on official long or short stay sites or on unofficial sites, and circus, fairground and bargee families. Previously nomadic Travellers settled in housing within the previous two years are also included'.
>
> (DFE Circular 11/92, *Education Reform Act 1988: Specific Grant for the Education of Travellers and of Displaced Persons*, para 11).

So far as displaced persons are concerned, the DFE draws a distinction between, for example, homeless persons who have been provided with bed and breakfast accommodation and persons who are refugees or similarly displaced persons living in a special camp or other discrete accommodation. The former are considered to be outside the scope of the grant, since their accommodation is not provided exclusively for displaced persons (see reg 4(c)).

The Education (Grants) (Travellers and Displaced Persons) Regulations 1993 (SI 1993 No 560) provide the scheme under which the grants are paid. Grants are paid at the rate of 75 per cent of the approved expenditure (reg 5). The Schedule to the regulations lists the items in respect of which grants are payable. Included are the cost of providing distance learning or outreach work and transport and uniform grants. LEAs and GM schools have to bid for section 210 grants. The overall amount available for distribution to applicants is limited in accordance with the Government's public expenditure plans for the year in question.

GM schools may be paid special purpose grants for similar purposes to the above (Education (Grant-Maintained Schools) (Finance) Regulations 1993).

5. Section 11 funding

The Home Secretary is empowered by section 11 of the Local Government Act 1966 to pay grants to local authorities:

> 'who in his opinion are required to make special provision in the exercise of any of their functions in consequence of the presence within their area of substantial numbers of immigrants from the Commonwealth whose language or customs differ from those of the community'.

The Home Secretary may determine which kinds of expenditure the grants may cover and, with the consent of the Treasury, the amount available for distribution. Section 11 funds may also be allocated to governing bodies of GM schools, proprietors of CTCs and further education corporations (sixth-form colleges and FE colleges) (ERA 1988, s 211, as amended by FHEA 1992, Sch 8 para 47). The overall amount provided to LEAs via section 11 funding was cut back quite severely in 1994 (see *The Guardian*, 15 March 1994).

Chapter 4

School government

1. Introduction

School governing bodies had their role changed dramatically under the education legislation of the 1980s. LEAs' powers and responsibilities with regard to the running of schools were restricted. In many areas over which traditionally the LEA had, in the majority of schools, been autonomous, such as staff appointments, the school day, use of school premises, exclusion of pupils and, most significantly, expenditure, governing bodies gained considerable sovereignty.

By taking much of the decision-making away from LEAs, the Government hoped, amongst other things, to reduce the influence of local party politics (especially those of the Left) in education. But this object could not have been achieved had local councillors retained their full power on school governing bodies. So the Government sought to dilute the influence of local authority governors, first via a requirement that all school governing bodies should have parent governors (EA 1980, s 2(5)), secondly, via a limitation in the number of schools at which a person could serve as a governor (currently two – Education (School Government) Regulations 1989, reg 5), and thirdly by placing LEA members firmly in the minority on governing bodies (E(No 2)A 1986, ss 3 and 4).

With their role to be expanded considerably (the E(No 2)A 1986 (s 16(1)) states, for example, that the conduct of a school is to be 'under the direction of the governing body'), it was clearly important for governing bodies to become more accountable. This was achieved through, *inter alia*, election of parent governors, a requirement that governors publish various matters (including 'performance-related' information and their policy on the secular curriculum) and through the establishment of a system of reporting and meetings – all of which aimed to provide a bridge between the school and the local community (especially parents).

The purpose of this chapter is not to examine the numerous functions of governing bodies (which are described in the specific chapters on finance, discipline, the employment of teachers, etc, although the powers which arise on incorporation are listed in Part 9 of this chapter). Instead, the chapter aims to set out the legal framework for the conduct of school government. Changes to this framework made by the EA 1993 include provision for sponsor governors of certain secondary schools and core governors for grouped GM schools. Consideration must also be given to the significance of the conferment of corporate status on governing bodies of county, voluntary and maintained special schools (EA 1993, s 238). Grant-maintained schools' governing bodies enjoyed this status from the start, under the ERA 1988.

2. Instrument and articles of government

Every county, voluntary and maintained special school is required by the E(No 2)A 1986 to have:

'(*a*) an instrument providing for the constitution of a governing body of the school (to be known as the *instrument of government*); and

(*b*) an instrument in accordance with which the school is to be conducted (to be known as the *articles of government*)'.

(E(No 2)A 1986, s 1(1)).

Grant-maintained schools are also to have such instruments (EA 1993, s 55(1)).

The *instrument of government* is to refer to such matters as the size and composition of governing bodies and the procedures for electing members and filling vacancies (E(No 2)A 1986, s 1(3), referring to Pt II of the Act). In grant-maintained schools, the instrument of government is to have a broader function. For example, it is to make provision as to meetings and proceedings of governing bodies (EA 1993, Sch 5 para 13). In county, voluntary and maintained special schools, such provision is to be made via regulations made by the Secretary of State (E(No 2)A 1986, s 8(6)) (Education (School Government) Regulations 1989 – see below).

The *articles of government* are to be concerned with, amongst other things, the way that a school is to be conducted and the allocation of functions between governors, head teacher and LEA (or Secretary of State and funding authority, where GM schools are concerned) (E(No 2)A 1986, s 1(4), and EA 1993, ss 55 and Sch 6 (GM schools)). Also covered by the articles are responsibilities in relation to admissions, discipline, reports and meetings, and certain other matters.

In the case of LEA-maintained schools, the instrument and articles of government are to be made or altered by order of the LEA (E(No 2)A 1986, s 1(2)), after the prescribed procedure (in s 2) has been followed (this procedure was not required for alterations consequent on the introduction of financial delegation (see below)). Grant-maintained schools are also required to have instruments and articles of government, as prescribed by the Secretary of State (EA 1993, s 56(1); see the Education (Grant-maintained Schools) (Initial Governing Instruments) Regulations 1993, SI 1993 No 3102).

The instrument and articles of government form part of the legal framework for the operation of a school. They must not contain any provision which is inconsistent with any enactment (E(No 2)A 1986, s 1(5)(a)). For example, the model articles of government for county schools made in pursuance of the Education (No 2) Act 1986 (s 1(1)(b)) and set out in DES Circular 7/87, Annex 5, are required to contain various matters, including the statutory rules relating to the appointment and dismissal of staff. But within five years of the start of financial delegation (see Chapter 3) the articles must be amended to show that during financial delegation the paragraphs dealing with staff appointments and dismissal are superseded by those contained in ERA 1988, s 44 and Sch 3 (ERA 1988, s 44(4)). Moreover, during financial delegation, any provisions of the articles which are inconsistent with those of a delegation scheme shall be of no effect (*ibid*, s 51(3)); and the articles must, within five years, be amended accordingly (s 51(4) and (5)).

Some schools also operate under a trust deed. The articles and instrument of government must comply with any trust deed relating to the school (E(No 2)A 1986, s 1(5)(b); EA 1993, ss 55(3) (GM schools)). Where there is an inconsistency between statutory requirements concerning instrument and articles and the terms of a trust deed the Secretary of State may make modifications to the deed (E(No 2)A 1986, s 2(7); EA 1993, s 57(3) and (4)).

New instruments and articles had to be made to give effect to the important changes to the composition and functions of governing bodies which were introduced under the Education (No 2) Act 1986. The new system has applied in county and maintained special schools since 1 September 1988 and in voluntary schools since 1 September 1989.

3. Composition of governing bodies

(a) Introduction

Both the Plowden Report in 1967 and the Taylor Committee Report in 1977 recommended parental representation on school governing bodies, but this did not become compulsory until the Education Act 1980 (which also brought the title of members of primary schools' boards into line with those of secondary schools, changing it from 'manager' to 'governor' (EA 1980, s 1)) (for historical background, see J Sallis, *Schools, Parents and Governors: A New Approach to Accountability*, Routledge (1988)). The Education (No 2) Act 1986 now governs the composition of school governing bodies in LEA-maintained schools, although the EA 1993 has made provision for sponsor governors for aided secondary schools. The constitution of the governing bodies of GM schools is covered by the EA 1993, but the position is now far more complex than under the 1988 Act because of the different arrangements that apply in each of the differing situations in which, in effect, GM schools may come into existence.

(b) LEA-maintained schools

The composition of a governing body is to be in accordance with E(No 2)A 1986, section 3 (county, controlled or maintained special schools) or section 4 (aided and special agreement schools). It must be stated, in relation to each school, in its instrument of government. Adjustment in the number of governors in any particular category may be necessary if there is an excess of governors in that category (E(No 2)A 1986, s 14) (no-one may at any time hold more than one governorship of the same county, voluntary or special agreement school: E(No 2)A 1986, s 15(10)).

Composition of school governing bodies – county, controlled and maintained special schools (Education (No 2) Act 1986)

	Size of school (no of pupils)			
	Below 100	*100–299*	*300–599*	*600 or more*
Parents[a]	2	3	4	5
LEA[b]	2	3	4	5
Head teacher[c]	1	1	1	1
Teachers[d]	1	1	2	2
Co-opted[e] [or, in controlled school, foundation/co-opted[e]]	3 [2/1]	4 [3/1]	5 [4/1]	6 [4/2]
TOTAL	9	12	16	19

Notes

[a]Parent governors are to be elected in accordance with arrangements laid down in section 15. LEAs must arrange for elections. Where an insufficient number of parents stand for election (or where at least 50 per cent of a school's pupils are boarders and election would, in the opinion of the LEA, be impracticable), the governors are to *appoint* parents to the vacancies (s 5(1), (2) and (4)).

[b]These governors are appointed by the LEA.

[c]The head teacher can elect not to be a governor (ss 3(2)(d), (3)(d) and 5(d)). If he or she chooses to be a governor, he or she is to be treated as an *ex officio* governor (s 3(7)). Even if not a governor he or she generally has a right to attend governors' meetings (Education (School Government) Regulations 1989, reg 11 – see below). Note that where a school has more than one head teacher, each of them may be a governor (s 15(1)).

[d]Teacher governors are elected by teachers from their own number (s 15 – see below).

[e]It is the duty of the governors, when looking to co-opt any person to be a member of the governing body (otherwise than as a foundation governor), to, in effect, ensure that the local business community is represented on the governing body (if it is not already) (s 6). In maintained special schools with less than 100 registered pupils, a co-opted governor may be appointed by one voluntary organisation or two or more jointly (s 7). Two may be appointed if the school has 100 or more pupils (on co-opting, see further DES Circular 7/87, paras 5.3.9–5.3.12).

Composition of school governing bodies – aided and special agreement schools (Education (No 2) Act 1986)

	Size of school (no of pupils)	
	Below 300	*300 or more*
	at least . . .	
Parents[a]	1	1
LEA appointee	1	1
Teachers[b]	1	2
	plus . . .	
Head teacher[c]	1	1
Foundation governors[d]	6[e]	7[e]
TOTAL[e]	10 (plus)	12 (plus)

Notes

[a]To be elected in accordance with the arrangements laid down in section 15. Governing bodies are responsible for arranging the elections.

[b]Teacher governors to be elected from their own number (see s 15).

[c]The head teacher may choose not to be a governor (s 4(2)(g)), but whether or not he or she is one he or she will be counted as a governor for the purposes of calculating the required number of foundation governors (s 4(4)) (see note e below). Where the head teacher is a governor he or she is to be treated as an *ex officio* governor (s 4(6)). If the school has more than one head teacher, each may be a governor (s 15(1)).

[d]At least one of the foundation governors is to be, at the time of his or her appointment, a parent of a pupil at the school (s 4(3)(b)).

[e]This is not a prescribed figure. The law states that the instrument of government shall provide for such number of foundation governors as will lead to their outnumbering the other governors (plus a head teacher non-governor) by two, or three if the total number of governors is 19 or more (s 4(3)(a)). Note the effect of new section 4A(7), which applies where the instrument of government names a sponsor of the school (see below).

Note that aided secondary schools may if the governors consent or so request and the Secretary of State so directs, now have a sponsor or sponsors and up to four *sponsor* governors (E(No 2)A 1986, s 4A, added by EA 1993, s 271). If such arrangements are proposed by the governors where the school is to change from a controlled to an aided status, or is to be established or altered under EA 1980, the Secretary of State must make a direction (E(No 2)A 1986, s 4A(4) and (5)). If there is a sponsor for the school named in the instrument of government, the total number of foundation governors must be such that they will outnumber the other governors by two (s 4A(7)).

The rules governing eligibility are discussed below. It may be noted here that pupil representation on school governing bodies is not required by law, and although it is possible that a pupil could be co-opted, he or she would have to be at least 18 years old, for that is the minimum age at which a person may be appointed or elected a governor (s 15(14)).

(c) Grant-maintained schools

When it is proposed that a school is to become grant-maintained, an 'initial governing body' must be assembled, whose role will be 'to prepare it for the transition to its new status and to conduct it from the date of incorporation' (DES Circular 10/88, para 23). New GM schools, established by a funding authority or by promoters (see EA 1993, ss 48 and 49), also have an initial governing body. The next paragraph only applies to schools which acquired GM status by opting out of the LEA sector. Separate provision relating to schools established as 'new' GM schools under the 1993 Act is made in respect of the appointment of initial, first or foundation governors and the appointment and tenure of office of parent and teacher governors appointed before the date of implementation of the proposals for the establishment of the school (EA 1993, ss 60(6), 61(4) and 78; Education (Governors of New Grant-Maintained Schools) Regulations 1994, SI 1994 No 654; DFE Circular 18/93).

The composition of the 'initial governing body' and its successors will basically be the same, but the initial body may contain elected parent or teacher governors who were on the governing body before the school decided to become GM, whose term of office had not expired, and who were willing to continue as governors (they are defined in the 1993 Act as 'eligible governors': EA 1993, s 71(3); Sch 7 para 4). Where there are too many governors in these categories who are willing to continue, the matter may be decided by agreement between the eligible governors or, in default of agreement, by the drawing of lots (EA 1993, s 71(4)). Where there are fewer eligible governors than required, elections or appointments will be necessary (s 71(6)–(8)). The initial first or foundation governors will be those selected by the existing governing body when it published its proposals for GM status (EA 1993, s 73). Provision is made for the replacement of initial parent, teacher and first or foundation governors prior to incorporation in certain circumstances (death or resignation of the governor or his prospective disqualification for holding office as governor (EA 1993, ss 74 and 75)). GM schools may also have initial sponsor governors (selected under the arrangements set out in the Education (Grant-maintained Status) (Initial Sponsor Governors) Regulations 1993, SI 1993 No 3188) (EA 1993, s 77).

Note that separate provision is made in respect of governing bodies of GM special schools: see EA 1993, Sch 11; and the Education (Initial Goverment of Grant-maintained Special Schools) Regulations 1994 (SI 1994 No 2003).

Composition of school governing bodies – grant-maintained schools (Education Act 1993)[a]

Parents[b]	3–5 (primary school)	5 (secondary school)
Teachers[c]	1 or 2	
Head teacher[d]	1	
First[e] or foundation[f] governors	8 or 9[g]	
TOTAL[h]	15 or 17	

Notes

[a]The various categories of governor are defined in Schedule 7 to the EA 1993.

[b]EA 1993, section 60(2). These are to be elected (unless there are too few candidates, in which case an appointment must be made) under mostly identical arrangements to those applicable to LEA-maintained schools under section 15 of the E(No 2)A 1986 (EA 1993, s 60(5) and Sch 5, para 3).

[c]To be eligible, the governor must be a teacher at the school in question (EA 1993, Sch 7, para 6).

[d]The head teacher serves in an *ex officio* capacity. He or she does not have the option of choosing not to be a governor (EA 1993, s 62).

[e]A school which was a county school when deciding to become grant-maintained or which was established as a new GM school under proposals made by a funding authority has 'first' governors (EA 1993, s 63(1)). At least two of the first governors must be parents of pupils at the school (ss 63(3)(a) and 63(5)(a)). First governors must include in their number persons who are members of the local community; and the business community in particular must be represented (s 63(3)). The Secretary of State has new powers introduced under the 1993 Act to replace first governors where the governing body has been guilty of 'substantial or persistent failure to comply or secure compliance with any requirement imposed by or under any enactment', or if the school is failing to deliver an acceptable standard of education, or where action taken or proposed to be taken by the governing body, or any failure to act by it, 'is prejudicial to the provision of education by the school' (EA 1993, s 64(1)–(4)). The Secretary of State also has a power to fill any vacancies for first governor if it appears to him that the governing body is 'unable or unwilling' to do so (s 64(5)).

[f]A school which was a voluntary school immediately before it became GM, or which is established as a new GM school under proposals by promoters, is to have foundation rather than first governors (EA 1993, s 65(1)). At least two of the foundation governors must be parents of registered pupils at the school (s 65(6), (8) and (9)). The foundation governors may be appointed, in the case of a voluntary school which has opted out, by those who were entitled to appoint foundation governors to the governing body previously. However, in the case of a school established by promoters under section 49 of the 1993 Act, appointment will be made by the promoters (EA 1993, s 65(7)(b) and (c)).

[g]The first or foundation governors must outnumber the other governors (EA 1993, s 63(2) and 65(2)).

[h]The Secretary of State may appoint up to two additional governors 'if it appears to him that the governing body of the school are not adequately carrying out their responsibilities with respect to the conduct or management of the school' (EA 1993, s 67(1)). Additional first/foundation governors, equal in number to those additional governors appointed by the Secretary of State, may be appointed (s 67(2) and (3)).

4. Grouping

(a) LEA-maintained schools: Education (No 2) Act 1986

Subject in most cases to approval from the Secretary of State (E(No 2)A 1986, s 10), an LEA may resolve that two or more schools (excluding GM schools) be grouped for the purposes of school government (*ibid*, s 9(1)). If schools are grouped, they are treated as one school, with a single governing body, which will be constituted under a single instrument of government (s 9(2)). The grouped school will be treated as:

(i) an aided or special agreement school if one or more of the schools is of one of these types; or

(ii) as a controlled school if one of them is of that type and none of the others are aided or special agreement; or,

(iii) as a maintained special school if all of the schools are of this type and the others are all county schools; or

(iv) in any other case, as a county school.

(E(No 2)A 1986, s 9(3)).

Where certain changes or alterations are proposed to any school in the group, the LEA must review the need for the grouping. If it decides to continue with the grouping, it must refer the matter to the Secretary of State (provided his consent to the grouping was required in the first place under section 10) (s 9(4) and (5)). A grouping may be ended by the Secretary of State (s 9(6)). The LEA also has a power to end the grouping, simply by resolution if it does not include a voluntary school (s 9(7)(a)), or, in any other case (i) by resolution and with the governors' agreement or (ii) after expiry of one year's notice given by LEA or governors (s 9(7)(b)).

Provision is made as to the procedure on making the instrument of government and the election of parent and teacher governors in grouped schools (E(No 2)A 1986, Sch 1).

(b) Grant-maintained schools: Education Act 1993

Like LEA-maintained schools, grant-maintained schools can be conducted as a group by a single governing body, constituted under a single instrument of government (EA 1993, s 117 and 118) and with the same powers (under section 68 of the 1993 Act) as a governing body of a single GM school (EA 1993, s 125). Although the standard requirements for GM schools as to governorships, the conduct of governors' business and the articles of government (laid down in Schedules 5 and 6 to the 1993 Act) apply to a group, each school in the group must be conducted in accordance with any trust deed relating to it specifically (EA 1993, s 117(4)). Also, the individual schools in the group will retain their independent statutory obligations (for example, in relation to the curriculum) (s 117(6)). There is no prescribed limit to the number of GM schools which can form a group, but clearly there are practical limitations to operating a particularly large group. Generally the optimum number will be three or four, depending on the sizes of the schools.

The constitution of a grouped GM school's governing body will differ in some respects from that of a single GM school. First, the number of parent governors (who must be elected, or appointed by the governors if there is a shortfall) must not be less than three nor more than the number of schools in the group (if greater than three) (EA 1993, s 119). There must be one or two teacher governors, irrespective of the number of schools in the group (EA 1993, s 120). Each head teacher of schools in the group may elect to be a governor (*ex-officio*) (EA 1993, s 121) (remember that in single GM schools the head teacher *must* serve as a governor). Finally, the governing body must include 'core governors' (EA 1993, s 122). Core governors may be appointed by the governing body or may be externally appointed. The externally appointed core governors will be either appointed in respect of a particular school in the group, if the school was previously a voluntary school or was established by promoters as a new GM school, or will be appointed in respect of the group as a whole (EA 1993, Sch 8 para 2). The persons named in the instrument of government for the group as being entitled to appoint core governors will have the power to make appointments if, in effect, it is necessary to secure that the religious character of the school is maintained. Apart from externally appointed governors in respect of particular schools in the group, all core governors must be appointed 'from among persons who appear . . . to be committed to the good government and continuing viability of all schools in the group (Sch 8 para 2(5)). The total number of core governors depends on whether the schools in the group are either (i) voluntary schools which have opted out, (ii) new schools established by promoters, or (iii) other GM schools. In the case of (i) and (ii), the externally appointed core governors will be in the majority on the governing body (see Sch 8 para 3). In the case of (iii), one or two of the core governors must be parents of pupils at the school, and the total number of core governors (who must include representatives of the local business community) must be not less than five nor more than the number of schools in the group (if greater).

The Secretary of State has a power (in EA 1993, s 123) to replace core governors in the same circumstances as he may replace (under EA 1993, s 64) first governors of single GM schools. He also has a corresponding power (to that in EA 1993, s 67) to appoint up to two additional governors (see EA 1993, s 124).

Groups of GM schools can come into existence, and undergo a change of membership, in a variety of ways, set out in section 127 of the 1993 Act (although with regulations making the necessary provision):

(i) Two or more schools, each of which is eligible for GM status, may be able to acquire GM status as a group (sometimes referred to by the DFE as 'clustering': see *Choice and Diversity*, Ch 12) (there will have to be a ballot of parents in favour: s 127).

(ii) Two or more GM schools may join together to form a grouped GM school.

(iii) A school which is eligible for GM status may acquire it by joining a GM group; alternatively, a school which is a single GM school may join a GM group.

(iv) The schools in two or more existing groups may join together to form one group.

(v) A school which is a member of a GM group may leave the group and continue as a single GM school.

There are prescribed requirements in respect of each of these possibilities: the Education (Groups of Grant-Maintained Schools) Regulations 1994 (SI 1994 No 1041). These regulations also modify the rules on governors' terms of office (in Sch 5 to the EA 1993) and permit the dismissal of externally appointed core governors by those who appointed them. Provision is also made enabling grant-maintained special schools to form groups with other such schools or with GM schools (EA 1993, s 187 and the Education (Groups including Grant-Maintained Special Schools) Regulations 1994, SI 1994 No 779; see also SI 1994 No 2281).

5. Joint schemes for GM schools

An alternative, looser, arrangement to grouping is now also available for GM schools. Two or more GM schools may instead enter into a 'joint scheme', under which joint committees may be established and particular functions may be exercised jointly (EA 1993, s 69). The scheme could enable schools to have a single bursar or other administrative support, purchase services jointly and co-operate in ensuring that the necessary teaching expertise is available to support the curriculum across the schools. The Minister explained that a joint scheme would 'provide an additional route whereby small schools can come together and co-operate', providing them with greater security and an opportunity to benefit from the economies of scale (*Hansard*, HL, Vol 545, col 272 and Vol 546, col 1157, *per* Baroness Blatch). Schemes require the approval of the Secretary of State (s 70(1)). Provision is made for varying schemes (s 70(3)–(6)).

6. Election (and appointment) of parent and teacher governors

In the categories teacher governor (which excludes the head teacher) and parent governor election to the governing body is required, although in certain situations parent governors can be *appointed* to office by the other members of the governing body (E(No 2)A 1986, s 5(1)–(3); see, in relation to GM schools, EA 1993, ss 60, 61 and 71). For example, in county, controlled or maintained special schools not established in a hospital direct appointment may take place if, *inter alia*, the number of parents standing for election is fewer than the number of vacancies. When making such appointments, the governors who are not parent governors may appoint a parent of *any* pupil of compulsory school age, including, if necessary, a parent whose child attends another school (E(No 2)A 1986, s 5(4)(a); EA 1993, s 60(3) and (4), in the case of GM schools). But they may not appoint (i) an elected member of the LEA, (ii) an employee of either the LEA or the governors of an aided school, or (iii) a co-opted member of any committee of the LEA (E(No 2)A 1986, s 5(4)(b)).

Section 15 of the E(No 2)A 1986 contains the key provisions on election of governors. By virtue of sections 60(5) and 61(3) of the EA 1993, they apply also to GM schools. Responsibility for arranging elections rests, as noted earlier, with LEAs in the case of county, controlled and maintained special schools, and with the governing body in relation to other maintained schools (E(No 2)A 1986, s 15(2)(b)) (and in GM schools). Certain aspects of the conduct of the elections may be delegated to the head teacher, although the LEA/governors retain overall responsibility. The LEA/governors are also responsible for determining whether a person is a parent of a registered pupil or a teacher at the school for the purposes of their eligibility for candidature at an election to the governing body (s 15(2)(a)).

Elections must be by secret ballot (E(No 2)A 1986, s 15(4)). In the case of election of parent governors, an opportunity to vote by post or return a ballot paper via a registered pupil at the school must also be given (s 15(5)). Proper notice of the election must be given. The governors' annual report should contain information about forthcoming elections (E(No 2)A 1986, s 30(2)(g)). Furthermore, under section 15(6) of the 1986 Act, the LEA/governors must take:

> 'such steps as are reasonably practicable to secure that every person who is known to them to be a parent of a registered pupil at the school is:
>
> (*a*) informed of the vacancy and that it is to be filled by election;
>
> (*b*) informed that he is entitled to stand as a candidate, and vote, at the election; and
>
> (*c*) given an opportunity to do so'.

Letters to parents informing them of vacancies and setting out election arrangements should in appropriate cases be in languages other than English (see DES Circular 7/87, Annex 9, para 16).

There may be problems in determining who is eligible to vote as a parent. As noted in Chapter 1 (at Part 3), for the purposes of the Education Acts, a 'parent' means not only a child's natural parents, but also a person who has 'parental responsibility' for a child for the purposes of the Children Act 1989 or who has care for him/her (see EA 1944, s 114(1D)–(1F)). Thus it is quite possible for there to be more than two persons eligible to vote as parents of one registered child! LEAs and governors are advised that they are 'not required to track every person who might qualify under the . . . definition of a parent, but . . . cannot rule ineligible anyone known to them to be a parent' (DES Circular 7/87, para 12).

It is for the responsible authority, i.e. the LEA or governors, to decide whether candidates should be nominated, and if so, by how many others. They may also choose the method of election, e.g. first past the post or some form of proportional representation. (In the case of GM schools, the instrument of government *may* make provision 'as to the procedure for the election of members of the governing body' and 'for the determination of any questions arising in connection with, or matters relating to, such elections' (EA 1993, Sch 5, para 2).) Guidance on these and other matters relating to the conduct of elections, including what constitutes a secret ballot, is given in DES Circular 7/87, Annex 9 – 'The conduct of governor elections'. An extract appears in *Appendix 4* to this book.

If it is alleged that election of parent governors was carried out in a defective manner, complaint should be made to the Secretary of State under EA 1944, s 99, rather than via judicial review in the High Court (*R* v *Northampton County Council ex p Gray* [1986] The Times, 10 June).

Where, in the case of an LEA-maintained school, appointment of a governor is required (see above), the clerk must give written notice of the vacancy to the appointing authority so that they may fill it (Education (School Government) Regulations 1989, reg 18(1)). When the appointment is made, the authority must inform the clerk of the name and usual place of residence of the person they have appointed (reg 18(2)).

7. Governorship

(a) Term of office

Governors, other than those who are *ex officio*, hold office for not more than four years in county, controlled and maintained special schools (E(No 2)A 1986, s 8(2)). However, a governor may resign his or her office at any time (s 8(4)) or may become disqualified (s 8(3) and see below). A teacher governor may not continue as such once he or she ceases to be employed at the school (Education (School Government) Regs 1989, reg 15(2)). Where there is an excess of governors, elimination of the excess by removal of those with the longest service may be required (E(No 2)A 1986, s 14). Governors may be re-appointed or re-elected after the expiry of their term.

In GM schools elected governors hold office for up to four years at a time (EA 1993, Sch 5 para 5) and foundation or first governors generally for such term as is specified in the instrument of government, being not less than five nor more than seven years (*ibid,* para 6(2)). Similar rules to those in the 1986 Act relating to serving a further term, resignation and disqualification are laid down (*ibid,* paras 7–9). Additional first or foundation governors appointed to match the number of additional governors appointed by the Secretary of State (see EA 1993, s 67(2)) are to hold office for such terms as is specified in their terms of appointment (the maximum permitted period being five years) (EA 1993, Sch 7, para 6(4)). Replacement governors appointed by the Secretary of State under section 64 of the EA 1993 (on the ground that the governing body has failed in various respects) hold office for the period specified in their terms of appointment, being not less than five nor more than seven years (*ibid*, para 6(5)). On GM special schools see EA 1993, Sch 11 and SI 1994 No 2003.

(b) Disqualification

Governors in county, voluntary and maintained special schools may be disqualified from holding office only in the circumstances laid down in regulations 5–8 (and 15 (see above)) of the Education (School Government) Regulations 1989, as amended (SGR 1989) (reg 4). In GM schools, the instrument of government is to state the circumstances in which a person is to be disqualified (EA 1993, Sch 5, para 4). The Education (Grant-maintained Schools) (Initial Governing Instruments) Regulations 1993 (SI 1993 No 3102, Sch 1, paras 20–23) (and SI 1994 No 2104, re: GM special schools) make similar provision to the SGR.

The first rule concerning disqualification (in reg 5 of the SGR) aims to prevent a person from holding office as governor on more than *two* governing bodies. However, as the previous limit was four schools (the Education (School Government) (Amendment) Regulations 1991 made the reduction to two), there is transitional provision in the case of governors who were holding office immediately prior to 8 January 1992. If a person is appointed by the LEA as an 'additional governor' to a school requiring 'special measures' (under EA 1993, s 214; see Chapter 10), his or her appointment does not count towards the total number of school governorships he or she holds (reg 2 of the Education (School Government) (Amendment) Regulations 1993, SI 1993 No 3107).

A person may also be disqualified from holding or continuing to hold office as a governor if he or she is adjudged bankrupt or has made a composition or arrangement with creditors. In either case the governor must give notice of that fact to the clerk to the governing body (SGR 1989, reg 6(1)). In most cases the disqualification will cease on the person's discharge from bankruptcy or on annulment of the bankruptcy order (reg 6(2)). In the case of a composition or arrangement with creditors, the disqualification ends after three years, or after the debts are paid in full (if sooner) (see reg 6(3)).

An important aspect of disqualification concerns criminal convictions (excluding convictions outside the UK for offences involving conduct which would not amount to an offence in the UK: SGR 1989, reg 7(4)). A governor with relevant convictions must give written notice of them to the clerk to the governors (reg 7(3)). Convictions which disqualify a person from holding, or continuing to hold, office as a school governor (reg 7(1) and (2)) are:

(i) a conviction (in the UK or elsewhere) within the five years before election or appointment or while a governor, in respect of which a sentence of imprisonment (whether suspended or not) of not less than three months, and without the option of a fine, has been imposed;

(ii) a conviction as above, within the previous twenty years, for which a sentence of imprisonment of at least two-and-a-half years has been passed;

(iii) a conviction plus fine within the previous five years, or since being appointed or elected, for causing nuisance or disturbance on school premises (including those of a GM school) contrary to the Local Government (Miscellaneous Provisions) Act 1982, s 40 (as amended) (see Chapter 13, Part 3(f)(iii)).

A person is also disqualified from continuing to hold office as a governor if, without the consent of the governing body, he or she has not attended any governors' meeting for the previous six months (reduced from twelve months by the 1991 Amendment Regs, *op cit*) or more (SGR 1989, reg 8). However, he or she may be re-elected or reappointed to office (*ibid*).

(c) Resignation or removal – notice and other requirements

The clerk to the governing body must be given written notice of (i) resignation or (ii) removal of a governor. Notice should be given by, in the case of (i), the governor concerned, and (ii), by those removing the governor (SGR 1989, reg 17; see, in relation to GM schools, the Education (Grant-maintained Schools) (Initial Governing Instruments) Regulations 1993, SI 1993 No 3102, Sch 1, para 19) (see SI 1994 No 2104 re: GM special schools). Moreover, the governor concerned must be informed by the appointing authority of the proposed removal and the reasons for it and be given an opportunity to reply in writing to the complaints made against him or her (*R* v *Brent LBC ex p Assegai* (1987) The Times, 18 June (QBD)). The governing body may resolve to remove the chairperson from office, but the resolution is valid only if the possible removal was listed an agenda item (SGR 1989, reg 9(3A)). Moreover, in most cases the removal decision will stand only if it is confirmed by a second resolution not less than 14 days after the first meeting (*ibid*).

Appointing authorities (governors or LEAs) have the power to remove from office, where relevant:

(i) any foundation governor of an aided school;

(ii) any school governor other than:

- a co-opted governor who is not a co-opted foundation governor;
- an elected or appointed (by E(No 2)A 1986, s 5) parent governor or elected teacher governor;
- an *ex officio* governor (E(No 2)A 1986, s 8(5) – see also EA 1944, s 21(1)); in GM schools any foundation governor, other than one who holds office *ex officio*, and any sponsor governor may be removed from office by the person or persons who appointed him or her (Education (Grant-maintained Schools) (Initial Governing Instruments) Regulations 1993, *op cit*, Sch 1, para 19).

The Government hopes that the power of removal will be used 'only in exceptional circumstances' (DES Circular 7/87, para 5.5.1). But there have in the past been complaints about the use of the power of removal to achieve political ends. For example, it was alleged in 1989 that Humberside LEA had deliberately selected non-socialist governors for removal (*Guardian*, 25 October 1989). In *R* v *Governors of Haberdashers' Aske's Hatcham Schools ex p ILEA – sub nom Brunyate* v *ILEA* [1989] 2 All ER 417, the appeal courts held in turn that an LEA cannot remove governors in mid term solely because of their failure to further the authority's policies. The ILEA had removed two Conservative governors on a grouped governing body when they indicated that they were not prepared to support the authority's policy concerning the future of the schools (which involved opposing a possible application by the school for GM or CTC status) and an extended period of consultation thereon. In the House of Lords, Lord Bridge, giving the court's judgment, said (at p 421) that to remove a governor because of his or her 'non-compliance with the wishes (i.e. policy) of the authority is . . . a usurpation of the governors' independent function'. Thus as Woolf LJ had argued in the Court of Appeal, the power to remove a governor was 'limited to the extent that was necessary to prevent the policy of *the Act* being frustrated' (*per* Woolf LJ, (emphasis added)). In *R* v *Trustee of the Roman Catholic Diocese of Westminster ex p Andrews* [1989] The Times, 18 August (*sub nom Mars* (1987) 86 LGR 507 in QBD) the Court of Appeal, following the decision in *Brunyate*, held that the removal of two governors who would not support a trustee's scheme for reorganisation of the school had been an unlawful exercise of the power of removal.

The Secretary of State has powers to replace governors in certain circumstances where the governing body is not performing its role adequately, which were referred to above.

8. Governors' meetings

The position described below relates to LEA-maintained schools. For the (largely very similar) position in GM schools and GM special schools see the initial governing instruments prescribed by regulation: SI 1993 No 3102/SI 1994 No 2104.

(a) Requirement to hold a meeting

A governors' meeting must be convened at least once in every term (SGR 1989, reg 12(1)). However, in practice it has become increasingly difficult for the necessary business to be completed in three meetings a year, even with referral to subcommittees, and most governing bodies can expect to meet more frequently. (The governing body of a *new* school need meet 'as often as occasion may require' (reg 12(2)).) A meeting may be requisitioned by any three members of the governing body (reg 12(3)).

In some cases the power to make a decision may be delegated to a member of the governors, the head teacher, or a committee (SGR 1989, regs 25 and

26). Delegation is discussed further below (Part 9). The chairperson, or, if he or she cannot be contacted the vice-chairperson, may make decisions without the other governors where 'a delay . . . would be likely to be seriously detrimental to the interests of the school, or to the interests of any registered pupil at the school, his parent, or a person employed at the school' (reg 23(1) and (2)). 'Delay' is defined as 'a delay for a period extending beyond the date preceding the earliest date on which it would be reasonably practicable for a meeting of the governing body to be held' (reg 19(3)) (see further *R* v *Birmingham City Council ex p McKenna* [1991] The Times, 16 May (QBD)).

(b) Convening of meetings

The clerk to the governors convenes the meeting, although in doing so he or she must comply with any direction given by the governors at their previous meeting, or by the chairperson, or, in his or her absence, the vice-chairperson (SGR 1989, reg 19(1)). At least seven days before the date of the meeting a written notice of the meeting, signed by the clerk, and a copy of the agenda, should be given to every member of the governing body, the head teacher (assuming he or she is not a governor), and the chief education officer (reg 19(2)). However, a lesser period of notice of the meeting (plus agenda) may be given where the chairperson, or, in his or her absence, the vice-chairperson, so directs – on the ground that there are matters requiring urgent consideration (reg 19(2)). The written notice and agenda must either be sent to, or left at, the usual place of residence of those entitled to receive them (reg 19(3)). The fact that a member did not receive a written notice does not invalidate the proceedings of the meeting (reg 19(4)). Note the special requirements applicable to removal of the chairperson, referred to at p 95.

In an aided or special agreement school, if a decision is to be taken at a meeting to rescind or vary a resolution carried at a previous meeting of the governing body, such matter must be included as a specific item of business on the agenda for the meeting (SGR 1989, reg 20).

(c) Election of a chairperson and vice-chairperson

Generally speaking the governors must elect a chairperson and vice-chairperson from their number at the first meeting in the school year (SGR 1989, reg 9(1)). A subsequent casual vacancy may be filled at the next meeting after it occurs (reg 9(2)). A teacher governor is ineligible for election to either office (reg 9(5)). The chairperson or vice-chairperson may resign from office at any time (written notice to be given to the clerk) (reg 9(3)).

If the chairperson is absent from the meeting the vice-chairperson must take the chair. If neither the chairperson nor vice-chairperson are in attendance at a meeting, the other members present may elect one of their number (apart from a teacher governor) to chair the meeting (reg 9(4)) (separate provisions govern chairpersons and vice-chairpersons of temporary governing bodies: see SGR 1989, reg 10).

(d) Quorum

Generally the quorum for a meeting of the governing body (SGR 1989, reg 13(1) and (2)) is:

(i) Three governors, or, if greater, one-third of the total membership (rounded up where necessary); or

(ii) The quorum specified in the instrument of government for the school, if greater than the figure in (i) above, provided that it is not more than two-fifths of total membership (rounded up where necessary).

However, a larger quorum is required in a small number of prescribed circumstances, namely: appointment of parent governors under E(No 2)A 1986 (e.g. because there were fewer parents standing for election than the number of vacancies); co-option of non-foundation governors; co-option of temporary teacher governors; appointment of a committee with delegated functions (under reg 26 – see below) (reg 13(3)). The quorum in these cases is to be two-thirds (lowered from three-quarters by the 1991 Amendment Regulations: SI 1991 No 2845) of the governors entitled to vote on these particular matters (*ibid*). Where the governing body includes 'additional' governors (appointed by the LEA because of the failings of the school: see EA 1993, s 214), the quorum for removal of the chairperson is 50 per cent (SGR 1989, reg 13(4), added by the 1993 Amendment Regulations, SI 1993 No 3107, reg 4).

(e) The meeting

(i) Attendance and participation

Public access to governors' meetings is not specifically barred. The governing body is left with a discretion as to whether anyone who is not one of those entitled to attend (one of their number, a head teacher non-governor, and the clerk to the governors) should be admitted to the meeting (SGR 1989, reg 21).

In certain cases or circumstances any person present at a meeting, including a person present by right, may be required to withdraw from the meeting or be required not to take part in consideration or discussion of certain matters; sometimes he or she may simply have no right to vote on the matter (SGR 1989, reg 14). In any event, the governors are to have an unrestricted right, when conducting a disciplinary hearing or appeal in relation to a pupil's or a teacher's or other employee's alleged conduct, to allow such persons and others – the pupil's parent, the person making the allegation, or a material witness – to attend the meeting and be heard (SGR 1989, reg 14(4)).

Subject to the couple of exceptions in the preceding paragraph, the Schedule to the Education (School Government) Regulations details 'the only circumstances' in which withdrawal may be required (reg 14(2)) (it was held that the pre-1987 version of the regulations did not contain an exhaustive list of such circumstances (*Lockett* v *Croydon LBC* [1986] The

Times, 6 August (CA)), hence the specific limitation incorporated into the 1987, and now 1989, regulations). But note that further circumstances may be specified in the governing instrument for the school in relation to circumstances in which the governing body is considering the case of a registered pupil (reg 14(3)).

The first situation where withdrawal is necessary relates to pecuniary interest. Anyone present who has such an interest, whether direct or indirect, in any 'proposed contract or other matter' being considered by the governors must disclose that fact as soon as possible. He or she must take no part in the consideration or discussion of that matter and should withdraw from the meeting while the said matter is being considered – unless the governors decide otherwise. He or she must not vote on the matter nor on any question relating to it (SGR 1989, Sch, para 2(1)). What constitutes a direct or indirect pecuniary interest for this purpose is carefully defined. Certain changes have been made from the previous (1987) version of the regulations. Note that a person is to be taken to have a direct or indirect pecuniary interest if a 'relative' (including a 'spouse' – 'includes a woman who lives with a man as his wife': reg 3(a)) to his knowledge has such an interest (Sch, para 2(3)).

An indirect pecuniary interest would, for example, arise if a proposed contract for the benefit of the school was to be with a company or other organisation of which the governor was a member (with securities in it), or a partner, or an employee (with securities in it) (Sch, para 2(2)).

Governors are nowadays taking major decisions affecting the conduct of their schools. Such decisions can clearly have a major impact on the teaching staff. The governing body includes teacher governors and generally also the head teacher. The Schedule to the SGR 1989 lists the circumstances in which the teacher governors, and head teacher (whether a governor or not), shall *not* be deemed to have a direct or indirect pecuniary interest (para 2(4)):

(*a*) where he or she has an interest in a contract or other matter which is a greater interest than that of the generality of teachers at the school (note that conflict of interest concerning employment matters is covered elsewhere – see below);

(*b*) where the contract or other matter relates to the governors' exercise of their functions relating to the curriculum or management of the school's budget share following financial delegation; or

(*c*) where the decision being considered relates to the question whether or not to initiate the procedure for changing to grant-maintained status or to pass a resolution for opting out (see *Appendix 1* to this book). This confirms the decision of the Court of Appeal in *R* v *Governors of Small Heath School ex p Birmingham City Council* [1989] The Times, 14 August. In that case, decided under the previous version of the regulations which did not refer to this particular category of decision, it was held that there was no pecuniary interest because there was no evidence

> that the financial position of the teacher governors would alter if the school became grant-maintained. The court distinguished a decision in a previous case, *Bostock* v *Kay* [1989] The Times, 20 April, in which it was held that four teacher governors had a direct pecuniary interest in the outcome of proposals to turn their school into a city technology college (CTC). The Court of Appeal in *Small Heath* said that a change to GM status was far less fundamental than a change to CTC. In the latter circumstance the school would cease to exist and would be replaced by a completely new institution; staff might not be re-engaged, and if they did they might have to work longer hours, although for greater pay.

Governing bodies (or a selection panel thereof) may also have to consider the appointment, transfer, promotion or retirement of staff. If such a matter relates to a governor or his or her relative (including spouse – as above) the governor in question should take no part in the proceedings and should not vote. Indeed, he or she should not be present at all, unless the governors decide otherwise (Sch, para 3). Such restrictions on participation also apply if the governors are to consider the transfer, promotion, retirement, dismissal or suspension of a member of staff (teaching or otherwise), and one of the governors (or his or her relative) could be a candidate for any vacant post arising from the decision on the matter (para 4). A decision under the 1981 version of the regulations, admittedly concerned with appointment rather than promotion, is relevant here: *Noble* v *ILEA* (1984) 83 LGR 291. P, a senior teacher, applied for a deputy headship at his school. He was interviewed by the governing body. K, a teacher governor at the school, was present at the meeting. K voted in favour of P's appointment. P was recommended for the post and received a formal offer from the LEA, which he accepted. The LEA subsequently tried to repeat the selection process, but without K, who should not have been on the panel because he was eligible to be considered for P's post if P was appointed to the deputy headship. P tried to hold the LEA to the contract he had accepted. The Court of Appeal found for the LEA; the governors' proceedings were invalid.

The remainder of the Schedule to the SGR 1989 relates principally to withdrawal during consideration of disciplinary matters or the admission of pupils. A pupil or his parent must withdraw from a meeting if the admission of or disciplinary action against the pupil or against another pupil where the first pupil was involved in the incident, is being considered (Sch, para 5(1)(a) and (b)). A relative of the pupil other than a parent has, if in attendance, to disclose the relationship as soon as practicable after the commencement of the meeting (para 6). A person making allegations which might lead to disciplinary action against a pupil or teacher or other employee at the school must also withdraw, as must a witness of any alleged incident (para 5(1)(c), as qualified by para 5(2) – which enables the chief education officer or his or her representative to attend but not vote). In the case of disciplinary action against either a teacher or other employee or against the clerk to the governors, that person must also withdraw (para 5(1)(e)).

In all these cases in paragraph 5(1), the person concerned must withdraw during discussion or consideration of the matter in question and may not vote.

If the governors are hearing an appeal in respect of any disciplinary matter, anyone previously concerned with the matter, other than in the capacity of governor, must not take part in consideration of the appeal or any vote relating to it (para 5(1)(d)). This often results in the head teacher having to withdraw. However, he or she may nevertheless attend, but may not vote, in cases involving dismissal of staff (ERA 1988, Sch 3, para 8(9); SGR 1989, Sch, para 5(2)). In *Haddow* v *ILEA* [1979] ICR 202 the Employment Appeal Tribunal held that the proceedings of an LEA's disciplinary tribunal were not invalidated by the fact that the officer of the authority who had written the report on which the decision to dismiss was based was in attendance at the tribunal for consultation; but in *Hannam* v *Bradford Corporation* (1970) 68 LGR 498 there was a breach of natural justice (because reasonable people might suspect bias) where the education subcommittee which confirmed a teacher's dismissal contained three governors from his school, even though these three had not attended the governors' meeting at which the decision to dismiss was taken. See also *Simpson* v *Bradford Metropolitan District Council* [1974] The Teacher, 13 December. Nevertheless, it is, as the DES put it, 'in the interests of natural justice . . . when a head has, for example, previously suspended [a] member of staff, [that] he should withdraw while the governing body considers its decision' (Letter to Chief Education Officers and others re: *The Education (School Government) Regulations 1989*, 31 August 1989). In practice, disciplinary issues are generally dealt with by a disciplinary committee (see Part 9 below). Natural justice demands that the members selected to form the disciplinary panel should not have participated in the earlier stages in which evidence may have been submitted to the governing body as a whole (see the unreported case considered by Alliott J in October 1990, outlined in a paper by Peter Liell, solicitor and member of the Education Law Association (*Education (School Government) Regulations 1989 (As Amended) and the Rules of Natural Justice* (1993)). Liell reports that the case arose out of a decision by the governing body to set in motion the disciplinary procedure for possible suspension of a teacher from his duties at the school on the grounds of 'gross misconduct'. The disciplinary panel contained governors who had already received details of allegations against the member of staff concerned at the time that the governing body had been asked to initiate the disciplinary procedure, and this amounted to a breach of natural justice.

Finally, the Schedule to the SGR 1989 deals with cases where the governors are considering various matters relating to staff employed at the school, namely, their conduct, continued employment at the school, and the appointment of successors (para 7) (there appears to be some overlap but not inconsistency with para 5(1)(e)). Whether a governor or not, the member of staff should, unless the governors permit otherwise, withdraw from the meeting while consideration and discussion of the matter are taking place. If the member of staff has governor voting rights, he or she may not exercise them in respect of this matter.

(ii) Decisions: voting

Regulation 14(1) of the SGR 1989 states: 'Any question coming before the governing body of a school shall be decided by a majority of the members thereof voting on the question at a meeting of the governing body'. If equal numbers of votes for and against are cast, the chairperson is to have a second or casting vote. A decision for removal of the chairperson must be taken via 'the marking in secret of a voting paper by each member present and voting' (SGR 1989, reg 14(1A), added by the 1993 Amendment Regs, SI 1993 No 3107).

(iii) Minutes and record of persons present

Minutes of meetings are to be recorded in a minutes book and must be signed at the meeting, or at the next one, by the chairperson (SGR 1989, reg 14(5)). If entered on loose leaves, each sheet must be initialled by the chairperson (*ibid*). The chief education officer can, on request, insist on the LEA being furnished with a copy of the signed minutes of a meeting of the governing body (reg 14(6)). A record must be kept of governors and head teacher present at a meeting (reg 22).

As soon as they have been prepared, the draft minutes (if approved by the chairperson) or signed minutes of a meeting, plus a copy of the agenda and reports or other papers considered at the meeting, are to be made available at the school to persons wishing to inspect them (reg 24(1)). However, certain material may be excluded from the minutes before being made available – that relating to: a named teacher or other person employed at, or proposed to be employed at, the school; a named pupil or possible pupil; and 'any matter which, by reason of its nature, the governing body are satisfied should be dealt with on a confidential basis' (reg 24(2)). Note that temporary governing bodies of new schools are excepted from these requirements concerning publication of minutes, etc (reg 24(3)).

9. Delegation

(a) Introduction

The introduction of a detailed legal framework for delegation of decision-making to committees and individuals was the principal area of change to which the Education (School Government) Regulations 1989 gave effect. Previously, delegation was expressly empowered only in the two sets of circumstances laid down in the Education (No 2) Act 1986. The 1986 Act provides that governors can delegate to the head teacher responsibility for any sum of money made available to the governors by the LEA under section 29(1)(b) for expenditure on books, equipment, stationery etc (s 29(1)(d)). Also, the selection of permanent staff (other than a head or deputy head teacher) can be delegated to the head teacher and/or one or more governors (s 38(6)).

Section 8(7) of the E(No 2)A 1986 (as amended by ERA 1988, s 116) empowers the Secretary of State to make regulations providing for the establishment, by governing bodies, of committees of governors and/or others and for the delegation of functions of governing bodies to committees, individual governors and the head teacher. The present regulations came into force on 8 September 1989 (the Education (School Government) Regulations 1989, Part III). The Government has said that these provisions were needed:

> 'because of the greatly increased powers of governing bodies, which may render it impracticable for all decisions to be taken by the governing body . . . and the fact that governors may develop a particular interest or expertise in certain areas, such as finance, the curriculum or staffing, and . . . some decisions in those areas could most efficiently be taken by a small group of such governors' (DES Consultation Document, *Amendments to the Education (School Government) Regulations 1987*, May 1989, para 29).

The changes have also permitted the governors to invite experts on various matters to assist them in their decision-making (such experts will in almost all cases not have voting rights: see below).

Note that the provisions on delegation discussed in this part of the chapter do not apply in grant-maintained schools. However, it may be noted that the articles of such schools may make provision as to the establishment, by the governing body, of 'committees or other bodies of persons' to carry out such functions as may be determined by or under the articles (EA 1993, Sch 6 para 2(3)). Any delegation of functions allocated to the governing body, head teacher, etc must be provided for in the articles (*ibid*, para 2(2); see further, *R* v *Secretary of State for Education ex p Prior* [1994] ELR 231). Initial articles are set out in the Education (Grant-maintained Schools) (Initial Governing Instruments) Regulations 1993 (SI 1993 No 3102).

(b) Delegated functions

The SGR 1989 divide functions into three categories:

(i) those which may not be delegated;
(ii) those which may be delegated only to a committee; and
(iii) those which may be delegated to a committee, a member of the governing body or the head teacher.

All functions other than those listed in categories (i) and (ii) may be delegated as and when the governors think fit (reg 25(1)).

(i) Functions which may not be delegated

These are shown in the table below. These various functions are discussed elsewhere in this book.

Functions which may not be delegated by governing bodies (SGR 1989, reg 25(2), as amended)
Duty to hold a meeting at least once a term (reg 12).
Election of a chairperson and vice-chairperson of governing body (regs 9 and 10).
Convening of selection panel etc for appointment of head teacher or deputy head teacher (ERA 1988, Sch 3, para 1(8)–(10)).
Appointment or co-option of governors (E(No 2)A 1986, ss 3–6).
The power of delegation itself (reg 25(1)).
Functions relating to school admissions (EA 1980, ss 6–8 and ERA 1988, ss 26–32).
Various curricular matters in E(No 2)A 1986, ss 18 and 19 (as amended), including consideration of LEA curriculum policy, aims of secular curriculum for school, control of secular curriculum (subject to s 18(5)).
Responsibilities in relation to the basic curriculum, National Curriculum and collective worship and religious education, standing advisory council on religious education etc (ERA 1988, Ch I).
Responsibilities concerning the manner in which sex education is to be provided and governing the treatment of political issues and activities (E(No 2)A 1986, ss 44–46).
The provision of information (ERA 1988, s 22(1)).
Policies on charging for education and on remissions (ERA 1988, s 110).
Appointment by the governing body of a head or deputy head teacher (ERA 1988, Sch 3, para 1(8)–(10)).
Times of school sessions and the dates of school terms and holidays (E(No 2)A 1986, s 21(2) and (4), as amended).
Statement of governing body's general principles concerning pupil discipline (E(No 2)A 1986, s 22(b)(i)).
Approval of governing body's annual report to parents under E(No 2)A 1986, s 30.
Initiation of procedure for acquisition of grant-maintained status etc (EA 1993, Pt II Ch II).
Governors' role in discontinuance of voluntary schools (EA 1944, s 14) or in relation to their establishment or alteration (EA 1980, s 13).
Governors' role in relation to approval of school premises (EA 1980, s 14).

(ii) Functions which may be delegated only to a committee

In two situations functions may be delegated to a committee, constituted in the prescribed manner (under regulation 26 – see below).

Functions which may be delegated by the governors only to a committee (SGR 1989, reg 25(3) and (4))
Dismissal of member of staff and appeals relating thereto (ERA 1988, Sch 3, para 8).
Reinstatement of excluded pupils and appeals relating thereto (E(No 2)A 1986, ss 24–26).

(c) Committees exercising delegated functions

(i) Constitution etc

Save as otherwise provided in the 1989 regulations, the constitution, membership and proceedings of a committee to which functions have been delegated is to be determined by the governing body (SGR 1989, reg 26(1) and (2)). Most of the provisions of regulations 14, 19, 22 and 24 and the Schedule, which relate to proceedings and minutes of, and withdrawal from, meetings of the governing body (see above), apply also to committees (reg 26(7)). Persons who are *not* members of the governing body may be included on a committee, but shall have no voting rights, save where the committee is considering the question of the use of school premises outside school hours for the purposes of section 42 of the E(No 2)A 1986 (see Ch 2, Pt 4(b)) (reg 26(3) and (6A)).

Special provisions apply in the case of committees with delegated functions relating to (i) dismissal of staff (under reg 25(3)) and (ii) reinstatement of pupils (under reg 25(4)):

- *Dismissal.* The committee must include not less than three members of the governing body. Where this committee is taking an initial or preliminary decision in a dismissal case, no member of it may sit on the committee which hears any appeal (SGR 1989, reg 26(5)(a); see further *R* v *Secretary of State for Education ex p Prior* (1994)). The membership of the appeal committee must comprise no fewer numbers than that of the committee taking the first decision (reg 26(5)(b)). However, if there are fewer than six governors qualified for membership of either committee, or it is not practicable for there to be at least three governors on them, the committees may include fewer than three governors (*ibid*).

- *Reinstatement of a pupil.* The committee must include not less than three governors, none of whom may be the head teacher (reg 26(6)).

(ii) Disqualification

The provisions of regulations 6 and 7 relating to disqualification from membership of governing bodies on the grounds of bankruptcy and possession of criminal convictions (see above) apply also to membership of delegated committees (SGR 1989, reg 26(7)). Note that the House of Lords held that a police officer who was an elected parent governor could serve on an appointments committee without being in breach of police regulations (*R* v *Chief Constable of Gwent* [1989] 139 NLJ 754). It had been argued that such involvement might be viewed by the public as interference with a police officer's impartial discharge of his professional duties; but their Lordships disagreed with this.

(d) Reporting action or decisions

The person or committee to whom delegation has been made must report any action or decision taken to the governing body at their next meeting (reg 27).

10. Incorporation of governing bodies

Governing bodies of county, voluntary and maintained special schools are now, in common with those of GM schools, bodies corporate (EA 1993, ss 34(1), 52(1) and 238(1) and (2)). Governing bodies of schools which have acquired GM status have property, rights or liabilities attributable to the school transferred to them on incorporation (see Chapter 2, Part 4(d)(iv)), and similar transfers have occurred in county, voluntary and maintained special schools (s 238(3) and (4); and see Sch 13).

One of the effects of incorporation is that the governing body acquires a trading name, 'The governing body of (X School)' (s 238(5)). Its seal must be authenticated by the signature of the chairperson of the governing body and some other authorised member (s 238(6)). The specific powers of incorporated governing bodies are listed in sections 68 (GM schools) and 239 (county, voluntary and maintained special schools) of the EA 1993. There are also numerous powers in other provisions – for example the power to reinstate an excluded pupil or in some cases to charge for educational provision. The specific powers of incorporated governing bodies (see ss 68(4) and (5) and 239(1)–(3) of the EA 1993) include powers to:

- acquire and dispose of land and other property (on restrictions including, in some cases, a need for the Secretary of State's consent to dispose of land, see EA 1993, ss 68(7) and 239(3));
- enter into contracts (but only GM schools and, in certain circumstances, aided schools may enter into contracts of employment);
- invest sums not immediately required for the purposes of exercising their functions;
- accept gifts of money, land or other property and apply the

money, etc or hold and administer it on trust, for the above purposes; and

- do anything incidental to the conduct of the school or necessary or expedient in connection with the exercise of their functions.

In the case of county, voluntary and maintained special schools, the exercise of any of these powers must be consistent with the school's instrument and articles of government and the terms of any delegation scheme which applies to the school (EA 1993, s 239(3)).

Some of the key effects of incorporation on governors' potential liability are discussed in Part 11 below.

11. Governing bodies' appellate and complaints jurisdiction

Governing bodies act as appellate and complaints bodies for various purposes. For example, they (generally constituted as a special appeal committee) have appellate jurisdiction over a refusal to grant a parent access to a child's school record, a refusal to admit a child to a school (aided, special agreement or GM school) and the permanent exclusion of a child (aided, special agreement and GM schools). They have complaints jurisdiction in respect of formal complaints by parents that they have acted unreasonably, have or failed, in the performance of their statutory duties as regards the curriculum and the provision of information. These various functions are discussed in the relevant chapters to which they relate elsewhere in the book. This jurisdiction of governing bodies is important but is often overlooked, and has received nowhere near the degree of attention given to LEAs' appellate and complaints jurisdiction (but see N Harris, *Complaints About Schooling* (1992), National Consumer Council).

12. Accountability and legal liability of governors

(a) Introduction

As noted in Chapter 2 (in the course of discussion of Local Management of Schools), the accountability of governors has assumed considerable importance given the degree of autonomy now enjoyed by governing bodies and the wide range of legal responsibilities now resting with them. Accountability can be said to operate at three levels.

First, there is the broadly based accountability that flows from the requirements concerning the provision of information by governing bodies to parents and in some cases LEAs or the Secretary of State. This is discussed in Chapter 6. There is also the information that arises from school inspections under the framework provided by the E(S)A 1992 and EA 1993 (see Chapter 10). Reliance on any or all of this information, in particular information which relates to the 'performance' of a school, gives rise to a kind of 'market-place accountability' through the exercise of choice by parents in selecting a school. Also in this category is the information that must be provided to parents in the governors' annual report, for discussion at an annual meeting with parents (E(No 2)A 1986, ss 30 and 31: see Chapter 6). Accountability also flows from the involvement of elected parent governors on governing bodies and from the provision of information on financial matters (to the LEA), particularly under LMS (see Chapter 3).

Secondly, there are direct forms of intervention by which governing bodies can, in specific cases of default, be called to account by the Secretary of State or, in some cases, the LEA – through, for example, suspension of the right to a delegated budget, appointment of additional or replacement governors, or takeover of the overall management of a school by an Education Association.

Finally, there is the possibility of legal intervention via the courts under civil actions by parents and others. These can take the form of applications for judicial review (for example in respect of a decision to exclude a child: see Chapter 12) or actions for damages. There is also the possibility of personal or corporate criminal liability, for example in respect of breach of health and safety or environmental protection legislation or the misappropriation of funds.

The possibility of personal legal liability has given rise to a most deeply felt concern among individual governors. However, there is now (since the EA 1993) the reassurance that the corporate status of the governing body will offer protection from personal liability in most cases (see below).

(b) Aspects of liability of governors

Governing bodies are protected against personal liability for any act done in good faith for the purposes of expenditure of a school's delegated budget (ERA 1988, s 36(6)). This and other aspects of governors' liability following financial delegation were discussed in Chapter 3.

Prior to the conferment of corporate status on them, governing bodies holding a delegated budget under LMS who entered into a contract did so on behalf of the LEA, which was therefore liable under it (see DES Circular 7/88, para 183). But given the independent functions of governors under education law, as emphasised by the House of Lords in *Brunyate* (*op cit*), it had become increasingly difficult to argue that in general they acted in the capacity of agents for the LEA. Corporate status (previously held only by governing bodies of GM schools, under the ERA 1988) now means that governing bodies enter into contracts on their own behalf (see EA 1993, ss 68(5) and 239(2)).

Governing bodies may, of course, be liable for negligence in respect of certain activities carried on at the school for which they are responsible (e.g. using the school premises for a special event and not making safe arrangements). Premises liability is, however, a complex issue given the division of responsibility for maintenance of buildings between LEAs and governors following financial delegation (see pp 344–345).

Prior to incorporation, the position where governors were liable for negligence was that liability could be joint and several. Thus the negligent action of one governor acting in his or her capacity as such could render each governor personally liable as well as the governing body as a whole. In some cases, a governor who was liable could have been able to claim a contribution under the Civil Liability (Contribution) Act 1978 (ss 1 and 2) from another governor who, for example, perpetrated the negligence. Corporate status now means that liability for actions within the scope of a governor's express or implied authority would lie with the body corporate.

As noted in Chapter 3 (see p 76), LEAs have been required to arrange insurance cover for any personal liability in negligence towards staff or third parties incurred by governors in the exercise of their responsibilities. Such arrangements are to form part of the delegation scheme submitted by the LEA for approval by the Secretary of State (DFE Circular 2/94, *Local Management of Schools* (1994), para 235). However, it is possible that changes to this arrangement may be necessary as a result of incorporation.

Where a member of staff is negligent, the employer may be vicariously liable if the act or omission occurred, *inter alia*, while the employee was acting in the course of his or her employment. Where the governors are the employers they will need to ensure that insurance cover is arranged and that they comply with sections 2 and 3 of the Health and Safety at Work Etc Act 1974 (see pp 349–351). Under delegation schemes, governors will have responsibility for certain health and safety matters (*ibid*).

As shown at various points throughout the book, especially in the course of discussion of admissions, discipline and the curriculum, governing bodies also have responsibilities under the Sex Discrimination Act 1975 and Race Relations Act 1976.

13. Disputes with the LEA

Provision is made in the Education Act 1944 for the resolution of disputes between governors and LEAs. In its amended form the relevant provision (EA 1944, s 67(1)) states:

> 'Save as otherwise expressly provided by this Act, any dispute between a [LEA] and the governors of any school with respect to the exercise of any power conferred or the performance of any duty imposed by or under this Act, may . . . be referred to the Secretary of State; and any dispute so referred shall be determined by him'.

This provision is additional to several others dealing with disputes over particular matters, where the Secretary of State is to decide the issue – for example, over the instrument of government for a voluntary school (see E(No 2)A 1986, s 2(5)–(7)). The Secretary of State may also use powers in EA 1944, ss 68 and 99, where the governors or LEA are acting or proposing to act unreasonably (s 68) or in default (s 99) (these powers are discussed in Chapter 1 at p 5 and Chapter 2 at p 22).

LEAs have, until relatively recently, been able to exert considerable control over schools. LEA policy has shaped local provision. But while LEAs' role in areas such as special educational needs and the enforcement of school attendance is set to continue (DFE, *Choice and Diversity* (1992), paras 6.2–6.8), LEAs are increasingly having to share their diminishing powers and responsibilities. As their powers are stripped away, some LEAs will fight a rearguard action resulting in a short, disputatious era in education administration. As in the past, many of these disputes will result in litigation. However, many of the disputes will be with the new funding authorities rather than governing bodies. Nevertheless, school closures and opting out, sources of considerable, although localised, disputes in the past, will continue to bring LEAs and governing bodies into conflict.

One possible area of conflict between LEAs and governing bodies, highlighted in two cases which both received considerable media attention, has been removed. Section 24(1) of the Education Act 1944 gave the final say on dismissal of teaching staff at county schools (and of teachers, other than those employed to give religious instruction, at controlled schools) exclusively to the LEA. In two cases, both involving alleged racism by serving head teachers, the LEA chose to ignore a recommendation by the governing body against dismissal of the member of staff concerned. In the first of these cases, *Honeyford* v *Bradford City Metropolitan Council* [1986] IRLR 32 (CA), the court held that the articles of government of the school had to be construed in the light of section 24(1) under which the LEA had a residual power to dismiss. In the second case, *McGoldrick* v *Brent LBC* [1986] IRLR 67, the school governors unanimously decided that there was no evidence to substantiate allegations of racist remarks made by an infants school head teacher. She had been suspended by the LEA but the governors demanded her reinstatement. The LEA disciplinary subcommittee subsequently, and unexpectedly, confirmed her suspension at a meeting to which neither she nor her representative were invited. The subcommittee decided to hold a full investigation into the allegations and informed the head teacher of this. At this stage she commenced legal proceedings. In the High Court, Roch J held that the disciplinary subcommittee could not rehear the case and that the governors' findings of fact should stand. The Court of Appeal held that the subcommittee were only bound to follow the governors' findings if those findings supported disciplinary action, for that was what the articles of government and disciplinary code contemplated. Moreover, section 24(1) of the 1944 Act gave the final say on dismissal exclusively to the LEA.

Section 24(1) was repealed by the E(No 2)A 1986, Sch 6, but the LEA retained the final say on dismissals (E(No 2)A 1986, s 35), subject to consultation with the governors and (unless he or she was being dismissed) the head teacher (E(No 2)A 1986, s 41(1)). However, under the ERA 1988, Sch 3, para 8, if a financial delegation scheme is in operation the governors will have the final say on dismissals (see Chapter 5).

14. Expenses

Travelling expenses and subsistence allowances may be paid to governors of county, voluntary and maintained special schools if the LEA makes a scheme for this purpose (E(No 2)A 1986, s 58(1)), although the scheme can differentiate between different categories of school in the level of support offered, but not between different categories of governor of the same school (s 58(2)). However under an amendment made by the EA 1993 this provision for LEA schemes no longer applies to schools with delegated budgets (see EA 1993, Sch 19, para 106), and governors' expenses will therefore be expected to be covered by an LMS scheme instead. A governing body may not use their power (in ERA 1988, s 36(5)) to spend the school's budget share in order to 'pay to governors any allowances other than travelling and subsistence allowances' (ERA 1988, s 36(5B), added by EA 1993, Sch 19, para 125).

LEAs may pay travelling expenses and subsistence allowances to their representatives on the governing bodies of independent schools or special schools not maintained by them (E(No 2)A 1986, s 58(6)(b)). No other allowances may be paid to a governor (s 58(7)).

In a grant-maintained school, the governing body may pay their members such travelling, subsistence 'or other allowances' as may be determined by a scheme for this purpose approved by the Secretary of State (EA 1993, Sch 5, para 14(1)).

15. Information and training

LEAs must provide every governor of a county, voluntary and maintained special school with a copy of the instrument and articles of government for their school and such other information as they consider appropriate for a school governor (E(No 2)A 1986, s 57(a)). No charge may be made to governors for the supply of this information.

LEAs must also secure that 'such training as the authority consider necessary for the effective discharge of (their) functions' is made available (without charge) to every governor (E(No 2)A 1986, s 57(b)). LEAs have been expected to include arrangements for governor training in their proposed schemes for financial delegation (DES Circular 7/88, para 148). Grants are currently paid under the grants for education support and training (GEST) programme. In 1993–94, up to £7m of education expenditure on school governor training was supported by 60 per cent education support grant, and of the £25m maximum expenditure on General Support for School Management supported by ESG, there was a notional element of £8.3m allocated to governor training (see DFE Circular 10/92, *Grants for Education Support and Training 1993–94*).

16. Control of school session times and term and holiday dates

Under section 21 of the E(No 2)A 1986, governing bodies of aided and special agreement schools were to determine the times at which the school session was to begin and end on any day and the dates and times at which school terms and holidays were to begin and end. In county, controlled and maintained special schools, control of such matters lay with the LEA.

The ERA 1988, section 115, substituted a new section 21 of the EA 1944.

The position in aided and special agreement schools is unchanged (EA 1944, s 21(4)). In county, controlled and maintained special schools the LEA must determine term and holiday dates (EA 1944, s 21(2)), but the governing body is to determine the starting and finishing times of school sessions (s 21(2)). If they propose to change session times, the governors may institute the changes only at the start of the school year. They must provide opportunities for discussion of the proposals at the annual parents' meeting and must consult with the LEA and parents and give them three months' notice of the changes. Details of the proposals are to be provided in the governors' annual report; the LEA can insist on their comments being appended to the report. Note that information as to school hours must be made available to parents by the head teacher (Education (School Hours and Policies) (Information) Regulations 1989, SI 1989 No 1799, reg 3) and must be included in the school prospectus (e.g. Education (School Information) (England) Regulations 1994 (SI 1994 No 1421), Sch 2, para 13).

Recent government concern about wide disparities in the amount of teaching time provided in different schools across the country could result in new, prescribed minimum number of hours provision to be made for children at particular educational stages. Governing bodies would be constrained by such requirements when fixing the starting and finishing times of school sessions. Most of the minimum hours of secular instruction which were required to be given under the Education (Schools and Further Education) Regulations 1981, as amended (e.g. at least four hours per day for children over 8) were scrapped in 1991 because they bore little relation to current practice. In their place, guidance was issued in the form of a DES Circular (*Management of the School Day*). No change was made to the requirement (currently in reg 10(2) of the 1981 regulations) that a school year should consist of 380 half-day sessions. Publication of total curriculum time at a school is now required: see p 160.

A further change made by the ERA 1988 concerned the power (formerly in EA 1944, s 21(2), now in s 21(5)) to require a pupil in attendance at a school to receive secular instruction or training other than on the school premises. In county, controlled and maintained special schools this power rested with the LEA. Now the governors of these schools as well as those of voluntary aided and special agreement schools must have this power, under their articles.

Chapter 5

Teachers and other staff

1. Introduction

The employment of teachers is closely regulated – by general employment law and by specific legislation. The latter includes the Education (No 2) Act 1986, the Education Reform Act 1988, the School Teachers' Pay and Conditions Act 1991 and the Education Act 1993; there are also various regulations – in particular the Education (Teachers) Regulations 1993 (The Teachers Regs 1993) (as amended by the Education (Teachers) Amendment Regulations 1993, SI 1993 No 1969, and 1994, SI 1994 No 222). A key provision is section 222 of the ERA 1988, which empowers the Secretary of State for Education to:

> 'make such modifications in any enactment relating to employment and, in particular, in any enactment:
>
> (*a*) conferring powers or imposing duties on employers;
>
> (*b*) conferring rights on employees; or
>
> (*c*) otherwise regulating the relations between employers and employees;
>
> as he considers expedient in consequence of the operation of any of the provisions of this Act [relating to staffing following financial delegation]' (see the Education (Modification of Certain Enactments Relating to Employment) Order 1989).

As employees, teachers and other school staff are, for example, covered by the provisions of the Employment Protection (Consolidation) Act 1978 concerning unfair dismissal and redundancy, the Trade Union and Employment Rights Act 1993, with its amendments on maternity rights and redundancy consultation, and by the Sex Discrimination Act 1975 and Race Relations Act 1976. Trade union rights were affected dramatically by the Employment Acts 1980–90 and the Trade Union and Labour Relations (Consolidation) Act 1992. It is also important to be aware of the ever-increasing encroachment of European law in the field of employment rights, especially in relation to sex equality (and regulation of working conditions, which is discussed in Chapter 13) – although, as Anderman points out (below), the process will continue 'at a slower pace as a result of the UK opting out of the Social Chapter of the Maastricht Treaty'.

It is not really possible, in a work of this nature, to set out in detail major parts of general employment law. On these areas of general application, reference may be made to the specialist works on employment law – such as Wedderburn's *The Worker and the Law* (Penguin) (1986), *Employment Law* (loose-leaf service) and *Employment Handbook* (Tolley), Selwyn's *Law of Employment* (1993), Elliot and Wood's *Industrial Law* (1993) and Anderman's *Labour Law: Management Decisions and Workers' Rights* (2nd ed 1993) (all Butterworths). A particularly useful specialist legal work on teachers' employment is Leighton's *Schools and Employment Law* (1992) (Cassell) – a very practical guide.

The discussion below is of necessity selective and concentrates mostly on individual employer-employee relations.

2. Staffing levels in schools

The Education Act 1944 requires LEAs to ensure that there are for their area schools which are 'sufficient in number, character and equipment' for providing suitable education (s 8), a duty which may be shared with or transferred to a funding authority under section 12 of the EA 1993 (see Chapter 1, Part 2(d)). As we saw in Chapter 2, (at Part 2(b)), LEAs have a duty under section 8 to ensure that not only are school buildings and equipment available, but also essential personnel – although where there are teacher shortages due to unavoidable recruitment difficulties or financial constraints an LEA will not be in breach of this 'target' duty (*ibid*; see in particular *R* v *Liverpool City Council ex p Ferguson* [1985] The Times, 20 November and *R* v *ILEA ex p Ali and Murshid* [1990] The Times, 21 February).

In any event, section 218(1)(d) of the ERA 1988 empowers the Secretary of State to prescribe as to staffing in schools. The Education (Teachers) Regulations 1993 (the Teachers Regs 1993) provide that:

> 'At any school (or further education institution) there shall be employed a staff of teachers suitable and sufficient in numbers for the purpose of securing the provision of education appropriate to the ages, abilities, aptitudes and needs of the pupils (and students) having regard to any arrangements for the utilisation of the services of teachers employed otherwise than at the school (or further education institution in question)' (reg 6(1)).

The staff of teachers employed at the school must include a head teacher (reg 6(2)). Teachers at the school (or FE institution) must be suitably qualified (see below) (*ibid* and reg 6(3)).

Section 34 of the Education (No 2) Act 1986, which applies only to schools which do not have a delegated budget, requires schools to have a 'complement of teaching and non-teaching posts' (including part-time posts) determined by the LEA. In schools which have a delegated budget, LEAs have no power to set a required complement 'but may wish to give governing bodies advice about the staffing levels which it judges would be broadly consistent with the school's budget and with the delivery of the National Curriculum' (DFE Circular 2/94, para 169a). In such a school it is for the governors to decide how many staff should work at the school; advice from the head teacher will clearly be necessary (*ibid*).

3. Qualification for employment as a teacher

(a) Introduction

As the National Curriculum continues to be brought into effect, one of the biggest threats to its success appears to be the shortage of suitably qualified teachers, especially in certain subject areas, such as mathematics and modern languages. Government and teacher-union surveys have also highlighted teacher shortages in certain parts of the country, especially the South-East and inner London, where pay levels are lower than elsewhere, relative to living costs. Shortages of subject specialists have already prompted the Government to empower governing bodies to offer incentive allowances to attract teachers qualified in these subjects to their schools. As a response to the overall shortage of teachers, the Government has also made provision (initially via the Education (Teachers) Regulations 1989) for the employment of 'licensed' teachers and teachers from other European Union countries. Because the licensed teacher scheme involves recruiting as teachers persons without the normal entry requirements, the Government has been accused of hypocrisy by advocating improved quality of educational provision whilst at the same time compromising on teaching qualifications. But shortly before the introduction of the scheme, an education minister (Mrs Angela Rumbold) argued that:

> 'Streamlining the routes to qualified teacher status will help schools and LEAs secure the teachers they need. It will allow mature, well-qualified people who want to turn to teaching in mid-career to do so without having to return to life as a full-time student. The new route will also make it easier for teachers from overseas to take up posts in our schools – their skills and expertise are welcome'.
>
> (DES Press Release 260/89, 17 August 1989).

These new provisions are the latest under which Secretaries of State have exercised their power to control teacher qualifications. The Secretary of State also exercises control over teacher training but the new Teacher Training Agency may be conferred accreditation powers (see the Education Act 1994, Part I). Plans for a 'mums army' of teacher assistants were abandoned by the Government in 1993, but new Teachers Regulations were introduced, making changes to the requirements on employment of teachers at schools (and FE institutions).

(b) The Education (Teachers) Regulations 1993

These regulations apply, in the case of schools, to the employment of teachers in schools maintained by LEAs, non-maintained special schools and grant-maintained schools (reg 3(1)(a)). In addition to prescribing qualifications to teach, they:

(i) prescribe health and physical capacity standards necessary for employment, or continued employment, as a teacher or worker with children or young persons (regs 7–9); and

(ii) give the Secretary of State a power to bar a person from teaching, or to make his or her employment subject to certain conditions:
- on medical grounds;
- on the grounds of a person's misconduct (whether or not he or she has been convicted of a criminal offence in respect of it); or
- on educational grounds (teachers only).

(See further regs 7 and 10).

So far as teaching in a school is concerned, a person may be:

(i) qualified to teach; or
(ii) unqualified, but able to be employed (in some cases as a 'licensed' teacher); or
(iii) unqualified and not able to be employed.

The general rule, laid down in regulation 13 of the Teachers Regs 1993, is that save in specified circumstances 'no person shall be employed as a teacher at a school unless he is a qualified teacher in accordance with Schedule 3'.
The requirement to serve a *probationary* period (previously in Sch 6 to the Teachers Regs 1989) was abolished as from 1 September 1992 (Education (Teachers) (Amendment) Regulations 1992, SI 1992 No 1809; see further DES Administrative Memorandum No 2/92). Nevertheless, for those whose period of probation commenced before that date the requirement to complete a probationary period (which could be extended beyond the normal one year or, in the case of a part-time teacher, two years) will continue (by virtue of the transitional arrangements in the Teachers Regs 1993, Sch 1 para 7).

(i) Qualified to teach

A person cannot be a qualified teacher until he or she has received notification to that effect from the Secretary of State (Sch 3 para 1), or was qualified on 31 March 1993 by virtue of Schedule 5 of the Teachers Regulations 1989. This latter group includes teachers of the mentally handicapped who possess a prescribed diploma (or recognition), who at any time before 8 April 1982 served as teachers in special schools, and who completed three years' satisfactory service in such a school before 1 September 1989 (Teachers Regs 1989, Sch 5, para 2(2)(e)). In such a case, the LEA/governors (as appropriate) must have issued a recommendation in respect of such person to the Secretary of State. Also qualified under Schedule 5 to the 1989 regulations are those who made an application for qualified teacher status under prescribed categories laid down in the 1982 Teachers Regulations and whose application was under consideration by the Secretary of State on 31 August 1989. They were qualified if the Secretary of State decided that they fell within one of the said categories (Teachers Regs 1989, Sch 5, para 2(3)).

The date from which the person is qualified to teach will be as specified in the notification. In an appropriate case, qualified teacher status may be conferred retrospectively: the date of qualification can be stated to commence one year prior to the date of notification (Teachers Regs 1993, Sch 3, para 1(2)). Where a licensed teacher is concerned, the date of qualification must be after the completion by him or her of a prescribed period of service (*ibid*, para 2(6) – see below).

The normal route into teaching is via a Bachelor of Education (B.Ed.), Certificate in Education (Cert.Ed.), or Post-graduate Certificate in Education (PGCE) course. Provided such course is approved for the purposes of initial training of teachers (schools may now provide courses: EA 1994, s 12(1)) and may only be followed by those who have attained grade C standard in English and mathematics at GCSE level (or equivalent), a person will be qualified to teach (Sch 3, para 2(2)).

Those whose qualification to teach was obtained in Scotland or Northern Ireland or who are (i) registered as teachers in Scotland or (ii) recognised as teachers in schools in Northern Ireland by the DFE (Northern Ireland Office), are qualified to teach in schools in England and Wales (Teachers Regs 1993, Sch 3, para 2(2)–(4)). The regulations (like the 1989 regs) also give effect to the requirements of EC Council Directive 89/48 which requires Community Member States to recognise each others' teaching qualifications where any such qualification is obtained after a minimum of three years' training (Sch 3, para 2(5)) (see also EA 1994, s 14(2)).

There are further requirements concerning teachers of pupils who are (i) *hearing impaired*, (ii) *visually impaired*, or (iii) *who suffer from both forms of disadvantage*. Unless he or she has an approved qualification for teaching hearing impaired or visually impaired children (as appropriate), a qualified teacher is qualified to give instruction to such children in a craft, trade or domestic subject only (Teachers Regs 1993, regs 15 and 16). The same applies to a teacher of pupils with both forms of disadvantage (reg 16(1)). However, where the teacher has an approved qualification for the purposes of *either* (i) *or* (ii), he or she is qualified to teach pupils with *both* forms of disadvantage provided the employing authority is satisfied that no person with an approved qualification for teaching them is available (reg 16(2)).

(ii) Unqualified, but able to be employed

Certain teachers can be employed to teach at a school even though they are not qualified (Teachers Regs 1993, Sch 2). In the majority of cases such employment as an unqualified teacher may only be temporary.

One such category refers to persons temporarily employed at special schools as teachers of the visually impaired, hearing impaired, or both, whilst not qualified for such teaching. Any such person may be employed for up to three years (in aggregate), with the proviso that their employing authority is satisfied that it is their intention to obtain an approved qualification for the teaching of such pupils (Teachers Regs 1993, reg 17). Other categories are prescribed in Schedule 2:

(i) existing unqualified teachers permitted by the 1982 Teachers Regs to work as teachers in nursery classes at nursery schools and employed there immediately before 1 September 1989 – they can continue in their employment (but presumably cannot be further appointed after that date);

(ii) student teachers (persons aged 18 or over who have been accepted onto an approved initial training course but are waiting to take up their place, or whose completion of their period of training has been delayed by up to one year (because they have failed satisfactorily to complete their course)) – they can be employed for an aggregate period of up to two years (or longer if authorised by the Secretary of State), provided they are required 'neither to take responsibility for a class nor to teach a subject which is not also taught by a qualified teacher at the school';

(iii) persons employed to give instruction in any art or skill, or in any subject or group of subjects (including any form of vocational training) the teaching of which requires special qualifications or experience; such a teacher may be employed if no suitable qualified teacher, licensed teacher or overseas-trained teacher is available for appointment or to give the instruction, provided that the LEA or governors (as appropriate) are satisfied as to his or her qualifications or experience (see para 3(1)).

The licensed teacher scheme. This came into operation on 1 September 1989. As indicated above, the scheme is intended to provide a more direct route into teaching for mature persons with appropriate experience and qualifications.

Application for a licence may not be made by individuals, but by the 'recommending body', which is defined in reg 3(2)) as:

- the LEA, for maintained schools without delegated budgets and maintained special schools,
- the governing body of a school with a delegated budget, provided the LEA consents (if it does not it must inform the Secretary of State of its reasons: Sch 2, para 5(2)),
- the governing body of a grant-maintained school and a non-maintained special school.

The application is made to the Secretary of State, who is empowered to grant licences to teach to persons named in recommendations (Sch 2 para 5(1)). A recommendation must contain such particulars as the

Secretary of State may determine (Sch 2, para 6), some of which are prescribed by the regulations.

First, there must be a statement by the recommending body that the proposed licensee:

(i) is in their opinion a 'suitable person to be a teacher';
(ii) has grade C in GCSE mathematics and English;
(iii) has completed not less than two years' full-time higher education in England or Wales or comparable full- or part-time education in England and Wales or elsewhere;
(iv) is aged at least twenty-four at the date at which his or her employment is to commence (unless trained outside the UK).

(Sch 2, para 7).

Secondly, particulars of the training proposed to be given to the licensed teacher must be set out (para 7(2)). Not surprisingly, in view of the criticism of the licensed teacher scheme from teaching unions, to the effect that professional standards for teachers would be compromised (as noted above), considerable emphasis is placed on training. Responsibility for ensuring that the licensee receives training rests with the recommending body and, in the case of schools with delegated budgets, the LEA (para 9). DES Circulars 18/89 and 13/91 contain guidance on training and specify the knowledge and competences which the licensee is expected to acquire. Particulars of the means for assessing, after his or her training and the completion of the licence period, the licensee's competence overall are to be submitted with the licence application (18/89 para 26). Circular 18/89 advises that the LEA or governors (as appropriate) should make appropriate arrangements for such assessment (para 28).

Thirdly, there must be a statement detailing prescribed particulars of the post (or, if he or she is to work at two or more schools, the posts) in which the licensed teacher is to be employed. It must state, *inter alia*, the name(s) of the school(s) in which he or she will work, the age range of pupils he or she will teach and the subject(s) in which he or she will specialise (Sch 2 para 7(2)(b)).

The licence is to be granted for a period of two years in the first instance or, in the case of a part-time post or subsequent licence, for such period as may be specified in the licence (Sch 2, para 8(1)). In most cases the teacher would be expected to remain with the recommending school or, where the LEA makes the recommendation, a named school (DES Circular 18/89, *op cit*, para 34). In certain cases the licence may lapse if the teacher ceases to be so employed; the Secretary of State may have to be informed of the facts of the case by the recommending body (Sch 2, para 11).

If a licensed teacher is to attain qualified teacher status a recommendation must be made by the recommending body. If the recommending body is the governing body of a maintained school with a delegated budget, the LEA must give its consent (Sch 3, para 2(6)). The recommendation is made to the Secretary of State. The recommendation should be accompanied by a statement stating that the licensed teacher has successfully completed the necessary licence period in his or her case and his or her training. The minimum period of service as a licensed teacher for this purpose is (*ibid*):

(i) in standard cases, two years full-time or the period of part-time service specified in the licence; or

(ii) one year, where the teacher is aged at least twenty-four and has at least two years' prior teaching experience in independent schools or city colleges or in further or higher education or as an instructor or education officer in the armed forces and in whichever case was not dismissed for reason other than redundancy; or

(iii) one term, in the case of an overseas-trained teacher (see below) or in the case of a person who has successfully completed a course in initial teacher training of at least three years' duration, or a first degree course plus a PGCE course, outside England or Wales.

Special rules apply in Guernsey (see para 2(7)).

Registered teachers in city colleges. A scheme similar to that for licensed teachers (above) has been introduced for persons employed as 'registered' teachers in CCTs and CCTAs (para 2(8)).

Overseas trained teachers. As with licensed teachers (see above), the 'recommending body' (defined above) can grant authorisation for an overseas-trained student to be employed at a school. The recommendation must state that the person named is suitable to be employed as a teacher, has the requisite qualifications (English and mathematics to at least GCSE grade C standard, a university or equivalent degree plus PGCE qualification or a degree in education from a university) and has been employed for not less than one year as a teacher or lecturer and was not dismissed other than for redundancy (Teachers Regs 1993, Sch 2 para 15). Particulars of the post, including subjects and age range of pupils to be taught, must be stated (*ibid*). For the duration of authorisation see para 16.

4. Appointment of staff

The powers and required procedures concerning the appointment of staff to work at a school are found in the ERA 1988, in the case of schools with delegated budgets, in the E(No 2)A 1986, in the case of other LEA-maintained schools, and in the EA 1993 and regulations, in the case of GM schools (delegated budgets, under LMS, are discussed in Chapter 3). The three sets of arrangements are described below, preceded by a discussion of anti-discrimination law.

(a) Anti-discrimination law

The Sex Discrimination Act 1975 outlaws direct or indirect discrimination against women and men on the grounds of sex or marital status as well as victimisation of a person who has complained of an infringement under the Act. There is also the EC Equal Treatment Directive (76/207/EEC), which states that, subject to certain exceptions, 'there shall be no discrimination whatsoever on grounds of sex either directly or indirectly by reference in particular to marital or family status'.

The 1975 Act refers to discrimination against women, although by virtue of section 2(1) applies also to discrimination against men. Direct discrimination falls under section 1(1)(a) of the Act. It involves treating a woman 'less favourably' on the ground of her sex. The sex of the complainant must be a 'substantial cause' of the less favourable treatment: *James* v *Eastleigh Borough Council* [1989] 3 WLR 123 (CA) (and [1990] 2 AC 751, HL), *per* Sir Nicolas Browne-Wilkinson V-C. Indirect discrimination arises if a person applies to a woman:

> 'a requirement or condition which he applies or would apply equally to a man but–
>
> (i) which is such that the proportion of women who can comply with it is considerably smaller than the proportion of men who can comply with it, and
>
> (ii) which he cannot show to be justifiable irrespective of the sex of the person to whom it is applied, and
>
> (iii) which is to her detriment because she cannot comply with it.'
>
> (s 1(1)(b)).

The Race Relations Act 1976 contains similar provisions. It applies to discrimination against a person on the grounds of their 'colour, race, nationality or ethnic or national origins or nationality' (ss 1 and 3(1)). It does not apply to discrimination on religious grounds *per se* (see *Nyasi* v *Ryman* [1988] 367 IRLIB 115 and *Dawkins* v *Crown Suppliers PSA* [1993] IRLR 284 (CA)). There is at present no specific provision proscribing age discrimination, although where age discrimination results from sex or race discrimination there might be a remedy (see, in this context, *Price* v *Civil Service Commission (No 2)* [1978] IRLR 3 and *Jones* v *University of Manchester* [1993] IRLR 218 (CA), discussed below).

There is no need for the discrimination to have been intentional:

> 'The intention or motive of the defendant to discriminate, though it may be relevant so far as remedies are concerned (see section 66(3) of the 1975 Act), is not a necessary condition to liability; it is perfectly possible to envisage cases where the defendant had no such motive, and yet did in fact discriminate on the grounds of sex' (*per* Lord Goff in *Equal Opportunities Commission* v *Birmingham City Council* [1989] 1 All ER 617 at p774).

Discrimination (on the grounds of sex or race) in the arrangements for the recruitment of staff, the terms on which employment is offered and in deciding whether to employ is generally unlawful under the Sex Discrimination Act (s 6, and see Equal Opportunities Commission, *Avoiding Sex Bias in Selection Testing* (1988)) or the Race Relations Act

1976 (s 4). It may, however, be lawful to discriminate in certain situations. Indirect discrimination may be lawful if it is 'justifiable', which requires 'an objective balance between the discriminatory effect of the condition and the reasonable needs of the party who applies the condition' (*per* Balcombe LJ in *Hampson* v *DES* [1989] 2 All ER 294; see further the discussion at pp 221–222 below). In schools this is most likely to arise in the context of the desire to discriminate in favour of particular ethnic groups or a particular gender. In such cases the excuse of 'genuine occupational qualification' might be applicable. If the preference is expressed in terms of religion, the justifiability test alone may determine the issue: see *Board of Governors of St Matthias Church of England School* v *Crizzle* [1993] ICR 407 (EAT), discussed below.

This excuse is based on a test of whether gender or race is a 'genuine occupational qualification' for the post in question (see RRA 1976, s 5 and SDA 1975, s 7). In *Lambeth LBC* v *Commission for Racial Equality* [1990] The Times, 24 April advertisements for management posts in a housing benefit department specifying that applicants from particular racial groups were required were held to constitute a breach of the Race Relations Act 1976, on the basis that belonging to one of these groups was not a genuine occupational qualification because although more than half of the tenants of the council were of Afro-Caribbean or Asian origins, the officer would have little personal contact with them. However, there may be situations where a teacher from an ethnic minority background, perhaps a speaker in a particular language, is needed, and discrimination in recruitment may not be unlawful. In the case of gender, the 1975 Act cites the need for the job to be done by a person of a particular sex 'to preserve decency or privacy' (this may be particularly relevant to PE teachers) or where 'the holder of the job provides individuals with personal services promoting their welfare' (s 7(2)(b) and (e)). The latter exception also appears in the Race Relations Act 1976 (s 5). In *Tottenham Green Under Fives' Centre* v *Marshall (No 2)* [1991] ICR 320, a white person had applied for a post, vacated by an Afro-Caribbean person, as a nursery assistant at a centre where the children were predominantly of Afro-Caribbean origin. In the advertisement, reference was made to an express requirement that a personal awareness of Afro-Caribbean culture was required. The Centre's defence that there was a genuine occupational qualification was rejected by the industrial tribunal because although personal services were provided to the children, maintaining their cultural link, and although the duties included discussion with parents, reading and talking in West Indian dialect and covering skin and health care, all of these, with the exception of knowledge of West Indian dialect, could be provided by any trained nursery assistant. However, the Employment Appeal Tribunal upheld the Centre's appeal. It was considered that, *inter alia*, the service of reading and speaking in West Indian dialect had given rise to a genuine occupational qualification irrespective of the fact that most aspects of the post could be performed by a person of any race (but see *Meer* v *Tower Hamlets LBC* [1988] IRLR 399 (CA) below).

Employers may insist on various requirements, and some of these may be lawful. For example, to insist that a teacher has a good command of the English language would not amount to indirect racial discrimination, either because it is justifiable (see above) in the context of the employer's business (the provision of education) or because it is not the overriding requirement where selection is concerned (*Perera* v *The Home Office* [1980] IRLR 233). Moreover, an act of race discrimination carried out in pursuance of regulations (for example, governing qualified teacher status) might be lawful (*Hampson* v *DES* [1990] 2 All ER 25), because section 41 of the Race Relations Act 1976 excludes from race discrimination an act in pursuance of a statutory requirement.

The onus is on the employer to show that the condition or requirement is justifiable (*Mandla* v *Dowell Lee* [1983], 1 All ER 1062, discussed at p 221 below). But the burden of proving discrimination rests with the complainant (see e.g. *Barking and Dagenham LBC v Camara* [1988] The Times, 18 July), and may present him or her with great difficulties because, taking as an example race discrimination:

> 'there is normally not available to him any evidence of overtly discriminatory words or actions used by the respondent. All that the applicant can do is to point to certain facts which, if unexplained, are consistent with his having been treated less favourably than others on racial [or sex] grounds' (*Chattopadhay* v *Headmaster of Holloway School* [1981] IRLR 487 *per* Browne-Wilkinson, President, EAT).

To be unlawful as indirect discrimination, the requirement or condition must affect one sex or racial (etc) group more than another. In *Price* v *Civil Service Commission (No 2)* [1978] IRLR 3 a maximum age limit of 28 was held to be unlawful sex discrimination because in practice many women spend a period out of work during their twenties in order to bring up children whereas far fewer men do. But in *Jones* v *University of Manchester* [1993] IRLR 218 (CA) it was held that advertising a post for a graduate aged 27–35 did not amount to sex discrimination, because there was no evidence that, among all graduates with the necessary experience, disproportionately more women than men would be deprived of the chance to secure the post as a result of the age stipulation. In *Meer* v *Tower Hamlets LBC* (1988) (*op cit*) an unsuccessful applicant for a legal post with a local authority complained that, as he was a recent immigrant to the UK, a requirement by the authority that an applicant should have local knowledge amounted to indirect race discrimination. The Court of Appeal rejected this argument, because there were a large number of stated requirements and it could not be shown that absence of local knowledge would, alone, have swayed the matter. Nevertheless, subject to the 'justifiability' principle, such a requirement could, in different circumstances (especially where it is the only requirement or the principal one) amount to racial discrimination. A good example of this issue arose in *Board of Governors of St Matthias Church of England School* v *Crizzle* [1993] ICR 407 (EAT), where the governors of a Church of England school specified, in their advertisement for a head teacher, that they wanted to select from 'committed, communicant Christians'. This was clearly thought by the governing body to be justifiable given the religious ethos of the school. The Employment Appeal Tribunal applied the justifiability principle articulated in *Hampson* (see above) and felt that justifiability could be considered in the broad context of the school's provision of education (i.e. including the religious ethos and not confined to the statutory requirements on curricular provision) and the reasonable needs of the governing body in relation to it. The EAT held that the test of justifiability was satisfied in this case.

Complaint may be made to an industrial tribunal (SDA 1975, s 63; RRA 1976, s 54), which may award compensation if a case is made out. Compensation will include an element for restitution (concerning pecuniary loss arising out of non-appointment etc) and, although probably attracting less weight in the assessment, injury to feelings (see *Alexander* v *The Home Office* [1988] IRLR 190). Indeed, in *Murray* v *Powertech (Scotland) Ltd* [1992] IRLR 257 the Employment Appeal Tribunal concluded that a claim for hurt feelings is almost inevitable in any case of sex discrimination; being shocked about being dismissed for being pregnant may be sufficient evidence under the claim. As to the amount that should be awarded in compensation, this will obviously depend on the circumstances of the case. In *Sharifi* v *Strathclyde Regional Council* [1992] IRLR 259 (EAT) it was concluded that in a case of race discrimination £500 would be around the minimum that should be awarded. Although the 1975 and 1976 Acts imposed a ceiling (in the region of £10,000) on the amount that could be awarded (see, for example, s 56(2) of the RRA 1976 and s 65(2) of the SDA 1975), an important ruling of the European Court of Justice suggested that, so far as public-sector employees were concerned, the upper limit set by domestic law conflicted with the requirement to provide a remedy which helped to establish a situation of equality as required by the EC Equal Treatment Directives (76/207/EEC (see above) and 75/117/EEC). This ruling, in *Marshall* v *Southampton and West Hampshire Area Health Authority (No 2)* [1993] 4 All ER 586, was concerned with compensation for dismissal, although it was suggested that the ruling could successfully be applied to other discriminatory acts (B Napier, 'Community law and awards for discrimination' [1993] NLJ 1184). In November 1993 the limit on awards for sex discrimination was removed by the repeal of section 65(2) of the 1975 Act (see the Sex Discrimination and Equal Pay (Remedies) Regs 1993, SI 1993 No 2798). Corresponding amendment of the Race Relations Act 1976 required primary legislation, and the Race Relations (Remedies) Act 1994 has removed the limit imposed by section 56(2).

The tribunal may also make a recommendation that action is taken to stop a discriminatory practice in order to prevent further harm to the applicant. Anti-discrimination legislation is discussed further below, in the context of equal pay, maternity rights, dismissal and redundancy.

(b) Appointments to schools without delegated budgets

(i) County, controlled, special agreement and maintained special schools

Appointments procedures for county, controlled, special agreement and maintained special schools not covered by LMS (which, as all schools in these categories are now covered by delegation schemes – see Chapter 3 – presumably now means only schools whose budget has been suspended) are laid down in sections 36–39 of the E(No 2)A 1986 (and see Sch 2 in the case of new schools). They apply only to posts within the school's 'complement', as determined by the LEA under section 34. The complement is to include all full-time teaching posts, all part-time teaching posts specific to the school, and other non-teaching staff at the school apart from persons employed by the LEA solely in connection with the provision of meals and/or the supervision of pupils at midday (E(No 2)A 1986, s 34(2) and (3)). The LEA has a duty to consult with the governing body and head teacher before appointing a person to work full-time at the school but not as a member of its complement or meals or supervision staff (*ibid*, s 35(2)).

So far as the appointment of head teachers and deputy head teachers is concerned, a selection panel is to be convened (*ibid*, s 36). The panel is to comprise equal numbers of LEA and governor members, being not less than three from each category. LEA and governors may replace one or more of their appointed members at any time. Regulation 29(1) of the Education (School Government) Regulations 1989 states that the panel must make its decision by majority (no casting vote). The panel may decide who is to attend the meeting (*ibid*, reg 29(3)).

Specific rules concerning the appointment of *head teachers* and, by virtue of section 39(1)(a), *deputy head teachers*, are contained in section 37 (E(No 2)A 1986. If a post is vacant it must be advertised nationally. (In the meantime the LEA must appoint an acting head teacher, after consulting with the governing body, but there is no duty to appoint an acting deputy head teacher: s 39(3).) Suitable applicants are to be interviewed. If the panel are unable to agree on the applicants they wish to interview, up to two candidates each may be selected by the governor and LEA factions. An appointment may only be made if the selection panel have recommended the candidate concerned. If the panel feel unable to recommend an appointment they may reinterview such of the candidates as they wish or require the LEA to readvertise the post. These repeat steps should occur if the authority declines to appoint the person recommended by the panel (as it has the power to do).

The chief education officer or his or her nominee has the right to attend all proceedings of the panel, including interviews, for the purpose of giving advice to members of the panel. In the case of interviews for deputy headships, the head teacher is also entitled to be present (whether as a member of the panel or not) and, if not a member of the panel, may give advice to panel members (E(No 2)A 1986, s 39(2)(a)). Whether or not he or she attends selection panel proceedings, he or she is entitled to be consulted before the panel offers a recommendation to the LEA concerning an appointment of a deputy head teacher (s 39(2)(b)).

Appointments to other posts forming part of the complement of the school are not subject to the selection panel procedure. Where there is a vacancy in an existing post, the LEA must decide whether or not it should be retained (s 38(1)(a) – this applies also to vacancies at deputy head level, by virtue of s 39(1)(b)). If the post is to be filled, the LEA must advertise the vacancy, unless the intention is that the post should be filled by an employee who is currently in post with the authority (s 38(1)(b) and (c)). The procedure for making appointments (other than to the post of head or deputy head teacher or to a temporary appointment pending either the return to work of a member of staff or formal selection in accordance with the articles) is laid down in section 38(3). The LEA must advertise the post in such a way as will bring it to the attention of persons qualified to fill it. The governing body must interview any suitable candidates and recommend an appointment (if they can agree and if they consider a candidate suitable – if they cannot agree or do not wish to appoint they may re-interview or ask the LEA to re-advertise the post, which normally it must do: see s 38(3)(e)). The LEA cannot appoint a person to a post which has been advertised in accordance with the requirements of section 38(3) unless the appointment has been recommended by the governors or the person appointed is already an employee of theirs (s 38(5)). But the authority may decline to appoint a person recommended by the governors.

If the intention is to fill a vacancy from among persons already employed by the authority (or appointed and waiting to take up a post), the post does not have to be advertised (s 38(1)(c) – see above). In such a case, the governing body may determine a specification for the post, in consultation with the head teacher, and must send a copy to the LEA (s 38(4)(b) and (c)). The LEA must consult with the governing body and head teacher over the appointment it makes. Consultation with the governors is not required where the appointment is required urgently and the chairperson or vice-chairperson cannot be contacted (Education (School Government) Regulations 1989, reg 31). If it is an appointment with which the governing body disagree, the LEA must report that fact to the next meeting of the appropriate education committee (s 38(4)(c)).

Delegation of functions concerning appointments of staff under section 38 (i.e. not head teachers, deputy head teachers and certain temporary appointments) may be made to (i) one or more governors, (ii) the head teacher, or (iii) a combination of (i) and (ii) (s 38(6)).

The appointment of *clerks* to governing bodies of county, controlled, special agreement and maintained special schools is also regulated (s 40).

(ii) Voluntary aided schools

In voluntary aided schools teachers are employed by the governing body, although, subject to agreement between the LEA and governors, the articles of government may provide that the LEA may prohibit the appointment, without its consent, of staff to give secular instruction at the school (EA 1944, s 24(2)).

Power over the appointment of persons to give religious instruction at voluntary schools remains substantially in the hands of governing bodies (EA 1944, ss 27 and 28; E(No 2)A 1986, s 35(1)(g)).

Note that the requirements of the Education (School Government) Regulations 1989, concerning governor withdrawal from a meeting where matters in which he or she (or his or her spouse) has a pecuniary interest, apply also to meetings concerned with appointment of staff to all maintained schools (see further Chapter 4).

(c) Appointments to schools with delegated budgets

(i) Schools other than aided schools

The provisions of the 1986 Act, noted above, concerned with a 'complement' of staff and staff appointments (and also those concerned with suspensions and dismissals – see below) in county, controlled or special agreement schools do not apply where the school has a delegated budget (ERA 1988, s 44(2)). Within five years of the beginning of a financial year in which a school first has a delegated budget, the articles of government must be amended to include a statement to that effect and also to the effect that section 44 of and Schedule 3 to the ERA 1988 govern staffing matters (ERA 1988, s 44(4)).

Appointment of staff is to be in accordance with Schedule 3, which places appointments firmly in the hands of governing bodies, with increased powers and duties, although the required procedures do not differ markedly from those contained in the 1986 Act.

Where *headships* are concerned, the governing body must notify the LEA of any vacancy or prospective vacancy before it can proceed to select a candidate. While the vacancy remains open, the governing body is to recommend a person for appointment as acting head teacher, and the LEA must appoint him or her unless he or she is not qualified (on academic, professional, physical capacity, etc grounds: para 1(6)) (para 1(4)) – in which case the governors must choose another acting head (para 1(12)). Unlike under the 1986 Act, the governors have the same power in relation to appointing acting *deputy head* teachers (para 1(5)). The governors (not the LEA) must ensure that any vacant headship or deputy headship is advertised nationally (para 1(7)). Candidates whom the governors consider worthy of consideration for the post must be interviewed by a selection panel consisting of at least three governors (para 1(8) and (9)). If the selection panel choose a suitable candidate they must recommend that person to the governing body. If the governing body approves the recommendation, it must recommend the applicant for appointment by the LEA (para 1(9)). If, on the other hand, the panel or governing body do not wish to recommend a candidate, the governors may readvertise the vacancy and/or reinterview the candidates (para 1(10)). The LEA has no power to veto a recommended appointment to a headship or deputy headship other than on qualification grounds (as defined in para 1(6) – see above) (para 1(11)).

Note that the LEA's chief education officer (or his or her nominee: para 11(3)) and, in the case of deputy head appointments, the head teacher, may attend, to give advice, all proceedings of the governing body or selection panel (para 3(1) and (4)). The chief education officer or his or her nominee (or head teacher where a deputy headship is concerned) is under a duty to offer such advice as he or she considers appropriate in relation to appointments of head and deputy head teachers and of those who are to act in such capacity (para 3(2)). If such advice is offered, the selection panel or governors must give consideration to it (para 3(3)).

Appointment of *other teachers* is governed by paragraph 2 of Schedule 3. The governors once again have virtually total control. Note that they may delegate any of their functions in the selection process to (i) one or more governors, (ii) the head teacher or (iii) a combination of (i) and (ii). The first stage in the selection process involves the drawing up by the governors of a specification for the post, in consultation with the head teacher, following which a copy is to be sent to the LEA (para 2(4)). The authority is entitled to nominate for consideration a person already employed by them and, with the permission of the governors, a person employed by the governing body of an aided school maintained by the LEA (para 2(5)). The governors are required to advertise the post unless they decide to recommend a person already employed at the school or a person nominated by the LEA (under para 2(5) – see above) (para 2(6)). The governors are not required to advertise the post nationally, but must advertise it in a manner likely to bring it to the attention of persons who are qualified for it (para 2(7)). Candidates, including those put forward by the LEA (as above) are to be interviewed (para 1(8)(a)). If a candidate is selected, the LEA must appoint him or her unless he or she lacks a necessary qualification (as above) (para 1(10)) – in which case the governors must repeat any of the steps in the above selection process they deem necessary in the circumstances (para 1(11)). Note that as in the case of senior appointments, the chief education officer (or his/her nominee) and head teacher may attend various proceedings in the selection process to give advice – which advice must be taken into consideration by the relevant person(s) (para 3, *op cit*).

There is a simple procedure for the appointment of temporary staff. If the appointment is for a period not exceeding (or not likely to exceed) four months the LEA must appoint the person recommended by the governors (or their delegate – see below) unless he or she does not meet any applicable staff qualification requirements (as defined earlier) (para 2(2) and (3)).

Provision is also made in respect of the appointment of *non-teaching staff* (para 4). The governors are able to select staff for non-teaching posts, and normally the LEA will be required to appoint them (para 4(4)). The governors must, in recommending an appointment (in writing), state the duties to be performed (including the hours, where the appointment is part time), grade considered appropriate, and remuneration (where the LEA has discretion over pay: see para 4(5)) (para 4(2)). The governors must consult the head teacher (and, if the post involves more than 16 hours' work per week at the school, the chief education officer) before selecting (para 4(3)).

The governors may select a person for appointment as their clerk, after consultation with the LEA. The LEA must appoint the person recommended (para 5). But the governors have no control over the appointment of school meals staff where less than 50 per cent of their pay is to be met from the school's budget share (para 10).

(ii) Voluntary aided schools

There are separate provisions governing voluntary aided schools, in section 45 of the ERA 1988. They supersede the arrangements contained in the school's articles under EA 1944, s 24(2) referred to above. The articles must be amended to contain a statement to that effect within five years of the start of financial delegation at the school (ERA 1988, s 45(11)).

The governors have full powers over appointment of staff. The chief education officer may give advice on staff appointments (as under Sch 3 above) if either a voluntary (written) agreement has been struck by the governors with the LEA concerning advisory rights or if the Secretary of State orders that the officer should enjoy such rights (ERA 1988, s 45(4) and (6)). Such advice may, *inter alia*, be in respect of the appointment of head teachers and deputy head teachers alone or of all teachers at the school (s 45(5)).

(iii) Community schools

The financial delegation staffing rules in sections 44 and 45 and Schedule 3 (all of which were outlined above) may apply to persons employed to work at 'community schools', which are maintained schools of the type to which financial delegation may apply (s 47(1)). A 'community school' is one where (a) non-school activities are carried on on the school premises, and (b) all such non-school activities are carried on under the managing control of the school's governing body (ERA 1988, s 47(2)). A delegation scheme may, for the purposes of these staffing rules, treat positions involving work solely or partly for the purposes of non-school activities carried out on the school premises as though such activities were school activities (s 47(3)), thus enabling the staffing provisions to apply.

(d) Grant-maintained schools

In grant-maintained schools, the governing body has a power to appoint teachers and other staff (EA 1993, s 68(5)(d)). Schedule 2 to the Education (Grant-maintained Schools) (Initial Governing Instruments) Regulations 1993 (SI 1993 No 3102, as amended), which sets out the initial articles of government for GM schools, lays down separate procedures for the appointment of (i) head and deputy head teachers (para 17) and (ii) other staff (para 18).

For head and deputy head teacher appointments, the governing body must advertise the vacancy in appropriate publications in England and Wales. Shortlisting and interviews are to be conducted by a selection panel of at least three governors. The final decision on the appointment rests with the governing body as a whole; thus the selection panel may only make a recommendation. The governing body may appoint an acting head teacher or deputy head teacher pending the filling of the vacancy.

Decisions on the appointment of other staff also rest with the governing body, but the selection of staff may be delegated to one or more governors, including the head teacher. In any event, the head teacher must be consulted over any selection. Posts must be advertised, unless it is decided to fill a vacancy from among persons already working at the school.

5. Discipline, detriment and dismissal

As is the case where appointments are concerned, different arrangements concerning discipline and dismissal of staff will apply to schools which have and those which do not have delegated budgets. It is clear that the shift towards even greater control by governing bodies over appointments (see above), which LMS has brought, has occurred with equal intensity in relation to discipline and dismissal. The most remarkable of the changes is the power of governing bodies of county, controlled or special agreement schools to require LEAs to dismiss members of staff. This has removed a cause of conflict between LEAs and governors, which was highlighted in the *Honeyford* and *McGoldrick* cases in 1986 (see Chapter 4, at p 110). There are separate disciplinary provisions covering GM schools (see below).

Staff discipline in the context of allegations of child abuse at school is discussed in Chapter 13 (Part 4(d)(iii)).

(a) Sex and race discrimination and harassment

All schools are subject to anti-discrimination law as it affects staff discipline. The Sex Discrimination Act 1975 (s 6) and Race Relations Act 1976 (s 4), discussed above in relation to appointment of staff, outlaw discrimination when dismissing an employee (which includes making them redundant) or subjecting them to 'some other detriment'. As noted above, also relevant to sex discrimination is the Equal Treatment Directive 76/207/EEC, which states that, subject to certain exceptions, 'there shall be no discrimination whatsoever on grounds of sex either directly or indirectly by reference in particular to marital or family status'. The Directive clearly applies to dismissal.

The scope of 'detriment' in the context of the Race Relations Act seems to be somewhat limited, as *De Souza* v *Automobile Association* [1986] IRLR 103 illustrates. Here an employee referred to a black colleague in a racially insulting manner. Despite the obvious offence caused to the woman concerned, the Employment Appeal Tribunal held that the words 'or other detriment' had to be taken to refer to a detriment of a similar type to dismissal. In their opinion the insult did not. It is clear, however, that sexual (or racial) harassment can amount to other detriment (*Porcelli* v *Strathclyde Council* [1985] ICR 177; *Snowball* v *Gardner Merchant Ltd* [1987] ICR 719), but the employer will have a defence if he or she or it has taken reasonable steps to prevent the action concerned (see *Balgobin* v *Tower Hamlets LBC* [1987] ICR 829). In a survey by the NAS/UWT in 1987, 72 per cent of female secondary school teachers reported that they had been sexually harassed at work. An important development in this area is the Recommendation and Code of Conduct on sexual harassment issued by the EC in 1991. The Recommendation condemns sexual harassment and calls on employers to take steps to ensure that it does not occur. The Code states that harassment covers any unwanted conduct of a sexual nature, including 'unwelcome' physical, verbal and non-verbal conduct. Such conduct is considered unacceptable if it is used to influence decisions on the employee's status or prospects within the organisation or if it 'creates an intimidating, hostile or humiliating working environment'. Conduct will, for this purpose, be unacceptable if it is 'unwanted, unreasonable and offensive' (see further Lester [1993] NLJ 1473).

So far as sex discrimination is concerned, one area of difficulty for the law has been pregnancy of female employees. An important question has been whether the dismissal of an employee because she is pregnant is dismissal on the grounds of sex and, if it is, if it amounts to direct or indirect discrimination for the purposes of the Sex Discrimination Act 1975. The case law suggests that it would be *direct* discrimination, on the basis that the discrimination would not have occurred but for the fact that the person discriminated against is a woman. In *Berrisford* v *Woodford Schools* [1991] ICR 364 an unmarried assistant school matron was dismissed when she became pregnant and refused to marry. The EAT accepted that she had been dismissed not for pregnancy *per se* but rather the message it conveyed to pupils. Also, if a male teacher had engaged in extra-marital sex he would have been dismissed. In *James* v *Eastleigh Borough Council* [1990] 2 AC 751 (HL), a local authority's reduced charge for entry into the municipal swimming pool applied to persons once they reached state retirement age (60 for women, 65 for men). Although the local authority had not sought to discriminate between men and women, and were following a long-standing policy on concessionary rates, the discrimination against the complainant would not have occurred if she were not a woman. There had been direct discrimination. This case was distinguished in *Bullock* v *Alice Ottley School* [1993] ICR 138, where the Court of Appeal found that there had not been direct discrimination when an employer operated a retirement policy under which teaching and domestic staff retired at 60 and maintenance staff (all of whom were men) retired at 65, since the two groups did not fall to be compared for the purposes of the 1975 Act because of the different selection procedures, which in neither case based selection on gender but rather on skills and recruitment difficulty. In *Dekker* v *SVJV* [1991] IRLR 27 the ECJ found that there had been direct discrimination where a pregnant interviewee, who was considered the best candidate for the job, was not appointed. However, in *Webb* v *EMO Air Cargo (UK) Ltd* [1992] 4 All ER 929 (HL), where a female employee, engaged by the firm to replace another employee who was taking maternity leave, became pregnant and was dismissed, the House of Lords held that the employee had been dismissed not because of her pregnancy *per se*, but rather because it 'had the consequence that she would not be available for work during the critical period' (*per* Lord Keith at p 934). But the ECJ ([1994] 4 All ER 115) held that Directive 76/207/EEC had been breached; yet the position might have differed if her contract had been fixed term (see *Napier* [1994] NLJ 1020). (See further p 143 below.)

Female staff who wish to resume work following maternity leave, under the right to return (see below), may also face discrimination. In *Hughes* v *Leeds City Council* ((1994) *Education Law Monitor* 11), a college typist who wished to return following maternity leave asked to be taken back on a job-share or part-time basis, which the employer (the LEA) generally agreed to in such cases. However, the college principal was opposed to this and the authority turned down the woman's request. A tribunal, which heard the woman's complaint of sex discrimination, felt that the authority was in breach of the 1975 Act because the proportion of men who could carry out the work on a full-time basis was greater than the proportion of women who could do so. The imposition of the condition (namely, of working full time as opposed to part time) was thus indirect sex discrimination, and the tribunal felt that this could not be objectively justified. In another case, *Clay* v *Governors of the English Martyrs School* ((1994) *Education Law Monitor* 12), which concerned a female English teacher with eight years' service at the school, who was denied the opportunity to return to work on a job-share basis following maternity leave, the employers sought to justify their decision by arguing that there were sound educational reasons for preferring full-time teaching staff, in that job-sharing caused disruption. However, with evidence that the LEA had a job-share scheme for teachers, the tribunal were not convinced that job sharing by teachers could be regarded as causing detriment to children's education. Thus it was concluded that there had been unlawful sex discrimination (see further p 143 below).

Another tribunal case on a closely related issue has also seen the Sex Discrimination Act 1975 invoked to protect part-time workers' rights (which are considered further at pp 138–139 below). In this case, *Tickle* v *Governors of Riverview School and Surrey County Council* ((1993) *Education* 229) a part-time teacher employed on a fixed-term job-share basis, was informed in February 1992 that at the expiry of her contract in September of that year she would be replaced by a full-time (and, as it happened, newly qualified) teacher. As in the previous case, the tribunal could not accept that there was any reason justifying the decision to replace her with a full-timer and found that there was unlawful sex discrimination. The selection of part-time workers for redundancy, when part-time workers are more likely to be females than males, may also give rise to a breach of the SDA 1975 (see *Clarke and Powell* v *Eley (IMI) Kynock Ltd* [1983] ICR 165 (EAT) and *Bhudi and Others* v *IMI Refiners Ltd* [1994] The Times, 7 March (EAT)).

The role of industrial tribunals, to whom complaints may be directed, was discussed earlier in relation to appointments (above, Part 4(a)). For the purposes of relevant parts of the Sex Discrimination Act 1975 and Race Relations Act 1976, the governing body is the employer following financial delegation (Education (Modification of Enactments Relating to Employment) Order 1989, arts 2(2) and 3(1)) (but see below as to the LEA's liability to meet the cost of dismissals and redundancies).

(b) Discipline and dismissal of staff in schools without delegated budgets

County, controlled, and special agreement schools are required to incorporate the provisions of section 41 of the E(No 2)A 1986 into their articles of government (see DES Circular 7/87 Annexes 5–7 for *Model Articles*). The section applies to staff employed in a post which forms part of the 'complement' of the school (as defined in s 34 – see above, Part 4(b)) and to staff employed to work solely at the school in any other post, apart from one involving only the provision of meals or midday supervision of pupils (s 41(3)).

The power of dismissal rests with the LEA as employer. But under the section, the LEA must consult the head teacher (except where he or she is the person concerned) and governors before dismissing a member of staff (other than a reserve teacher at a controlled or special agreement school – who can be dismissed by the foundation governors: EA 1944, s 27(5) and 28(4)). Such consultation is also required where the LEA otherwise requires a person to cease to work at the school or allows a person to qualify for premature retirement compensation by taking early retirement (s 41(1)(a)).

The governing body is entitled to recommend that a person should cease to work at a school. In such a case the LEA must consider the governors' recommendation (s 41(1)(c)). There is also a power, resting with the governors and the head teacher, to suspend (without loss of pay) a teacher or other member of staff employed to work at the school (s 41(1)(d) and (2)). The head teacher or governors (as the case may be) must be notified by the party suspending the member of staff, and so must the LEA (s 41(1)(e)).

Disciplinary and grievance procedures are generally drawn up by the LEA in consultation with trade unions.

(c) Discipline and dismissal of staff in schools with delegated budgets

(i) County, controlled and special agreement schools

Suspension and dismissal of staff working at county, controlled and special agreement schools with delegated budgets are governed by ERA 1988, Sch 3 (s 44(3)). The requirement to amend the articles within five years from the start of financial delegation, to incorporate the Schedule 3 provisions (see above), refers also to such disciplinary matters (s 44(4)). Other provisions, which remain operative, are those giving foundation governors of controlled or special agreement schools the right (under

EA 1944 ss 27(5) and 28(4)) to insist on the dismissal of unsatisfactory reserve teachers (s 44(5)).

So far as discipline is concerned, the position is that:

> 'The regulation of conduct and discipline in relation to the staff . . . and any procedures for affording to members of the staff opportunities for seeking redress of any grievances relating to their employment, shall be under the control of the governing body'.
>
> (ERA 1988, Sch 3, para 6(1)).

The governing body is required to establish disciplinary rules and procedures and grievance procedures and take steps to make them known to staff at the school (*ibid*, para 6(2)). DFE Circular 2/94 (*Local Management of Schools*, para 175) urges governing bodies to ensure that the procedures are fair. As the Circular also points out (whilst offering little guidance on the point), the governing body may delegate the handling of disciplinary and grievance procedures to the head teacher, an individual governor or a committee (see the Education (School Government) Regulations 1989, in Chapter 4, Part 9(b); note that decisions and appeals relating to dismissals may be delegated only to a committee: reg 25 of the 1989 Regs).

If the governing body is not empowered by the Schedule to take the particular measures which it considers are necessary in the given case, it may request the LEA to exercise its powers and the LEA must comply (para 6(3)). The governors and head teacher will continue to enjoy the power to suspend a member of staff (without loss of pay) (para 7(1)), as under the 1986 Act previously. As before, they must inform each other of any decision to suspend (para 7(2)). In schools without delegated budgets, the governors or head teacher must end the suspension of a member of staff when required to do so by the LEA (E(No 2)A 1986, s 41(1)(e)); but in schools with delegated budgets a suspension may only be ended by the governing body (ERA 1988, Sch 3, para 7(3)). The governors must inform the head teacher and LEA of their decision, immediately (*ibid*)).

The power to order the dismissal of a member of staff (or the clerk to the governing body) rests basically with the governing body, although the LEA must be informed of their decision (paras 8(1), (6) and (9)). A person employed to work solely at the school concerned must be given an opportunity to resign; if he or she does not do so, then within 14 days from being notified of the governors' decision the LEA must terminate his or her contract of employment – if entitled by law to do so (para 8(2)). If the employee is not employed to work solely at the school, the LEA must take him or her away from it, whereupon the cost of his or her salary shall cease to be included in the school's budget share (para 8(3), (4) and (5)).

A person threatened with dismissal must be given an opportunity to make representations (orally, if he or she wishes) and to appeal against the decision; the governors are required to make appropriate arrangements (para 8(7) and (8)). As noted above, regulation 25 of the Education (School Government) Regulations 1989 requires the committee to consist of at least three governors, appointed by the governors (see further *R* v

Secretary of State for Education ex p Prior [1994] ELR 231, discussed in (d) below). Persons who took part in the original decision should not sit on the appeal committee, as such involvement would give rise to a breach of natural justice (as in *Ridge* v *Baldwin* [1964] AC 40). The chief education officer (or his or her nominee) and, unless it is he or she who is threatened with dismissal, the head teacher, are entitled to attend in an advisory capacity any meetings or hearings at any stage of the dismissal process under paragraph 8 (para 8(9)).

Note that the LEA may only dismiss on the grounds of failure by the teacher to satisfy prescribed standards of health, physical capacity, qualifications, etc required to teach (para 9(2)).

(ii) Aided schools

In aided schools with delegated budgets the power to suspend or dismiss rests with the governing body (ERA 1988, s 45(3)). If they decide to dismiss a member of staff the governors must notify the LEA of their decision in writing (s 45(9)). If the governors agree with the LEA that the chief education officer shall enjoy advisory rights, or if the Secretary of State requires such rights to be conferred, the chief education officer may attend the meeting and give advice on the suspension or dismissal of a teacher. Advisory rights may be limited to dismissals of certain grades of personnel (e.g. head and deputy head teachers) (s 45(4)–(8)). Where the member of staff who is to be suspended or dismissed is employed by the LEA, the provisions of ERA 1988, Sch 3, paras 8 and 9, outlined in (i) above, apply (s 45(10)). Within five years of the school receiving a delegated budget, the articles of government must be amended to include a statement that the above provisions are applicable while the school has such a budget (s 45(11)).

(d) Discipline and dismissal of staff in GM schools

The requirements on staff disciplinary matters in GM schools are laid down in schools' articles of government (see Sch 2 to the Education (Grant-maintained Schools) (Initial Governing Instruments) Regulations 1993, SI 1993 No 3102 as amended by SI 1994 No 2094). The governing body is required to establish disciplinary rules and procedures, but the control of all disciplinary matters rests with a Staff Committee, which the governing body is required to establish (it must have not less than three members who are governors, but may also have non-governor members: *ibid,* instrument of government, para 36), although it must consult the head teacher before taking disciplinary action ('disciplinary action' is defined as including 'any action relating to the suspension or dismissal of any person employed to work at the school' (art 19)).

An important decision relating to the organisation or conduct of Staff Committees is *R* v *Secretary of State for Education ex p Prior* (1994). Here the Staff Committee in a GM school, which was convened to hear a disciplinary matter in respect of a teacher, Mr P, included a chairman,

Mr C, appointed by the chairman of the governing body. The teacher complained about this and about the fact that the school's disciplinary procedures stated that it should be the head teacher who should present the complaint against a member of staff, rather than, as was planned for the hearing concerned, the chairman of governors. The Staff Committee rejected these complaints. After the teacher and his representative left the meeting, the hearing continued in their absence. When the Secretary of State refused to use his powers in sections 68 or 99 of the EA 1944 to intervene, the teacher successfully sought judicial review to quash the Secretary of State's decision. Brooke J concluded (at p 250):

> 'I . . . do not understand how he [the Secretary of State] could reasonably have directed himself that the invalidity of Mr C's presence did not appear to give cause to challenge the decisions which were then made. The Secretary of State seems to have completely overlooked the fact that Mr P refused to recognise those who purported to be clothed with the powers of the staff committee, as he was legally entitled to do; and that in those circumstances if the three people on the panel proceeded with a hearing as if they had legal authority to conduct one, their proceedings, and the proceedings of any subsequent appeal committee which proceeded on the basis that their decision was *intra vires*, were fundamentally flawed. In these circumstances the observation that the default did not appear to give cause to challenge the decision of the staff committee was not one which in my judgment any Secretary of State properly directing himself on the facts and the law could reasonably have arrived at'.

Both the Staff Committee and the head teacher have a power to suspend a member of staff. If the head teacher suspends he or she must inform the Staff Committee of the decision plus reasons immediately. Only the Staff Committee have a power to end a suspension. If they exercise this power the Committee must immediately inform the head teacher (art 20).

Only the governing body may dismiss a member of staff, whether summarily (if the circumstances justify it in law) or by giving notice. But the prescribed procedure is such that before matters get to that stage the Staff Committee must have considered the matter and made a determination, and the member of staff concerned must have had an opportunity to exercise his or her right of appeal. When the Staff Committee are to consider a case where dismissal is a possibility they must give the member of staff concerned at least seven days' written notice of the meeting at which the dismissal is to be considered and inform him or her of his or her right to make written and/or oral representations to the Committee (which the Committee are required to take into account). The head teacher may attend the meeting and, apart from in a case where the head teacher's dismissal is under consideration, any advice he or she gives to the Committee must be taken into account by them. Before reaching a final decision on the matter the governing body must consider the Staff Committee's determination and give the member of staff concerned a right of appeal against it. The appeal lies to an appeal committee.

It must be stressed that the appeal committee is quite a separate entity from the Staff Committee and the governing body. The constitution of the appeal committee is prescribed by the instrument of government (SI 1993 No 3102, *op cit*, para 43). The committee must comprise an odd number of persons (not less than five) drawn from the governing body – but the head teacher and members of the Staff Committee are not eligible to serve on the appeal committee. The appeal committee members must appoint a chairperson from amongst their number and a select a clerk (who must not be drawn from among appeal committee members). Note that joint appeal arrangements may be made between the governing bodies of two or more schools (art 12(2)).

An appeal procedure is laid down in Appendix 2 to the articles. (Rules on withdrawal of committee members from proceedings in the event of personal interest in the outcome etc, similar to those contained in the Education (School Government) Regulations 1989 in relation to other schools (see Chapter 4), are set out in para 38 of the initial instrument of government.) The procedure laid down in Appendix 2 to the articles states that the appellant may attend the hearing and/or make representations. The head teacher and a member of the Staff Committee may make written representations. The appellant and the Staff Committee member may be represented. In the event of disagreement between the appeal committee members as to the decision which should be taken, voting may be by majority, with the chairperson having a second or casting vote in the event of a tie. The appeal must be heard in private, although a member of the Council on Tribunals may attend. The appeal committee's decision must be communicated in writing to the appellant, the governing body and the head teacher.

Finally, account ought to be taken of Brooke J's comment in *ex p Prior* (*op cit*) (at p 251):

> 'I should add . . . how important it is that the governors of a grant-maintained school should have access to good legal advice before they set in motion dismissal procedures'.

(e) Period of notice to terminate employment

The statutory minimum period of notice, laid down in the EPCA 1978, s 49, is one week for a person with one month to two years' service, plus one further week for each further completed year of service up to twelve years. Twelve weeks is the maximum notice that need be given therefore. Where teachers are concerned, the usual requirement (laid down in the teacher's contract of employment) is for two months or one half term's notice – or three months if the appointment is to end at the end of August.

(f) Unfair dismissal and redundancy

When exercising the power of dismissal, governors and LEAs should bear in mind the provisions of the Employment Protection (Consolidation) Act 1978 concerning unfair dismissal. This is distinguishable from 'wrongful dismissal', which refers to summary dismissal without notice in breach of the employment contract – for which damages, *inter alia*, may be obtained at common law. Note the employee is entitled to a written statement of his or her terms and conditions of employment within two months of commencing employment with the employer (EPCA 1978, s 1). The written 'contract of employment' must contain the prescribed information (on pay, hours, holiday, sickness etc; see s 1(3)). The teacher's responsibilities will need to be spelt out. General responsibilities are prescribed under the School Teachers' Pay and Conditions Document – see below.

Dismissal occurs where an employer terminates an employee's contract of employment, or fails to renew a fixed-term contract, or where an employee resigns because of the employer's conduct which amounts to a repudiation of the contract of employment. This last type of dismissal is known as 'constructive dismissal'.

Unfair dismissal is a complex area and warrants considerably more space than this book can provide. Moreover, over-simplification could be potentially misleading. Consequently it is only desirable here to inform the reader who is unfamiliar with this area of a few basic principles which may assist in identifying possible cases of unfair dismissal.

An important point to note here is that by virtue of the Education (Modification of Enactments Relating to Employment) Order 1989, the employer for the purposes of unfair dismissal is in every case the governing body (art 4(b); for guidance, see DES Circular 13/89). But any award made by an industrial tribunal against an 'employer' is treated as made against the LEA (or the funding agency in the case of GM schools), not the governors. In other words, the position seems to be that if the governors sack unfairly, the LEA (or funding agency) must foot the bill! However, in the arrangements concerning financial delegation spelt out in DES Circular 7/88, LEAs were advised that they could withhold from a school's budget share the cost of any dismissal which the LEA considered was 'likely to be found unfair before an Industrial Tribunal' (para 167).

The EPCA 1978 provides that rights in respect of redundancy and unfair dismissal only apply to staff:

(i) who work for at least 16 hours per week and who have at least 2 years' continuous service; or
(ii) in the case of those who work less than 16 hours but at least 8 hours per week, 5 years' continuous service, with the LEA or governors or with them and other LEAs or governors, although if their hours have changed from 16 or more to below 16 but at least 8, they are treated for 26 weeks as being employed for 16 hours per week.

(EPCA 1978, s 64 and Sch 13).

However, the House of Lords recently held that the differing thresholds in the EPCA 1978 referred to above were incompatible with Article 119 of the EEC Treaty and the Equal Pay and Equal Treatment Directives:

Equal Opportunities Commission and Another v *Secretary of State for Employment* [1994] 1 All ER 910. The court concluded that the Secretary of State had not shown that the differences were objectively justified. More part-time workers were women rather than men, so the provisions clearly discriminated indirectly, and yet no evidence had been presented to show that the beneficial social policy aim of the discriminating rule – to increase employment opportunities by providing employers with an incentive to make part-time work available – had been achieved as a result of the provisions.

Note that an employee cannot, for the purpose of the weekly hours thresholds (above), add together the hours worked under separate concurrent employment contracts with the employers if they truly are separate (*Lewis* v *Surrey County Council* [1987] 3 All ER 64).

So far as continuity of employment is concerned, breaks between successive fixed-term temporary contracts, as used quite often by LEAs, could be construed as temporary cessations of work such as would not break continuity of employment (*Ford* v *Warwickshire County Council* [1983] IRLR 126). In a recent industrial tribunal case, reported in the *TES* (2 April 1993), a home economics teacher who had been employed on four successive one-year contracts was shortlisted for, but not offered, a permanent post at the school concerned. She complained that she had been unfairly dismissed. The tribunal, by a majority, rejected the employer's argument that the contracts had, over the past two years, been genuinely temporary in view of the uncertainty over the National Curriculum requirements. Note that if an LEA-maintained school becomes grant-maintained, continuity of employment is preserved (EA 1993, s 39). A period of maternity leave (see below) will not break continuity of employment.

For dismissal not to be classifiable as unfair the employer must first show that it was for one or more of the reasons set out in section 57 of the EPCA 1978:

(i) This refers to the employee's capabilities or qualification for the post for which he or she is employed. Capability here refers to skill, aptitude, health or other physical or mental qualities (see, in particular, the requirements concerning qualified teacher status discussed in Part 3 above). Lying about one's qualifications to the employer could amount to 'some other substantial reason' which justifies dismissal (see (v) below).

(ii) This relates to the employee's conduct, in work (e.g. persistent and unjustified lateness or absenteeism, assault of pupils, sexual harassment of member of staff etc) or outside – if capable of prejudicing the employer's business (e.g. (a) *Gardiner* v *Newport County Borough Council* [1974] IRLR 262 – art college teacher's gross indecency with another man in a public convenience so regarded; see also *Wiseman* v *Salford City Council* [1981] IRLR 202; (b) *Tabor* v *Mid-Glamorgan County Council* [1982] COIT 1/65/7 – teacher of teenagers allowed others to grow cannabis in his garden and was convicted of possession of the drug; even though he did not use cannabis his dismissal was regarded as fair (cf *Norfolk County Council* v *Bernard* [1979] IRLR 220); (c) *Vogler* v *Hertfordshire County Council* [1975] The Times, 7 and 8 November – teacher had sexual intercourse with 16-year-old pupil and his dismissal was fair).

(iii) Redundancy is another reason. It occurs where a dismissal is 'attributable wholly or mainly' to either one of two factors:

(*a*) that the employer has 'ceased or intends to cease, carrying on the business for which the employee was employed by him, or . . . to carry on that business in the place where the employee was so employed' (EPCA 1978, s 81(2)(a)); or

(*b*) 'that the requirements of that business for employees to carry out work of a particular kind, or for employees to carry out work of a particular kind in the place where he was so employed, have ceased or diminished, or are expected to cease or diminish' (s 81(2)(b)).

In *Murphy* v *Epsom College* [1985] ICR 80, the college, which already employed one plumber to help run the boiler and carry out plumbing work, employed a second (M). The boilers were modified but caused a good deal of trouble, and eventually the college decided to hire a heating engineer and retain only one of its two plumbers. M was dismissed. He claimed that his dismissal was unfair. But it was held that he was redundant, because of a change in the requirements of the business for work of M's kind. A heating engineer was needed for the new system and could assist with the plumbing too. Guidance on redundancy selection in LMS schools was given in *Cooke* v *Governors of Horsell High School* [1994] IRLIB (503) 9/10.

If the employee unreasonably refuses an offer of suitable alternative work from the employer he or she will not be redundant and so will qualify for no redundancy payment regardless of length of service (e.g. *Taylor* v *Kent County Council* [1969] 3 WLR 156).

Consultation and notice (in some cases to the Secretary of State) concerning proposed redundancies are required under both national agreement and statute (see the Trade Union and Labour Relations (Consolidation) Act 1992, ss 188–192, subject to the EC Acquired Rights Directive (77/187/EEC); see also *National Union of Teachers* v *Avon County Council* [1978] IRLR 58).

Statutory redundancy pay is calculated on the basis of the number of complete years of continuous service (up to a maximum of 20 years) multiplied by weekly pay at the date that redundancy occurs (subject to a ceiling, currently set at £205 per week). In the calculation, account is taken of the age of the person being made redundant. If he or she is between the ages of 18–21 (inc), each year attracts half a week's pay; if he or she is aged 22–40 each year attracts one week's pay; for persons over this age each year attracts one-and-a-half weeks' pay. For example, a person made redundant at the age of 60 after 19 years' continuous service, who earns £250 per week, will be entitled to £5,842.50 in statutory redundancy pay. He or she may also qualify for additional sums under a collective agreement. Persons made redundant when aged 64 lose one-twelfth of their entitlement for each month that they have continued to be employed after their sixty-fourth birthday. Persons made redundant after their sixty-fifth birthday do not qualify for a statutory redundancy payment (EPCA 1978, s 81, as amended).

Fredman and Morris explain that where a teacher is able to take advantage of early retirement provisions, the benefits will be offset against redundancy compensation, 'with the effect that a teacher who has received the maximum of ten years' enhanced superannuation will not receive any redundancy compensation' (Mansell, *The State as Employer: Labour Law in the Public Services* (1989), p 301).

Account may, in redundancy cases, have to be taken of the Transfer of Undertakings (Protection of Employment) Regulations 1981, which seek to give effect to the EC Acquired Rights Directive (*op cit*). The regulations, which were amended by section 33 of the Trade Union Reform and Employment Rights Act 1993, provide that where a 'relevant transfer' of an undertaking occurs the employees will be transferred to the employment of the new employer (as stated in Chapter 2, under the EA 1993, an employment transfer occurs where a school becomes GM and the employers become the governing body in place of the LEA). Where services to schools and/or LEAs are privatised, especially in the context of compulsory competitive tendering, staff may in some instances be transferred to the employment agency which takes over the work (see Department of the Environment Circular 10/93). In *Kenny* v *South Manchester College* [1993] IRLR 265 (QBD), the High Court held that the transfer of prison education services following competitive tendering was a transfer of undertakings within the terms of the EEC Directive. See also *Dines and Others* v *Initial Health Care Servies Ltd and Another* [1994] The Times, 28 May (CA). Anderman (*Labour Law: Management Decisions and Workers' Rights* (1993), Butterworth, p 181) notes that:

> 'following recent decisions of the [European Court of Justice] it is quite clear that the directive is meant to apply to a wide variety of transfers including those between non-commercial ventures and those involving the initial contracting out of services or part of an operation from one employer (public or private) to another, as long as the business has retained its identity and the operation is continued'.

If there is a 'relevant transfer' for this purpose, one of the effects will be that the transferee employer will have the statutory obligations vis-à-vis redundancy that the previous employer would have had had the transfer not taken place.

(iv) Another reason is that the employee could not continue to be employed without the employer breaking the law (e.g. the employee is employed as a driver but has been disqualified from driving).

(v) There is some other substantial reason justifying an employee's dismissal. In *Saunders* v *Scottish National Camps* [1980] IRLR 174 the dismissal of a man from his job as a maintenance handyman in a children's camp when he was discovered to be homosexual was held to be fair – even though he was not a danger to children nor worked in close proximity to them.

If the employer can prove that one of the above applies, the dismissal will be fair provided that he or she acted reasonably in the circumstances (having regard to the size of the employer's business and its administrative resources) in treating the reason as sufficient to warrant dismissal (EPCA 1978, s 57(3)). The question of whether or not the employer did act reasonably is to be determined 'in accordance with equity and the substantial merits of the case' (*ibid*). According to Anderman (*Labour Law: Management Decisions and Workers' Rights* (1993), Butterworth, pp 134–135), an industrial tribunal will ascertain whether the employer acted reasonably in forming his or her view of the facts, 'in the sense of having reasonable grounds for his belief that the employee had committed an act of misconduct or was incapable as alleged'. In *ILEA* v *Gravett* [1988] IRLR 497 (EAT) for example, the industrial tribunal found that the employer had genuinely believed that a swimming instructor had indecently exposed himself to a 13-year-old girl and had indecently assaulted her. They dismissed him. But the objective test of reasonableness was not satisfied because the employer's investigation had not been sufficiently thorough and had not produced adequate conclusive evidence that would have led a reasonable employer to effect a dismissal (contrast the case of *Dick* v *University of Glasgow* [1993] IRLR 581). In *P* v *Nottinghamshire County Council* [1992] ICR 362 the Court of Appeal found that it was reasonable, where an assistant school groundkeeper had pleaded guilty to indecently assaulting his daughter, for the employer to have believed that he had committed the offence and to have concluded that the risk to children at the school justified his dismissal.

If the employer acted reasonably in reaching his or her conclusions on the facts the next question will be whether a reasonable employer would, on those facts, have concluded that dismissal was warranted. This will, of course, depend on the gravity of the 'offence', etc. The question of procedural fairness will come into the reckoning. Here it will be a question of whether a reasonable employer would have given adequate warnings, a 'second chance', etc, if the circumstances justified it, before deciding to dismiss. Anderman (*op cit*, p 143) concludes from the cases that 'the only excuse for a procedural omission is that the step would have been futile in any event judging from the time of the dismissal'.

Note that if a tribunal finds that dismissal was unfair they may award compensation and/or (although rarely ordered) re-engagement or reinstatement. Compensation may consist of a 'basic award', which is calculated in exactly the same way as statutory redundancy pay and takes into account the employee's age, length of service and rate of pay on dismissal (subject to a statutory maximum); there may also be a 'compensatory award' of an amount up to a prescribed maximum, currently £10,000 (EPCA 178, ss 72–75) (higher awards are possible in discrimination cases). More generous compensation (under a special award) can be awarded if the employee is dismissed for belonging to, or refusing to join, a trades union. Both compensatory and basic awards can be reduced on various grounds, including the employee's conduct.

Payment of compensation will be the responsibility of the LEA, in the case of LEA-maintained schools, the funding agency, in the case of GM schools, and the proprietor, in the case of independent schools.

(g) Pregnancy/maternity

There is general protection against dismissal for pregnant workers and those on maternity leave (see also p 131 above). For example, an employee may not lawfully be dismissed on the grounds of pregnancy (or childbirth during a period of maternity leave) unless her pregnancy means that she would not be capable of carrying out her duties adequately or even if she could her employment would be in breach of another statutory provision (e.g. prohibiting expectant mothers from working with radioactive substances) (EPCA 1978, s 60). It is also unfair dismissal to dismiss an employee for, *inter alia*, availing herself of maternity leave (*ibid*, which has been substituted by section 24 of the Trade Union Reform and Employment Rights Act 1993) (see also EPCA 1978, ss 45–47, on the circumstances in which an employee may be suspended from work on maternity grounds and the employee's rights on such suspension). If an employee is on maternity leave and has a right to return to work (Part 8 below) the employer must either permit her to resume her post or offer her an alternative one. Failure to offer an alternative would amount to unfair dismissal, unless the employer can show that there is no suitable vacancy (see *John Menzies GB Ltd* v *Porter* (1992) (EAT)).

The employee may be entitled to statutory maternity leave (see Part 8 below).

6. School teachers' pay and conditions

(a) Introduction

The system of free collective bargaining through which teachers' pay and conditions in state schools were determined prior to 1987 was replaced in that year. Parliament replaced the Remuneration of Teachers Acts and the Burnham Committee forum for the negotiation of pay and conditions with a system through which the Secretary of State can impose a pay award on teachers. Under the Teachers' Pay and Conditions Act 1987 the Secretary of State was able to give legal effect to teachers' pay and conditions by Order. Although the Secretary of State received advice from an Interim Advisory Committee of between five to nine persons with knowledge of or experience in education, and despite a statutory consultation process in which LEAs, teachers' unions, governors' organisations and others could make representations, at the end of the day the Secretary of State could determine these matters as he thought fit.

The 1987 Act was repealed by the School Teachers' Pay and Conditions Act 1991, which established a review body of five to nine members (see Sch 1) (appointed by the Prime Minister) to examine and report on matters relating to the statutory conditions of employment of school teachers in England and Wales. The Secretary of State may give directions to the review body as to the matters they are to consider. The review body must consult with prescribed interested parties (including LEA associations, governors of GM schools and teaching associations). The review body must report its recommendations to the Secretary of State and the Prime Minister (s 1). Teachers' pay scales, allowances and conditions are laid down in the *School Teachers' Pay and Conditions Document*, which is presently issued, in revised form, annually. Legal effect is given to this by the relevant School Teachers' Pay and Conditions Order. Before these are given legal force, there must be further consultation with the above-mentioned interested parties (s 2). This secondary legislation can lay down a wide range of matters, including a limit on the number or proportion of teachers at a school who may be paid on the specified scales. It will contain in particular the relevant pay scales, London allowances, incentive allowances and other discretionary allowances and increments, including incentives to aid recruitment of teachers in areas of subject shortage. Note that a governing body of a GM school may apply for exemption from the Order (s 3).

The method of calculating pay, the rates and scales of remuneration and the conditions of employment (including professional duties of head teachers, deputy head teachers and others) are, at the time of going to press, set out in the *School Teachers' Pay and Conditions Document 1994* (see the Education (School Teachers' Pay and Conditions) (No 2) Order 1994, SI 1994 No 1673) (see DFE Circular 7/94)).

(b) Pay

(i) Statutory pay scales, allowances and increments

As noted above, these are currently laid down in the *School Teachers' Pay and Conditions Document*. The powers and duties of governing bodies and LEAs with regard to payment of allowances, including the five rates of incentive allowance and the discretion to award additional increments for excellence in teaching, are all set out in the Document, to which reference should be made. Note, however, the effect of equal pay legislation, discussed below.

(ii) Equal pay legislation

Every contract of employment contains an implied equality clause under which employers must *inter alia* provide employees with equal pay for 'like work', work rated as equivalent by a job evaluation study and 'work of equal value', save where there is a 'genuine material difference (other than sex)' between the two workers being compared (Equal Pay Act 1970, s 1, and Equal Pay (Amendment) Regulations 1983, SI 1983 No 1794). Article 119 of the Treaty of Rome (with Directive 75/117 and 76/207) lays down a principle of 'equal pay for equal work'.

Implementation of the provisions gives rise to a number of problems for schools. Firstly, the basis of comparison might involve not only comparing, say, one teacher with another, but also comparing people employed in posts which are different but which might be considered to be of equal value (e.g. female dinner ladies and male council workers: see *North Yorkshire County Council* v *Ratcliffe and Others* [1994] The Times, 11 May (CA)). It may also involve comparing specific terms of the contracts concerned, such as basic rates of pay and overtime, even if the contracts as a whole are no more or less favourable than each other (*Hayward* v *Cammell Laird Shipbuilders Ltd* [1988] 2 All ER 257 (HL)).

Secondly, justification for differential pay for people performing like work or work of equal value may depend not only on experience and qualifications for the job, but also on 'red-circling', where persons are in effect demoted but kept on protected salaries (this seems to be lawful, at least in the short term), and situations where a higher rate of pay is offered to attract teachers to areas of subject shortage. The latter seems to be lawful, by analogy with a case where the court felt there had been no breach of the 1970 Act where a health authority had to offer higher pay to mostly male workers who previously worked for a subcontractor carrying out work for the authority (*Rainey* v *Greater Glasgow Health Board* [1987] IRLR 26 (HL)). Indeed, in *Ward* v *Cheshire County Council* (1991) (cited in Leighton, *Schools and Employment Law* at p 63) the fact that statistics showed that there were fewer applicants for music-teacher posts than for drama-teacher posts justified not paying a head of drama an incentive allowance whilst paying one to a head of music. In *Enderby* v *Frenchay Health Authority* [1994] ICR 112 the European Court of Justice, on a reference from the Court of Appeal, held that in relation to Article 119 of the Treaty of Rome (see above), it was to be left to the national court to determine whether the need to offer higher pay due to a likely shortage of candidates for a post constituted an objectively justified economic ground for the difference in pay between two jobs of equal value, and that if the national court could determine what proportion of the higher pay was attributable to market forces, it had to accept that the pay differential was objectively justified (to the extent of that proportion). In *North Yorkshire County Council* v *Ratcliffe and Others* (1994) (*op cit*) dinner ladies' and male council workers' work had been established to be of equal value. However, when a competitive tendering process was followed it was necessary to pay the dinner ladies a lower rate of pay in order to compete with the commercial rates. These rates did discriminate against the women, but it was held that because they were due to the operation of market forces, the 'material factor' defence under section 1(3) of the 1970 Act was available.

When finances are tight, schools can clearly seek to recruit staff as cheaply as possible. But this may lead to inequalities between two workers which, in the short term, may be justified by the financial constraints, but in the longer term may be more difficult to justify, especially where no efforts have been made to increase the pay of the disadvantaged worker (see *Benveniste* v *University of Southampton* [1989] IRLR 122).

(c) Conditions

The precise scope of teachers' professional duties was always unclear. Some aspects, such as lunch-time supervision, were highly contentious. One work written before the Teachers' Pay and Conditions Act 1987 noted that: 'In over a century of public education, there has been no agreement between LEAs and their teacher employees on what teachers are required to do in order to earn their salaries' (D Nice (ed), *Education and the Law* (1986), p 136). Often teachers argued that certain activities, such as those taking place outside school hours, were voluntary, while their employers argued that they were contractual. Now these duties are spelt out in detail in the *School Teachers' Pay and Conditions Document*. While there may still be argument over matters of interpretation, the scope of teachers' duties and the extent of their paid working time are generally clear. In some cases, the precise duties to be performed by main-scale and deputy head teachers will depend in part on the particular duties from time to time assigned to them by the head teacher.

The *School Teachers' Pay and Conditions Document* sets out separately the conditions of employment of head teachers, deputy head teachers and other school teachers. The conditions contained in the 1994 Document are set out in full in *Appendix 3* to this book.

Various matters, such as a teacher's timetable, class contact time, entitlement to travel expenses and sick-leave arrangements, will continue to be determined locally – either by LEA-wide or school-based negotiation. While 'consultation' has largely superseded 'negotiation' over teachers' conditions (which produced the *Burgundy Book* spelling out teachers' conditions of service), there is still scope for national agreement.

7. Pay and conditions of non-teaching staff

Pay and conditions for non-teaching staff employed by local authorities are almost entirely determined via collective bargaining and national agreement between employers and unions. Local authority services tend to be heavily unionised, the major unions being UNISON (formed in 1993 through an amalgamation of NUPE, NALGO and COHSE, and representing administrative and clerical staff such as school secretaries but also education welfare officers and social workers), the National Union of Public Employees and the General, Municipal and Boilermakers' Union (which represent, *inter alios*, school caretakers, delivery drivers, school meals staff and others). Reference should be made to the various 'books', such as the *Purple Book* governing town hall workers' pay and conditions. Local agreement, on various matters such as manning levels, overtime, supervision and other work arrangements, also plays a role. The privatisation of certain services to schools and LEAs has had an impact on the pay and conditions of some workers.

So far as the pay and conditions of administrative, professional, technical and clerical (APTC) staff and manual workers following financial delegation are concerned the position is explained in DFE Circular 2/94 (para 173) as follows:

> 'Pay and conditions of non-teaching staff will continue to be on a non-statutory basis. For new non-teaching staff, the governing body will be able to specify the duties to be performed and the appropriate grade within the scale of grades currently applicable to employment with the LEA. In most cases these grades will be those resulting from the national agreements . . . It is for the governing body to select the grade that it considers appropriate for the post. The governing body will also be able to exercise any discretion over remuneration which the LEA has in making the appointment. An example would be the point of entry to a scale for APTC staff. Other conditions of service are for the LEA and will usually be those which are defined in the relevant national or local collective agreement . . .'.

So far as appointments are concerned, the LEA will make the appointment but selection will often be made by the governing body (see pp 127–129). When making the appointment the LEA will have to take account of statutory provisions and national and local collective agreements, except where they conflict with the legal powers enjoyed by the governors. For example, governors are responsible for disciplinary procedures (ERA 1988, Sch 3, para 6) (see further DFE Circular 2/94, para 174).

8. Maternity leave and pay

Under the statutory maternity leave provisions (see EPCA 1978, ss 33, 45–48 and Sch 2), the employee may be absent for a period of up to twenty-nine weeks after the birth (and a further four weeks on certain grounds, e.g. illness – s 47) and eleven weeks before the expected week of confinement (or less if she so elects – see *ILEA* v *Nash* [1979] ICR 229), and has a right to return to work, although not necessarily the same post, thereafter. The employee must, however, give three weeks' written notice of her return (see EPCA 1978, s 40). The employer may postpone her return for up to four weeks (s 42). If on her return, the employee's post is no longer available, the employer is (unless he or she employs five or fewer employees) required to offer a suitable alternative, and if this is turned down dismissal would not be unfair (s 56A). The employee must be offered work of a similar nature which she is capable of doing and which is in the same place (see s 153(1)).

An employee only qualifies for the right to return if, no more than eleven weeks before the expected week of confinement, she has been continuously employed (see above) for at least two years and gives notice (at least twenty-one days, unless impracticable) to her employer that she will be absent due to pregnancy and wishes to return. Note that the employee may be required by her employer to confirm that it is her intention to return to work at the end of her leave. Seven weeks after the birth the employer may demand an answer on this question from the employee, who has two weeks in which to reply (s 33(3A)).

(*Note:* section 35 used to give an employee who qualified for the right to return the right to maternity pay, whether or not she intended to return. It was paid for six weeks at the rate of 90 per cent of a week's earnings minus state maternity allowance. Payment fell due from the beginning of the eleventh week before the expected week of confinement or later if the start of leave was delayed by the employee. Now the employee must generally claim statutory maternity pay under the Social Security Contributions and Benefits Act 1992 (s 166). For the first six weeks this is paid at the rate of nine-tenths of the woman's normal weekly earnings, broadly the same amount as would have been available under the previous system. From the seventh week the standard rate, set at £48.80 from April 1994, is payable. Statutory maternity pay is paid (by the employer) for eighteen weeks in all.)

These rights are additional to any maternity rights available to the employee under the terms of her contract of employment. If there is any overlap or conflict between the rights under the contract and those in the statute, the employee may choose whichever she considers are the more favourable (EPCA 1978, s 48; see *Bovey* v *Board of Governors of the Hospital for Sick Children* [1978] IRLR 241).

9. Time-off rights

(a) Trade union activities

Time off for trade union activities is available to trade union officials and trade union members in certain circumstances (TULRCA 1992, ss 168–170; see also ACAS, *Code of Practice (No 3): Time off for Trade Union Duties and Activities* (1991)).

Officials of trade unions which are recognised for the purposes of the Trade Union and Labour Relations Consolidation Act 1992 are entitled to paid time off work in certain circumstances. Basically, paid time off must be granted to enable them to receive training or to carry out their union duties where related to negotiations with an employer or a matter concerned with a trade dispute, provided the activity relates to the kind of matter for which the union is recognised by the employer. Clearly, if a union official is mediating in a disciplinary matter involving a member of his or her union or is attending a meeting with his or her national officials in connection with a dispute at a school, he or she would be entitled to paid time off in connection with such activities (see G Pitt, *Employment Law* (1992), Sweet and Maxwell, pp 102–103). Note that in *Hairsine* v *Kingston-upon-Hull City Council* [1992] IRLIB 10 (EAT) it was held that only trade union duties performed during contractual working hours attract the right to paid time off.

Members of trade unions are entitled to unpaid time off during working hours to participate in union activities. Industrial action does not count as a union activity for this purpose, although an official may have a right to time off in respect of his or her role (see above). Union elections or meetings to consider an employer's offer in the course of a dispute would most probably be a union activity. In one case, *Luce* v *Bexley LBC* [1990] ICR 591, the EAT had to decide whether the attendance of officials of the NUT to lobby Parliament over the Education Reform Bill counted as a union activity for the purposes of the right to time off. The EAT felt that in the circumstances it was not such an activity since it was more in the form of a protest action rather than an attempt, through the use of persuasive argument, to persuade Parliament to vote in a particular way.

There is no prescribed limit to the amount of time which those entitled to time off for union duties or activities may take, but the cases suggest that only a reasonable amount of time may be taken (see Pitt *op cit*, p 104).

(b) Public duties

The EPCA 1978 (s 29) permits persons to take reasonable time off work to perform certain public duties, including service as a school or college governor, a member of a statutory tribunal (this would include education appeal committees as well as social security appeal tribunals etc), or a magistrate. Employees may be *required* to be absent from work for jury service or, if served with a *subpoena*, to attend court as a witness.

10. Teacher appraisal schemes

Statutory machinery exists for the regular appraisal of the performance of teachers in the discharge of their duties (E(No 2)A 1986, s 49(1)). Appraisal is to be carried out by LEAs or other prescribed persons (*ibid*); in GM schools the governing body is the appraising body. Under regulations made by the Secretary of State (the Education (School Teacher Appraisal) Regulations 1991 (SI 1991 No 1511)) governing bodies are obliged to ensure that appraisal arrangements are complied with and that LEAs receive proper assistance (s 49(3)). Provision may also be made for teachers to be informed of the results of an appraisal and given an opportunity to make representations.

So far as schools are concerned, appraisal regulations may apply to teachers, including head teachers and deputy head teachers, at any maintained school (including one which is grant-maintained) and any non-maintained special school; they may also apply to unattached teachers employed by an LEA (*ibid*, and ERA 1988, Sch 12, para 36). Detailed guidance on appraisal is given in DES Circular 12/91 (*School Teacher Appraisal*). Appraisal is carried out on a two-year cycle. Teachers employed part time on contracts involving less than 40 per cent of full-time hours, and certain others such as licensed teachers, are not covered by statutory appraisal under section 49 at present.

11. Retirement

Under national agreement, male and female teachers alike must generally retire at the age of 65 and may retire, on full benefits which have accrued by then, at the age of 60. Pressurising a teacher into taking early retirement could amount to constructive dismissal leading to a claim for unfair dismissal. Pensions entitlement and compensation for premature retirement are governed by the Superannuation Act 1972, the Teachers' Superannuation (Consolidation) Regulations 1988 (SI 1988 No 1652), as amended, and the Teachers' (Compensation for Redundancy and Premature Retirement) Regulations 1989 (SI 1989 No 298), as amended.

Chapter 6

Publication and provision of information

1. Introduction

In the four years since the previous edition of this book, the range of legal requirements concerning the publication and provision of information about schools and schooling has grown significantly. The Government argues that the consequential administrative burden on schools and LEAs is justified by the need to inform parental choice of school and promote greater accountability on the part of education providers. Promising to build on the existing information provision regime, the Government indicated in its *Parent's Charter* in 1991 that parents would be able to enjoy access to 'five key documents', which comprised 'A report about your child . . . Regular reports from independent inspectors . . . Performance tables for all local schools . . . A prospectus or brochure about individual schools . . . An annual report from your school's governors'. Requirements relating to the first three of these documents have been introduced over the past couple of years, whilst publication of school prospectuses and annual governors' reports has been mandatory since the 1980s (see below).

The Education (Schools) Act 1992 and regulations made under it require information relating to school performance to be published in comparative tables (often known as examination 'league tables'). These, and the long-standing requirement that schools publish their examination results in prospectuses, have proved to be highly controversial aspects of the policy on publication of information, because of concern about the distorting effect of raw data on judgements about the worth of a particular school. The Government has begun to look at the inclusion of information showing 'value added', which offers a more accurate picture of attainment levels; indeed, one Secretary of State announced that such an element would be phased in, starting in 1995 (see House of Commons Education Committee, Session 1992–93, *Publication of Examination Results, Minutes of Evidence,* 25 November 1992, Annex A). Truancy rates have been added to the range of performance information to be published. In due course there will also be requirements to publish information on pupil 'destinations' (university, college, training, employment etc). Institutions in the FEFC sector (see Chapter 2) are now covered by similar requirements on publication of performance-related information (see FHEA 1992, s 50, and the Education (Further Education Institutions) (Information) (England) Regulations 1993, SI 1993 No 1993 and (Same)

(Wales) Regulations 1993, SI 1993 No 2169; see also DFE Circular 3/93, *The Parent's Charter: Publication of Information About the Performance of Colleges in the Further Education Sector in 1993*).

2. Information on school admissions arrangements

The Education Act 1980 (s 8(1)) requires LEAs and governing bodies to publish annually particulars of the arrangements:

(i) for admission of pupils to maintained schools;

(ii) for the provision of education at schools maintained by another LEA or not maintained; and

(iii) for enabling a parent to express a preference for a particular school (under s 6(1) of that Act) and to appeal against the appropriate authority's decision on admission to a school (under s 7(1)).

Other information which the 1980 Act requires to be provided includes the *admission number*, i.e. the standard number applicable to admissions to a school (EA 1980, s 8(3)(a), as substituted by ERA 1988, s 31(2)), and the policy followed in deciding admissions (EA 1980, s 8(3)(c)). Regulations made under section 8 of the 1980 Act require the publication of various forms of information about schools, which parents might wish to consult when exercising their right to express a preference for a school (see below).

Where *grant-maintained* schools are concerned, their articles of government are to require the governing body to publish, for each school year, details of admissions and appeal arrangements (EA 1993, Sch 6 para 6).

3. Information on educational policy and provision

In addition to the power to make regulations under section 8 of the EA 1980 (as amended) on the provision of information about schools, the Secretary of State has a power, in section 22(1) of the ERA 1988, to make regulations requiring LEAs, and governing bodies and head teachers of maintained schools, to make certain forms of information available 'either generally or to prescribed persons, in such form and manner and at such times as may be prescribed'. This information may relate to the educational provision and syllabuses followed at maintained schools, and to the educational achievements of pupils (s 22(2)) (but not the result of the assessment of an individual pupil, under the National Curriculum or otherwise: s 22(5)). The information may also convey the contents of various documents – reports and policy statements such as the LEA's statement of curricular policy; the governors' statement of how, if at all, the LEA's statement should be modified; the governors' statement of curricular policy for their school; and the governors' annual report (s 22(3)). Regulations may authorise charges for the provision of documents supplied (s 22(6)) (see below).

Some of the information on educational policy and provision must also relate to schools' performance (with inclusion of examination results in prospectuses). In addition, there are separate regulations specifically governing school performance information, discussed in Part 4 of this chapter.

There are currently four main sets of regulations on the publication of information on educational policy and provision:

(i) The Education (School Information) Regulations (England) 1994, SI 1994 No 1421 and (Wales), SI 1994 No 2330;

(ii) The Education (School Curriculum and Related Information) Regulations 1989, SI 1989 No 954, as amended;

(iii) The Education (Special Educational Needs) (Information) Regulations 1994, SI 1994 No 1048; and

(iv) The Education (Individual Pupils' Achievements) (Information) Regulations 1992, SI 1992 No 3168 (reg 8 only); (Same) 1993, SI 1993 No 3182 (all); and (Wales) Regulations 1993, SI 1993 No 835.

The Education (Information as to Provision of Education) (England) Regulations 1994 require LEAs and the FAs to provide each other and the Secretary of State with prescribed information on school capacity and accommodation etc.

(a) LEA information to be sent to parents of prospective pupils

The information which falls under this heading is policy and arrangements in respect of primary, secondary and special education (Education (School Information) Regulations (above), Sch 1). Under this category, LEAs must, in advance of a school year and (except where the information relates exclusively to primary education or special educational provision) at least six weeks before parents may express a preference for a school, send parents of prospective pupils information about their schools and make it available at schools, libraries and LEA offices. The information is to include schools' names and addresses, numbers on the roll and any religious affiliation. Also to be included are statements as to LEA policy on such matters as examination entry, transport to and from school, and special educational needs.

In addition, from 1 August 1995 governing bodies will have a duty to send a copy of the prescribed information on special educational provision at the school to parents who request it (Education (Special Educational Needs) (Information) Regulations 1994 (SI 1994 No 1048), reg 3). A copy must also be sent to an LEA, funding authority or District Health Authority who requests one (*ibid*).

(b) Information for inclusion in a school's 'prospectus'

Certain types of information about individual schools must be published by the governors in a 'school prospectus', which must be made available to parents on request and for reference by parents and others (Education

(School Information) (England) Regs, *op cit*, reg 11, and (Wales), *op cit*, reg 9 and Sch 2; see also EA 1993, s 153(1)).

The categories of school-specific information required to be included in the prospectus have broadened considerably since the first publication requirements were introduced in the early 1980s.

Information concerning the curriculum for inclusion in school prospectuses
Name, address, telephone number of school.
Names of head teacher and chair of governors.
Classification of the school (county/voluntary aided etc; primary, middle or secondary; comprehensive, secondary modern, grammar or bilateral; co-educational or single-sex; etc).
Admissions policy.
Arrangements for visits by parents of prospective pupils.
Secondary schools: number of places for pupils at normal age of entry; number of written applications or expressions of preference for places.
Statement on curriculum and organisation of education and teaching methods at the school, including special arrangements for statemented pupils and others.[a]
A statement on 'the ethos and values of the school'.
In the case of any county, voluntary or maintained special school (other than a special school established in a hospital) information on the procedure for curriculum etc complaints under section 23 of the ERA 1988.[b]
A summary of the content and organisation of sex education.
Particulars of careers guidance and arrangements for work experience (if any).
Religious affiliation of the school, if any, and particulars of religious education and parental right to withdraw their child from it.
A summary of charging policy and policy on remission of charges.
Dates of school holidays, including half-term holidays; and the times at which each school session begins and ends on a school day.
Changes relating to any of the above as compared with the previous year.
Various prescribed particulars on the level of attainment achieved by pupils in relation to the National Curriculum are subjects, and, in some cases, local and national averages; in a secondary school, prescribed information on GCSE, A/AS level and vocational qualification results and the destinations of pupils who have left (e.g. employment, further or higher education, training etc).
In Wales, particulars of the Welsh language at the school.
Various prescribed particulars relating to the level of unauthorised absences of pupils.

Notes

[a]From August 1995 school prospectuses for 1996–1997 onwards must summarise the school's special educational needs policy. See DFE Circular 6/94 *The*

Organisation of Special Educational Provision (1994) and the Education (Special Educational Needs) (Information) Regulations 1994 (SI 1994 No 1048).

[b]In one survey in 1992, only 18 per cent of primary school prospectuses and 28 per cent of secondary school prospectuses were shown to contain this information: N Harris, *Complaints About Schooling* (National Consumer Council, 1992), p 121.

(c) Information to be published with the governing body's annual report to parents

School governors in LEA-maintained schools and grant-maintained schools must prepare, and, where reasonably practicable, distribute to parents copies of, an annual report (E(No 2)A 1986, s 30; EA 1993, Sch 6 para 8). The report must set out, *inter alia*, the manner in which the governors have exercised their various functions, the dates of the beginning and end of each term and of half-term holidays, and a summary of any changes to the school prospectus (Education (School Curriculum and Related Information) Regulations 1989, reg 4(1) and (Same) (Wales) Regulations 1991, reg 8; the Education (Grant-maintained Schools) (Initial Governing Instruments) Regulations 1993 (SI 1993 No 3102)). Amendments made by the Education (Pupils' Attendance Records) Regulations 1991 (SI 1991 No 1582) have added a requirement to include in the report information relating to attendance at the school (which information must also be published in the prospectus, under the School Information Regs, *op cit*). A further requirement, in section 161(5) of the EA 1993, is that the governing body's annual report 'shall include a report containing such information as may be prescribed about the implementation of the governing body's policy for pupils with special educational needs'. The prescribed information comprises:

(i) 'the success of the governing body's special educational needs policy since the last annual report';
(ii) 'significant changes' to the policy since the last report;
(iii) the outcome of any consultation on co-ordinating provision for pupils with special educational needs, which has involved the school;
(iv) 'how resources have been allocated to and amongst pupils with special educational needs since the last annual report'.

(Education (Special Educational Needs) (Information) Regulations 1994 (SI 1994 No 1048), reg 5, Sch 4).

Note that the articles of government of LEA-maintained schools must:

(i) enable the governing body to produce their report 'in such language or languages (in addition to English) as they consider appropriate' (E(No 2)A 1986, s 30(3)(a)); and
(ii) require them to 'produce it in such language or languages (in addition to English and any other language in which the governing body propose to produce it) as the local education authority may direct' (s 30(3)(b)).

The governors' annual report is among the matters to be laid down for discussion at the annual parents' meeting (required by E(No 2)A 1986, s 31 and EA 1993 Sch 6 para 9 – see below). DES Circular 8/86 explains that the report 'is intended to be a straightforward factual document for reference by parents of pupils at the school and to inform the annual meeting' (para 10(c)).

(d) Documents and information to be available for public access

Under the Education (School Curriculum and Related Information) Regulations 1989 and (Wales) Regulations 1991 public access information falls into two distinct categories:

(i) Statements of curricular policy which LEAs and governors are required to prepare under the E(No 2)A 1986, as amended. Copies of these statements must be available to head teachers, governors and LEAs.

(ii) Prescribed types of information which the head teacher of every maintained school must make available on request 'at all reasonable times' (but not in relation to nursery classes in primary schools) (reg 6 (England) Regs and reg 11 (Wales) Regs).

The head teacher *must*, on request, supply a copy of any document within (i) above, and *may* supply a copy of a document (other than one subject to copyright) within (ii). He or she may make a charge, not exceeding the cost of producing the copy.

Information to be made available at school to parents and others 'at all reasonable times' on request[a]
Relevant statutory instruments, departmental circulars and administrative memoranda relevant to Chapter I, Part I of the ERA 1988 (the curriculum).[b]
Any published school inspection reports relating to the school.
Schemes of work in current use at the school.
Syllabuses followed at the school.
Arrangements for complaints under ERA 1988, s 23 or under the articles of government of a grant-maintained school.
The agreed syllabus for RE adopted by the LEA and, in the case of a voluntary school, the arrangements for RE in that school as specified in its trust deed or other document.

Notes

[a]Regulation 6(3) and, in Wales, regulation 11(3) of the (Wales) Regulations.

[b]The Secretary of State has given an undertaking that enough copies of these documents will be sent to schools for the purpose of public access (DES Circular 14/89 *The Education (School Curriculum and Related Information) Regulations 1989*, para 25).

There are separate duties concerning the availability, for public inspection at the school, of prescribed information about the school's special educational provision, its policies for the identification, assessment and provision for all pupils with special educational needs and on staffing, and partnerships with bodies beyond the school (see Education (Special Educational Needs) (Information) Regulations 1994 (SI 1994 No 1048), regs 2 and 3 and DFE Circular 6/94 *The Organisation of Special Educational Provision* (1994)).

(e) Information on FE and on other institutions

(i) Requests by schools providing secondary education for provision of information about their schools by primary schools

Section 264 of the EA 1993 deals with the situation where an individual secondary school requests that information about itself is made available to parents of children at a primary school. The governing body of the school providing primary education must ensure that a request by one school is treated no less favourably than a request by another.

(ii) Provision of information, by schools providing secondary education, about FE provision

Regulations may require schools, city technology colleges and city colleges for the technology of the arts to provide information about further education provision plus the achievements and career (etc) destinations of students on completion of their courses and certain other information (EA 1993, s 265; the Education (Distribution by Schools of Information about Further Education Institutions) (England) Regulations 1993 (SI 1993 No 3197) and (Same) (Wales) Regulations 1994 (SI 1994 No 1321)).

(f) Translation of documents

Translation of documents may be necessary in the following circumstances:

> 'If it appears requisite to an education authority or, as the case may be, the governing body of a maintained school, that any such document should be translated into a language other than English, it shall be so translated and the translated document shall be published or made available in such manner as appears to the governing body to be appropriate' (Education (School Curriculum and Related Information) Regulations 1989, reg 13(2); and (Same) (Wales) Regulations 1991, reg 14(3), which refers to documents published other than in English or Welsh).

5. Information on school performance

As noted above, the *Parent's Charter* (1991) contained a number of undertakings by the Government to ensure that information on school performance would be published in such a way that parents could compare one school with another effectively (see also DES, *Implementing Parent's Charter Requirements in 1992, Documents 1–3* (1992)). The principal performance indicator is public examination performance, which is based on the information which individual schools must include in their prospectuses. So far, the undertaking that National Curriculum test results will be included in the comparative tables has not been fulfilled, largely due to the boycott of testing by most of the teaching unions. Fundamental revisions to the assessment arrangements in the light of the Dearing Report (published in January 1994 – see Chapter 8) may delay this further. Truancy rates were published in the tables for the first time in November 1993. In due course pupil destinations may be included.

The law is presently contained in section 16 of the Education (Schools) Act 1992, the Education (School Performance Information) (England) (No 2) Regulations 1994 (SI 1994 No 2077) (SPI Regs) and the Education (School Performance Information) (Wales) (No 2) Regulations 1994 (SI 1994 No 2254) (SPI(W) Regs). Guidance for 1994 was given in DFE Circular 4/94 (*The Parent's Charter: Publication of Information About Secondary School Performance in 1994*) and 5/94 (. . . *Information about Primary Schools in 1994*). The requirements apply to LEA-maintained schools but also, in some cases, independent schools and non-maintained special schools (see ESA 1992, s 16(1)). The regulations must be made with a view to assisting parents choose schools for their children, increasing public awareness of the quality of educational provision by the relevant schools and of educational standards achieved in them, and assisting 'in assessing the degree of efficiency with which the financial resources of those schools are managed' (ESA 1992, s 16(3)(c)). Apart from this, the Secretary of State is given considerable discretion in relation to the kind of information to be published, the manner and timing of publication and the persons/bodies to be responsible for publication (see ESA 1992, s 16(4)–(8)). A proprietor of an independent school who fails to comply with any regulations may, if regulations so provide, be struck off the Register of Independent Schools (ESA 1992, s 16(9)).

The prescribed information (see below) must be provided by the head teacher to the governing body, for the purposes of enabling the governors to comply with their obligations under the SPI Regs (reg 5) and SPI(W) Regs 1993 (reg 6).

The relevant information and the requirements as to the manner and timing of its publication are as described in (a)–(e) below.

(a) General information to be provided to the Secretary of State

This must be provided, if requested, to the Secretary of State by the governors of all maintained secondary schools (except, in England, a middle-deemed secondary school) and by the proprietors of independent and non-maintained special schools (in England, only if they have some pupils aged fifteen) (SPI Regs, reg 10 and Sch 5 and SPI(W) Regs 1994, reg 7 and Sch 1, Pt VI). The information must be provided within two weeks of a request and must give details of, *inter alia*, the number of registered pupils, the age range of pupils, the number of pupils for whom there are statements of special educational needs, the classification of the school and whether it is mixed or single-sex, whether the school is selective, and, in the case of an independent school other than a CTC, whether the school participates in the assisted places scheme.

(b) Provision of assessment results to the Secretary of State

Only the SPI Regulations require National Curriculum assessment results to be supplied to the Secretary of State, and only in relation to Key Stage 1 and (in relation to maintained schools and CTCs only) Key Stage 3 results (reg 6 and Sch 1). At the time of writing only the core subjects (English, Mathematics and Science) apply for this purpose in relation to Key Stage 1 and Key Stage 3. Changes will be made consequent on the Dearing report (see Chapter 8). At present, the information that must be sent to the Secretary of State must show the number of pupils who, as regards each subject (in relation to constituent attainment targets and, in respect of technology, each constituent profile component):

- reached each level of the 10-level scale; or
- were assessed as working towards level 1 on the scale; or
- were exempted from the assessment under sections 18 or 19 of the ERA 1988.

In relation to Key Stage 3, the information must also show the number who missed the assessment by reason of unauthorised absence or who failed to register a level on being assessed. Various annual deadlines, in July, are prescribed (SPI Regs, reg 6).

(c) Information on school examination results (and, in England, vocational qualifications) to be provided to the Secretary of State

In *England* this information relates, *inter alia*, to the number of pupils aged 15 years, GCSE subject entries and results achieved (including percentages of pupils achieving certain grades), the number of pupils who were entered for prescribed vocational qualifications in the school reporting year and the number who obtained the relevant vocational qualifications. It also relates to the A level entries and grades for 16–18 year-olds entered for one A level or equivalent or two or more A levels or equivalent, and the number of entries and names for the International Baccalaureate Diploma, BTEC National Certificate or Diploma and Diploma in Vocational Education (SPI Regs, Sch 2). There are similar requirements in *Wales* (see SPI(W) Regs). All of this information must be provided by governing bodies/proprietors within two weeks of receipt of a written request.

(d) Information about authorised and unauthorised absences to be provided to the Secretary of State

In England, governing bodies of maintained schools must provide to the LEA, in respect of the reporting school year, information on authorised and unauthorised absences (showing, *inter alia*, the number of pupils who have had at least one unauthorised absence during each term and the number of unauthorised absences per year). Furthermore, the LEA (in respect of the information) and the governing body of a GM school (or maintained school in Wales) or proprietor of an independent or non-maintained special school in respect of information on unauthorised pupil absences, must supply such information to the Secretary of State within two weeks of a request from him (SPI Regs, reg 8 and SPI(W) Regs 1994, reg 3).

(e) Provision of information about lesson time

A new requirement in England relates to the provision of information to the Secretary of State (via the LEA, in the case of LEA-maintained schools) on 'the amount of lesson time provided for the majority of relevant pupils during a normal school week' (SPI Regs, Sch 4 and reg 9).

(f) Publication of local and national performance information about secondary schools

The Secretary of State is empowered to publish some of the information on school performance compiled under the regulations. In England, this includes the general information referred to in (a) above plus examination results, success rates in vocational qualifications, lesson time and truancy rates in secondary schools, and the local averages in these categories (SPI Regs, reg 11) (see, e.g., DFE Circular 14/94). In Wales, only the general information and examination results have been included (SPI(W) Regs, reg 11), but 1994 SPI(W) Regs (SI 1994 No 1186) make separate provision as to publication of truancy rates and taught lesson time.

In England, the duty resting on governing bodies to provide this information to parents extends only to parents of final-year primary school pupils, although it must be made generally available for reference at the school, as is the case in Wales. In Wales, governors/proprietors and the LEA have a duty to provide this information to parents of final-year primary school pupils and of year 11 secondary school pupils. They must also make it available at primary and secondary schools in the area and in libraries (SPI(W) Regs, reg 11).

In practice, the information has attracted considerable media interest and has been published in 'league table' form in national and local newspapers. There is no legal requirement to publish the information in league tables – indeed the Secretary of State lists the schools alphabetically. It is the newspapers that place schools in descending order of pupil GCSE (etc) performance.

6. Publication of school inspection reports and action plans

School inspection reports offer further school performance information (see below), but are covered by separate provisions. As noted earlier, there is a duty on the head teacher of every maintained school, under the Education (School Curriculum and Related Information) Regulations (*op cit*), to make copies of any school inspection reports relating to the school available to parents and others, on request. In addition, the governing body (or LEA, in the case of an LEA-maintained school which does not have a delegated budget) must make sure that an inspection report on the school and a summary of it are available for inspection by members of the public at such times and places as may be reasonable (EA 1993, s 209(4)(a)). Copies must be provided when requested (EA 1993, s 209(4)(b); E(S)A 1992, Sch 2 para 9C) (a charge can be made in some cases: see the Education (School Inspection) (No 2) Regulations 1993 (SI 1993 No 1986) reg 8 and (Wales) (No 2) Regulations 1993 (SI 1993 No 1982), reg 8). 'As soon as is reasonably practicable', parents of registered pupils are to be provided with a copy of the summary of the inspector's report (s 209(4)(c); ESA 1992 Sch 2, para 9C). Copies of plans of action by governing bodies to deal with problems highlighted by school inspectors must be made generally available to the public and must be provided to parents and to any others who request them (EA 1993, s 210(6); E(S)A 1992 Sch 2 para 10; a charge may be made in some cases ((School Inspection) Regs, *op cit*).

7. Information on individual pupils' achievements

In its *Parent's Charter* (1991) the Government indicated a commitment to ensuring that parents are given information on their child's progress at least once a year, in the form of a written report on the child's achievements under the National Curriculum. There was also an undertaking to ensure that parents are made aware of how their child's performance compares with that of other children of the same age. The process of reporting on a pupil's progress is facilitated by the requirements on maintaining records of achievement for individual pupils (see below).

Separate regulations apply to England and to Wales (the Education (Individual Pupils' Achievements) (Information) Regulations 1992 (SI 1992 No 3168) (reg 8 only) and 1993 (SI 1993 No 3182) (all) and the (Same) (Wales) Regulations 1993 (SI 1993 No 835) (reg 8 only) and 1994 (SI 1994 No 959)). The head teacher is required to provide a written report to parents of all registered pupils and to pupils aged 18 or over (and their parents, if special circumstances warrant it). The report must contain information relating to the pupil's educational achievements and in particular must refer the matters prescribed in Schedules 1 and 2 to each of the sets of regulations in relation to the particular stage that the pupil has reached (for example, the report in the final year of Key Stage 3 must give a brief account of the progress made in the core subjects and results of National Curriculum tests, plus brief particulars of achievements in other areas of the curriculum and success rates for other pupils at the school). It must be sent 'by post or otherwise', at least once per school year, by the end of the summer term. In some cases, where examinations or assessments are wholly or partly externally assessed and the results are not available by the relevant date (above), the report may be sent out by 30 September.

All school leavers who have ceased to be of compulsory school age must be provided with a report. This must give their most recent National Curriculum formal assessment results and the results of public examinations and examinations for vocational and other qualifications. It must also indicate their progress and achievements in relation to other curricular activities. The report has to be provided to the pupil by the 30 September after he or she leaves the school. The school is required to ensure that pupils sign the parts of their reports which refer to their name, school and brief particulars of their progress (see further Sch 3 to each of the sets of regulations).

The above regulations also require a report to be prepared by a head teacher of a school when a pupil transfers to another school. This report, containing prescribed information on academic performance, must be sent to the head teacher of the receiving school within 15 days of the pupil's departure. In Wales, this report need not be prepared and sent if the pupil was with the school from which he has transferred for less than four weeks.

8. The keeping, disclosure and transfer of pupil records

Since September 1989, when the Education (School Records) Regulations 1989 (SI 1989 No 1261) (ESR Regs) (which have been subsequently amended) came into effect, LEA-maintained schools, special schools (maintained or not) and grant-maintained schools have been required to maintain a curricular record for each pupil, permit access to the record in specified circumstances, and transfer the record when a pupil moves to another school or college.

(a) 'Curricular record'

The regulations apply to a pupil's 'curricular record'. This is defined as 'a formal record of a pupil's academic achievements, his other skills and abilities and his progress at school' (ESR Regs, reg 4(1)). Where disclosure is concerned, 'other educational records' relating to the child, including a 'teacher's record', are to be treated as part of the pupil's curricular record (reg 7). The Circular on the regulations (17/89) explains that 'other educational records' (a phrase not defined in the regulations) refers to 'any other information which schools might find it helpful to keep for their own purposes' even though they are not legally required to do so (para 16). Included, as mentioned above, is information contained in a 'teacher's record'. The 'teacher's record' is defined as 'any record kept at the school by a teacher other than a record kept and intended to be kept solely for that teacher's own use' (ESR Regs, reg 7(2)). No guidance on how the distinction between what is or is not intended for the teacher's own use is offered by the Circular. This part of the regulations seems certain to have caused confusion and, in leaving the matter to be decided by individual teachers, has to some extent negated one of the major overall purposes of the regulations as a whole, namely to provide greater certainty over questions of record-keeping and access to records.

(b) Duty to keep curricular records

School governing bodies are required to ensure that in respect of every registered pupil there is a curricular record (defined above) and that it is updated at least once a year (ESR Regs, reg 6(1)(a)).

(c) Disclosure

(i) Those entitled to disclosure

The regulations provide that an 'entitled person' may, on making a request in writing, see a pupil's record and (provided he or she is willing to pay the cost of producing it) receive a copy of it. Where appropriate, the record should be provided in a language other than English – at no extra cost to the entitled person (ESR Regs, reg 14). Access to the record must take place within 15 days of receipt of the request (reg 6(2)).

The following are entitled persons (reg 4(1)):

(*a*) the parent of a pupil, where the pupil is aged under 16;

(*b*) the pupil or his/her parent where the pupil is aged 16 or 17;

(*c*) the pupil, if aged 18 or over.

Various persons might have rights as parents (see Chapter 1, Part 3) for this purpose, including those who do not have day-to-day care of the pupil – a separated or divorced parent, a legal guardian, or a foster parent, or any others who have parental responsibility under the Children Act 1989 (see EA 1944, s 114(1D)–(1F)). Local authority social services departments or voluntary organisations in which parental responsibility has been vested may also qualify (see Circular 17/89, *op cit*, para 22).

(ii) Correction and removal of inaccuracies

If the entitled person (above) submits a written notice to the school pointing out any alleged inaccuracies in the record, the governing body must either correct the record accordingly, or leave it as it is but append the parent's notice to it (ESR Regs, reg 6(c)). However, this does not apply to that part of a curricular record consisting of any assessment of a pupil's achievement, for example under the National Curriculum (reg 6(4)).

(iii) Exceptions to the duty of disclosure

A number of exceptions to the general rule on disclosure are prescribed. Most are concerned with situations where disclosure might be detrimental to the child (see Box below). In the case of these exceptions, the regulations do not authorise or require disclosure.

Information which is excluded from the duty of disclosure (regs 9–13)
Information originating from or supplied by or on behalf of a person who is not (i) employed by the LEA, or (ii) an educational welfare officer, or (iii) the person requesting disclosure, or (iv), in the case of a GM or voluntary aided school, a teacher or other employee engaged at the school.
Information which would reveal its source (except where the source is the pupil or person referred to in the above category).
Where disclosure would, in the opinion of the holder, 'be likely to cause serious harm to the physical or mental health or emotional condition of the pupil or any other person'.
Where, in the opinion of the holder, the information 'is relevant to the question whether the pupil to which it relates is or has been the subject of or may be at risk of child abuse'.
A reference given by a teacher in respect of a pupil's application to a school or to further or higher education.
Educational records which are data for the purposes of the Data Protection Act. (The School Records Regulations apply to the keeping, disclosure and transfer of manual records only.)
Statements of special educational needs.
Any report prepared for the purposes of certain court proceedings.
Information as to the racial group to which a pupil belongs, the language spoken in his home, and his or her religious persuasion – except to an 'entitled person'.
Anything recorded before 1 September 1989.

(iv) Transfer

When a pupil changes school or moves to a college or other institution the person responsible for the conduct of that institution is entitled to receive, without charge, the pupil's records or a copy thereof, on request in writing (ESR Regs, reg 6(1)(d)). Educational records kept before 1 September 1989 should also be transferred, if the governors consider it appropriate (reg 6(5)). On a change of school, details of the pupil's temporary exception (if any) from the National Curriculum should be transferred as well. However, the institution is not entitled to receive details of assessment results at the stage where the pupil is being *considered* for admission to it (reg 6(3)).

(v) Appeals

The governing body must make arrangements for parents to appeal against any decision relating to disclosure, transfer, correction or supply of a copy (reg 8). Nothing in the Education (School Government) Regulations 1989 prohibits the delegation of the hearing of appeals to a committee of governors (see Chapter 4). It may be advisable (in the interests of natural justice) that neither the head teacher nor teacher governors are present at appeal hearings on such a matter.

9. The Data Protection Act 1984

The Data Protection Act 1984 regulates the keeping of *computerised* data. Schools should be registered with the Data Protection Registrar as data users – this is the LEA's or governors' responsibility. Failure to register is a criminal offence.

Data users must indicate to the Data Protection Registrar that they hold information and the purpose for which it is held. The 1984 Act establishes 'data protection principles' (s 2) which require, *inter alia*, such data to have been lawfully obtained, relevant, accurate, and kept for no longer than is necessary. The data must only be used and disclosed for the purpose for which it was obtained (s 5).

Subject to certain exceptions, individuals (including pupils) have a right of access (s 21) to the information personal to them and may insist on amendments and deletions in appropriate cases (s 24). Data users must make appropriate security arrangements and may be liable for damage caused as a result of loss or unauthorised disclosure of data (s 23). Pupils are entitled to see the marks on which their examination results are based, although disclosure may be delayed until forty days after they are published, or five months after the request, whichever is the earlier (s 35) (see further M Staunton, 'Caught in the Act', *Times Educational Supplement*, 29 November 1985).

10. Annual parents' meeting

The articles of most maintained schools require their governing bodies to hold a meeting once in every school year – the 'annual parents' meeting' – which shall be open to:

'(*a*) all parents of registered pupils at the school;

(*b*) the head teacher; and

(*c*) such other persons as the governing body may invite'.

(E(No 2)A 1986, s 31(1)).

The articles for grant-maintained schools must make similar provision, although the meeting is to be open to parents and to governors' invitees, and not expressly to the head teacher (EA 1993, Sch 6 para 9).

Teachers, other than the head teacher, have no legal right to attend the annual parents' meeting, unless invited by the governors to do so. The official guidance is that there 'may . . . be a case for inviting a few non-governor members of the teaching and non-teaching staff to the meeting' (DES Circular 8/86, para 13(b)).

The meeting is intended to consider the governors' report and the discharge by the governors, head teacher and LEA of their functions in relation to the school (E(No 2)A 1986, s 31(2); Education (Grant-maintained Schools) (Initial Governing Instruments) Regulations 1993, SI 1993 No 3102). The Government believes that these meetings should 'give the whole parent body the opportunity to become more closely involved in the life of the school, to mutual benefit' (Circular 8/86, para 13), although, obviously, attendance at the meeting could only be a small element of parental involvement.

Chapter 7

School admissions

1. Introduction

For nearly two million children and their families each year, decisions on admissions to individual schools are eagerly awaited. Often there is great anxiety. Yet since 1980 the Government has sought to capitalise politically on the majority of parents' concern about securing a place for their child at a suitable school by introducing what it has perceived to be popular measures designed to facilitate the exercise of parental choice. A right to express a preference, which has to be granted save on specific grounds, was introduced under the EA 1980, along with important appeal rights. The ERA 1988 introduced the concept of 'open enrolment' (DES Circular 6/91 in fact refers to it as 'more open enrolment') under which admissions authorities ceased to be able to set admissions targets designed to keep pupil numbers below the level of the school's physical capacity. The EA 1993 has made changes to the appeals system to deal with certain specific criticisms of its operation.

A recent survey reported in *The Times* (31 December 1993) revealed that although 90 per cent of parents secure a place for their child at their first-choice school, 94 per cent had done so in the previous year. This decline reinforces the argument that despite the increase in parental rights in this area, and the tighter legal framework within which admissions authorities are now required to operate, the conflict between parental choice and central planning of local schools has tended, perhaps inevitably, to be resolved in overall favour of the latter. As we shall see, parental 'choice of school' is a misleading concept, and is some way from being a legal reality, because popular schools will always be oversubscribed and rationing of places will be required. This has led to the Government placing far greater emphasis over the past couple of years on the creation of greater diversity of provision as a means of giving greater credence to its choice-of-school policy. Thus, as shown in Chapter 2, we have seen an impetus towards city technology colleges and specialist schools and expansion of the GM schools sector. We have also seen moves to facilitate the reintroduction of selection by ability or aptitude in school admissions (see, for example, *Choice and Diversity*, para 1.49).

2. Admissions arrangements

(a) Responsibility for admissions arrangements

Admissions policy is a matter for the LEA or, in the case of GM schools and voluntary schools, the governing body (see below). Independent schools' admissions policies are usually determined in accordance with the trust deed for the school. In GM schools, the governing body must make its own arrangements for admissions (EA 1993, Sch 6, para 4(a)). Admissions arrangements for GM schools have had to be 'independent of, but similar in nature to, the arrangements operating for local authority schools in the area' and 'consistent with the previous character of the school' (DES Circular 10/88). In aided and special agreement schools the arrangements will also be made by the governing body (in accordance with the articles of government and, in some cases, the trust deed), but it is common for agreements as to admissions to be entered into between the LEA and governing bodies. Under section 6(6) of the EA 1980, such agreements may be entered into with a view to preserving the religious character of a voluntary aided or special agreement school by enabling parental preference to be overridden in the case of a child who does not belong to the denominational group served by the school. The EA 1993 has made provision for modification or replacement of such agreements by one party (or as directed by the Secretary of State) where the other disagrees (EA 1980, s 6(7)–(9), added by EA 1993, s 270).

Local problems have arisen from a lack of co-ordination over admissions between the expanding GM schools sector and the LEA. However, under the EA 1993 it is now possible for co-ordinated arrangements for admissions to be introduced by agreement between admissions authorities or under a scheme ordered by the Secretary of State (EA 1993, s 260).

As noted in Chapter 6 (in Part 2), those responsible for admissions arrangements have a duty under section 8 of the EA 1980 (EA 1993, Sch 6, para 6 in the case of GM schools) to publicise them.

(b) Requirement to admit a child

The EA 1993 has introduced a power to direct a school to admit a child to a school (ss 13 and 14) if, *inter alia*, he or she has been refused admission to any school which is a reasonable distance from his or her home and which provides suitable education. The power may also be used where a child has been permanently excluded from a school. The principal purpose of this power is to ensure that children whom a school considers undesirable for whatever reason but who might suitably be educated there are not kept in limbo for many months while the LEA struggles to find a school willing to accept them. The power may be exercised by the 'appropriate authority' – the LEA or, if the school is the subject of an order transferring responsibility for school places in an area to a funding authority, the funding authority. Before exercising the power the appropriate authority must consult with the child's parent, the school to which the authority wishes to have the child admitted and the authority which maintains the school (if different from themselves). If the direction is given by the LEA it must name the school to which the child must be admitted. The governing body of the school which the appropriate authority intends to name in the direction must be given notice (under EA 1993, s 14); the governors may refer the matter to the Secretary of State within 15 days of receiving the notice. On such a reference the Secretary of State is to determine which school is to be required to admit the child, and he must specify the school in his direction.

Children will also have to be admitted to a school named in a statement of special educational needs (EA 1993, s 168(5)(b)) or in a school attendance order (EA 1993, s 192(6)).

(c) Duty not to charge for admission to maintained school

No charge may be made for admission to any maintained school, including one which is grant-maintained (ERA 1988, s 106(1)).

(d) Providing an opportunity for the expression of parental preference: LEA-maintained and GM schools

A parent is entitled to express a preference for a particular school for his or her child. The relevant provisions so far as LEA-maintained schools are concerned are in the Education Act 1980, as amended. LEAs must make arrangements for such a preference to be expressed and for the parent(s) to give reasons (EA 1980, s 6(1)). Subject to the exceptions in sections 6(3) (and the operation of the admissions policy criteria: see below), LEAs and governors have a duty to comply with any preference expressed (s 6(2)). It is the exceptions in section 6(3) which provide the major barrier to parental choice. They are discussed in detail below. So far as GM schools are concerned, admissions arrangements are to be as laid down in the articles of government (EA 1993, Sch 6, para 4). The model articles of government for GM schools state that any application to the school for admission shall be accepted unless the child's admission to the school would be incompatible with the school's religious character or arrangements for selecting by ability or aptitude, or would prejudice efficient education or use of resources (but see Part 6(c)(i) below), or if a different school is named in the child's statement of special educational needs (Education (Grant-maintained Schools) (Initial Governing Instruments) Regulations 1993 (SI 1993 No 3102), Sch 2, art 8). On the position vis-à-vis outstanding applications for admission on the date that the school becomes incorporated as a GM school, see DFE Circular 6/93, *Admissions to Maintained Schools* (1993), paras 21–28.

3. Admissions limits for LEA-maintained schools: the 'standard number'

(a) Introduction

New arrangements for admissions to LEA-maintained primary and secondary schools have been phased in under the ERA 1988. The 'open enrolment' arrangements provided for by the 1988 Act are clearly designed to enable popular schools to admit as many pupils as the physical capacity of the school will allow, rather than any limit the LEA might wish to set (perhaps with a view to spreading pupil numbers evenly around the authority's schools).

(b) Admissions limits in LEA-maintained schools – 'the standard number'

Every LEA-maintained school will have a 'standard number', and the authority responsible for admissions to the school must not restrict its intake of pupils in the 'relevant age group' below that number (ERA 1988, s 26(1)). 'Relevant age group' is defined in ERA 1988, s 32(2) (see also Circular 11/88, para 9). Authorities responsible for admissions may, however, decide to have an admissions total *higher* than the relevant standard number (s 26(3)) (see below).

The standard number *for secondary schools* is to be *whichever is the greater* of the following two numbers:

(i) The 'appropriate pre-commencement number' (s 27(1)(a)): i.e. 'in the case of a secondary school . . . the standard number applying to the school under section 15 of the 1980 Act in relation to the age group in question in the school year immediately preceding the commencement year' (s 27(2)(a)). This normally means the total number of pupils admitted to the 'relevant age group' (i.e. the age group at which children are normally admitted to the school) in the whole of the school year 1979–80 (see DES Circular 11/88, para 8).

(ii) The 'number of pupils in that age group admitted in the school year immediately preceding the commencement year' (s 27(1)(a)). So, if admissions in 1989–90 exceeded the standard number under section 15 of the EA 1980 (see above), the 1989–90 admissions figure would be the new standard number.

Note that admissions of pupils at ages other than the normal age or ages of admission do not count towards a standard number.

The standard number for *primary schools* is calculated using a totally different, and highly complex, method which cannot easily be summarised (see the Education (Variation of Standard Numbers for Primary Schools) Order 1991, SI 1991 No 410, and DES Circular 6/91, para 27). In essence, the standard number will be the highest of the following:

(i) The total number of pupils on roll as at 1 May 1991 divided by the number of age groups in the school, rounded down to the nearest whole number.

(ii) The number produced by applying a formula laid down in the Order (and see Annex A to DES Circular 6/91). The formula is said to provide 'a notional assessment of the physical capacity of the school . . . and from this an admission number'.

(iii) The number of pupils which it was intended to admit in 1990/91, published under statutory requirements.

(iv) If applicable, the number of pupils in the age group intended to be admitted to the school as stated in the most recent proposals published under sections 12 or 13 of the EA 1980, which were fully or partly implemented by 1 May 1991.

For the purposes of defining admission numbers for primary schools, children admitted to a primary school for nursery education must be disregarded. Their admission will be deemed to take place when they are transferred to a reception class. Children admitted into a reception class are, even if they are not yet five years old, included in the calculation of the standard number (ERA 1988, s 29). The standard number will thus reflect the actual numbers at the school more accurately than under the EA 1980.

(c) Increasing admissions levels

Admissions in excess of the standard number may take place in basically two ways:

(i) The authorities responsible for admissions may, subject to certain requirements (including the duty under E(No 2)A 1986, s 33 to consult over varying admissions arrangements) admit pupils in excess of the standard number, *provided the buildings are adequate to accommodate the new number* (see Education (School Premises) Regs 1981 - Chapter 13, Part 3(b) below p 346). DES Circular 11/88, para 10 advises that schools are not required to expand physically to meet demand and that if the LEA or governors wish to enlarge the premises so that they may accommodate more pupils, proposals for school changes should be published in the normal way. At present the Government is keen to offer assistance to enable popular schools to expand physically.

(ii) A proposal may be made by (a) the governors, if the LEA is the admissions authority, or (b) the LEA, if the admissions authority is the governing body, for:

'fixing as the number of pupils in any . . . age group it is intended to admit . . . a number which exceeds both–

(*a*) the relevant standard number; and

(*b*) any number fixed or proposed to be fixed for that purpose by the authority responsible for determining the arrangements for admission of pupils . . .'.

(ERA 1988, s 26(4)).

The proposer may make a formal application (in writing) to the admissions authority, asking for a higher admissions limit and specifying how many should be admitted (s 26(6)). If the admissions authority does not reject the proposal in writing within two months of the day after it was received, the authority must adopt it (s 26(7)). If the admissions authority does so object, the proposer has twenty-eight days in which to make an application to the Secretary of State to increase the relevant standard number (s 26(8)). The information the Secretary of State would wish to have before him when considering a proposal to increase the standard number (under his power in section 27(5)) is set out in the Circular (11/88, para 13). On an application to increase the standard number the Secretary of State may refuse to make the order, or order the number to be increased to that proposed, or, after consultation with the LEA and governing body, set the number at a lower number than that proposed (s 27(7)).

Physical capacity. There is a standard form to be used in calculating a school's physical capacity (Annexes to Circulars 11/88 and 6/91). The form should be completed and submitted to the Secretary of State with any application for a variation in the standard number. In the case of proposals to reduce the standard number, the completed form should accompany the published proposals and should be made available for inspection by relevant parties. Further guidance, including advice as to completion and submission of the form, is in the Circulars and in each case is set out on the *pro forma* itself.

(d) Reductions in admissions limits – setting a lower standard number

Applications for a reduction in the standard number may be made, but only by the authority responsible for admissions (ERA 1988, s 28(1)). The appropriate authority must first consult with the LEA or governors (as appropriate) (s 28(8)). The Secretary of State may only make an order if he considers that:

> 'reduction is necessary, having regard to any reduction in the school's capacity to accommodate pupils as compared with its capacity at the beginning of the school year to which the current standard number first applied in relation to that age group' (s 28(7)).

DES Circular (11/88, para 14) explains that reduction in the standard number would be necessary if:

'(*a*) the amount of accommodation available at the school at the time the standard number was determined is no longer physically available, or

(*b*) the use to which the accommodation has subsequently been put has reduced the school's capacity to accommodate pupils, or

(*c*) admitting pupils up to the existing standard number would lead to the school having to exceed the number of pupils for whom accommodation could be provided under the current school premises regulations' (see also DES Circular 6/91, para 31).

It will be important for the admissions authority to assess the likely demand for places at the school in question. As Circular 11/88 states, if the level of demand is likely to be short of the standard number, the authority 'may consider it unnecessary to seek a reduction, believing they can safely have an admissions limit which will not in practice be reached'.

Any proposal to reduce the standard number must be published by the admissions authority together with a statement as to the effects of the proposals. Regulations lay down requirements as to the manner of publication of proposals (Education (Publication of Proposals for Reduction in Standard Number) Regulations 1991, SI 1991 No 411). If objections to the proposals are raised by ten or more local government electors or by the governing body or LEA (etc) (ERA 1988, s 28(3) and (5)), the admissions authority must refer them, within specified time periods, to the Secretary of State. The Secretary of State may reject outright or confirm the proposals, or he may set a higher standard number than that proposed (s 28(6)) (for further information, see DES Circular 11/88, paras 14–20, and Circular 6/91, Annex C).

(e) Keeping the standard number under review

The admissions authority is required to:

> 'keep under review any standard numbers . . . having regard to any change in the school's capacity to accommodate pupils as compared with its capacity at the beginning of the school year to which those standard numbers first applied' (ERA 1988, s 27(8)).

4. Grant-maintained schools: the 'approved admissions limit'

The admissions limit set by the governors of a GM school must be not less than the approved admission number for the relevant age group which they intend to admit (EA 1993, s 149(1); s 155(4)). Generally, unless it is varied in consequence of the implementation or partial implementation of proposals for a significant change in the character or significant enlargement of premises or a transfer to a new site, or is varied with the approval of the Secretary of State, the approved admissions number will be the number of pupils which the proposals for the acquisition of GM status of the school, or for the establishment of a new school as a GM school, stated that the school intended to admit in its first year as a (GM) school. In calculating the admissions limit, pupils intended to be admitted for nursery education shall be disregarded (s 149(5)); those who were so admitted but are now transferring to a reception class are to be included. Circular 10/88 states that it is the Secretary of State's intention that the admissions limit should normally be set at the physical capacity of the school.

The approved admission number may be increased by order of the Secretary of State, but not if the increase would constitute a significant change in the character of the school or necessitate any alteration of the school's premises (EA 1993, s 150(2) and (3)). Only the first of these limitations is imposed on a funding authority when exercising its corresponding power to direct an increase in the approved admissions number (EA 1993, s 151(1)–(3)). The funding authority can exercise this power only if either form of transfer order has been made under section 12(1) of the EA 1993 (see Chapter 1 at pp 9–10) (s 151(1)). If the premises will require alteration as a result of its direction, the funding authority must give particulars of the required alteration (s 151(2)(b)). The governing body must ensure that any alteration is carried out; the funding authority must make a grant to the governors of an amount equal to the reasonable expenses incurred or to be incurred in doing so (s 151(8)). Before it can issue a direction to the governing body the funding authority must serve them with a draft of the proposed direction. Once this is done the governors have 15 days in which to refer the matter to the Secretary of State if they are dissatisfied with some aspect of the direction (s 151(5) and (6)). The Secretary of State can authorise the direction as stated or as modified by him or her (s 151(7)).

As in LEA-maintained schools, the governing body can fix as the admissions limit a number in excess of the approved admission number, as long as the school's physical capacity permits it (see DFE Circular 6/93, para 10).

5. Admissions policy

(a) Introduction

An admissions policy lays down the criteria which are applied in determining, in the case of LEAs, which children are admitted to which schools, and in the case of schools where the governing body is the admissions authority, whether a child should be admitted to the school. Admissions policies should clearly be designed primarily to ensure that a child is able to attend the right school for him or her; but now that the legal framework builds in a degree of parental choice in relation to admissions, the admissions policy may be seen as providing a degree of objectivity in the rationing of places at popular schools. In the case of denominational schools and those that select by ability, the admissions policy will be designed to preserve the character of the school. Admissions policies must, as discussed in Chapter 6, be published by admissions authorities. The duty to publish the policy, the need to conform not only to the public law requirement of reasonableness but also to statutory non-discrimination duties, the duty to comply with parental preference save on specific grounds, and the right for parents to appeal against a decision, have combined to foster a considerable tightening up of admissions policies. Nevertheless, admissions authorities still have a fairly wide discretion over framing and applying their policy.

(b) Legal constraints on admissions policies

Admissions authorities have considerable discretion over the policy they follow in deciding admissions. They will, however, be subject to the overriding public law requirement of reasonableness (see below), and are barred by statute from practising discrimination on the grounds of race, ethnicity or nationality/national origins (Race Relations Act 1976, ss 17 and 18) or, apart from in relation to single-sex schools, sex (Sex Discrimination Act 1975, ss 22, 23 and 26). A complaint of race discrimination was upheld in the case of *Mandla* v *Dowell Lee* [1983] 1 All ER 1062 (HL) (which progressed to the House of Lords over the question, answered in the affirmative, whether Sikhs are an ethnic group for the purposes of the Race Relations Act 1976). The head teacher had refused to admit a Sikh boy who wore a turban to the school. The reason given was that the wearing of the turban was contrary to school rules, which, so far as school uniform was concerned, were in part designed to promote the school's policy of downplaying racial and cultural differences. The House of Lords confirmed that this reason was not a 'justifiable' reason within the terms of section 1 of the 1976 Act (see p 123 above) and the refusal to admit was unlawful (see also the *Cleveland* case, on the applicability of section 18 of the Act, discussed below). In *R* v *City of Bradford Metropolitan Borough ex p Sikander Ali* [1994] 2 ELR 299 (QBD) the court rejected an argument that there had been indirect discrimination (contrary to s 1(1)(b) of the 1976 Act) resulting from the fact that a school admissions policy left Asians in the Manningham district of Bradford with a far smaller chance of securing a place for their child at a chosen school than non-Asians living in other districts. Jowitt J said that when one compared Manningham Asians' and Manningham non-Asians' chances of having their preference upheld, which he said was the basis of comparison the 1976 Act required (see s 3(4)), one found that 31.4 per cent of the former and 37.5 per cent of the latter did not secure a place at their preferred school. Thus, Jowitt J concluded, there was no imbalance unfavourable to Asians.

The argument that an admissions policy is constrained by the need to have regard to the general principle contained in section 76 of the EA 1944 that there should be adherence to the wishes of parents in matters of their child's education has been shown by a number of court decisions to be weak (see in particular *Watt* v *Kesteven County Council* [1955] 1 QB 408 and *Cumings* v *Birkenhead Corporation* [1972] Ch 12). However, a policy might be challenged on the basis that it is so unreasonable that no reasonable LEA would have adopted it, or where irrelevant considerations feature in the admissions criteria or relevant ones have been ignored. The charge of unreasonableness would generally have to be pursued via complaint to the Secretary of State under section 68 of the EA 1944 (see Chapter 1) (see further *Secretary of State for Education and Science* v *Tameside Metropolitan Borough* [1977] AC 1014 and *Bradbury* v *Enfield LBC* [1947] 3 All ER 434). A policy in Wirral and Lancashire that a lower priority for a place at county secondary schools be given to Roman Catholics, on the basis that Roman Catholics have guaranteed places at RC schools in the district, has been challenged via complaint to the Secretary of State under section 68 and judicial review (see Part (c) below).

In the case of *Choudhury* v *Governors of Bishop Challoner Roman Catholic Comprehensive School* [1992] 3 All ER 277 (HL), Lord Browne-Wilkinson said (at p 282) that 'the governors' admissions policy has to be reasonable, but apart from the express statutory provisions of section 6 of the 1980

Act, there is no requirement as to the criteria to be adopted'. Section 6 of the 1980 Act requires admissions authorities to comply with parental preference save in specified circumstances (which are prescribed by section 6(3)) and to ensure that those living outside the LEA area are not accorded a lower priority for admission to a school merely because they live extra-district (see below). In *Choudhury* (above), Lord Browne-Wilkinson (at p 285) acknowledged the necessity, where there is an excess of demand over supply of places at any school, for there to be a schools admissions policy 'in order to select from those who have expressed . . . preference which of them is to be accepted and which rejected'. It is clear that in framing that policy the admissions authority is not limited to the factors in section 6 of the 1980 Act, which, in essence, enable admission to be denied on the grounds that it would prejudice efficient education or the efficient use of resources, or would be incompatible with the admissions arrangements made between the governing body and the LEA (in the case of an aided or special agreement school) designed to preserve the character of the school, or would be incompatible with admissions arrangements where pupils are selected by ability and aptitude (see EA 1980, s 6(3), discussed below).

It is important for admissions authorities to avoid operating an admissions policy or admissions criteria which is/are too rigid. Parker LJ put the matter succinctly in the High Court in *R* v *Greenwich LBC ex p Governors of John Ball Primary School* [1989] The Times, 16 November:

> 'Every council has to have some policy regarding school admissions, particularly in the case of oversubscription. The creation of the policy is a matter of discretion for the local authority but the discretion is not to thwart the law. A policy has to be prepared to consider exceptions'.

(c) Acceptable and unacceptable admissions criteria

Circular 11/88 advises LEAs and governors that they may apply 'any reasonable criteria they wish for deciding which pupils should have priority of admission' subject to various legal requirements, such as the Race Relations Act 1976 and Sex Discrimination Act 1975 (para 49). Criteria commonly adopted by admissions authorities include: attendance of siblings at the preferred school; home to school distance; attendance at a particular 'feeder' primary school; medical reasons; and other social or domestic reasons. In one case the court implicitly endorsed the adoption of sibling connection and geographical proximity criteria in admissions policies (*per* Farquharson LJ in the Court of Appeal in the *Greenwich* case ((1990) 88 LGR 589 at p 602)). In another case, the court accepted a religious criterion as an equally legitimate reason for denying admission in an oversubscribed denominational school (*Choudhury* (1992), *op cit* and see p 182 below). But there has generally been little to guide admissions authorities in framing their policies. In consequence, the DFE issued fairly detailed guidance in 1993, in DFE Circular 6/93, *Admissions to Maintained Schools*. This states that the criteria adopted must be 'set in unambiguous priority order' and gives examples of acceptable or unacceptable criteria, highlighting particular points to watch.

The Circular (Annex C) favours objective criteria, such as sibling links, home-to-school distance, catchment areas, feeder primary schools and (in the case of selective schools) ability. These are regarded as most appropriate because they 'leave least room for confusion and dissatisfaction on the part of parents' (Annex C, para 1). Points to watch include the *Greenwich* judgment, which confirmed that an admissions policy should not discriminate against those living outside the district simply on the basis that they are extra-district (see below).

'Flexible' catchment areas are not dealt with directly in the Circular, but were considered by the High Court in *R* v *Bradford Metropolitan Borough ex p Sikander Ali* (1994), *op cit*. Here the LEA operated an admissions policy for its secondary schools under which the catchment areas for schools, which were based largely on traditional links between certain residential areas and the schools in question, were adjusted to take account of the number of parents expressing a preference for the particular schools. Thus the larger the number of preferences for a school, the wider its catchment area. After the sibling factor, the next priority under the admissions policy related to residence in the catchment area. The applicant lived in the Manningham area, which did not have any community link with any particular school. He did not secure a place for his son at any of the three schools he preferred, and appealed (unsuccessfully) in respect of his first choice to the local education appeal committee. It was found that Manningham was not in any school's catchment area for 1993/94, with the result that children from this area were mostly being allocated to undersubscribed schools. The applicant challenged this system as unlawful. It was argued that 'traditional links' between the area and the school provided too nebulous a factor to provide a basis for rational decision-making, an argument dismissed by Jowitt J, who said (at p 308) that while all matters of judgement are potentially contentious, it could not be argued that this was an arbitrary factor when the 'education department was well qualified to make the assessment called for by this criterion'. It was also argued for the applicant that it was wrong to consider traditional links when it was known that the substantial immigrant population in the LEA's area was only sparsely represented in the catchment areas, an argument also rejected by Jowitt J, who said that basing catchment areas on traditional community links did not of itself render the policy *Wednesbury* unreasonable.

A further argument presented on behalf of the applicant was that by having regard, in defining a catchment area, to traditional links, the LEA was seriously undermining parental choice for parents who were not fortunate enough to live in the relevant catchment areas. In some ways any catchment area policy limits parental choice, but the argument here was confined to the more narrow issue of whether the fact that an admissions policy could operate in such a way as to leave an applicant for a school place not living in any catchment area was contrary to section 6 of the EA 1980. The argument was based on the dictum of Lloyd LJ in the

Greenwich case (discussed below); he said that all applicants, whether living inside or outside the LEA's area, must be at the 'starting gate' at the same time. However, Jowitt J distinguished *Greenwich* on the facts, since that case was concerned with parity (as required by s 6(5) of the 1980 Act) between those living inside the LEA's area as a whole and those living outside it, in a different LEA area. He also concluded (at p 312) that a policy could not be construed as *Wednesbury* unreasonable 'simply because all applicants do not contend on equal terms, though the nature of the inequality may make it so'. The LEA's policy was merely a means of rationing places, and, as the *Greenwich* case had also held, the policy was not confined to the factors listed in section 6(3) (see below).

Criteria involving 'an element of judgment', which some admissions authorities may favour because they allow more flexibility in individual cases, are also acceptable, but need to be approached with care. The following examples are given in the 1993 Circular: medical, social or compassionate grounds, travelling time, educational reasons/contribution to the life of the school/pastoral benefit, religious affiliation and a wish for single-sex/co-education. One of the difficulties with the last of these criteria is how to assess the relative strength of different parents' wishes when a number of parents are relying on it. The Circular advises that the admissions arrangements should make it clear how such judgments will be made (see para 11). However, in practice this is likely to prove quite difficult.

Finally, the Circular highlights unacceptable criteria, described as criteria which 'seem to the Secretary of State to interfere unacceptably with the operation of an open and fair system such as the law requires' (para 13):

(i) Governors' reserved right (in other words, giving the governors (or LEA) a discretion which enables them to circumvent the published criteria when they see fit to do so).

(ii) Exclusion of the potentially disruptive (although schools are reminded that head teachers have the power subsequently to exclude a pupil for serious misbehaviour). As noted above (at p 168) section 13 of the EA 1993 in any event provides LEAs and funding authorities with a power to direct a school to admit a child.

(iii) Exclusion of those with special needs. Pupils for whom there are statements must in any event be admitted to the school named in the statement (see p 169 above).

(iv) Fees. Fees may not be charged for admission to a maintained school (see *ibid*).

(v) Lot. The Government argues that 'decisions made by lot cannot be tested, and leave no basis for appeal', but there is also the argument that deciding in this way could be unlawful since the authority would be failing to exercise any discretion at all.

(vi) Date of application/length of time on a waiting list.

(vii) Distinguishing between applicants on religious grounds in non-denominational schools, as in the Wirral complaint referred to on p 175; the LEA's action would seem to fall foul of this advice. A similar policy to that of Wirral has been operating in Lancashire. In 1993 the policy there was that where parents whose children attended Roman Catholic (RC) primary schools wanted them to attend a non-RC secondary school then children could be admitted if places were available. The LEA's policy continued: 'It should be borne in mind, however, that if the preferred school is oversubscribed then places will normally be allocated firstly to children in the non-Roman Catholic sector'. A few weeks prior to the publication of Circular 6/93 the DFE wrote to the authority asking it to reconsider its policy, a policy which ministers had found unjustifiable. The appeal committee had this letter before it when considering the appeal of a Roman Catholic couple who had been denied their preference for a school as a result of the application of the policy. Popplewell J said that as things stood at the relevant date, the appeal committee had been entitled to apply the LEA's long-established policy: *R* v *Lancashire County Council ex p M* [1994] ELR 478 (QBD). More recently, in *R* v *Lancashire County Council ex p Foster* [1994] The Times, 24 May (QBD), Kennedy LJ took the view that Lancashire's policy was not unlawful. In his Lordship's view, the particular arrangements of the diocese meant that there were very few places at Roman Catholic schools for non-Roman Catholic children. He said that if equal preference were to be given to Roman Catholic children to attend non-denominational schools some children might be left without places in the areas in which they live.

6. The exercise of parental preference

(a) The duty to comply with parental preference

Before the Education Act 1980, some parents seeking a degree of choice in the education system sought to rely on section 76 of the 1944 Act (children to be educated according to the wishes of parents if it is 'compatible with the provision of efficient instruction and training and the avoidance of unreasonable public expenditure'). But the courts showed section 76, which, incidentally, is still in force, to be somewhat limited in scope; parental wishes were only one of a number of factors to which LEAs had to have regard when exercising their powers and duties (*Watt* v *Kesteven County Council* (1955); *Wood* v *London Borough of Ealing* (1967); *Cumings* v *Birkenhead Corporation* (1972); *Smith* v *ILEA* (1978)). Recently this position was reaffirmed in a Scottish case, concerned with the application of the identical provision in Scottish education legislation – Education (Scotland) Act 1980, s 28(1). Parental wishes were only one of the factors to be taken into account when plans to close a school were being considered: *Harvey* v *Strathclyde Regional Council* [1989] Public Law 160.

The Education Act 1980 lays down a requirement that admissions authorities give parents an opportunity to express a preference for a school (s 6(1)). (Note that neither this duty nor the right of appeal provided for by section 7(1) of the Act applies to special schools nor in respect of the under-fives, apart from those aged four-and-a-half plus who are admitted to a reception class: EA 1980, s 9.) The parent's request under section 6(1) must be complied with unless one of the grounds in section 6(3) applies (see s 6(2)), although where there is competition for a place the admissions criteria will determine the final outcome. In *R* v *Cleveland LEA and Others ex p Commission for Racial Equality* [1992] The Times, 25 August the Court of Appeal held that because the duty to comply with parental preference is mandatory, it must be complied with even if the admission of a child to a particular school may technically amount to racial discrimination. In this case a mother had requested that her white child be moved from a school with a high proportion of Asian children because, *inter alia*, the child had few white friends there and was being taught Pakistani songs. The Divisional Court accepted that her request was not racially motivated and rejected the argument that the LEA was acting racially by merely complying with the request. The Court of Appeal held that in any event, since section 41 of the Race Relations Act 1976 permits what might otherwise amount to unlawful discrimination under the Act where it is carried out in the course of fulfilling other mandatory statutory requirements (in this case the duty to comply with parental preference under s 6 of the EA 1980), there could be no breach of section 18 of the 1976 Act (which prohibits race discrimination by LEAs when carrying out certain functions). (For further discussion of this case, see N Harris, *Law and Education: Regulation, Consumerism and the Education System* (Sweet and Maxwell, 1993), pp 141–145.)

In relation to admissions to GM schools, the governors must admit a child unless, *inter alia*, one of the factors in article 8(1)(a)–(c) of the Initial Articles of Government applies (see (d) below).

Parental choice in respect of schools named in statements of special educational needs is governed by separate provisions in Schedule 10 to the EA 1993 (discussed in Chapter 9).

(b) The general principle that LEAs should give equal preference to those living inside and outside their area

Section 6(5) of the EA 1980 states that the duty to comply with parental preference:

> 'shall also apply in relation to . . . any application for admission to a school maintained by a local education authority of a child who is not in the area of the authority . . . and references in subsection (3) . . . to a preference and a preferred school shall be construed accordingly'.

What was not clear from this was whether it meant that an LEA had to apply a general principle of equal preference in relation to school admissions as between those living in its area and those living outside it. The Court of Appeal in *R* v *Greenwich LBC ex p Governors of John Ball Primary School* (1990) (*op cit*) confirmed that equal preference was to be given, other things being equal. Greenwich's education committee approved an admissions policy which favoured children residing in the borough over and above those living in neighbouring Lewisham. Under relatively long-standing reciprocal arrangements between the boroughs, a number of children attending seven named primary schools in Lewisham had in the past been allocated places at Greenwich secondary schools. But the effect of Greenwich's revised policy would have been the removal of the opportunity for Lewisham children to attend Greenwich secondary schools. In the High Court Greenwich's policy decision was declared invalid. Explaining the duty of the LEA, Parker LJ said:

> 'All parental preferences are to be complied with unless it is shown that compliance would prejudice efficient education. It was the same for children in or out of the area. The schools admission policy should have been designed to create such a result . . . The policy was invalid for, far from advancing the purpose of the 1980 Act, it was seen and recognized to be a policy which did not further the purpose but went against the statute'.

When the LEA appealed to the Court of Appeal (1990) the appeal was dismissed. Lloyd LJ said (at p 597) that section 6(5) was designed to ensure that when an LEA exercised its discretion over school admissions 'all children from within or outside the area rank *pari passu*, that they all come from the starting gate at the same time'.

Bromley LEA's school admissions policy, revised following the *Greenwich* decision, was also subject to a legal challenge (*R* v *Bromley LBC ex p C and Others* [1992] 1 FLR 174). The authority had sought to make their policy subject to an overall proviso that they might depart from their standard admissions criteria (based on sibling, proximity and other factors) where they believed that there was a threat to their ability to guarantee a school place for any of their own residents, under their statutory requirement to ensure the provision of sufficient schools to meet the needs of residents in their area (see ss 7 and 8 of the EA 1944, discussed above, Chapter 2, Parts 1 and 2). Whilst acknowledging the LEA's difficulties, the court felt that in the light of *Greenwich* it had no option but to declare the policy unlawful. In a separate decision on the same day, the Kingston upon Thames LEA's revised school admissions policy, under which equal preference was to be given to Kingston and non-Kingston residents, was challenged because the changes to the policy meant that a Kingston resident's chances of securing a place at a single-sex school in Kingston had diminished as compared with the situation which applied previously. The court held that the authority's policy was in compliance with section 6(5) (*R* v *Kingston upon Thames ex p Kingwell* [1992] 1 FLR 182).

Note that the above equal preference rule does not mean that an LEA's admissions policy is required to ensure that persons living in different zones *within* its overall area have the same degree of choice: see *R* v *Bradford Metropolitan Borough ex p Sikander Ali* (1994) (*op cit*), and the discussion of catchment areas above.

(c) When the LEA or governors need not comply with parental preference (county and voluntary schools)

(i) Where compliance with parental preference '. . . would prejudice the provision of efficient education or the efficient use of resources' (s 6(3)(a))

If the admission of the pupil would not take the total number of admissions above the school's standard number for the relevant age group or any higher admissions number fixed for the school (see pp 170–171 above), such admission shall not be taken to 'prejudice . . . efficient education' (etc) for the purposes of section 6(3)(a) (s 26(9)) and the pupil could not be denied a place on this ground. The initial articles of government for GM schools make similar provision in relation to admission of pupils within the approved admissions limit total: art 8(2).

This basis for denying preference is the most important, since it can be expected to be applied in virtually all cases of oversubscription. Naturally, the admissions authority will apply it in conjunction with its own admissions criteria to determine which of the limited number of pupils it can admit should have priority. That is exactly what had happened in the *Choudhury* case 1992 referred to earlier (pp 175–176). A Roman Catholic girls' secondary school was oversubscribed. It applied its admissions policy under which, *inter alia*, priority was to be given to Roman Catholics. Parents of two girls, one Muslim and the other Hindu, were denied admission under this criterion. Lord Browne-Wilkinson said that a religious criterion could lawfully be applied in relation to such a school. He accepted that an admissions authority had to apply its policy where there was oversubscription, since 'compliance with the performance of *all* applicants would prejudice proper education at the school through overcrowding' (at p 285).

However, when the matter comes before an appeal committee they will have to apply the prejudice test to each individual case. In doing so they should apply the two-stage test laid down by Forbes J in *R* v *South Glamorgan Appeals Committee ex p Evans* [1984] 10 May, Lexis Co/197/84 (for discussion see Tweedie [1986] PL 407). Forbes J said that the committee should first consider whether the admission of one child would prejudice the provision of efficient education at the school, with the onus being on the LEA to show that it would. If that question was answered in the negative, the child should not be denied a place under section 6(3)(a). If, however, it was concluded that the admission of the child *would* prejudice efficient education (etc), the committee would have to consider whether the prejudice was sufficient to outweigh the arguments presented by the parents and/or the circumstances known to the committee. In *R* v *Local Commissioner for Administration ex p Croydon LBC* [1989] 1 All ER 1033 Woolf LJ (at p 1041) said that whilst the onus was on the LEA at the first stage to show that there would be prejudice, at the second stage the committee had to balance up the arguments and prejudice factor. See also *W (A Minor)* v *Education Appeal Committee, Lancashire* [1994] ELR Issue 530 (CA). The application of the Evans test has not proved all that easy (see the discussion in the AMA/ACC seminar report, *Education Appeals Code of Practice* (1992)). The Council on Tribunals' *Code of Practice on Appeals* (1992) (currently being revised) refers to stage one of the *Evans* approach as applied to the, now common, practice (following its approval in the *Croydon* case (*op cit*)) of hearing all appeals in relation to a particular school before making a decision. The Code suggests that in such a case the committee should form a view as to how many children can be admitted to the school without this causing prejudice to efficient education.

(ii) If, in the case of aided or special agreement schools, it 'would be incompatible with any arrangements between the governors and the local education authority made under subsection (6)' (s 6(3)(b), as amended by ERA 1988, s 30(2))

Section 6(6) requires LEAs to make arrangements with the governors of these schools 'for preserving the character of the school', where so requested by the governors. DES Circular 11/88 advised that 'the arrangements might, for example, safeguard the particular character of a church aided school by stipulating what percentage of the intake has to be of the denomination concerned' (11/88, para 40). But this is put rather differently in Circular 6/93 (para 14), which states that the arrangements 'may for example allow a child of a different faith from that supporting the school to be refused admission to an empty place once a fixed proportion of places have been offered to pupils of different faiths'.

If agreement on the arrangements cannot be achieved by the LEA and governors, the arrangements will have to be determined by the Secretary of State. Provision is also made for modification of the agreement by the consent of the parties or, at the request of one party, as ordered by the Secretary of State (s 6(7)–(9), inserted by s 270 of the EA 1993).

(iii) If entry to the preferred school is selective in terms of a child's ability and aptitude, and compliance would be incompatible with selection under these arrangements (s 6(3)(c)) – even if the school is not full (see DES Circular 6/93, para 14)

Admissions policies for selective schools will almost always include other criteria, for example catchment areas or distance from home to school. Such a policy was unsuccessfully challenged in *R* v *Kingston upon Thames Royal LBC ex p Emsden* (1993) 91 LGR 96 (QBD). Schiemann J said that section 6(3)(c) implicitly sanctioned the employment of a policy under which home-to-school distance would be used to determine priority once a pool of those who met the required academic standards, which contained more applicants than there were places, had been formed. In the Wirral a zoning policy is in operation, under which the LEA, which has selective schools in only one of its three zones (Bebington/Deeside), gives priority, as between those passing the eleven-plus examination, to those living in the zone which has the selective schools. The policy was outlined in some detail in *R* v *Wirral Metropolitan Borough ex p Pickard* [1991] Lexis

CO/1735/91, although its legality was not ruled on because, in the event, the girl, who lived outside Bebington/Deeside and whose parents mounted a legal challenge to the admission decision, had failed to achieve the necessary mark in the examination to be in contention for a place.

(d) When the governors of a GM school need not comply with parental preference

The initial articles of government for GM schools (art 8; see also *R* v *Governors Pate's GMGS ex p T* [1994] COD 297) state that the governors need not comply with parental preference if:

(i) the child's admission to the school would be incompatible with the admissions arrangements, including in particular any arrangements for preserving the religious character of the school and those based on selection with reference to ability or aptitude; or

(ii) the child's admission to the school would 'prejudice efficient education or the efficient use of resources at the school' (the same wording as in EA 1980, s 6(3)(a) – see (c)(i) above).

This does not apply where an LEA maintains a statement of special educational needs in respect of the child (art 12A).

7. School admission appeals

(a) Schools other than those which are grant-maintained

The appropriate admissions authority – LEA or governors – must make arrangements for parents to appeal against the school allocated for their child (EA 1980, s 7). Authorities may have informal procedures for resolving disputes over choice of school. These are quite legitimate and, as the DES pointed out in Circular 11/88 (at para 53), can be useful although they cannot override statutory rights of appeal.

(i) Constitution of the appeal committee

Appeal lies to an appeal committee constituted in accordance with Schedule 2 to the 1980 Act, as amended by Schedule 16 to the EA 1993 (after much criticism by the Council on Tribunals and others about these committees' relative lack of independence) (references below are to paras of Sch 2, unless stated otherwise). Guidance on procedure before, during and after the hearing is contained in a Code of Practice (not legally binding) drawn up by local authorities in association with the Council on Tribunals, the latest edition of which (1992) is being amended to incorporate changes made by the EA 1993.

In relation to *county and controlled schools* each committee must have three, five or seven members, drawn from two broad categories:

(*a*) One must be nominated by the LEA from the panel of persons eligible to be lay members (para 1(2)(a), as substituted by

EA 1993, Sch 16 para 2). A person is eligible to be a lay member if 'he is a person without personal experience in the management of any school or the provision of education in any school (otherwise than as a governor or in any other voluntary capacity)' and if he meets certain other conditions. These conditions are that he does not have, or has not at any time had, any connection with either the LEA or a member or employee of it 'of a kind which might reasonably be taken to raise doubts about his ability to act impartially in relation to the authority' (para 4A(2), added by EA 1993, Sch 16 para 4). Those who may be appointed under (*b*) (below) or who are employed by the LEA are not eligible to be nominated as lay members (para 1(2A), as inserted). Note that regulations (made under section 267 of the EA 1993) have introduced from 6 June 1994 a requirement that LEAs advertise for lay members on or before 1 September 1994 and at intervals of not more than three years thereafter (Education (Lay Members of Appeal Committees) Regulations 1994 (SI 1994 No 1303)).

(*b*) Apart from the lay member, there must be two, four or six other members appointed by the LEA (who may not appoint persons who are LEA employees other than those employed as teachers) (para 1(2)(b), as substituted by EA 1993, Sch 16 para 2). The persons appointed by the LEA must comprise LEA or education committee members and people who have experience in education, have knowledge of local education conditions or are parents of pupils registered at a school (but not the school in respect of which the appeal is being made) (Pt I, para 1(3), as amended). Of LEA employees, only teachers are permitted to sit as appeal committee members, but not where the appeal relates to their own school. LEA members must not outnumber the other members (para 1(4), as amended).

Note that the chairperson of the appeal committee must not be a member or employee of the LEA (para 1(5), as substituted). The Code of Practice on Appeals warns against the selection of a committee too large in number, in case this proves too daunting for parents. Sufficient persons may be appointed by the LEA to enable two or more committees to sit at the same time (para 1(2B), as substituted).

The constitution of the appeal committee is slightly different for *voluntary aided and special agreement schools* (para 2), although the total number of panel members required is the same (i.e. three, five or seven):

(1) One must be nominated from the governors from a panel of those eligible to be lay members (para 2(2)(a), as substituted by EA 1993, Sch 16). A person is eligible to be a lay member if he does not have, or has not at any time had, any connection (of a kind that might reasonably be taken to raise doubts about his ability to act impartially) with the school in question or with a member or employee of the governing body of that school (para 4A(2)(b), as inserted). Those who may be appointed under

(2) below or who are employees of the LEA are not eligible to be nominated as lay members (para 2(2A), as inserted). Note that regulations (made under section 267 of the EA 1993) have introduced a requirement that governing bodies advertise for lay members from 1 September 1994 (see above).

(2) There must be two, four or six others (as appropriate), who may include governors, but not anyone employed by the LEA otherwise than as a teacher, and must include the appropriate number of persons drawn from a list compiled by the LEA (para 2(3)) (the appropriate number being three, in the case of a panel of seven, two, for a panel of five, and one, for a panel of three: para 2(4)). The chairperson may not be a governor (para 2(5)).

In the case of *county and voluntary schools* the appellant must give notice of appeal setting out the grounds on which the appeal is made (para 5). The appellant can address the appeal committee and can be accompanied by a friend or be represented (para 6). The hearing must be held in private except where the LEA or governors direct otherwise (para 10). However, an LEA observer, or a member of the Council on Tribunals, may attend (*ibid*). There are, in fact, very few procedural rules laid down by the Act, and reference to the Code of Practice should be made for guidance on such matters as adducing evidence, adjournments, the role of the clerk, the decision-making process, and the applicability of the rules of natural justice (a complaint that a woman who appealed to a Rochdale appeal committee had not been given an adequate opportunity to state her case and was frequently interrupted by the chairman was upheld by the Local Government Ombudsman (Complaint No 388/C/83)). The courts have endorsed the practice of hearing all appeals in relation to one particular school before deciding (*Croydon* – (*op cit*), p 182). When this practice is followed, but the proceedings have to be adjourned, natural justice demands that the reconvened panel consists of the same persons who heard the appeals in respect of the school in question (*R* v *Camden LBC ex p S* (1990) 89 LGR 513).

The matters that the appeal committee must take into account when reaching their decision include:

(A) any preference expressed by the parent(s) (under EA 1980, s 6);

(B) the arrangements for admission published in accordance with section 8 (para 7).

Consideration of other relevant factors is not precluded.

In the event of disagreement, the committee may decide by majority, with the chairperson having a second or casting vote if the voting is equal (para 8). The committee's decision must be sent in writing to the appellant and LEA (or governors, in respect of an aided or special agreement school); the grounds for the decision must be stated (para 9). There must be an adequate statement of the reasons for the decision. In judging the adequacy of such reasons, the courts have taken account of the type of adjudicating body on whom the duty lies:

> '[Counsel] submits . . . that, in effect, the Appeal Committee should have spelt out in detail their assessment of the several grounds put forward by the Appellant and weighed them individually and in aggregate against the reasons put forward by the Authority. I reject this contention which would have placed an undue and unwarrantable burden on this lay Committee' (*per* Hirst LJ in *W (A Minor)* v *Education Appeal Committee, Lancashire* (1994) (*op cit*); followed by Popplewell J in *R* v *Lancashire County Council ex p M* (1994) (*op cit*)).

The decision of the appeal committee is binding on the LEA or governors (EA 1980, s 7(5)). These committees fall within the jurisdiction of the Local Government Ombudsman (*R* v *Commissioner for Local Administration ex p Croydon LBC* [1989] 1 All ER 1033).

(b) Grant-maintained schools

In GM schools the articles of government must include provision as to arrangements for appeals over admissions decisions to be made to an appeal committee constituted in accordance with the instrument of government (EA 1993, Sch 6 para 5; Education (Grant-maintained Schools) (Initial Governing Instruments) Regulations 1993 (SI 1993 No 3102), Sch 1, App 3). In common with other admissions appeal committees (above) they have three, five or seven members, one of whom must be a lay member. Of the other two, four or six members, half must have educational experience, be acquainted with educational conditions in the area or be parents of registered pupils (but not of a pupil at the school in question) but may not be appointed if they have ever been a member of the school's governing body. Otherwise members of the governing body are eligible for appointment to the appeal committee (other than as lay members); but 'A person shall not be appointed . . . if he is employed as a teacher or otherwise at the school'.

The appeal committees will, in common with those established under the Education Act 1980 for LEA schools, fall within the jurisdiction of the Council on Tribunals (ERA 1988, Sch 12, para 12) and the Local Government Ombudsman (see EA 1993, s 269). Separate guidance on appeal procedure for GM schools was issued by the Council on Tribunals for the first time in December 1992 and is currently being revised. Appeal procedure is set out in Appendix 2 to the model Initial Articles of Government.

The governors must publish details of the school admission appeal arrangements (EA 1993, Sch 6, para 6 and the 1993 Regs, *op cit*, as amended Sch 2, arts 8A and 8B).

Chapter 8

The curriculum

1. Introduction

The Education Act 1944 laid down a legal framework for religious education and collective worship at school but left the secular curriculum almost unregulated by statute. The secular curriculum was placed in the overall control of individual LEAs and the teaching profession. Both were able to determine its content (with the exception of the detailed content of examination board syllabuses) and, in the case of teachers, methods of delivery. This autonomy was increasingly exerted during the 1960s and 1970s. By the late 1970s the DES was taking an increasing interest in the school curriculum (see, for example, DES/Welsh Office, *Local Arrangements for the School Curriculum* (1979)), at a time when the 'Great Debate' over standards in schools was underway and the William Tyndale affair (arising out of what was seen as an excessively liberal approach to teaching and an overly child-centred ethos at an Islington School) was bringing progressive teaching practices into public disrepute. But the Government publicly rejected calls for stricter legislative powers to enable it to control provision, and in particular to intervene when the local curriculum was under threat (as was becoming increasingly prevalent at a time when local authorities were being subjected to intense public expenditure restraint). It argued that the traditional relationship between central government and LEAs, particularly on matters of curriculum, would be undermined (*Initial Observations on the Second Report from the Education Science and the Arts Committee, Session 1981–82 Cmnd 8551*).

But the political climate was changing under the Thatcher government, which wanted to assert greater central authority over the education system as a whole. Ministers expressed concern about the activities of left-wing LEAs and teachers. Singled out for particular criticism was alleged political indoctrination in the classroom; the White Paper *Better Schools* (Cmnd 9469 (1985)) highlighted, for example, the spread of 'Peace Studies' at school. With blame for falling standards, and claims of ideological excesses and abuse of professional autonomy, directed at teachers and LEAs, greater control and regulation were inevitable, and they soon arrived, in the form of the Education (No 2) Act 1986 and the Education Reform Act 1988. There was also the abolition of the teacher-dominated Schools Council, a curriculum and policy advisory body, in 1985. According to Sheila Lawlor, deputy director of the right-wing Centre for Policy Studies, 'politicians have tried to unpick parts of the web which educational professionals, teachers' unions, departmental officials and the curriculum and examination quangos had managed to weave around them' (*The Times,* 10 January 1994).

The Education (No 2) Act 1986 removed much of LEAs' power to control the secular curriculum, giving governing bodies more autonomy on curricular matters, although requiring account to be taken of LEA curriculum policy. But the most dramatic change of all came with the introduction of the National Curriculum, under the Education Reform Act 1988, an Act which also made important changes to the law governing religious education and collective worship and which provided parents with a right of complaint over the way that governing bodies and LEAs exercised their statutory functions with regard to the curriculum and the provision of information.

When the previous edition of this book was published, in 1990, the National Curriculum had only just come into operation. It is still being phased in, but much has happened over the past four years. Naturally, there has been a proliferation of statutory instruments, bringing into operation attainment targets, programmes of study and assessment arrangements for various of the foundation subjects, in relation to the 'key stages'. Numerous such orders are currently in force. The past four years have also witnessed controversy over the content of the National Curriculum, with Ministers having sometimes disagreed with, and ignored, the advice of the National Curriculum Council (see D Graham and D Tytler, *A Lesson for Us All – The Making of the National Curriculum*, Hodder and Stoughton (1992)). There has been a teachers' strike over the administration of National Curriculum tests; in a court case, which reached the Court of Appeal, it was held that teachers are not under a statutory duty to test pupils (*Wandsworth LBC* v *NAS/UWT* (1994)).

In 1993 the Government asked Sir Ron Dearing to chair an investigation into the National Curriculum and its assessment regime. The interim report was published in August 1993 and a final report in January 1994 (*The National Curriculum and its Assessment – Final Report*). The Dearing recommendations include streamlining the National Curriculum, in particular the core subjects of English, mathematics and science, to give teachers more flexibility and, by cutting down on the number of detailed points of knowledge against which pupils' progress will be checked, more time. More choice at Key Stage 4 (14–16) was also recommended (history and geography, for example, would cease to be compulsory during this stage). Most of these reforms will not come into operation until September 1995. Specialist subject committees were appointed to conduct a review of each of the foundation subjects. Proposals were published during the spring of 1994, and the changes were settled by the autumn. The timetable for instituting the reforms has, as Sir Ron Dearing himself said, been 'tough and demanding' (House of Commons Education Committee, *The National Curriculum and Its Assessment (The Dearing Report), Minutes of Evidence,* 19 January 1994, Q13).

The Dearing reforms to the National Curriculum formed the basis for changes announced by the SCAA in November 1994 (see *Appendix 7*). They will necessitate a wide range of legal changes. Nevertheless, the legal framework has already changed as a result of the EA 1993, which, for example, has extended schools' power to charge for music tuition, has established a School Curriculum and Assessment Authority and has made important changes to the law governing sex education. This 1993 Act has also changed the framework governing religious education, particularly as regards the preparation of agreed syllabuses. The changes made by Part III of the 1993 Act in relation to special educational needs are discussed in Chapter 9.

2. Basic principles

The general duty resting with the Secretary of State for Education to 'promote the education of the people of England and Wales', first laid down in section 1 of the EA 1944, is now enshrined in section 1 of the EA 1993. For their part, LEAs retain their general duty to 'contribute towards the spiritual, moral, mental and physical development of the community' (EA 1944, s 7). There is now also a specific overall duty resting on the Secretary of State, LEAs, governing bodies and head teachers (of public-sector schools), to exercise their functions with a view to securing that the curriculum of a school:

> 'is a balanced and broadly based curriculum which –
>
> (*a*) promotes the spiritual, moral, cultural, mental and physical development of pupils at the school and of society; and
>
> (*b*) prepares such pupils for the opportunities, responsibilities and experiences of adult life'.
>
> (ERA, s 1(2) and (3)).

This is referred to as the 'whole curriculum', which goes beyond the National Curriculum. It also 'goes far beyond the formal timetable', involving:

> '. . . a range of policies and practices to promote the personal and social development of pupils, to accommodate different teaching and learning styles, to develop positive attitudes and values, and to forge an effective partnership with parents and the local community'.
>
> (National Curriculum Council, Circular No 6 (1989), para 6).

There is an important cross-curricular aspect to the 'whole curriculum', involving the inculcation of various skills and emphasising themes such as economic and industrial understanding, careers education and guidance, environmental education, health education and citizenship. Such themes 'make links between different parts of the curriculum' and may be taught through other subjects (*ibid*, paras 15 and 16). One particular initiative in support of a cross-curricular theme (supported by the Government) concerns the spiritual and moral dimension. The paper on this subject by the National Curriculum Council (NCC), *Spiritual and Moral Development* (1993), emphasised the need for schools to aim to inculcate moral values such as self-discipline, telling the truth, keeping promises, and respecting the rights and property of others (see, for another example, the NCC's Circular (No 8) on *Education for Citizenship* (1990)).

3. Control of the secular curriculum

LEAs were given control of the secular curriculum by section 23 of EA 1944. But this section was repealed by the E(No 2)A 1986 (Sch 6). Now the 'determination and organisation of the secular curriculum' in county, voluntary controlled and maintained special schools is in the hands of the head teacher (E(No 2)A 1986, s 18(5)). However, he or she must, in some cases, ensure that the curriculum is compatible with the governors' policy on sex education (see below) and the LEA's statement on curricular policy – as modified by the governors' own statement on the curriculum for the school. The head teacher must also ensure that the curriculum is compatible with other enactments relating to education: '(including, in particular, those relating to children with special educational needs)' (s 18(6)(c)) (the major statutory duty concerns implementation of the National Curriculum – see below).

In voluntary aided schools, control of the secular curriculum is placed in the hands of governors, although they must have regard to, *inter alia*, LEA curricular policy (E(No 2)A 1986, s 19(1) and (2)).

In GM schools the governing body has similar responsibilities, under the articles of government.

4. Statements of curricular policy (secular)

(a) The LEA's statement

The LEA is obliged to publish and keep under review its policy on secular provision, and, in doing so, must consider the range and balance of content in the curriculum (E(No 2)A 1986, s 17(1) and (2)).

(b) The governors' statement

The governing body must make and keep up to date a statement of curricular policy for the school – referring to content and organisation and (in primary schools only) whether sex education should form part of the secular curriculum (E(No 2)A 1986, s 18(1) and (2)). Governing bodies of secondary schools must make and keep up to date a policy on sex education and must make it available for inspection by parents (EA 1993, s 241(5)). In all maintained schools there is also a duty on the governing body to have regard to representations made to them by persons connected with the community served by the school, and by the chief officer of police, in relation to curriculum policy for the school (E(No 2)A 1986, s 18(3) and 19(2), and EA 1993, Sch 6 para 7(3)). In LEA maintained schools there is also a duty to have regard to the LEA's statement on the curriculum (see (a) above).

5. The 'basic curriculum'

Every maintained school must have a basic curriculum which meets the requirements of section 2(1) of the ERA 1988 (as amended by EA 1993, s 241(1)). The basic curriculum must include:

'(*a*) provision for religious education for all pupils at the school;
(*aa*) in the case of a secondary school, provision for sex education for all registered pupils at the school;
(*ab*) in the case of a special school, provision for sex education for all registered pupils at the school who are provided with secondary education; and
(*b*) a curriculum for all registered pupils at the school of compulsory school age (to be known as "the National Curriculum")'.

Note that (*a*) does not apply to special schools (ERA 1988, s 2(3)).

6. The National Curriculum

(a) The broad structure

Chart 1 **The National Curriculum**

I. Core subjects	*II. Other foundation subjects*
(ERA, s 3(1)) Mathematics, English and Science (and Welsh in Welsh-speaking schools)	(ERA, s 3(2)) History*, Geography*, Technology*, Music, Art, PE and a modern language** (in secondary years 1–3 or equivalent) (and Welsh in non-Welsh speaking schools in Wales) **Key Stages 1–3 only (at present), plus 4 (Technology only for pupils who entered this key stage in 1993)* ***Key Stage 3 only (at present)*

I and II each to have:

'Attainment targets'	'Programmes of study'	'Assessment arrangements'
'the knowledge, and understanding which pupils of different abilities and maturities are expected to have by the end of each key stage' (ERA, s 2(2)(a))	'the matters, skills and processes which are required to be taught to pupils of different abilities and maturities during each key stage' (ERA, s 2(2)(b))	'the arrangments for assessing pupils in respect of each key stage for the purpose of ascertaining what they have achieved in relation to the assessment targets for that stage' (ERA, s 2(2)(c), as amended by EA 1993, s 240(1))

The National Curriculum comprises 'core' and 'other foundation' subjects (see *Charts 1* and *2*), as prescribed for each of the four 'key stages' (see *Chart 3* on p 194). LEAs, governors and head teachers are under a legal duty to ensure that the National Curriculum, as in force at the relevant time, is implemented in their schools (ERA, s 10(2); EA 1993, Sch 6, para 7(1)). Individual teachers, however, are not under an independent statutory duty to implement the National Curriculum (*Wandsworth LBC* v *NAS/UWT* (1994) (*op cit*), which was concerned with the union's boycott of testing), although may in any event be in breach of their contract of employment for failing to do so.

Attainment targets (ATs) and programmes of study (PS) are prescribed by Order – many such Orders (some of which now incorporate amendments) have been made, e.g.: Education (National Curriculum) Attainment Targets and Programmes of Study in (Subject X) Orders:

> Art (SI 1992 No 598); English (SI 1989 No 907); Geography (SI 1991 Nos 678 and 2562); History (SI 1991 No 681); Mathematics (SI 1989 No 308 and SI 1991 No 2896); Music (SI 1992 No 597); Physical Education (SI 1992 No 603); Science (SI 1991 No 1520); Technology (SI 1990 No 424); Welsh (SI 1990 No 1082).

Changes will be made to many, if not all, of these SIs as and when the Dearing recommendations are phased in from autumn 1995. Dearing wants to free up about 20 per cent of curriculum time for use at the discretion of the school, and acknowledges that achieving this will 'mean some hard decisions about what should remain as a statutory requirement in the programmes of study' (Dearing, *The National Curriculum and its Assessment: Final Report* (1994) para 4.16). Dearing also recommends that as much as 40 per cent of curriculum time should be made available in this way at key stage 4 (para 5.26), with Modern Foreign Languages and Technology becoming compulsory short courses (but available as optional full courses as well) (paras 5.20–5.22). *Stop Press*: (see *Appendix 7*).

The Act permits the ATs and PS to be set out in a separate document published by HMSO, provided the Order makes appropriate reference to it (s 4(4)). One example is *Science in the National Curriculum* (1989) (ISBN 0 11 2706673). ATs and PS are prescribed for different 'key stages' of compulsory schooling (see *Chart 3* on p 194).

Chart 2 **Prescribed modern foreign languages (National Curriculum)**

I. Languages unconditionally specified as foundation subjects:
Danish, Dutch, French, German, Greek (Modern), Italian, Portuguese and Spanish
II. Languages which may be offered as foundation subjects provided that the school also offers pupils the opportunity of studying one or more of the languages in I above:
Arabic, Bengali, Chinese (Cantonese or Mandarin), Guijerati, Hebrew (Modern), Hindi, Japanese, Punjabi, Russian, Turkish and Urdu

Source: The Education (National Curriculum) (Modern Foreign Languages) Order, SI 1991 No 2567 (as amended by SI 1994 Nos 1815 and 1818)

Chart 3 **The 'key stages'**

Stage 1 *ages 5–7*	From attainment of compulsory school age to the end of the school year that the majority of pupils in the class reach the age of seven
Stage 2 *ages 8–11*	From the school year when the majority of pupils in the class reach the age of eight until the end of the year in which the majority reach the age of eleven
Stage 3 *ages 11–14*	From the school year when the majority in the class reach the age of twelve to the end of the year that the majority reach the age of fourteen
Stage 4 *ages 15–16*	From the school year when the majority in the class reach the age of fifteen to the year when the majority cease to be of compulsory school age

(ERA, s 3(3)).

Note: A definition of 'school year' for the purposes of the definitions of the key stages was added to section 3(6) of the ERA 1988 by section 240(3) of the EA 1993: 'the period beginning with the first school term to begin after July and ending with the beginning of the next school year'.

(b) Assessment

Assessment of pupils is integral to the National Curriculum. The ERA 1988 enables the Secretary of State to prescribe 'assessment arrangements' (s 4(2)(c)). As the definition shown in *Chart 1* makes clear, these arrangements relate to assessment at or near the end of each key stage (for the definition of which, see *Chart 3*). At the time of writing, the latest of these Orders include the Education (National Curriculum) (Assessment Arrangements for the Core Subjects) (Key Stage 1) Order 1993 (SI 1993 No 1983) as amended, (Key Stage 2) Order (SI 1994 No 2110) and (Key Stage 3) Order 1994 (SI 1994 No 2101). It must, however, be emphasised that the assessment arrangements have been changed rapidly in the light of experience and that they will be streamlined considerably following the Dearing recommendations (*op cit*; see paras 3.31, 3.42 and 7.10). It is expected that SATs (standard assessment tasks – the standard national tests) will continue to be required at the end of Key Stages 1–3, and in the core subjects only (at Key Stage 1, in English and mathematics only). Nevertheless, teachers' own assessments have also formed an important part of the regime, and Dearing recommends that they should continue to do so (indeed, outside the core subjects, they will form the main basis of assessment) and that teachers should be guided by national criteria (Dearing, *op cit*, paras 7.6–7.11). As teachers have, up until now, been expected to keep a record of each pupil's progress in relation to each attainment target throughout the child's period of schooling, with records of achievement chronicling individual pupils' attainment within the National Curriculum, implementation of the Dearing proposals (see *Appendix 7*) on modifying the ten-point scale used for assessment, and reducing the level of record-keeping, could prove to be of considerable practical significance.

Although *Wandsworth* v *NAS/UWT* (see (a) above) clarified that LEAs, headteachers and governing bodies are under a duty to secure that tests are carried out, by virtue of their general duty in section 10 to secure the full implementation of the National Curriculum (as in force at the time) in their schools, the Government was concerned to ensure that more specific obligations could be placed upon them. The 1993 Act (s 240(4)) has amended section 4 of the ERA 1988 to enable the Secretary of State, when prescribing assessment arrangements under section 2(2)(c) of the ERA 1988, to impose specific functions on the governing body and the head teacher and (in the case of maintained schools) on the LEA (ERA 1988, s 4(5)). Furthermore, the Secretary of State is now able to specify arrangements for auditing and verifying standards of assessment; the governing body, head teacher and (in LEA-maintained schools) the LEA are under a duty to permit the person carrying out the audit and moderation to enter the school premises, observe the implementation of the arrangements and inspect documents and other articles and take copies of them (ERA 1988, s 4(6) and (7)). (Assessment arrangements for 1995 including provision for external marking at Key Stage 3 are set out in DFE Circulars 20/94 and 21/94.)

(c) Reports to parents

Schools have to ensure that parents receive an annual report on their child's progress in relation to the various components of the National Curriculum. The requirements are described in Chapter 6 (at Part 7).

(d) Exception from the National Curriculum

Exception from the National Curriculum may be possible, under three separate provisions:

(i) If the head teacher thinks fit, individual pupils' education can be excepted from the National Curriculum (ERA 1988, s 19(1)) – in circumstances prescribed by regulation and for a certain period (not more than six months at a time). The child's parents, the LEA and the school governors are to be given information on this (including reasons) by the head teacher. Parents have a right of appeal to the governors against the head's direction (or any revocation or variation of it) (ERA 1988, s 19(7)–(10)). The head must comply with the governors' ruling in such a case.

Regulations have been made under section 19 – the Education (National Curriculum) (Temporary Exemptions for Individual Pupils) Regulations 1989. These state that for there to be a temporary exception the head teacher must consider that it is inappropriate for the child to follow the National Curriculum for the time being and that *either*:

(*a*) circumstances giving rise to that opinion are likely to change within the next six months; *or*

(*b*) the pupil may have special educational needs requiring modification of the National Curriculum, and temporary exception is necessary while those needs are assessed.

If the head's direction is given under (*a*) it is called a 'general direction', and if under (*b*) it is a 'special direction'. A general direction could be necessary, for example, in respect of a recently immigrated child who speaks little English and who needs intensive language support (see DES Circular 15/89 *The National Curriculum: Temporary Exceptions for Individual Pupils*).

(ii) Where a child has special educational needs for the purposes of Part III of the Education Act 1993, any special educational provision specified in a statement under section 168 of that Act (see Chapter 9 of this book) may include provision excluding the application of the National Curriculum or modifying it in his or her particular case (ERA 1988, s 18). This is clearly intended as a longer term form of exception to that in (i) above.

(iii) There is also a wide discretionary power to provide by regulation for all or part of the National Curriculum not to apply, or to apply in a modified form, in specific cases (ERA 1988, s 17). This power has been used to disapply, for pupils in Wales at Key Stage 1 who receive more than half their teaching in Welsh, the requirements concerning the implementation of the National Curriculum relating to English (Education (National Curriculum) (Exceptions) (Wales) Regulations 1989). Regulations have also disapplied section 10(3) of the ERA 1988 (which requires National Curriculum subjects to be taught for a 'reasonable time' each week prior to the implementation of specific attainment targets and programmes of study in the subject and key stage concerned) with regard to the teaching of Welsh – where not more than half the pupils in the school in 1987/88 or 1988/89 were taught Welsh (Education (National Curriculum) (Exceptions) (Wales) Regulations 1990). Further exceptions regulations applicable to Wales have disapplied section 10(3) (see above), as regards Welsh, in respect of pupils admitted to a school in Wales in the final year of Key Stage 3 or any year of Key Stage 4, unless within three years prior to their admission to the school they studied Welsh at school for at least 38 weeks (Education (National Curriculum) (Exceptions) (Wales) Regulations 1991). From 1 August 1994 there is also an exception from the provisions of the National Curriculum in Welsh (including Welsh Second Language) for pupils in Key Stage 4 (apart from pupils who commenced the first year of this Key Stage in 1993); the exception applies until 31 July 1999 in the case of pupils entering the first year of the Key Stage and 31 July 2000 in respect of those entering the second year of the Key Stage: Education (National Curriculum) Exceptions in Welsh at Key Stage 4) Regulations 1994 (SI 1994 No 1270).

Regulations under section 17 have also been used to enable schools to offer combined humanities and science courses for GCSE and presently to disapply any National Curriculum subject in the case of, *inter alia*, pupils who take their examination a year early (SI 1992 Nos 155, 156, 157). All of these have been revoked by the Education (National Curriculum) (Exceptions) Regulations 1994 (SI 1994 No 2112) (see also SI 1994 No 2206), which except all elements of specified foundation subjects in respect of pupils taking GCSE courses in prescribed subjects (see DFE Circular 4/94, paras 12–17).

(e) Implementation of the National Curriculum

The phasing in of the National Curriculum began on 1 September 1989. The Secretary of State is obliged to introduce it 'as soon as it is reasonably practicable (taking first the core subjects and then the other foundation subjects)' (ERA 1988, s 4(1)). From 1990 all core and foundation subjects were to be covered for a reasonable amount of time during the week (ERA 1988, s 10(3)) (*note:* the Secretary of State is prohibited by ERA, s 4(3) from prescribing periods of time or proportions of school timetables to be allocated to programmes of study).

Specific attainment targets and programmes of study in respect of each of the foundation subjects were in place for at least the first year of Key Stages 1 to 3 by Autumn 1992. The National Curriculum attainment targets and programmes of study presently extend to all years of all key stages in the three core subjects and are still being phased in for the other foundation subjects (or, so far as compulsory inclusion of certain subjects is concerned, are being phased out). Under existing arrangements, phasing-in will not be complete until 1997, but Dearing contemplates new Orders across the board (*op cit*, para 4.3), which will undoubtedly change aspects of the timetable for implementation. The Dearing Report will also lead to changes in the implementation of the SATs. In 1994, it was planned that SATs in only the three core subjects would be held at the end of Key Stages 2 and 3, and, in mathematics and English only, at the end of Key Stage 1.

The Government's timetable for the implementation of Dearing indicates that following publication of the revised curriculum requirements in November 1994, implementation will occur, in the case of Key Stages 1–3, in September 1995 and, so far as GCSE syllabuses are concerned, September 1996 (see DFE, *Final Report on the National Curriculum and its Assessment: The Government's Response* (1994)).

(f) The School Curriculum and Assessment Authority

Section 244 of the EA 1993 established the School Curriculum and Assessment Authority (SCAA) in place of the National Curriculum

Council (NCC) and the School Examinations and Assessment Council (SEAC). The 1993 Act has also extended the role of the Curriculum Council for Wales (see s 252) and renamed it Awdurdod Cwricwlwm ac Asesu Cymru or the Curriculum and Assessment Authority for Wales (CAAW) (see s 253 and Sch 15).

The establishment of the SCAA is intended to bring 'new coherence' to the advisory and developmental work being carried out in relation to the school curriculum (see the White Paper *Choice and Diversity* (1992), para 2.4). According to the Financial Memorandum to the Education Bill in 1992, the establishment of the SCAA and the transfer of certain functions to the CAAW 'will lead to reductions in public service manpower' and 'significant recurrent savings'.

Property, rights and liabilities of the NCC and SEAC were transferred to the SCAA by virtue of the National Curriculum Council and School Examinations and Assessment Council (Transfer of Property) Order 1993 (SI 1993 No 2195), made under section 247(1) of the EA 1993. The transfer of the NCC's and the SEAC's staff to SCAA was effected by the National Curriculum Council and School Examinations and Assessment Council (Designation of Staff) Order 1993 SI 1993 No 2231 (made under section 248(1) and (5) of the Act).

The SCAA has 10–15 members, all of whom are appointed by the Secretary of State (EA 1993, s 244(2)). Included among their number must be persons with experience and demonstrated capacity in the provision of education, including experience and capacity in positions of responsibility (s 244(4)). The operation of the SCAA is governed partly by the requirements of Schedule 14 to the 1993 Act (which covers tenure of office, payments to members and various operational matters) and section 245, which sets out the powers of the Authority. These powers include reviewing the school curriculum and examinations and assessment, advising the Secretary of State, assisting with the conduct of research for him, and carrying out ancillary functions as directed.

The functions of CAAW (which is to have 8–12 members) are concerned with the curriculum and assessment arrangements with regard to Welsh schools and Welsh as a taught language. But Key Stage 4 and GCSEs are the responsibility of the SCAA throughout England *and* Wales.

(g) Complaints

The ERA 1988 requires LEAs to establish complaints procedures for the consideration and disposal of complaints about various curricular matters, including the implementation of the National Curriculum and decisions about whether to grant exemption from its requirements in individual cases (s 23(1)). The complaints procedure is explained below (pp 223–229).

7. Political issues

The Education (No 2) Act 1986 proscribes political bias in the curriculum in various ways.

First, LEAs, head teachers and governing bodies are required to forbid the pursuit, at a school, of:

(i) 'partizan political activities' by junior school pupils (the side note refers to 'political indoctrination'), and

(ii) with reference to pupils at all stages, 'the promotion of partizan political views in the teaching of any subject in the school'.

(E(No 2)A 1986, s 44(1)).

Secondly, teachers must not make arrangements for junior pupils to engage in partizan political activities off the school premises (E(No 2)A 1986, s 44(2)). Finally, LEAs, head teachers and governing bodies must take reasonable steps to secure that:

> '. . . where political issues are brought to the attention of pupils while they are:
>
> (*a*) at the school; or
>
> (*b*) taking part in extra-curricular activities which are provided or organised for registered pupils at the school by or on behalf of the school;
>
> they are offered a *balanced presentation of opposing views*' (s 45, emphasis added).

These provisions were a response in the mid-1980s to what the Government saw as an unbalanced treatment of issues, or politically motivated selection of issues for coverage, by teachers in some LEA schools – especially those offering 'Peace Studies' or where pupils were allegedly being radicalised by 'Left-wing' teachers.

The question of what is or is not a 'political' issue is important. It would seem to be appropriate to extend its meaning beyond the merely party political. Nuclear power or other 'green' issues can clearly be political, depending on the context in which they appear.

8. Sex education

The Government's White Paper on *The Health of the Nation* (1992) (Cm1986) set as a target a 50 per cent reduction in pregnancy among the under 16s by the year 2000. Sex education is seen as playing a key role (see DFE Circular 5/94, *Education Act 1993: Sex Education in Schools* (1994), para 9).

(a) Must sex education be provided?

Prior to the Education Act 1993 there was no specific legal duty on schools or education authorities to provide sex education. Nevertheless, some aspects of sex education featured in the National Curriculum attainment targets for Science. The DES Circular (11/87) on sex education in schools stated (at para 7) that while a governing body was free to decide that sex education should not be provided at a school (which choice, in fact, became doubtful after its subsequent inclusion in the National Curriculum Science attainment targets), the Secretary of State expected that governors would accept that 'schools have a responsibility to their pupils to offer at least some education about sexual matters'. In fact, it was doubtful whether schools could adequately 'prepare . . . pupils for the . . . responsibilities and experiences of adult life', as required by ERA 1988, s 1(2)(b), without providing sex education.

Section 241 of the EA 1993 has amended section 2(1) of the ERA 1988 to include sex education as part of the basic curriculum that must be provided (subject to the parental right to withdraw a child: see below) in all maintained *secondary* schools and to all pupils receiving *secondary* education in special schools (the relevant provisions are set out on pp 191–192 above). Sex education is defined as including education about Acquired Immune Deficiency Syndrome (AIDS) and Human Immunodeficiency Virus (HIV) (EA 1944, s 114(1), as amended by EA 1993, s 241(2)). As noted below, however, schools are advised to make decisions on coverage of AIDS/HIV and other sexually transmitted diseases taking account of pupils' age and maturity (DFE, Circular 5/94, *Education Act 1993: Sex Education in Schools* (1994, para 11).

At the same time, the Secretary of State is required to use his power in section 4 of the ERA 1988 to revise the content of the National Curriculum in such a way as to remove sex education from the science syllabus (EA 1993, s 241(4); see now the Education (National Curriculum) (Attainment Targets and Projects of Study in Science) Amendment Order 1994, SI 1994 No 1520). The true purpose of this provision can only be understood with reference to the right of parents to withdraw their children from sex education, other than where it is provided under the National Curriculum (see below). The Minister explained that 'it would be quite wrong to legislate for the possibility that some children might leave secondary education without a clear knowledge of the basic biological and physical facts of life' (*Hansard*, House of Lords, Vol 547, cols 1290–1291, *per* Baroness Blatch).

Sex education has not been made compulsory in *primary* schools. Indeed, section 18(2)(a) of the E(No 2)A 1986 continues to require governing bodies of primary schools 'to consider . . . the question whether sex education should form part of the secular curriculum for the school'. Again, it could be argued that education in preparation for adult life demands some basic sex education at the primary education stage.

(b) The parent's right to withdraw a child from sex education

Until the EA 1993, parents had, on the face of it, no right to withdraw their children from sex education lessons. However, it was possible that a parent might have had a choice by virtue of EA 1944, s 76, which states that provided it is compatible with the provision of efficient education and the avoidance of unreasonable public expenditure, 'children are to be educated in accordance with the wishes of their parents'. The courts have considered the scope of section 76 (see Chapter 2, Part 8(d), and Chapter 7, Part 6(a)), but not yet in this context. This argument has to be balanced against the European Court of Human Rights' conclusion (in *Kjeldsen, Busk Masden and Pedersen* (1976)) that compulsory sex education for all pupils in Denmark did not constitute a breach of Article 2 to the First Protocol to the European Convention on Human Rights, 1950. This Article provides that 'no person shall be denied the right to education', and in this regard state educational provision must be in conformity with parents' religious and philosophical convictions. The Court held that the parents' wishes were subject to the state's overriding duty to present information and knowledge, objectively, pluralistically and critically.

In any event, schools in England and Wales had a discretion to permit parents to withdraw their children from sex education, and the DES advised schools to recognise the strong religious objections felt by some parents towards sex education and to bear these views in mind when exercising their discretion (see DES Circular 11/87, *Sex Education in Schools* (1987)).

But the EA 1993 has now provided parents in England and Wales with a right to withdraw their children from sex education. Section 241(3) inserts section 17A into the ERA 1988. This new section provides that if a parent requests that his or her child be wholly or partly excused from receiving sex education at school, the request must be granted. The exemption will apply to that child until the parent withdraws his or her request. Section 17A does not permit withdrawal of the child from any sex education comprised in the National Curriculum. There is no requirement for the parent to express any reasons for the request, and the right of withdrawal is unconditional. Indeed, the DFE's guidance on sex education (Circular 5/94 (*op cit*, para 37)) warns head teachers to 'avoid putting any pressure on parents who decide to exercise this right'.

(c) Information about sex education

Under the Education (School Information) Regulations 1994, LEAs and governors have a duty to include in the published information about their schools, details of the manner and context in which sex education is given (see Chapter 6, Part 3(b)).

(d) What kind of sex education?

LEAs and governing bodies have, since 7 January 1987, been charged with a duty to:

> 'take such steps as are reasonably practicable to secure that where sex education is given to any registered pupils at a school it is given in such a manner as *to encourage those pupils to have due regard to moral considerations and the value of family life*' (E(No 2)A 1986, s 46, emphasis added).

The recent DFE Circular on sex education (*op cit*) advises that at the *primary* school level, teaching should 'aim to prepare pupils to cope with the physical and emotional challenges of growing up, and to give them an elementary understanding of human reproduction' (para 10). In responding to pupils' questions, the circular advises, 'due consideration should be given by teachers to any particular religious or cultural factors bearing on the discussion of sexual issues' (*ibid*) and to parental wishes. At *secondary* schools, sex education should encompass facts as to human reproductive processes and behaviour and also give consideration to the 'broader emotional and ethical dimensions of sexual attitudes' (*ibid*, para 11). As noted above, the Circular advises that AIDS/HIV and other sexually transmitted diseases should be covered only when pupils are sufficiently mature. Guidance for *special* schools acknowledges the 'particularly sensitive' role they must play in relation to sex education (para 12).

According to the Government, section 46 is important in establishing a 'moral framework' for sex education. Sex education, the Government says, should present the facts and encompass the law on sexual behaviour. But it should be 'set within a clear moral framework' in which pupils are:

> 'helped to consider the importance of self-restraint, dignity, respect for themselves and others, acceptance of responsibility, sensitivity towards the needs and views of others, loyalty and fidelity. And they should be enabled to recognise the physical, emotional and moral implications, and risks, of certain types of behaviour and to accept that both sexes must behave responsibly in sexual matters' (para 8).

So far as 'physical' risks are concerned, teaching about sexually transmitted diseases is obviously important; this is now provided for by virtue of the definition of sex education in section 114(1) of the EA 1944 (see above).

The moral framework for sex education also involves teachers emphasising the 'value of stable family, marriage and the responsibilities of parenthood' (Circular 5/94, *op cit*, para 8). But at the same time the Circular stresses the importance of recognising that because some pupils come from backgrounds in which there is no such stability, sensitivity will be needed to avoid causing hurt and offence to them and their families (*ibid*).

(e) Advice about contraception

The legal and ethical problems surrounding the giving of contraceptive advice highlighted by the *Gillick* case (*Gillick* v *West Norfolk and Wisbech AHA* [1985] 3 All ER 402 (HL)), in which Mrs Victoria Gillick unsuccessfully challenged the provision of advice about contraception given by doctors in certain circumstances to under-age girls without parental consent, could well arise in a school situation. Teachers may be giving information about contraception as part of sex education lessons or possibly may be approached by individual pupils for advice. The recent DFE Circular 5/94 (like DES Circular 11/77 before it) warns teachers never to allow their concern for the well-being of pupils to 'trespass on the proper exercise of parental rights and responsibilities' (*op cit*, para 38).

If a teacher is approached for advice by a pupil, the teacher should, according to the Circular (para 40), encourage the pupil to seek help from his or her parent or, alternatively, a health professional. If the teacher believes that the pupil 'has embarked upon, or is contemplating a course of conduct which is likely to place him or her at moral or physical risk or in breach of the law' the teacher should warn the pupil of the implications and advise the pupil to obtain advice.

The Circular suggests that in some cases the head teacher should be informed. The question whether to involve specialist support services, including school health professionals, is said to be a matter to be judged with reference to 'the particular circumstances and the professional judgement of the staff' (*ibid*). The head teacher is advised to arrange counselling where appropriate. The Circular really ought to go further here, although it does, for example, link with guidance on identification and referral in cases of child abuse (see DES Circular 4/88 and the inter-agency guidance by the Department of Health, *Working Together under the Children Act 1989* (1991); for general discussion, see Lyon and de Cruz, *Child Abuse* (2nd ed) (1993) Family Law, p 95). The guidance also states that head teachers should, if the pupil is under age, ensure that the parent is made aware of the matter (preferably by the pupil himself or herself).

An implication of the *Gillick* decision (for analysis of which, see Bainham, *Children: The Modern Law* (Family Law 1993) pp 276–280) is that giving advice on contraception to under-age pupils without parental consent could be considered to be 'an inappropriate exercise of a teacher's professional responsibilities' (para 39). In fact teachers are placed in a difficult position that, most probably, no amount of guidance can adequately resolve. Some teachers or head teachers may feel compelled not to commit a 'breach of confidence', given the importance of retaining the trust and respect of pupils or out of concern for their welfare. The DFE seems to be rather uncertain as to the precise effect of the *Gillick* decision on the provision of contraceptive advice by teachers. References to *Gillick* in the 1987 Circular were scaled down to a mere mention in a replacement draft issued in April 1993; the recently issued Circular (*op cit*) makes no reference to *Gillick* at all. The guidance states merely that 'Teachers are not health professionals, and the legal position of a teacher giving advice in such circumstances has never been tested in the courts' (*ibid*). Nevertheless, *Gillick* (as applied in *Re R* [1992] 1 FLR 190) is clearly being viewed as limiting the scope for the provision of contraceptive advice by teachers to the under-16s. The Family Planning Association has criticised the DFE's approach as liable to leave 13–15 year-olds without proper guidance: see *The Times*, 30 March 1994. The Sex Education forum, having obtained legal opinions, believes that a teacher would not incur criminal liability for giving an individual pupil contraceptive advice if genuinely acting in the child's best interest; but the legal position remains unclear. The crucial question in determining whether contraceptive advice would, in the absence of parental consent, be lawfully given is whether the child is competent to receive it. According to Bainham (*op cit*, p 283) 'both *Gillick* and *Re R* require a high level of understanding, extending beyond the mechanics of the medical procedure involved, to the wider medical, moral and family considerations of what is proposed'.

Note that although the Government believes that subjects like contraception and, indeed, abortion, would normally be covered by sex education, it accepts that where schools are founded on specific religious principles this will have a direct bearing on how these subjects are presented.

(f) Homosexuality and sex education

See 9 below.

(g) Complaints about sex education

The curriculum complaints procedure, referred to earlier and considered more fully below (see Part 13), applies also to sex education. For an example of how one such complaint was handled, see N Harris, *Complaints About Schooling – The Role of Section 23 of the Education Reform Act 1988* (National Consumer Council, 1992), at pp 87–91.

9. Homosexuality

The Government's concern about some teachers' alleged portrayal of homosexual relationships as 'normal' resulted, controversially, in its forceful rejection of such practices. Paragraph 22 of the DES Circular on sex education (11/87 (1987) – see above) told teachers that:

> 'There is no place in any school in any circumstances for teaching which advocates homosexual behaviour, which presents it as the "norm", or which encourages homosexual experimentation by pupils'.

The Government did not seek to ban all references to homosexuality in the course of teaching. But it told schools that unless the subject was handled with sensitivity by teachers, 'deep offence' might be caused to those, especially members of various religious faiths, for whom 'homosexual practice is not morally acceptable' (*ibid*). The fact that the age of consent for male homosexuals is to be reduced from 21 to 18 strengthens the case for coverage of homosexuality in sex education. The 1994 Circular omits homosexuality altogether, although the law on buggery is summarised in Annex B.

Section 28 of the Local Government Act 1988 (which inserts s 2A into the Local Government Act 1986) forms part of the relevant legal context. It states that local authorities shall not:

> '(*a*) intentionally promote homosexuality or publish material with the intention of promoting homosexuality;
>
> (*b*) promote the teaching in any maintained school of the acceptability of homosexuality as a pretended family relationship'.

The section applies to local authorities, rather than their employees, e.g. teachers. A local authority that failed to prevent a teacher from 'promoting' homosexuality might be in breach of section 28.

It is clear that fears that certain works of literature (e.g. Mann's *Death in Venice*) might have to be taken out of the school curriculum, and possibly removed from examination syllabuses, because of section 28, were unfounded.

10. Collective worship and religious education

(a) Introduction

All maintained schools must provide religious education (in many cases under the local 'agreed syllabus', drawn up by a 'conference', as required by the EA 1944) as part of the 'basic curriculum' of the school (ERA 1988, s 2(1)). There is also a general requirement that all pupils should take part in daily collective worship. These duties were first laid down in the EA 1944, but significant changes were made by the ERA 1988, including an emphasis on Christianity in collective worship and the establishment of local standing advisory councils on religious education (SACREs). The EA 1993 has now made further important changes – for example, in the procedure for preparing the agreed syllabus for religious education once an area is well represented by GM schools, in requiring conferences and SACREs to reconvene, in requiring agreed syllabuses to be reconsidered, in empowering the Secretary of State to give directions to defaulting or unreasonable SACREs, and for providing for public access to meetings of conferences or SACREs.

(b) The statutory advisory councils on religious education

Each LEA is required to establish a standing advisory council on religious education (with a somewhat appropriate acronym of SACRE) for its area. The council's function is to:

> 'advise the authority upon such matters connected with religious worship in county schools and the religious education to be given in accordance with an agreed syllabus as the authority may refer to the council or as the council may think fit' (ERA 1988, s 11(1)(a) – a copy of the advice must be sent to head teachers of certain GM schools: subs (11) and (12), added by the EA 1993),

and to consider whether, on an application by the head teacher of a county school, it is appropriate for the requirement for Christian collective worship (see below) to apply in the case of that school, or in the case of any class or description of pupils at that school (ERA, ss 11(1)(b) and 12(1)).

The SACREs are to consist of various representative groups:

(i) such 'Christian and other denominations and other religions and other denominations of such religions' as reflect the 'principal religious traditions' in the area;

(ii) the Church of England (except in Wales);
(iii) teachers' associations; and
(iv) the LEA.

They may also include co-opted members and must include a nominee of the governors of a grant-maintained school which is following an agreed syllabus adopted by the LEA (ERA, s 11(3) and (4), as amended by EA 1993, Sch 19 para 116). In relation to representative group (i), the number of members appointed to represent each denomination or religion required to be represented must, so far as practicable, 'reflect broadly the proportionate strength of that denomination or religion in the area' (EA 1993, s 255(2)). The phrase 'principal religious traditions', referred to in relation to this group, is nowhere defined in the Act, nor is it explained in the relevant DFE Circular (*Religious Education and Collective Worship*, 1/94, *op cit*). The LEA is required to take all reasonable steps to assure itself that a person seeking to represent a particular denomination on the SACRE is a true representative of that denomination (EA 1993, s 13(1)).

SACRE meetings are to be generally open to the public. Public notice of the meetings must be given and copies of agenda and reports are to be provided (a charge may be made) and, along with minutes of the meeting, made available for public inspection (EA 1993, s 258; Religious Education (Meetings of Local Conferences and Councils) Regulations 1994 (SI 1994 No 1304)).

LEAs must reconstitute SACREs within six months of the commencement of section 255 of the EA 1993 (which occurred on 1 April 1994). A SACRE must also be reconstituted once six months have elapsed following the making of an order in respect of an area's schools under section 12(1)(b) of the EA 1993 (under which sole responsibility for ensuring sufficient school places is transferred to a funding authority) (EA 1993, s 16(1)). The purpose of this rule, introduced by the EA 1993, is to ensure proper representation of relevant GM schools on the SACRE, as is warranted by the fact that (in most cases) where a section 12(1)(b) order is made, at least 75 per cent of children at state schools in the area will be registered at GM schools.

As noted above, the EA 1993 has given the Secretary of State a power to issue directions to SACREs which act unreasonably when deciding whether all or some pupils should be covered by the requirement as to broadly Christian collective worship in section 7 of the ERA 1988 (EA 1993, s 257, adding s 12A to the ERA 1988). There is a corresponding power in relation to any failure by a SACRE to carry out the requirements of section 12 of the 1988 Act (relating to granting and reviewing exemptions from the Christian collective worship requirement) (*ibid*). Each SACRE is required to publish an annual report (ERA 1988, s 11(9) and (10)).

(c) Collective worship

Section 25 of the Education Act 1944, which provided for an act of collective worship at the start of each school day (and for religious instruction at each county and voluntary school) was repealed with effect from 1 January 1989 (ERA 1988, Sch 13). In its place are carefully worded and rather more prescriptive provisions. However, recent evidence suggests that not all of the legal requirements are being complied with (Office of HM Chief Inspector of Schools/OFSTED, *Religious Education and Collective Worship 1992–1993* (HMSO, 1994)). A recent survey of head teachers has revealed that seven out of ten are unable to comply with the requirement to hold a daily act of worship (*The Independent*, 1 June 1994).

(i) What form of act?

Section 6 of the ERA 1988 provides that in each maintained school (including a grant-maintained school), on each school day, all children present at the school must take part in an *act of collective worship* – whether a single act of worship for all pupils or separate acts for different age groups or other school groups. 'Worship' is not defined in the Act, but is defined in the OED with reference to a divine being or deity. DFE Circular 1/94 (*Religious Education and Collective Worship* (1994), paras 57–59) suggests that worship 'should be concerned with reverence or veneration being paid to a divine being or power', but that its form in the school context 'will necessarily be of a different character from worship amongst a group with beliefs in common' and that it should be capable of eliciting a response from pupils (even if an individual's participation cannot be guaranteed). In 1993 an important test case was brought in which the requirements of the 1988 Act as to the 'Christian' aspect of collective worship were considered: *R* v *Secretary of State for Education ex p R and D* [1993] Lexis CO/2202/92. An extract from the judgment of McCullough J (who refused leave to apply for judicial review) is set out at *Appendix 5* to this book.

(ii) Whose responsibility?

Governing bodies and, in relation to LEA-maintained schools, LEAs, must exercise their functions with a view to ensuring that the requirement for there to be collective worship is carried out (ERA 1988, s 10(1)(a)). Responsibility for making the necessary arrangements for the act of collective worship rests with the head teacher, after consultation with the school governing body, in the case of a county school, and vice versa in the case of a voluntary school (ERA 1988, s 6(3)). Generally the act of collective worship is to take place on the school premises; the governors can, if they consider it desirable, make appropriate arrangements for it to take place elsewhere 'on a special occasion' (ERA 1988, s 6(4) and (5)).

(iii) The act to be of a broadly Christian character

The ERA states that the act should be 'wholly or mainly of a broadly Christian character' – i.e. it should reflect 'the broad traditions of Christian belief without being distinctive of any particular Christian denomination' (ERA 1988, s 7(1) and (2)). Note that from time to time acts of collective worship do not have to comply with the above requirements, provided most of them do (s 7(3)).

This requirement as to Christian collective worship only applies in *county* schools. In *voluntary* schools the character and content of collective worship will continue to be determined by governing bodies and/or trust deeds. The position of a GM school will depend basically on whether or not it has been established as a denominational school or was a voluntary school immediately before it acquired GM status (see EA 1993, ss 138–141). Non-denominational GM schools, whether they were established as such or were formerly county schools, are covered by similar requirements to sections 6 and 7 of the ERA 1988 (see above) (EA 1993, s 138). City technology colleges and colleges for the technology of the arts are exempt from the legal requirements regarding collective worship (and RE).

(iv) Alternative collective worship and withdrawal

The head teacher of a county school may, if he or she considers that alternative collective worship is appropriate in respect of the whole school or any class or description of pupils at the school, apply to the local SACRE to lift or modify the requirements as to Christian collective worship where such pupils are concerned (ERA 1988, s 12(1)). By December 1992, around 300 schools had been granted permission not to comply with the Christian collective worship requirement of the 1988 Act, including 98 per cent of the schools in Brent, but only 2 per cent of those in Wolverhampton (*Sunday Times*, 6 December 1992).

The right of parents to withdraw pupils from acts of collective worship, without having to give reasons, (previously in the Education Act 1944) is re-enacted in section 9(3) of the ERA 1988 (and EA 1993, s 188(6), in the case of special schools).

Various circumstances are to be taken into account by the SACRE when deciding on whether broadly Christian worship is appropriate for the pupils concerned, including pupils' family backgrounds (ERA 1988, s 12(2)). SACREs must review their decisions on this matter within five years of their previous determination, or at any time if an application for review from the head teacher (after he or she has consulted with the governing body) is received (s 12(5)).

One problem arising from departure from blanket Christian collective worship is that in schools of a multi-ethnic composition there might have to be a form of segregation for acts of collective worship. Segregation on the basis of religion often results in segregation by race. This could constitute unlawful discrimination under section 1 of the Race Relations Act 1976; however, section 41 of that Act permits discrimination in furtherance of compliance with mandatory statutory duties (in this case in the ERA 1988). The kind of ecumenical approach prevailing in many school assemblies at present, and often something of a tradition, is probably lawful, for the most part, by virtue of the fact that not all acts of collective worship have to be of a broadly Christian character provided that in any school term most are.

If, in any particular school, the numbers requiring alternative collective worship are very small, the SACRE may decide not to permit it, and parents will simply have the option of withdrawing their children from the Christian act. If alternative collective worship for a minority religious group *has* been authorised by the SACRE, the collective worship must 'not be distinctive of any particular Christian or other religious *denomination* (but this shall not be taken as preventing that worship from being distinctive of any particular *faith*)' (ERA 1988, s 7(6)(b), emphasis added). In some schools teachers will undoubtedly experience great difficulty in drawing the required distinction.

Nothing in the ERA 1988 prevents a school from allowing participation in RE or worship in a particular faith or denomination by individual pupils whose parents have withdrawn them from approved RE or collective worship (see DFE Circular 1/94, para 88). This non-statutory provision need not be provided free of charge, according to the Minister of State for education (*TES*, 5 January 1990). Note that it cannot be a condition of attendance at a maintained school (including a GM school) that a pupil attends, or abstains from attending, any Sunday school or place of worship (ERA 1988, s 9(1)).

(d) Religious education

(i) Introduction

The law governing religious education (RE) in state schools in England and Wales is now contained in three separate statutes: the EA 1944, the ERA 1988 and the EA 1993. Despite the range of statutory provisions regulating RE, the content of RE has varied between one LEA and another and between different schools in each area. Such diversity has always been accepted as necessary and desirable, not only because of religious diversity of schools and the diverse demands of the different religious denominations for schools that uphold their particular religious traditions, but also, in part, because of the different ethnic and cultural make-up of the population in each locality. In many LEA areas, the perceived importance of a truly multicultural approach to the school curriculum has led to attempts to secularise RE or to broaden it to embrace elements of all major religions. This approach has been made possible, at least in relation to county schools, by the 1944 Act (as amended), under which an agreed syllabus on RE for an area is to be drawn up by a local conference of representatives of the principal religious traditions in an area, the Church of England (apart from in Wales), teaching associations and the LEA. These conferences are constituted under Schedule 5 to the 1944 Act. The ERA 1988 required a greater emphasis on Christianity in agreed syllabuses (see below). But evidence suggested that compliance with this requirement was patchy, with significant numbers of Schedule 5 conferences failing to review their syllabuses and bring them into line with the 1988 Act (see *The*

Independent, 11 March 1993). Research suggests that an overwhelming majority of parents want their children to learn about other faiths in addition to Christianity (see *The Independent*, 6 September 1993), and the Government has been keen to emphasise that while Christianity should 'predominate', other religions must also be covered (DFE Circular 1/94, *Religious Education and Collective Worship* (1994), para 35–see below). Government concern to ensure that local syllabuses reflect that balance, as required by the 1988 Act, has led to attempts by it to tighten up on RE.

RE is not part of the National Curriculum, and the Secretary of State has no power to prescribe attainment targets or programmes of study in relation to it. Nevertheless, the Government asked the National Curriculum Council (NCC) to draw up model syllabuses, offering local committees a choice of which syllabus to adopt after carrying out the review required by the 1993 Act. In their 1991 guidance (*Religious Education–A Local Curriculum Framework*) the NCC had tried to demonstrate how local syllabuses could be drawn up using the National Curriculum framework of attainment targets (ATs) and programmes of study (PS). At that time the NCC's view was that no attempt should be made to prescribe national ATs and PS for RE, nor to offer models, 'since if it is decided to draw up such a framework, it will need to be specific in each case to the local agreed syllabus and the local needs which it is intended to meet' (*ibid*, p 11). Nevertheless, the idea that local syllabuses should be based around ATs and that they should conform to a particular model (from a choice of different models) has persisted. In January 1994 two model syllabuses were published by the SCAA, which by then had taken over the work of the NCC. (For the background to the development of these syllabuses, see SCAA, *Model Syllabuses for RE – Consultation Document – Introduction* (1994) pp 1–2.) Revised versions of the syllabuses were published in July 1994, following consultation with, amongst others, representatives of the six main religious faiths in England, who have approved them. There are two Model Syllabuses, both of which are 'intended for use by agreed syllabus conferences' and 'are not intended as schemes of work by schools' (SCAA, *Religious Education – Model Syllabuses: Model 1 – Living Faiths Today; Model 2 – Questions and Teachings* (July 1994)). Thus changes in the law will not be needed. Model 1 'is structured around the knowledge and understanding of what it means to be a member of a faith community'. Model 2 'is structured around knowledge and understanding of the teachings of religions and how these relate to shared human experience' (*ibid*). The coverage of the syllabuses is based around attainment targets. There is wider scope for local flexibility than was offered by the earlier versions. Study of Christianity still predominates, but one or two other religions would also be studied at each key stage, and by the end of Key Stage 4 pupils would be expected to have been taught about Buddhism, Hinduism, Islam, Judaism and Sikhism in addition to Christianity. The presence locally of other religions could mean that they might also be taught.

Evidence suggests that many schools are failing to meet the legal requirements on RE (see Office of HM Chief Inspector of Schools/

OFSTED, *Religious Education and Collective Worship 1992–1993* (HMSO, 1994)).

However, now a tougher approach to ensuring compliance with the law on RE has also been taken via new provisions on inspections of denominational education and collective worship (ESA 1992, s 13, as amended by EA 1993, s 259 – see Chapter 10, Part 5).

(ii) Local conferences

Local conferences are constituted under Schedule 5 to the EA 1944, but, as with SACREs, the requirements on their constitution vary depending upon whether a full transfer order has been made under section 12(1)(b) of the EA 1993 (see p 206 above). If there is no such order, the conference comprises persons representing the following groups:

(i) such 'Christian and other denominations and other religions and other denominations of such religions' as reflect the 'principal religious traditions' in the area;
(ii) the Church of England (except in Wales);
(iii) teachers' associations; and
(iv) the LEA.

Public access rules applicable to SACREs apply to meetings of Schedule 5 conferences (see p 206 above).

Section 15 of the EA 1993 provides that if an order under section 12(1)(b) of the 1993 Act has been made, the Schedule 5 conference must be reconvened within six months, unless in that period it has agreed a syllabus. When it is convened or reconvened, the conference must include persons representing denominational GM schools (see EA 1993, ss 138 and 139). Where a GM school was formerly a voluntary aided or special agreement school, and the parents of any pupils there wish them to be taught RE under the agreed syllabus for the area, the conference's general duty to consult GM schools in the area who use the syllabus, when reconsidering the agreed syllabus (a duty set out in EA 1993, s 146), will be applicable (EA 1993, s 15(4)(b)). A person appointed to represent GM schools may resign from the committee or, if no longer considered to be acceptable as a representative to the majority of GM schools in the area, may be withdrawn by the LEA (s 15(6)). Any such person must be replaced (*ibid*). Similar provision is made in Schedule 5 to the EA 1944 in respect of other members of the conference.

(iii) Religious education syllabuses

Religious education in *county* schools must be in accordance with an 'agreed syllabus' established by a Schedule 5 conference (EA 1944, s 26(1); see p 209 above). All agreed syllabuses adopted on or after 29 September 1988 must (ERA 1988, s 8(3)):

'reflect the fact that the religious traditions in Great Britain are in the

> main Christian whilst taking account of the teaching and practices of the other principal religions represented in Great Britain'.

The phrase 'principal religions' is nowhere defined in the Act.

It is important to bear in mind that the requirement in section 26 of the EA 1944, that RE should not be given 'by means of any catechism or formulary which is distinctive of any religious denomination', is preserved in the amended version of that section. However, the amended section goes on to state (EA 1944, s 26(2)) that 'this provision is not to be taken as prohibiting provision in a syllabus for the study of such catechism or formularies'. So pupils can, subject to the parental right of withdrawal (see below), be required to learn about religions other than their own during RE lessons.

In *voluntary* schools RE must be in accordance with the agreed syllabus or the school's trust deed or in accordance with the practice which was observed before the school became a voluntary school (EA 1944, ss 27(1) and 28(1), as amended).

GM schools will, in effect, be treated in the same way as county or voluntary schools so far as RE syllabus requirements are concerned. A school which is established by a funding authority or as a non-denominational school by promoters, or which was a county school before it became GM, must follow the 'appropriate agreed syllabus' for the area (EA 1993, s 138(9)). This is basically the local agreed syllabus or any another agreed syllabus adopted by another LEA on or after 29 September 1988 (EA 1993, s 142). In former controlled schools, RE must be in accordance with the appropriate agreed syllabus or, if the parents of any pupils request that it be such for their children, the school's trust deed or the practice before the school became GM (s 139(3)). Changes to RE in the aforementioned GM schools are possible, under the procedure in sections 96 and 98 of the EA 1993. If approval is given for denominational RE the requirements on RE are the same as for the following types of school (EA 1993, s 141), which have denominational RE. These are GM schools which were voluntary aided or special agreement schools immediately before becoming GM or which were established by promoters as a denominational school (to provide RE in accordance with a trust deed or the terms of a statement as to denominational education published simultaneously with the proposals for the school to acquire GM status) (see EA 1993, s 140). In the case of a voluntary aided school which acquires GM status, RE will be in accordance with the trust deed or, where the trust deed does not specify provision for RE, in accordance with the practice before the school became GM. In some circumstances, where parents of children at such schools want their children to receive RE in accordance with the agreed syllabus, the governors must make appropriate arrangements (EA 1993, s 140(3) and (4)).

(iv) Parental rights

Parents may exclude their children from religious education at a school and have their children receive a particular form of such education away from the school premises but during school hours (ERA 1988, s 9(3) and (4)). Moreover, it cannot be a condition of attendance at a maintained (including a grant maintained) school that a pupil attends, or abstains from attending, any Sunday school or place of worship (*ibid*, s 9(1)). In one recent survey it was found that less than 1 per cent of secondary school parents had exercised the right of withdrawal (Office of HM Chief Inspector of Schools/OFSTED, *Religious Education and Collective Worship 1992–93* (HMSO, 1994), para 42).

(e) Opting out by teachers

Teachers in most state schools are not to be disqualified, on the grounds of failing to participate in collective worship or RE teaching, from being employed there, and, if appointed, must not be discriminated against (in terms of pay, promotion etc). These basic rules apply to all schools apart from aided or certain GM schools (those which offer denominational religious education and/or which were voluntary schools before becoming GM), and in respect of reserved teachers in voluntary controlled or special agreement schools (EA 1944, s 30; EA 1993, s 143–145). Note that if a voluntary school becomes GM, the position of a teacher who was employed at the school before GM status commenced will remain the same for as long as this employment continues (EA 1993, s 144(4)). The DFE argues that these provisions do not prevent an appointments committee from taking account of a candidate's willingness to lead collective worship or teach RE in making an appointment, although it advises further that such willingness cannot be made a requirement for appointment (DFE Circular 1/94, *op cit*, para 145).

In *Ahman* v *ILEA* [1978] QB 36 a teacher of the Moslem faith was employed at an LEA-maintained school. He attended a mosque on Fridays. Of the time that he spent at the mosque each week, three-quarters of an hour coincided with school hours. The minimum weekly cover for him that could be arranged was a half day. The LEA therefore sought to change the teacher's contractual commitment to four-and-a-half days per week, on a part-time basis, with a consequential reduction in salary. The teacher argued that the LEA was in breach of section 30 of the EA 1944 (see above) and also Article 9 of the European Convention on Human Rights 1950 (freedom of religion). The Court of Appeal held that section 30 did not authorise a teacher to break his contract and that as the teacher had been aware of the school timetable and the extent of his duties when he accepted the post, and had not disclosed his intention to be absent for religious observance, the section could not help him. The majority also rejected the claim that Article 9 of the European Convention applied in this situation.

Many teachers are, in fact, opposed to compulsory collective worship for pupils. The circular (1/94, *op cit*, paras 146 and 147) states that where there are insufficient teachers who are prepared to lead an act of collective worship, the head must take all reasonable steps to find suitable persons *not* employed at the school who would be willing to conduct such acts, perhaps initially taking advice from their LEA and SACRE. The circular also states that senior pupils could lead acts of collective worship in appropriate cases (para 148).

11. External qualifications and examination entry

(a) External qualifications

Courses leading to qualifications authenticated by an outside body cannot be offered to pupils of compulsory school age unless the syllabus has been approved or meets approved criteria (ERA 1988, s 5(1)). Approval, for this purpose, must be given by the Secretary of State or a 'designated body' (i.e. one designated by the Secretary of State). Before the introduction of the School Curriculum and Assessment Authority (SCAA), the School Examinations and Assessment Council (SEAC) performed this role. DFE Circular 2/93 is the latest circular to explain the approval arrangements.

(b) Examination entry

Pupils at maintained schools must be entered by the school for any public examinations for which they have been prepared by the school, unless either the parent requests in writing that the pupil should not be so entered (but see the exception below) or there are 'educational reasons' for not entering him or her (ERA 1988, s 117(1) and (2)). It has always been unsatisfactory that a parent has been able to insist that his or her child is not entered for a public examination taken as part of the National Curriculum, and an amendment to section 117(2) made by section 240(5) of the EA 1993 disapplies both exceptions in the case of examinations which form part of Key Stage 4.

The governing body is required to notify parents in writing of its determination relating to the entry of pupils for public examinations, 'as soon as practicable' after such determination (ERA 1988, s 117(5)).

12. Charging for education

The charging provisions in the Education Reform Act 1988 have been in effect since 1 April 1989. The law is complex and, not surprisingly, has caused confusion in schools.

(a) Lessons and materials

Section 61(1) of the Education Act 1944 provided that 'No fees shall be charged in respect of admission to any school maintained by a local education authority . . . or in respect of the education provided in any such school'. So charging in such schools for, for example, music tuition was illegal (*R* v *Hereford and Worcester LEA ex p Wm Jones* [1981] 1 WLR 768). But section 61 has now been repealed.

In its place are sections 106 to 111 of the Education Reform Act 1988. As previously, no charge is possible in respect of admission to a maintained school (s 106(1)), and the EA 1993 (Sch 18, para 9) prohibits charging for admission to a pupil referral unit. But charges are possible for education provided during school hours for individual and small-group (up to four pupils) music tuition (s 106(3), as amended by EA 1993, s 280). No charge may be made in respect of RE or the National Curriculum (of which music, as a foundation subject, is part) (ERA 1988, s 106(2)), nor in respect of anything required as part of a syllabus for a prescribed public examination (see the Education (Prescribed Public Examinations) Regulations 1989) which is a syllabus for which the pupil is being prepared at the school (s 106(4)), nor for entry to the examination itself (s 106(5)) (the legal position with regard to charging for examinations is considered further below). Charging for 'materials, books, instruments or other equipment' (except, perhaps, in connection with individual or small-group music tuition), or for transport, in respect of all of the above, would be unlawful (s 106(6) and (7)). Nevertheless, parents may be invited to provide these voluntarily (ERA 1988, s 118) as long as no child is put 'at a disadvantage because of a parent's unwillingness or inability to contribute in this way' (DES Circular 2/89, para 15).

Moreover, parents may be required to pay for materials to be used by pupils to produce, in the course of education provided to them, an article which the parent or child wishes to keep (provided the parent indicated this beforehand). This clearly has implications for art and craft lessons, although it is unlikely that parents will make a prior request to keep the painting or other article, other than where it is a major piece of work (for a school art exhibition etc). Home economics is another problem area – the circular refers, in this context, to the cost of 'ingredients'.

The prohibitions against charging for education provided, save in specified circumstances, also operate in the case of children being educated in pupil referral units (EA 1993, Sch 18, para 9).

(b) Public examinations

Although, as noted above, no charge may be made for entry to a prescribed public examination for which the pupil is being prepared by the school, the amount of relevant fees may be recovered from the parent of a pupil who 'fails without good reason to meet any examination requirement for that syllabus' (ERA 1988, s 108(1)). It is for the authority concerned to decide what is or is not a 'good reason' for this purpose (s 108(2)). It would clearly be unreasonable for the LEA or governors to recover the fee where the pupil has simply 'failed' the examination (in whatever way that 'failure' may be defined). The circular (2/89, *op cit*) does not deal with examination failure, but advises that failure to complete necessary coursework or failure to sit the examination without good reason might constitute grounds for recovery of a fee.

(c) School trips

Charges may be made for residential trips (in respect of the entire period of the trip), provided that more than 50 per cent of the half days spent away fall outside normal school hours, and the trip involves at least one night away from the pupil's usual accommodation (ERA 1988, s 107(3)–(6)). 'Half day' is defined as 'any period of twelve hours ending with noon or midnight on any day' (s 107(4)). If six or more of the hours of a half day are spent on the trip that half day is to be treated as occurring during the trip (DES Circular 2/89, *op cit*, para 31).

In relation to classes in general, education provided partly in and partly out of school shall be treated as falling within school hours (and so attracting no charge) if at least 50 per cent of the time (including travelling) falls within school hours (ERA 1988, s 107(1) and (2)). If more than 50 per cent falls outside school hours, then a charge may be made.

(d) 'Optional extras'

Where the lesson or public examination does not fall within the terms of section 106 of the ERA 1988 (above) (e.g. it is not a 'prescribed public examination': s 106(5)) it is known as an 'optional extra' for which the education, examination entry and transport (and board and lodging if the provision is a residential trip) may be charged for, provided the parents have agreed to such provision being made for their child (ERA 1988, s 109(1) and (2)). A 'regulated charge', up to, but not exceeding the cost of providing the optional extra(s) to that child, can be made to a parent. Governors may, however, meet all or part of such costs from their own funds (s 109(10)).

Apparently, reasonable charges may be made by schools for the use, by pupils, of lockers. According to the Education Secretary, provision of lockers is extra-curricular; it is for 'convenience' rather than a 'necessity'. This announcement was made after doubts arose over plans by a school in Brighton to charge pupils £3 a year for the hire of lockers to be purchased by the school's Parent-Teacher Association (*TES*, 26 January 1990).

If it is necessary, because there is no other suitable provision, for a child to be educated at a maintained (including grant-maintained) school as a boarder, the parents will not have to bear the cost (ERA 1988, s 111(2)-(4)). In any other case where a child is so educated, the LEA or governors have a discretion to remit up to 100 per cent of boarding charges, to avoid financial hardship to the parent (ERA 1988, s 111(5) and (6)). In some cases LEAs have obligations to meet the fees and charges for board and lodging for pupils being educated at non-maintained schools because of a shortage of places or because the schools offer special educational provision particularly appropriate to particular children's special educational needs (see the Education (Miscellaneous Provisions) Act 1953, s 6(2), and EA 1993, s 190(2)).

(e) LEA/governors' policy on charging

Governing bodies and LEAs are required to determine and keep under review a policy on charging for optional extras and board and lodging, including the circumstances where they would remit all or part of the charges (ERA 1988, s 110(1) and (2)). The remissions policy must provide for a complete remission of a permitted boarding charge for a residential trip (under s 106(9)) in the case of pupils whose parents are in receipt of income support or family credit during any part of the period encompassed by the trip (s 110(3)). There is no requirement to remit on the grounds of parental income any other permitted charges, although there is nothing to stop governors and LEAs making provision for this in their policies.

13. Equal opportunities

The concept of equal opportunities has become firmly embedded in educational philosophy and practice, and has assumed great importance. Inequality is a concept that is broad enough to encompass various forms of disadvantage that can affect differentially pupils' educational experience, and indeed the degree of access to education. The broad legal definitions of sex and race discrimination are outlined in Chapter 5 (on the employment of teachers), and the legal context to discrimination in relation to the provision of schools and school discipline are discussed in Chapters 2 and 12 respectively. Legal issues relating to disability in the educational context are discussed in Chapter 9 (special educational needs) and Chapter 13 (health, safety and welfare – including access to, and use of, premises). Assistance for the financially disadvantaged is discussed in Chapter 11 (on attendance at school). The discussion below focuses on the provisions in the Sex Discrimination Act 1975 and Race Relations Act 1976 which are relevant to the school curriculum.

(a) Sex Discrimination Act 1975

(i) Discrimination by the responsible body under section 22

Under section 22 of the Sex Discrimination Act 1975, direct or indirect discrimination on the grounds of sex is unlawful if committed by an LEA (or governors) ('the responsible body') in relation to:

- the admission of a pupil to an educational establishment;
- what is provided at the school (the 'benefits, facilities and services'); and
- exclusion 'or other detriment'. It might reasonably be supposed that 'detriment' refers here to some form of punishment akin to exclusion rather than a wholly different form of detriment (see *De Souza* v *Automobile Association* (1986) which deals with the phrase 'or other detriment' in the Race Relations Act 1976).

Responsibility under section 22 rests with the appropriate 'responsible body' – i.e. the governors or LEA, depending on which is responsible for the particular function in question. Institutions must be designated under the Sex Discrimination (Designated Institutions) Orders 1975 and 1980, made under section 24 of the 1975 Act (as amended by ERA 1988). The proprietor of an independent school is also a 'responsible body'. In a grant-maintained school the responsible body is the governing body (SDA 1975, s 22, as amended by ERA 1988, Sch 12, para 15).

Discussion of discrimination within schools ensues below, but it may be noted here that in a co-educational school discrimination might occur in relation to subject choices, since this clearly falls within the definition of 'benefits, facilities or services'.

The general non-discrimination duties resting on LEAs and governing bodies under sections 23 and 25 of the 1975 Act, which relate principally to the provision of schools, are discussed in Chapter 2, Part 2(b).

(ii) Sex discrimination in schools

Sex discrimination could occur in relation to subject choice and the way that subjects are taught. More often than not, such discrimination occurs unintentionally (Equal Opportunities Commission, *Formal Investigation Report: West Glamorgan Schools* (1988)). Despite positive efforts to eradicate it, including repeated emphasis on equal opportunities in DES/DFE guidance (e.g. Circular 2/76) and reports (e.g. *Science Education in Schools* (1982)), there is evidence that it is still a problem. For example, in the formal investigation into discrimination in West Glamorgan schools (*op cit*), the Equal Opportunities Commission found conclusive evidence of discrimination in relation to access to classes for craft, design and technology. Separate curricular provision for boys and girls, which was the problem in West Glamorgan, is surprisingly commonplace (HMI, *Secondary Schools. An Appraisal by HMI* (1988), p 43). The Equal Opportunities Commission (1988, *op cit*, p 47) explains that the Sex Discrimination Act 1975 'does not prohibit separate facilities for boys and girls within a co-educational school, provided that the facilities afforded to each sex can justifiably be regarded as equal'. It is clear that the 1975 Act applies to equal access to specific learning opportunities across the curriculum. Thus, schools are advised that:

> 'Equal opportunities does not mean that all pupils will study all subjects on offer, but it does mean that they should have an equal chance to study all such subjects. Care should be taken in the structuring of the timetable to make this choice real, particularly with respect to non-traditional subjects. The way in which options are devised is of crucial importance'.

It has been argued that while the National Curriculum (as originally structured) improved the prospects of gender equality by ensuring that males and females studied the same subjects (in particular, all girls would receive the full science curriculum which many had traditionally shied away from), it could be expected to have little impact on the entrenched social and economic inequalities that women experience beyond school (S Miles and C Middleton, 'Girls' Education in the Balance: The ERA and Inequality', in M Flude and M Hammer, *The Education Reform Act 1988: Its Origins and Implications* (Falmer, 1990) p 187).

Discrimination might also occur in the way that classes are organised. In one case, a primary school in Bromley, faced with shortage of space for a fourth-year class, sent only boys up to this class. The LEA admitted contravention of the Act, and three girls affected by the authority's decision were each awarded compensation of £500 by the county court (*Debell and Teh* v *Bromley LBC* (1984) – cited in Milman, *Educational Conflict and the Law* (1986), p 52).

In limited circumstances segregated PE or sport might be lawful–'where the physical demands of a particular competitive sport would place girls at an undue disadvantage. Thus inter-sex rugby could quite justifiably be banned' (Milman and de Gama, 'Sexual Discrimination in Education: One Step Forward, Two Steps Back?' (1989) (1) *JSWL* 4, 12). However, it has been argued that banning boys from netball or girls from soccer would, most probably, be unlawful (*ibid*).

(iii) Enforcement

For breaches of section 22 (or 23), redress may be sought in the county court, where, in these cases, High Court remedies, e.g. unlimited damages, are obtainable (SDA 1975, ss 62 and 66). Before proceedings can be brought (there have in fact been very few education cases), the complainant must give notice to the Secretary of State who then has two months to consider the complaint (s 66(5)). Damages, which can include an amount for injury to feelings, cannot be awarded if indirect discrimination was unintentional (s 66(3)). Complaint to the Secretary of State under sections 68 and 99 of the EA 1944, on the ground that the responsible body is acting (or proposing to act) unreasonably or has acted in default of its duty (see p 5 above), is also possible, and, indeed, is the only way of enforcing the duty under section 25 of the 1975 Act (SDA 1975, s 25(4)). If the complaint is upheld by the Secretary of State, he can issue directions to the responsible body to desist from the discriminatory practice.

Judicial review procedure has proved a useful option in sex discrimination cases and has been pursued in various reported cases (see Chapter 2, Part 2(a)). In the *Birmingham* case (discussed on p 23 above), for example, the court was able to make a declaration that the LEA's arrangements for secondary education were unlawful. The Equal Opportunities Commission is recognised by the court as having *locus standi* (i.e. having a legitimate right to bring the case) for this purpose.

The Commission can also conduct a formal investigation (SDA 1975, s 57) and, if it does so, must make any recommendations it considers necessary or expedient and prepare a report (SDA 1975, s 60).

It is not clear whether complaints of sex discrimination under the curriculum fall within the scope of the local complaints procedure which LEAs (and governors of grant-maintained schools) have to establish. In relation to LEA schools, the procedure applies, *inter alia*, to 'any . . . enactment relating to the curriculum' (ERA 1988, s 23(1)(a)(ii)). If this includes complaints of sex discrimination in relation to curricular provision, then section 23(2) of the 1988 Act will presumably apply. This states that before a complaint falling within section 23(1) of that Act can be considered by the Secretary of State, it must have first been taken through the local complaints procedure (see p 223 below).

(b) Race Relations Act 1976

(i) The non-discrimination duty

In parallel provisions to those covering sex discrimination (see above), the Race Relations Act 1976 provides that direct or indirect discrimination in education on the grounds of 'colour, race, nationality or ethnic or national origins' (ss 1 and 3(1)) (but not specifically religion – see *Nyasi* v *Ryman Ltd* [1988] 367 IRLIB 15) is unlawful:

- under section 17 (non-admission or the terms of admission to a school, access to benefits, facilities or services at the school, exclusion or other detriment) (LEA or governors responsible, as appropriate – see Table in s 17);
- under section 18 (the carrying out by an LEA of any of its functions under the Education Acts); and
- under section 19 (general duty in public sector of education – facilities for education and/or any ancillary benefits or services).

Sections 17–19 are identical in scope to sections 22, 23 and 25 of the Sex Discrimination Act 1975 (see above).

There are some exceptions to these basic requirements – positive discrimination in the form of greater access of an ethnic or racial group to certain educational facilities because of their special educational needs, is permissible (RRA 1976, s 35).

There is also a general duty on local authorities to carry out their various functions, which include provision of education, with due regard to the need to eliminate racial discrimination and promote equality of opportunity and good relations between persons of different racial groups (RRA 1976, s 71). Anti-racism strategies have been adopted by a large number of LEAs. The Commission for Racial Equality issued a *Code of Practice for the Elimination of Racial Discrimination in Education* in December 1989. This highlights the need for the avoidance of discrimination in school admissions, teaching, assessment, discipline, careers advice and work experience placements. In the Code's foreword, the Secretary of State for Education reminds LEAs and schools of their 'important responsibility to work towards the promotion of equality of opportunity for the different ethnic groups who are part of our national life'.

Inequalities in educational attainment as between different racial and ethnic groups remain pronounced, despite improvements in recent years, according to Modood (*Racial Equality: Colour, Culture and Justice* (IPPR 1993)). As Modood says, however, 'these inequalities are produced by a plurality of factors, interacting in a complex way' (*ibid*, p 3). This issue cannot be explored within the context of this book, but remains a key factor in approaches to racial equality in education. The law provides a broad framework within which, and with reference to which, strategies for tackling inequality may be developed.

(ii) Specific issues

A. Dress

Insistence by a school or LEA that a particular form of dress and no other be worn by pupils could amount to indirect racial discrimination under section 1 of the Race Relations Act 1976, although it would be a defence for the governors or LEA to show that the requirement is 'justifiable' under section 1(1)(b)(ii). The proportion of, for example, girls of Asian origin belonging to a particular ethnic group who 'can comply' with a condition that they should wear skirts for school may be less than the proportion of girls of other (e.g. non-Asian) groups who can so comply. Although the former are physically able to comply, they may be unable to do so for cultural reasons.

In *Mandla* v *Dowell Lee* [1983] 1 All ER 1062 (also discussed at p 175 above), a head teacher of a private school had refused to admit a Sikh child unless he went without his turban and had his hair cut. The wearing of the turban was alleged to be inconsistent with the school's policy on uniform and its policy of de-emphasising religious and cultural differences. The House of Lords decided that the ban on the boy was discrimination and that discrimination for the reasons given was not 'justifiable' under the terms of the statute – because it had to be 'justifiable' irrespective of the race, colour, ethnic origins, etc, of the person to whom it applied (*per* Lord Fraser, at p 1070).

Restrictions on type of dress could possibly be 'justifiable' indirect discrimination on public health or safety grounds (e.g. wearing of jewellery in school). The safety argument was put forward by Altrincham Girls Grammar school to justify the suspension of two Muslim girls, aged 14 and 15, for wearing traditional head scarves contrary to school rules. The governors, accused by some of committing indirect discrimination, subsequently acceded to the girls' request to wear the head coverings. The compromise reached was that the scarves would be in the school's colour of navy and would be tucked inside the girls' collars.

Justification based on practical inconvenience may be insufficient (see Poulter, *English Law and Ethnic Minority Customs* (1986), pp 181–8). In *Steel* v *Union of Post Office Workers* [1977] ICR 181 it was held that a discriminatory condition or requirement would have to be justified 'by the need – not the convenience – of the business or enterprise'. The necessity test in *Steel* was further articulated in *Rainey* v *Greater Glasgow Health Board* [1987] IRLR 26 (HL). In *Ojutiku* v *MSC* [1982] ICR 661 (CA) the emphasis had been on whether reasonable people would find the condition 'sound and tolerable'. But, as noted earlier at p 122, in *Hampson* v *Department of Education and Science* [1990] 2 All ER 25 Balcombe LJ said that '"justifiable" requires an objective balance between the discriminatory effect of the condition and the reasonable needs of the party who applies the condition'. It is difficult to apply this 'reasonable necessity' test, laid down in these employment cases, to education. The principal 'needs' of a school would comprise the provision of a sound curriculum and the maintenance of discipline, health and safety. It is hard to imagine any situation, apart from, perhaps, where there is a risk to health or safety (see above), in which racial discrimination in a school would be 'justifiable'. Of course, if a condition or requirement which has a discriminatory effect can be shown to be on balance justifiable irrespective of that effect, it would not be unlawful under the Act. In any event, the question of restrictions on type of dress is for the LEA or, rather, the governors of a school, to consider both carefully and objectively. The onus is on the discriminator to show that the condition is justifiable and, moreover, justifiable irrespective of race, ethnic origins (etc) (see *Mandla* v *Dowell Lee, op cit*).

B. Language and culture

So far as the language in which pupils are taught is concerned, the fact that it is not a pupil's mother tongue would probably not be a ground for complaint under the Act or the European Convention on Human Rights (see the *Belgian linguistics* case, Series A Volume 6). However, claims that languages such as Urdu, Bengali and Arabic should at least be offered as subjects by schools have been met. These and a few other such languages have been prescribed as ones which can be offered under the National Curriculum, provided one of the official EC languages (French, German, Spanish etc) is also available as an alternative (Education (National Curriculum) (Modern Foreign Languages) Order 1991) (see above, at Part 6(a) *Chart 2*).

The Commission for Racial Equality has advised that the placement of children for whom English is their second language in separate centres and their removal from mainstream schooling would constitute indirect discrimination (Commission for Racial Equality, *Code of Practice for the Elimination of Discrimination in Education* (1989), para 32). There is a particular risk of indirect discrimination in methods of assessing pupils' abilities, resulting from cultural bias. The *Code of Practice* advises (at para 44) that:

> 'Indirect discrimination in assessment will occur if the criteria or procedures applied are culturally biased and result in lower assessments being given to a considerably higher proportion of pupils or students from particular racial groups and those criteria cannot be justified on educational grounds. Culturally biased assessment criteria are those that assume a uniformity in children's cultural, linguistic, religious and lifestyle experiences'.

(iii) Enforcement

In relation to a complaint of breach of section 17 or 18, civil proceedings may be instituted by a complainant in a designated county court (RRA

1976, s 57), within six or eight months of the discrimination (RRA 1976, s 68). Notice must be given to the Secretary of State, as under the Sex Discrimination Act (see above) (RRA 1976, s 57(5)). Similarly, damages awarded may take account of, *inter alia*, injury to feelings but cannot be awarded if the indirect discrimination was unintentional (s 57(3)). Complaint to the Secretary of State under sections 68 and 99 of the Education Act 1944 is also possible (see *Sex Discrimination Act – Enforcement* (above, at (a)(iii))). Whether or not proceedings have been brought in respect of a breach of section 19, the Commission for Racial Equality can, following the carrying out of a formal investigation (under RRA 1976, s 48), issue a non-discrimination notice requiring the person in breach to desist from the discriminatory acts(s) and to inform the Commission of the completion of changes in practice required in response to the notice (s 58(2)).

Where the claim is for breach of section 19 only, civil proceedings are not possible (see RRA 1976, s 19(4)), and complaint lies to the Secretary of State under section 68 or 99 of EA 1944. The Commission for Racial Equality cannot issue a non-discrimination notice in section 19-only cases, but should refer any such cases of which they become aware to the Secretary of State (RRA 1976, s 58(6)).

14. Complaints

(a) Scope of the statutory complaints provisions

A complaint may be made via the local complaints machinery, which must be established by LEAs under section 23 of the ERA 1988, about the way that governing bodies and LEAs have performed their duties and exercised their powers concerning the curriculum and the provision of information. The Secretary of State may not entertain a complaint about any matter within the scope of section 23 under his jurisdiction in section 68 or section 99 of the EA 1944 unless it has first been pursued under the local arrangements (ERA 1988, s 23(2)). The section 23 procedures apply to county, voluntary and maintained special schools (other than those established in hospitals). Separate complaints arrangements must be made by governing bodies of GM schools (see (c) below).

A survey by the author revealed widespread uncertainty among those who hear section 23 complaints (governing bodies and LEAs) about their precise remit under the section (see N Harris, ***Complaints About Schooling: The Role of Section 23 of the Education Reform Act 1988*** (National Consumer Council, 1992)). Section 23 itself states that complaints about the following are covered:

> 'that the authority, or the governing body of any county or voluntary school maintained by the authority or of any special school so maintained which is not established in a hospital –
>
> (*a*) have acted or are proposing to act unreasonably with respect to the exercise of any power or the performance of any duty imposed on them by or under–

(i) any provision of [sections 1–25 of the ERA 1988, which are concerned with the school curriculum and the provision of information]; or

(ii) any other enactment relating to the curriculum for, or religious worship in, maintained schools other than grant-maintained schools; or

(*b*) have failed to discharge any such duty'

(s 23(1)).

It is, at least, clear, that any function relating to any statutory provision imposing a duty or conferring a power relating to the curriculum or the provision of information may be the subject of a complaint under section 23. But there are, of course, numerous such provisions, which partly accounts for the ignorance about the scope of the section revealed by the survey.

(b) The procedures

(i) Arrangements for approval of the section 23 local complaints procedures

Section 23(1) of the Education Reform Act 1988 required complaints procedures to be operative as from 1 September 1989 (London LEAs taking over from the Inner London Education Authority were given until 1 April 1990 to get their procedures up and running). The procedures require the approval of the Secretary of State. DES Circular 1/89 (*Education Reform Act 1988: Local Arrangements for the Consideration of Complaints*) was issued on 9 January 1989, followed a few weeks later by the circulation to all LEAs of a model, prepared on behalf of the Association of Metropolitan Authorities and Association of County Councils (the 'AMA/ACC model'), with accompanying guidance from the associations. Under section 23(1) of the Act, LEAs had, before submitting proposals, to consult with the governing bodies of aided and special agreement schools. The DES also required LEAs to consult with the governing bodies and head teachers of all *other* schools maintained by them (Circular 1/89, Annex A, paragraph 1).

An overwhelming majority of the authorities in the author's survey (68 LEAs sent procedure documents) had followed very closely the AMA/ACC model, the final version of which was drafted with reference to the guidance contained in the DES Circular 1/89. In particular, it sought adherence to the basic principles set out in paragraphs 4–6 and Annex A to the Circular (see below).

(ii) Incorporation into a general complaints procedure

Although not dealt with specifically by the DES Circular nor by the AMA/ACC guidance or model, some LEAs decided to incorporate their section 23 complaints procedures within their general education complaints procedure. Such a practice would appear to be quite lawful, and indeed quite sensible in view of the difficulties in drawing distinctions between section 23 complaints and others.

(iii) Basic principles

The DES laid down certain basic principles around which LEAs were required to base their proposed arrangements. These principles were incorporated into, or otherwise formed the underlying basis to parts of, the AMA/ACC model:

Informal resolution of complaints. The Government's intention was that most 'concerns' felt by parents over the school curriculum and related matters at the school level should continue to be dealt with via *informal* discussion between parent and teacher or head teacher. Only where informal resolution was not possible should the formal procedure be invoked (DES Circular 1/89, para 4). Evidence suggests that most complaints are dealt with informally.

Separate stages to the formal complaints procedure. The Circular contemplates separate stages to the complaints procedure, with complaints being dealt with initially by 'those with direct responsibility for the matters involved' (DES Circular 1/89, para 5) and thereafter by the governing body and subsequently the LEA (*ibid*, para 7). The AMA/ACC model refers to (i) preliminary discussion; (ii) formal complaint to the governing body; and (iii) formal complaint to the LEA. A complaint could normally proceed through these three stages, although might go directly from (i) to (iii) where the complaint relates 'to something which is solely the responsibility of the LEA and a complaint to the governors would therefore not be appropriate' (AMA/AC Model, para 23).

Complaints to be investigated speedily, efficiently, fully and fairly, with all aspects of a case given proper consideration. These principles were set out in DES Circular 1/89, Annex A, para 4 and in a section entitled 'General Principles' in the AMA/ACC model.

Complainants to be kept informed of progress in the investigation of their complaint. Both DES Circular 1/89 and the AMA/ACC model state that complainants should be kept informed of progress during, as well as at the end of, each stage (see below).

The complaints procedure document should refer to a clear first point of contact in the LEA for formal section 23 complaints. In fact, very few LEAs have included the name of the designated officer in their procedure documents, presumably because of the possibility of personnel changes making the document out of date in this respect.

There should be a mechanism for filtering out complaints not within the scope of section 23. The AMA/ACC model provides that the LEA designated officer or the clerk to the governing body should determine whether or not a complaint falls within the scope of section 23.

At the end of each stage the complainant should be informed of the decision and the reasons for it, the action proposed (if any) and of the further recourse available. This principle, set out in paragraph 5(ix) of Annex A to DES Circular 1/89, is dealt with in paragraphs 22 and 29 of the AMA/ACC model.

(iv) The complainant

Section 23 refers only to complaints, not to complainants. However, it is fair to assume that the intention was that the same people who would be able to use section 68 and 99 of the EA 1944 Act would be able to utilise section 23. Complaints under section 68 may be made to the Secretary of State by 'any person'. Those falling under section 99 may be made by 'any person interested'. During the passage of the Education (Reform) Bill the Government referred to the rights of 'parents and others' to make complaints under what is now section 23 (*Hansard*, House of Commons, Standing Committee J, col 429, 12 January 1988, Mrs A Rumbold, Minister of State), a phrase also used in DES Circular 1/89 (para 4) and in the AMA/ACC model complaints procedure document (para 4). Although there is no reference in the legislation, guidance or model procedures to child complainants (in contrast to Children Act 1989 complaints: see s 26 of that Act), it is submitted that complaints by children under section 23 should be entertained. The National Consumer Council has suggested that all pupils aged 16 or over should be given a statutory right of complaint (*When Things Go Wrong at School: Grievance Procedures in the Education Service* (1992)).

(v) The procedure

The procedure is almost always in three stages, commencing with an informal stage, at which complaints tend not to be recorded. Only a very small number of complaints proceed to the formal stages, and the total actually declined in successive years between 1989–90 and 1991–92 from 89 to 75 to 73 (DFE statistics supplied to the author). In 1991–92, only 6 out of 68 complaints reaching Stage 2 (governing body) and 1 out of 26 complaints reaching Stage 3 (LEA) were upheld.

Stage 1: Informal or preliminary discussion. As noted above, the AMA/ACC model suggests that there should be informal discussion with the head teacher or other staff of the school or, where the complaint is about the LEA, with appropriate officers of the authority. Most LEAs have incorporated this principle into their approved procedure documents. Generally the head teacher is to be approached before a formal complaint is registered. There is, however, a question as to whether this is appropriate in cases where the complaint is directed at the governing body, as head teachers would generally be members of that body. A few of the documents specify LEA subject advisers or other officers as persons with whom informal discussion might take place.

Stage 2: Formal complaint to the governing body. General practice, as revealed from the author's survey of 68 procedure documents, appears to be that a formal complaint will first be referred to the designated officer of the LEA. The officer will consider whether or not the complaint falls within section 23. If he or she determines that it does, the officer will decide whether or not the complaint concerns an area of responsibility of the governing body. Assuming that it is such a complaint, the officer will be expected to refer the complaint to the governing body. A subcommittee of the governing body (some of the documents refer to a 'complaints panel'), consisting generally of 3 (or in a few cases 5) governors, will meet to hear the complaint. The complainant is to be invited and given an opportunity to speak and submit a written statement. The governing body proper may be represented and the head teacher may attend. Some of the approved procedures provide for cross-examination by the complainant and the governing body's representative. Others simply make reference to all parties being given an opportunity to speak. In some cases there is reference to the provision of an interpreter. Some of the procedures, but by no means all of them, state a time within which the subcommittee (etc) must be convened after the receipt of a complaint (e.g. 10, 15 or 21 days). Some seek to distinguish between urgent and non-urgent cases (for example 14 days for non-urgent cases and 7 days for urgent cases).

However, none of the documents specify a time within which the complainant should be notified of the decision of the subcommittee or panel. This is perhaps understandable given that in some cases there is provision for further investigation into the matter before the decision is taken. It will not be possible to predict the duration of the investigation at the outset. When the decision is communicated (in writing and with reasons) to the complainant, information concerning the opportunity to take the complaint to the LEA (or simply about 'further recourse') is generally to be given.

Stage 3: Formal complaint to the LEA. Complaints will reach Stage 3 in basically one of two ways:

- (i) where the complaint lies against the governing body and the complainant is not satisfied with the outcome achieved at Stage 2; or
- (ii) where the complaint lies against the LEA and it has not therefore been necessary for it to proceed via Stage 2.

In addition, the AMA/ACC model (para 10) provides that where there has been a statutory appeal to a governing body, for example over a decision about temporary exception from all or part of the National Curriculum or perhaps about access to a school record, further complaint may be made to the LEA under the section 23 arrangements.

The LEA has no jurisdiction over complaints concerning denominational religious education or collective worship in voluntary aided or special agreement schools. Generally the investigation of these complaints will be conducted by diocesan advisers; in some cases, most particularly where the complaint centres on RE in accordance with the locally agreed syllabus (see above), advice will be sought from the local standing advisory council on religious education (SACRE).

The AMA/ACC model provides for the LEA's designated officer to play a key role in the administration of complaints at Stage 3. Among the designated officer's administrative tasks are: identifying urgent complaints and arranging for them to be dealt with as a priority; arranging for the complaints to be investigated; and keeping the complainant informed of various matters including the decision of the LEA panel (see below), the reasons for the decision and the action proposed in the light of it.

So far as the investigation of the complaint is concerned, the AMA/ACC model simply states (para 26) that 'the designated officer will arrange for the complaint to be investigated and the investigating officer will seek such information or advice as he or she considers appropriate in so doing'. It is not clear who the 'investigating officer' should be. Following an investigation the complaint will be considered by a panel, generally consisting of the designated officer and two or more LEA members. It seems to be the intention that the designated officer shall be present only to advise the panel and not to participate as a member of it. The procedure documents reveal general uniformity in the composition of panels, with three LEA members being the norm (with additional members for complaints about religious education or collective worship). However, a small number state that one of the three panellists shall be an independent person or a person who is not an education committee member. Many LEAs have established a sub-committee of the LEA for the purposes of section 23 complaints at Stage 3 (19 out of 31 in the survey).

The complaints procedures specify that the complainant is entitled to use representation and to make an oral presentation. Some of the documents make specific reference to the LEA's willingness to make arrangements for an interpreter to be present if required. Generally the arrangements also make provision for the governing body to make representations. Provision similar to that referred to above in relation to the information to be provided to the complainant after the decision at Stage 2 has been reached applies in relation to Stage 3 decisions. Just under one-third of the LEAs in the survey said that the decision might be notified to the complainant in person at the conclusion of the hearing, although of these most stated or implied that this would be the exception rather than the rule. Another third said that the complainant would definitely not be informed in person.

The AMA/ACC model (para 28) provides that in a case which has proceeded via Stage 2 (complaint to governing body), a representative of the governing body may attend the hearing and make an oral presentation. A small number of the procedure documents also refer specifically to the right of a head teacher or representative of the LEA to attend and speak, but many are silent on this point. Nevertheless, the survey revealed that nearly two-thirds of LEAs would definitely permit the head teachers to attend and address the panel. Almost as many LEAs would also permit advisers to do these things.

Complaint upheld – remedial action. As regards remedial action in consequence of decisions taken at Stages 2 and 3, the model states (paras 22 and 29) that at the conclusion of both stages complainants whose complaint is upheld should be informed of any action taken or any recommended remedial action. The model also states (*ibid*) that the complainant should be informed of 'any request made to those complained against to take particular action to resolve the complaint'.

What is missing, however, is any requirement to inform the complainant subsequently of the progress being made towards rectification of the problem which led to his or her complaint.

Complaint to the Secretary of State. Once a complainant has pursued his or her case via the local complaints arrangements under section 23, he or she may, if dissatisfied, then refer the complaint to the Secretary of State, who will consider whether to use his or her powers under section 68 or 99 of the Education Act 1944 (see Chapter 1, Part 2(a)). Such avenue of redress does not form part of the local arrangements for the consideration of complaints, but the DES stipulated that the arrangements should include the provision of information to complainants about further recourse available (DES Circular 1/89, para 5(ix)(c)).

(c) Grant-maintained schools

The requirements of section 23 of the ERA 1988 concerning complaints arrangements do not extend to GM schools. Nevertheless, the articles of a GM school must make provision as to the arrangements for the 'consideration and disposal of complaints relating to any matter concerning the curriculum followed within the school including, in particular, the discharge by the governing body of [the duties imposed under Ch I, Pt I of the ERA 1988 (the curriculum)]' (EA 1993, Sch 6, para 7(2)). The initial articles of government for GM schools require the arrangements to require complaints to be considered by the head teacher in the first instance and, if the complainant remains dissatisfied, by the governing body (Education (Grant-maintained Schools) (Initial Governing Instruments) Regulations 1993, Sch 2, art 5(2)). As with complaints under section 23 of the ERA 1988 (see above), the arrangements require the approval of the Secretary of State (art 5(3)).

(d) Complaint to the Local Commissioner for Administration

The existence of a new statutory complaints procedure does not preclude investigation of maladministration by one of the Local Commissioners for Administration (under the Local Government Act 1974). For example, Derbyshire County Council's practice of charging parents for A-level field trips and the authority's refusal to refund fees of up to £75 charged for certain trips were condemned by the Local Commissioner in her report into the matter (see *The Times,* 8 July 1988). The Commissioners cannot examine matters pertaining to the internal affairs of an individual school, however, including the curriculum (1974 Act, Sch 5).

Commissioners' reports can put pressure on LEAs to improve their practices. Nevertheless, a Commissioner's recommendations are not legally enforceable. The Commissioner (or 'Ombudsman' has to decide whether there was maladministration and, if there was, whether it amounted to an injustice. It is not uncommon, in cases where there is maladministration and injustice, and a detriment to a child's education as a result, for the Local Ombudsman to recommend payment of a specified sum in compensation. Local authorities are empowered to incur expenditure in making such a payment (1974 Act, s 31(3)). (On the relevant procedures, including local authorities' duties to take action in response to the Local Ombudsman's recommendations, see S Bailey (ed), *Cross on Local Government Law,* paras 4.109–4.118.)

15. Copyright law

Copyright restrictions may affect the way that teaching and learning materials are prepared. They thus can have an influence over the way the curriculum is delivered. With teaching increasingly being influenced by technology – computers, video, and so on – it is important to be aware of the way copyright law affects these areas as well as the more traditional methods of teaching.

Copyright law takes up over 150 sections of the Copyright, Designs and Patents Act 1988. References below are to that Act, unless stated otherwise.

(a) What is copyright?

Copyright is defined as a 'property right' subsisting in:

'(*a*) original literary, dramatic, musical or artistic works,
(*b*) sound recordings, films, broadcasts or cable programmes, and
(*c*) the typographical arrangements of published editions'.

(s 1(1)).

Copyright protection only applies if certain requirements as to the author (a British citizen or other as prescribed) and the country in which the work was first published (the UK or other, as prescribed) are satisfied (ss 1(3), 153 and 155).

First ownership of copyright generally rests with the 'author' (ss 9 and 10) of the work (s 11(1) and (3)). Where a literary, dramatic, musical or artistic work is made by an employee in the course of his/her employment, his/her employer is the first owner, subject to any agreement to the contrary (s 11(2)). The Crown owns the copyright in works written by civil servants in the course of their duties and in Acts of Parliament (see ss 163 and 164).

Like any property, copyright can be transferred by its owner. Where books are concerned, the usual practice is for the author to retain copyright in the text but to grant an exclusive right to print and publish the work to the publisher, under the agreement between them. The makers of broadcasts and films own a copyright in them which is separate to the copyright owned by the author. Copyright in 'published editions' of works – typographical arrangements of them – belongs to the publisher.

The kinds of works (etc) in which copyright may be owned are defined in sections 3–8 of the Act. A 'literary' work comprises any work, other than a dramatic or musical work, which is written, spoken or sung. A computer program is a literary work (s 3(1)). A 'dramatic' work includes a work of dance or mime. Copyright does not subsist in a literary, dramatic or musical work unless and until the work is recorded, in writing or otherwise (s 3(2)). 'Artistic' works are defined as: graphic works, photographs, sculptures or collages, irrespective of artistic quality; works of architecture, whether buildings or models of buildings; and works of 'artistic craftsmanship' (s 4). There are also definitions of sound recordings, films ('a recording on any medium from which a moving image may . . . be produced') (s 5), broadcasts (s 6), cable programmes (s 7) and published editions (s 8).

(b) Duration of copyright

Copyright in a work is not of unlimited duration. It subsists for a prescribed period, set out in sections 12–15. Where literary, dramatic, musical or artistic works are concerned, copyright expires 50 years (likely to be extended to 70 years from July 1995, under EU harmonisation provisions) after the end of the calendar year in which the author (or the last of known joint authors) dies (s 12(1) and (4)) (see s 12(2) and (4) for the position concerning unknown authorship). The name purporting to be that of the author and appearing on the work when published or made is presumed to be that of the author unless the contrary is proved (s 104(2)).

If the work is 'computer generated', copyright subsists for 50 years from the end of the year in which it was made (s 12(3)). Crown copyright lasts for 50 years from the date on which the work was first published commercially (if the work was so published within the first 75 years after it was made) or, if not so published, for 125 years from the end of the calendar year in which it was made (s 163(3)). In the case of sound recordings, films and broadcasts, copyright subsists, basically speaking, for 50 years (ss 13 and 14) – which period runs, where a broadcast is concerned, from the end of the year in which it was first made, not from any repeat broadcasts (s 14). Copyright in a typographical arrangement of a published edition subsists for 25 years (s 15). Although the copyright to Barrie's *Peter Pan* expired on 31 December 1987, all royalties from the work's public performance or commercial publication belong exclusively to the Hospital for Sick Children, Great Ormond Street, London (s 301, Sch 6).

(c) Infringement of copyright

Under copyright law, the copyright owner has the exclusive right to copy the work, issue copies of it to the public, perform, show or play the work in public, and make certain other uses of it (e.g. broadcasting) (ss 17–21). Anyone who, without licence of the copyright owner, does any of these things, directly or indirectly and in relation to the work as a whole or *a substantial part of it*, infringes copyright (s 16(2) and (3)). The question of substantiality is one on which no guidance may be found in the legislation. It seems that it is a question to be determined by quality as much as quantity (*Ravenscroft* v *Herbert* [1980] RPC 193), so that if making a copy is worthwhile, in the sense that doing so perhaps obviates the need to purchase a copy of the work, the test of substantiality is satisfied.

Infringement of copyright may lead to the owner (or exclusive licence holder) pursuing the remedies available (see ss 96–102). The remedies are damages and/or injunction and/or delivery up of the infringing article (ss 98 and 99). Additional damages may be awarded to take account of the flagrancy of the breach and the benefit accruing to the defendant from the illegal copying (etc). Subject to certain strict conditions, infringing copies of works may be seized (s 100). A court may order the destruction or other disposal of infringing copies (s 114). In some cases, for example where a person sells copies commercially or makes an article to be used for making copies of a work with copyright protection, there can be criminal liability (s 107). Those responsible for, *inter alia*, the public showing or playing of a film or sound recording, or the public performance of a literary or dramatic work, may be guilty of an offence – if they had reason to believe that copyright would be infringed (s 107(3)).

This is the general position. But the infringement provisions are specifically modified in certain cases (s 16(4)), of which the most relevant to schools are: research and private study (s 29), education (ss 32–36) and libraries (ss 37–43 – see below).

(d) Research and private study

'Fair dealing' with a literary, dramatic, musical or artistic work for the purposes of research or private study does not infringe any copyright in the work or, in the case of a published edition, in the typographical arrangement (s 29(1)). 'Fair dealing' is not defined in the Act, but would be taken to restrict the usage to that which would be justifiable for the purposes of the research or private study. If the usage might interfere with the normal commercial exploitation of the work, it might not amount to fair dealing.

Where the copying is by a librarian (including a school or college librarian – see below) it can only amount to fair dealing in specific defined circumstances (in ss 38 and 39 – see below) (s 29(3)(a)). If the copying is by any other person carrying it out on behalf of the student or researcher, there will be no fair dealing if the person doing the copying knows or has reason to believe that it will result in copies of substantially the same material being provided to more than one person at substantially the same time and for substantially the same purpose (s 29(3)(b)).

(e) Education

Even though copyright legislation has traditionally relaxed some of its rules where schools are concerned, the scope for legal copying of published material for use in teaching has been limited. There has, of course, been illegal copying on a wide scale. To schools experiencing shortages of learning resources, copying from works may at times seem the only answer. Some help has been offered by licensing, now dealt with by

Chapter VII or Part I of the 1988 Act. Licensing schemes are expected to increase in number consequent on, for example, the increasing competition in, and commercialisation of, broadcasting (see V Porter, 'The Copyright Designs and Patents Act 1988: The Triumph of Expediency over Principle' (1988) 16 *Law & Society* 340). A licence agreement between the Copyright Licence Agency and local authorities for copying from books, periodicals and journals in schools and colleges was first concluded in 1984.

Copying, for use in instruction, of literary, dramatic, musical or artistic works, does not cause an infringement if the person copying is giving or receiving instruction and the copying *is not by means of a reprographic process* (s 32(1)). Copying, by a person giving or receiving instruction, of a sound recording, film, broadcast or cable programme, is also permissible, if being done for the purposes of instruction (s 32(2)).

Copying for the purposes of examinations, including the making of a reprographic copy of a musical score which a candidate will perform for an examination, will not infringe copyright (s 32(3) and (4)). Permission for copying is sometimes given by the copyright holder via a statement in the document itself (see for example, some SCAA publications).

The legislation now permits multiple reprographic copying by educational establishments (or on their behalf) of passages from published works – for the purposes of instruction and provided *not more than 1 per cent* is copied in any quarter (running from 1 January, April, July and September) (s 36(1) and (2)). However, such copying is not authorised where a licence is in force and the person doing the copying knew or ought to have been aware of that fact (s 36(3)). However, a licence is of no effect in so far as it restricts the proportion of the work that may be copied to less than that authorised by section 36 (see above). Recording of broadcasts and cable programmes for educational purposes at an educational establishment is also permissible, under section 35 of the Act; but if a licence scheme which makes provision for licence agreements has been certified, it will determine the right to record programmes (see the Copyright (Certification of Licensing Scheme for Educational Recording of Broadcasts) (Open University Educational Enterprises Ltd) Order 1993 (SI 1993 No 2755); and the Copyright (Certification of Licensing Scheme for Educational Recording of Broadcasts and Cable Programmes) (Educational Recording Agency Ltd) Order 1990 (SI 1990 No 879), as amended by the (Same) (Amendment) Orders 1992 (SI 1992 No 211), 1993 (SI 1993 No 193) and 1994 (SI 1994 No 247)).

The 1988 Act also enables extracts (a 'short passage') from certain literary or dramatic works to be used in anthologies intended for use in educational establishments (and so described in the title etc), provided that the anthologies consist mainly of material in which no copyright subsists. It is necessary that the work from which the extract was taken is not intended for use in such an establishment. Also, no more than two extracts from copyright works by the same author may appear within a space of five years in the same publisher's collections (s 33).

Pupils, teachers and others (where the purpose is to instruct) may perform literary, dramatic or musical works without infringing copyright (s 34). The performance must be to an audience consisting of 'teachers and pupils . . . and any other persons directly connected with the activities of the establishment'. Parents of pupils are not automatically to be taken to be directly connected with the activities of the establishment for this purpose (s 34(3)). If the performance is by persons other than teachers or pupils, it has to be at the relevant educational establishment (s 34(1)). The playing of a sound recording, film, broadcast or cable programme to such an audience does not amount to a showing of the work in public for copyright purposes (s 34(2)).

(f) Libraries (including school libraries)

Subject to tight restrictions, the Copyright, Designs and Patents Act 1988 enables copying in libraries to take place without infringement. School libraries in all LEA-maintained and grant-maintained schools are amongst the classes of library covered (Copyright (Librarians and Archivists) (Copying of Copyright Material) Regulations 1989, reg 3(1) and Sch 1, para 3).

Only the librarian may make and supply the copy under these provisions. A single copy of an article in a periodical may be made, but no more than one article from the same issue (s 38). Also, a single copy of no more than a 'reasonable proportion of any work' may be made (s 39). In both cases the person for whom the copy is made must be either a student or researcher and must be required to pay the librarian 'not less than the cost (including a contribution to the general expenses of the library) attributable to . . . production' (ss 38(2)(c) and 39(2)(c)).

Regulations (*op cit*, reg 4(2)(a)) provide that the copy may not be supplied until the librarian has obtained a signed declaration (substantially in accordance with Form A set out in the regulations) from the person requesting the copy. The declaration is to state, *inter alia*, that the student (etc) has not previously obtained a copy of the same material from a librarian and that he or she will not use the copy for any purpose other than research or private study nor will he or she supply a copy of it to any other person. To prevent members of a class from obtaining individual copies of a work which is on their syllabus, thus defeating the restrictions against multiple copying, the librarian must be satisfied that the requirements of the person making the request and that of any other person are not similar (i.e. that, in effect, such persons are not following the same course of study for which the copy is required (*ibid*, reg 4(2)(b) and 1988 Act, s 40)).

(g) The moral right

Finally, it may be noted that the 1988 Act recognises the moral right of the author to ensure that his or her reputation is not sullied through the exploitation of his or her work by others (see especially ss 77–81). Basically speaking, the author has a right (i) to be identified whenever the work is performed in public, broadcast or published, and (ii) to object to a derogatory treatment of the work by others. There are exceptions to (i) and (ii). For example, neither apply to computer programs, and (ii) does not apply to literary work written for and published in newspapers, magazines or similar periodicals. So far as (i) is concerned, the author does not need to be identified when (by virtue of s 32(3) of the Act) his or her work may be used without infringement for the purposes of examination questions (s 79(4)(c)).

Chapter 9

Special educational needs

1. Introduction

The Education Act 1981 aimed to change fundamentally the whole approach to the education of children with special educational needs, who constitute about one-fifth of the school population. Modelled on the report by the committee chaired by Mary (now Lady) Warnock, *Special Educational Needs* (Cmnd 7212 (1978)), it aimed to identify children who needed special help under the education system not by reference to their physical or mental disability *per se*, but rather to the way in which that disability affected both their capacity to learn and their general educational development. It also aimed to establish clear procedures for assessing such children's needs and for setting out in a clear statement the provision that was required in cases of particular learning difficulty. The Act included in its provisions a duty to educate children for whom there were such statements in mainstream schools alongside other children, wherever possible. It also gave parents a number of important rights, including a right of appeal, for example against the educational provision proposed for the child in a statement. Parents had to be consulted over the statement and be permitted to make representations. Among their other rights, all of which could be said to be aimed at facilitating their involvement in their children's education and decisions concerning it, was a right to request a reassessment of their child's needs. Finally, the Act aimed for greater inter-agency co-operation in general and a multi-professional approach in the assessment of needs.

This Act placed much of the responsibility for pupils with special educational needs with LEAs; but governing bodies were given a duty to ensure that such pupils were identified and given appropriate provision and that the head teacher made all those who were to teach these children aware of their needs. So far as assessment and statementing requirements were concerned, flesh was placed on the bones represented by the Act by the Education (Special Educational Needs) Regulations 1983 (SI 1983 No 29). Guidance was issued via DES circular.

Amendments to the Act were made by the ERA 1988 to extend its coverage to grant-maintained schools. The 1988 Act also introduced the National Curriculum (see Chapter 8). It was envisaged that pupils with special educational needs would participate in it, although statements could modify provision. It was also recognised that exception from it would be advantageous in certain situations (for example, while a child's needs were being assessed or where a child was suffering from a temporary disability while recovering from hospital treatment etc), and the law provided for such exception (see below). Further amendment to the Act was made by the Children Act 1989, which empowered LEAs to provide funds to enable a statemented child to receive special educational provision outside England and Wales and imposed duties on local authorities and LEAs to co-operate or assist each other in various ways: LEAs had to comply with requests for assistance from local authorities in respect of the latter's exercise of their functions concerning support for children and families under Part III of the 1989 Act, while, for their part, local authorities had to assist LEAs in respect of the provision of services by them for children in their area with special educational needs. Local authorities were also given duties under the 1989 Act to ensure the availability of day-care provision for under-fives 'in need' (N Harris, 'The Children Act 1989: the Education Provisions' (1992) 4(2) *Education and the Law* 61).

The Education Act 1981 did not establish any kind of coherent monitoring system concerning its implementation. However, various aspects of its operation came under review. The House of Commons Education Select Committee issued a report in 1987 which explained that many parents did not feel that the system enabled their views on their child's education to be taken into account properly, that inter-agency co-operation was often deficient, and that there were unjustifiably wide inconsistencies between LEAs in the proportion of children who were statemented. It also found that insufficient resources were being allocated to special educational needs (so that, for example, there was a serious shortage of speech therapists) (*Third Report, Special Educational Needs: Implementation of the Education Act 1981* (1987) HC 201–1). Disparities between LEAs in the extent of statementing were also highlighted in a report by the Audit Commission and HMI in 1992, who felt that the explanation lay in differences in interpretation of the Act rather than in different local conditions (*Getting in on the Act – Provision for Pupils with Special Educational Needs – the National Picture* (1992) HMSO). This report also called for parents of children with special educational needs to be given more opportunities over choice of school.

In 1992–93 the House of Commons Education Select Committee carried out a follow-up review to its earlier study and found that, despite certain improvements, parents had not been brought into 'partnership' with schools and LEAs over the special education of their children as had been hoped and that statementing was in need of reform, being far too prevalent (there are presently around 170,000 children with statements) and subject to too many delays (Third Report, Session 1992–93, *Meeting Special Educational Needs: Statements of Needs and Provision* (1993)). Complaints about delays in issuing draft or final statements of special educational needs and provision feature prominently in the caseload of the Local Government Ombudsman on this issue (see N Harris, *Law and Education: Regulation, Consumerism and the Education System* (Sweet and Maxwell, 1993, p 243). In one case the court refused to grant a remedy for such delay, because although it had been 'unreasonable' it had not been 'reprehensible' (*R* v *Gloucestershire County Council ex p P* [1994] ELR 334 (QBD), where the delay was in respect of obtaining a medical report and issuing an amended or redrafted statement).

The DFE's consultation paper (*Special Educational Needs – Access to the System*) in 1992 also highlighted delays in statementing and suggested that time limits should be introduced. It also recommended improvements to the appeals system (which it found to be failing to meet parents' expectations of a timely and effective means of redress), including extended appeal rights and a new, fully independent, Special Educational Needs Tribunal. Despite the deficiencies in the procedures that these various reports indicated, there was at least evidence that children with special educational needs were benefiting from the National Curriculum (HMI, *National Curriculum and Special Needs* (1991)); indeed teachers tended to be against excepting children with special educational needs from it, reinforcing National Curriculum Council policy on the issue (National Curriculum Council, *Special Needs and the National Curriculum* (1992) and *A Curriculum for All* (1989)).

The new legal regime formed largely by Part III of the EA 1993, the Code of Practice made under it and regulations, shows that many of the problems with the system provided for by the 1981 Act have been addressed. Partnership with parents and involvement of the child are being promoted more directly and more forcibly (via the Code of Practice – see also the DFE's *Special Educational Needs: a guide for parents* (1994)), time limits for various stages of the procedure are being introduced, stricter guidance is being laid down, appeal rights have been extended and a new Special Educational Needs Tribunal has been established (with jurisdiction from September 1994). Nevertheless, it is a testament to the vision of Lady Warnock and her committee that many of the key concepts built into the 1981 Act, including 'learning difficulty' and integration, remain firmly embedded in the legislative framework.

Part III of the EA 1993 Act has replaced almost all of the 1981 Act. References in this chapter are to the 1993 Act unless stated otherwise. The transitional arrangements are summarised in *Appendix 6* to this book. The duties concerning the publication of a school's educational needs policy (under the Education (Special Educational Needs) (Information) Regulations 1994 (SI 1994 No 1048)) were discussed at pp 153–155.

2. The Code of Practice on special educational needs

A new element in the law governing special education is the statutory *Code of Practice*. The Secretary of State must issue such a Code, and may from time to time revise it, after consulting appropriate persons and considering any representations made by them (EA 1993, ss 157(1) and 158(2)). The draft Code must be laid before both Houses of Parliament and can only be issued if both Houses approve it by affirmative resolution (s 158(3) and (4)). The approved Code must be published (s 157(4)).

The Code must provide 'practical guidance in respect of the discharge by local education authorities and the governing bodies of maintained or grant-maintained schools, or grant-maintained special schools, of their functions under [Part III of] this Act' (EA 1993, s 157(1)). It was clear from the ministerial statements made during the 1993 legislation's passage through Parliament that the Code would deal with the full range of responsibilities of schools and LEAs under Part III and that it would be premised on the following principles (adumbrated in a speech by Baroness Blatch (*Hansard*, House of Lords, Vol 545, col 489)):

(i) there is a need for early identification of children with special educational needs (see also (iii));
(ii) provision for children with special educational needs should be made by the most appropriate agency (usually a mainstream school);
(iii) clear guidance for schools is required on the steps they should take to identify, assess and monitor children with special educational needs;
(iv) schools and LEAs should be given clear criteria as to when a statutory assessment may be necessary and when a statement should follow;
(v) LEAs should receive clear guidance on assessments (reference being made to time limits, inter-agency co-operation and the need to take into account the wishes and the feelings of the child concerned, considered in the light of his or her age and understanding, all of which would be dealt with in the Code or in regulations);
(vi) there is a need for guidance on writing clear, thorough and specific statements of special educational needs and on enabling parents to express a preference for a school to be named in a statement.

The Minister further explained that the Code would also cover the role of parents. A draft version of the Code was issued at the end of October 1993 (DFE and Welsh Office, *Draft Code of Practice on the Identification and Assessment of Special Educational Needs*). It contained similar statements of principle and indications of essential practices and procedures. The final version of the Code, revised in the light of numerous representations made to the DFE, was published in May 1994 and came into effect on 1 September 1994 (Education (Special Educational Needs Code of Practice) (Appointed Day) Order 1994 (SI 1994 No 1414)). The *Code of Practice* sets out (at para 1:2) its fundamental principles thus:

- the needs of all pupils who may have special educational needs either throughout, or at any time during, their school careers must be addressed; the Code recognises that there is a continuum of needs and a continuum of provision, which may be made in a wide variety of different forms
- children with special educational needs require the greatest possible access to a broad and balanced education, including the National Curriculum

- the needs of most pupils will be met in the mainstream, and without a statutory assessment or statement of special educational needs. Children with special educational needs, including children with statements of special educational needs, should, where appropriate and taking into account the wishes of their parents, be educated alongside their peers in mainstream schools
- even before he or she reaches compulsory school age a child may have special educational needs requiring the intervention of the LEA as well as the health services
- the knowledge, views and experience of parents are vital. Effective assessment and provision will be secured where there is the greatest possible degree of partnership between parents and their children and school, LEAs and other agencies'.

Practice and procedures are to be designed with these principles in mind, and the Code is to be read subject to them. The essential practices and procedures (set out in para 1:3 of the *Code of Practice*) will involve:

— early identification of needs;
— provision by the most appropriate agency (in most cases a mainstream school, working in partnership with the child's parent);
— assessments and statements, where needed, to be carried out within the prescribed time limits;
— statements to be clear, and specific as to needs, provision, objectives and arrangements for monitoring and review;
— 'special educational provision will be most effective when those responsible take into account the ascertainable wishes of the child concerned, considered in the light of his or her age and understanding';
— close agency co-operation and a multi-disciplinary approach.

The Act requires LEAs and governing bodies exercising functions under Part III, and others exercising such functions on their behalf, to 'have regard to the provisions of the Code' (EA 1993, s 157(2)). Where there is an appeal to the Special Educational Needs Tribunal, the Tribunal must have regard to any provision of the Code 'which appears to the tribunal to be relevant to any question arising on the appeal' (s 157(3)). The precise legal status of the Code was a subject of some debate in the House of Lords. For example, Lord Simon supported an amendment proposed by Lord Campbell which would have made it more clear that what was being expected of LEAs, governors and the Tribunal was that the Code would be taken into account and, so far as practicable, would be applied. Baroness Blatch explained the position thus:

> 'By law, those who must have regard to the Code cannot ignore it. If they do so, they will be in breach of a duty. They do not, however, have to follow the Code to the letter and in every particular. But any departure from the Code will be challenged, require justification – to parents in the first instance and then, depending on the circumstances,

> to the . . . new special needs tribunal if the matter at issue is the subject of an appeal. In justifying their actions, those to whom the Code applies will have to show that the alternative action produced results which were at least as beneficial as those which would have resulted from their following the Code' (*Hansard*, HL, Vol 545, col 487).

The *Code of Practice* must therefore be regarded as an integral part of the legal regime governing special educational needs and provision. Much of the Code is structured around its staged model, which it recommends for general adoption while acknowledging that there is scope for differences of definition in respect of the stages and for variation in the number of stages which individual schools and LEAs actually adopt. It may be helpful, when using the breakdown in the rest of the chapter, to bear in mind the five stages set out in the Code (at para 1:4):

> 'Stage 1: class or subject teachers identify or register a child's special educational needs and, consulting the school's SEN (special educational needs) co-ordinator . . . take initial action
>
> Stage 2: the school's SEN co-ordinator takes lead responsibility for gathering information and for co-ordinating the child's special eductional provision, working with the child's teachers
>
> Stage 3: teachers and the SEN co-ordinator are supported by specialists from outside the school
>
> Stage 4: the LEA consider the need for a statutory assessment and, if appropriate, make a multi-disciplinary assessment
>
> Stage 5: the LEA consider the need for a statement of special educational needs and, if appropriate, make a statement and arrange, monitor and review provision'.

The first three stages are school based. Responsibility at Stages 4 and 5 is shared between schools and LEAs.

3. Definitions

(a) 'Child'

Part III of the EA 1993 applies to children with special educational needs. A 'child' is defined as 'any person who has not attained the age of nineteen years and is a registered pupil at a school' (EA 1993, s 156(5)). This differs from the definition of 'child' under the Children Act 1989, an Act which also has some relevance to special educational provision, which defines a child (for most purposes) as a person under the age of 18 (CA 1989, s 105(1)).

(b) 'Special educational needs'

A child has special educational needs if he or she 'has a learning difficulty which calls for special educational provision to be made for him' (EA 1993, s 156(1)). A child is not to be taken to have a 'learning difficulty' merely because the language or form of language in which he is being, or will be, taught is different from the (form of) language 'which has at any time been spoken in his home' (s 156(3)). A child will have a 'learning difficulty' if:

'(*a*) he has a significantly greater difficulty in learning than the majority of children of his age,

(*b*) he has a disability which either prevents or hinders him from making use of educational facilities of a kind generally provided for children of his age in schools within the area of the local education authority, or

(*c*) he is under the age of five years and is, or would be if special educational provision were not made for him, likely to fall within paragraph (*a*) or (*b*) when over that age' (s 156(2)).

This follows exactly the wording of section 1(2) of the 1981 Act. Two contentious areas under the 1981 Act, dyslexia and speech difficulties requiring speech therapy, were both held to give rise to a learning difficulty within (*a*) and (*b*) calling for special educational provision (*R* v *Hampshire Education Authority ex p J* (1985) 84 LGR 547; and *R* v *Lancashire County Council ex p CM* [1989] 2 FLR 279, disapproving *R* v *Oxfordshire Education Authority ex p W* [1986] The Times, 20 November). In conclusion, subsections (1) and (2) of section 156 require that in order to fall within the scope of Part III of the EA 1993 a child must have a learning difficulty within section 156(2) (e.g. defective hearing), being a difficulty/need which requires special educational provision.

(c) Special educational provision

Special educational provision is, in relation to a child aged two or over:

> 'educational provision which is additional to, or otherwise different from, the educational provision made generally for children of his age in schools maintained by the local education authority (other than special schools) or grant-maintained schools in their area' (s 156(4)(*a*)).

The previous version of this provision (in s 1(3) of the EA 1981), the key elements and substance of which were identical to the current version, was interpreted as meaning that even if each of an LEA's schools had, say, a deaf unit, such provision would still amount to 'special educational provision' (*R* v *Hampshire Education Authority ex p J* (1985) (*op cit*)). 'Special educational provision' can thus be any generally available provision other than that made for what Taylor J in *ex p J* referred to as 'the general run of normal children, the normal majority' (today regarded as politically incorrect terminology, although the meaning is clear). Hampshire LEA's argument, that any provision for children who were deaf, or partially blind, or disturbed etc, which was generally available in its schools was not special educational provision, was rejected by the court.

So far as children aged under two are concerned, any educational provision is special educational provision (EA 1993, s 156(4)(b)). Such children will not be receiving education at school, but the LEA is under a duty to assess the special educational needs of a child in their area aged under two (at the parent's request or with the parent's consent) if the LEA is of the opinion that the child has special educational needs and it is necessary for the authority to determine the special educational provision which his or her needs call for (EA 1993, s 175) (see further Part 5 of the *Code of Practice*).

4. General duties

(a) Review of arrangements

LEAs must keep their arrangements for special educational provision under review (EA 1993, s 159). To the extent that it appears necessary or desirable for the purpose of co-ordinating provision for children with special educational needs, their review of arrangements must involve consultation with the funding authority and governing bodies of maintained and GM schools in the area (*ibid*).

(b) Integration

Increasingly, since the implementation of the EA 1981, children with even quite severe learning difficulties have been educated in ordinary schools rather than special schools (for the definition of 'special school', see p 28 above). The 1981 Act laid down (what is often known as) the integration principle in respect of pupils with statements, and the 1993 Act has extended this to *all* pupils with special educational needs. All those with responsibility under Part III have a duty to ensure that a child with special educational needs is, if the prescribed conditions are satisfied, educated in a school which is not a special school, 'unless that is incompatible with the wishes of his parent' (EA 1993, s 160(1)). The prescribed conditions for integration are that educating the child in an ordinary school would be compatible with:

(i) his or her receiving the special educational provision his or her needs call for;
(ii) the pupils with whom he or she will be educated receiving efficient education; and
(iii) the efficient use of resources.

(EA 1993, s 160(2)).

There has been some debate about whether or not section 160(1) of the EA 1993 (see above) gives parents a veto over an LEA's decision to place a child in any non-special school or a particular school. This was not the Government's intention and is certainly not its view, but education lawyers have advised the Independent Panel on Special Education Advice that this is the case (see further Part 6(d) below).

The same prescribed conditions ((i)–(iii) above) apply in respect of the duty in section 161(4) to ensure that, where a child with special educational needs is being educated in a maintained school (including a maintained nursery school) or GM school, he or she 'engages in the activities of the school together with children who do not have special educational needs'.

On the special difficulties which arise in this context in connection with pupils with emotional and behavioural difficulties, see DFE Circular 9/94, *The Education of Children with Emotional and Behavioural Difficulties* (1994), which, while advocating arrangements for such children in mainstream schools and presenting various strategies, notes that these children's emotional and behavioural difficulties may be such that they 'cannot be taught effectively in mainstream schools, or without serious disruption of the education of others' (para 61).

LEAs may, in fact, arrange for all or part of the special educational provision for a pupil with special educational needs to be made otherwise than in a school if they are satisfied that it would be 'inappropriate' for this provision to be made in school (EA 1993, s 163). The 1993 Act also continues the power, first introduced via an amendment of the EA 1981 by the Children Act 1989, for LEAs to make arrangements (including payment of fees and travelling and living expenses for the child and any person accompanying him or her) for a child for whom there is a statement to attend an institution outside England and Wales which specialises in providing for children with special needs (EA 1993, s 164).

(c) General duty to identify children with special educational needs and make the necessary special educational provision

LEAs have a general duty to exercise their powers with a view to securing that they identify those of the children for whom they are responsible who have special educational needs and in respect of whom it is necessary for the LEA to determine the special educational provision which any learning difficulty they have may call for (EA 1993, s 165). For this purpose, the LEA is responsible for children registered at maintained, GM or GM special schools (or at another type of school but at the LEA's or funding authority's expense). It is also responsible for other children who are registered pupils at a school, and children aged between two and school-leaving age who are not registered pupils, who in either case have been brought to the LEA's attention as having, or probably having, special educational needs (s 165(3)). In practice, children with special educational needs will often be identified by teachers as a result of general monitoring of progress and assessment under the National Curriculum. The Code advises use of appropriate screening or assessment tools and suggests that the 'trigger' for invoking the school-based stages of action will be the registration of concern about the child's learning difficulties along with evidence from teachers or another professional such as a health or social services worker (Code, para 2:71).

There is a general duty on District Health Authorities and NHS trusts (EA 1993, s 176) to notify parents of a child aged under five years whom they identify as having, or probably having, special educational needs, of their opinion that the child has such needs. After giving the parent an opportunity to discuss that opinion with them, the health authority or trust must bring their opinion to the attention of the LEA. The health authority or trust also have a duty to inform the parent of any voluntary organisation that is likely to be able to give him or her advice or assistance in connection with the child's special educational needs.

There is a duty on governing bodies, and LEAs in the case of maintained nursery schools, to use their 'best endeavours' to ensure that children with special educational needs receive the special educational provision that their learning difficulty calls for (EA 1993, s 161(1)(a)). There is also a duty on them to make the child's needs known to all those who are likely to teach him or her; the duty arises once the child has been identified to the 'responsible person' by the LEA (s 161(1)(b)). The 'responsible person' is the head teacher in the case of nursery schools, and the head teacher or appropriate governor (chair or delegate) in the case of other schools (s 161(2)). In rare circumstances LEAs may supply goods and services to the governing bodies of GM and GM special schools and to the governing bodies of county, voluntary and maintained special schools in other areas to assist them in the performance of the 'best endeavours' duty in section 161(1)(*a*) (above) (see EA 1993, s 162 and the Education (Payment for Special Educational Needs Supplies) Regulations 1994 (SI 1994 No 650), as amended by SI 1994 No 2156).

The governors or, in the case of a nursery school, the LEA, also have a general duty to 'secure that teachers in the school are aware of the importance of identifying, and providing for, those registered pupils who have special educational needs' (s 161(1)(c)).

(d) Agency co-ordination and co-operation

Agency co-ordination and co-operation has always been an important principle in the field of special educational needs but, as studies have pointed out, both elements have often been lacking in practice (see, for example, House of Commons Education, Science and the Arts Select Committee, Session 1986/87, Third Report, *Special Educational Needs: Implementation of the Education Act 1981*, Vol 1 (1987) *op cit*; CM Lyon, *The Implications of the Children Act 1989 on Children and Young People with Learning Difficulties* (Barnardos, 1991)). One of the responsibilities of the special educational needs co-ordinator, which the Code of Practice recommends that each school should have, will be to liaise with external agencies including the educational psychology service and other support agencies, medical and social services and voluntary bodies (see para 2:14 of the Code). The Code also recommends (para 2:54) that social services departments should designate an officer or officers to be responsible for working with schools and LEAs on behalf of children with special educational needs. For schools, the need to have links with social services departments should enable them to register concern about a child's welfare, put into practice any local procedures relating to child protection issues, liaise with the local authority where the child is accommodated by that authority and obtain information on services provided by that authority for children in need (see below) (Code, para 2:57). Co-operation with child health services is also important (Code, paras 2:41–2:52).

(i) The Children Act 1989

The Children Act 1989 has aimed to foster greater co-operation between agencies concerned with the welfare of children, in particular local authorities and LEAs. LEAs are, for example, required (by s 27(1)–(3) of the 1989 Act) to comply with requests for assistance from local authorities in respect of the functions concerning support for children and families in Part III of the 1989 Act (including the duties centring on the need to safeguard and promote the welfare of children within their area who are 'in need' and to provide day-care facilities for such children if aged five or under and not yet attending school (see CA 1989, ss17(1) and 18(1); for further duties, see Sch 2, paras 1, 2, 4 and 6)). A child is in need in any one of three possible circumstances, which are such that these children are highly likely to have special educational needs for the purposes of the EA 1993. The first of these is where the child is unlikely to achieve or maintain, or to have the opportunity of achieving or maintaining, a reasonable standard of health or development without the provision of such services (CA 1989, s 17(10)(a)). 'Development' is defined for this purpose as 'physical, intellectual, emotional, social or behavioural development' (CA 1989, s 17(11)). 'Health' covers physical or mental health. The second circumstance in which a child is in need is where his or her health or development is likely to be significantly impaired, or further impaired, without the provision to him or her of such services (CA 1989, s 17(10)(b)). Finally, a child is in need if disabled (s 17(10)(c)). 'Disabled' is defined for this purpose as being 'blind, deaf or dumb or suffering from a mental disorder or being substantially and permanently handicapped by illness, injury or congenital deformity (or such other disability as may be prescribed)' (s 17(11)).

As remarked earlier, many, if not most, of the children who are 'in need' for the purposes of Part III of the Children Act 1989 will have special educational needs for the purposes of Part III of the Education Act 1993. The Children Act provides that a local authority may assess a child's needs in conjunction with an assessment of his or her special educational needs under the 1993 Act (CA 1989, Sch 2, para 3, as amended).

Note that section 27(4) of the 1989 Act, which required local authorities to assist LEAs in connection with the provision of LEAs' services relating to special educational needs, has been repealed (by EA 1993, Sch 19, para 147). In its place is section 166 of the EA 1993 (see (ii) below).

(ii) The Education Act 1993

An LEA may request the help of a District Health Authority (DHA) or local authority (defined for this purpose in EA 1993, s 166(5)) in connection with any of the LEA's functions under Part III of the 1993 Act

(EA 1993, s 166(1)). The request must be complied with save on specified grounds:

- the authority to whom it is made considers that its help is 'not necessary' for the purpose of the exercise by the (LEA) of its functions under Part III;
- in the case of a DHA only, the DHA, having regard to the resources available to it for the purpose of exercising its functions under the National Health Service Act 1977, considers that 'it is not reasonable' for it to comply with the request;
- in the case of a local authority only, the authority considers that the request made to it 'is not compatible with (its) own statutory or other duties and obligations or unduly prejudices the discharge of (its) functions'.

(EA 1993, s 166(2) and (3)).

In relation to requests which must be complied with, and which relate to assessment or statementing, regulations can set time limits for compliance (EA 1993, s 166(4)).

The 1993 Act also imposes consultation duties on governing bodies and, in the case of nursery schools, LEAs, which apply 'to the extent that it appears necessary or desirable for the purpose of co-ordinating provision for children with special educational needs' (s 161(3)). Consultation must be carried out in exercising functions relating to provision for children with special educational needs. Governing bodies must consult the LEA, the funding authority and the governing bodies of other maintained schools (apart from nursery schools). LEAs must consult the funding authority and governing bodies of county, voluntary and GM schools.

5. Assessment of needs

(a) Introduction: from school-based assessment to formal assessment

The duty to identify children who have special educational needs was described earlier. In the *Code of Practice* three 'School-based stages of assessment and provision' are identified and described in some detail. There are two further stages, statutory assessment and statementing.

The school-based stages may be outlined briefly here. They are not really regulated apart from under the Code, although such matters as record-keeping and assessment under the National Curriculum are governed by statute or statutory instrument, as noted in other chapters. **Stage 1** (see Code, paras 2:70–2:83) involves the child's teacher gathering various pieces of relevant information about the child, relating to the child's academic record (e.g. National Curriculum attainments), overall progress (as noted in records of achievement and reports on the pupil in school settings), behaviour (from teachers' observations) and known health or social problems (as noted, e.g., in school records). Information should also be obtained from the parent and the child as to their perceptions of any difficulties experienced by the child and how they may be addressed. The teacher or tutor and special educational needs co-ordinator would then have to decide whether any information should be sought from medical, social or education welfare services. A decision would have to be taken about whether to continue the child's current educational arrangements (without further help), to seek further advice and support or to give the child special help by differentiating the curriculum and monitoring and reviewing the child's progress. Whatever action is decided upon, a review should be undertaken, by a review date set by the teacher or tutor. At **Stage 2** (Code, paras 2:85–2:98) the co-ordinator will take prime responsibility for managing the child's special educational provision and assessing further the child's needs. Stage 2 is triggered by a decision at a Stage 1 review or where the co-ordinator decides that early intensive action is necessary. In the light of his or her assessment the co-ordinator will be expected to seek further advice and/or draw up an individual education plan. Again progress will be reviewed. If the child's progress is not satisfactory or early intensive action with external support is needed, the child will move up to **Stage 3** (Code, paras 2:99–2:118), when external specialist support will be called upon to help the child.

The one in five schoolchildren with special educational needs will mostly be catered for by the school-based stages outlined above. In some cases, involving only about 2 per cent of school pupils, it will be necessary to conduct a formal, statutory assessment of the child's needs (the Code refers to this as **Stage 4** (Code, Part 3)). This will be where the LEA concludes that a child has, or probably has, special educational needs and that 'it is necessary for the LEA to determine the special educational provision which any learning difficulty he may have calls for' (EA 1993, s 167(1) and (2) and s 174), provided that (in the case of children aged over two) the authority has served the required notice and taken into account the representations made to it (see below). Other children's needs might be met through provision determined by the school itself – for example, through remedial teaching. In some circumstances (see (b) below) the duty to assess arises from a request by parents or the governing body of a GM school. **Stage 5** follows on from Stage 4 and involves consideration by the LEA of the need for a statement of special educational needs and, where considered appropriate, the making of a statement and arranging, monitoring and reviewing provision (Code, Part 4).

An important change made by the EA 1993 is the tighter regulatory framework for the carrying out of assessments. Not only will regulations make provision for time limits for the carrying out of assessments, but the LEA will have to have regard to the provisions of the Code of Practice (Part 3). Statutory assessment procedure is outlined in (c) below.

(b) Assessment at request of parent or governing body of GM school

Parents had a right under the EA 1981 to request an assessment of their child. LEAs had to comply with such a request, in the case of a non-statemented child, unless an assessment had been carried out in the previous six months or it was 'unreasonable' (see EA 1981, s 9(1) and *R* v

Hampshire County Council ex p W [1994] ELR 460 (QBD)). In the case of a statemented child, the LEA was obliged by the EA 1981 to comply with a request for an assessment provided that an assessment had not been carried out in the previous six months and unless it was satisfied that an assessment would be 'inappropriate' (EA 1981 s 9(2)). Now the LEA must comply with either such request for a formal statutory assessment provided the authority considers it 'necessary' to make an assessment (or, in the case of a statemented child, a further assessment) under section 167 and no assessment has been carried out in the previous six months (EA 1993, s 172 and 173; see also Code, paras 3:17–3:21). Under the 1981 Act the assessment carried out in response to the parental request did not have to be a formal statutory assessment in every case (*R* v *Surrey County Council ex p G; ex p H* [1994] The Times, 24 May (QBD)).

If such an assessment is indeed 'necessary' under section 167, the LEA would be under an independent duty to carry out the assessment, so the value of this provision reveals itself in situations where there has been a failure to identify children as requiring an assessment or further assessment. If the authority decides not to carry out an assessment following such a request, the parent has a right of appeal to the Special Educational Needs Tribunal, and the LEA must inform the parent of this right when informing him or her of its decision (EA 1993, ss 172(3) and (4) and 173(2) and (3)).

Governing bodies may be directed to admit a child under the new power, in section 13 of the EA 1993, for LEAs to order schools to admit particular pupils who have been refused admission to schools or who have been permanently excluded from a school (which is not the school which is the subject of the direction). Where the governing body of a GM school so directed to admit a child asks the LEA to arrange for a formal assessment of the child's special educational needs the authority must carry out such an assessment provided that no such assessment was carried out within the six months prior to the date of the request (EA 1993, s 174). Before the assessment is carried out various procedural steps must be taken, including the giving of notice to the parents of the proposed assessment and the provision of information to them concerning the assessment procedure, the name of the officer from whom information may be obtained and the right to make representations and submit written evidence. The parent and governing body must be informed by the LEA of its decision whether or not to carry out an assessment (EA 1993, s 174(6)). If the assessment is to go ahead, it will proceed as under section 167 (see below).

Separate provision is made in respect of children aged under two. An LEA must also carry out, at the request of the parent, an assessment of the educational needs of such a child if it is of the opinion that the following applies, or probably applies, to him or her:

(i) the child has special educational needs; and
(ii) it is necessary for the authority to determine the special educational provision which any learning difficulty he or she may have calls for.

(EA 1993, s 175(1) and (2)).

Unlike assessments of children aged two or over, the statutory procedure discussed below (in (c)) does not apply. The assessment must simply be carried out 'in such manner as the authority consider appropriate' (EA 1993, s 175(3)).

(c) Statutory assessment procedure

(i) Notice

The first stage in the statutory assessment procedure under section 167 is the service of a notice on the child's parent informing him or her of the following:

- that the LEA proposes to make an assessment of the child's educational needs;
- the procedure that will be followed;
- the name of the officer of the LEA from whom further information can be obtained; and
- the parent's right to make representations and submit written evidence (within a period stipulated in the notice, of at least 29 days from the date on which the notice is served).

(EA 1993, s 167(1)).

For the definition of 'parent', see EA 1944, s 114(1D)–(1F), as amended. Chapter III of the Code recommends that parents should also be supplied with information on independent sources of advice such as national and voluntary organisations and local support groups. The regulations (Education (Special Educational Needs) Regulations 1994 (SI 1994 No 1047, as amended), regs 5(1) and (3)) require the LEA to send a copy of the proposal to assess to various persons, including the head teacher of the school. The Code (para 3:16) recommends that a copy should also be sent by the LEA to its educational psychology section and other relevant agencies, such as the education welfare service, who might be asked for advice should the assessment proceed.

The duty to serve this notice arises where the LEA is of the opinion that a child for whom they are responsible (see p 244 above) falls, or probably falls, within the following category: 'he has special educational needs, and . . . it is necessary for the authority to determine the special educational provision which any learning difficulty he may have calls for' (EA 1993, s 167(2)).

(ii) Duty to assess

The LEA must make an assessment of the child's needs if:

- they have served a notice under EA 1993, s 167(1) (see (i) above);
- the period specified in the notice for representations to be made, or written evidence to be submitted, by the parent has expired; and

- having taken into account any such representations or submissions, the LEA remains of the opinion that the child's needs are such that it should determine the special educational provision that should be made.

(EA 1993, s 167(3)).

Reference should be made to the detailed guidance on the criteria for deciding whether to make a statutory assessment which is offered by the *Code of Practice* (paras 3:46–3:94).

(iii) Informing the parent of the LEA's decision whether to assess

Having decided whether or not to make an assessment, the LEA must give notice in writing to the child's parent of its decision and, in most cases, its reasons for making it (EA 1993, s 167(4); in the case of a request by a governing body of a GM school directed to admit the child, s 174(5) and (6); in the case of a request by parents for an assessment, ss 172 and 173). This information must be given within six weeks of service of the notice (reg 11(1)–(3) of the Education (Special Educational Needs) Regulations 1994).

(iv) Assessment

Like the 1981 Act before it, the EA 1993 requires the multi-professional approach advocated by the Warnock Report. The 1993 Act stipulates that except in any prescribed circumstances the LEA should seek medical, psychological and educational advice and such other advice as may be prescribed (EA 1993, Sch 9 para 2). The Education (Special Educational Needs) Regulations 1994 (regs 6–9) make further provision as to the advice which LEAs are to take into account in making assessments. The regulations (reg 6(1)(a)) require the LEA to seek advice from the child's parent (this is a new requirement, and the Code contains important guidelines for parents on their contribution to their child's statutory assessment: paras 3:100–3:102), the head teacher or other person responsible for educational provision for the child over the previous 18 months (3:103–3:105), a fully registered medical practitioner (via the district health authority) (3:106–3:112), an educational psychologist (3:113–3:115), the social services authority (3:116–3:119) and any other appropriate source (3:121). The advice must be in writing and must relate to the child's educational needs, referring to the educational, medical, psychological or other features of the case (according to the nature of the advice sought), how those features could affect the child's educational needs, and the provision which is appropriate for the child in relation to those features (excluding any matter which must be specified in a statement by virtue of s 168(4)(b) – the name of a school or other institution). The Code recommends that the child's views are ascertained so that they can be taken into account (para 3:120).

In some cases there is a time limit for the provision of professional advice. A district health authority or social services authority must normally comply with a request for advice within six weeks from the date that they receive the request; they need not comply with the time limit if it is impracticable for them to keep to it in various prescribed circumstances (Education (Special Educational Needs) Regulations 1994, *op cit*, reg 11(7) and (8)).

The assessment must be carried out within the prescribed period and in the manner laid down in the regulations (EA 1993, Sch 9, para 3). The prescribed period is ten weeks from the date that notice was given to the parent of the decision to make an assessment, unless it is impracticable to complete the assessment within ten weeks for one or more prescribed reasons (Education (Special Educational Needs) Regulations 1994, reg 11(5) and (6)). These prescribed reasons include: exceptional circumstances making it necessary for the authority to seek further advice; the parent indicates, after the expiry of six weeks from when advice from the parent is requested, that he or she wishes to provide it; exceptional personal circumstances have affected the child or his parent during the ten-week period; and the child fails to keep an appointment for an examination or a test during the ten-week period.

LEAs must take into account, when making an assessment, the advice obtained under regulations 6–9 (see above), any representations made by the child's parent and any evidence submitted by the parent at his or her request (in both cases, for the purposes of s 167(1) of the 1993 Act) (reg 10).

Examination of the child will generally form part of the assessment. The parent has a legal right to be present at an examination (EA 1993, Sch 9, para 4). The Act states that where the LEA proposes to carry out an assessment it 'may' serve a notice on the parent requiring the child's attendance for examination (*ibid*). The notice must state the purpose of the examination, the time and place at which the examination will be held and the name of the officer of the authority from whom further information may be obtained; it must also inform the parent of his or her rights to submit information to the authority and be present at the examination (*ibid*). A parent commits an offence for failing without reasonable excuse to comply with any requirements of the notice, if the child who is the subject of the notice is over compulsory school age at the date for the examination stipulated in the notice (EA 1993, Sch 9, para 5). Parents have no right to attend any case conference which is convened, but the advantages of inviting parents to attend, in terms of maintaining parents' trust and encouraging their co-operation, have long been emphasised by the Department.

6. Statements of special educational needs

Following the assessment, the LEA must decide whether a statement of special educational needs is called for. The purpose of the statement is, essentially, to set out details of the child's special educational needs and the provision which is considered necessary in respect of them. If the LEA decides to make a statement, it must follow the fairly complex procedure laid down in Schedule 10 and the regulations (apart from statements made under s 175 of the EA 1993 in respect of children aged under two).

(a) When is a statement necessary?

The EA 1981 (s 7(1)) gave the LEA considerable discretion over whether to issue a statement of special educational needs. It required the LEA to make and maintain a statement if, in the light of the assessment and representations made, it was 'of the opinion' that it should determine the provision that was needed. Under the EA 1993, s 168(1), this duty arises where the LEA considers a statement is 'necessary'. The change of emphasis seems intended to foster a reduction in LEAs' propensity to make statements (as noted earlier (in Part 1), in 1993 the House of Commons Education Committee strongly urged such a reduction). The Act thus distinguishes clearly between (i) a child who has special educational needs *per se*, and (ii) a child who has special educational needs which are such that the LEA may consider that it is necessary to determine the provision that should be made for him. Where only (i) applies, it will be left to the school to determine the provision that should be made for the child (see further *R* v *Secretary of State for Education and Science ex p Lashford* [1988] 1 FLR 72). One of the aims of the new *Code of Practice* is to ensure greater consistency of practice between LEAs on determinations for the purposes of section 168(1).

The Code (paras 3:48 and 4:7) advises LEAs to establish local 'moderating groups' to oversee statementing, the aim being to ensure greater local consistency. It also (in Part 4) offers detailed guidance on when a statement should be made, the aim here being to ensure greater national consistency and, it seems, a reduced incidence of statementing. It suggests (para 4:2) that an LEA may decide that it must make a statement if it concludes that all the special educational provision necessary to meet the pupil's needs cannot reasonably be provided within the resources normally available to mainstream schools in the area. Relevant examples are given in the Code (at para 4:12). If, for example, the LEA concludes that the child's learning difficulties call for occasional advice to the school from an external specialist, or a particular piece of equipment such as a portable computer, or minor building alterations, 'the LEA may well conclude that the school could reasonably be expected to make such provision from within its own resources'. On the other hand, if the child is found to need regular direct teaching by a specialist teacher, a significant piece of equipment such as closed circuit television, more expensive computer equipment, or a major building adaptation such as the installation of a lift, the LEA may conclude that the provision should be set out in a statement, although the conclusion reached must 'depend on the precise circumstances of each case'. The Code advises that if the child needs to be moved to a specialist unit in his or her school or another school or requires a day or residential special school placement, the LEA should, especially in the case of a placement, draw up a statement.

As discussed below, LEAs must serve a copy of the proposed (draft) statement on parents and provide them with an opportunity to make representations. The LEA may then issue the statement in identical terms to the draft or in a modified form. It is also clear that the LEA may decide at this stage that (for the purposes of section 168) a statement is not necessary at all (see *R* v *Isle of Wight County Council ex p RS and ex p AS* [1993] 1 FLR 634 (CA)). Parents may appeal to the Special Educational Needs Tribunal against a decision not to make a statement (EA 1993, s 169). The *Code of Practice* acknowledges the sense of disappointment frequently felt by parents when the LEA decides not to issue a statement in respect of their child's needs (para 4:17). Parents may regard the decision as a denial of additional resources for their child. The Code advises that LEAs should aim to combat this view by making parents aware that 'resources are available within all maintained schools to meet the majority of special needs of their pupils' and of the three school-based stages of assessment and provision 'which will ensure that their child's needs are met by the school, with external support if necessary, in the appropriate way'. Whether or not parents will be satisfied with this kind of explanation is another matter. The fact that the parent is dissatisfied in the first place is no doubt the result of his or her perception that the provision within the school has not been adequate.

(b) Form and content of statements

The statement must be in the prescribed form and contain the prescribed information (EA 1993, s 168(2)–(4)). In particular, it must give details of the LEA's assessment of the child's special educational needs and specify the special educational provision to be made for the purpose of meeting those needs, including the following particulars:

- (i) the *type* of school or other institution which the LEA considers would be appropriate for the child;
- (ii) if the LEA is not required by Schedule 10 to the EA 1993 to specify a school selected by the parents (see p 257 below), the *name* of any school or institution (in the UK or elsewhere) which it considers would be appropriate for the child and should be specified in the statement; and
- (iii) any provision for the child *other than at school* which the LEA considers to be appropriate for the child (under the power in s 163: see 4(b) above).

The statement must be in a form 'substantially corresponding to that set out in Part B of the Schedule' to the Education (Special Educational Needs) Regulations 1994, contain the information specified in Part B and be dated and signed by an authorised officer of the LEA (1994 Regulations, reg 13). Some changes have been made to the prescribed form and content of the statement. The 1983 regulations, as amended, required the statement to be in five parts, with up to seven appendices (containing the parental representations and evidence, professional advice and information furnished by the district health authority and/or social services authority). The five parts were:

- I–Introduction;
- II–Special Educational Needs;
- III–Special Educational Provision;
- IV–Appropriate School or Other Arrangements; and
- V–Additional Non-Educational Provision.

The new form of the statement has the statement divided into six parts, with up to eight appendices to contain the representations, evidence and advice which were taken into account in accordance with the Act and regulations in the course of the assessment. The first four parts correspond to those contained in the previous version. However, new Part 3–Special Educational Provision, is more prescriptive than old Part III as to what must be included: the objectives of the provision, the special educational provision needed to meet those objectives and the child's needs and the arrangements made for monitoring progress in meeting the objectives, including any modification of the National Curriculum (this had to be included under the previous version as well). Part IV is retitled 'Placement' (new Part 4) and must contain the name or type of school and, where relevant, the provision for the child's education otherwise than at a school. There is a new Part 5, which covers Non-Educational Needs. New Part 6 covers Non-Educational Provision (with a new requirement to specify the objectives of the provision and the arrangements for monitoring progress in meeting them) and Part 7 relates to Other Arrangements.

The changes to the prescribed form and content of statements made by the 1994 regulations are not all that fundamental. Much of the previous case law on statements will therefore have continuing relevance.

As regards the precise extent of the duty to specify in the statement the special educational provision to be made for a child, two decisions, although somewhat in conflict, clarified the position. In *R* v *Secretary of State for Education and Science ex p E* [1992] 1 FLR 377 a 13-year-old boy had been assessed and found to have learning difficulties as a result of dyslexia and discalcula. Part II of the statement which had been issued referred to his needs as arising from his difficulty with numeracy and literacy. Part III of the statement, which specified the provision to be made in respect of his needs, referred only to literacy. The LEA's explanation of the absence of a reference to numeracy provision in Part III was that it had decided that assistance with numeracy could be determined by the school itself and, in consequence, it did not require inclusion in the statement. The Court of Appeal, affirming the High Court's decision, held that the LEA was required to specify the provision to be made in respect of each of the needs which were identified in Part II of the statement, so that teachers would not know exactly what was needed as regards the curriculum for the child concerned.

Nevertheless, the court in a subsequent case urged a cautious application of the *ex p E* approach. In *Re L* (1994) Leggatt LJ said (at p 22) that when the court had said that the purpose of Part III was to set out details of the provision needed to match the needs set out in Part II:

> 'the court was not inviting a line by line examination of the parts in order to gauge the degree of correspondence between them. Inelegant or even imperfect matching, whether or not the product of poor draftsmanship, would not be enough. Only if there were a clear failure to make provision for a significant need would the court be likely to conclude that there was such a dereliction of duty by a local education authority as called for the intervention of an appeal committee or, in default, of the Secretary of State or, indeed, of the High Court. In short, the case does not justify a detailed comparison between the parts of a statement in support of a challenge to its sufficiency'.

Glidewell LJ took a similar view. Leggatt LJ (at p 22) also rejected the argument that had been raised in the case that the reference to occupational therapists' advice on handwriting skills in Part V of the statement (Part V covered 'additional non-educational provision') rather than, as should have been the case, in Part III of the statement, was of such consequence as would warrant the intervention of the court, although it may be noted that a more serious error of this nature might have been viewed somewhat differently.

As regards specifying in the statement the name or type of school, LEAs have a wide discretion, although the 1993 Act gives parents an opportunity to express a preference for a school to be named in the statement and to appeal (see p 257 below). The cases demonstrate that the courts are unwilling to exercise a function entrusted in an LEA by Parliament and that a challenge to the LEA's choice of school cannot be founded merely on the argument that a superior form of education is available in a different school, if the school selected by the LEA for inclusion in the statement offers suitable provision (see *R* v *Surrey County Council ex p H* (1985) 83 LGR 219, *per* Slade LJ at p 235 and *R* v *Mid-Glamorgan County Council ex p Greig* (1988) The Independent, 1 June).

The statement must include (in Part 4) any provision to be made otherwise than at school (see point (iii) on p 254 above). It seems that this need not be set out in precise detail; only the general nature of the provision needs to be specified (*R* v *Hereford and Worcester County Council ex p P* [1992] 2 FLR 207).

On the content of statements in respect of the under-fives, see the *Code of Practice*, paras 5:20–5:22.

(c) Consultation with parents on the proposed statement

LEAs must serve a copy of the proposed statement on the parent(s) of the child concerned. They must also provide the parents with a written notice explaining the arrangements under which the parents may express a preference for a school to be named in the statement and the right of the parent(s) to make representations and to appeal against the contents of the statement under section 170 (EA 1993, Sch 10, para 2). These documents must be supplied to the parent within two weeks of the date on which the assessment was completed (Education (Special Educational Needs) Regulations 1994, reg 14(1)).

Unlike the final statement, the proposed statement must not specify any of the matters referred to in section 168(4) (name of school, type of school and provision otherwise than in a school). The notice is to be in a form 'substantially corresponding' to that set out in Part A of the Schedule to the Education (Special Educational Needs) Regulations 1994 and must contain the information specified therein (reg 12).

Leaving aside the rights over choice of school to be named in a statement, which are discussed in (d) below, parents in receipt of a proposed statement have a right to make representations to the LEA and to demand a meeting with an officer of the authority to discuss the matter. Subsequently, a further meeting can be called at the request of the parent at which the advice included in the statement following the assessment of the child can be discussed with the person who gave it (EA 1993, Sch 10, para 4). This right would be exercised where the parent disagreed with the advice.

The LEA may not make the statement until it has considered the representations made to it (*ibid*, para 5).

(d) Parental choice of school to be named in the statement

The Government made a commitment in the White Paper *Choice and Diversity* (1992) (para 9.3) to giving parents some choice over the school to be named in the statement, after this had been recommended by the Audit Commission/HMI report *Getting In On the Act – Provision for Pupils with Special Educational Needs – the National Picture* (1992).

As noted above, the proposed (draft) statement must not name a school (EA 1993, Sch 10, para 2). The parent on whom a copy of the proposed statement has been served must be given an opportunity to express a preference, with reasons, as to the maintained, GM or GM special school at which he or she wishes the child to be registered (EA 1993, Sch 10, para 3(1)). The parent has 15 days in which to express his/her preference, beginning with the date on which the proposed statement was served or, if the parent has requested a meeting under the right in paragraph 4 of Schedule 10 (see (c) above), the date of the meeting or the last of the meetings (*ibid*, para 3(2)). If the LEA proceeds to make a statement, it must name the school for which the parent has expressed a preference unless:

- (i) the school in unsuitable to the child's age, ability or aptitude or to his special educational needs, or
- (ii) the attendance of the child at the school would be incompatible with the provision of efficient education for the children with whom he would be educated or the efficient use of resources.

(EA 1993, Sch 10, para 3(3)).

This Code suggests (at para 4:42) that the LEA's duty under section 160 of the EA 1993 will come into play if the parent's request for a place at a mainstream school is denied on grounds (i) or (ii) above. Section 160 lays down a general duty (subject to conditions) to ensure that a child is educated in a mainstream school. The duty does not apply if placing the child in a mainstream school is incompatible with the wishes of the child's parent. The Code states (para 4:43), that this does *not* give the parents 'a veto on mainstream education'. The selection, by the parents, of a special school for their child must, however, result in that school being named unless conditions (i) or (ii) above apply.

Before specifying any maintained, GM or GM special school in the final version of the statement, the LEA must consult the governing body of the school concerned. If the school is maintained by another LEA, that authority must also be consulted (Sch 10, para 3(4)).

Parents also have a right, once twelve months have elapsed since the statement was made or amended or an appeal against the contents of the statement (under EA 1993, s 170) was determined, to request that an alternative school be named in a statement (EA 1993, Sch 10, para 8: see below).

(e) Making the statement

As noted above (see (a)), the LEA may make the statement in the form originally proposed (with the inclusion of the matters referred to in section 168(4), such as the name/type of the school, which had to be excluded from the proposed (draft) statement), or they may make it in a modified form, or they may chose not to make the statement at all if they consider that a statement is not necessary. Where the LEA is required to make the statement it must be in the required form (see (b) above) and must be made within any prescribed time limits (EA 1993, Sch 10, para 5). Delays in issuing statements have been a frequent cause of complaint to the Local Government Ombudsman, but there are now to be strict time limits. The LEA must serve a copy of the statement on the parent of the child concerned within eight weeks of the date on which the proposed (draft) statement was served (Education (Special Educational Needs) Regulations 1994, reg 14(2)), but there are exceptions to this time limit (see reg 14(3)), for example where exceptional personal circumstances have affected the child or his parent during the eight-week period, or the child or parent have been absent from the area for a continuous period of at least four out of the eight weeks or where the parent has requested any additional meeting(s) with the appropriate person (see (c) above). The LEA must, within the same eight-week time limit (and subject to the same exceptions) also give the parent written notice of his or her appeal rights under section 170(1) against the description of the child's special educational needs as assessed by the LEA, or the special educational provision specified in the statement or, if no school is named in the statement (remember that the LEA may specify the *type* of school or institution the child should attend rather than the name of a school or institution), that fact (EA 1993, Sch 10, para 6).

(f) Once the statement is made and served

Once an LEA maintains a statement of special educational needs it must, unless the child's parent has made 'suitable arrangements' ('if the parents themselves make suitable arrangements they effectively relieve the local education authority of its duty' – *per* Glidewell LJ (*obiter*) in *R* v *Governors of Hasmonean High School ex p N and E* [1994] ELR 343 (CA) at p 355), arrange that the special educational provision specified in the statement is made for the child and that any non-educational provision specified in the statement is made in an appropriate manner (EA 1993, s 168(5)(a)). The governing body of any maintained, GM or GM special school specified in the statement must admit the child, but this is without prejudice to the head teacher's power subsequently to exclude the child once registered at the school (s 168(5)(b) and (6)).

Requirements as to the keeping, disclosure and transfer of statements must be complied with (see EA 1993, Sch 10, para 7, and regs 18 and 19 of the Education (Special Educational Needs) Regulations 1994). The statement must be reviewed periodically and in certain other circumstances (see below).

(g) Review of statements

LEAs must review a statement whenever an assessment of the child under section 167 occurs and, in any event, within the period of twelve months beginning with the making of the assessment or, as the case may be, the previous review (EA 1993, s 172(5); see the *Code of Practice*, Part 6). Regulations are to make provision as to various matters relating to reviews of statements: the manner in which they are to be conducted, the participation of persons in them and such other matters as may be prescribed (s 172(6)). The Education (Special Educational Needs) Regulations 1994 make separate provision for review of statements of children attending school either in years in which their fourteenth birthday does not fall (reg 15) and the year in which is does (reg 16).

A review of a statement of a child *who will not attain the age of fourteen in the academic year concerned*, when required by section 172(5) (above), begins with the LEA serving a notice on the head teacher requiring him or her to send the authority a report by a specified date (not less than two months from the date of the notice) and to send a copy of the notice to the parent of the child. The head teacher's report will be based partly on the written advice (obtained from prescribed persons) on the child's progress and other matters such as the appropriateness of the statement. The head teacher must invite various persons to a meeting, to be held prior to the date by which the report must be submitted. Those who must be invited (these include the child's parent, the child's teacher(s) and other appropriate persons: see reg 15(5)) must also be sent, at least two weeks before the meeting is to be held, copies of the advice obtained by the head teacher, and they must be invited to submit written comments on the advice to him or her. The meeting must make recommendations on, for example, whether the statement should be amended or terminated and/or on any targets that should be set as to the child's progress in relation to objectives specified in the statement. The head teacher's report (see above) must be completed after the meeting and should refer to the recommendations of the meeting and the head teacher's conclusions, if different to those of the meeting. The LEA must then review the statement (under EA 1993, s 172(5)) in the light of the report and any other relevant information or advice. In some cases they must prepare a transition plan (see below). The LEA must, within one week of the review of the statement, send copies of their recommendations and any transition plan to prescribed parties (including the child's parent, the head teacher, the persons who contributed advice and persons who attended the meeting which preceded the submission of the headteacher's report). A transition plan is a plan setting out suitable arrangements for the 14–19 year-old, including not only education but also work, designed 'to facilitate a satisfactory transition from childhood to adulthood' (reg 2(1); see *Code of Practice*, paras 6:45–6:47).

Reviews (again under s 172(5)) of children *who will attain the age of fourteen during the academic year* in which the review is required to be completed are subject to a similar procedure (reg 16). The range of persons who must be invited to attend the meeting with the head teacher is, however, wider. For example, a careers officer and a representative of the social services authority are also to be invited.

There is a separate procedure for children who do not attend a school (1994 regs, *op cit*, reg 17). It is similar to the above procedures, but as the child does not attend a school the report and meeting are the responsibility of the LEA rather than a head teacher.

(h) Changes to statements

Changes to statements may be required in several different sets of circumstances.

(i) Amendment of statement on appeal

If a parent appeals under EA 1993, s 170, against the contents of the statement, the Special Educational Needs Tribunal may order the LEA to amend the statement 'so far as it describes the authority's assessment of the child's special educational needs or specifies the special educational provision' and to make 'such other consequential amendments to the statement as the Tribunal think fit' (EA 1993, s 170(3)).

(ii) Amendment of statement on revocation of school attendance order

If a parent of a statemented child who is the subject of a school attendance order asks for that order to be revoked on the ground that the parent has made suitable arrangements for the child to be educated otherwise than at school, the LEA refuses to comply with the request, and the parent refers the matter to the Secretary of State, the Secretary of State can direct the LEA to amend the statement (EA 1993, s 197).

(iii) Substitution of name of school in statement at request of parent

A parent may request that a different maintained, GM or GM special school be named in a statement. The LEA must comply with the request (and thus amend the statement accordingly) –

(i) provided it is made less than twelve months after either a previous request, or service of a copy of the statement, or receipt of notice of amendment or the conclusion of an appeal by the parent under section 170; *and*

(ii) unless the school is unsuitable having regard to the child's age, ability and aptitude or his special educational needs, or the child's attendance at the school would be incompatible with the provision of efficient education for the children with whom he would be educated or the efficient use of resources.

(EA 1993, Sch 10, para 8).

The parent has a right of appeal to the Special Educational Needs Tribunal against a refusal of the LEA to comply with the request. The Tribunal has a power to order that the school requested by the parent be substituted for the one named by the LEA in the statement (*ibid*).

There is a time limit of eight weeks, which runs from the date that the parent makes the request as to the school to be named in the statement, within which the LEA must either comply with the request, or give notice that it has decided not to do so and provide the parent with information of his or her right to appeal (reg 14(4) of the Education (Special Educational Needs) Regulations 1994).

(iv) LEA's decision to amend statement

The LEA may decide, following a review of the child's statement or following a reassessment (see above), that it should amend the statement (EA 1993, Sch 10, para 10; see *Code of Practice*, para 6:34–6:35). If it decides to do this it must inform the parent of its proposal and of the parent's right to make representations. These representations may be made within fifteen days beginning on the date on which the LEA's notice of proposed changes to the statement is served. The LEA must consider the representations. Once it has done so and made its decision it must inform the parent of that decision. Where the LEA amends the description of the child's special educational needs or the special educational provision it must give the parent notice of his or her right to appeal under section 170(1) (see below). The LEA may not amend the statement until the expiry of eight weeks from the date on which it served notice under Schedule 10, paragraph 10 (see above) of its proposal to amend the statement (reg 14(6) of the Education (Special Educational Needs) Regulations 1994).

(i) Cessation of statement

As Part III of the EA 1993 applies only to a child (as defined in s 156(5) – see p 241 above), a statement will cease to have effect when a person ceases to be one. The LEA may in any event be ordered to cease to maintain a statement by a Special Educational Needs Tribunal following an appeal under section 170(1) (EA 1993, s 170(3)(c): see below). In other circumstances the LEA may simply conclude, following, for example, a review of the child's educational needs or an assessment requested by the parents, that a statement is no longer necessary. The parent must be given notice of the LEA's proposal to cease to maintain a statement and be informed of the right to appeal to the Special Educational Needs Tribunal (but there is no specific right to make representations to the LEA) (EA 1993, Sch 10, para 11). On appeal, the tribunal can dismiss the appeal or order that the LEA continues to maintain the statement in its existing form or in an amended form (*ibid*; see 7(b)(vi) below). Regulations provide that the LEA may not cease to maintain the statement before the end of the period during which the parent may appeal to the tribunal or within four weeks from the end of that period (Education (Special Educational Needs) Regulations 1994, reg 14(7)).

7. Appeals to the Special Educational Needs Tribunal

(a) Introduction

New appeal arrangements came into operation on 1 September 1994 (although there are transitional arrangements in respect of cases or procedures in progress at that date: see *Appendix 6*, para 5). They replace a bifurcated system under which both the Secretary of State and local appeal committees (constituted and operated in the same way as LEA appeal committees with jurisdiction over school admissions and permanent exclusions) had jurisdiction. Appeals lay to the Secretary of State over a decision by an LEA not to make a statement; the Secretary of State could, if he thought fit, direct the LEA to reconsider its decision (EA 1981, s 5(7) and (8)). If, however, the appeal was brought under section 8 of the 1981 Act, in respect of the special educational provision proposed in a statement following a first or any subsequent assessment of a child, or against any amendment to an existing statement by the LEA, the appeal lay to the appeal committee, constituted under Schedule 2 to the EA 1980. The committee's decision was not binding on the LEA; the committee could only confirm the provision specified in the statement or remit the case to the LEA for reconsideration in the light of the committee's observations. Parents could appeal to the Secretary of State against the committee's decision or the LEA's decision on the remitted case. He could confirm, amend, or order the cessation of, a statement. Cases established that the Secretary of State could only consider the provision to be made (he could not look at past provision) (*R* v *Secretary of State for Education and Science ex p Davis* [1988] The Guardian, 12 December (DC)) and that he was not under an obligation to disclose to appellants details of any specialist advice he had sought on the case (for example from HMI: *R* v *Secretary of State for Education ex p S* [1994] The Times, 15 July (CA)). Although appeals to the Secretary of State under the EA 1981 more than trebled between 1984 and 1991, there were, in 1991, only 72 under section 5 and 78 under section 8 (DFE statistics).

Despite the relatively small number of appeals, delays were a common occurrence. The Audit Commission/HMI reported (*Getting In On the Act – Provision for Pupils with Special Educational Needs – the National Picture* (HMSO, 1992) para 37) that it generally took six to twelve months for appeals to be determined by the Secretary of State. The DFE concluded (in its 1992 consultation paper, *Special Educational Needs – Access to the System*) that a two-stage process for some of the appeals was unnecessary, caused delays and hindered the effectiveness of the system for appellants. The DFE explained the need for a new appeals system, especially in the light of the considerable extension of the grounds of appeal that was also proposed. In place of the previous arrangements there is now a single appeals system, involving appeals to an independent Special Educational Needs Tribunal (SENT). The DFE's Consultation Document on the SENT (*Special Educational Needs Tribunal – Consultation Paper on Draft Regulations and Rules of Procedure* (1994), Appendix B) suggested that the period from the date that the appeal is lodged until the date that the parties are informed of the tribunal's decision should, if the planned time limits are not exceeded, be no more than 130 days, but the guide, based on the Regulations, offers a timescale of 95 working days (DFE, *Special Educational Needs Tribunal, How to Appeal* (1994) (pages 18–19). (Note that provision for extending particular time limits in exceptional circumstances is made in the regulations.)

The SENT comprises a legally qualified chairman and two lay members drawn from a panel of persons with experience of special educational needs or experience of local government. Decisions of the SENT will be binding on LEAs (see below). Thus two of the other criticisms of the previous system, namely that 'local appeal committees have been unable effectively to enforce their recommendations' and that the system lacked independence, because, for example, 'those committees are established and maintained by LEAs themselves' (Consultation Paper, *op cit*, para 6), have been addressed.

The DFE emphasises that one of the objectives of the new legal regime governing special educational needs, including the *Code of Practice*, 'is to keep the number of appeals to a minimum' (*ibid*, para 9). But the number of appeals in special educational needs cases may be expected to increase under the new system, not least because of the additional grounds of appeal (see (b) below). At the same time the opportunities for judicial review may be more limited since, particularly as appeals will have to be heard within prescribed time limits, the courts may be expected to apply more strictly the principle that alternative remedies, especially statutory rights of appeal, should be pursued first (*R* v *City of Salford ex p L* [1991] (QBD) (unreported); but see *R* v *Governors of Hasmonean High School ex p N and E* [1994] ELR 343 (CA) at p 355 (Glidewell LJ) and *R* v *London Borough of Camden ex p B* [1993] 17 December (QBD) (unreported)). In *E* v *Dorset County Council; Christmas* v *Hampshire County Council*; *Keating* v *Bromley LBC* [1994] ELR 416, the Court of Appeal held that actions for breach of statutory duty in respect of alleged failures to comply with the legal requirements on special educational needs by education authorities, teachers and others, which were claimed to have resulted in damage to the children concerned, could not be sustained. The Court said that the appropriate remedy for such complaints lay through the statutory appeal structure or by way of judicial review (*per* Sir Thomas Bingham MR). It may be noted that the Court refused to strike out common law negligence actions against LEAs concerned, in respect of the LEAs' failure – more particularly that of their psychologists, teachers and officers – to ascertain learning difficulties and make appropriate provision, including advice and support. This may prove to be a landmark decision in this respect (see also *Holtom* v *London Borough of Barnet and St Christopher's School* [1993] The Times, 30 September).

(b) Jurisdiction of the SENT, under the Education Act 1993

(i) Where the LEA decides not to make a statement (s 169)

The parent of a child for whom there is no statement can appeal to the SENT when the LEA decides, following a formal statutory assessment of the child (under s 167), not to propose a statement. In such a case the SENT may dismiss the appeal (s 169(3)), order the LEA to make or maintain a statement, or remit the case to the LEA to consider whether, having regard to the SENT's observations, it should make a statement.

(ii) Where the LEA makes, amends or decides not to amend a statement (s 170)

The parent may appeal to the SENT under section 170 against:

- the description in the statement of the LEA's assessment of the child's special educational needs;
- the special educational provision specified in the statement; or
- if no school is named in the statement, that fact.

This right of appeal under section 170 arises when the LEA first makes a statement or when it amends or decides not to amend a statement. But it does not apply to amendment of a statement under Schedule 10, paragraph 8 or 11, because such amendment gives rise to a separate right of appeal under each of those paragraphs (s 170(2) – see below). Furthermore, the general right of appeal conferred by section 170 itself does not extend to a decision by the LEA to amend, or not to amend, the description in a statement, under Schedule 10, paragraph 10 (see s 170(2)). However, the separate right of appeal under that paragraph offers the parent a right of appeal under section 170 once the amendment is made (EA 1993, Sch 10, para 10(4)).

On appeal under section 170 (s 170(3)) the SENT may either:

- dismiss the appeal;
- order the LEA to amend the statement (so far as it describes the child's special educational needs or specifies the special educational provision) and make other consequential amendments to the statement as they see fit; or
- order the LEA to cease to maintain the statement.

The tribunal cannot order the LEA to specify the name of a school in the statement (or to substitute the name of the school in the statement) unless either the parent has expressed a preference for the school in pursuance of the arrangements in Schedule 10 (see p 257 above), or, in the proceedings themselves, the parent, the LEA or both have proposed the school (s 170(4)).

Any deficiency in the statement can be corrected by the tribunal before the appeal is determined, if the parties agree (s 170(5)).

(iii) Where the LEA decides not to comply with a request by a parent of a child for whom a statement is maintained that the child be further assessed (s 172)

A parent may appeal to the SENT against a refusal by the LEA to comply with his or her request to carry out a further assessment of his or her statemented child (see 5(b) above). The tribunal may dismiss the appeal or order that an assessment under section 167 be carried out (s 172(4)).

(iv) Where the LEA decides not to comply with a request, by a parent of a child for whom no statement is maintained, for the assessment of the child (s 173)

In the case of a child who has not been statemented, the parent may appeal against the LEA's decision not to comply with a request for an assessment (see 5(b) above). The tribunal may dismiss the appeal or order the LEA to carry out an assessment under section 167 (s 173(3)).

(v) Where the LEA decides not to comply with a request by a parent of a child for whom there is a statement, specifying the name of a school, for the name of a different school to be substituted (Sch 10, para 8)

If the parent's request for a different school to be specified in a statement in place of the one included in it is turned down, the parent may appeal to the SENT (EA 1993, Sch 10, para 8(3)(b)) (see p 261 above). On appeal the tribunal may either dismiss the appeal or order the LEA to comply with the parent's request as to the school to be named in the statement.

(vi) Where the LEA decides to cease to maintain a statement (Sch 10, para 11)

LEAs may cease to maintain a statement where they consider that the statement is no longer 'necessary' (see 6(i)). A parent may appeal against the LEA's decision to the SENT, which may either dismiss the appeal or order that the LEA continues to maintain the statement in its existing form or in an amended form ('with such amendments of the description in the statement of the authority's assessment of the child's special educational needs or the special educational provision specified in the statement, and such other consequential amendments, as the Tribunal may determine': Sch 10, para 11(3)).

(c) Constitution of the SENT

There is a SENT President (EA 1993, s 177(2)(a) (presently Trevor Aldridge QC)), appointed by the Lord Chancellor (s 177(3)) from among persons with a seven-year general qualification for the purposes of the Courts and Legal Services Act 1990 (EA 1993, s 178(1); generally this means a solicitor or barrister of seven years' standing, but persons who qualified professionally after January 1991 have to have held a right of audience in the higher courts for at least seven years). Separate panels of chairmen and lay members must be appointed (s 177(2)(b) and (c)). A chairman must be appointed by the Lord Chancellor from among persons with a seven-year general qualification (s 177(3) and 178(1)). Lay members must be appointed by the Secretary of State (s 177(4)). A person is not eligible for appointment as a lay member unless he or she satisfies the prescribed requirements (s 178(2)).

To be eligible for *appointment* as a lay member, to the lay panel, a person must have knowledge and experience in respect of children with special educational needs or in respect of local government (Special Educational Needs Tribunals Regulations 1994, reg 3).

The Secretary of State has a power to pay remuneration and expenses to persons who serve on the tribunal (EA 1993, s 179). The President, chairmen and lay members may resign and shall be eligible for re-appointment if they cease to hold office (EA 1993, s 178(5)).

The tribunal for any hearing must consist of a chairman and two members of the lay panel; but if one of the lay members is absent the appeal may, with the consent of both parties at the hearing, be heard by the chairman and the other member (SENT Regs, *op cit*, regs 5(1) and 29(5)). The chairman for each hearing must be either the President or a member of the chairman's panel (reg 5(2)).

The SENT Office has a Secretary (see SENT Regs, *op cit*, reg 2). The SENT Secretary is 'responsible for the day to day management of its business' (DFE, *Special Educational Needs Tribunal – Consultation Paper on Draft Regulations and Rules of Procedure* (1994), para 17). His or her functions may be carried out by other persons authorised by the President (reg 39). Administration is to be centralised, with a small secretariat of seconded civil servants from the DFE based at the Office of the Tribunal in central London. Clerks for individual tribunal hearings will be drawn from this secretariat (*ibid*) and will be appointed for this purpose by the

Secretary (see reg 2 of the SENT Regs). At present there are no plans for regional offices of the SENT, presumably because the overall number of appeals is considered unlikely to be sufficient to warrant them. However, persons appointed to chairmen's and members' panels will be expected to serve in Wales or particular English regions. The consultation paper stated that the idea is that tribunal members will have regional knowledge and face reduced travelling time. It will also help to minimise costs (Consultation Paper, *op cit*, para 21). Tribunals 'will sit, as and when required, in places which are easily accessible to both the parents and the LEA', normally 'within a few miles of the parents' home' if suitable accommodation is available (*ibid*). But the procedural guide (*Special Educational Needs Tribunal – How to Appeal* (1994)) merely states that the hearing will take place 'as near to your home as we can arrange', with all London and South-East cases being heard in the SENT headquarters in Central London (page 12).

SENTs fall under the direct supervision of the Council on Tribunals under the Tribunals and Inquiries Act 1992 (EA 1993, s 181(1)).

(d) Procedure

Rules of procedure for SENTs, made under the power in section 180 of the EA 1993, are laid down in the Special Educational Needs Tribunal Regulations 1994 (SI 1994 No 1910). The rules are detailed, in marked contrast to the procedural requirements governing the operation of the local appeal committees hearing appeals under the EA 1981. All references below are to the 1994 regulations, unless indicated otherwise. There is also a procedural guide, published by the DFE: *Special Educational Needs Tribunal – How to Appeal* (1994), to which reference is also made.

(i) Prior to the hearing

The appeal process begins with the appellant delivering to the Secretary of the Tribunal a signed notice of appeal. The Secretary must enter details of it in the records, acknowledge its receipt (giving the correspondence address of the SENT and Secretary) and inform the appellant that advice on the appeal may be obtained from the SENT Office (reg 17(1)(a) and (b)). To be effective the notice must contain the required information, be accompanied by the prescribed documents (see below) and be received by the Secretary not later than the first working day after the expiry of two months from the date on which the LEA gave the appellant notice that he or she could appeal (reg 7). The various circumstances in which the LEA must give information on the right of appeal were discussed earlier.

The notice of appeal must state that it is such a notice and must include the name and address of the appellant, the name of the child, the name of the LEA whose decision is being appealed against and the date that the parent was notified of the decision. The notice must also state the grounds of the appeal (reg 7(1)(a)). It must be accompanied (as appropriate) by a copy of the LEA's notice of the decision under dispute and a copy of the statement of special educational needs (reg 7(1)(b)). The appellant may also give details of any representative to whom the tribunal should send notices or replies (reg 7(1)(c)). Doing so does not preclude the parent from selecting or changing a representative and notifying the tribunal accordingly (reg 11(1)–(2)).

The LEA must be sent a copy of the notice of appeal (if it was delivered within the time limit or a time extension was granted by the President under reg 42) by the SENT Office. The Office must also supply to the LEA copies of papers accompanying the notice and state the SENT's and the Secretary's correspondence address: see reg 17(1)(b). The LEA may deliver a written reply, which must be sent to the appellant by the Office (see below). The appellant is entitled to deliver a written response to the LEA's reply within 15 working days of receiving it (reg 8(1)–(2)). In addition, the appellant is entitled, in 'exceptional circumstances', to amend the notice of appeal or the LEA's response to it, or to deliver or amend a supplementary notice of appeal, provided he or she delivers the relevant amendment (etc) to the SENT Secretary before the hearing (reg 8(4)). Permission to make the amendment or to lodge a supplementary notice must be obtained from the President, at any time before the hearing, or from the tribunal at the actual hearing (reg 8(3)).

The appellant must supply further information requested by the Secretary, relating to such as matters as whether he or she intends to attend the hearing, be represented (and if so by whom) and call witnesses at it, will require an interpreter for him or herself or for a witness, and wishes the hearing to be held in public (regs 10(1) and 18(a)). The appellant must also be asked for the name of any person he or she wishes to admit to the hearing if it is to be in private (reg 18(b)).

If the appellant indicates that he or she will not be attending or be represented at the hearing, he or she may supply written representations to the Secretary, for the tribunal's consideration, provided that this is done not less than five working days before the hearing (reg 10(2)).

The appellant may withdraw his or her appeal at the hearing or by written notice to the Secretary in advance of the hearing (reg 9).

Turning to the LEA, once it receives the appellant's notice of appeal it must acknowledge service by SENT Office. The authority must, in so doing, state whether it intends to oppose the appeal. If it does intend to oppose it must state the grounds. The authority must also state its address for service of papers and the name and profession of its representative (reg 12(1)). A summary of the facts relating to the disputed decision and any separate reasons for the disputed decision must also be provided to the tribunal by the LEA (reg 12(2)). All this must be delivered to the tribunal within 20 working days after the date on which a copy of the appellant's notice of appeal was received (reg 12(3)). The LEA must also supply to the Secretary the same type of information (about witnesses, whether the hearing should be public etc) which may be requested of appellants under regulation 18 (see above) (reg 16(2)).

If the LEA considers that the SENT lacks jurisdiction to hear the appeal, it may serve notice to that effect on the Secretary, stating grounds (reg 14(1)). This must then be sent to the appellant by the Secretary (reg 14(2)). The tribunal can consider the LEA's contention regarding jurisdiction as a preliminary point of law or at the beginning of the appeal hearing itself (reg 14(3)). It should be noted that provision is made for the Secretary to notify the appellant where the Secretary considers that the tribunal is being asked to do something that it cannot do (see reg 17(2)).

An LEA's failure to reply in time or its indication that it does not oppose the appeal does not mean that the appellant will succeed purely by default. The tribunal may either determine the appeal on the basis of the notice without a hearing, or may (without notifying the LEA) hold a hearing at which the LEA is not represented (reg 15).

Provision is made for directions to be issued by the President, of his own motion or at a party's request (regs 19–22). These may include directions for the provision of further particulars or supplementary statements and the disclosure of documents and other material – 'such discovery or inspection of documents (including the taking of copies) as might be granted by a county court' (reg 22(2)). The parties may also apply for the issuing of witness summonses by the President; a summons will require any identified person in England and Wales to attend and answer questions or produce documents etc (reg 23).

Various powers arise where there is a failure to comply with directions within the specified time. The tribunal may proceed to hold a hearing at which the person in default is not represented, dismiss the appeal without a hearing (if it is the appellant who is in default) or hold a hearing without notifying the LEA (if it is in default) (reg 24).

The Secretary must fix the time and place of the hearing 'with due regard to the convenience of the parties' (reg 25(1)) (on location, see further (c) above). Generally the notice of the hearing must be delivered at least ten working days in advance. The Secretary must include with the notice various information and guidance on prescribed aspects of procedure, including information on the right to representation and assistance and on the consequences of non-attendance (reg 25(2)). In some circumstances the hearing date can be altered at relatively short notice (reg 25(4)). Provision is made for the proceedings to be transferred to another tribunal where it is more convenient (reg 35).

Note that proceedings may be struck out at any time on the application of the President or the LEA, on the grounds of lack of jurisdiction, or that the appeal or appeal notice is 'scandalous, frivolous or vexatious', or want of prosecution (reg 37(1)). An opportunity must be provided for representations to be made by the appellant (reg 37(2) and (5)). The President can also order that a response or statement should be struck out because it is scandalous (etc) (reg 37(3)). Again opportunities to make representations must be afforded (reg 37(4) and (5)).

(ii) At the hearing

A party who will not be attending or be represented at the hearing may send the Secretary additional representations in support of their appeal/reply, provided this is done at least five working days before the hearing (regs 10(2) and 16(3)). Where a party fails to attend or be represented at a hearing of which he or she has been properly notified the tribunal can adjourn the case or hear and determine the appeal in the party's absence (giving consideration in such a case to the written submissions, notice and reply etc), 'unless it is satisfied that there is sufficient reason for such absence' (reg 28(1)). Alternatively, the tribunal may adjourn the hearing (*ibid*; see also the general power in reg 25(5) at p 271 below). In either case the tribunal can make 'such order as to costs and expenses as it thinks fit' (*ibid*). Costs are discussed below in (*iii*).

The appellant and the LEA may each be represented by one person at the hearing, although permission may be sought for representation by more than one person (regs 11(3) and 16(1)). Such permission must be obtained either from the President before the hearing or from the tribunal at the hearing itself. So far as legal representation is concerned, the Regulations state that a party may be represented by a person whether that person is 'legally qualified or not' (regs 11(3) and 16(1)). It should be borne in mind, however, that legal aid will not be available, although the appellant may be able to obtain advice and assistance (including the preparation and submission of the notice of appeal and written representations) under the Green Form scheme. The DFE's view is that 'the use of lawyers be kept to a minimum' (*Special Educational Needs Tribunal – Consultation Paper on Draft Regulations and Rules of Procedure* (1994), para 36). One possibility it discusses is for 'concordats' under which LEAs would agree to dispense with legal representation at a hearing if appellants did so. However, there is clearly a risk that parents could be put, or at least feel, under pressure to dispense with legal representation, when doing so could ultimately be prejudicial to their case.

The procedural guide (*op cit*, p 10) advises appellants that 'Neither you nor the LEA should need a legal representative, as the hearing will be straightforward and the tribunal members will not use legal jargon'. It is submitted that contrary to this suggestion, legal issues will arise quite frequently and that legal skills may in any event be needed in cases where the evidential issues may be difficult.

Hearings will be in private unless either both of the parties request a public hearing or the tribunal deems that there should be one (reg 27(1)). Nevertheless, various persons, in addition to the parties and representatives, are entitled to attend (reg 27(2)):

- persons named in advance by the appellants (in response to the enquiry made prior to the hearing by the Secretary (see above));
- a parent of a child who is not a party to the appeal (note that he or she may be permitted to address the tribunal: see reg 27(7));
- the clerk to the tribunal and the SENT Secretary;*
- the President and any member of the chairmen's or lay panel (observing rather than sitting as a member of the panel);*
- a member of the Council on Tribunals;*

- any person undergoing training as a tribunal member or chairman or as a clerk to the tribunal;*
- any person acting on behalf of the President in the training or supervision of clerks to tribunals;
- an interpreter.

(Persons in the categories marked (*) are the only persons, apart from the members of the tribunal, who may be present when the tribunal is deliberating and reaching its decision.)

The tribunal may, with the consent of the parties or their representatives, permit any other person to attend the private hearing (reg 27(3)). The tribunal also has a power to exclude from the hearing any person whose conduct has disrupted, or is likely, in the tribunal's opinion, to disrupt, the hearing (reg 27(4)).

The tribunal decides the order in which the parties are heard and the issues determined (reg 29(3)). The tribunal chairman must explain the order of proceedings which the tribunal proposes to adopt; he or she must do this at the beginning of the hearing (reg 29(1)). The consultation document (*op cit* para 39) suggested that the hearing should be conducted under an 'informal and flexible' procedure. Thus the Regulations require the tribunal to 'conduct the hearing in such a manner as it considers most suitable to the clarification of the issues and generally to the just handling of the proceedings' (reg 29(2)); and they also state that the hearing should, so far as appears appropriate, be conducted in a way that avoids formality (reg 29(2)). The tribunal has a power to enable a party to raise at the hearing issues not referred to in the notice, reply or response and to adduce evidence not presented to the LEA at the time it reached the decision which is being challenged (reg 29(4)). Subject to the provisions of the 1993 Act and the Regulations, the tribunal has the power to regulate its own procedure (reg 36(1)).

If the tribunal is, after the commencement of the hearing, one member (other than the chairman) short, the hearing may be conducted by the two members present, whose decision should not be invalidated by being taken by them alone (reg 29(5)).

The tribunal may require evidence to be given on oath or affirmation or may require written evidence to be given by affidavit (reg 30(4)). The parties may give oral evidence, call up to two witnesses (or more, if the President has given prior permission) and question each other's witnesses as well as their own (reg 30(1)). The child whose education is at issue is not a party to the proceedings but may be called as a witness. The procedural guide (*op cit* p 11) advises parents thus:

> 'Your child does not have to attend the hearing. But if you or your child want his or her views to be taken into account separately from your own views, your child can attend the hearing and answer questions as a witness, or make a written statement'.

The length of time a hearing will last will obviously vary from one case to the next. The procedural guide (*op cit* p 14) states that most hearings will last for no more than half a day.

The tribunal has a power (reg 26) to determine a case without a hearing if the parties agree in writing to this or in certain cases of default by the parties (regs 15 and 24 – see above). It also has a general power to adjourn a hearing (reg 25(5); see also the power in reg 28(1) at p 269 above).

(iii) Deliberation and decision

Only the clerk or an interpreter may take part in the deliberations of the tribunal (reg 27(6)), and this should be a limited, technical involvement only, as the decision is the tribunal's alone. The tribunal decides by majority; in the case of a two-member panel, the chairman will have a second or casting vote (reg 31(1)). The tribunal's decision must be recorded in writing in a document with an annexed or incorporated statement of reasons (in summary form) (reg 31(2)). For no clear reason the Regulations state that neither the fact that a decision was by majority nor the minority reasons must be referred to in the record (reg 31(3)). A separate record of the decision must be kept (reg 31(4)).

The decision may be given orally at the end of the hearing or may be reserved (reg 31(2)). As soon as practicable the document (decision plus reasons) must be sent to each party along with guidance on the right of further appeal (to the High Court) and the procedure involved (reg 31(5)).

The Regulations permit the tribunal to make orders for costs and expenses in certain circumstances, although they state that 'the tribunal shall not normally make [such an] order' (reg 34(1)). These circumstances are where the conduct of a party in relation to the proceedings has been vexatious or frivolous or where 'his or her conduct in making, pursuing or resisting an appeal was wholly unreasonable' (reg 34(1)(a)). The tribunal can also make an order against an LEA which has not replied to the notice of appeal or where the LEA's decision which is disputed was 'wholly unreasonable' (reg 34(1)(b) and (c)) (as to what counts as costs and expenses, see reg 34(2)). An order may not be made until the parties have been given an opportunity to make representations against the making of it (reg 34(3)). Provision is made for taxation of costs in the county court (reg 34(5)).

The procedural guide (*op cit* p 16) explains that neither party will normally have to pay any costs, but that they may be required to do so '(i)n very exceptional circumstances, if the tribunal thinks that [they] have acted unreasonably, or deliberately wasted the tribunal's time'. Unfortunately, this reassurance could actually leave some parents anxious as to possible liability for costs and deter potential appellants. It should be borne in mind that people often fail to appeal to tribunals in general, despite in reality having good grounds for appealing, because they do not want to cause trouble or waste a tribunal's time. Nevertheless, to be accurate, the guide obviously had to point out the possibility of liability for costs.

(iv) Review and correction of errors

The tribunal may review its decision (on the application of a party or of its own motion) on prescribed grounds (reg 32):

- the decision was wrongly made as a result of an error by tribunal staff;
- a party who had been entitled to be heard at the hearing but had failed to attend or be represented, had had good and sufficient reason for not appearing;
- the interests of justice require.

An application for review may be refused by the President or the chairman of the tribunal which decided the case if, in his or her opinion, the application has no reasonable chance of success (reg 32(3)). The review shall, where practicable, be determined by the tribunal which decided the case (reg 32(4)). In consequence of the review, the chairman may by certificate set aside or vary the decision (reg 32(1)). Decisions of the President in relation to a case (for example, on whether to permit a party more than two witnesses) may also be reviewed – by the President – on the grounds that the decision was wrongly made because of an error by tribunal staff or where the interest of justice so require (reg 33).

There is separate provision for correction of errors in documents recording decisions of the tribunal or President or the President's direction(s) in a case, and for curing or waiving irregularities resulting from failure to comply with the Regulations or any direction (see reg 40).

(e) Appeal from SENTs to the High Court

There is a right of appeal on a point of law to the High Court against the decision of a SENT (Tribunals and Inquiries Act 1992, s 11(1), as amended by EA 1993, s 181(2)).

8. Special educational needs and the National Curriculum

(a) The general approach

The Government's policy is that *all* pupils, including those with special educational needs, should have the opportunity of benefiting from the National Curriculum. There can be no departure from the duty, in ERA 1988, s 1, to offer a balanced and broadly based curriculum to all pupils, including those with special educational needs. This was emphasised in the National Curriculum Council's guidance on special educational needs in the National Curriculum (*A Curriculum for All* (1989)). The *Code of Practice on Special Educational Needs* (*op cit*, para 4:8) emphasises that a statement should give 'details as to how a broad, balanced curriculum is to be maintained'.

In certain situations, however, exception from the National Curriculum will be necessary, especially for pupils with statements (see (b) below). The general power in section 17 of the ERA 1988 to prescribe modification or non-application of all or part of the National Curriculum has not been applied specifically to children with special educational needs (see p 196), despite the suggestion made by the DES in its 1989 Circular on special educational needs assessments and statements (Circular 22/89, *Assessments and Statements of Special Educational Needs: Procedures within the Education, Health and Social Services* (1989)) that there were situations where general exception would be desirable:

> 'For example, where the National Curriculum requirements would involve certain kinds of physical or practical work, alternative arrangements might be prescribed for those whose physical disabilities could put at risk their own safety or that of others. Such arrangements might apply to pupils with or without statements'.

Exception in other circumstances has, however, been provided for (see (b) below).

(b) Exception from the National Curriculum

(i) Temporary exception

Under section 19 of the ERA 1988, temporary exception in individual cases may be ordered by head teachers, in circumstances prescribed by regulations: see the Education (National Curriculum) (Temporary Exceptions for Individual Pupils) Regulations 1989. So far as special educational needs are concerned, a head teacher may make such an order, in the form of a 'special direction', on the ground that it is for the time being inappropriate for a child to follow the prescribed National Curriculum, and that the National Curriculum should be modified in his or her case while he or she is being assessed for special educational needs or while a statement is being prepared. The circular on these regulations (DES, Circular 15/89, *Education Reform Act 1988: Temporary Exceptions from the National Curriculum* (1989), para 17) states, however, that:

> 'a special direction will not always be necessary when a head teacher refers a pupil for assessment. Head teachers should consider in each case if there is a clear case for a direction, and should not assume that this will be the case or prejudge the outcome of the assessment procedures'.

(ii) Exception specified in a statement

Section 18 of the ERA 1988 provides that the special educational provision specified in a statement under section 168 of the EA 1993:

> 'may include provision–
>
> (*a*) excluding the application of the provisions of the National Curriculum; or
>
> (*b*) applying those provisions with such modifications as may be specified in the statement'.

Such modifications will be set out in Part 3 of the statement. As from September 1995, statements will no longer have to include modification of the National Curriculum to enable a child to pursue studies at a lower level on the ten point scale (used for assessment under the National Curriculum and to be changed following the Dearing report: see pp 194–195) than that which applies to most of the pupils who are working within the same key stage (see *Code of Practice*, para 4:28).

Chapter 10

School inspections and 'special measures'

1. Introduction

Prior to the Education (Schools) Act (ESA) 1992 formal school inspections were the responsibility of Her Majesty's Inspectorate of Schools (HMI). LEAs also carried out inspections of schools (under the power in s 77(3) of the Education Act 1944). Dissatisfied with the scale of the school inspection system (for example, only 150 of the 24,000 schools in England and Wales were receiving formal HMI inspections each year) and with aspects of HMI's *modus operandi*, the Government pushed through quite fundamental reforms via the 1992 Act. The first important change has been to make the office of Chief Inspector (CI) statutory. The CI (there are in fact two, one for England and one for Wales) may be appointed by the Secretary of State for up to five years at a time and must provide advice to the Secretary of State and monitor and review the conduct of school inspections and standards being achieved in schools (ESA 1992, ss 2 and 5). The CI's office has been given by the Government the non-statutory title of the Office for Standards in Education (OFSTED). The role of OFSTED and the CI and the appointment of Her Majesty's Inspectors were discussed briefly in Chapter 1. A new CI for England, in place of Stewart Sutherland, was appointed from 1 September 1994: Christopher Anthony Woodhead (The Education (Chief Inspector of Schools in England) Order 1994, SI 1994 No 1633).

A major part of the CI's role involves ensuring that schools are inspected at prescribed intervals – once every four years in England and once every five years in Wales (see below). One important function involves the maintenance of the register of school inspectors (registered inspectors, or RIs). School inspections must generally be carried out by RIs under section 9 of the 1992 Act (these are known in the legislation as 'section 9 inspections': EA 1993, s 204(2)). The important point about the RI system is that it enables private individuals to become involved in school inspections, either as RIs or as inspection team members. RIs contract with the Office of the CI to carry out inspections, and so the system has thus been largely privatised. However, the 1992 Act also empowers the Chief Inspector to arrange for inspections by one or more members of HMI (under sections 3(1) and 7(1)) and empowers the Secretary of State to order HMI to inspect a school (ss 2(2)(b) and 6(2)(b)).

Despite quite severe reservations about the RI system expressed at the time the ESA 1992 was progressing through Parliament, a report by Coopers and Lybrand (*A Focus on Quality* (OFSTED, 1994)) has concluded that the new system 'has made a remarkably good start' (para 89), although improvements are needed in the standard of the written reports and summaries (para 90). Nevertheless, OFSTED is believed to favour streamlining of primary school inspections in the face of a growing backlog (see *The Times*, 26 September 1994).

A separate system of inspection of denominational religious education has also been established under the 1992 Act (see s 13 and Sch 2 Pt II) (see below).

LEAs retain a power of inspection of schools they maintain, but the 1992 Act has circumscribed it (ESA 1992, s 15). They may also offer a 'school inspection service', on a full costs basis, providing inspections for schools in their area, whether or not maintained by them (ESA 1992, s 14).

The 1992 Act has placed an onus on governing bodies to formulate plans for remedial action if there is a damning report on the school by the inspectors. However, under changes introduced under Part V of the EA 1993, matters have now been taken a significant stage further. The powers to ensure that problems are put right had, according to the Government, previously been too limited (White Paper, *Choice and Diversity*, para 11.5).

2. Section 9 inspections

The majority of school inspections are to be carried out by RIs under section 9 of the 1992 Act. RIs must be assisted by an inspection team (see below).

(a) Registered inspectors

The Chief Inspector maintains the register of inspectors and may not register a person unless 'it appears to him that that person (a) is a fit and proper person for discharging the functions of a registered inspector and (b) will be capable of conducting inspections under this Act competently and effectively' (ESA 1992, s 10(3)). Registration may be granted with or without conditions or it may be refused (s 10(5) and (6)). A person's registration may be terminated if the CI is satisfied that the inspector is no longer a fit and proper person to carry out the role of inspector, or is no longer capable of conducting inspections competently and effectively, or has significantly failed to comply with any conditions attached to his or her registration, or has knowingly or recklessly produced a report of an inspection which is, in whole or in part, seriously misleading (ESA 1992, s 11(2)). Conditions of registration may be varied (s 11(3)). There is a right of appeal (s 12(1)) against the imposition or variation of conditions attached to registration, a refusal to renew a registration and the removal of an RI's name from the register. Appeal lies to a tribunal consisting of a chairman (a lawyer with a seven-year general qualification for the purposes of s 71 of the Courts and Legal Services Act 1990, appointed by the Lord Chancellor) and two others (for whom there are no prescribed qualifications, appointed by the Secretary of State) (see ESA 1992, Sch 3; see also the Education (Registered Inspectors of Schools Appeal Tribunal) (Procedure) Regulations 1994, SI 1994 No 717). A person cannot (save in prescribed circumstances) conduct an inspection of a school unless he or she has completed an approved training course (ESA 1992, Sch 2, paras 4 and 5).

(b) Inspection teams

School inspections under section 9 must (apart from where they are carried out by HMI: see EA 1993, s 205) be 'conducted by a registered inspector with the assistance of a team (an "inspection team") consisting of persons who are fit and proper persons for carrying out the inspection' (ESA 1992, Sch 2, para 3(1)). The selection of team members is the responsibility of the RI. He or she must ensure that at least one member of the team has *no* personal experience in the management of a school or the provision of education in a school (other than as a governor or in a voluntary capacity) and 'whose primary function on the team is not that of providing financial or business expertise'; 'insignificant' experience can be ignored for this purpose (*ibid*, para 3(4)). The RI must also ensure that the inspection team should not include anyone who has, or has had at any time, any connection with:

(*a*) the school in question;
(*b*) any person who is employed at the school;
(*c*) any person who is a member of the school's governing body; or
(*d*) the proprietor of the school (in the case of an independent school) (para 3(5)).

(c) Section 9 inspections by HMI

If the CI is satisfied that it is not reasonably practicable for a section 9 inspection to be carried out by an RI, he must ensure that it is carried out by a member of HMI (EA 1993, s 205(1)). In any event, where the Chief Inspector arranges for HMI to inspect a school (under the power in ESA 1992, ss 3(1) and 7(1)), or where an inspection of a school by HMI has been carried out on the order of the Secretary of State (ESA 1992, ss 2(2)(b) and 6(2)(b)), the inspection must be treated as though it were a section 9 inspection by an RI (EA 1993, s 205(2) and (3)).

(d) Schools presently covered by section 9

Inspections must be carried out in the following categories of school:

- county;
- voluntary;
- special;
- grant-maintained;

- independent schools approved for children with statements;
- city technology colleges;
- city colleges for the technology of the arts; and
- maintained nursery schools.

(e) Frequency of section 9 inspections

The 1992 Act provides that inspections must be carried out at such intervals as may be prescribed. All English secondary schools must be inspected at any time between 1 September 1993 and 31 July 1997 (inclusive) and thereafter within four school years from the end of the school year during which last inspection took place. Other English schools must receive their first inspection under the 1992 Act between 1 September 1994 and 31 July 1998, with subsequent inspections within the next four years, as in the case of secondary schools (Education (School Inspection) (No 2) Regulations 1993 (SI 1993 No 1986), reg 4). In Wales, where the maximum interval between school inspections is five years, the first inspection for each secondary school must occur between 1 September 1993 and 31 July 1998 and, where all other Welsh schools are concerned, between 1 September 1994 and 31 August 1999 (Education (School Inspection) (Wales) (No 2) Regulations 1993 (SI 1993 No 1982), reg 4). Schools which were or are likely to be at risk of failing to deliver an acceptable standard of education have been targeted for early coverage under the new inspection regime.

(f) Pre-inspection procedure

A wide range of bodies (including, in prescribed cases, the LEA, funding authority, persons who appoint foundation or core governors, the local TEC and selected employers) must, so far as is practicable, be informed of the time when the inspection will take place (ESA 1992, Sch 2 para 6(a)(ii) and the English and Welsh Inspection (No 2) Regulations *op cit*, reg 5 in each). Such steps as are reasonably practicable must also be taken to notify parents and pupils (ESA 1992, Sch 2, para 6(a)(i)).

In addition, in every case a meeting between parents and inspectors must be held (*ibid*). Responsibility for arranging the meeting generally rests with the governing body. The School Inspection Regulations for England and Wales (*op cit*) provide that this meeting must be held at a time before the inspection is to begin. In selecting the time and place of the meeting regard must be had to the convenience of parents. Three weeks' notice of the meeting must be given to parents if possible. The only persons who may be present at this meeting are the RI and inspection team and persons they require for administrative or clerical support, parents (or an appropriate officer of the local authority if a pupil is in care), an officer of the FEFC or LEA, in the case of a pupil attending a special school whose fees they are paying, and any member of HMI who is monitoring the inspection itself.

(g) Content of inspection

The 1992 Act says very little about the content of inspections. It merely requires the RI to report on 'the quality of education provided'; 'the educational standards achieved'; 'whether financial resources . . . are managed efficiently'; and 'the spiritual, moral, social and cultural development of pupils' (ESA 1992, s 9(4)). Nevertheless, all inspectors must, as a condition of their registration, conduct the inspection in accordance with the *Framework for the Inspection of Schools* laid down by the CI. This spells out the wide range of factors to be considered in the evaluation. There is also a *Handbook for the Inspection of Schools*, which runs to 500 pages, prepared by OFSTED. The RI's report will need to focus on: the curriculum; teaching and assessment; special educational needs and provision; equal opportunities; discipline; welfare; accommodation; parental and community links; and so on. Teaching will be observed and rated; each session observed will be evaluated using a standard form. Pupils' achievement will be monitored.

Section 9 inspections, other than those by a member of HMI, must be carried out within prescribed time limits (EA 1993, s 208(1) and (2)). The regulations (*op cit*) set a time limit of two weeks.

3. After a section 9 inspection: reports and action plans

It is important to bear in mind that the provisions of Schedule 2 to the 1992 Act which deal with the aftermath of an inspection no longer apply to county, voluntary, maintained special, and grant-maintained schools (nor do they apply to the new category of school created by the 1993 Act: grant-maintained special schools). Instead, sections 206–210 of the 1993 Act apply. As these (detailed) provisions therefore apply to the majority of schools it is intended to focus on them rather than on the parallel provisions in the 1992 Act.

The way that the matter proceeds after an inspection will depend on whether it is concluded that 'special measures' are required to be taken in relation to the school. The 1993 Act states that such measures are required 'if the school is failing or likely to fail to give its pupils an acceptable standard of education' (s 204(3)) (see below).

(a) The inspection report

A registered inspector must prepare a full report and summary following an inspection. If the inspector has concluded that 'special measures are required' he or she must submit a draft of the report to the CI (EA 1993, s 206(2)). The CI must then inform the inspector whether or not he or she agrees with the inspector's opinion (s 206(4)). One of the consequences where the CI disagrees with the inspector's conclusion is that the report must contain a statement of the CI's disagreement (s 206(5)–(7)). If the section 9 inspection follows an earlier inspection in which it was concluded by the CI or (if the inspection was carried out by HMI) HMI that special measures were needed, but this time the section 9 inspector does not consider this to be the case, the report must contain the inspector's opinion (s 206(8)).

Where a school inspection is carried out by a member of HMI who concludes that 'special measures' are needed, that report must state this conclusion. If the member of HMI is not of this opinion but a previous report concluded that special measures were needed, and that report was by HMI or the CI agreed with the conclusion, the report must state HMI's view that special measures are not needed (EA 1993, s 207).

All reports of section 9 inspections must be completed within the prescribed period of time (EA 1993, s 208(1) and (2)), set at five weeks (or, in Wales, seven weeks if a Welsh translation in is needed) (School Inspection Regulations *op cit*, reg 7(2) of each). As under the 1992 Act, the deadline may be extended by up to three months by the CI (EA 1993, s 208(2) and (3)).

There is provision (EA 1993, s 209) for dissemination of reports and summaries. The Secretary of State must be sent all reports where the CI or member of HMI is indicating that special measures are needed in relation to the school. He must also be sent all reports relating to GM and GM special schools. There is also provision for the CI (unless the report was by a member of HMI), head teachers, schools and LEAs to receive inspection reports. Other recipients should include, in relevant cases, persons who appoint foundation governors for the school, any sponsors of the school and persons entitled to appoint an externally appointed core governor. Dissemination to parents, and public access, are also provided for.

(b) Action plan

As under Schedule 2 to the 1992 Act, the EA 1993 imposes a duty on the 'appropriate authority' to respond to a report by preparing a written statement of any action they propose to take in the light of the report and the period of time within which they propose to take it (EA 1993, s 210(1)). If the school is a county, voluntary or maintained special school the appropriate authority is the school's governing body, unless the school does not have a delegated budget, in which case it will be the LEA. In the case of GM and GM special schools, the appropriate authority is always the governing body. Usually the statement (referred to as an 'action plan') must be prepared within a prescribed period (s 210(2)). The prescribed period, which runs basically from the date of receipt of the inspection report, is forty days (or, in Wales, forty-five days if a Welsh translation is needed) (School Inspection Regulations *op cit*, reg 7(3)). However, in certain cases of urgency the Secretary of State can require it to be completed in a shorter period (s 210(2)). As under the 1992 Act, there is a requirement to send copies of the statement to various persons (s 210 (3)–(5)), including the CI, LEA, governors, parents and any 'other persons . . . prescribed' (includes all persons employed at the school). These persons must be sent a copy of it within five days of its completion, or, if the report indicated that special measures were needed in respect of the school and the report was by HMI or the CI agreed with the inspector's conclusion as to the need for such measures, within two days of the statement's completion or forty-two days from when the report was received (whichever occurs first) (School Inspection Regulations, *op cit*, reg 7(4) and (5), as substituted by the Education (School Inspection (No 2) (Amendment) Regulations 1993 (SI 1993 No 2973); see also (Same) (Wales) Regulations 1993 (SI 1993 No 2968)). In the case of a GM or GM special school, the Secretary of State is also to receive a copy (EA 1993, s 210(3)(c)).

The 1992 Act was fairly vague as to what should happen to ensure that the appropriate authority's plan of action was implemented. It made provision for monitoring by prescribed persons and reporting on progress made. LEAs could exercise powers under the Education Reform Act 1988 to suspend the right to a delegated budget if the governing body was mismanaging the school's finances. But, as the White Paper pointed out, there was little scope for effective local action to secure that governors were compelled to rectify serious problems identified by the inspector (*Choice and Diversity*, *op cit*, para 11.5). LEAs have now been given a power to appoint additional governors and enhanced powers to suspend a delegated budget (see below). Provision is made for monitoring any action taken under an action plan in response to a finding that special measures are needed, and for reporting on such action (EA 1993, s 212).

(c) Additional special measures by the LEA

The LEA has to consider what special measures it needs to take in relation to any school with a delegated budget which has been identified as requiring special measures (as confirmed, in the case of an inspection which was not carried out by HMI, by the CI) (EA 1993, s 211). This duty in effect arises when the LEA receives the governing body's statement of the action it proposes to take in the light of an inspector's report (see above). The LEA must prepare a statement of proposed action or of its reasons for not taking any action, and must send it to prescribed persons within ten days (or such shorter period as the Secretary of State directs because of the urgency of the situation) (EA 1993, s 211(3) and the School Inspection Regulations, *op cit*, reg 7(6) in each case).

4. Particular action and prohibitions in respect of schools requiring special measures

(a) Introduction

The powers and prohibitions below apply only to county schools, voluntary schools and (but only in respect of (i)–(iv) below) maintained special schools. They are as follows:

(i) the appointment of additional governors by the LEA;

(ii) suspension of the right to a delegated budget by the LEA;

(iii) a power to bring to an end a grouping of schools, and prohibition against a school joining a group;

(iv) a prohibition on balloting parents on GM status for the school;
(v) an order that overall control be given to an Education Association.

(b) General conditions

The *basic* conditions for each of (i)–(iv) (above) only are (EA 1993, s 213):

(*a*) that the inspector stated in his or her school inspection report that special measures were needed; and
(*b*) the inspector was a member of HMI or the CI agreed with his or her opinion; and
(*c*) the school has not been given the all-clear by a subsequent inspection; and
(*d*) the Secretary of State has not appointed an Education Association to have responsibility for the school (see pp 283–286 below).

In relation to bringing in an Education Association, general conditions (*a*)–(*c*) apply plus a further one: that the Secretary of State has received a copy of the statement of proposed action prepared by the appropriate authority or the time within which the report should be prepared has expired (see below). There are also specific conditions applicable to each of the special measures (see below).

(c) Appointment of additional governors by the LEA

When new special measures were first announced, they included a power to appoint additional governors in respect of failing county, controlled or maintained special schools. However, in the case of voluntary aided and special agreement schools the White Paper said that consultation with the Churches was underway 'on whether they see a need for any additional powers to assist them to improve schools which are found to be failing' (White Paper, *Choice and Diversity*, para 11.5). Thus in the Education Bill 1992/93 parallel provisions (subsequently amended in the House of Lords during the passage of the Bill) to those applicable to county, voluntary controlled or maintained special schools were laid down for voluntary aided and special agreement schools.

The basic conditions for appointing additional governors were outlined above. In addition, section 214 of the EA 1993 contains specific procedural requirements in the case of both broad categories of schools.

As the LEA may 'appoint such number of additional governors as they think fit' (s 214(1)), the composition of the governing body could change quite significantly. Indeed, this might be what is needed if the new governors are going to be able to make any kind of impact on the school. Generally, in relation to the exercise of the power to appoint additional governors, the requirements of the Education (No 2) Act 1986 on the constitution of governing bodies must be read as including the appointment of additional governors, so far as the school's instrument of government is concerned. This means that the additional governors will have full voting rights and the same standing as other governors. Normally LEA-appointed governors hold office for a term of four years, but it is not clear whether such term of office applies to additional governors appointed under this new power. DFE Circular 17/93, *Schools Requiring Special Measures*, states merely that they 'will remain in office until their term of appointment expires'.

(d) Suspension of the right to a delegated budget

Before the LEA can exercise the power to suspend a delegated budget, the general conditions (see above) must be satisfied and the LEA must have served a copy of the statement of the action proposed by them (as required by section 211 of the 1993 Act) and received an acknowledgement from the Secretary of State (EA 1993, s 215(1) and (2)). Furthermore, at least ten days must have elapsed since the date of the notice of acknowledgement. The suspension will take effect as though made under section 37 of the Education Reform Act 1988, but without the governors' right of appeal over the imposition of the suspension itself (EA 1993, s 215(4)). However, the power to suspend in section 215 of the 1993 Act is clearly additional to the powers in section 37 of the 1988 Act, which may be exercised on various grounds of financial mismanagement or gross incompetence etc.

(e) Grouping and degrouping

When the general conditions apply (see above), there is a prohibition on the LEA passing a resolution under section 9 of the Education (No 2) Act 1986 grouping two or more schools under one governing body (EA 1993, s 216(1)). Also, if a school requiring special measures is a member of an existing group, the Secretary of State may make an order removing it from the group (s 216(2)).

(f) Prohibition on ballot of parents on GM status for the school

Schools which require special measures and in respect of which the general conditions (above) apply are prohibited from conducting a ballot of parents on whether the school should seek GM status, or in the case of a maintained special school, GM special school status (EA 1993, s 217). However, Part V of the 1993 Act contains other provisions which could result in failing schools acquiring GM status, irrespective of whether or not the parents or governors prefer the school to have it (see below).

(g) Overall control given to an Education Association

According to the Government, the aim of bringing in an Education Association is 'to put the school under new management until its performance has reached a satisfactory level' (White Paper, *Choice and Diversity*, para 11.7). It is not intended to be a permanent arrangement. In due course either the governing body would be put back in control, but the school would become GM, or the school would be closed.

An Education Association can be brought in if general conditions (*a*)–(*c*) (above) apply and if the Secretary of State has already received a statement prepared by the appropriate authority (usually the governing body) of the action that that authority proposes to take, or the time for making such a statement has passed (EA 1993, s 220(1) and (2)). The school concerned must be a county, voluntary or special school. In the case of special schools some of the provisions discussed below are modified or disapplied – see the Education (Special Schools Conducted by Education Associations) Regulations 1994 (SI 1994 No 1084). There must also be prior consultation, in the case of a voluntary school, with the appropriate diocesan authority or the person who appoints the foundation governors (EA 1993, s 218(4)). According to the White Paper, if the Secretary of State considers that the action proposed by the governing body and LEA seems 'effective', he will allow them up to one academic year to improve the school; but 'if at any time in the course of that period or at the end of it, it became clear that the plan was not working, the Secretary of State would have the option to place the school under the management of an EA' (*Choice and Diversity*, *op cit*, para 11.8). An Education Association can be brought in right from the start if the Secretary of State judges that the governors' plan of action and the LEA's supporting plan would not secure the necessary improvement.

An Education Association is brought in via an order by the Secretary of State 'for the school to be conducted by an education association named in the order from such date as may be specified in the order (. . . the "transfer date")' (EA 1993, s 220(2)). On the transfer date the LEA ceases to have a duty to maintain the school. If the school is a special agreement school, the special agreement will cease to have effect (s 220(4)). On making the order the Secretary of State must give notice of it in writing to the head teacher, governors, LEA and the funding authority (s 220(3)). Once an Education Association is supervising one school in an area, the Association could be given responsibility for 'as many schools in the area, including neighbouring LEAs, as were found to be failing' (*Choice and Diversity*, *op cit*, para 11.9).

The 1993 Act defines an Education Association as a body corporate established under section 218. It is to have not less than five members appointed by the Secretary of State, one of whom must be appointed as its chairman. The Government says that a 'small and cohesive body' would be assembled, and the likelihood is that the Association will have a chairman and 'five other part-time members' (*Hansard*, Official Report, Standing Committee E, col 1249, 2 February 1993, *per* Mr T Boswell MP, Under-Secretary of State). At least one of the appointments to the Association must be a person who has experience and capacity in the provision of, or in holding responsibility for, primary or secondary education (EA 1993, s 218(5)(a)). If the school is a voluntary school or special school, at least one member of the Association (he or she may be the same person as the aforementioned member) must have experience of, and capacity in, educational provision in voluntary schools or for pupils with special educational needs, respectively.

During the Committee Stage of the Education Bill in the House of Commons, the Under-Secretary of State explained that members of the Education Association would mostly be drawn from the local community and that they would include people from business, the professions (including head teachers or former head teachers) and, possibly, parents (*Hansard*, Official Report, Standing Committee E, cols 1245–1246, *per* Mr T Boswell MP, Under-Secretary of State). It was also explained that a member (or members) with appropriate expertise would be sought in relation to a specific problem afflicting a particular school. For example, in cases of poor management, skills in accountancy or personnel management might be needed by the Association. In a case where the curriculum is in difficulty, a person with experience of the National Curriculum might be required (*ibid*). In some cases such expertise and experience can be harnessed via recruitment to an Association's committees (if it has any). The 1993 Act empowers an Education Association to establish such committees, which may include non-members of the Association (Sch 12, para 5), and enables functions to be delegated to them or to the chairman of the Association (*ibid*, para 6).

The White Paper stated that an Education Association would 'effectively be in the position of a grant-maintained governing body' (*Choice and Diversity op cit*, para 11.9), a position confirmed by the regulations setting out the relevant articles of government (the Education (Schools Conducted by Education Associations) (Initial Articles of Government) Regulations 1993 (SI 1993 No 3101) as amended by (Amendment) Regulations 1994 (SI 1994 No 1085)). As noted above, the LEA ceases to have responsibility for maintaining the school on the transfer date in the same way that this responsibility ceases when a school acquires GM status (EA 1993, s 34(3)). But, more significantly, the Association is to be treated, for the purposes of nearly all statutory provisions, as a governing body of a school which was a county or voluntary school but has now acquired GM status (EA 1993, s 221(5) and (6); regulations can make further provision in this regard (s 238(1)(a)) – see the Education (Schools Conducted by Education Associations) Regulations 1993 (SI 1993 No 310) as amended by (Amendment) Regulations 1994 (SI 1994 No 1083)). The Education (Special Schools Conducted by Education Associations) Regulations 1994 (SI 1994 No 1084) make separate provision for special schools. It is expected that schools under an Education Association will be funded in the same way as GM schools, with an appropriate adjustment to the LEA's funds, and that there will be corresponding access to grants for special purposes (which may well be needed in order to facilitate the required improvements). Where the Association is responsible for more than one school, 'it will determine the allocation of funding between them' (*Choice and Diversity*, para 11.10).

Relevant statutory powers and duties normally resting with governing bodies vest in an Education Association when a transfer order is made (EA 1993, s 218(7)). In addition, an Education Association will have the general function prescribed by the 1993 Act: to 'conduct the school . . . so as to secure, so far as it is practicable to do so, the elimination of any deficiencies in the conduct of the school identified in any report made by a registered inspector or member of the Inspectorate' (EA 1993, s 222 (1) and (2)). Its power to conduct the school is a power 'to conduct a school of the same description as the school immediately before that date'. An Education Association will also have a power, equivalent to one enjoyed by GM schools (see EA 1993, s 68(8)), to provide further education or part-time education for junior pupils (EA 1993, s 222(4)). While under the control of the Association, the school must be conducted in accordance with the prescribed articles of government (see above) and the school's trust deed (EA 1993, s 223(1)–(3)).

The stewardship of a school by an Education Association can end only when the school becomes grant-maintained (under EA 1993, s 224) or is discontinued (under s 225) (EA 1993, s 221(2)). According to the White Paper, before deciding whether to bring the Association's role in the school to a conclusion, the Secretary of State will take advice from the CI in judging the extent to which the Association has brought about the necessary improvement to the school. Where the Association has been successful, the school will become GM (see *Choice and Diversity*, *op cit*, para 11.13). Before he or she can make an order for a school conducted by an Education Association to acquire GM status, the Secretary of State must have received a report of an inspection of the school by a member of HMI indicating that special measures are not required (note that schools under the control of an Education Association may not be inspected under s 9 of the Education (Schools) Act 1992: EA 1993, s 227(4); thus, instead of a s 9 inspection, the school will be inspected by order of the CI under ESA 1992, ss 2 or 6 (England) or 3 or 7 (Wales)). Having received the HMI report, the Secretary of State may, if he or she is of the opinion that the school should become a GM school, give notice of this opinion to the head teacher, the LEA, the Education Association and the funding authority. Once in receipt of this notice, the Education Association has up to three months in which to publish proposals for the acquisition of GM status. The matter will then proceed in the way that applications for GM status generally do, subject to any modifications in the procedure provided for by statutory instrument (EA 1993, s 224(3)(b)).

The Secretary of State also has a power to order the discontinuance of a school conducted by an Education Association at any time (EA 1993, s 225). It is assumed that this would not happen unless the Education Association had not secured the necessary improvement to the school. The Act and the White Paper are silent on this point, presumably because by highlighting the possibility that an Education Association might not succeed in its designated task, it would imply a lack of complete confidence in the system on the part of the Government.

When the school becomes GM or is discontinued, the Education Association is to be wound up and its property, rights and liabilities may be transferred to the Secretary of State (EA 1993, s 226).

5. Inspections of denominational education and collective worship

As noted in the introduction to this chapter, a separate system of inspection of denominational education and collective worship has been established under the ESA 1992 (see s 13 (as amended by s 259 of the EA 1993) and Sch 2).

The governors of both voluntary schools and denominational GM schools (see ESA 1992, s 13(3)) in which denominational education (see below) is given to pupils must ensure that the required inspection takes place (s 13(1)). 'Denominational education' is religious education which is required to form part of the basic curriculum of the school and which is provided otherwise than under the agreed syllabus for the area (see pp 211–212 above) (s 13(3A)). It will be provided in many voluntary schools and GM schools which were formerly voluntary schools. The ESA 1992 (Sch 2, para 14) provides that these inspections must be carried out within a prescribed period. The inspection itself must be carried out during a period not exceeding two weeks (Education (School Inspection) (No 2) Regulations 1993 (SI 1993 No 1986), reg 11(1) and the Education (School Inspection) (Wales) (No 2) Regulations 1993 (SI 1993 No 1982), reg 11(1)). Unless denominational education was inspected in September 1993, secondary schools have to receive their first inspection under section 13 between 1 October 1993 and 31 July 1997 (England) or 31 July 1998 (Wales). In other schools, the starting and end dates for the period in which the inspection is to take place are in each case one year later than the equivalent dates for secondary schools (*ibid*, reg 10).

Inspections of collective worship and religious education must be conducted separately (ESA 1992, s 13(7)), although they can be timed to coincide. The inspector may also report on 'the spiritual, moral, social and cultural development of pupils at the school' (*ibid*). There is no registration scheme for inspectors of denominational education and no prescribed qualifications. The inspector, who is to be selected by the governing body, must produce a written report and summary within five weeks (or seven weeks if a translation into Welsh is needed) (English Welsh School Inspection Regs, *op cit*, reg 11(2)) and send it to the governors of the school without delay (see ESA 1992, Sch 2, para 14). The report plus summary must be made available to the public and the summary must in any event be provided to the parent of every child who receives denominational education at the school. The governing body must prepare an 'additional action plan' within forty days (or forty-five, if a Welsh translation version needs to be prepared) (School Inspection Regulations, *op cit*, in both cases reg 11(3)). This plan must show the action that the governors propose to take in the light of the inspector's report.

6. LEA inspections

The Government had wanted the Education (Schools) Bill, when enacted, to remove LEAs' power to inspect schools. But a defeat in the House of Lords, where Lord Richie and others argued that it was unjustifiable to take away from LEAs the power to inspect schools maintained by them and for which they have responsibility, preserved an, albeit, restricted power of inspection for LEAs. LEAs may cause an inspection to be made by one or more of their officers with the object of obtaining information about any matter in connection with any school maintained by them 'for the purpose of enabling them to exercise any function of theirs' (ESA 1992, s 15(1)(a)). However, this power is subject to the proviso that it is 'not reasonably practicable' for the information required to be obtained in any other manner.

As noted earlier, LEAs may also establish a school inspection service (ESA 1992, s 14) to participate in section 9 or 13 inspections (see above) of schools which are maintained by the LEA and/or of those which are not, subject to the service being provided on a full cost basis and to any required tendering arrangements.

Chapter 11

School attendance

1. Introduction

It is now clear that truancy is endemic in schools, is caused by many different factors, and requires new approaches by education authorities, teachers and government (see, e.g. D O'Keefe, *Truancy in English Secondary Schools* (HMSO, 1994)). The present political climate supports ever tougher measures to combat non-attendance at school. Moral condemnation of truancy is underpinned by an increasing emphasis, by the Government in particular, on links between truancy and criminality and on the need for parents to take greater responsibility. It is true, however, that in recent years Government money has supported initiatives designed to tackle the problems of alienation and lack of motivation among pupils that are often at the root of truancy. For example, in 1993–94 the Government provided, within the 'Reducing Truancy' initiative, a 60 per cent grant towards expenditure of nearly £8.7 million by 64 English LEAs. The funding was provided within the GEST scheme (see Chapter 3), and the programme was described by the Government as 'the most ambitious assault on truancy yet mounted in this country' (*per* E Forth MP, Schools Minister, DFE Press Release 6/93, January 1993). Although some of the projects supported under this programme have been concerned with the use of information technology in recording and monitoring attendance and absences, many are concerned with curricular initiatives. There is some evidence that such financially supported initiatives have produced improved attendance rates compared with previous years (see OFSTED, *Access and Achievement in Urban Education* (1993), para 35). The impetus has continued with further GEST support (see DFE Circular 18/94) and the announcement in January 1994 that £14 million of central government funds will be allocated for initiatives to tackle truancy.

A perhaps greater emphasis on the causes of truancy is particularly reflected in the education supervision order (ESO) procedures provided by the Children Act 1989. Since the previous edition of this book was published in 1990, the relevant parts of the 1989 Act have (from 14 October 1991) provided a wholly new form of legal response to individual cases of truancy, in which the paramountcy principle (i.e. that the welfare of the child shall be the paramount consideration for the court in deciding what order to make, or whether to make an order, in respect of a child) shall apply (see the Children Act 1989, s 1(1)). But just as it would be wrong to associate Government-supported developments at school or LEA level with a retreat from the legalistic responses to truancy, so it would be wrong to assume that all such legal responses are necessarily wholly welfare-orientated. A parent's failure to ensure his or her child attends school or receives efficient full-time education other than at school remains a criminal offence, punishable as such by a fine (although no longer with imprisonment, which was rarely imposed in any event). It is clear that the availability of the alternative ESO procedure to the education welfare service is not considered by the DFE to obviate the need for swift prosecution as a potentially effective weapon in an appropriate case (see DES, *Education Supervision Orders – Guidance* (1991)). Note that prosecution and an application for an ESO are both possible in respect of the same child's truancy: see EA 1993, s 202(1), discussed below. At the same time, resort to non-statutory enforcement measures, such as police/LEA 'truancy patrols', in which an EWO-police officer team tours the streets looking for truants and attempts to discuss their truancy with them if they find them, has become a popular option in some areas (see T Thomas, 'Police truancy patrols' (1994) NLJ 82). (As no offence is committed by the child by merely truanting, he or she cannot be arrested but simply encouraged to go to school.)

The law on school attendance has been substantially consolidated in Part IV of the EA 1993. However, the requirements as to registration of pupils continue to be found in (recently amended) regulations. In the past couple of years requirements on reporting on attendance and non-attendance in individual pupils' reports and on publishing truancy rates in school prospectuses, annual reports and comparative tables, all discussed in Chapter 6, have also been introduced.

2. Registration of pupils

Pupils' names will be registered at a school on the first day they attend – in the *admissions register*. (Their parents' names and address(es), and certain other information, must also be recorded: see Pupils' Registration Regulations 1956, as amended, reg 3(2).) Thereafter, their attendance and failure to attend will be recorded in the *attendance register*, of which there must be one for each form or class. The rules concerning the keeping of this register are laid down in the Pupils' Registration Regulations 1956, as amended, made under EA 1944, s 80. Responsibility for the maintenance of the register rests with the 'proprietor' of the school, which in the case of a county, voluntary or grant-maintained school means the governing body (EA 1944, s 114(1), as amended by ERA 1988, Sch 12 Pt I, para 7).

(a) What must be shown on the register?

Guidance on the marking of attendance registers is at present still a matter for the discretion of the LEA. The LEA's guidelines are usually printed on the inside cover of the register. Apparently, these guidelines are of variable quality (HMI, *Attendance at School*, Education Observed 13 (1989), para 13). Guidance has recently been issued by the DFE, to ensure more accurate and consistent marking of registers, and, in particular, better recording of absences (DFE, *School Attendance – Policy and Practice on Categorisation of Absence* (1994)).

The following information must be shown (1956 regs, as amended):

(i) The names of all pupils in the class and a record (in ink, with alterations clearly identifiable) of their attendance at the beginning of each morning and afternoon session. This does not apply to independent schools all of whose pupils are boarders. Pupils receiving medical or dental treatment on a particular day should be marked present unless in hospital (Pupils Registration Regulations 1956, *op cit*). In the case of pupils of compulsory school age, the register should state whether a particular absence is or is not authorised (this information should be recorded as soon as practicable after it has become known to the school if it was not known at the time the register was taken). Absence is not to be treated as unauthorised if it is by reason of: sickness; unavoidable cause; day of religious observance; no suitable transport or boarding arrangements have been made by the LEA where the school is not within walking distance of the child's home; or attendance at another school at which he or she is also registered (e.g. a PRU).

(ii) 'The name and address of every person known to the proprietor of the school to be a parent of a pupil at the school' (EA 1944 s 80(1A)) must be shown in all school registers. There is a separate rule in the regulations requiring the parent with actual care of the child to be identified and his or her emergency contact number set out in the admissions register (see DES Administrative Memorandum 1/88 (July 1988)) (on the definition of 'parent', see Chapter 1, Part 3).

(b) Use of information technology

Amendments made to the Pupils' Registration Regulations 1956 by the Education (Pupils' Attendance Records) Regulations 1991 (SI 1991 No 1582) lay down requirements as to the keeping of admissions and attendance registers in computerised form (see DES Circular 11/91). The substituted regulation 10 of the 1956 regulations makes it clear that the duties in the regulations as a whole can be fulfilled with the use of information technology, provided the practice conforms to certain requirements: the attendance register must be printed out at least once a month and the admissions register at least once a year; print outs made after correction of the register under regulation 8 (see (d) below) must clearly distinguish between the original and the corrected entry; and monthly (etc.) print outs of the attendance register for each school year must, for the purposes of regulation 9 (see (c) below), be collected in a single volume which must be kept for a period of three years from the end of the relevant school year.

(c) Legal significance of the register

It is often said that the register 'is a legal document'. What this emphasises is the importance of the register as evidence of non-attendance when legal action is brought against parents, and the fact that failure to comply with the regulations concerning registers amounts to a summary offence (level 1 fine, Criminal Justice Act 1982) (EA 1944, s 80(2), as amended). Registers must be retained for three years after their period of use (1956 regulations, *op cit*, reg 9). The admissions and attendance register must be available for inspection during school hours by inspectors (*ibid*, reg 5).

(d) Alteration/correction of the register

Any correction to the register must 'be made in such a manner that the original entry and the correction are both clearly distinguishable' (1956 regulations, *op cit*, reg 8). In prescribed circumstances a pupils' name must be deleted from the admissions register (and it follows that it should also be removed from the attendance register), such as where the pupil transfers to a different school, dies or has been permanently excluded from school (but not until after the pupil has had a chance to appeal against the exclusion) (regs 4 and 4A, added by SI 1994 No 2128).

(e) Returns

LEAs have their own systems for monitoring school attendance. In any event, the law requires schools to make returns to their LEA indicating absences of named pupils, of two weeks or more, without medical certification, and the cause of absence where this is known (reg 7). In addition, LEAs or governing bodies have a duty to provide, annually, certain information about unauthorised absences to the Secretary of State (see further p 160 above).

3. A parent's legal duty to cause his or her child to receive efficient full-time education

(a) The general duty

> 'It shall be the duty of the parent of every child of compulsory school age to cause him to receive efficient full-time education suitable to his age, ability and aptitude and to any special educational needs he may have either by regular attendance at school or otherwise'.
>
> (EA 1944, s 36).

'Parent' includes anyone who has parental responsibility for a child or who has care of him (see EA 1944, s 114(1D)–(1F)). This means that the duty in section 36 of the 1944 Act may rest with several individuals (see Chapter 1, at pp 16–17).

'Child of compulsory school age': 'Child' is defined for the purposes of the Education Acts as 'a person who is not over compulsory school age'

(EA 1944, s 114(1)). 'Compulsory school age' is defined in section 277 of the EA 1993 (the previous definition was in s 35 of the EA 1944, which has been repealed by the 1993 Act). A person reaches compulsory school age on his or her fifth birthday. Someone under the age of five is therefore a child who is not of compulsory school age (EA 1993, s 277). A person ceases to be of compulsory school age on the official school leaving date (determined by the Secretary of State by order under ss 277(4)), but only if he or she has reached the age of sixteen between the start of the school year and that date, or is sixteen on the school leaving date, or will reach the age of sixteen between the end of the school leaving date and the start of the next school year. There is a special exemption from the duty in section 36 of the 1944 Act in the case of a child who attains the age of five years during a school term, if arrangements have been made for his or her admission to the school during the next school term. In such a case, during the period between the child's fifth birthday and the start of the next school term, the parent's duty in section 36 of the 1944 Act will not apply in respect of the child (Education (Miscellaneous Provisions) Act 1948, s 4 and (in respect of GM schools) EA 1993, s 203).

'Efficient' in section 36 has never been defined, but arguably would have to be considered both in conjunction with 'suitable' and in the context of the provisions of the National Curriculum. In other words, the quality of education provided must of a suitable standard, bearing in mind the presence of a legally defined curriculum, including the National Curriculum.

'Full-time' is not defined in the Act, but the Education (Schools and Further Education) Regulations 1981, reg 10 in the past prescribed at least three hours of secular instruction per day for classes of under-eights and four hours for over-eights, in schools operating a five day week. Although guidance on the management of the school day has been issued (DES Circular 7/90, *Management of the School Day* (1990)), new regulations promised by the Government to prescribe the minimum number of hours of class contact pupils should receive have not yet materialised (regarding publication of total lesson time see p 160).

'Regular' attendance is not defined, but is generally taken to mean frequent attendance at times prescribed by the governing body (E(No 2)A 1986, s 21(2), added by ERA 1988, s 115) (formerly the LEA), not including times of arrival after the register has closed (*Hinchley* v *Rankin* [1961] 1 All ER 692).

'Or otherwise' permits parents to make their own arrangements for their children's education, including home schooling. LEAs may be entitled to inspect the child's home in such a case (*R* v *Surrey Quarter Sessions Appeals Committee ex p Tweedie* [1963] 61 LGR 464). Many LEAs question the suitability of the curriculum likely to be provided by parents. The introduction of the National Curriculum renders 'education otherwise' extremely questionable in a legal as well as an educational sense (but see further AJ Petrie, 'Education at home and the law' (1993) 5(3) Education and the Law 139).

Note that governors have a power to require a pupil at a school to attend for secular instruction and training other than on school premises (EA 1944, s 21(5)). Moreover, LEAs have a duty to make full-time or part-time provision (at school or otherwise) for pupils of compulsory school age who, by reason of illness, exclusion from school or otherwise, would or may not otherwise receive suitable education (EA 1993, s 298). This provision may, for example, be made at a school established specifically for such pupils, known as a 'pupil referral unit' (see p 41). Long-term attendance problems are one of the reasons pupils are referred to such units. A recent report notes that year 10/11 pupils referred to units 'usually had not attended school for considerable periods of time, often for more than six weeks and in some individual cases as much as two years prior to referral' (OFSTED, *Education for Disaffected Pupils* (1993), para 20). A parent will fulfil his or her duty under section 36 of the EA 1944 if the child concerned attends the unit. If, however, the child does not attend the unit as he or she is supposed to, the unit could be named in a school attendance order served on the parent under section 192 of the EA 1993 (EA 1993, Sch 18 para 14, which also modifies the procedure in such a case).

(b) Breach of section 36 of the 1944 Act – school attendance orders

Although, as noted above, various strategies are being advised for improvement of school attendance, from closer monitoring to rewarding attendance (see HMI, *Attendance at School*, Education Observed 13 (1989), and O'Keefe, *Truancy in English Secondary Schools* (1994) HMSO), the legal framework remains important. This framework is, apart from section 36 itself, contained in Part IV of the EA 1993.

(i) Notice to parent requiring him or her to satisfy LEA that child is being suitably educated

If it appears to the LEA that a parent is failing to comply with his or her section 36 responsibilities, the LEA must serve a notice requiring the parent to satisfy the authority within a specified time (being not less than 15 days beginning on the date that the notice is served) that the child is being suitably educated (EA 1993, s 192(1) and (2)). 'Suitable' education means 'efficient full-time education suitable to [the child's] age, ability and aptitude and to any special educational needs he may have' (s 192(8)).

(ii) School attendance order

If the parent does not satisfy the LEA that the child is being suitably educated, and the LEA is of the opinion that it is 'expedient' that the child should attend school, the authority must serve a school attendance order (SAO) in the prescribed form, requiring the child to attend the school named in the order (EA 1993, s 192(3)).

Provision is made for parents to exercise a degree of choice over the school to be named in the order. In the case of a child for whom there is no statement of special educational needs, the LEA must, before serving the SAO, serve a written notice on the parent informing him or her of the intention to serve the SAO and specifying the school to be named in the order plus any suitable alternatives (EA 1993, s 193(2)). An LEA-maintained or GM school could be named in the notice, but where the admission of the child who would be the subject of the notice would take the number of pupils on roll above the admissions limit, the LEA may not specify a school in the notice unless it is responsible for admissions to the school (EA 1993, s 194(1) and (2)). If none of the schools that could, under the above provisions, be named in the notice is within a reasonable distance of the child's home, another maintained or GM school which is within a reasonable distance of the child's home may be specified (EA 1993, s 194(3)). No school may be specified in the notice if the child is permanently excluded from it (s 194(4)). Before deciding to specify a school in the notice, the LEA must consult the governing body and, if the school is maintained by a different LEA, that LEA (s 194(5)). These bodies, plus the head teacher of the school concerned, must be informed of the decision once it is made (s 194(6)). An LEA or governing body so informed may, within 15 days of receiving the notice, ask the Secretary of State for a direction as to the school to be specified in the notice (s 194(7)). Such a direction will be binding.

The notice must explain the parent's right to select a school to be named in the SAO. This right operates as follows (see EA 1993, s 193(3)–(6)): first, if within 15 days of the notice the parent selects one of the alternative schools specified in it, that school must be named in the SAO; secondly, if the parent applies for and secures a place for his or her child at an LEA-maintained or grant-maintained school, and the LEA responsible for the school chosen by the parent (if it is not the LEA which served the notice) or grant-maintained school informs the LEA which served the notice of the parent's application, that school shall be named in the SAO; and finally, if the parent secures a place for the child at a school other than an LEA-maintained or grant-maintained school and either the LEA is to meet the cost of the fees (under s 6 of the Education (Miscellaneous Provisions) Act 1953) or in any event the school is suitable to the child's age, ability and aptitude and any special educational needs he or she may have, that school is to be named in the SAO.

If there is a statement of special educational needs in respect of the child concerned, the school specified in the statement must be named in the SAO; alternatively, if the statement does not name a school it must be amended to name the school specified in the SAO. The procedure for amending statements set out in EA 1993, Sch 10, para 10 (see Chapter 9, p 261), must be applied (s 196(1)–(3)).

(iii) Once a school attendance order is made

The governing body and head teacher must be informed once a maintained or grant-maintained school is named in an SAO (EA 1993, s 192(5)), and the child must be admitted to the school (s 192(6)), without prejudice to the right subsequently to exclude him (for serious misbehaviour etc) once he or she is registered there (s 192(7)). The duty to issue an SAO does not apply while an ESO is in force in relation to the child (Children Act 1989, Sch 3 para 13(2), as amended by EA 1993, Sch 19 para 152).

Non-compliance with an SAO is a punishable offence (see below), although a parent must escape liability if he or she is ensuring that the child is receiving a suitable education otherwise than at school (EA 1993, s 198(1)).

(iv) Amendment of school attendance order at request of parent of child for whom there is no statement of special educational needs

If a parent wants his or her child to attend a different school to the one named in the SAO, and he or she secures a place for the child at the desired school (which is LEA-maintained or grant-maintained), the LEA must comply with a request by the parent for this school to be named in the order (EA 1993, s 195(1) and (2)). The SAO will thus apply to this chosen school instead of the one previously named in the order. A similar amendment may be made at the parent's request if he or she secures a place for the child at a school which is neither LEA-maintained nor grant-maintained and (i) in respect of which the LEA is to pay the fees (under s 6 of the Education (Miscellaneous Provisions) Act 1953 – for example because it is not able to make the provision needed in one of its schools) (EA 1993, s 195(3)) or, (ii) the school is suitable having regard to the child's age, ability and aptitude and any special educational needs he or she may have (s 195(4)).

On the position of pupils with statements of special educational needs, see section 196 of the EA 1993 (discussed at the end of (ii) above).

(v) Duration of school attendance order

Once made, the SAO remains in force until the child has reached compulsory school age, unless the order is revoked by the LEA or a direction is made under section 198(2) or 202(5) of the 1993 Act because the parent is acquitted by the court of a charge of non-compliance with an SAO or the court refuses an application for an ESO on the ground that the child is being properly educated for the purposes of section 36(3) of the Children Act 1989. A parent can also apply for an SAO to be revoked by the LEA. The LEA must revoke the order if the parent shows that arrangements have been made for the child to receive suitable education otherwise than at school (EA 1993, s 197(1) and (2)). This does not apply where the named school is specified in a statement of special educational needs relating to the child (s 197(5)).

(c) Absence of registered pupils: parents' liability

Under EA 1993, s 199 (formerly s 39 of the EA 1944), a parent commits an offence for failing to ensure the regular attendance of his or her child who is registered as a pupil at a school, unless one or more of the prescribed excuses apply. The excuses (which do not apply in respect of boarders) are (s 199(3) and (4)):

(i) leave (being defined as 'leave granted by any person authorised to do so by the governing body or proprietor of the school' (s 199(8));

(ii) sickness (the child's not the parent's);

(iii) Unavoidable cause, being a cause affecting the child and generally involving an emergency (see *Jenkins* v *Howells* [1944] 1949 1 All ER 942 (DC) and *Jarman* v *Mid-Glamorgan Education Authority* [1985] 82 LS Gaz 1249 (DC));

(iv) day exclusively set aside for religious observance by the religious body to which his parent belongs; and

(v) the school at which the child is registered:

> 'is not within walking distance of the child's home . . . and no suitable arrangements have been made by the [LEA] or the funding authority for [the child's] transport to and from school . . . boarding accommodation for him at or near the school . . . [or] enabling him to become a registered pupil at a school nearer to his home'.

Note that (v) does not apply to children of no fixed abode, although in respect of these children the parent must be acquitted if he proves that the child is aged six or over and has made at least 200 attendances in the previous twelve months, and the parent is engaged in a trade or business that requires him to travel from place to place and the child has attended school 'as regularly as the nature of that trade or business permits' (s 199(6)).

The question of what are 'suitable arrangements' for the purposes of (v), and, in particular, whether parental preference should come into the reckoning in determining whether arrangements are suitable, was considered in *R* v *Rochdale Metropolitan Borough ex p Schemet* [1994] ELR 89 and *R* v *Essex County Council ex p C* [1994] ELR 54 and 273. These cases are discussed below (pp 304–305).

'Walking distance' is defined as two miles, or three miles if the child is aged eight or over, 'measured by the nearest available route' (s 199(5)). A route does not cease to be 'available' simply because it would not be possible for an unaccompanied child to walk it without risk of danger (*Rogers* v *Essex County Council* [1986] 3 All ER 321 (HL)). In furtherance of his or her duty to ensure a child attends school, a parent should, where reasonably practicable and prudent to do so, accompany a child to school when it would be unsafe for the child to go unaccompanied (*George* v *Devon County Council* [1988] 3 All ER 1002). However, in deciding whether to provide transport for a child, LEAs must now have regard (amongst other things) to 'the age of the pupil, and the nature of the route, or alternative routes, which he could reasonably be expected to take' (EA 1944, s 55, as amended by E(No 2)A 1986, s 53; see further pp 303–304).

The courts have refused to extend the previous version of the above list (*Spiers* v *Warrington Corporation* [1954] 1 QB 61), unduly strain their interpretation of it (e.g. *Happe* v *Lay* (1977) 76 LGR 313) or apply international law (the European Convention on Human Rights) (*Jarman* v *Mid-Glamorgan Education Authority* (1985) 82 LS Gaz 1249).

Section 39 of the 1944 Act was held in *Crump* v *Gilmore* (1969) 68 LGR 56 to have created an absolute offence, which meant that a parent could not rely on his or her lack of knowledge of the child's absence as a defence. The decision appears applicable to the excuses in section 199 of EA 1993.

In the case of children who are boarders, excuses (i)–(v) do not apply directly, but the parents of such a child can only be prosecuted for an offence under section 199 if the child is absent from school without leave during any part of a school term, unless he was prevented from being present by reason of sickness or any unavoidable cause (s 199(7)).

Note that pupils may be absent with permission during term time for the purposes of going on an annual holiday with their parents (two weeks maximum) (Education (Schools and Further Education) Regulations 1981, reg 12).

(d) Court action in non-attendance cases

Official guidance recommends that 'all reasonable efforts' should be made to avoid the need for proceedings and argues that 'many attendance difficulties can be overcome by schools and the Education Welfare Service' (DES, *Education Supervision Orders – Guidance* (1991), para 1.18). If proceedings are taken, they may be of the following types:

(i) Criminal proceedings in the magistrates court

If a parent commits an offence under EA 1993, s 198, of failure to comply with an SAO, or under section 199, of failure to secure his or her child's regular attendance at school, the parent will be liable, on summary conviction, to a fine (level 3 on the Criminal Justice Act 1982 scale – currently £400 maximum) (EA 1993, s 201(2)). Fines imposed generally average around £50 (the average fine in twelve convictions in Barnsley in 1992 was £45: *The Times*, 11 March 1993), but the actual amount depends on local factors and, more importantly, on whether it is a first or subsequent offence. The power to impose a prison sentence in such cases was removed by Schedule 15 to the Children Act 1989, but imprisonment for non-payment of the fine is still a possibility. A prosecution under section 198 or section 199 may only be brought by an LEA. For the purposes of the proceedings under these sections, a child is to presumed to have been of compulsory school age (see above) at any relevant time unless the parent proves otherwise (EA 1993, s 200(2)).

Before instituting proceedings, the LEA must consider whether it would be appropriate to apply for an education supervision order (ESO) as well as or instead of instituting the proceedings (EA 1993, s 202(1)). If a person is convicted by a court under section 198 of the EA 1993 for breach of section 36 of the EA 1944, or is being prosecuted before a court for breach of section 199 of the EA 1993, the court concerned may direct the LEA to apply for an ESO, unless the LEA considers that the child's welfare will be satisfactorily safeguarded without one (EA 1993, s 202(2)). However, even if directed by the court to apply for an ESO, the LEA may decide not to apply for one, although it must provide the court with its reasons (s 202(3) and (4)), normally within eight weeks of the direction.

Once there has been a prosecution in respect of non-compliance with a particular SAO, no further prosecution may be brought in respect of that SAO (*Enfield LBC* v *Forsyth* [1987] 2 FLR 126), although a further SAO must be issued if there is a fresh or continuing breach of section 36 of the EA 1944 (see above) (EA 1993, s 198(3)).

(ii) Education supervision orders under the Children Act 1989

The Children Act 1989 empowers the magistrates court to make an education supervision order (ESO) in respect of a child, on the application of the LEA, on the ground that the child 'is of compulsory school age and is not being properly educated' (CA 1989, s 36(3) – see *Essex County Council* v *B* [1993] 1 FLR 866). A child is not being properly educated unless 'he is receiving efficient full-time education suitable to his age, ability and aptitude and any special educational needs he may have' (CA 1989, s 36(4)), the same test laid down in section 36 of the Education Act 1944, referred to above. An order may not be made where the child is already in the care of an LEA (CA 1989, s 36(6)). The effect of the order, discussed more fully below, is to require that a supervisor should 'advise, assist and befriend, and give directions to' the supervised child and anyone who has parental responsibility for him or her, in such a way as will ensure that the child is 'properly educated' (CA 1989, Sch 3 para 12(1)). The Act does not specify the type or designation of supervisor. However, it is generally assumed that he or she will be an education welfare officer or an education social worker who may already have had dealings with the family (DES, *Education Supervision Orders - Guidance* (1991)). Once made, the order will remain in force for one year. However, at any time within three months before its expiry date an application for its extension may be made to the court, which has the power to extend the order for up to three years, with the possibility of further extensions should they be necessary. The order will in any event terminate when the child ceases to be of compulsory school age or is no longer in care (CA 1989, Sch 3, para 15), or where the court discharges the order on the application of the child concerned, his or her parent or the LEA (*ibid*, para 17). Parents have a right of appeal to the High Court against an order (CA 1989, s 94).

Before instituting proceedings for an ESO, the LEA must consult with the local authority (CA 1989, s 36(8), as amended, and (9)). The chief purpose of this requirement is to enable the local authority to consider whether it should provide any child or family support under Part III of the 1989 Act.

When an ESO is in force, the LEA is barred from issuing school attendance orders (SAOs) in respect of the child (indeed, any SAO which is in force at the time the ESO is made will cease to have effect) (see above). One of the options available to a parent who is served with an SAO is that of selecting a school other than the one named in the order, applying for admission under the parental preference provisions of the EA 1980 and appealing if unsuccessful. This option is, in fact, open to a parent irrespective of any SAO. But once an ESO is made not only will any SAO lapse in relation to the child in question, but the parental preference and appeal provisions of the EA 1980 and the general duty under section 76 of the EA 1944 to comply with parental wishes will not apply (CA 1989, Sch 3 para 13). The supervision will thus be more likely to proceed unencumbered by any parental attempts to effect changes to the child's education. However, it may be that the child would benefit from a change of school, and supervisors are advised that 'parents' temporary loss of rights in this matter need not prevent a change of educational provision should it be necessary' (DES, *Education Supervision Orders – Guidance* (1991), *op cit*, para 1.30). Moreover, before a direction (see below) is issued the supervisor must, so far as is reasonably practicable, ascertain the wishes and feelings of the child and his or her parents – 'including, in particular, their wishes as to the place at which the child should be educated' (CA 1989, Sch 3, para 12(2)).

Whilst the Government clearly anticipates that the supervisor will play a non-authoritarian and, especially where the child has special educational needs, supportive role, seeking to foster co-operation between parents and school, there is an emphasis on strengthening the exercise of parental responsibility. Supervisors are under a duty to issue directions to the parent and child in such a way as will, in their opinion, secure that the child is 'properly educated' (CA 1989, Sch 3, para 12(1)). The official guidance recommends that such directions be given in writing. The 1989 Act does not specify the kind of directions which should be issued. Although it would appear from the wording of the statute that the issuing of directions should be the norm, the guidance suggests that directions should be used 'only where necessary'. Illustrative examples are given:

> 'Directions might include, for example, a requirement for the parents and the child to attend meetings with the supervisor or with teachers at the school to discuss the child's progress. They may need to cover such areas as medical treatment or examination, or assessment by an educational psychologist' (DES (1991), *op cit*, para 1.32).

Sanctions for non-compliance with directions were introduced at the Report stage of the Children Bill. A *parent* who persistently fails to comply with a reasonable direction, with which compliance was reasonably practicable and was not inconsistent with directions given under another supervision order, is guilty of an offence, punishable with a fine of up to £400 (CA 1989, Sch 3 para 18). Where a *child* persistently fails to comply with a direction the LEA must notify the local authority (social services), who must investigate the circumstances of the child (*ibid*, para 19) and may decide to take action in the interests of the child's welfare under Parts III or IV of the 1989 Act.

It should be noted that the child's welfare is the 'paramount consideration' when the court is considering an application for an ESO (this is the 'paramountcy principle', which applies also to other family proceedings under the 1989 Act) (CA 1989, s 1(1)). The court will also have to consider whether making the order would be better for the child than making no order at all (the 'non-intervention principle') (s 1(5)) and consider the checklist of factors (see s 1(3)) to be taken into account in any contested proceedings under Part IV of the Act, which includes ESO applications under section 36. These factors include the child's physical, emotional and educational needs and the child's own wishes (considered in the light of his or her age and understanding). In one recent case the High Court found that the magistrates had not fulfilled their duty as regards the statutory checklist properly: *Essex County Council* v *B* [1993] 1 FLR 866 (FD) (see further *Re P (A Minor) (Education)* [1992] 1 FLR 316; *Re S (Minors)* [1992] 2 FLR 313 (CA) and *M* v *M (Minors) (Removed from Jurisdiction)* [1993] The Times, 1 August).

(iii) Care proceedings

Where non-attendance is a symptom of deeper difficulties, for example parental indifference or neglect, it is possible that local authority social services will become involved and care proceedings may be warranted on the ground that the child is suffering or is likely to suffer 'significant harm' (see Children Act 1989, s 31; 'harm' is defined in subs (9) – see p 361). In *Re O (A Minor) (Care Proceedings: Education)* [1992] 1 WLR 912 the magistrates court considered an application by a local authority for a care order in respect of a girl aged 14. The local authority wanted her removed from her family to a children's home. They saw the care order as offering the only effective means of dealing with a situation where the girl was truanting persistently. She had developed school phobia. Her parents had already been prosecuted and fined in respect of her non-attendance at school. The magistrates decided to make a care order on the ground that the girl would suffer lasting harm to her intellectual and social development if she continued to miss out on her education. The girl appealed. On her behalf it was argued that as failure to receive an education was no longer a specific ground for taking a child into care (following repeal of s 1, and in particular s 1(2)(e), of the Children and Young Persons Act (CYPA) 1969), application for an ESO should have been made by the LEA, and that in any event the threshold condition for a care order under section 31 of the Children Act 1989 (that a child was suffering or was likely to suffer significant harm if the order was not made) had not been satisfied. Ewbank J rejected this latter argument, saying that compared with another (hypothetical) child of equivalent intellectual and social development who was attending school, there was little doubt that the girl's truancy would result in significant harm and that the girl (who was by now aged 15) was beyond her parent's control (as in the CYPA 1969, s 1(2)(e), case of *Re DJMS (a minor)* (1977)) or the harm was attributable to the parent's failure to give the care that might be expected of a reasonable parent. Ewbank J also agreed that all the steps that would have to be taken if an ESO were in force, such as daily EWO visits, had already been taken but had not succeeded. Thus it was inappropriate in a case such as that to expect the LEA to apply for an ESO.

If care proceedings are brought, the statutory checklist and the non-intervention and paramountcy principles (discussed in (ii) above) will have to be applied by the court.

4. Aiding attendance

Every pupil in England and Wales has the right to a free education (but see the rules on charging for education introduced by the ERA 1988, discussed in Chapter 8). Nevertheless, there are expenses associated with the upbringing of children that are a consequence of a child's attendance at school and which can prove extremely burdensome for many parents, especially those who are on low incomes. In order that pupils from poorer families are not educationally disadvantaged as a direct consequence of their parents' low income, the law has provided for free milk and school meals, transport, and a framework for the provision of grants and education allowances. Provision is not, however, generous. The assisted places scheme covering fees and incidental expenses in respect of attendance at an independent school, was discussed in Chapter 2, pp 43–44.

(a) Transport

LEAs are under a duty to make appropriate arrangements for the provision of free transport for the purpose of facilitating the attendance of pupils at school, including boarding school (EA 1944, s 55(1)). As shown above (p 298), a parent is not obliged to send his or her child to school if 'the school . . . is not within walking distance . . . and no suitable arrangements have been made by the LEA for [the child's] transport . . .' (EA 1944, s 39(2)(c)). The factors which LEAs may be obliged to take into account in determining whether arrangements are suitable were considered in two recent cases (*R* v *Rochdale MBC ex p Schemet* [1994] ELR 89 and *R* v *Essex County Council ex p C* [1994] ELR 54 and 273, both discussed below). 'Walking distance' is defined as two miles, or three miles if the child is aged eight or over, measured by the 'nearest available route'. (For judicial interpretation of this, see *Rogers* v *Essex County Council* [1986] and *George* v *Devon County Council* [1988] 3 All ER 1002, cited at p 298 above.) Section 55(3) of the EA 1944 (added by E(No 2)A 1986, s 53, following the *Rogers* decision) provides that:

> 'In considering whether or not they are required [under s 55(1)] . . . to make arrangements in relation to a particular pupil, the local education authority shall have regard (amongst other things) to the age of the

pupil and the nature of the route, or alternative routes, which he could reasonably be expected to take . . .'.

Section 55(3) (as amended by EA 1993, Sch 19, para 15) now also requires the parents' religious preferences to be taken into account for this purpose (see below).

The introduction of grant-maintained schools has necessitated further amendment of section 55 – the addition of a new subsection ((4)), which provides that transport arrangements made by a LEA under section 55(1) must include:

> 'provision for pupils at grant-maintained schools which is no less favourable than the provision made in pursuance of the arrangements for pupils at schools maintained by a local education authority' (added by ERA 1988, s 100(3)).

Transport for pupils not covered by section 55(1) *may* be paid for, in whole or part, by the LEA (EA 1944, s 55(2)).

Two recent cases have clarified the law governing LEAs' responsibilities vis-à-vis school transport arrangements. In *R* v *Rochdale Metropolitan Borough ex p Schemet* (1994) the applicant and his wife lived in Rochdale with their two children, a son aged twelve and a daughter aged fourteen. They were members of the Church of England and wanted their children to attend C of E secondary schools when they left middle school. In 1989 the daughter moved to a C of E school in the borough of Oldham. The school was 4.55 miles from their home, via the nearest available route. Rochdale LEA paid for the daughter's travel to school by issuing her with a pass. In 1991 Rochdale ceased to pay for the girl's transport and did not pay for the son, who that year started at the same school that the daughter attended. The LEA's decision not to pay was the result of a policy change arising from the need to make economies. No exceptions to the general policy of not paying for pupils' transport to extra-district schools would be granted on denominational grounds alone. The parents challenged the LEA's decision, arguing that they should have been consulted over the change to the LEA's school transport policy and that the policy itself was unlawful, in part because there was a duty to have regard to parental preference in determining the suitability of the arrangements. Roch J held that the parents of children who were receiving transport passes had a legitimate expectation that such provision would continue unless and until they had been informed of, and given an opportunity to comment on, rational arguments for a change in policy. Some parents would be quite seriously affected by such a change, and might have to move their children to a different school in consequence. He also said that the LEA was required to take into account parental preferences when deciding whether or not suitable arrangements could be made for the child to attend a school nearer to his or her home, although the wishes of the parents were not to be regarded as the sole consideration. If the LEA wanted to avoid having to pay for or to provide free transport by making arrangements for the child to attend a school nearer to his or her home, they had to show that the school was suitable for the particular pupil (cf *R* v *East Sussex County*

Council ex p D (15 March 1991) where Rose J said that 'suitable' related to the 'arrangements' alone, in this context; in *R* v *Essex County Council ex p C* (1994) (*op cit*) in the Court of Appeal, Staughton LJ agreed with Roch J's interpretation in *Schemet*).

Since the decision in *Schemet*, and apparently in response to it, the law has been changed. LEAs must now also take into account, for the purposes of deciding whether they are required to make transport arrangements for a child to attend a particular school, 'any wish of his parent for him to be provided with education at a school or institution in which the religious education provided is that of the religion or denomination to which his parent adheres' (EA 1944, s 55(3), as amended by EA 1993, Sch 19 para 15).

This still begs the question of how a conflict between parental wishes and the LEA's choice should be resolved. In *R* v *Essex County Council ex p C (Re C)* [1994] ELR 54 QBD and 273 (CA) the parents of a boy with special educational needs arranged for their son to attend a school (school M) which was 14 miles away from their home. The LEA refused to meet the transport costs, arguing that the EA 1944, section 55(1), read with section 39(2)(c), entitled it to do so in cases where the LEA was willing to make suitable arrangements for the child to attend another school (in this case) which was nearer to his home. For the parents, it was argued, in essence, that the law required the conflict between the principle of parental choice and the choice of the LEA to be resolved in favour of the former. The High Court and Court of Appeal found for the LEA. In the Court of Appeal Steyn LJ (at p 279) confirmed the extent of the LEA's discretion, saying that, in his view:

> 'section 39(2)(c) of the Education Act 1944, as amended, contemplates that a local education authority is entitled to make arrangements for a child registered at one school to become a registered pupil at another school nearer her home. I am far from saying that parental choice is irrelevant to such a decision. On the contrary, it seems to me a factor to be taken into account together with all other relevant factors including the financial implications . . . But . . . an acceptance of the appellant's argument would emasculate the local education authority's power under section 39(2)(c) to nominate an objectively suitable school nearer the child's home'.

(b) Grants and allowances

The payment of grants and allowances is provided for under a variety of provisions.

(i) Payment of expenses

Payments to enable pupils to participate in educational activities, including those taking place outside school hours, and scholarships, may be provided by LEAs (EA 1944, s 81; Scholarships and Other Benefits Regulations (SI 1977 No 1443), as amended), provided that any such payment is warranted by virtue of low parental income. Payment could cover the cost of fees at an independent school (see also (iii) below). An LEA would act illegally if it fettered its discretion by excluding consideration of exceptional circumstances with regard to payment of fees under this discretionary power (*R* v *Hampshire Education Authority ex p J* (1985) 84 LGR 547). Payments for children above compulsory school age are covered instead by grants and awards paid under the Education Act 1962 (see (iv) below).

(ii) Clothing

LEAs may provide clothing (which includes footwear) to, *inter alios*, pupils who are:

- boarding at educational establishments maintained by the LEA or at a GM school; or
- in maintained nursery schools or classes; or
- receiving special educational provision and for whom the LEA is providing board and lodging otherwise than at a maintained educational institution.

(Education (Miscellaneous Provisions) Act 1948, as amended, s 5(1)). Clothing may also be provided to those who do not fall into the above categories but who attend a maintained school or special school (including one that is not maintained) and would not be able to take full advantage of the education provided at the school because of the inadequacy or unsuitability of their clothing (*ibid*, s 5(2)). Arrangements for such provision to pupils may also be made with the proprietor of a school which is not maintained by the LEA and which is not a special school or GM school (*ibid*, s 5(4)). Clothing for use in physical training may also be provided, to pupils at maintained schools (s 5(3)).

Where the recipients are granted ownership of the clothing, the LEA may charge for it as much as the parents can bear without financial hardship (s 5(6); Education (Provision of Clothing) Regulations, SI 1980 No 545).

(iii) Fees and board and lodging

LEAs have a power to make arrangements for a child to receive primary or secondary education at a non-maintained school (Education (Miscellaneous Provisions) Act 1953, s 6(1)). The LEA must pay the fees (i) where the child has to be placed at such a school because of a shortage of places at suitable maintained schools or (ii) where the pupil fills a place at the school which its proprietors have put at the disposal of the LEA and the school is one which receives a grant under section 100 of the EA 1944 for educational provision. The LEA must also pay for board and lodging if it is necessary to enable the child to attend a school that is suitable for his or her educational needs, including any special educational needs (Education (Miscellaneous Provisions) Act 1953, s 6(2), as amended). LEAs have a similar duty (under EA 1993, s 190) to pay the fees and expenses and, if they are satisfied that board and lodging for the child is necessary if he is to receive the appropriate special educational provision, meet board and lodging charges for a child with special educational needs at a non-maintained school. The child concerned must be attending a non-maintained school which is named in a statement of special educational needs or which it is in the child's interests and appropriate for him to attend to receive special educational provision which is available there.

Where board and lodging is provided but its provision is not necessary for the pupil to receive an education suitable to his or her age, ability and aptitude, the parent may be required to pay as much as he or she can manage without financial hardship (ERA 1988, s 111).

(iv) Educational Maintenance Allowances/Minor Awards

Educational Maintenance Allowances are paid by LEAs in respect of pupils who have reached the end of their period of compulsory schooling but are staying on at school (Scholarships and Other Benefits Regulations 1977, as amended, reg 4(e)(i), made under EA 1944, s 81). The payments must be required to prevent or relieve financial hardship and must be related to the pupil's parents' means (reg 6). They are generally paid to the parents rather than the pupil. LEAs have a discretion as to both the assessment of need and the amount paid. There has always been a considerable disparity in levels of provision across different LEAs.

Most awards are very low. Nevertheless, the importance of these allowances in encouraging participation in education beyond the age of 16 has long been recognised (e.g. House of Commons Expenditure Committee (Education and Arts Sub-Committee) *Third Report 1974,* HC306). They were seen as essential to attract those with special educational needs to continue in education (*Warnock Report* (1978), para 10.103). In the light of the current inadequacy of EMA provision, various proposals for an improved, national system of allowances have been made over the years; but all would involve considerable amounts of additional public expenditure, and reform has been resisted by government.

Discretionary (or 'Minor') awards may also be made (EA 1962, s 2, incorporated into the EA 1980, s 19 and Sch 5). They are payable in respect of persons over compulsory school age attending a full- or part-time course, other than a course of secondary education or a course 'designated' for mandatory awards. They are usually paid direct to the young person concerned. In *R* v *London Borough of Lambeth ex p G* [1994] ELR 206 the applicant argued that the decision of the Lambeth LEA not to make him a Minor Award to enable him to study for A levels at his existing school, which was outside the LEA's area, was, *inter alia*, contrary to the provisions on parental choice in section 6 of the Education Act 1980 and unlawful. He had previously been in receipt of a maintenance grant while studying for GCSEs at the school. Potts J held that the purpose of a Minor Award was to enable persons from low income families to carry on studying beyond compulsory school age and into a sixth form. He said that the LEA's policy that, if appropriate provision was available in one of its schools, a Minor Award should not be made to a person to attend an extra-area school, had the effect of curtailing freedom of choice for no good reason.

Some LEAs give applicants an opportunity to appeal to an appeal panel when, for example, they are refused an award (see *Local Government Ombudsman Report on an Investigation No 92/B/3112 Against Berkshire CC* (1994)).

(c) School milk and meals

Although less directly connected with the theme of access to education discussed in this part of the chapter, provision of school milk and free school meals can conveniently and appropriately be discussed here.

Lady Thatcher attracted the nickname 'milk-snatcher' for proposing the Bill which became the Education (Milk) Act 1971. This Act, in effect, relieved LEAs of the duty to provide milk for a child after the school year in which he or she reached the age of seven. Only children at the primary stage, or at a special school, or who needed milk for health reasons, were entitled to school milk. LEAs had the *power* to provide milk to older pupils, but had to charge for it. The Education Act 1980, restated LEAs' power to provide milk, meals and other refreshments. But it stipulated that they were only to be provided free of charge to pupils whose parents were in receipt of supplementary benefit or family income supplement (FIS) (EA 1980, s 22(2)). In all other cases the LEA could make 'such charges as they think fit', although they could remit charges 'if, in the particular circumstances of any pupil or class or description of pupils, they consider it appropriate to do so' (EA 1980, s 22(3)(b)).

Free provision is, following the introduction of section 77(2) of the Social Security Act 1986 (which amended s 22 of the EA 1980), restricted to pupils who are, or whose parents are, in receipt of income support (the replacement, along with the social fund, for supplementary benefit – which was abolished in April 1988) (see EA 1980, s 22(2) and (3)). Family credit (FC) replaced FIS as the main social security benefit intended for those families dependent on a low wage, and the Government sought to deflect the criticism that the lack of entitlement to free school milk and meals for those receiving FC would cause hardship, by pointing out the higher rate of benefit paid under FC than under FIS.

LEAs are required to ensure that there are such facilities as they consider appropriate for the consumption of any meals or other refreshments brought to school by pupils (EA 1980, s 22(1)).

Chapter 12

Discipline

1. Introduction

The importance of discipline in schools lies not only in its contribution to a better learning environment. It also contributes to the protection of pupils from the physical and psychological effects of bullying (see DP Tattum and DA Lane (eds) *Bullying in Schools* (1989)). Recently a civil action was brought by a former school pupil who sued her LEA alleging that the school's failure to prevent her from being bullied at school, which she alleged had caused psychological damage, amounted to a breach of the duty of care owed to her (see pp 338–339). Comprehensive DFE guidance for schools on how best to deal with bullying has recently been issued: *Bullying: Don't Suffer in Silence* (1994). More generally DFE Circular 8/94 urges schools to act, and be seen to be acting, firmly against bullying and to ensure that school behaviour and discipline policies and rules of conduct make specific reference to it. Similar guidance is offered in respect of racial and sexual harassment (paras 56–61). In respect of less serious forms of misconduct, there is an emphasis not only on punishment but also on rewards – to encourage good behaviour (paras 36–38). This has been recommended for some time now (see e.g. HMI, *Education Observed 5: Good Behaviour and Discipline in Schools* (1987)), although some schools still place too much emphasis 'on external control, with little expectation that pupils might develop self-discipline' (OFSTED, *Access and Achievement in Urban Education*, (1993) para 36). Schools continue to apply a wide range of sanctions in cases of misbehaviour (for a review of the law and practice, see N Harris, 'Discipline in Schools: the Elton Report' (1991) JSWFL 110). Their selection may be left to the good sense of the school, provided that due regard is given to the constraints imposed by the law and the school's disciplinary policy.

A review of the law governing pupil discipline and, more especially, disciplinary practice, was undertaken by a committee of enquiry chaired by Lord Elton, which reported in 1989 (*Discipline in Schools* (HMSO)). Changes have been introduced in line with some of the committee's recommendations (guidance issued in the form of DFE Circular 8/94 (above) 'draws on the findings and recommendations of the Elton Committee' and contains, *inter alia*, recommendations on the preparation of a 'whole school behaviour policy'). The committee called for greater liaison between teachers, parents, education welfare officers and other agencies, but this has resource implications, as it requires more education welfare officers and more of teachers' time; so far insufficient additional resources have been found. One of the recommendations of the committee was that the Government should provide funds for the training of staff and additional support for dealing with the more difficult of pupils. Provision has been made under the LEA Training Grants Scheme and the Education Support Grant Scheme, although the amounts available have been small. The GEST programme for 1995–96 will provide grants in respect of 'The Truancy and Disaffected Pupils' which may fund, *inter alia*, discipline training. The Elton Committee also recommended monitoring of the operation of the exclusion and reinstatement provisions of the Education (No 2) Act 1986. The Government established a National Exclusion Reporting System which operated for two years. This found, *inter alia* (for a summary of findings, see DFE, *Exclusions: A Discussion Paper* (1992) para 16), that there was a substantial increase in the number of permanent exclusions from school (from 2,910 in 1990–91 to 3,833 in 1991–92). Changes to the law, via the Education Act 1993, have provided for: a downwards adjustment in the funding of a school from the date of the pupil's permanent exclusion (s 262; see DFE 17/94), in a bid to discourage permanent exclusion; a new duty on LEAs to make provision otherwise than at school for excluded pupils (s 298); and, in the light of the continuing delays in the resumption of many permanently excluded pupils' education (see OFSTED, *Education for Disaffected Pupils* (1993), para 12), a requirement (see pp 168–169 above) for a school to admit a child when directed by the LEA to do so.

The Elton Report also called for the teacher's disciplinary authority to be set in statute. This was not acted upon (see DES Press Release 141/90, 2 May 1990). Another possible legal change, concerning civil liability for parents in respect of their children's acts in school, was also rejected by the Government. The Elton Report also urged against racial stereotyping of certain ethnic groups as troublemakers (R 91 and p 159); there was evidence of over-representation of Afro-Caribbean pupils in the exclusion statistics from 1990–92 (see DFE, *Exclusions: A Discussion Paper, op cit*; OFSTED, *Education for Disaffected Pupils* (1993) para 9). This issue has yet to be fully tackled, although it has at least been recognised officially (see p 316 below).

A further problem, addressed in particular by OFSTED, has concerned the practice of excluding pupils indefinitely from school. OFSTED recommended the abolition of the power to exclude indefinitely (OFSTED, *Exclusions* (1993), pp 1–2), and the Education Act 1993 effected this reform. Emphasising the DFE's general view that schools should use the power of exclusion 'sparingly and as a last resort' (*Exclusions: A Discussion Paper*, *op cit*, para 17), the 1993 Act will limit the power of fixed term exclusion by restricting the number of days in any term for which a pupil can be excluded.

The Education (No 2) Act 1986 in effect took away from most teachers the power to inflict corporal punishment. In respect of certain pupils in independent schools it may still be used: but the 1993 Act has constrained the power, with reference to the test for lawful chastisement laid down in the European Convention on Human Rights 1950.

The law governing discipline in schools has become increasingly complex. In addition to the amendments to the 1986 Act and additional provision made by the Education Act 1993 and recent regulations, there are parts of the Children Act 1989 that may be relevant to the action that may be taken and procedures invoked in the case of pupils who misbehave. There is also the framework provided by the UK's international treaty obligations, notably the European Convention on Human Rights (see below) and the United Nations Convention on the Rights of the Child 1989. The latter provides, for example, that 'States parties shall take all appropriate measures to ensure that school discipline is administered in a manner consistent with the child's human dignity and in conformity with the present Convention' (Art 28). Furthermore, there have been a number of important court cases over the past few years and fresh, and more detailed, guidance from the DFE (including a portfolio of circulars – *Pupil Behaviour and Discipline* (8/94) referred to above, *The Education of Children with Emotional and Behavioural Difficulties* (9/94), *Exclusions from School* (10/94) and *The Education by LEAs of Children Otherwise than at School* (11/94) – issued in May 1994, which are discussed in the relevant places in this chapter). Increasing attention has also been focused on the appeals procedures in exclusions cases, which the Council on Tribunals' guidance on *Education Appeals* also covers.

This, then, is a very broad area, and one in which the law provides the framework for an important and difficult area of practice. Inevitably, the following exposition concentrates on the legal issues, but it seeks to relate them to some of the practical and policy issues, drawing on the recent guidance from the DFE.

2. Responsibility for disciplinary matters

(a) General responsibility for discipline

Overall responsibility for the conduct of a county, controlled or maintained special school rests with the governing body, since the school must be conducted 'under their direction' (E(No 2)A 1986, s 16(1)). In a grant-maintained school, the school must be conducted in accordance with the articles of government, which must spell out the responsibilities of the governing body, head teacher and others (see EA 1993, s 55 and Sch 6, para 2). The initial articles for GM schools are prescribed and contain a similar general provision stating that overall responsibility for the conduct of the school should rest with the governing body (Education (Grant-maintained Schools) (Initial Governing Instruments) Regulations 1993).

(b) The role of head teachers

In respect of county, voluntary and maintained special schools there are a number of specific rules dealing with discipline, placing day-to-day responsibility in the hands of head teachers:

'The articles of government for every county, voluntary and maintained special school shall provide:

(*a*) for it to be the duty of the head teacher to determine measures (which may include the making of rules and provision for enforcing them) to be taken with a view to–

(i) promoting, among pupils, self-discipline and proper regard for authority;

(ii) encouraging good behaviour [and respect for others] on the part of pupils;

(iii) securing that the standard of behaviour of pupils is acceptable; and

(iv) otherwise regulating the conduct of pupils;

(*b*) for it to be the duty of the head teacher, in determining any such measures–

(i) to act in accordance with any written statement of general principles provided for him by the governing body; and

(ii) to have regard to any guidance that they may offer in relation to particular matters;

(*c*) for it to be the duty of the head teacher to make any such measures generally known within the school;

(*d*) for the standard of behaviour which is to be regarded as acceptable at the school to be determined by the head teacher, so far as it is not determined by the governing body;

(*e*) for it to be the duty of the governing body and the head teacher to consult the local education authority, before determining any such measures, on any matter arising from the proposed measures which can reasonably be expected–

(i) to lead to increased expenditure by the authority; or

(ii) to affect the responsibilities of the authority as an employer;

(*f*) for the power to exclude a pupil from the school (whether by suspension, expulsion or otherwise) to be exercisable only by the head teacher'.

(E(No 2)A 1986, s 22; the words in square brackets in para (a)(ii) were added by EA 1993, Sch 19 para 95).

Note that under the Education (School Government) Regulations 1989, the governors cannot delegate to the head teacher, or to anyone else, the role of agreeing their written statement on pupil discipline (see p 104, above). Similar provision to that in section 22 (above) (apart from (*e*), for which there is no equivalent) is made in respect of discipline in GM schools by these schools' articles of government (see Schedule 2 to the Education (Grant-maintained Schools) (Initial Governing Instruments) Regulations 1993, at art 9).

(c) Teachers' disciplinary authority

Individual classroom teachers have disciplinary authority, which can be enforced through the use of sanctions (although these have become more limited since the changes to the law governing corporal punishment – see below). This authority is now widely recognised as being independent rather than derived from the *in loco parentis* principle (which was regarded as giving teachers disciplinary authority through expressed or implied parental delegation: see *Cleary* v *Booth* [1893] 1 QB 465 *per* Collins J at p 468 and *Ryan* v *Fildes* [1938] 3 All ER 517 *per* Tucker J at p 521). The Elton Report (1989, *op cit*), for example, noted (para 72) that the 'case law is probably sufficient to inhibit litigation by parents opposed to particular actions, such as putting a child in detention'. However the Elton Committee wanted the teachers' disciplinary authority to be enshrined in statute to remove any scope for doubt, although this has not happened. There have been circumstances in respect of which the court has held that the teacher's disciplinary authority extends to a pupil's misbehaviour outside school, for example where a pupil was smoking in a public place contrary to school rules or hitting another pupil on the way to or from school (see *R* v *Newport (Salop) JJ ex p Wright* [1929] 2 KB 416 and *Cleary* v *Booth, op cit*). But this was on the basis that the teacher's disciplinary authority derived from the *in loco parentis* principle, and it is unclear whether teachers now have this authority outside the school context. Mention should also be made of the Children Act 1989. This provides for certain individuals to hold parental responsibility in respect of a child; parental responsibility is defined in section 3(1) of the 1989 Act as including 'all the rights, duties, powers, responsibilities and authority which by law a parent has in relation to the child and his property' and is taken to include disciplinary authority. Those with parental responsibility can arrange for others to exercise it on their behalf (Children Act 1989, section 2(9)). In any event, a person caring for a child may 'do what is reasonable in all the circumstances of the case for the purpose of safeguarding or promoting the child's welfare' (*ibid*, s 3(5)). Either way, the 1989 Act probably authorises a teacher to exert disciplinary authority over a pupil either to promote the child's welfare or that of fellow pupils (see further the discussion at pp 357–358 below).

One question that arises from this is how any conflict between the parent and the teacher over how a pupil should be disciplined should be resolved. There are several legal provisions which support a degree of parental choice over the matter, notably section 76 of the Education Act 1944, which lays down the general principle that 'children are to be educated in accordance with the wishes of their parents', and Article 2, First Protocol, United Nations Convention on Human Rights 1950, which, in the context of the right to education, calls upon states to uphold the religious and philosophical convictions of parents. The latter was successfully invoked in a case where Scottish parents had kept their children away from school because of their opposition to corporal punishment (*Campbell and Cosans* v *UK* [1982] 4 EHRR 293). Parental wishes need only be upheld under section 76 of the 1944 Act if, *inter alia*, it would be compatible with the provision of efficient education. Surely giving individual parents of pupils some choice over disciplinary matters would be unworkable and hardly compatible with the smooth running of a school. Indeed, that is why the Government dropped its plans, enshrined in the 1985 Education Bill following the *Campbell and Cosans* ruling, to give individual parents a choice about whether their children might receive corporal punishment. The European Convention on Human Rights also states that public authorities should not interfere with the individual's private and family life (Art 8); but it has been held that inflicting a form of punishment at school, in particular corporal punishment, does not normally constitute unlawful interference with private life if it does not entail adverse effects for the person's physical or moral integrity, bearing in mind that 'the sending of a child to school necessarily involves some degree of interference with his or her private life' (*Costello-Roberts* v *UK* [1994] ELR 1 at p 12).

3. Enforcing discipline

(a) 'Excessive' punishment

Excessive punishment is clearly outside the scope of a teacher's or head teacher's authority. What is excessive for this purpose is punishment that would give rise to liability for assault, battery or false imprisonment under civil and/or criminal law. One of the guiding principles is that all punishment given to pupils must be 'reasonable', not 'for the gratification of passion or rage' or overly protracted or too severe (*R* v *Hopley* [1860] 1862 F&F 202, *per* Cockburn CJ). 'Inhuman or degrading treatment or punishment' is contrary to the European Convention on Human Rights, whether inflicted in a state school or independent school (*Costello-Roberts* v *UK* (1994); this case is discussed in (c) below).

(b) Exclusion of pupils

(i) Who may exclude?

As noted above (p 312), the power to exclude a pupil rests exclusively with the head teacher. A person acting in the head's absence may exercise this power (by virtue of delegation, as provided for in *The School Teacher's Pay and Conditions Document*: see *Appendix 3*).

(ii) When to exclude

The law has never prescribed the kinds of behaviour in respect of which the power of exclusion may be exercised. The only guidance has derived from decisions such as *R* v *Hopley* (1860) on the need for punishment to be a moderate and reasonable response to the relevant behaviour. However, in one recent case the High Court granted leave for a pupil to apply for judicial review of the decision of the head teacher of a secondary school in Cheshire to exclude him for allegedly telling a supply teacher to 'f--- off' ('Court to review boy's f-word expulsion', *The Independent*, 8 September 1993).

Case law has established that unjustifiable exclusion, whilst not an actionable tort (*Hunt* v *Damon* (1930) 46 TLR 575), can, in the case of a child excluded from a private or independent school, constitute a breach of contract (*Price* v *Wilkins* (1888) 58 LT 680). In *Fitzgerald* v *Nothcote* (1865) 4 F&F 656 the implied contract between parent and private school was held to impose on the school an obligation to provide education for the child provided the child did not misbehave in such a way as to justify his exclusion from school. In fact, the normal basis for a challenge to an exclusion from an independent school, based on arguments as to unfairness, lies in suit for breach of contract, since public law remedies are not available (*R* v *Fernhill Manor School ex p A* [1994] ELR 67; on the contractual basis to private schooling, see further *Mount* v *Oldham Corporation* [1973] 1 QB 309 and *Price* v *Dennis* (1988) Court of Appeal, 29 January 1988). Public law remedies may, however, be available, in respect of exclusion from a maintained school (*R* v *Board of Governors of London Oratory School ex p R* [1988] The Times, 17 February). However, it must be emphasised that in judicial review proceedings the basis of the challenge to exclusion is more likely to succeed if it concerns questions of procedural fairness (see below) rather than the merits of the decision to exclude; moreover a question of reasonableness would generally be one for the Secretary of State to consider first (under s 68 of the EA 1944: see p 5 above), on complaint by the parent or pupil. In relation to the question whether an excluded child should be reinstated, Potts J said in a recent case that 'that is essentially for those who are concerned with the administration of the school and the education of (the) child. Educational factors will have to be taken into account, which are outside the province of this court' (*R* v *The Board of Governors of Stoke Newington School and Others ex p M* [1994] ELR 131, at p 138).

The DFE's Circular 10/94 (*Exclusions from School* (1994)) lays down guidance as to when a school might be justified in excluding a pupil, emphasising that exclusion should be considered as 'a last resort' (para 5). It advises that permanent exclusion should only be used when 'the school has taken all reasonable steps to avoid excluding the child; and allowing the child to remain at school would be seriously detrimental to the education or welfare of the pupil, or to that of others at the school' (*ibid*). The circular later indicates the factors to be taken into account in determining the need for, and duration of, any exclusion. These include: the age, intellectual ability and state of health of the pupil; the pupil's previous record; the pupil's domestic situation and any family changes (e.g. greater tolerance may be needed for pupils who have been the victims of child abuse or whose parents have divorced); any parental or peer group pressure leading to the committal of the misbehaviour, the degree and severity of the offence and the likelihood of it recurring; and whether the pupil acted alone or was part of group (scapegoating being particularly undesirable) (para 21). Children whose misbehaviour may be a symptom of emotional and behavioural difficulties may need to be treated differently, under the procedures set out in separate guidance (see DFE, *Code of Practice on Identification and Assessment of Children with Special*

Educational Needs (1994) and DFE Circular 9/94, *The Education of Children with Emotional and Behavioural Difficulties* (1994)).

(iii) Restrictions on the power of exclusion

The Education Acts impose certain restrictions on the power of exclusion. In addition, practising unjustifiable race or sex discrimination when subjecting a pupil to exclusion (or indeed to 'any other detriment') would be unlawful under section 17 of the Race Relations Act 1976 or section 22 of the Sex Discrimination Act 1975. The DFE's Circular (*Exclusions from School*, *op cit*, para 32) recommends that head teachers should take 'particular care to ensure that they apply disciplinary procedures objectively and consistently across all cultural groups'. The exclusion of a pupil who cannot comply with uniform or dress requirements for cultural or religious reasons is now specifically warned against (para 26), partly on the basis that it could constitute indirect race discrimination contrary to the Race Relations Act 1976 (above) (see *Mandla* v *Dowell Lee* (1983), discussed at p 175).

A pupil may be excluded for a fixed term or permanently, but now that section 261(1)(a) of the Education Act 1993 is in force a head teacher is not permitted to exclude a pupil for an indefinite period. Under transitional arrangements, the exclusion of any pupil standing indefinitely excluded at the date the section came into operation (1 September 1994) terminated within one month of that date (EA 1993, s 261(3)(b)). In practice, 75 per cent of exclusions are fixed term, usually for two to three days (OFSTED, *Education for Disaffected Pupils* (1993), para 6). Section 261(1)(b) (in force) provides that a pupil may not be excluded for one or more fixed periods totalling more than 15 school days in all in any school term. This limit does not apply to a pupil whose exclusion began before the section came into effect, but any further periods of exclusion after the commencement date will be covered by the 15-day limit, and periods of exclusion prior to the commencement date but in the same term as that date will count towards the total (EA 1993, s 261(4)). Note that section 261 above applies to grant-maintained and grant-maintained special schools as well as LEA-maintained schools.

(iv) Procedural requirements when exercising the power of exclusion

1. The head teacher must (E(No 2)A 1986, s 23), without delay (which the DFE's Circular 10/94 *Exclusions from School* states should be interpreted as on the day of the exclusion if possible):

- (i) inform the pupil's parents (if pupil is under 18) of the period of exclusion (including where the exclusion was originally for a fixed period and the head teacher subsequently decides to make it permanent) and the reasons for it; and
- (ii) inform the parents, and the pupil if 18 or over, of the right to make representations about the exclusion to the governing body and the LEA (see *R v Newham LBC ex p X* [1994] The Times 15 November).

The Circular (*op cit*) states that the notification should be given in writing and, if appropriate, orally. In cases of permanent exclusion, the guidance recommends that the head teacher should explain parents' rights of access to the pupil's curricular record under the Education (School Records) Regulations (discussed at pp 162–165 above). The Circular also recommends that parents should be informed that they should notify the governing body/disciplinary committee and/or LEA in writing of their intention to make representations (see paras 44 and 45).

2. In the case of a fixed-term exclusion the head teacher must also (E(No 2)A 1986, s 23), again without delay, inform the LEA of his or her decision (including the period of exclusion in relevant cases) and the reason for it (i) if it will involve exclusion for an aggregate of more than five days in any one term, or the pupil would miss an opportunity to take a public examination; or (ii) if a fixed period of exclusion is to be made permanent. The Circular (*op cit*, at para 45) recommends that it is 'in any case good practice for the head teacher to notify the governing body and LEA of all exclusions regardless of their duration' because 'it provides them with the opportunity to intervene' if they are not content with the head teacher's action. In the case of permanent exclusions, the LEA must be informed in every case.

Similar rules apply under the articles of government of GM schools, but the need to notify the LEA only arises if the exclusion is permanent and when the disciplinary committee (established by the governing body to make decisions on reinstatement) decides not to reinstate (arts 10 and 11 of Sch 2 to the Education (Grant-maintained Schools) (Initial Governing Instruments) Regulations 1993).

3. What should happen next depends on the type of school that is involved:

A. *County, controlled and maintained special schools*

The articles of government must contain the requirements regarding reinstatement laid down in section 24 of the E(No 2)A 1986. These may be summarised thus (note the time limits laid down mostly in the Education (Exclusions from Schools) (Prescribed Periods) Regulations 1994 (SI 1994 No 2093) (ESPP Regs)):

Permanent exclusion: The DFE Circular 10/94 (*op cit*) (paras 48, 49 and 58) advises that in all cases of permanent exclusion the governing body (or, in the case of GM schools, the disciplinary committee) should convene a meeting within a maximum of 15 school days of the notification by the head teacher of the exclusion. The purpose of this meeting is for the governing body to consider the case and any representations by the parents. The parents must be given an opportunity to 'make written and oral representations in an environment which avoids intimidation and excessive formality'. As the governing body may delegate this function, the circular recommends that a committee of at least three members of the governing body, excluding the head teacher, should consider the matter. In GM schools the disciplinary committee must contain a minimum of three governors, excluding the head teacher. The panel in all schools should not include a teacher who has been responsible for the pupil whose exclusion is the subject of the meeting. In *R* v *The Board of Governors of Stoke Newington School and Others ex p M* [1994] ELR 131 the teacher concerned was a governor who, in his capacity as teacher, had been the excluded girl's head of year and had had previous dealings with her. The panel, which included the teacher, confirmed the head teacher's decision to exclude the child. In quashing the panel's decision, Potts J said that in the view of the reasonable man there was a real likelihood of bias against the pupil as a result of the presence on the exclusion panel of the teacher, by virtue of the teacher's relationship to the child.

Parents and pupils should be advised that they may, if they so desire, bring someone with them to represent them. It is clear that the rules of natural justice apply to the proceedings: 'It must be right that a [pupil] facing possible expulsion should know the nature of the accusation made against him, that he should have an opportunity to answer, and he should appear before a tribunal that acts in good faith' (*per* McCullough J in *R* v *Board of Governors of the London Oratory School ex p Regis* [1988] The Times, 17 February; Lexis).

The Circular advises that the parent and pupil be informed of the outcome of the meeting 'without delay'. Once informed, the LEA must consider, after giving the governing body an opportunity (15 school days, running from the date the LEA was notified of the exclusion: ESPP Regs, *op cit*, Sch 1) to express its views and after considering any such views expressed within the prescribed period, whether the pupil should be reinstated. If it decides he or she should be, it should (within 20 school days of being notified of the exclusion: *ibid*) give an appropriate direction to the head teacher. The direction will not take effect for 5 school days (or until the governors indicate they will not be appealing, whichever is the sooner) (E(No 2)A 1986, Sch 3 para 3(1), as amended). If the LEA decides not to reinstate, it must inform the pupil (if aged 18 or over) or his or her parent(s) (E(No 2)A 1986, s 24(a)) within 20 school days from the date the head teacher informed it (the LEA) of the exclusion (ESPP Regs, *op cit*, Sch 1). The head teacher is bound by any direction made under section 24(a) (s 24(f)). If the governors (who have a separate power to) order the reinstatement of a pupil who has been excluded from the school by the head teacher (see s 22(f)) for any period during which he would have taken a public examination, and the exclusion is permanent, the head teacher must comply with their directions (s 24(b)) (as to LEA's and governors' directions conflicting, as to the date of reinstatement, see below). The parent or pupil (if aged 18 or over) has a right of appeal to an appeal committee in respect of a decision not to reinstate the pupil (E(No 2)A 1986, s 26 – see below). When notifying the parent or pupil of the decision not to reinstate, the LEA or governing body (as appropriate) must inform the parent or pupil (as appropriate) of this right and of the time limit for an appeal (E(No 2)A 1986, Sch 3 paras 1 and 2, as substituted by the Education (No 2) Act 1986 (Amendment) (No 2) Order 1994 (SI 1994 No 2092)) (see below at p 320). The governing body also has a right of appeal, where the LEA directs the child's reinstatement (E(No 2)A 1986, s 26). The parent or pupil (as appropriate) must be informed of their right to make representations to the appeal committee (E(No 2)A 1986, Sch 3 para 3(2)) (see further *Duty to inform* below).

Fixed-term exclusion: Reinstatement here may be ordered by the governors or LEA. Where the LEA propose to order reinstatement, they must first consult with the governors (E(No 2)A 1986, s 24(d)). The head teacher must comply with the order, provided that the pupil has been excluded for more than five school days (in aggregate) in any school term or in circumstances in which the pupil will miss the opportunity to take a public examination (s 24(b)). There is no right of appeal against the decision on reinstatement in the case of a fixed-term exclusion. Before the governing body or LEA takes a decision on reinstatement the parents must, if they wish to make representations, be given an opportunity to do so (see s 24(a)(iii)). Similar provision as is recommended in the case of permanent exclusions, for a committee of the governing body to meet as soon as practicable to consider these representations and make the decision on reinstatement (see above), is recommended for fixed-term exclusions (Circular 10/94, *op cit* para 48). The case law on natural justice is equally applicable.

Time limits: Time limits within which the governing body should decide whether a pupil should be reinstated, set by the articles of government, have been held not to be mandatory, as a number of factors, including educational factors, may bear on the speed within which such a decision may be taken: *R* v *Board of Governors of Stoke Newington School and Others ex p M* [1944] ELR 131 (QBD). It would appear that the time limits now laid down in the ESPP Regulations (above) do not themselves have to be incorporated into the articles. But whether or not a court would regard them as mandatory in every case is unclear. Note that there are separate time limits.

Conflicting directions: Where the directions of the LEA and governors conflict as to the date of reinstatement, the head teacher must 'comply with that direction which will lead to the earlier reinstatement of the pupil' (E(No 2)A 1986, s 24(g)).

Duty to inform: The governors and LEA are required to inform each other and the parents of the pupil (and the pupil if 18 or over) of any direction as to reinstatement made under section 24 of the 1986 Act (see s 24(h)). These parties must be informed within one school day from the date on which the direction was given (ESPP Regs 1994, *op cit* Sch 1) under section 24 of the 1986 Act (above).

Note also the rules on delegation and withdrawal discussed in C below.

B. *Voluntary aided and special agreement schools*

Similar rules to those applicable in county, controlled and maintained special schools (see A above) apply to aided and special agreement schools (E(No 2)A 1986, s 25 and the ESPP Regs 1994, *op cit*, Sch 2)), with one significant difference – the corresponding duty to that in section 24(a) (duty to consider reinstatement etc.) in cases of permanent exclusion rests with the governing body and not the LEA (E(No 2)A 1986, s 25(a)). Appeal arrangements must be made by the governing body; the parent must be informed of them at the same time that notification is given on the decision not to reinstate (E(No 2)A 1986, Sch 3 para 2). The DFE's guidance, referred to at various points in (i) above, applies also to voluntary aided and special agreement schools. Note also the rules on delegation and withdrawal discussed in C below.

C. *Delegation of decisions (LEA-maintained schools)*

Governing bodies cannot delegate to an individual consideration (under sections 24 and 25 of the E(No 2)A 1986 (see above)) of whether to direct the reinstatement of an excluded pupil or the consideration of representations made in exclusion cases (Education (School Government) Regulations 1989, reg 25(4)), but may delegate such matters to a committee of at least three governors (excluding the head teacher) (reg 26(6)). Note that when governing bodies or their delegates are considering any disciplinary matter relating to a pupil they should bear in mind the rules on withdrawal from meetings and voting laid down in the Education (School Government) Regulations 1989 and, in the case of GM schools, the articles of government (discussed in Chapter 4, at pp 98–101).

D. *Grant-maintained schools*

In GM schools the disciplinary committee of the governing body considers reinstatement. The committee may order the head teacher to reinstate an excluded pupil in parallel circumstances to those applicable in the case of LEA-maintained schools (see C and D above) (see art 11 of the prescribed Initial Articles of Government as amended by SI 1994 No 2094; note the time limits in art 11(3A) introduced from 1 September 1994).

(vi) Appeals

Arrangements for appeals against failure to reinstate are required in cases of *permanent exclusion only*. These arrangements must be made by the LEA, in the case of county, controlled and maintained special schools (E (No 2)A 1986, s 26(1)), and by the governing body in the case of aided and special agreement schools (s 26(2)). Appeals may be made by the pupil himself or herself if aged 18 or over and in other cases by the parent(s). The appeal must be lodged within 15 school days of notification of the right of appeal by the governing body and LEA (E(No 2)A 1986, Sch 3 para 3A).

In the case of county, controlled and maintained special schools, the governors may also appeal – if the LEA has ordered the reinstatement of a permanently excluded pupil. There is separate provision for GM schools (see below).

Appeal lies to an appeal committee which should normally meet within 15 school days of the lodging of the appeal (E(No 2)A 1986, Sch 3 para 6A; DFE Circular 10/94, para 70). The decision of the appeal committee is binding (E(No 2)A 1986, s 26(5)). The appeal committee is constituted under Schedule 2 to the Education Act 1980 and is the same one that hears appeals concerning school admissions (see Chapter 7, Part 7), although under a separate procedure (see E(No 2)A 1986, Sch 3, as amended). Guidance is offered by *Education Appeals: Code of Practice on Procedure* (prepared on behalf of the Council on Tribunals), which is currently being revised.

The articles of government require the LEA, in the case of county, controlled and maintained special schools, and the governors, in the case of aided and special agreement schools, to inform the parents (or pupil, if aged 18 or over) of their right of appeal, and the time limit for appealing, when informing them of the decision on reinstatement (E(No 2)A 1986, Sch 3, paras 1 and 2, as substituted). If the governors appeal against an LEA's decision to reinstate (under s 24(a)), the parent (if pupil aged under 18) or pupil (if aged 18 or over) must (within four school days) be informed of their right to make representations to the appeal committee (*ibid*, para 3(2)) (note that reinstatement ordered by the LEA is suspended for five school days whilst the governors decide whether or not to appeal (*ibid*, para 3(1))).

Written notice, setting out the grounds of appeal, must be given (para 6). The appeal committee must meet within 15 school days of the day on which the appeal was lodged (para 6A). All parties can attend, be represented and offer oral or written submissions (*ibid*, paras 7 and 8, as amended by the Education (No 2) Act 1986 (Amendment) Order 1993, SI 1993 No 2709 and (Same) (No 2) Order 1993, SI 1993 No 2827). The Council on Tribunals' 1992 Code of Practice on Appeals (currently being revised) (note that there is a separate Code of Practice for GM schools) suggests that legal representation may be 'unnecessary and could be counter-productive'; however, it advises that 'it will seldom be appropriate' to prevent the parent from using it. It should be added that it might also be contrary to natural justice and international law to do so. Governors with a personal involvement in the case must withdraw.

The running order is a matter for the panel, but the Code of Practice by the Council on Tribunals suggests an appropriate order of hearing. Appeals should be disposed of 'without delay' (E(No 2)A 1986, Sch 3, para 9); extension of any time limit set by the governors may be permitted (*ibid*, reg 9(2)). The appeal hearing must generally be held in private, but LEA observers or members of the Council on Tribunals are entitled to be present (E(No 2)A 1986, Sch 3, para 13). Two or more appeals may be heard together where 'the issues raised by the appeals are the same or connected' (*ibid*, para 14). The decision plus reasons must (generally within 17 school days) be communicated by the committee in writing to the parent, the pupil (if aged 18 or over), the LEA and the governing body (*ibid*, para 12).

Appeals against permanent exclusion from a *grant-maintained school* may be made by the pupil (if aged 18 or over) or the parent (Education (Grant-maintained Schools) (Initial Governing Instruments) Regulations 1993, Sch 2, art 11, as amended). Appeals lie to the governing body's appeal committee (constituted in accordance with App 3 to Sch 1 to the above regulations). The procedure is laid down in the articles of government and there are corresponding time limits, notice requirements etc, to those for LEA-maintained schools (see 1993 Regs above, Sch 2, as amended). As noted above, there is also a separate Code of Practice on Education Appeals in respect of GM schools, published by the Council on Tribunals. The EA 1993 enables appeal arrangements to be made jointly with the governing body of one or more other GM schools (Sch 6, para 5).

(vii) Alternative provision for excluded pupils

Arrangements for suitable full-time or part-time education must be made by LEAs for pupils who have been excluded from school and who, in consequence, will not otherwise receive the education they need (EA 1993, s 298(1)). This duty (which replaces a discretion in EA 1944, s 56) applies to pupils of compulsory school age. LEAs have a discretion to make this provision for 16–19 year-olds (*ibid*, s 298(4)).

(c) Corporal punishment

Despite the general ban on the use of corporal punishment in state schools (E(No 2)A 1986, s 47 – see below), it may still be inflicted in independent schools, but certainly not independent schools funded under the Direct Grants Regulations 1959, schools maintained by the Ministry of Defence and central government funded city technology colleges and colleges for the technology of the arts (E(No 2)A 1986, s 47(5)(a)(iii) and the Education (Abolition of Corporal Punishment) (Independent Schools) Regulations 1987 and (Amendment) Regulations 1989). In independent schools where corporal punishment may still be used, it may not be given to any pupil whose fees in respect of attendance are paid by a local authority or education authority (Scotland) or the Education Board (Northern Ireland) (E(No 2)A 1986, s 47(6)(b) and (7), and the Education (Abolition of Corporal Punishment) (Independent Schools) (Prescribed Categories of Persons) Regulations 1989).

The cases sanctioning the use of corporal punishment in schools have, since 15 August 1987, been relevant only to independent schools. The common law sanctions corporal punishment provided it is not inflicted 'for the gratification of passion or rage', or is not 'excessive in its nature or degree, or . . . protracted beyond the child's powers of endurance' (*per* Cockburn CJ in *R* v *Hopley* (1860) (*op cit*); see also *R* v *Grey* [1666] Kel J 64; *Ryan* v *Fildes* [1938] 3 All ER 517 (CA); and *R* v *Gilchrist* [1961] The

Times, 11 July) – otherwise the teacher may be guilty of an assault and could be made the defendant in a civil suit or criminal action. However, inflicting corporal punishment where the parents are philosophically opposed to it is a breach of Article 2 to the First Protocol to the European Convention on Human Rights 1950 (*Campbell and Cosans* v *UK* (1982)). Corporal punishment which amounts to 'torture or inhuman or degrading treatment or punishment' is contrary to Article 3 of the Convention. In *Costello-Roberts* v *United Kingdom* (1994) the applicant, aged seven, received three strikes on his bottom through his shorts with a rubber-soled gym shoe administered in private by the head teacher. The European Court of Human Rights (ECHR) reviewed the authorities and concluded that the question whether a breach of Article 3 had occurred depended on such factors as the nature and context of the punishment, the manner and method of its execution, its duration, its physical and mental effects and, in some instances, the sex, age and state of health of the victim. The Court held (by a majority of 5–4) that on the evidence the applicant's punishment had been insufficiently severe to constitute a breach of Article 3. It was also held that the treatment meted out to the applicant did not entail the kinds of adverse effect on his physical or moral integrity as would bring it within the scope of Article 8 (which calls for respect for private and family life), although the Court did not rule out the possibility that in some circumstances greater protection might be afforded by Article 8 than by Article 3. Finally, the Court considered whether the applicant had available an adequate route to a remedy under domestic law (as required by Art 13) and concluded unanimously that he did.

So far as Article 3 is concerned, the Government decided in the light of the *Costello-Roberts* decision to amend the law on corporal punishment still further, to ensure that any such punishment meted out in English, Welsh and Scottish schools conforms to the standard laid down in the Convention, as interpreted by the ECHR. Accordingly, it is now provided that 'where, in any proceedings, it is shown that corporal punishment has been given to a pupil by or on the authority of a member of the staff, giving the punishment cannot be justified if the punishment was inhuman or degrading' (E(No 2)A 1986, s 47(1A), added by EA 1993, s 293(2) (in England and Wales); and Education (Scotland) Act 1980, s 48A(1A), added by s 294(2) of the 1993 Act (in Scotland)). In determining whether or not such punishment is inhuman or degrading, 'regard shall be had to all the circumstances of the case, including the reason for giving it, its nature, the manner and circumstances in which it is given, the persons involved and its mental and physical effects' (E(No 2)A 1986, s 47(1B), added by EA 1993, s 293(2)). This means that the kinds of factors which the cases, and in particular *Costello-Roberts*, state should be applied in determining whether there has been a breach of Article 3, are to be applied in judging whether there has been inhuman or degrading corporal punishment for the purposes of the relevant education legislation.

Corporal punishment in state schools, including grant-maintained schools, is no longer lawful (E(No 2)A 1986, s 47) – other than where it is necessary:

> 'for reasons that include averting an immediate danger of personal injury to, or an immediate danger to the property of, any person (including the pupil concerned)' (s 47(3)).

No specific offence of unlawful corporal punishment is created by section 47 (s 47(4)); the section merely seems to remove a defence of lawful chastisement in any proceedings brought against a teacher. 'Corporal punishment' means, for the purposes of the section:

> 'anything [done] for the purposes of punishing the pupil concerned (whether or not there are also other reasons for doing it) which, apart from any justification, would constitute battery' (s 47(2)).

On an attempt, prior to the 1986 Act, by an LEA to ban corporal punishment in schools, see *R* v *Manchester City Council ex p Fulford* (1984) 81 LGR 292 (DC).

(d) Detention

Detention is not unlawful as a form of punishment of pupils, but teachers need to use it sparingly and with care if they are to avoid illegality. The general principle (in the criminal case of *R* v *Hopley* (1860)) which holds that all punishment must be reasonable and moderate surely applies to detention as well. Detention for improper reason is false imprisonment (*Fitzgerald* v *Northcote* (1865) (*op cit*)). Detention by a parent of his or her own child is unlawful if it is 'for such a period or in such circumstances as to take it out of the realm of reasonable parental discipline' (*per* Lane LCJ in *R* v *Rachman* [1985] 81 Cr App Rep 349). The position of the teacher who detains is surely analogous to this, especially given the traditional emphasis on the *in loco parentis* principle (see above) in providing the justification for various forms of disciplinary action by teachers. There is, of course, an overriding duty on teachers as regards the safety of pupils. Therefore parents should be notified in advance if younger pupils are to be detained or if the detention is going to be for more than 5–10 minutes. There is a county court decision (*Terrington* v *Lancashire County Council* (1986) (unreported)) which suggests that the detention of a whole class, where there is known to be only one culprit, may be unlawful. DFE Circular 8/94, *Pupil Behaviour and Discipline* (para 41) advises that 'it is general good practice to provide parents with at least twenty-four hours' written notice for detentions lasting longer than thirty minutes'. This, it is submitted, probably misrepresents by overestimation, the extent of the teacher's authority in matters of detention. Furthermore it should be noted that in extreme cases, school detention could amount to child abuse (see pp 362–363 below).

Children who are a danger to themselves and/or others or to property in the way they are behaving, may require physical restraint. DFE guidance is at present rather brief (see DFE Circular 9/94, *The Education of Children with Emotional or Behavioural Difficulties*), recommending minimum force and the presence of more than one adult; but reference is made to Department of Health guidance on *Permissible Forms of Control in*

Children's Residential Care (1993). Recent Mental Health Foundation guidance outlines the circumstances in which detention or restraint of a child presenting severe challenging behaviour may be legally justified under civil or criminal law – for example to prevent a serious risk of harm to other children or to the child himself or herself (See C Lyon and E Ashcroft, *Legal Issues arising from the care and control of children with learning disabilities who also present severe challenging behaviour: A guide for parents and carers* (Mental Health Foundation, 1994)). The guidance in effect emphasises that detention or restraint, where justified, should continue only for so long as the serious risk exists (see also Professor Lyon's report for the Mental Health Foundation (*Legal Issues* (etc) (1994), Chapter VI); see further Chapter 13, Part 4(d)(iii)).

(e) Confiscation of property

Confiscation is not unlawful, and in some cases is a necessity, e.g. if a pupil has a dangerous object, weapon (etc). These items, or drugs, or obscene material, should be handed to the Police as soon as possible. Deliberate destruction by a teacher of a confiscated item could amount to a trespass to goods, leading to possible civil liability, unless perhaps the destruction was necessary in the interests of safety. Retention by a teacher of confiscated items for his or her own use may amount to theft (Theft Act 1968, s 1). To avoid any possible liability, the item should be returned to the pupil or his or her parent at an early opportunity – preferably at the end of the school day.

(f) Breakdown of discipline: LEAs' reserve power

LEAs are empowered to

> 'take such steps in relation to any county, controlled or special school maintained by them as they consider are required to prevent the breakdown, or continuing breakdown, of discipline at the school' (E(No 2)A 1986, s 28(1)).

The power can only be exercised if, in the LEA's opinion, the behaviour of pupils, or the action taken by them or their parents, is such that 'education of any pupils is, or is likely in the immediate future to become, severely prejudiced' (s 28(3)). Just what form of action Parliament anticipated LEAs might decide to take in these circumstances is not at all clear.

Chapter 13

Safety and welfare

1. Introduction

Many head teachers, governors and LEAs confess that of all their responsibilities, those relating to the health, safety and welfare of pupils cause them the greatest concern. This concern is fuelled not only by the occasional tragedy which receives considerable media attention – examples over recent years include the deaths arising from the fall of pupils in the Austrian Alps, the incident at Land's End, when several pupils were swept into the sea by waves, and the canoeing tragedy at Lyme Bay – but also by the deep awareness of the poor physical state of, and the overcrowding in many school buildings, which present clear risks to pupil safety. The fact that governing bodies now have responsibility for certain day to day repairs to school buildings (under LMS) (see *Appendix 2* to this book for a list), means that even more attention is likely to be given to health and safety issues. As the DFE's guidance on LMS states:

> 'though LEAs generally retain liability for capital and grant related expenditure in county and controlled schools, many day to day responsibilities associated with health and safety may lie with school governing bodies. It is therefore essential that these responsibilities are set out clearly in the LMS scheme or the health and safety policy which may form an accompanying annex' (DFE Circular 2/94, *Local Management of Schools* (1994) para 239).

Moreover, the range of legal responsibilities for health and safety has grown over recent years, although the law probably still does not go far enough (see, for example, D Brierly and B Matthews, *Pupils and Students and Health and Safety Law: Second Class Citizens?* (1992)). Pupil welfare has also (rightly) assumed greater importance. The Children Act 1989 has introduced important responsibilities in the areas of child protection and the welfare of pupils in independent schools. Moreover, as shown in previous chapters, the law now pays greater attention to areas such as school attendance, discipline and special educational needs.

Schools and LEAs are now faced with an ever increasing volume of key guidance on health, safety and welfare matters, including:

- Department of Health, *Working Together under the Children Act 1989* (1991)

- Open University (for the DES), *The Children Act 1989: A Guide for the Education Service* (1991)
- Health and Safety Commission, *The Responsibility of School Governors for Health and Safety* (1992)
- Same, *The Management of Health and Safety in Schools* (1994).

Unfortunately, the law governing health and safety of staff and pupils remains complex and, at times, less than clear-cut. One reason for the complexity of the law is that it emanates from a variety and combination of sources. First there is the common law, deriving from the judgments of the courts over many years, which establishes negligence as a tort – a civil wrong giving rise to entitlement to compensation for the person wronged. Then there is statute law (often supplemented by regulations) covering, for example, civil liability in respect of premises ('occupier's liability') and criminal liability in respect of unsafe or unhealthy working conditions and the general physical environment. All of these are areas of the law of wide application. They apply to various workplaces, buildings and other places, and to people engaged in all kinds of activities. Thus in order to describe the legal position as it applies to schools in particular, it is necessary to extract carefully the relevant principles from the general law. Where questions of liability for negligence are concerned, a substantial part of the task may be to consider the wealth of relevant case law, on the care and supervision of pupils in particular, although it has to be appreciated that the teaching environment of the 1990s, like the current attitudes of many of the judges, differs in many respects from the way that it was when some of the cases were decided. Furthermore, no two cases are exactly alike, and for this reason, amongst others, it is not always possible to state with certainty the legal position in a particular situation. As Stephenson LJ said in *Porter* v *City of Bradford Metropolitan Council* [1985] Lexis 14 January: 'It is quite clear what the duty of an education authority and of its teachers is; the difficulty is to apply the law correctly to the facts of any particular case'. The question of whether there has been negligence, and that of the appropriate remedy – be it damages or otherwise – will, at the end of the day, often have to be resolved via litigation.

Health, safety and welfare in schools is an enormous subject, of which legal issues are merely one part. This chapter necessarily concentrates on the legal issues (for further reading, see the excellent guide to the health and safety issues, as well as coverage of legal issues, by D Brierly, *Health and Safety in Schools* (1991)). The first area examined below is negligence in the care and supervision of pupils (the author wishes to acknowledge the influence of the work of the late Geoffrey Barrell in clarifying the general principles of negligence in this context: see, in particular, his *Legal Cases for Teachers* (1970) and his *The Teacher and the Law* (Methuen, 1985) (the latter co-written with JA Partington; previous editions were by Barrell alone)). There is then a discussion about school premises and the physical environment. The final section of the chapter deals with pupil welfare under the Children Act 1989.

2. Negligence in the care and supervision of pupils

(a) Introduction

The tort of negligence is very familiar to lawyers, but less so many to others. Negligence rests on three concepts: duty, breach and damage. Negligence arises when someone who owes a duty of care breaches that duty and as a result damage is occasioned to another person (known as the 'plaintiff'). As negligence is based around the notion of reasonable care, it follows that an injury which no reasonable amount of care could have prevented and which was completely unforeseeable will not give rise to negligence liability. For example, in *Webb* v *Essex County Council* [1954] TES 12 November, a pupil jumped from a stool being used as part of the 'agility apparatus'. Although the stool was surrounded by rubber mats, the boy, aged five, was injured. The court found that the apparatus itself was sound and that the teachers were not negligent: there was nothing further they could have done to prevent the injury, which resulted from a pure 'accident'.

It will be noted that the *Webb* case concerned an action against a local education authority. Under the principle of 'vicarious liability' an employer may be liable for, *inter alia*, the negligence of his or her employee occasioned while the employee is acting in the course of his or her employment. Where a teacher is concerned, this applies to anything undertaken as part of his or her contractual duties. There has always been some doubt about the application of the principle to voluntary duties (on which, see M Jones, *Textbook on Torts* (4th ed 1994) pp 276–279)) – a relevant example here is rugby coaching on a Saturday morning – and the teacher concerned should, in any event, always ensure that the employers have insurance cover. A critical question may be whether the teacher is expected by the employer to carry out the tasks concerned (*Stenner* v *Taff Ely* (1987), cited in Brierly, *op cit*, p 2). Furthermore, in some cases a person will be acting in the course of his or her employment by doing something which is not expressly part of his or her contract but which he or she may be deemed to have implied authority to do (as in the case of *Poland* v *Parr and Sons* (1927) 1 KB 236, where an off-duty employee took action to stop boys stealing from his employer's wagon). If, on the other hand, an employee performs an act which he or she is expressly forbidden by the employer to do, he or she will not be acting within the course of his or her employment. Note that the fact that a pupil assists with one or two routine tasks around the school does not make him or her an 'employee' for the purposes of vicarious liability: *Smith* v *Martin and Kingston-upon-Hull Corpn* [1911] 2 KB 397; *Watkins* v *Birmingham City Council* [1975] The Times, 1 August (CA).

In theory, the plaintiff may sue either the employer or the employee or both of them jointly – although it is rare for the teacher alone to be sued since the LEA's financial resources are far greater. If negligence is found, the employer may then be entitled to a contribution from the employee. In practice this might occur only rarely in relation to teachers (see D Nice *Education and the Law* (1986), p 194).

Although under LMS governing bodies will enjoy many of the rights of an employer, the LEA will retain the responsibility of an employer for the purposes of vicarious liability (except in aided and GM schools, where the governing body is the employer). Governors will, under LMS, acquire responsibilities in respect of certain activities under their remit, however, although ERA 1988, s 36(6) offers some protection from liability arising from their spending of the school budget (see pp 108–109 above). Governors' liability under health and safety legislation and under the Occupier's Liability Act 1957 is discussed below.

(b) The duty of care

The scope of the duty of care may be understood initially with reference to the 'neighbour principle' enshrined in the dictum of Lord Atkin in the well-known case of *Donoghue* v *Stevenson* [1932] AC 562 (HL) (at 580). His Lordship stated that a person owes a duty of care to his 'neighbour'. For this purpose neighbours are 'persons who are so closely and directly affected by my act that I ought reasonably to have them in contemplation when I am directing my mind to the acts or omissions that are called in question'. The test for determining the existence of a duty of care is not found in this dictum alone, despite Lord Reid's view, in *Home Office* v *Dorset Yacht Co* [1970] 2 All ER 294 (HL), that the neighbour principle should apply unless there was a valid reason justifying its exclusion. The courts have struggled to develop this area in a clear and authoritative manner in recent years (see *Street on Torts* (9th ed 1993) by M Brazier, p 174 *et seq* and *Textbook on Torts* by M Jones, *op cit*, pp 26–30). However, it now seems (*Caparo Industries plc* v *Dickman* [1989] 1 All ER 568 (HL) *per* Bingham LJ at 802–4) that the existence of a duty of care depends on three factors:

(i) the foreseeability of harm;

(ii) 'proximity', or 'neighbourhood' as *per Donoghue* v *Stevenson* (above); and

(iii) the court considers it just and reasonable to hold that there is a duty,

although (ii) and (iii) were described by Lord Bridge (pp 573–574) as 'little more than convenient labels to attach to the features of different specific situations which, on a detailed examination of all the circumstances, the law recognises as giving rise to a duty of a given scope'.

In any event, it is now well-settled that among the 'numerous and extensive categories of situations which are treated by the courts as imposing a duty of care . . .[is that whereby] a teacher owes a duty of care to his child-pupil' (*Street on Torts, op cit*, p 174).

Of course, it will still be necessary to show that the harm resulted from a breach of the duty of care which occasioned the damage.

(c) The standard of care

The general rule is that breach of the duty of care is judged by the standard of care expected of the reasonable person (e.g. *Blyth* v *Birmingham Waterworks Co* [1856] 11 Exch 781, *per* Alderson B). In the case of a person performing professional duties, the classic view of Winfield, much cited, is that the law expects such a person to demonstrate the 'average amount of competence associated with the proper discharge of the duties of that profession'. But in *Wilsher* v *Essex Health Authority* ([1986] 3 All ER 801 (CA) and [1988] 1 All ER 871 (HL)) the court (whose members approached the matter in slightly different ways) held that the standard should be that which might be reasonably expected of a person in the particular post, or at least involved in carrying out the particular function, in question. In the Court of Appeal, Glidewell LJ (at p 831) said that 'the law requires the trainee or learner to be judged by the same standard as his more experienced colleagues. If it did not, inexperience would frequently be urged as a defence to an action for professional negligence'. This implies that a lower standard of care may not be expected of a probationer or other inexperienced teacher, but leaves the position somewhat ambiguous as regards a trainee teacher. But one point to bear in mind is that where an employer gives an inexperienced employee a task to perform which the employee is not competent or qualified to undertake, the employer may be directly liable in negligence (see *Jones* v *Manchester Corporation* [1958] 2 QB 852 and *Wilsher op cit*, cited by M Jones *op cit* at p 127).

In the medical context the doctor might have a defence if he or she is acting in accordance with general and approved practice. If there are two conflicting opinions, the adoption of one practice will be justified if it is accepted as proper by a 'responsible body of medical men skilled in that particular art' (*per* McNair J in *Bolam* v *Friern Hospital Management Committee* [1957] 2 All ER 118 at p 122). According to Jones (*op cit* p 124), the authorities show that the *Bolam* test is of general application to professions or callings requiring special skill, knowledge or experience (see *Gold* v *Haringey Health Authority* [1987] 2 All ER 888 at 894 and *May* v *Messenger May Baverstock* [1990] 1 All ER 1067).

Where teachers are concerned, a general and approved practice is easier to prove than it is in the case of doctors. In *Conrad* v *ILEA* (1967) 65 LGR 543 it was recognised that there were two schools of thought as to appropriate initial instruction in judo. In *Chilvers* v *London County Council* [1916] 80 JP 246 a child was injured when a lance on a toy soldier he was playing with poked his eye. The court held the local authority not liable because it was common for children to be allowed to play with these toys in schools. Similarly, when a child was injured taking part in gymnastic exercises, the fact that the teacher had been following general and approved practice in instructing other pupils to assist in the safety procedure led to a finding that he was not negligent (*Wright* v *Cheshire County Council* [1952] 2 All ER 789 (CA)). But in *Fryer* v *Salford Corporation* [1937] 1 All ER 617 Slesser LJ thought that the fact that it was educational practice at the time not to guard stoves used in domestic science was an insufficient reason for not installing a guard.

Where teachers are concerned a special test governing the standard of care has been applied. The courts have held that a teacher is *in loco parentis*, which means that he or she acts in place of a parent. In an early decision, *Williams* v *Eady* [1893] 10 TLR 41 (CA), the court held that the teacher should show the same standard of care as that of a 'careful' parent. This test was applied in the case of *Rich* v *London County Council* [1953] 1 WLR 895, where it was held that an LEA was under no obligation to take measures to keep boys away from an unfenced pile of coal in the school playground. Similarly, in *Martin* v *Middlesborough Corpn* (1965) 63 LGR 385 (CA) a child slipped on some ice and cut her hand on the pieces of a broken milk bottle which was lying on top of a drain in the playground. Willmer LJ felt that the risk of this injury occurring was foreseeable and that better arrangements for the disposal of empty milk bottles should have been made. He did not think that the arrangements made were such as would be approved of by a reasonably prudent parent.

But the test has been modified. In *Lyes* v *Middlesex County Council* (1962) 61 LGR 443, it was held to be important to apply the careful or prudent parent test in the context of a school rather than the home. In the school situation a teacher has the care of far more children than a parent ever has to deal with (although the fact that the risk of injury arising from an activity which is considered safe in the home is no greater in school when more children are participating will mean that there may not be liability (see *Smart* v *Gwent County Council* (1991) below)). In *Beaumont* v *Surrey County Council* [1968] 66 LGR 580 Geoffrey Lane J (as he then was) (at p 585) preferred the 'ordinary language of the law of negligence' to the test laid down in *Williams* v *Eady* (above). Thus a head teacher was bound to take 'all reasonable and proper steps to prevent any of the pupils under his care from suffering injury from inanimate objects, the actions of their fellow pupils, or from a combination of the two. That is a high standard'. It may be that the courts will incline more closely towards 'the reasonable professional' standard, outlined earlier, these days, although when *Van Oppen* v *Clerk to the Bedford Charity Trustees* [1989] 3 All ER 389 was in the High Court (see p 333 below), the court adopted a similar approach to the one in *Lyes* v *Middlesex* (above).

One of the key factors in determining whether there is a breach of the duty of care concerns the degree of risk involved in the conduct which has caused the damage. Although it is a general principle that foreseeable damage must be guarded against, it does not follow that every conceivable risk must be avoided. In *Bolton* v *Stone* [1951] AC 850 Lord Oaksey said (at p 863) that a reasonable person should take precautions 'against risks which are reasonably likely to happen'. The kinds of precautions that will be necessary will depend on: the magnitude of the risk; the practicability of, and resources required in, guarding against the risk; and the social utility of the defendant's activity. In school situations often the only practicable way of guarding against the risk of foreseeable harm is to provide appropriate levels of supervision for children, in respect of particular activities and in general (see below). So far as the magnitude of the risk in school activities is concerned, the case of *Smart* v *Gwent County*

Council (1991) Lexis offers a useful illustration of the approach taken by the courts. Here a girl aged three was injured at her nursery school when she trapped her hand in the wooden door of a Wendy House and lost the fleshy tip of her thumb. The judge accepted that there had been a reasonably foreseeable risk of injury to a small digit by its being caught in the nip of the door, either between the door and the door jamb or in the part where it was hinged. However, he concluded that the local authority was not unreasonable in exposing the child to the risk and that the risk was no greater than it would have been in the child's own home. On appeal, counsel for the plaintiff argued that while a Wendy House of this type might be safe to use at home, there were intrinsically greater risks of using it in the school context, where a larger number of children were taking part in the activity (30 children in all), and so the standard of care was higher. In the Court of Appeal, Stuart-Smith and Nicholls LJJ agreed with the trial judge. Stuart-Smith LJ said that the children were not out of control, nor were all 30 of them playing in the Wendy House at the same time. He was 'wholly unpersuaded that the risk in this nursery school, supervised as it was by a competent teacher, was significantly greater than in an ordinary home'. Moreover, the risk of injury 'was not an unacceptable risk, that is it was one which a prudent parent would not say that it was unreasonable to expose this child to, notwithstanding the fact that they were in a class of 30 rather than in their own home'. Stuart-Smith LJ also gave examples of the kinds of similar everyday injuries, with which he appeared to equate the injury from the Wendy House door, which were equally as likely to happen at school as at home:

> 'Drawers, cupboard doors and windows can be a source of trapped fingers and can from time to time cause quite nasty injuries. Injuries from falling off chairs, tables and other common or garden everyday objects are foreseeable risks to small children, but no-one suggests that they should not be subjected to them providing, of course, that they are properly supervised according to their age'.

There is clearly a trade-off between inhibiting activities which are known to carry some risk of injury, and permitting children to benefit from the lesson of experience in the course of growing up and from the enjoyment of childhood. As Salmon LJ said in *Ward* v *Hertfordshire County Council* (1969) 114 Sol J 87 (CA), it is wrong to try to protect children against minor injuries such as grazed knees caused by falling down when running in the playground, 'by forbidding them the ordinary pleasures which school children so much enjoy'.

Another factor governing the standard of care, and one which was relevant to the determination in *Smart* (above), concerns the social utility of the defendant's act. In *Daborn* v *Bath Tramways Motor Co Ltd* [1946] 2 All ER 333 (CA) Lord Asquith said (at p 336):

> 'In determining whether a party is negligent, the standard of reasonable care is that which is reasonably to be demanded in the circumstances. A relevant circumstance . . . may be the importance of the end to be served in behaving in this way or that . . . [I]f all the trains in this

country were restricted to a speed of five miles an hour, there would be fewer accidents, but our national life would be intolerably slowed down'.

The importance of having to balance the social utility of the act with the need to demonstrate care has been recognised by the courts when considering the standard of care required of a teacher. In the case of children, some relaxation in supervision has been condoned on the grounds of its desirability in encouraging children to take increasing responsibility for their own actions as they grow up. In *Jeffrey* v *London County Council* (1954) 52 LGR 521 McNair J said (at p 523) that a balance had to be struck 'between the meticulous supervision of children . . . and the very desirable object of encouraging their sturdy independence'. Similarly, in another case, Hilbery J dismissed an action brought against the governors and a teacher, following an incident in which boys who were using a cricket pitch roller caused it to roll onto one of their number, saying that 'If boys were kept in cotton-wool, some of them would choke themselves with it' (*Hudson* v *Governors of Rotherham Grammar School* [1938] LCT 303). In *Simkiss* v *Rhondda BC* [1983] 81 LGR 460 (CA) the Court of Appeal (*per* Dunn LJ at 465) confirmed that one had to balance the robustness which would make children take the world as they found it and the tenderness which would give them nurseries wherever they went. Social utility (of using a Wendy House in a nursery school) was also relevant in *Smart* (above). The county court judge in that case had said that 'the purpose of the Wendy House must be, I think, to provide a thing with which the children can play so that they can relate their play to everyday life . . . [I]nside the Wendy House are beds, a doll in one of the beds, a dressing table . . . , telephones and so on'; and he said everyday 'skills . . . like using a telephone and a dressing table and a pushchair, . . . and opening and shutting doors' would be learnt.

It is clear that in some situations it is not practicable to eliminate or even to reduce significantly the risk other than by desisting from the activity concerned altogether. Many of these situations are ones arising from activities which carry intrinsically greater risks, such as sporting activities and outdoor activities in general, and it is here that the question of social utility may become particularly important. In *Van Oppen* v *Clerk to the Bedford Charity Trustees* (1989) Ralph Gibson LJ said, in the High Court (at 291, cited with approval by Balcombe LJ in the Court of Appeal at 410–12):

> 'It is fundamental to the relationship between school and pupil that the school undertakes to educate him in as wide a sense as it reasonably can. This involves the school having the pupils in its care and it involves the pupils in various activities in the classroom, in the chapel, in the gymnasium, on the sports field and so on. There are risks of injury inherent in many human activities, even of serious injury in some. Because of this, the school, having the pupils in its care, is under a duty to exercise reasonable care for their health and safety. Provided due care is exercised in this sphere, it seems to me that the school's duty is fulfilled'.

The above judicial statement demonstrates that it is accepted by the courts that although various educational activities carry risks, they need not be avoided for this reason alone. Provided reasonable care towards pupils is shown, such activities may proceed. Indeed they are necessary if a pupil is to be educated in the widest sense (something towards which the 'whole curriculum' concept in section 1 of the ERA 1988 (see Chapter 6) seems to be particularly directed). This is, once again, the social utility argument referred to earlier – the end justifying the means.

Nevertheless, even if the activity itself is acceptable regardless of the dangers, it is incumbent on teachers to minimise the risks by ensuring that the activity is carried out in a safe manner. They should do all that is reasonable to guard against any reasonably foreseeable risks. A run through some of the decided cases will give an indication of the standard of care which is expected.

In *Barnes* v *Bromley LBC* [1983] The Times, 16 November, a male pupil was dismantling a rusty bicycle in the metal workshop. The bicycle was to be used as part of a sculpture. The boy was using an old and somewhat brittle riveting tool which splintered when he hit the bicycle with it, causing the injury. There was held to be negligence, in view of the condition of the tool. But damages were reduced by one-third to take account of the boy's negligence in using the tool in that manner.

Fryer v *Salford Corporation* (1937) (*op cit*) concerned an injury to an eleven year old girl whose apron was ignited by the flame on an unguarded cooker. It was held that it was perfectly natural for the children to crowd round the stove 'having witnessed the final transfiguration of their own puddings' (*per* Slesser LJ (at p 621)). The danger was one which ought reasonably to have been anticipated and which reasonable precautions – in this case the provision of a guard – would have prevented.

In *Van Oppen* v *Clerk to the Bedford Charity Trustees* (1989) (*op cit*), the plaintiff was aged sixteen and a half at the time of the crippling injury he received in the course of a tackle while playing rugby at school. Initially he claimed damages both in respect of the school's negligence in coaching and in respect of their failure to advise his father of:

(*a*) the inherent risks in the game;
(*b*) the need to take out accident insurance for his son; and
(*c*) the fact that the school had no such insurance cover.

It was also alleged that there had been negligence in the school's failure to have such insurance cover at the material time. In the High Court the plaintiff's claim was unsuccessful on all counts. He pursued only the insurance aspect of the case in the Court of Appeal but was unsuccessful there as well. The Court held that while it might be desirable for the school to arrange insurance and/or to inform parents of the need to take out independent personal accident insurance, this went beyond the school's duty in respect of the welfare of the pupils. The claim of negligent coaching was not taken to the Court of Appeal, but Boreham J's comments in the High Court (at p 277) are instructive:

> 'It is accepted on all sides that the Bedford School, being *in loco parentis*, owed a general duty to the plaintiff and to all pupils to exercise reasonable care for his and their safety both in the classroom and on the games field. It is also accepted that injury is more likely if the correct techniques are not followed by the players, particularly in tackling. It follows therefore that it was the school's duty by teaching or by coaching or by correction to take reasonable care to ensure that the plaintiff in playing the game of rugby football applied correct techniques while tackling . . .
>
> 'I am satisfied that the defendants, through staff "taking" rugby, were well aware of the inherent risks in playing rugby football and of the need for the application of correct techniques and the correction of potentially dangerous errors and lapses. I am also satisfied that the standard of supervision was high, that the refereeing was vigilant and strict and that . . . there was at the school an emphasis on discipline, which meant playing the game correctly. There is therefore no substance in the allegations of negligence . . .'.

In the context of rugby instruction, it may be noted that the participation by a teacher in a game with pupils, notwithstanding that it is for the purpose of demonstration, should be avoided, in the light of the decision in *Affutu-Nartoy* v *Clarke and ILEA* [1984] The Times, 9 February. Here, the teacher tackled a teenage boy in a legitimate manner under the rules of the game, but, in law, unlawfully and dangerously. Hodgson J, in awarding damages, warned against teachers having physical contact with pupils in such circumstances. Here the risk of injury was unacceptably high.

It is clear that if the pupil is told or encouraged to perform an activity which is beyond his or her reasonable capabilities and the teacher should have known this, and an injury ensues, there may be negligence. In such a situation the risk of injury to the pupil is clearly too great to warrant his or her participation in the activity concerned. In *Moore* v *Hampshire County Council* (1981) 80 LGR 481 (CA), the plaintiff, aged twelve, broke her ankle while attempting a handstand in a PE lesson at the secondary school she attended. She was awarded £500 in damages. She had a medical history of congenital dislocation of the hips and had wrongly persuaded the mistress that she was allowed to take PE. The teacher in question had in any event been told that the girl was not to take PE. The Court of Appeal unanimously held that although teachers' tasks of supervision were often very difficult, there had not been adequate supervision of the girl. In *Tillotson* v *Harrow BC* (1984) (unreported) £9,000 was awarded to a girl whose weight increased by 50 per cent following a leg fracture she sustained when jumping a hurdle. Negligence had been admitted by the LEA.

Supervision of pupils and the special dangers of out of school activities are considered further below.

(d) Children and negligence

As shown below, teachers or LEAs or governing bodies may be liable in negligence for failing to prevent harm caused by one pupil to another. Indeed several of the cases referred to above were concerned with this. If the child is old enough to foresee the consequences of his behaviour the courts might find him or her to have been contributorily negligent, so the damages against the LEA or governors would be reduced accordingly (see *Barnes* v *Bromley LBC* (1983) p 334 above). In other cases the pupil may be wholly liable, assuming there was no breach of duty by the teacher, if he or she fails to demonstrate the standard of care expected of a reasonable child of his or her age. In *Staley* v *Suffolk CC and Dean Mason* (26 November 1986, unreported but cited in *Street on Torts* 9th Ed 1993, p 226) a boy aged twelve was held liable for throwing a tennis ball into a classroom at another boy and hitting the dinner lady, causing injury. If the act of the child could have been prevented by the exercise of reasonable supervision by the teachers, the school or LEA may be held liable, depending on the age of the child concerned.

A pupil's age is relevant to the question of whether the supervision or instructions given to children in a school are adequate. The courts are prepared to accept that as they get older pupils may be assumed to be more responsible; and, as we have seen, the standard of care expected of a teacher may be influenced by the need to balance careful supervision on the one hand with the encouragement of a pupil's progressive social and personal development on the other.

In *Smerkinich* v *Newport Corporation* [1912] 76 JP 454 a youth aged 19 was injured when using a circular saw at a technical institute. The local authority was held not to be liable but the judge (Lush J) said that the decision might have been different had the plaintiff been a child. In *Butt* v *Cambridgeshire and Ely CC* [1970] 68 LGR 81 a large class of nine and ten year olds were using scissors and one child accidently poked another child in the eye with his pair. The LEA was held not liable. But in *Black* v *Kent County Council* [1983] The Times, 23 May, the court awarded over £13,000 in damages against the LEA when a child aged seven was jabbed in the eye by a pair of sharp pointed scissors he was using in an art class. Sir John Donaldson MR said that it was reasonably foreseeable that the use of sharp pointed scissors as compared with blunt ended ones involved quite a degree of risk where children of this age were concerned. The staff should avoid such risks. In *Porter* v *Barking and Dagenham LBC* [1990] The Times, 9 April, there was no liability arising from the failure to supervise two 14 year old boys who were practicising their shot-putting.

The age of the pupil will also be relevant in determining whether any warning of risks involved in a particular activity may be effective to negate liability. It is difficult to apply the principle *volenti non fit injuria* – a willing party suffers no wrong – in a school situation, since most activities are compulsory and it is hard to show that children were fully cognisant of the risks involved and were legally competent to accept them. Clear warnings given to a class may absolve the teacher from liability, depending on the age of the class and on whether the class might be expected to be well-behaved as opposed to being given to horse-play or carelessness (*Crouch* v *Essex County* [1966] 64 LGR 240). Warnings of the *specific* dangers involved in a particular activity should be given. For example, if a dangerous substance is being used in the laboratory, a more graphic and specific warning than simply 'don't touch' is required (*Noonan* v *ILEA* [1974] The Times, 14 December).

(e) Special aspects of negligence in the school context

(i) Responsibility outside lessons

Break times/lunch time

Lunch-time supervision is not part of a teacher's contractual duties. Head teachers are responsible, under the articles of government, for the internal organisation and management of the school. Under the School Teachers' Pay and Conditions Document (see *Appendix 3* to this book), a head teacher is entitled to a break during the school day but must arrange for a suitable person to take responsibility for his or her functions during it. In most schools at present the LEA provides care assistants or 'dinner ladies' to carry out lunch-time supervision of pupils, under the control of the head teacher. It almost goes without saying that the LEA must provide suitable staff for this role. Following financial delegation to schools under LMS governors may be responsible for the appointment of these ancillary employees (ERA 1988, Sch 3, para 4), although in the majority of schools they will be 'employed' by the LEA.

The kind of supervision demanded during lunch-time and other breaks is often different to that required during lesson times. For example, in *Beaumont* v *Surrey County Council* (1968) a heavy duty piece of elastic had been discarded into a bin in the playground and was discovered by some pupils who played about with it. Unfortunately one pupil was struck in the eye and suffered a serious injury. Unusually, the two members of staff assigned to playground supervision were absent from the playground at the time of the incident. Various prefects were also required to assist in the supervision. But the defendants were held liable because supervision was lacking at the time. The court found the *system* of supervision adequate, but felt that it had not been working properly. In *Pettican* v *Enfield LBC* (1970) Kilner-Brown J emphasised that where lunch-time supervision was concerned, staff could not be expected to perform as 'policemen or security guards'. He rejected the plaintiff's suggestion that a teacher should have been on duty in each classroom when the children were sent indoors on wet days. The plaintiff had been injured on one such day when struck in the eye by a piece of chalk during horseplay. The LEA was found not liable. This case contrasts with another, *Blasdale* v *Coventry CC* (1981) (unreported, but referred to in the *Times Educational Supplement*, 13 November 1981), in which Sir Basil Neild J awarded a boy £6,500 damages after his eye was damaged by a paper clip fired at him by another pupil during a lunch-time in which the children were allowed indoors because of rain. One dinner lady had been given the task of supervising two classrooms, and this was found to have been inadequate supervision.

When pupils absent themselves from school during the course of the school day it is not only their education that may suffer. There is also an increased risk of injury, especially where young children are concerned. While the duty to cause children to attend schools rests with their parents (see Chapter 11), the school has a responsibility to ensure that pupils are left in no doubt that they must not wander off. Moreover, supervision of pupils must be adequate so that the opportunities for straying are minimised. In *Ricketts* v *Erith Borough Council* (1943) 42 LGR 471 a ten-year-old child left the school premises during the lunch break and returned with a bow and arrow which he fired causing injury. But there was held to have been no failure of supervision. In *Carmarthenshire County Council* v *Lewis* [1955] 1 All ER 565, a boy aged four who was a pupil at a nursery school was made ready to go for a walk with one of the teachers and another child. The teacher left the room to get herself ready, and while out of the room had to attend to an injured child. She was away for about ten minutes. During her absence the two children got out of the classroom and wandered through an unlocked school gate and on to a busy road. A lorry driver had to swerve to avoid hitting one of the children, and as a result his vehicle collided with a telegraph pole. The driver was killed and his widow sought damages from the LEA. The case progressed eventually to the House of Lords, where it was held that irrespective of the lack of negligence on the individual teacher's part, the LEA was liable for the failure to take adequate precautions to avoid what was a foreseeable accident. Lord Goddard said that if it was possible for these young children to escape into a busy street so easily when the teacher was not with them, this implied a lack of care and of precautions that might reasonably be required.

If the school has not been negligent, but the children leave the premises and an injury to the child or a third party away from the school occurs, the teacher or LEA or governors should not be liable. However, the school should ensure that absences without permission are notified to parents or others as soon as possible. If a child complains of feeling ill the school should arrange for the parents to collect the child, rather than simply sending him or her home. What if the child, when crossing the road on his or her way home, collapsed and was injured? The parents would undoubtedly feel entitled to compensation for negligence on the part of the school, although liability would depend on a number of factors.

It is difficult to draw any firm guidance from these cases. In view of the fact that the courts say that no more than 'reasonable supervision' is in every case required (e.g. *Clark* v *Monmouthshire County Council* (1954) 52 LGR 246 (CA), *per* Denning LJ), all will depend on the particular circumstances involved.

Recently a new dimension to this issue arose as a result of a case brought by a 20-year-old woman who sued her LEA in respect of her school's failure, when she was a pupil, to prevent her from suffering repeated bullying from some of the other pupils, both during and outside lessons, which she claimed caused her psychological damage. It was argued by her counsel that there had been a breach of duty of care owed to her by staff at her school. The claim was unsuccessful (*Walker* v *Derbyshire County Council* The Times, 7 June 1994).

Supervision of pupils prior to the start of the school day

The general rule is that there can be no responsibility for the supervision of pupils prior to the start of the school day; but where pupils are allowed on to the premises at a certain time there may be responsibility. In *Ward* v *Hertfordshire County Council* (1969) 114 Sol J 87 the school's practice was to allow children into the playground before the start of the school day, but not to supervise them. One day an eight-year-old boy crashed into a wall during a race and injured his skull. The school staff knew that children frequently raced in the playground. The head teacher stated that he would not have prevented the racing had he been present. The trial judge decided that the jagged wall in the playground was inherently dangerous and there should have been supervision. But in a unanimous decision, the Court of Appeal found that there was no negligence. The accident had occurred in the ordinary course of play. Denning MR said: 'It often happens that children run from one side of the playground to the other. It is impossible so to supervise them that they never fall down and hurt themselves. I cannot think that this accident shows any lack of supervision by the school authorities'.

In *Mays* v *Essex County Council* [1975] The Times, 11 October a child was injured five minutes before the start of the school day when he fell while sliding on ice in the playground which had not been salted. The boy suffered permanent brain damage. The school gates were generally opened quite early, but most pupils arrived only about ten minutes before the start of school. The head teacher had sent a circular to parents requesting them not to send their children to school too early. The judge felt it perfectly reasonable for children of the plaintiff's age (14) to be allowed to slide on the ice in an orderly fashion whilst unsupervised. No average prudent parent in the playground at that time would have thought it necessary to stop the children playing on the ice. Furthermore, it would have been impracticable to salt an area as large as the playground in question every time there was a frost. The judge also felt that parents could not impose responsibility on teachers outside the ordinary school hours. Only if the school voluntarily accepted responsibility for children arriving early (as opposed to opening the gates for the convenience of parents and in the interests of the safety of pupils) would it be under a duty to provide supervision. But on the question of icy playgrounds, it could well be that a court today would take a stricter line. Failure to clear snow from a school step or path leading to a school, resulting in injury where there was a fall, *has* been held to be negligence (see *Woodward* v *Mayor of Hastings* [1944] 2 All ER 505 (CA) and *Murphy* v *Bradford Metropolitan Council* [1991] ICR 80 (CA)). Liability here will probably arise under the common duty of care owed to pupils as 'visitors' (licensees) under the Occupiers' Liability Act 1957 (see pp 344–346 below).

Responsibility after school hours

After school hours the school's responsibility is to ensure that there is an adequate system for handing children over to their parents. This is especially important where very young children are concerned. If the parents simply fail to collect or meet the child the school will not be liable (*Jeffrey* v *London County Council* (1970) *op cit*), although the position is, in reality, not all that clear cut. If a child remains on the premises after school hours, and if the parents cannot be contacted, the head teacher ought to ensure that the child is handed over to social services or the police to avoid any claim that he or she knowingly allowed a young child to wander out alone on to a public street with all its dangers. Remember that the teacher may generally do what is reasonable in the circumstances of the case for the purposes of safeguarding or promoting the welfare of the child (CA 1989, s 3(5)) (see further p 359 below).

Barnes v *Hampshire County Council* [1969] 1 WLR 1563 (HL) concerned the situation where children are let out of school early. The normal procedure at the school in question involved handing pupils over to their parents or guardians at 3.30 pm. On one occasion pupils were released early, and one child, a five-year-old, wandered out into the street because her mother had not yet arrived at the school gate. She was injured on the road nearby at 3.29 pm. It was held that the risk of such injury was foreseeable, and the LEA was liable.

In *Good* v *ILEA* [1980] 10 Fam Law 213 (CA) a child was injured when another pupil threw sand into his eye. The incident occurred after the end of the school day at 4.00 pm, but while both children were still on the school premises. The sand was in an area of the grounds which had been roped off and where a swimming pool was to be constructed. The children had been warned to keep away. It was normal for some children to be on the premises after school hours. Most children were collected by a parent at the end of the school day. But there was a play centre across the playground, to which the remaining children could go while waiting for their parents. The children who were playing near the sand were unnoticed. The plaintiff claimed damages for negligence, arguing that the children should have been supervised. It was held that there was no breach of duty on the part of the school for not supervising the whole of the children's journey from the infants school building to the play centre.

It is important that if the arrangements at the end of the school day are to change – for example if the children are to be released early on a particular day – parents are informed well in advance.

(ii) Responsibility for pupils outside school: educational visits and transport

School trips

Where pupils are in their care, teachers and LEAs or governing bodies are responsible for their safety. As the previous discussion indicated, all reasonable steps to avoid foreseeable injury must be taken. When pupils are away from school on trips, the risk of injury may be greater. For example, hill-walking or sailing carry inherent risks. But as we have seen, the courts accept that activities of this nature are permissible, provided reasonable safety can be assured, because they help a child's proper development. Nevertheless, teachers must ensure that the arrangements for supervision of pupils during all visits are appropriate in the light of the ages of the pupils concerned and other factors (e.g. if there are children with disabilities who need special care). When booking equipment or accommodation they should, wherever possible, keep to approved companies (usually the LEA will keep a list) and ensure that the authorities have arranged appropriate insurance cover. Parents should be advised to arrange independent cover in appropriate cases.

The accidents in recent years at Land's End, when pupils from Stoke Poges school were swept into the sea and drowned, and in the Austrian Alps, when four teenage boys fell 300 feet down a mountain, have prompted a reappraisal of the precautions necessary for school trips. Many schools are now extremely wary about taking pupils away, especially abroad. But there seems no reason why trips should be curtailed, provided sensible arrangements are made (including insurance) and proper precautions are taken. Valuable guidance has been issued by various authorities and professional organisations (e.g. the National Association of Head Teachers; and see below). Specific recommendations were made by the panel conducting the inquiry into the accident on the Austrian Alps (see *The Times*, 27 January 1989 for a summary).

The accident in the Austrian Alps occurred in 1988 during a visit to Austria by pupils from a school in Maidenhead. Some pupils had been left by teachers to play in the snow in a 'safe area' on top of a mountain that the party were visiting via cable car. Later, several unsupervised pupils wandered off to play in another area and four slid to their deaths. One of the surviving pupils said that they had been warned to keep to the paths and not to wander off. The Coroner recorded a verdict of death by misadventure (report in *The Times*, 7 July 1988). Berkshire Education Authority's report into the incident concluded: 'Telling the pupils what to do and trusting them to obey was not enough . . .; the teachers should not have allowed the pupils to go unsupervised for some fifty minutes; their presence might have discouraged the pupils from leaving the path' (report in *The Times*, 27 January 1989).

A case in 1985 raised similar issues to those in the above case. The case, *Porter* v *City of Bradford Metropolitan Council* (14 January 1985 (CA) unreported, but available via Lexis), arose out of an incident during an outing by a dozen 15- and 16-year-old pupils, and their geology teacher, to Shipley Glen. One boy, X, had been rolling large stones down a slope at the bottom of which were five pupils from the group. No-one was hurt, but the teacher saw the boy and told him to desist. Later, the teacher proceeded up the glen with a number of the pupils who had a keener interest in geology, and he was out of sight and sound of the children who were involved in the first incident. X started to drop or throw stones from a bridge. After perhaps 15 minutes of doing this he dropped a stone which landed on the head of a girl pupil, fracturing her skull. In the High Court, Bennett J held that the teacher had been negligent. In the light of the earlier incident in which he had learnt of X's propensities, there was a foreseeable danger and he should have used his best endeavours to keep the party together.

The LEA appealed to the Court of Appeal. Giving the Court's judgment, Stephenson LJ said that he did not wish to impose on teachers a duty of supervision which went beyond that of a reasonable parent (in the context of a school trip of this nature); but

> '. . .looking at the admitted facts of this case and looking at what [X] did such a short time before, I think . . . that on this occasion [the teacher], faced with the difficult task of trying to instruct pupils, some of whom were keen and some of whom were obviously not, failed in his duty to supervise this particular set of pupils. In my judgment he ought not to have relied on the obedience of [X] as negativing any reasonable possibility that he might try something of the same sort again; he ought to have kept the pupils, willing and unwilling, together and he ought not to have gone out of sight and sound of this group, including as it did the boy [X], although I sympathise with him and appreciate the difficulty of his task . . .'.

Activity centres

There are a number of legal issues arising out of the use of activity centres, including important safety issues. Some people consider that the fact that many of these centres are privately run makes it particularly important to ensure adequate safeguards. Although companies or proprietors owning or managing centres owe a duty of care to any children they are supervising (teachers accompanying the children will also have responsibility for their care, safety and welfare), and have responsibilities under the Occupier's Liability Act 1957 and Health and Safety at Work (etc) Act 1974 (see Part 3(a) and (e) below), proper licensing arrangements are presently lacking (see e.g. S Trotter, 'Activity holidays and the law' (1994) NLJ 454). The fact that schools and LEAs could be liable for exercising proper care in selecting a reputable centre does little to assuage genuine public concern, especially with regard to outdoor activities. Of course, many centres are known to be well run and to pay a high regard to safety in various settings and may be subject to inspections under Health and Safety at Work (etc) Act 1974. Even so, greater regulation of activity centres and holidays is needed.

The DFE has issued guidance on *Safety in Outdoor Activity Centres* (Circular 22/94) to LEAs and schools, which they are urged to follow in planning and making visits to such centres. The new guidance puts the onus on schools and LEAs to satisfy themselves that centres are properly staffed, equipped and managed, as judged by consideration of specified criteria, and to make appropriate arrangements for insurance and parental consent and for providing parents and children with appropriate information. Risk assessment is also recommended, at the planning stage of any visit. The guidance also recommends that schools will need to obtain various undertakings and assurances concerning safety, activity management and staffing. The Activity Centres Advisory Committee, which was set up by the English Tourist Board in March 1993, has drawn up a Code of Practice for outdoor adventure activity providers, and it plans to introduce an accreditation scheme, to which the Code of Practice will be integral. The DFE hopes that the operation of the scheme in due course will 'provide a reliable guide for schools about the safety compliance of member centres' (Circular 22/94, para 69). Whether the Government will bow to public pressure to introduce a comprehensive inspection and licensing system, remains to be seen.

Transport

There have been various cases concerned with liability for injuries sustained on transport provided by the LEA. It is clear that children on school buses must be supervised (*Shrimpton* v *Hertfordshire County Council* [1911] 104 LT 145) and that the careful or prudent parent test (above) is relevant to determining the standard of care required (*Ellis* v *Sayers Confectioners* (1963) 61 LGR 299). In *Jacques* v *Oxfordshire County Council* (1967) 66 LGR 440, a child was injured by a pellet fired at him by another pupil while they were both travelling on a school bus. The LEA was held not to be negligent, even though supervision had been left to prefects. Where pupils are using public transport to get to and from school the bus company will be responsible for ensuring the safety of these passengers.

Where teachers transport pupils in their own vehicles they should ensure that they are covered by their own car insurance policies for doing so. Many a teacher has rushed a child with a cut to hospital without considering the question of whether he or she is covered should a crash occur and an injury to the passenger ensue. LEAs or governors generally give instructions to staff on such matters and may arrange cover.

It is advisable that when the school's or the authority's own vehicles are used there should be comprehensive insurance cover. Teachers should make sure that the particular use to which the vehicle is to be put is covered by the policy and that the teacher concerned is authorised to drive the vehicle. If the vehicle in question is a school minibus, the provisions of the Transport Act 1985 may apply. Under the Act, vehicles seating between eight and sixteen passengers (i.e. excluding the driver) ('small buses') and larger vehicles, i.e. those adapted to carry more than sixteen passengers, may be excluded from the requirement that the driver has a public service vehicle licence (*ibid*, s 18(a)). The vehicle must, *inter alia*, not be used for carrying members of the public at large nor with a view to profit (Transport Act 1985, s 19(2)). In the case of a 'small bus', the permit may be granted to a school (or others) by the LEA (s 19(3) and (7)) or traffic commissioners (s 19(4)). In the case of a 'large bus' the permit may be granted by the traffic commissioners to an LEA or co-ordinating body for religion, social welfare (etc), (s 19(6)) – provided that there will be 'adequate facilities or arrangements for maintaining any bus under the permit in a fit and serviceable condition'. A permit holder may hold more than one permit – but needs a separate permit in respect of each vehicle (s 19(9)). Restrictions may be imposed as to the use of the vehicle, by way of conditions attached to the granting of a permit (ss 19(7)(a) and 20(4)). Conditions as to fitness for use (small buses) and other matters relating to the driving of buses (small and large) shall be as prescribed (s 21). (See further, JR Dunford and M Livesey, 'School transport: a question of safety or cost?' (1991) 3(4) *Education and the Law* p 187.)

3. School premises and environment

(a) The Occupier's Liability Act 1957

The Occupier's Liability Act 1957 imposes a duty of care on the occupier of premises (s 1(1)). An occupier is a person in control of the premises. In the case of a public sector school, it would appear that the occupiers will generally be the governing body and/or LEA (for it is possible for there to be more than one occupier for the purposes of the Act). Under LMS the LEA will generally retain ownership of school buildings and be responsible for major repairs, whereas governing bodies will be responsible for management of the premises and routine maintenance (see p 68 above and *Appendix 2*). In *Wheat* v *E Lacon & Co Ltd* [1966] 1 All ER 582 (HL), both the owners and the manager of a public house were held to be occupiers. Liability may depend on who has control for the purposes of the particular defect which has caused the damage. In *Collier* v *Anglian Water Authority* [1983] The Times, 26 March, the plaintiff sustained an injury while on a seaside promenade. The water authority had responsibility for the structure of the sea defences of which the promenade formed part. The local authority, on the other hand, had responsibility for keeping the promenade, which was on land which it owned, clear of rubbish etc. The water authority was liable for the injury caused, as it had responsibility for the structure of promenade, but if the plaintiff had been injured by something which was within the local authority's area of control, such as a broken bottle, it would have been liable instead. LEAs and governing bodies are, therefore, likely both to be occupiers of a school, with liability dependent on which of them has responsibility for the particular aspect of the premises which has caused the damage.

There is also a duty owed by those 'occupying or having control over any fixed or movable structure, including any vessel, vehicle or aircraft' (s 1(3)). According to *Street on Torts* (9th ed 1993, by M Brazier, p 295) this subsection probably applies to playground swings. If a 'portakabin' is not covered by section 1(1) of the 1957 Act, it is surely covered by section 1(3).

The duty is owed to 'visitors' – basically persons entitled to enter the premises by express or implied licence. A trespasser is not a visitor. (On liability in respect of trespassers and non-invited entrants, who might include pupils who enter school grounds outside school hours without permission, see the Occupier's Liability Act 1984 and Jones, *Textbook on Torts*, *op cit*, pp 196–205.) So far as a school is concerned, 'visitors' would include pupils (*Woodward* v *Hastings Corpn* (1944) (*op cit*) and *Ward* v *Hertfordshire County Council* (1970) (*op cit*)), parents (*Griffiths* v *Smith* [1941] AC 170) and teachers. The duty applies to the state of the premises and 'things done or omitted to be done on them'. For example, in *Woodward* v *Mayor of Hastings* (1944) there was liability when a pupil slipped on frozen snow on a step which had not been cleared. The case was decided under the previous common law, but today would be covered by the 1957 Act. In *Murphy* v *Bradford MBC* [1991] The Times, 11 February there was liability when the plaintiff slipped on a frozen path into school which had not been gritted. In *Gillmore* v *London County Council* [1938] 3 All ER 31 (DC) a child slipped on a highly polished school hall floor. The injury was held to have been foreseeable. The floor had been polished to such an extent that there was a serious risk of injury.

The duty that is owed is 'the common duty of care'. This is

> 'a duty to take such care as in all the circumstances of the case is reasonable to see that the visitor will be reasonably safe in using the premises for the purposes for which he is invited or permitted by the occupier to be there' (Occupier's Liability Act 1957, s 2(2)).

Among the factors to be considered in determining whether or not the duty has been fulfilled is the degree of care which might be expected of the visitor. The Act specifically states that 'an occupier must be prepared for children to be less careful than adults' (s 2(3)(a); see further *Phipps* v *Rochester Corporation* [1955] 1 QB 570 and *Simkiss* v *Rhondda* (1983) *op cit*). Thus in *Williams* v *Cardiff Corpn* [1950] 1 All ER 250 (decided under the previous common law but still relevant) it was held that a child aged four might be at risk of injury where there was a grassy slope with broken glass at the bottom. If a child was unaccompanied by a parent or guardian, the fact that the occupier might reasonably have expected the child to have been accompanied might be taken into account (*Bates* v *Parker* [1954] 1 All ER 768). This might be relevant if a school has a system for the delivery of children to school by their parents which envisages the parents accompanying the children to a certain place on the premises, and an injury occurs to a child who is unaccompanied. A further point to note is that an occupier is entitled to expect that a person entering in the exercise of his or her calling will appreciate and guard against any special risks ordinarily incidental to his work (1957 Act, s 2(3)(b)).

A warning may be given to visitors, but it will not be sufficient to absolve the occupier from liability unless it was specific as to the danger or could reasonably be acted upon (s 2(4)(a)). If a risk is willingly accepted as his by the visitor concerned, the occupier will not be liable (s 2(5)); where pupils are concerned there may be doubts about their capacity to accept risks in view of their age. This may also be true where the occupier seeks to restrict his common duty of care to his visitors by notice (under s 2(1)) (see M Jones *op cit* p 195).

If the damage is caused by a danger resulting from the faulty execution of work by contractors, the occupier will not be liable if he or she can show that he or she acted reasonably in entrusting the work to an independent contractor, took reasonable steps to ensure that the contractor selected was one who was competent, and checked that the work was properly done (s 2(4)(b)).

(b) The Education (School Premises) Regulations 1981

These regulations (as amended) impose minimum standards for school premises. They are made under section 10 of the EA 1944, and apply to all LEA-maintained schools and (by virtue of amendment regs (SI 1989 No 1277)) grant-maintained schools. Sixth form colleges count as schools for this purpose (reg 3(1)). It may be argued that despite the existence of these minimum standards, many school buildings are in a very poor condition and facilities are sometimes lacking, as, for example, the Senior Chief Inspector of Schools reported in 1992 (*Education in England 1990–91, The Annual Report of HM Senior Inspector of Schools* (1992)); deficiencies in school premises were found in 30 per cent of the schools inspected. Facilities for sport are also poor, with many playing fields and other facilities badly maintained and/or in need of upgrading (see House of Commons Education Committee, *Sport in Schools* (1991) HC 155–1, para 27). In a 1990 survey by HMI (*A Survey of Work in Physical Education in 16 Secondary Schools* (1990) DES), many school playing fields and gymnasia were found to pose a threat to pupil safety.

The regulations apply to all aspects of school premises, starting with the land itself – which must be 'adequate' to permit the provision of not only buildings, recreation areas and playing fields of the required standard, but also of ancillary facilities such as service roads, delivery bays and vehicle parks (reg 4). Recreation areas (i.e. outdoor areas for 'recreation, play and outdoor education') and playing fields (an outdoor area suitable, and laid out, for team games) must conform to the requirements as to size (area) determined under Schedules 2 and 3 (regs 5 and 6). The requirements are based on formulae which take account of the various ages of the pupils who may use the facilities and the kind of school involved. Recreation areas must consist partly (e.g. at least one-third of the total recreation area, in the case of infants schools) of paved areas and/or areas with hard porous surfaces.

School buildings must be adequate to permit (reg 7):

(i) the convenient passage of persons and movement of goods within the buildings;

(ii) the storage, in or near teaching accommodation, of apparatus, equipment and materials used in teaching;

(iii) the storage, elsewhere than in the teaching accommodation, of furniture and certain other items not presently required;

(iv) the separate storage of any fuel required for the purposes of the school;

(v) the storage and drying of pupils' outdoor clothing and for storing their other belongings; and

(vi) the preparation of food and drinks and the washing of crockery and other utensils.

The school buildings must also provide not less than the prescribed minimum area of teaching accommodation (which, in the case of a nursery class or school, includes playroom area) (reg 8). The minimum is calculated with reference to, in essence, the ages of the pupils at the school (Sch 4). Where the school has pupils who are aged sixteen or over, accommodation must be provided for 'private study and social purposes' (reg 9). School buildings must also contain not less than the prescribed minimum washroom facilities (reg 10(1)–(3)), with washbasins and sanitary fittings of a prescribed number and type (e.g. two-thirds of those provided for boys should be urinals). In some cases there must be changing facilities for the over-eights, including showers for the over-elevens (reg 9(5)–(7)). Staff washrooms and cloakrooms, and changing facilities for staff teaching PE to the over-eights, must also be provided (reg 11(2) and (3)).

There should be suitable accommodation at the school for medical and dental examination and treatment of pupils, and for the care of pupils during school hours (reg 12).

So far as staff accommodation is concerned, schools are to have a head teacher's room and room for use by staff 'both for the purposes of work (otherwise than in teaching accommodation) and for social purposes' (reg 13). In a special school, and in a school with more than 250 pupils (which number is to be calculated with reference to reg 3) or where the majority of pupils are aged 11 or over, there is also to be a room for the senior assistant teacher.

(Note that Part IV of the regulations (regs 14–21) prescribes minimum accommodation (including sleeping accommodation) for staff and pupils at boarding schools.)

School buildings must be of a design and construction that reasonably assures the safe escape of occupants in the case of fire, and their health and safety in other respects (reg 24(1)–(2)). In fulfilling this requirement, regard must be had to the likely rate at which flames might spread, the resistance to fire of materials and structures, and the means of escape in case of fire (reg 24). The design and construction of the building should be of an approved standard with regard to acoustics, lighting, thermal environment and, where new buildings are concerned, energy conservation (reg 25). The standard is that laid down in Design Note 17 (2nd ed), *Guidelines for Environmental Design and Fuel Conservation in Educational Buildings* (note that these requirements are additional to others, e.g. under the Health and Safety at Work (etc.) Act 1974 – see below).

Other provisions are concerned with: load bearing structures (reg 22); weather protection ('reasonable resistance to penetration by rain, snow and wind and . . . moisture rising from the ground') (reg 23); water supplies (so far as practicable to be drawn from the mains) (reg 26); and drainage (reg 27).

Under transitional arrangements introduced on 1 August 1991 (Sch 1, paras 3–9), a small number of the requirements do not come into effect until 1 September 1996 (a date substituted for the original date of 1 September 1991, and thereby extending the transition period by a further five years, by the Education (School Premises) (Amendment) Regulations 1990 (SI 1990 No 2351)).

The Professional Association of Teachers argues that 'the Regulations are in practice unenforceable because there are so many schools that fall short of the standards they presuppose' (D Brierly and B Matthews, *Pupils and Students and Health and Safety Law: Second Class Citizens?* (1992), para 10). LEAs' and schools' difficulty in complying with the existing regulations may be another reason why the review of the regulations in 1991–92 has so far failed to precipitate any Government action to improve standards.

If injury results from a breach of these regulations individual parents may have a private law claim for breach of statutory duty (e.g. (i) *Reffell* v *Surrey County Council* [1964] 1 All ER 743 – girl badly cut when her hand went through a glass panel on a swing door in a school corridor – the glass was too thin; (ii) *Ching* v *Surrey County Council* [1910] 1 KB 736 – hole in school playground surface – child injured – damages awarded for breach of statutory duty; (iii) *Morris* v *Carnarvon County Council* [1910] 1 KB 858 – child caught hand in door which was too highly sprung and represented a danger – authority held liable).

Finally, it may be noted that a private members' bill, which if passed would have made provision (via regulations) for compulsory safety standards for equipment, layout and surfaces in children's playgrounds, was unsuccessfully put forward under the 'ten minute rule' in 1989 (the Safety in Children's Playgrounds Bill). It is not clear whether this three clause Bill would have applied to playgrounds in or attached to schools.

(c) The Environmental Protection Act 1990

The Environmental Protection Act 1990 (s 87) makes it an offence punishable on conviction by fine (current maximum £2,500) for a person to throw down, drop or otherwise deposit litter on, *inter alia*, relevant land of a designated educational institution (land in the open air which is under the direct control of the governing body of a school, other than an independent or nursery school: s 86(7) and the Litter (Designated Educational Institutions) Order 1991 (SI 1991 No 561)). A local authority must, with a view to promoting the abatement of litter, make the fact that such an offence exists known to the public in their area (s 87(6)).

The Act also imposes a duty on the governing body of a school, in respect of the land under its control, and the 'principal litter authority' (generally the local authority), in respect of land under its direct control and to which the public have access, 'to ensure that the land is, so far as is practicable, kept clear of litter and refuse' (s 89(1)). The Secretary of State has the power to extend the meaning of 'refuse' for this purpose to include animal droppings (such as dog excrement). In determining the standard to be met by the governing body or litter authority, 'regard shall be had to the character and use of the land, highway or road as well as the measures which are practicable in the circumstances' (s 89(3)). Guidance on the duty in section 89, in the form of a Code, is issued by the Secretary of State; regard to the Code (Code of Practice) must be had by those with the duty (s 89(7) and (10)). The Code gives governors 24 hours (or a week out of term-time) to remedy any fall below the required standard, although it acknowledges that it is not practicable for schools to be kept litter free at all times and that whilst governing bodies should aim to achieve such a state, it is not absolutely necessary to remove all small pieces of rubbish.

Any person may make a complaint to the magistrates court of a failure, by the person who has the duty to keep the land clear, to comply with the requirements of section 89(1) – complaining, for example, that a governing body has not kept school premises sufficiently clear of litter or refuse (s 91(1) and (4)). If there has indeed been a failure to comply with the duty in section 89(1), the magistrates court can impose on the governing body (etc) a 'litter abatement order', requiring it to clear the litter or refuse away (not necessarily in person!) within a specified time (s 91(6)). A person who, 'without reasonable excuse', fails to comply with the order is liable on summary conviction to a maximum fine of (presently) £2,500 plus a further £125 for each day on which the offence continues after the conviction (s 91(9)). If the magistrates were satisfied that there were reasonable grounds for bringing the complaint and that when it was made the land was defaced by litter or refuse or was wanting in cleanliness, the court can order the defendant to pay some or all of the expenses incurred in bringing the complaint (s 91(12)). This last provision is clearly intended to encourage members of the public to bring complaints that they consider are warranted.

Governing bodies might, alternatively, face compliance with a 'litter abatement notice' issued by the principal litter authority (under s 92). Such a notice (breach of which gives rise to criminal liability attracting a fine of up to £2,500 plus £125 per day (as above): s 92(6)) may be served on the governing body where the litter authority (other than a county council, regional council or joint board) is satisfied that the land is defaced by litter or refuse or that such defacement is likely to recur (s 92(1) and (3)). The notice may require clearance of the litter or refuse within a specified time or impose a prohibition on permitting the land to be defaced by litter or refuse (s 92(2)). The authority serving the notice can, in default, enter and clear the litter or refuse and recover all necessary expenditure in doing so (s 92(9)).

The DFE has argued that the above fines or costs may be levied against individual governors, but this is disputed in a well reasoned critique by Celia Wells ((1993) 5(3) *Education and the Law* 135). The DFE's argument is based principally on the absence of corporate status for governing bodies (apart from in GM schools) and the fact that section 91 imposes a duty on the 'person' responsible for keeping the land clear under section 89(1). However, governing bodies of county, voluntary and maintained special schools are now incorporated (since 1 January 1994: EA 1993, s 238, Education Act 1993 (Commencement No 2 and Transitional

Provisions) Order 1993 SI 1993 No 3106)). As a result, it seems that individual governors should not incur liability under the above provisions.

(d) The Chronically Sick and Disabled Persons Act 1970

The Chronically Sick and Disabled Persons Act 1970 provides for the needs of the disabled to be met in relation to access to and within, parking at and toilets in, universities, schools and colleges (s 8) and workplaces (s 8A) in so far as it is in the circumstances both practical and reasonable. Notices must be displayed for facilities provided under, *inter alia*, sections 8 and 8A of the 1970 Act (Disabled Persons Act 1981, s 5).

If and when amendments via the Disabled Persons Act 1981 are brought into effect, the facilities will have to be 'appropriate' to the needs of persons using the building who are disabled, unless a prescribed body concludes that in the circumstances 'it is either not practicable to make such provision or not reasonable that such provision should be made'. For the purposes of section 8 of the 1970 Act, facilities would have to conform to the standards laid down in Design Note number 18, 'Access for the Physically Disabled to Educational Buildings'. Improvements are likely with a bill to tackle discrimination against disabled people being announced in the Queen's Speech in November 1994.

(e) The Health and Safety at Work Etc Act 1974

(i) The Act and its enforcement

The 1974 Act aims, *inter alia*, to secure the health, safety and welfare of persons at work and to protect persons who are not at work against risks to their health and safety arising out of or in connection with the activities of workers (see s 1(1)). The Secretary of State may make regulations (s 15) dealing with, for example, particular hazards. Some of the most important ones are as follows:

The Control of Substances Hazardous to Health Regulations 1988

These impose safety standards and procedures in respect of chemical substances, including photocopier toner.

The Health and Safety Information for Employees Regulations 1989

These require, *inter alia*, an employer to ensure that an 'approved' poster is displayed, in a readable condition, at a place which is reasonably accessible to an employee while at work (regs 4 and 5). The 'approved' poster outlines the provisions of the 1974 Act as they affect employees, and gives other relevant information.

The Management of Health and Safety at Work Regulations 1992
(SI 1992 No 2051) (implementing EC Directive 89/391/EEC)

These lay down general health and safety duties on employers (including risk assessment duties) and impose specific legal duties on employees. Employees must act in accordance with safety training or instructions and must report situations which present an immediate hazard to health and safety and anything which a person with the particular employee's training and instruction would reasonably regard as a shortcoming in the employer's protection arrangements for health and safety, insofar as it affects the employee or arises in connection with his or her activities and has not already been reported. There is an Approved Code of Practice on *Management of Health and Safety at Work* (1992).

The Display Screen Equipment Regulations 1992

These introduce health and safety standards for visual display unit (VDU) workstations, including screens and furniture (seats and backs must be adjustable in terms of height from the floor, backs must be adjustable in tilt and there must be adequate leg-room and comfort). They apply to all new workstations used after 1 January 1993; in respect of those already in use at that date, compliance will be necessary by 31 December 1996 or earlier if there is an immediate threat to health and safety. (See further J Harnett, 'Are you sitting comfortably?' (1994) *Sol J* 210.)

The Health and Safety at Work Etc Act 1974 provides for the appointment of a Health and Safety Commission and a Health and Safety Executive (HSC and HSE). The HSC can issue Approved Codes of Practice (s 16): see, for example, the Code on *Workplace health, safety and welfare* (1992). It can carry out research into health and safety matters and is responsible for the provision of information to employers, government departments and others (s 11). The HSE is responsible for the administration and enforcement of the law (s 18). Suitably qualified inspectors are to be appointed (s 19), with a wide variety of powers to enter premises, take measurements and samples and seize anything likely to cause imminent danger and render it harmless (ss 20 and 25). It is an offence to hinder an inspector (s 33). If they find that the Act has been broken, inspectors may prosecute. The court can impose a large fine and, in some cases, a term of imprisonment not exceeding two years (*ibid*). What inspectors are most likely to do is to issue an 'improvement notice', requiring the wrongdoer to carry out specified action to remedy the contravention within a specified period (s 21), or, where there is, or potentially is, a risk of serious personal injury, a 'prohibition notice' ordering that a particular activity ceases until the contravention is remedied.

(ii) Duties under the Act

Duties are owed under the 1974 Act by employers to their employees and others (ss 2 and 3) and by employees to themselves and others (s 7). Manufacturers, designers, importers and suppliers are also under duties as regards the design, construction, and testing of any article for use at work and the provisions of information as to use (s 6).

For the purposes of sections 2 and 3 the LEA, or, in aided schools, the governing body, is the employer and will remain so after financial delegation (see DFE Circular 2/94, para 237). Certain aspects of health and safety provision will fall to governing bodies under LMS schemes, such as purchase and maintenance of equipment (including fire fighting equipment), non-structural repairs and indoor and outdoor cleaning (of, for example, school swimming pools) (*ibid*, para 239). As controllers or partial controllers of school premises, governing bodies could be subject to the requirements in section 4(2) of the 1974 Act, that such persons make sure that the premises, means of access to or egress from buildings, and any plant or substance in the premises, are safe for persons other than their employees (see s 4(1) and (4)). In *Moualem* v *Carlisle City Council* [1994] The Times, 8 July (QBD), the Divisional Court held that the protection of section 4 extended to children who attended a play centre; so it clearly must extend to school pupils.

The question of whether the LEA or the governing body or both of them has or have responsibility under s 4(2) 'depends on the degree of control they have' (Health and Safety Commission, *The Responsibilities of School Governors for Health and Safety* (1992) para 13). This is bound to lead to some uncertainty, apart from in GM schools, where the governors have exclusive responsibility. In voluntary aided schools, the governing body is the employer and, consequently, it has primary responsibility for health and safety under the 1974 Act. As regards other schools, it is important that LMS schemes clarify the extent of governing bodies' responsibility for health and safety matters (see DFE Circular 2/94, para 239).

An employer must 'ensure, so far as is reasonably practicable, the health, safety and welfare at work of all his employees' (1974 Act, s 2(1)). Particular regard must be had to various matters (in s 2(2)). These include the need to provide, 'so far as is reasonably practicable': (i) plant, work places and systems of work, and arrangements for handling, transporting and storing substances and articles, that are safe and without risks to health; and (ii) information, instruction, training and supervision to ensure health and safety of employees. As noted above, these duties in the Act are supplemented by requirements laid down in regulations. The employer must also provide a working environment which is, so far as is reasonably practicable, safe, without risks to health, and has adequate facilities for employees' welfare at work. The phrase 'so far as is reasonably practicable' means that the employer may balance the degree of risk against any sacrifice in terms of money, time or trouble (*Edwards* v *National Coal Board* [1949] 1 QB 704; *Marshall* v *Gotham Co Ltd* [1954] AC 360; *West Bromwich Building Society* v *Townsend* [1983] ICR 257).

In prescribed cases, safety representatives may be appointed by recognised trades unions from amongst the employees (s 2(4)), and safety committees may be established to keep under review the measures taken by the employer to ensure the health and safety of the employees (s 2(7)) (see further the Safety Representatives and Safety Committees Regulations 1977). Save in certain exceptional cases, the employer must also prepare a health and safety policy statement and bring it to the notice of the employees (s 2(3)). An LEA's health and safety policy will be a key document, since the LEA will expect governing bodies to comply with it; and governing bodies of voluntary aided schools may be expected to base their policy on it (Health and Safety Commission, *The responsibilities of school governors for health and safety* (1992) *op cit*, para 22). The HSC has recommended (*ibid* para 23) that the LEA's policy should contain:

(i) a declaration (signed by the director of education) of the employer's commitment to provide safe and healthy working conditions for employees;
(ii) an acknowledgement that the employer has responsibilities for the health and safety of pupils and visitors;
(iii) details of the organisation for implementing the policy (stating what officials of the LEA, the governors and head teachers are responsible for);
(iv) details of the arrangements for implementing the policy;
(v) details of monitoring arrangements; and
(vi) a section for supplementary statements of organisation and arrangements for implementing the policy in different schools or departments.

Duties concerning health and safety, although less specific than those owed to employees, are owed by employers to persons other than their employees (s 3). This clearly protects school pupils.

Furthermore, teachers and other staff are, as employees, under a duty, while at work, to take reasonable care for their own safety and that of others who may be affected by their acts or omissions at work (s 7(a)). They must also co-operate with an employer as regards the performance of the employer's duties concerning health and safety (s 7(b)). An employer may not charge its employee for anything provided in furtherance of its statutory duties vis-à-vis health and safety (s 9). But under tens cannot be criminally liable; ten- to thirteen-year-olds can be: see in particular *C* v *DPP* [1994] 3 All ER 190 (QBD).

Note that 'any person', which would include a pupil, must not 'intentionally or recklessly interfere or misuse anything provided in the interests of health, safety or welfare' (e.g. safety notices, fire extinguishers, first aid kits, etc) (s 8).

Section 47 of the Act specifically excludes any right of action in *civil* proceedings to arise from a breach of ss 2–8. So breaches of the duties do not create statutory torts.

Work placements

Trainees on government training schemes may be 'employees' for the purposes of the 1974 Act (SI 1983 No 1919; Health and Safety (Training for Employment) Regulations 1988, reg 4). However, although pupils in their final year of compulsory schooling may be given work experience (Education (Work Experience) Act 1973), such pupils are not 'employees' for the purposes of section 2 of the 1974 Act, although may be protected by the duty in section 3 of that Act (see also (f) below).

(f) Miscellaneous

(i) Reporting of injuries etc

Regulations (the Reporting of Injuries, Diseases and Dangerous Occurrences Regulations 1985) require employers to notify the Health and Safety Executive as quickly as possible of a death or prescribed category of serious injury to an employee (e.g. bone fracture other than in the hand or foot, burn from electric shock, amputation of a finger, loss of sight in an eye etc) (reg 3). Dangerous occurrences (set out in Sch 1 and referring to such matters as the unintended collapse of a wall or floor in a workplace) must be reported by the person having control of the premises (which, in schools, presumably means the governing body or LEA) (regs 2 and 3). A record of all reportable injuries must be kept by the employer; and a record of dangerous occurrences must be kept by the person in control of premises (reg 7). The record generally must be kept at the workplace. Schedule 3 prescribes the information which must be recorded.

Certain diseases suffered by employees carrying out prescribed categories of work must also be notified (reg 5). Few of these are relevant to teachers, but certain infections such as tuberculosis have to be notified.

(ii) Compulsory insurance of employees/defective equipment

Employers have a common law duty to take reasonable care for the safety of their workers, by providing competent co-workers, adequate premises and equipment and a proper system of working (see *Street on Torts* 9th ed (1993) by M Brazier, Chapter 17). Regardless of this, there is a statutory duty on an employer to have insurance cover in respect of liability for injuries to, or diseases suffered by, employees arising out of or in the course of their employment (Employers' Liability (Compulsory Insurance) Act 1969). Pupils on work experience are not employees for this purpose, and LEAs or governors should ensure that if the employer is not willing to take out insurance cover for such pupils they do so.

Where the employer provides any plant, equipment or vehicle for his employees to use in their work, and the employee is injured because the equipment (etc) is defective, the employer may be liable (Employers' Liability (Defective Equipment) Act 1969). The employee must show that the fault in the equipment resulted from the negligence or other tort of a third party (e.g. the supplier, manufacturer etc). If this is shown, 'the injury shall be deemed to be also attributable to negligence on the part of the employer' (s 1(2)). In *Knowles* v *Liverpool City Council* [1993] The Times, 15 October 1993, the applicant, a labourer, was injured when a flagstone he was manoeuvring broke due to a defect in its manufacture. He recovered damages of £3,092 from his employer, who appealed over the question, answered in the affirmative by both the Court of Appeal and

House of Lords, whether a flagstone could be 'equipment' for the purposes of the Act.

(iii) Danger from unwelcome visitors to school premises and others

Schools may be under a duty to take reasonable precautions to protect teachers and pupils from the unlawful intentions of unwelcome visitors to school premises. In *West Bromwich Building Society* v *Townsend* (1983) (*op cit*) McNeill J rejected counsel's argument that the risk of injury from criminals was outside an employer's obligations under the Health and Safety at Work Etc. Act 1974 (above), although that was in relation to the lack of a 'bandit screen' at a building society office. If a parent or pupil is violent towards a teacher, the teacher, no doubt backed by his or her trade union, will be able to bring a suit for trespass to the person.

A person who causes a nuisance or disturbance on school premises commits a summary offence under the Local Government (Miscellaneous Provisions) Act 1982, section 40 (as amended). A police constable or person authorised by the LEA may enter school premises to remove such a person.

To avoid any possible claim against a school for not taking reasonable steps to prevent the theft of belongings (in practice, unlikely to succeed), parents and pupils should be advised that valuables and more than small amounts of money should not be brought on to the premises. LEAs will generally not accept responsibility for loss of or damage to pupils' property; they should so advise parents and pupils.

(iv) Tampered-with equipment – an exceptional case?

The case of *DPP* v *K* [1990] 1 All ER 331 (DC) offers a salutary lesson to pupils who enjoy tampering with equipment. A 15-year-old pupil, K, had been attending a chemistry lesson at which sulphuric acid was being added to chlorine water and ammonia to test its effects. The pupils had been given an instruction sheet advising great care when working with acid. K asked to go to the toilet, and, unbeknown to the teacher, took a test-tube of concentrated acid with him. He tested it on some toilet paper, and then, hearing footsteps approaching, he panicked and poured the acid into the hot air hand dryer, the nozzle of which was pointing upwards. K left, intending to return to the toilet after his lesson to wash out the drier. However, before he could return another pupil turned on the drier and acid was ejected onto his face, causing a permanent scar. It was alleged that K's behaviour had been reckless and that he was guilty of committing an assault occasioning actual bodily harm contrary to section 47 of the Offences Against the Person Act 1861. In the Divisional Court, Parker LJ said that K knew either that there was a risk that someone might use the machine before he could return to remove the acid, or he gave no thought to that risk. K's conviction stood, although it seems that the wrong test for recklessness was applied (see *R* v *Spratt* [1991] 2 All ER 210 (CA)).

The injured boy would probably also have had a strong case for compensation in a civil court. In conclusion although injuries caused by a pupil to a fellow pupil rarely give rise to criminal liability, injuries resulting from tampered with equipment and misused substances are all too common and this prosecution should, perhaps, be cited by teachers in order to discourage such behaviour.

4. Pupil welfare under the Children Act 1989

(a) Introduction

The Children Act 1989 as a whole is concerned with the welfare of children in a variety of contexts, including particular residential settings. These residential settings may include schools. The Act lays down safeguards for children's welfare in residential schools, some of which are classed as 'children's homes' under the Act (as amended by the EA 1993) and are subject to the requirements as to registration and inspection laid down in the Act and regulations. Of concern to many more schools are the Act's provisions on child protection and parental responsibility (discussed in Chapter 1, but revisited here in the specific context of pupil welfare).

(b) The welfare of children in independent schools

During the 1980s there were a number of *causes célèbres* involving misdeeds at a small number of independent residential schools. The problems which were revealed generated well-founded and legitimate concern about whether the safeguards for the welfare of children in these schools were adequate (the potential for abuse of children in residential institutional settings in general was also highlighted recently by the 'Pindown' inquiry in Staffordshire and the *Report of the Inquiry into Police Investigation of Complaints of Child and Sexual Abuse in Leicestershire Children's Homes* (1993)). But the Children Act 1989 has sought to provide a number of safeguards.

Note that the powers of inspection referred to below are vested in local authorities, but the Secretary of State may also arrange for inspections of, and/or demand information relating to, children's homes and independent schools which provide accommodation for a child (CA 1989, s 80(1)(a) and (1), (4) and (5)). Registered independent schools may, of course, be inspected by Her Majesty's Inspectorate of schools.

(i) Schools which are children's homes

Prior to its amendment under section 292(1) of the EA 1993, the Children Act 1989 provided that, with the exception of special schools making provision for pupils with statements of special educational needs, any independent school providing accommodation for not more than 50 children was a 'children's home' for the purposes of the Act. Under the amended version of the Act (CA 1989, s 63(6)), an independent school at which children are provided with accommodation is a children's home if either:

(i) in each of the two previous years prior to the relevant date accommodation was provided (at the school or under arrangements made by the proprietor) for more than three children for more than 295 days in the year, or

(ii) it is intended that such accommodation should be provided for three or more children for more than 295 days of the year.

By virtue of being a children's home, any such school will be subject to Part VIII of and Schedule 6 to the 1989 Act, and the relevant regulations (the Children's Homes Regulations 1991 SI 1991 No 1506, as amended). Provision is made for registration of children's homes (CA 1989, s 63(1), (2), (10) and (11) and Sch 6), the disqualification of certain persons from running or being employed at such homes (s 65) and offences for breach of the relevant requirements. There is also provision which aims to safeguard the welfare of children at such homes (s 64). The duties owed in respect of such schools actually apply irrespective of whether or not a particular child in question resides at the school. The information which proprietors of independent schools may be required to provide to the Registrar of Independent Schools now includes such information as may be needed by the local authority for the purpose of determining whether a school is a children's home under the 1989 Act (EA 1944, s 70(4A), added by EA 1993, s 292(2)).

(ii) Schools which are not children's homes

Any independent school which provides accommodation for any child and which is not classed as a children's home (above) is covered by separate provisions (CA 1989, s 87). A duty to safeguard and promote a child's welfare is imposed on the proprietor and anyone else who is responsible for conducting the school (CA 1989, s 87(1); 'proprietor' is defined, in s 87(10), with reference to the Education Act 1944). The local authority in whose area the school is located is required to take such steps as are reasonably practicable to enable it to determine whether the welfare of any child being accommodated at the school is being adequately safeguarded and promoted there (CA 1989, s 87(3)). The local authority can, for this purpose, authorise a person to enter and carry out an inspection of the premises, children and records, as prescribed by regulations (s 87(5) and (6), and the Inspection of Premises, Children and Records (Independent Schools) Regulations 1991 SI 1991 No 975). When seeking to exercise his powers, the inspector must, if asked to do so, produce a duly authenticated document certifying his or her authority (s 87(7)). That person may at any reasonable time have access to computer equipment and any associated material (s 87(8)). Presumably access is thus given to computerised records for this purpose. It is an offence intentionally to obstruct a person exercising any power under section 87 or regulations made under it (s 87(9)).

If the local authority is of the opinion that there has been a breach of the duty to safeguard or promote a child's welfare it must notify the Secretary of State of it (s 87(4)). As noted in Chapter 2 (see p 42), the Secretary of

State has a duty under the Education Act 1944 to serve a notice of complaint on the proprietor of a registered or provisionally registered independent school if he is satisfied that the school is 'objectionable' on certain grounds. The complaint may be referred to the Independent Schools Tribunal, with appeal against its decision to the Secretary of State. A failure to put right any problem could lead to the school being struck off the register (EA 1944, ss 72–74).

(iii) Independent schools approved for children with statements of special educational needs

Special considerations may apply to independent schools which have been approved (under EA 1993, s 189 and the Education (Special Educational Needs) (Approval of Independent Schools) Regulations 1994 (SI 1994 No 651)) as suitable for the admission of pupils with statements of special educational needs, where such children have emotional or behavioural difficulties. DFE Circular 9/94 (which is also DoH Circular DH LAC (94)9), on *The Education of Children with Emotional and Behavioural Difficulties*, is mostly concerned with organisation of provision. However, detailed and comprehensive guidance has recently been published by the Mental Health Foundation, together with a report, to which reference is particularly recommended (Report: C Lyon, *Legal Issues Arising from the Care, Control and Safety of Children with Learning Disabilities who also present Severe Challenging Behaviour* (1994), Mental Health Foundation. Guidance: C Lyon and E Ashcroft, *Legal Issues* (etc.) . . . *A Guide for Parents and Carers* (1994)). This (as noted in Chapter 12 at p 325), is particularly concerned with the difficult legal questions arising out of the control and management of challenging behaviour in an institutional setting, but it also deals with various welfare issues (including the administration of medicines and medical care).

(iv) Residence during school holidays

Where a child aged under 16 attends a school not maintained by an LEA and lives there for at least two weeks during school holidays, he or she is treated as being a privately fostered child during the period while living at the school (CA 1989, Sch 8, para 9). Although requirements relating to private fostering may not be set by the local authority in such a case, Part IX of the Children Act 1989, which concerns, *inter alia*, the welfare of children who are subject to private fostering arrangements, will apply. Any person who proposes to care for and accommodate at an independent school at least one child who is to be treated as a privately fostered child, as above, must give at least two weeks' prior notice to the local authority, unless exempted from doing so by the authority (*ibid*).

(c) 'Parental responsibility'

As discussed in Chapter 1, the Children Act 1989 has introduced the important concept of 'parental responsibility'. Those who have parental responsibility in respect of a child – parents of the child who were married to each other when he or she was born, unmarried mothers, unmarried fathers granted it via a parental responsibility agreement or order of the court, a guardian appointed by the court (see s 5(6)) or anyone else acquiring it via a residence order (which confers parental responsibility automatically: see s 12) or a local authority (if a care order is in place) – have vested in them 'all the rights, duties, powers, responsibilities and authority which by law a parent has in relation to the child and his property' (CA 1989, s 3(1)). These are taken to include the power to direct the child's conduct, such as by exercising reasonable control over his or her behaviour (for example, to order the child to wash mud off his face or to desist from swearing) or to control more fundamental matters such as the child's religion (but note the limitation on local authorities in s 33(6)(a)) or consent for medical treatment. A person who has parental responsibility for a child may not surrender any aspect of it to anyone else but may arrange for someone else to exercise it on his or her behalf (CA 1989, s 2(9)). The guide to the 1989 Act for those in the education service, prepared for the DES by the Open University (*The Children Act 1989: A Guide for the Education Service* (1991), p 11), notes that the effect of this provision is that 'parents may give authority to schools to, act *in loco parentis*, much as before'. If, therefore, a parent agrees that his or her child should go away for several days on a school trip, the supervising teachers would be acting *in loco parentis* for this purpose and could therefore control such matters as bed time and making one's bed in the morning!

It would be a nonsense if, by virtue of the fact that they do not have parental responsibility *de jure*, teachers were precluded from having authority to take action in emergencies, such as where a child is injured at school. The Act provides that a person who does not have parental responsibility for a particular child but who has care of the child 'may (subject to the provisions of this Act) do what is reasonable in all the circumstances of the case for the purpose of safeguarding or promoting the welfare of the child' (s 3(5)). This general authority clearly extends to teachers and, presumably, lunchtime supervision staff. It confers authority to give consent to medical treatment in an emergency, if the parent cannot be contacted, although the mature adolescent may have some freedom to make decisions on his or her own behalf (see Open University, *op cit*, p 11; see also A Bainham, *Children: The Modern Law* (1993) pp 275–290).

(d) Child protection

(i) Introduction

Child protection measures under the Children Act 1989 are relevant to schools in two particular contexts: first, in relation to the identification of children who may have been abused or sexually abused outside school and reporting that suspicion; and, secondly, in dealing with the situation where a child may have been abused at school, by school staff.

(ii) The role of schools in child protection

As with the identification of pupils who have learning difficulties, the detection of child abuse is something in which teachers may be expected to play an important role. Both the DFE's and the Welsh Office's Circulars (4/88 and 25/88 respectively) emphasise the need for schools to play a role in notifying social services departments, the National Society for the Protection of Cruelty to Children (NSPCC) and, in some cases, the police, where there is concern for the safety and welfare of a child, although, pending a key House of Lords ruling, it is not clear whether civil liability could be incurred for failing to do so: *X* v *Bedfordshire County Council* [1994] 2 WLR 554; cf *E* v *Dorset County Council* [1994] ELR 416 *per* Evans LJ. The circulars pre-date the Children Act 1989, but the Department of Health's *Working Together* (1991) guidance, which schools are expected to follow, calls on schools to liaise closely with the various child protection agencies. LEAs are recommended (Open University, *Children Act 1989: A Guide for the Education Service* (1991), pp 25–26) to keep and maintain up-to-date registers of designated staff and ensure that they receive appropriate training and support (see also *Working Together* (1991) *op cit*, para 4.37). In terms of who should be designated, *Working Together* states (*ibid*) that 'the head teacher or another senior member of staff should be designated as having responsibility for liaising with social services and other relevant agencies in cases of child abuse'. Lyon and de Cruz (*Child Abuse* (2nd ed) (1993), Family Law, p 95) comment that 'staff in educational establishments often feel extremely vulnerable because of their ignorance on what they deem to be a very important subject'. They note that training of staff in educational establishments on the subject of child abuse has not occurred on a wide scale (see also S Adams, 'Close contact', *The Guardian*, 31 May 1994). Under the GEST Programme for 1995/96. LEAs will now be able to bid for grants for training in child protection for senior teachers with designated responsibility (see DFE Circular 18/94, paras 147–157).

Note that if the child's school record contains information which, in the opinion of the holder, 'is relevant to the question whether the pupil to which it relates is or has been the subject of, or may be at risk of, child abuse', the obligation to grant access to the contents of the record to parents will not apply (see Education (School Record) Regulations 1989, noted at p 164 above).

The term 'child abuse' is all-embracing, but 'as yet, there is still no universally agreed, all-encompassing definition of child abuse which has been formulated by either researchers, Parliament or the courts' (Lyon and de Cruz, *op cit*, p 2; for one useful typology, see B Whitney, *The Children Act and Schools*, TCAS, 1993, p 38). Instead, the Children Act 1989 uses the concept of 'significant harm' as the key basis for legal intervention (s 31; see below). An indication of the kinds of circumstances in respect of which authorities ought to consider whether protective intervention is necessary is given in *Working Together* (at para 6.40), when it refers to the criteria for considering whether to place a child on the child protection register:

'*Neglect*: the persistent or severe neglect of a child, or the failure to protect a child from exposure to any kind of danger, including cold or starvation, or extreme failure to carry out important aspects of care, resulting in the significant impairment of the child's health or development, including non-organic failure to survive.

Physical injury: actual or likely physical injury to a child, or failure to prevent physical injury (or suffering) to a child, including deliberate poisoning, suffocation and Munchausen's syndrome by proxy.

Sexual abuse: actual or likely sexual exploitation of a child or adolescent. The child may be dependent and/or developmentally immature.

Emotional abuse: actual or likely severe effect on the emotional and behavioural development of a child caused by persistent or severe emotional ill-treatment or rejection'.

The guidance goes on to note (at para 6.41) that these categories 'do not tie in precisely with the definition of "significant harm" in section 31 . . . which will be relevant if court proceedings are initiated. For example, with a case of neglect it will be necessary to consider whether it involves "ill-treatment" or "impairment of health or development" (in each case defined by the Act)'. A court may make a care or supervision order if a child is suffering, or is likely to suffer, significant harm, and that harm is attributable either to the care, or likely care, not being what it would be reasonable to expect a parent to give the child or to the child being beyond parental control (CA 1989, s 31(2); see *Re M (A Minor) (Care Order; Threshold Conditions*) [1994] 2 FCR 871 (HL)). 'Harm' is defined as 'ill-treatment or the impairment of health or development'. 'Health' is defined as 'physical or mental health', and 'ill-treatment' includes 'sexual abuse' (a term not defined in the Act) 'and forms of ill-treatment which are not physical'. All these definitions are in section 31(9). The child's health or development must, for this purpose, be compared with that which could reasonably be expected of a similar child (s 31(10)). The Children Act guidance suggests that 'the "significance" could exist in the seriousness of the harm *or the implications of it*' (emphasis added) (Department of Health, *The Children Act 1989: Guidance and Regulations*, *Vol 1. Court Orders* (1991) para 3.19). 'Significant', the guidance suggests, means 'considerable, noteworthy or important' (*ibid*). For discussion of the concept of 'significant harm', see Lyon and de Cruz, *op cit*, pp 98–100 and B Hoggett, *Parents and Children – the law of parental responsibility* (4th ed) (1993) Sweet and Maxwell, pp 180–182. A finding of 'significant harm' will also provide a key part of the basis for a child assessment order (CA 1989, s 43) or emergency protection order (s 44), the power of the police to remove the child to suitable accommodation (s 46), and a duty on the local social services authority to make enquiries to determine whether it should take any action to safeguard or promote the child's welfare (s 47). Teachers may be called as witnesses in civil or court proceedings arising out of child abuse.

Area Child Protection Committees are responsible for co-ordination, monitoring and guidance (see Lyon and de Cruz, *op cit*, pp 147–148, who provide a full list of ACPC functions). Lyon and de Cruz report (*ibid*, p 95) that LEAs all over the country have received guidance from ACPCs and have, in turn, issued guidance to staff on the legal requirements and child protection procedures.

In addition to reporting possible abuse, those working in the education service may be required to contribute to child protection case conferences, whose official purpose is to determine whether or not abuse has taken place, although not to decide what to do (see Hoggett, *op cit*, p 187). The conference may, however, decide whether the child's name should be placed on the child protection register.

The guidance suggests that social services departments should notify schools (including nursery schools) if a pupil's name has been included on the child protection register, or when a child whose name is on the register starts school (Open University, *op cit*, p 26). The guidance states that the notification 'should include information about whether the pupil is subject to a care order, the name of the key worker on the case, and what information may be made known to the parents' (*ibid*). The school should inform the custodian of the register if the child moves to another school.

Children whose names are on the child protection register require close monitoring by schools. The guidance states that 'schools should pay particular concern to the attendance and development of such pupils, and report any cause for further concern to the local authority' (*ibid*). The guidance also suggests that schools have an important role to play in preventing abuse, not only through adopting effective policies and systems for managing child abuse issues but also through the 'whole curriculum' approach advocated by the Education Reform Act 1988 (see Chapter 8, at p 190). This was interpreted by the National Curriculum Council as warranting coverage of personal health and safety issues, within the foundation subjects and generally.

(iii) Abuse of children by staff

The Open University guidance ((1991), *op cit*, p 26) states that 'LEAs, school governors and proprietors of independent schools must make sure their procedures cover cases where a member of staff is alleged to have abused a pupil'. Considerable publicity attended the case of the primary school head teacher who was suspended after sitting a pupil on his knee (after alleged previous incidents of the same conduct), and there have been reports of 'a rise in the number of teachers suspended pending investigations arising from commonplace incidents such as comforting a distressed child or breaking up a playground fight' and of guidance from one teaching union 'not to shout in class to avoid allegations of abuse' (The Times, 5 March 1994). Teaching unions have recently drawn up guidelines for staff (see below). It is not possible to consider this issue at length, but a few observations may be made.

Extreme cases, such as locking up children or subjecting them to sexual abuse (as in the 'Pindown' or Leicestershire cases respectively), are those where significant harm is likely. Excessive corporal punishment will generally constitute abuse (see the discussion in Lyon and de Cruz, *op cit*, at pp 242–244), and corporal punishment is in any event unlawful at most schools (see Chapter 12, Part 3(c)). On the other hand, detention of (especially older) pupils at school as a form of punishment for a reasonable period or in reasonable circumstances is not likely to cause significant harm to a child although there is often a fine line to be drawn between what is lawful and unlawful detention or restraint (see Chapter 12, Part 3(c) and (d)). Neglecting to seek to control a child's behaviour (in a moderate manner) could in fact, be likely to cause more harm than good so far as his or her proper social development is concerned. For example, the Children Act guidance suggests that 'a child that is failing to control his anti-social behaviour' would be included within the scope of the definition of impaired development (DoH, *The Children Act 1989: Guidance and Regulations, Vol 1. Court Orders* (1991), para 3.20). In the case of infant school children being cuddled by teachers, this may be important in providing security, and thus be necessary to meet the child's emotional needs; failure to comfort an injured or bullied child in this way might be to neglect such needs. On the other hand, children are in a vulnerable position and could be unaware that, for example, they are being stroked or cuddled for the sexual gratification of the teacher. As *Working Together* notes (above), sexual abuse may take the form of 'sexual exploitation' of the child.

For the purposes of the 'threshold criteria' for care and supervisions orders under section 31 of the Children Act 1989, the significant harm to the child must, as noted above (in (ii)), be attributable either to the child's being beyond parental control or, alternatively, the fact that the care given is not what it would be reasonable to expect a parent to have given him. The latter may well provide a basis for judging the conduct of a teacher with regard to child abuse, especially given the applicability of the *in loco parentis* principle discussed above (Part 2(c)), although it should be noted that, as was shown, that principle now involves taking into account the context (school rather than home) in which care of pupils is administered.

Clearly a case of suspected child abuse by a member of staff presents a school with a difficult situation. There is a need to safeguard the welfare of the child concerned, while at the same time, and in the interests of the proper functioning of the school, ensuring that false or mistaken allegations are not permitted to damage the reputation of the individual teacher and the teaching staff in general. Head teachers (and deputy head teachers, especially where the allegations concern the head teacher) need to know when to involve an outside agency, in particular social services or the police. The must also be able to decide how to deal with the member of staff concerned: how and when to question him or her, when to suspend, and what records to keep of the alleged incident(s) and of the investigation. Involvement of the parents of the child concerned must also be handled delicately.

Recently, the six teacher organisations in England and Wales agreed and published a set of guidelines: *Teachers and Child Protection – Teachers Facing an Allegation of Physical/Sexual Abuse: Guidelines on Practice and*

Procedure (1994, NAS/UWT and others). These are clearly intended to supplement the guidance in the DoH's *Working Together* (above) and local authorities' own guidance, and are school-specific. The guidance points out that teachers are, because of their daily contact with children in a variety of situations, including the wider caring role, vulnerable to accusations of abuse. The guidance aims to ensure proper safeguards and natural justice to accused members of staff while not compromising the school's child protection role. Although the guidance is discussed below, readers are asked to bear in mind that some aspects of it are proving to be controversial. In particular, the Association of Chief Police Officers and several other organisations, including those representing local authority social service departments, are critical of what is seen as insufficient emphasis on calling in child protection agencies in any case of suspected child abuse. As will be shown below, the guidance puts the onus on the head teacher to decide whether or not to report the allegations to social services or the police.

It is not possible to include all of the guidance in this book. Nevertheless, some of the key features may be outlined, for information. First, the guidance emphasises the importance of child protection and the need to refer a case to the child protection investigation agencies (and to seek appropriate medical care, as necessary) if the child is at risk of significant harm and in need of protection (see above). It also stresses the importance of listening to the child. The guidance recommends that allegations should be recorded in writing and signed by the person(s) making them.

The head teacher is urged to act quickly in determining whether or not an allegation of child abuse warrants further investigation. What is perhaps a little surprising is that the guidance places this decision on the head teacher alone. In any event, the guidance suggests that what is required of the head teacher is not to form a view on the veracity or otherwise of the allegations made but simply to decide whether an investigation by an appropriate agency should be carried out. The guidance points out that in order to come to a decision on this matter confidential inquiries of staff or pupils may have to be made. The guidance emphasises that 'this assessment is not an investigation to determine guilt or innocence' (para 6.4). Interviewing children on such matters is something on which, it is submitted, much more careful guidance is needed. The sample questions which are given suggest that a pupil witness is merely going to be asked about the day, time or place that the teacher and the child making the allegation were together; but questioning on a one-to-one basis on sensitive matters of conduct would, it is submitted, be wrong and quite possibly be in breach of other official guidelines (see in particular *Working Together*). There is certainly a strong case for arguing that specialist child protection professional expertise should be involved even at this stage.

The guidance recommends that if the head teacher concludes that further investigation is not necessary, he or she must, *inter alia*, inform the relevant parties of this conclusion and prepare a report explaining it. Counselling or support for the child making the allegation may be desirable, it suggests. Where, on the other hand, the head teacher believes that further investigation of the allegation is warranted, he or she is recommended by the guidance to refer the matter to the police, social services or the NSPCC, or, where the child is not at risk of significant harm, to undertake further investigations at school level prior to considering the appropriateness of disciplinary action. In either case, the parents, the teacher against whom the allegation is made and the chair of governors should be informed.

The guidance deals specifically with the question of suspension of a member of staff, stating that this should not be undertaken in every case. It states that there would need to be a 'good reason' for doing so, such as where the allegation was so serious that dismissal for gross misconduct was possible, or it was necessary to enable the conduct of the investigation to proceed unimpeded, or where children were at risk (see para 8.2). The guidance sets out in some detail the procedure to be followed in relation to suspension.

In making recommendations on the conduct of an investigation, the guidance stresses that any internal investigation within the school should normally be held in abeyance until after an investigation by the police or child protection authorities. *Working Together* (*op cit*) recommends a Strategy Meeting, to plan the investigation, as part of the child protection procedures. The teaching unions' guidance suggests that it is desirable for head teachers to be involved in such a meeting where the alleged abuse concerns a teacher. The internal investigation may result in a disciplinary charge being brought against a member of staff or, alternatively, it may be decided not to proceed with disciplinary action. Either way, the child who made the allegations and his or her parents should be informed of the outcome. The guidance also states that a copy of the statement or record of the allegation plus details of the outcome should be kept in the section of the pupil's personal file 'which is not open to disclosure' (para 16.3). As noted in (ii) above, information in a child's school record which is relevant to a question of whether the child may have been subjected to child abuse is excepted from the general duty of disclosure under the Education (School Records) Regulations 1989.

Appendix 1

Procedure for the acquisition of grant-maintained status (Education Act 1993)

Until the EA 1993, the procedure for the acquisition of GM status by a county or voluntary school was laid down in the ERA 1988. The EA 1993 has replaced all the relevant provisions, making a number of important amendments in the process (EA 1993, Part II, Chapter II and Sch 3). Two significant changes are the abolition of the requirement for a second resolution of the governing body before a ballot of parents can take place, and a reduction (from six months to four months) in the period within which the governors must publish their proposals following a ballot in favour of GM status for the school. Further changes include greater regulation of campaigning on GM status – in particular, restrictions on the amount that LEAs can spend for the purpose of influencing the outcome of a ballot (see EA 1993, s 36) – and a duty on governing bodies to consider, at least once a year, whether a ballot of parents on GM status should be sought for the school (EA 1993, s 24; Education (Annual Consideration of Ballot on Grant-Maintained Status) (England) Order 1993, SI 1993 No 3115 and (Wales) Order 1994, SI 1994 No 1861) (for eligibility for GM status, see Chapter 2, at pp 34–35).

As under the 1988 Act, the procedure laid down in the EA 1993 (to which all section numbers below relate) may be initiated by a governors' resolution or a request from parents.

A. Initiation of the procedure

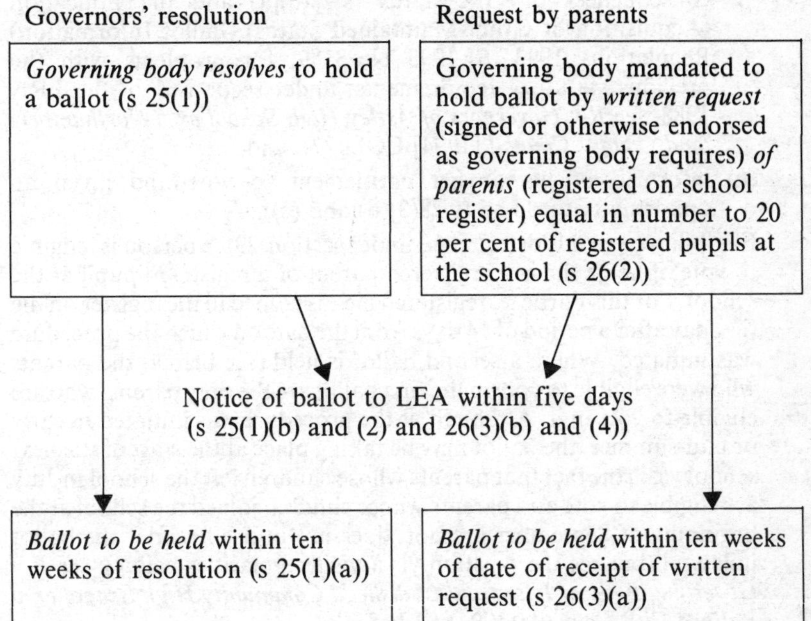

Notes:

1. The written request from parents must be delivered to the chairman of or clerk to the governors (s 26(6)).
2. No ballot may be held within twelve months of a previous ballot unless the Secretary of State gives written consent (ss 25(3) and 26(5)).
3 A parent is entitled, on request – in connection with the ballot – to a list of all parents of registered pupils; but any parent may request in writing non-disclosure of his or her name (s 27). A charge, not exceeding the cost of production, may be made by the governing body for supplying the list (s 27(4)).
4. The governors' resolution on whether to conduct a ballot must be made via a secret vote (Education (School Government) Regulations 1989, as amended, reg 14(1A)). Consideration of the question whether to conduct a ballot must be a specific agenda item (reg 19(2A)).

B. Before the ballot

1. Arrangements must be made for the ballot to be secret and postal (s 28(2)).
2. The governors are required to 'take such steps as are reasonably practicable to secure that every person eligible to vote in the ballot' is:

(*a*) given the prescribed information about the procedure and consequences of GM status (s 28(3)(a) and the Education (Acquisition of Grant-Maintained Status) (Ballot Information) Regulations 1993, SI 1993 No 3189; for problems with the previous statutory requirements, under section 61 of the ERA 1988, see *R* v *Governors of Astley High School ex p Northumberland County Council* [1994] COD 27); and

(*b*) informed of his or her entitlement to vote and given an opportunity to do so (s 28(3)(b) and (c)).

3. Eligibility to vote is determined under section 29. A person is 'eligible to vote' if he or she is a registered parent of a registered pupil at the school. For this purpose, registered means named in the register on the first day after a period of 14 days from the date on which the procedure was initiated. Where a second ballot is held (see below) the parents who were eligible to vote in the first ballot are the only parents who are eligible to vote in it. Although, if the procedure was initiated in early or mid-summer, the ballot may be taking place at the start of the next school year, the fact that parents whose children left the school in July are eligible to vote and parents whose children joined the school at the beginning of September are not, does not in itself render the ballot unlawful (but see the position vis-à-vis irregularities below): see *R* v *Governing Body of Irlam and Cadishead Community High School ex p Salford City Council* ([1994] ELR 81).
4. The prescribed information (see 2. above) is also to be made available to persons who work at the school (s 28(4)).
5. The governing body may 'promote (otherwise than as part of the arrangements made for the ballot) the case for seeking grant-maintained status for the school', and in doing so must take into account any guidance issued by the Secretary of State (s 28(6)). In *R* v *Governors of Small Heath School ex p Birmingham City Council* [1990] COD 23, Popplewell J said (*obiter*) that head teachers and governors were not barred from expressing their views as private individuals on GM status for the school. Presumably the Secretary of State's guidance, when issued, will explain this. Note that if voting is likely to have been influenced by false or misleading information the Secretary of State may declare the ballot void and order a fresh one (s 31(1)(g), 32(2)).

C. The ballot and publication of proposals

The governing body must ensure that the arrangements for the ballot are made by the prescribed body (s 28(1)). Presumably the Electoral Reform Society will be prescribed, as under the 1988 Act (see the Education (Parental Ballots for Acquisition of Grant-Maintained Status) (Prescribed Body) Regulations 1988 (SI 1988 No 1474)). The costs of conducting the ballot are recoverable from the Secretary of State (s 36(1) and (2)).

'First ballot'

Total no. of votes cast by persons eligible to vote is *less than 50 per cent* of the no. of such persons or the result of the first ballot is a tie (s 30(1)).	Total no. of votes cast by persons eligible to vote is *50 per cent or more* of the no. of such persons.

'Second ballot' (must be within 14 days of 'first ballot')

↓

Vote decided *by simple majority of those voting* (NB On the second ballot the result of the first ballot is disregarded) (ss 30(2) and 32(1)).

↓

Within 4 months of the ballot

↓

Governors to *publish proposals* and submit them to the Secretary of State (s 32(2)). Annexed to proposals or in an accompanying statement must be: result of ballot (votes for and against); classification of the school; description of the character of the school; number of pupils who can be accommodated; and other prescribed information. The proposals themselves must contain, *inter alia*, details of the initial governors; proposed admission and special educational needs arrangements; and arrangements for induction and INSET of teachers (Sch 3 paras 2–4).

Publication of the proposals:

The proposals are to be published

(i) by being posted at or near to the school's main entrance and at least one 'conspicuous place within the area served by the school'; and

(ii) by being made available for public inspection at the school or other convenient (to the public) place in the area (Sch 3 para 1(1)).

Also, a summary is to be published in at least one newspaper circulating in the area (Sch 3 para 1(2)).
(For the prescribed contents of the summary, see Sch 3 para 1(3).)

Irregularities

The Secretary of State may declare a ballot void for irregularity and order a fresh ballot. If the new ballot occurs on a date in the next following school year, only parents whose names are on the school register at that date may vote in it (s 31). An irregularity occurs if there is a failure to comply with any of the statutory requirements or to follow the guidance issued by the Secretary of State, or if the governing body has acted unreasonably in the discharge of its duties, or if persons not eligible to vote have purported to do so, or if voting is likely to have been influenced to a significant extent by the dissemination of information which appears to a material extent to be false or misleading (s 31(1)).

D. After publication of proposals

Within two months of publication of proposals the following may occur:

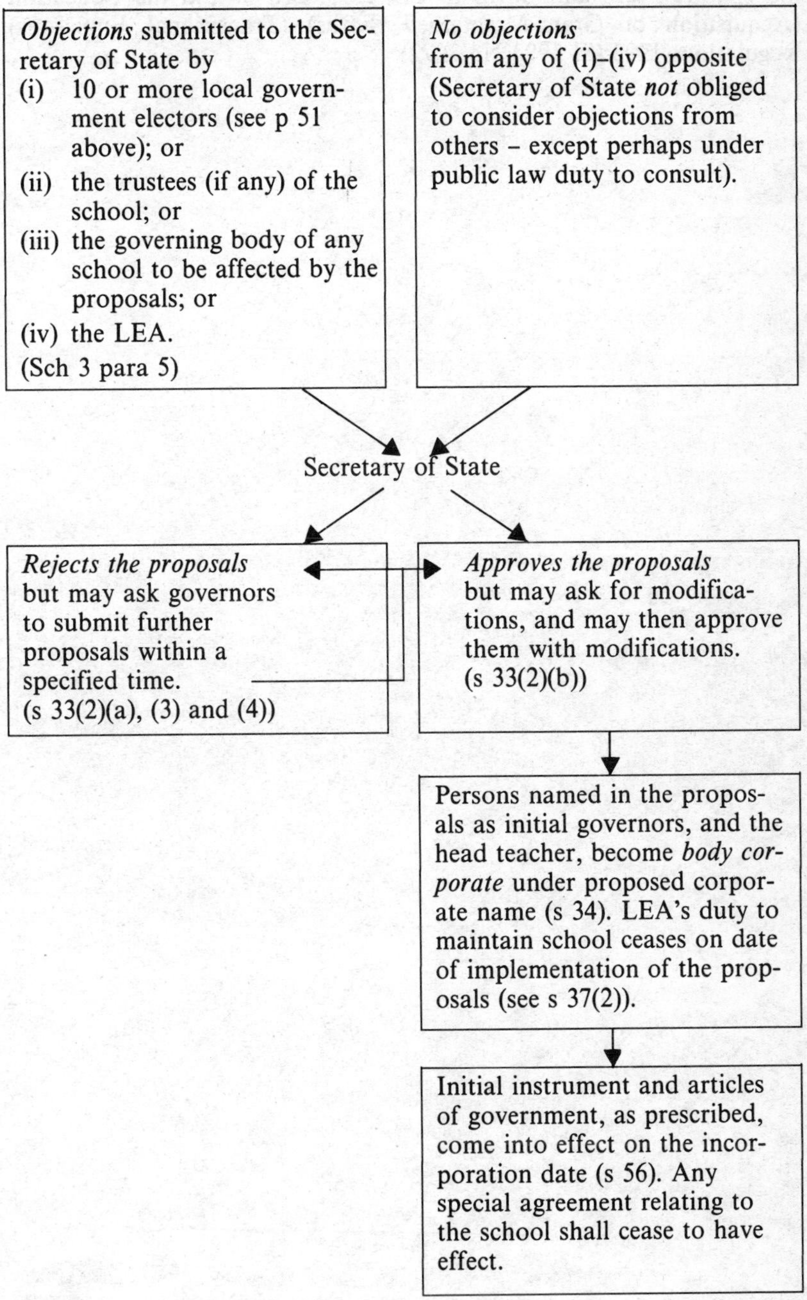

Objections submitted to the Secretary of State by
(i) 10 or more local government electors (see p 51 above); or
(ii) the trustees (if any) of the school; or
(iii) the governing body of any school to be affected by the proposals; or
(iv) the LEA.
(Sch 3 para 5)

No objections
from any of (i)–(iv) opposite (Secretary of State *not* obliged to consider objections from others – except perhaps under public law duty to consult).

↓

Secretary of State

↓

Rejects the proposals
but may ask governors to submit further proposals within a specified time.
(s 33(2)(a), (3) and (4))

Approves the proposals
but may ask for modifications, and may then approve them with modifications.
(s 33(2)(b))

↓

Persons named in the proposals as initial governors, and the head teacher, become *body corporate* under proposed corporate name (s 34). LEA's duty to maintain school ceases on date of implementation of the proposals (see s 37(2)).

↓

Initial instrument and articles of government, as prescribed, come into effect on the incorporation date (s 56). Any special agreement relating to the school shall cease to have effect.

Note:

Transitional arrangements for the period between approval and incorporation are laid down in EA 1993, Sch 5, and the Education (Acquisition of Grant-Maintained Status) (Transitional Functions) Regulations 1993 (SI 1993 No 3072).

Appendix 2

DFE Circular 2/94 Local Management of Schools, Annex G (extract)

This Circular replicates the suggested division of responsibilities for building and grounds maintenance set out in DES Circular 7/88 *Education Reform Act: Local Management of Schools* (Annex A).

DIVISION OF RESPONSIBILITY FOR BUILDING AND GROUNDS MAINTENANCE BETWEEN LEAs AND SCHOOLS

LEA responsibilities are described by overall headings for each item, with school responsibilities described in more detail.

LEA Responsibility	School Responsibility
A. STRUCTURE	
– Foundations	
– Structural frames	
– Floor structures (including ground floor slabs)	Repair or replacement of floor finishes
– Roof structures (including weather-proof coverings and insulation)	Repair of ceiling finishes
– Skylights, rooflights and verandahs	Minor repairs and repairs of glazing
– Rainwater goods	Clearing out gutters and downpipes
– Staircase and landing structures (including handrails and balustrades)	Repair of finishes and coverings
– External walls and surfaces (including insulation)	Repair of exposed internal finishes
– Internal walls, partitions and glazed screens	Repair of surface finishes and glazing
– Windows and fittings (including window walls)	Minor repairs, adjustment and glazing

– Doors and fittings	Minor repairs, adjustment and glazing
– Ceiling structures (including suspension systems)	Ceiling tiles/finishes and minor plaster repairs
	Glazing: to include all glazing throughout as indicated above
Timber preservation	
B. DECORATION	
– All external decoration	All **internal decoration:** including cleaning and preparation
C. WATER AND DRAINAGE SERVICES	
– Internal water supply services (including pumps, pipes, tanks and insulation)	
– Replacement of water supply including sanitary equipment	Minor repair and adjustment including taps and other fittings
– Waste and soil drainage services	Cleaning of pipes and maintenance of traps, wire guards etc
D. ELECTRICAL SERVICES	
– Servicing, repair and replacement of general electrical installations including switchgear, cables and conduits up to and including switches, sockets and other outlets	Replacing lamps, tubes and plugs
– All external lighting, including columns, floodlights and road lighting	
– Steel chimneys	
– Alarm, emergency and time systems (except for any systems purchased at school cost)	Reset of alarms and fire detection systems; minor repairs to clocks and bells; maintenance of any systems purchased at school cost
– Fan convectors and other fixed space and water heating equipment; fixed ventilation units	Portable heating and ventilation equipment; general cleaning; maintenance and replacement of fittings on all items
	Kitchen equipment: servicing and repair of fixed cooking equipment including ovens, ranges, fryers, boilers, steamers grills and mixers. Heated trolleys, refrigerators, cold rooms, fixed water boilers and sterilising sink heaters

Laundry equipment: servicing and repair of washing machines, tumble driers, spin driers, extractors and irons (excluding drainage systems)

- Lifts, hoists, barriers and electric door motors and controls
- Specialist external equipment (e.g. earthing, lightning conductors)
- Standby generators
- Temporary accommodation: all power supply and wiring

E. MECHANICAL SERVICES
- Servicing, repair and replacement of mechanical installations and plant including:
  - Boilers, including automatic controls and electrics
  - Ancillary boiler equipment: pumps and tanks
  - Heating and domestic hot water distribution systems, including replacement of radiators and other heat emitters, taps and shower fittings

Minor repairs and adjustments to heat emitters, taps and shower fittings

  - Gas distribution systems
  - Fixed air-conditioning and ventilation equipment
  - Direct oil and gas fired heater units
  - Sewage pumps and chambers

Kitchen equipment: servicing and repair of gas cooking equipment including motors and burners etc

- Swimming pools: including filtration plant, pumps pipes and boilers

Chemical dosing, cleaning and minor maintenance

Fire fighting equipment: extinguishers, fire blankets and fixed hoses

- Fume cupboards, including extractor fans and ductwork

F. FURNITURE & FITTINGS	
	Internal joinery fixtures: including cupboards, shelves, display boards, fixed benches and other internal seating with its coverings
	Gymnasium equipment: repairs of all fixed sports and gymnasium equipment and markings
	Supply, fixing and maintenance of all internal signs, blinds, curtain tracks etc
	Fires and fireplaces
G. EXTERNAL WORKS	
– Demolition of buildings and clearance of sites; sealing of services	
– Major repairs to hard-paved areas including roads, playgrounds, car parks and courts	Minor repairs to hard paved areas
– Perimeter and retaining walls; perimeter fencing and gates	Minor repairs to walls, fences and gates
– Major external fixtures	Minor external fixtures eg signs and notices
– Mature trees	**Upkeep of grounds:** maintenance of grounds, playing fields, amenities land, landscaped areas and boundary hedges (except mature trees)
– Mains drainage including traps, gullies and manholes	Cleaning and unblocking drainage systems
	Refuse containers and bins
	Pest control
– Gas, electric, water and heating mains	
– Maintenance of ancillary buildings including garages and huts, constructed at LEA cost	Maintenance of ancillary buildings constructed at school cost
H. MISCELLANEOUS	
– Asbestos removal or treatment	
– External maintenance on temporary buildings	Internal maintenance on temporary buildings; all glazing repairs

Appendix 3

Conditions of employment of head teachers, deputy-head teachers and teachers

(Source: *School Teachers' Pay and Conditions Document 1994* ISBN 011 270881 1.)

(Reproduced with the permission of the Controller of Her Majesty's Stationery Office.)

Part IX — Conditions of Employment of Head Teachers

Overriding requirements

29.1 A head teacher shall carry out his professional duties in accordance with and subject to:

(*a*) the provisions of the Education Acts 1944 to 1993;

(*b*) any orders and regulations having effect thereunder;

(*c*) the articles of government of the school of which he is head teacher, to the extent to which their content is prescribed by statute;

(*d*) where the school is a voluntary school or a grant-maintained school which was formerly a voluntary school, any trust deed applying in relation thereto;

(*e*) any scheme of local management approved or imposed by the Secretary of State under section 34 of the Education Reform Act 1988;

29.2 A head teacher shall carry out such duties in accordance with and subject to the following (to the extent to which they are not inconsistent with paragraphs 30 to 33):

29.2.1 provisions of the articles of government the content of which is not prescribed by statute;

29.2.2 in the case of a school which has a delegated budget:

(*a*) any rules, regulations or policies laid down by the governing body under their powers as derived from any of the sources specified in paragraphs 29.1 and 29.2.1; and (*b*) any rules, regulations or policies laid down by his employers with respect to matters for the governing body is not so responsible;

29.2.3 in any other case, any rules, regulations or policies laid down by his employers; and

29.2.4 the terms of his appointment.

General functions

30 Subject to paragraph 29.1 a head teacher shall be responsible for the internal organisation, management and control of the school.

Consultation

31 In carrying out his duties a head teacher shall consult, where this is appropriate, with the authority, the governing body, the staff of the school and the parents of its pupils.

Professional duties

The professional duties of a head teacher shall include:

32.1 *School aims:*

formulating the overall aims and objectives of the school and policies for their implementation;

32.2 *Appointment of staff:*

participating in the selection and appointment of the teaching and non-teaching staff of the school;

32.3 *Management of staff:*

32.3.1 deploying and managing all teaching and non-teaching staff of the school and allocating particular duties to them (including such duties of the head teacher as may properly be delegated to the deputy head teacher or other members of the staff) in a manner consistent with their conditions of employment, maintaining a reasonable balance for each teacher between work carried out in school and work carried out elsewhere;

32.3.2 considering in particular in relation to such allocation of duties how far the duties of the head teacher may be delegated to any deputy head teacher;

32.3.3 ensuring that the duty of providing cover for absent teachers is shared equitably among all teachers in the school (including the head teacher), taking account of their teaching and other duties; and

32.3.4 ensuring that teachers at the school receive information they need in order to carry out their professional duties effectively.

32.4 *Liaison with staff unions and associations:*

maintaining relationships with organisations representing teachers and other persons on the staff of the school;

32.5 *Curriculum:*

32.5.1 determining, organising and implementing an appropriate curriculum for the school, having regard to the needs, experience, interests, aptitudes and stage of development of the pupils and the resources available to the school; and his duty under sections 1(1) and 10(1)(b) and (2) of the Education Reform Act 1988;

32.5.2 securing that all pupils in attendance at the school take part in daily collective worship in pursuance of his duty under section 10(1)(a) of the Education Reform Act 1988;

32.6 *Review:*

keeping under review the work and organisation of the school;

32.7 *Standards of teaching and learning:*

evaluating the standards of teaching and learning in the school, and ensuring that proper standards of professional performance are established and maintained;

32.8 *Appraisal, training and development of staff:*

32.8.1 supervising and participating in arrangements made in accordance with The Education (School Teacher Appraisal) Regulations 1991[33] for the appraisal of the performance of teachers in the school; participating in arrangements made for the appraisal of his performance as head teacher, and that of other head teachers who are the responsibility of the same appraising body in accordance with such regulations; participating in the identification of areas in which he would benefit from further training and undergoing such training;

32.8.2 ensuring that all staff in the school have access to advice and training appropriate to their needs, in accordance with the policies of the maintaining authority or, in the case of a grant-maintained school, of the governing body, for the development of staff;

(33) S.I. 1991/1511.

32.8.3 ensuring that newly-qualified teachers and those returning to teaching after a break in service have access to adequate support in their first year of service or resumed service.

32.9 *Management information:*

providing information about the work and performance of the staff employed at the school where this is relevant to their future employment;

32.10 *Pupil progress:*

ensuring that the progress of the pupils of the school is monitored and recorded;

32.11 *Pastoral care:*

determining and ensuring the implementation of a policy for the pastoral care of the pupils;

32.12 *Discipline:*

32.12.1 determining, in accordance with any written statement of general principles provided for him by the governing body, measures to be taken with a view to promoting, among the pupils, self-discipline and proper regard for authority, encouraging good behaviour on the part of the pupils, securing that the standard of behaviour of the pupils is acceptable and otherwise regulating the conduct of the pupils; making such measures generally known within the school, and ensuring that they are implemented; and

32.12.2 ensuring the maintenance of good order and discipline at all times during the school day (including the midday break) when pupils are present on the school premises and whenever the pupils are engaged in authorised school activities, whether on the school premises or elsewhere;

32.13 *Relations with parents:*

making arrangements for parents to be given regular information about the school curriculum, the progress of their children and other matters affecting the school, so as to promote common understanding of its aims;

32.14 *Relations with other bodies:*

promoting effective relationships with persons and bodies outside the school;

32.15 *Relations with governing body:*

advising and assisting the governing body of the school in the exercise of its functions, including (without prejudice to any rights he may have as a governor of the school) attending meetings of the governing body and making such reports to it in connection with the discharge of his functions as it may properly require either on a regular basis or from time to time;

32.16 *Relations with authority:*

(except in the case of grant-maintained or grant-maintained special schools) providing for liaison and co-operation with the officers of the maintaining authority; making such reports to the authority in connection with the discharge of his functions as it may properly require, either on a regular basis or from time to time;

32.17 *Relations with other educational establishments:*

maintaining liaison with other schools and further education establishments with which the school has a relationship;

32.18 *Resources:*

allocating, controlling and accounting for those financial and material resources of the school which are under the control of the head teacher;

32.19 *Premises:*

making arrangements, if so required by the maintaining authority or the governing body of a grant-maintained or grant-maintained special school (as appropriate), for the security and effective supervision of the school buildings and their contents and of the school grounds; and ensuring (if so required) that any lack of maintenance is promptly reported to the maintaining authority or, if appropriate, the governing body;

32.20 *Absence:*

arranging for a deputy head teacher or other suitable person to assume responsibility for the discharge of his functions as head teacher at any time when he is absent from the school;

32.21 *Teaching:*

participating, to such extent as may be appropriate having regard to his other duties, in the teaching of pupils at the school, including the provision of cover for absent teachers.

Daily break

33 A head teacher shall be entitled to a break of reasonable length in the course of each school day, and shall arrange for a suitable person to assume responsibility for the discharge of his functions as head teacher during that break.

PART X — Conditions of Employment of Deputy Head Teachers

Professional duties

34 A person appointed deputy head teacher in a school, in addition to carrying out the professional duties of a teacher other than a head teacher, including those duties particularly assigned to him by the head teacher, shall:

34.1 play a major role under the overall direction of the head teacher in:

(*a*) formulating the aims and objectives of the school;

(*b*) establishing the policies through which they shall be achieved;

(*c*) managing staff and resources to that end; and

(*d*) monitoring progress towards their achievement;

34.2 undertake any professional duties of the head teacher delegated to him by the head teacher;

34.3 undertake to the extent required by the head teacher or the relevant body or, in the case of an aided school, the governing body, the professional duties of the head teacher in the event of his absence from the school; and

34.4 be entitled to a break of reasonable length as near to the middle of each school day as is reasonably practicable.

PART XI — Conditions of Employment of Teachers other than Head Teachers

Exercise of general professional duties

35 A teacher who is not a head teacher shall carry out the professional duties of a teacher as circumstances may require:

35.1 if he is employed as a teacher in a school, under the reasonable direction of the head teacher of that school;

35.2 if he is employed by an authority on terms under which he is not assigned to any one school, under the reasonable direction of that authority and of the head teacher of any school in which he may for the time being be required to work as a teacher.

Exercise of particular duties

36.1 A teacher employed as a teacher (other than a head teacher) in a school shall perform, in accordance with any directions which may reasonably be given to him by the head teacher from time to time, such particular duties as may reasonably be assigned to him.

36.2 A teacher employed by an authority on terms such as those described in paragraph 35.2 shall perform, in accordance with any direction which may reasonably be given to him from time to time by the authority or by the head teacher of any school in which he may for the time being be required to work as a teacher, such particular duties as may reasonably be assigned to him.

Professional duties

37 The following duties shall be deemed to be included in the professional duties which a teacher (other than a head teacher) may be required to perform:

37.1 *Teaching:*

In each case having regard to the curriculum for the school:

37.1.1 planning and preparing courses and lessons

37.1.2 teaching, according to their educational needs, the pupils assigned to him, including the setting and marking of work to be carried out by the pupil in school and elsewhere;

37.1.3 assessing, recording and reporting on the development, progress and attainment of pupils;

37.2 *Other activities:*

37.2.1 promoting the general progress and well-being of individual pupils and of any class or group of pupils assigned to him;

37.2.2 providing guidance and advice to pupils on educational and social matters and on their further education and future careers, including information about sources of more expert advice on specific questions; making relevant records and reports;

37.2.3 making records of and reports on the personal and social needs of pupils;

37.2.4 communicating and consulting with the parents of pupils;

37.2.5 communicating and co-operating with persons or bodies outside the school; and

37.2.6 participating in meetings arranged for any of the purposes described above;

37.3 *Assessments and reports:*

providing or contributing to oral and written assessments, reports and references relating to individual pupils and groups of pupils;

37.4 *Appraisal:*

participating in arrangements made in accordance with The Education (School Teacher Appraisal) Regulations 1991[34] for the appraisal of his performance and that of other teachers;

37.5 *Review: Further training and development:*

37.5.1 reviewing from time to time his methods of teaching and programmes of work; and

37.5.2 participating in arrangements for his further training and professional development as a teacher;

37.6 *Educational methods:*

advising and co-operating with the head teacher and other teachers (or any one or more of them) on the preparation and development of courses of study, teaching materials, teaching programmes, methods of teaching and assessment and pastoral arrangements;

37.7 *Discipline, health and safety:*

maintaining good order and discipline among the pupils and safeguarding their health and safety both when they are authorised to be on the school premises and when they are engaged in authorised school activities elsewhere;

37.8 *Staff meetings:*

participating in meetings at the school which relate to the curriculum for the school or the administration or organisation of the school, including pastoral arrangements;

37.9 *Cover:*

37.9.1 Subject to paragraph 37.9.2, supervising and so far as practicable teaching any pupils whose teacher is not available to teach them:

37.9.2 Subject to the exceptions in paragraph 37.9.3, no teacher shall be required to provide such cover:

(34) S.I. 1991/1511

(*a*) after the teacher who is absent or otherwise not available has been so for three or more consecutive working days; or

(*b*) where the fact that the teacher would be absent or otherwise not available for a period exceeding three consecutive working days was known to the maintaining authority or, in the case of a grant-maintained or grant-maintained special school or a school which has a delegated budget and whose local management scheme delegates to the governing body the relevant responsibility for the provision of supply teachers, to the governing body for two or more working days before the absence commenced;

37.9.3 The exceptions are:

(*a*) he is a teacher employed wholly or mainly for the purpose of providing such cover ('a supply teacher'); or

(*b*) the authority or the governing body (as the case may be) have exhausted all reasonable means of providing a supply teacher to provide cover without success; or

(*c*) he is a full-time teacher at the school but has been assigned by the head teacher in the time-table to teach or carry out other specified duties (except cover) for less than 75 per cent of those hours in the week during which pupils are taught at the school;

37.10 *Public examinations:*

participating in arrangements for preparing pupils for public examinations and in assessing pupils for the purposes of such examinations; recording and reporting such assessments; and participating in arrangements for pupils' presentation for and supervision during such examinations;

37.11 *Management:*

37.11.1 contributing to the selection for appointment and professional development of other teachers and non-teaching staff, including the induction and assessment of new and probationary teachers;

37.11.2 co-ordinating or managing the work of other teachers; and

37.11.3 taking such part as may be required of him in the review, development and management of activities relating to the curriculum, organisation and pastoral functions of the school;

37.12 *Administration:*

37.12.1 participating in administrative and organisational tasks related to such duties as are described above, including the management or supervision of persons providing support for the teachers in the school and the ordering and allocation of equipment and materials; and

37.12.2 attending assemblies, registering the attendance of pupils and supervising pupils, whether these duties are to be performed before, during or after school sessions.

Working time

38.1 A teacher employed full-time, other than in the circumstances described in paragraph 38.3, shall be available for work for 195 days in any school year, of which 190 days shall be days on which he may be required to teach pupils in addition to carrying out other duties; and those 195 days shall be specified by his employer, or if the employer so directs, by the head teacher.

38.2 Such a teacher shall be available to perform such duties at such times and such places as may be specified by the head teacher (or, where the teacher is not assigned to any one school, by his employer or the head teacher of any school in which he may for the time being be required to work as a teacher) for 1265 hours in any school year, those hours to be allocated reasonably throughout those days in the school year on which he is required to be available for work.

38.3 Paragraphs 38.1 and 38.2 do not apply to such a teacher employed wholly or mainly to teach or perform other duties in relation to pupils in a residential establishment.

38.4 Time spent in travelling to or from the place of work shall not count against the 1265 hours referred to in paragraph 38.2.

38.5 Such a teacher shall not be required under his contract as a teacher to undertake midday supervision, and shall be allowed a break of reasonable length either between school sessions or between the hours of 12 noon and 2.00pm.

38.6 Such a teacher shall, in addition to the requirements set out in paragraphs 38.1 and 38.2, work such additional hours as may be needed to enable him to discharge effectively his professional duties, including, in particular, the marking of pupils' work, the writing of reports on pupils and the preparation of lessons, teaching material and teaching programmes. The amount of time required for this purpose beyond the 1265 hours referred to paragraph 38.2 and the times outside the 1265 specified hours at which duties shall be performed shall not be defined by the employer but shall depend upon the work needed to discharge the teacher's duties.

Appendix 4

Governor elections

(Sections referred to are from the Education (No 2) Act 1986.)

DES Circular 7/87 The Conduct of Governor Elections (Annex 9)

(Reproduced with the permission of the Controller of Her Majesty's Stationery Office.)

PRE-ELECTION PUBLICITY

15. By virtue of section 30(2)(g) (see paragraphs 6 to 12 of Circular 8/86), the governors' annual report to parents is required to provide such information as is available about arrangements for the next election of parent governors.

16. Beyond that, section 15(6) (reproduced in paragraph 4 of this Annex), requires the responsible authority to give appropriate publicity to the election process when a vacancy needs to be filled. It is suggested that a letter should be sent to each household, perhaps using pupil post, (see paragraph 26 of this Annex) enclosing nomination forms and setting out the timetable for each stage. Where a substantial number of parents have a language other than English as their mother tongue, the letter (and all other documents relating to elections) should be translated into other languages.

17. Responsible authorities should frame their publicity to maximise participation, emphasising the importance conferred on school government by the Act. LEAs may also wish to consider measures, such as an authority-wide parent governor election week, in which governing bodies of aided and special agreement schools might also choose to participate.

NOMINATIONS

18. Responsible authorities are to decide how nominations are to be made, for example, whether a proposer and a seconder are required, or a larger number of sponsors. This should be explained clearly in the preliminary letter. Where participation has been low in the past, responsible authorities may wish to consider allowing self-nomination and nomination by a spouse. In any case, those nominated should signify in writing their willingness to stand for election. It is recommended that they should be invited to supply, with their nomination, a short personal statement for circulation to parents, either on the ballot paper or separately, if an election is required.

19. Proposers, seconders and other sponsors should, like the nominee, all be parents of registered pupils at the school. No parent should participate in more nominations than there are vacancies.

20. If the number of qualified nominees (see paragraphs 12 to 14 of this Annex) is smaller than or equal to the number of vacancies no voting is required: those nominated are simply declared to be governors. If there are vacancies remaining, the governing body is to appoint parent governors, see paragraph 5.3.5 of this Circular.

CONDUCT OF THE ELECTION

21. It is suggested that responsible authorities should appoint a PRESIDING OR RETURNING OFFICER for each school. In many cases this will be the head teacher, but the clerk to the governors or the chairman of the governors might also be appropriate.

22. The responsible authority is to select the ELECTORAL METHOD to be employed. This might be first-past-the-post or some form of proportional representation. If the latter is chosen, the responsible authority needs to ensure that the presiding/returning officer is familiar with the intricacies of the system.

23. It is for the responsible authority to determine whether a parent is to have one vote per child per vacancy or only one per vacancy. They should ensure that, whatever basis is chosen, it is made clear to the electorate.

24. The ballot paper should list the names of all the candidates, either in alphabetical order or at random. It may also include the short personal statement supplied by each candidate (see paragraph 18 of this Annex). Clear instructions for voting should be given, especially if proportional representation is to be used, and it should be stressed that no other mark should be made on the ballot paper. There must be at least one ballot paper per parent.

25. In operating the SECRET BALLOT required by section 15(4), it is necessary to ensure secrecy whilst also including some safeguards against voting in duplicate or by those not eligible to participate. A register of electors would in many cases be too time-consuming and complicated to make it worthwhile.

A REQUIREMENT THAT THE BALLOT PAPER BE SIGNED BY THE VOTER IS NOT CONSISTENT WITH A SECRET BALLOT. One possible method would be the use of a double envelope system.
The ballot paper would be sealed in the inner unmarked envelope which would be sealed in an outer envelope signed on the back by the voter. To ensure confidentiality, such a method would require a proper two-stage system of recording votes cast and opening ballot papers. The procedure might be that, on receipt of the ballot papers, the presiding/returning officer would check the name on the outer envelope for entitlement to vote and note the return on the ballot paper. The inner envelope containing the ballot paper would then be placed in the ballot box for counting at the appointed time later.

26. By virtue of section 15(5), parents have to be afforded the opportunity to vote by post. It will be for the responsible authority to decide how this requirement is to be combined with personal and proxy voting (if any). Any ballot where both postal and personal voting are allowed should be approached with caution since administration and verification could be complicated. In many cases, the responsible authority will no doubt wish to get ballot papers to and from parents by means of the pupils. However, where parents have more than one child in a school and voting is to be on the basis of one vote per parent per vacancy, some system will need to be devised to ensure that no parent receives more than one ballot paper. Ballot papers will also need to be posted or otherwise delivered, to parents whose child is absent from school when the ballot papers are issued.

27. It is suggested that ballot papers could be returned to the school, to a specified central point, over a period of days. During that period, candidates might also hold meetings for parents and the opportunity given for voting to take place in person. (This might coincide with the parents' annual meeting.)

28. The responsible authority should decide whether PROXY VOTING is to be allowed and, if so, who is to be entitled to act as proxy and how this is to be notified to the presiding/returning officer. The case for proxy voting is diminished by the requirement that postal voting be allowed, but it might be considered in schools where it is common for parents to be away for long periods of time, as for example in the case of service families.

29. If a ballot paper is inadvertently spoilt (or lost by a pupil) a duplicate may be issued by the presiding/returning officer. An election is not invalidated by an individual's failure to receive or to return a ballot paper.

THE COUNT

30. The count should be conducted by the presiding/returning officer at a time and place determined by the responsible authority. He may allow the candidate or their nominated representatives to be present. He should have responsibility for deciding the validity of dubious or spoilt ballot papers, but should be able to refer to a nominee of the responsible authority in difficult cases.

31. The responsible authority should decide, and announce well before the election, the method for deciding an election in the event of a tie. As a first step, the votes should be recounted. If the votes are then still equal, possible methods of deciding who is to become the governor include drawing lots, tossing a coin, or choosing the candidate with the youngest child at the school.

POST ELECTION

32. The result of the election (including any appointments – see paragraph 20 of this Annex) should be notified by the responsible authority to all parents, to the LEA and to the other members of the governing body. The ballot papers should be retained securely for, say, six months, in case the election result is challenged. The number of ballot papers issued and the

number returned at each election should be noted in order to monitor participation.

33. The responsible authority should review their election procedures from time to time, and particularly in the light of any problems found in their use.

Appendix 5

Collective worship: requirements of the ERA 1988

R v The Secretary of State for Education ex p R and D

Queen's Bench Division

26 February 1993

(Extract)

McCULLOUGH J: This application for leave to move for judicial review is refused. The reasons follow. They are at considerably greater length than I would normally think appropriate when refusing an ex parte application. This is for three reasons: first, out of respect for [counsel for the applicants'] argument; secondly, the question is one about which the applicants and their advisers feel keenly; thirdly, the applicants may want to appeal against my decision, and reasons may assist . . .

The first complaint is that the school 'does not have daily acts of collective worship wholly or mainly of a broadly Christian character, contrary to section 6 and 8 of the Education Act 1988'. The Secretary of State considered this complaint under four separate headings: (1) that the worship practised at the school was not worship; (2) that it was not an act of worship; (3) that the worship was so constituted by the school as to prevent some pupils from taking part; (4) that the multi-faith worship provided at the school was illegal.

The Secretary of State found that none of these complaints was made out. No challenge is made to his conclusions about the second and third headings. In relation to them it is necessary to say no more than that the Secretary of State recognised that on some occasions some of the pupils would not have been able to identify with the act of worship.

As to the first aspect, he said this: 'To constitute worship as normally defined in common English parlance, the courts would be likely to judge that collective worship in school must in some sense reflect something special or separate from ordinary school activities; that it should be concerned with reverence or veneration paid to a being or power regarded as supernatural or divine; and that the pupil, at his or her level, should be capable of perceiving this. The evidence suggests that the school has taken account of these points and does not bear out the complaint that the school is in breach of the Education Reform Act', the 1988 Act.

In accepting this definition of worship, the Secretary of State was, in essence, accepting the narrower of two definitions which had been under consideration in the material before him and, in particular, in [the LEA's Senior Inspector] Mr Molloy's report. The alternative and wider definition (to which the Secretary of State did not refer in his decision letter) was this: 'respect, admiration and devotion for an object of esteem or/and a sense of responsibility'.

Mr Molloy had concluded that the first definition could never be satisfied in what he called a meaningful and sensitive way by a collective act in which some pupils were of one faith, some of another and some had no belief in God.

Mr Molloy went on to conclude that collective acts of that kind could nevertheless meet the wider definition, and on this basis he concluded on the evidence before him that the acts of collective worship at the school were nearly all mainly of a broadly Christian character.

Two challenges are made to the Secretary of State's conclusions. The first is that although the Secretary of State is right to base his decision on the narrower definition, that in itself was not enough to satisfy the requirement for most of the acts of collective worship at the school to be of a broadly Christian character. To consider this question required the Secretary of State to identify the supernatural or divine being or power, and specifically to be satisfied that the being or power was God with a broadly Christian character.

In this connection, a letter was written to the Secretary of State on the 30 June 1992 by PACE – The Parental Alliance for Choice in Education. It asked the Department of Education specifically this: 'It would greatly help to know the identity of the being or power that was being revered or venerated in the act of worship at the school. It is clear that the Secretary of State, in establishing that worship was taking place, must have decided that some such being or power was the object of the worship'.

To this the Secretary of State replied on the 7 July 1992, saying that he did not have to discern the identity of the object of worship. It was sufficient to be reasonably satisfied that there was one.

Considered alone, the criticism made of the Secretary of State's approach in this supplementary letter would have substance, since without at least some consideration being given to the identity of the object of worship, the object might – in theory, at least – be the Man in the Moon.

The applicants' second criticism of the Secretary of State's approach to the first aspect of the first complaint is that he, having by implication rejected the sufficiency of the alternative and wider definition of 'worship', should have accepted Mr Molloy's conclusion that the collective worship at the school did not fulfil the narrower definition. It is submitted that on the evidence before him no other conclusion was reasonably open to him.

Mr Charles' response on behalf of the Secretary of State requires one to look at the Secretary of State's findings on the fourth aspect. These read as follows:

> 'For worship to be regarded by the courts as wholly or mainly of a broadly Christian character, as section 7(1) requires, it must contain some elements which can be related specifically to the traditions of Christian belief, and which accord some special status to the person of Jesus Christ, although it must not be distinctive of any particular Christian denomination. But broadly Christian worship under the Act is clearly intended to be such that pupils of a non-Christian background can take part. Section 7(1) of the ERA is regarded as permitting some non-Christian elements in the collective worship without this depriving it of its broadly Christian character. Nor would the inclusion of elements common to Christianity and one or more other religions be regarded as depriving it of that character. Section 7(3) provides that not every act of worship need comply with the broadly Christian requirement provided that, taking any term as a whole, most of such acts which take place at the school do so. In all these matters, however, any departure from the broadly Christian requirement must be justified in terms of the family backgrounds, ages and aptitudes of the pupils concerned. On this basis the evidence suggests that there are insufficient grounds to uphold the complaint that the school is not acting in accord with the provisions of the ERA 1988'.

The Secretary of State's conclusion can, in essence, be restated as follows: It is necessary for most of the acts of Christian worship to 'contain some elements which can be related specifically to the traditions of Christian belief, and which accord some special status to the person of Jesus Christ'. The evidence did not establish that this was not so.

The Secretary of State confined himself to a greater extent even than the first suggested definition of 'worship' defined.

Having regard to the Secretary of State's conclusion under the fourth aspect, it is, in my judgment, an irresistible inference that he must have been satisfied that on most occasions the object of worship at the school was God of a broadly Christian character.

That being so, the fact that the Secretary of State answered the question asked of him in the letter of 7 July 1992, as he did, gives no reason to believe that his decision could be challenged successfully on this account.

I detect no arguable error of law in his consideration of the fourth aspect. In argument Mr Knox laid stress on Mr Molloy's opinion that pupils from a variety of faith communities and pupils without any belief in God could not participate meaningfully and sensitively in one act of reverence or veneration to a divine or supernatural power.

Clearly, as the Secretary of State recognised, a pupil who has no belief in God could not meaningfully and sensitively revere or venerate any divine or supernatural being, but whether children from families with different traditions of monotheistic faith may be able to join together in a meaningful and sensitive way in some acts of worship is a matter of opinion. Much depends on the words 'meaningful' and 'sensitive'. How meaningfully? How sensitively? The more the adverbs are stressed, the more difficult it becomes to acknowledge that Christians of different denominations may join in a common act of worship. Yet section 7(2) contemplates that they will. The tenor of the legislation is against a doctrinal and divisive approach.

Mr Molloy was not, on my reading of his report, of the opinion that the majority of the acts of worship did not reflect the broad traditions of Christian belief. On the contrary, it related to the prayers, for example. He said that they all reflected Christian sentiments and were likely to have been written by Christians for use by Christians. There was nothing in them which was explicitly Christian or offensive to other faiths but, he continued, Christian prayers are not always explicitly or distinctively Christian.

Mr Molloy continues: 'If the daily act of collective worship in a county school could only use material which is explicitly and overtly distinctively Christian then there would be little to call on e.g. even some famous Christian prayers do not mention Christ or the Trinity by name. For instance "The Lord's Prayer" makes no reference to Christ or the Trinity'. He continues 'There are no explicity/overtly distinctive Christian concepts in well used hymns such as "God be in my head" from the Old Sarum Primer, and Psalm 23 "The Lord's My Shepherd"'.

In my judgment, the Secretary of State was unarguably right in his view that the Act permitted some non-Christian elements in the collective worship so long as these did not deprive it of its broadly Christian character, and that this character would not be lost by the inclusion of elements common to Christianity and to one or more other religions.

That being so, he was entitled to conclude (as it is plain that he did) that children of other faiths could participate in acts of worship which mainly reflected the broad traditions of Christian belief.

This reduces the possible basis of successful challenge to the Secretary of State's decision on the first aspect to the sufficiency of the evidence before him.

The Secretary of State had before him not merely Mr Molloy's conclusions but the evidence which Mr Molloy had considered, including a statement from the head teacher, a summary of the acts of collective worship between the 1 May to the 31 December, 1989, summarising in two lines or so the content of each day's act, a list of examples of the prayers used in the school and a report and a memorandum from Mr Bill Rodgers of the Schools Inspectorate about an act of worship which he had attended in July 1990. The Secretary of State also had Mr Molloy's own amplification of and comments upon this 'and other evidence'.

Having considered this material and Mr Knox's submission that it was insufficiently informative, I see no prospect of arguing that the Secretary of State reached a conclusion which no Secretary of State reasonably could have reached on the evidence before him.

Mr Knox's challenge to aspect (4) is, essentially, the same as to aspect (1), namely, that the Secretary of State should have said, but did not, that the object of worship had to be of a broadly Christian character and that there was no evidence to justify the conclusion that it was. Multi-faith worship, submits Mr Knox, can never be of an object having this character.

For the reasons I have already given, I see no more prospect of his submissions succeeding against aspect (4) than against aspect (1).

In conclusion, in relation to the way the Secretary of State dealt with complaint no 1, I see no realistic prospect of his decision being shown to have been reached unlawfully . . .

Author's note: this case has now been reported, with minor amendments, in [1994] ELR 495.

Appendix 6

Appendix to the Code of Practice on the Identification and Assessment of Special Educational Needs (Department for Education/Welsh Office, 1994)

Transitional Arrangements

1. Until 1 September 1994, the Education Act 1981 and the Education (Special Educational Needs) Regulations 1983, as amended and as made under the 1981 Act, will govern provision for children with special educational needs.
2. At 1 September 1994, the Education (Special Educational Needs) Regulations 1994, made under the Education Act 1993, come into effect. From that date, LEAs, governing bodies and those who assist them must have regard to this Code of Practice. Most provisions of the 1981 Act will be repealed.
3. Statements made under the 1981 Act and 1983 Regulations will remain valid legal documents under the new system. But to ensure a smooth transition between the old and new systems, some transitional arrangements are necessary. These arrangements apply to work in hand on assessments and statements at 1 September 1994; to the review of statements made before 1 September 1994; to statements transferred between authorities before 1 September 1994; and to the disclosure of statements. They are set out in regulation 21 of the 1994 Regulations.
4. In summary, Regulation 21 provides that:
   i. when, before 1 September 1994, an LEA have told parents that they are considering whether to make an assessment or have received a request from a parent for an assessment, the LEA must decide whether to make an assessment by 13 October 1994. If they do make an assessment, they must do so under the 1994 Regulations and within the time limits; (Regulations 21(5) and 21(6))

ii. where an authority are in the course of making an assessment under the 1983 Regulations at 1 September 1994, they will continue to make the assessment under those Regulations. If, however, they do not issue a proposed statement or tell parents that they will not make a statement by 1 January 1995, that assessment will lapse and a new assessment must be made under the 1994 Regulations and must be completed within ten weeks. Any relevant advice secured for the purpose of the 1983 Regulations assessment may be used to make the new assessment;
(Regulations 21(2)–21(4))

iii. where an authority have issued a proposed statement by 1 September 1994, that statement will be made under the 1983 Regulations;
(Regulation 21(7))

iv. where, as a result of an assessment in train at 1 September 1994, the authority issue a proposed statement before 1 January 1995, that statement will be made under the 1983 Regulations;
(Regulation 21(7))

v. the 1993 Act time limits on decisions to amend or cease to maintain a statement shall not apply where the relevant proposals were made before 1 September 1994;
(Regulation 21(8))

vi. reviews which must be completed by 1 December 1994 will not be subject to the 1994 Regulations;
(Regulation 21(9))

vii. when statements made under the 1983 Regulations are due to be received on or after 1 December 1994, they must be reviewed with reference to the 1994 Regulations. But, as there may be no objectives specified in those statements and no arrangements specified for the setting of targets, one of the tasks of the first review will be to establish such objectives and set such targets, which will then be considered in subsequent reviews. In the case of a child aged over 14, the first review must also consider a Transition Plan. LEAs must set out the new objectives, targets and, as appropriate, the Transition Plan in writing when making recommendations as a result of the review of the statement. It will not, however, be necessary to amend the statement on this account although LEAs will be free to do so if they wish;
(Regulation 21(10))

viii. the 1981 Act and 1983 Regulations continue to apply to statements transferred before 1 September 1994, except that:

a. when a statement has been transferred before 1 September and the receiving authority have not told parents whether they will make an assessment of the child, they must tell parents by 13 October 1994; and

b. where a statement has been transferred before 1 September, the receiving authority must review the statement by 30 November 1994 or within a year of the date of the last review, whichever is the later;

(Regulations 21(11)–21(13))

ix. statements made before 1 September 1994 may be disclosed for the purposes of appeals under the 1981 Act as well as any appeal under the 1993 Act.

(Regulation 21(14))

5. Transitional arrangements governing appeals will be specified separately. The principle will be that the SEN Tribunal will hear appeals against decisions made by LEAs on or after 1 September 1994, whether those decisions were made in the light of the 1983 or the 1994 Regulations. Appeals against decisions made before that date, and hence in the light of the 1983 Regulations, will continue to be dealt with under the system established by the 1981 Act.

Author's note: the arrangements referred to in paragraph 5 are specified in the Education Act 1993 (Commencement No 5 and Transitional Provisions) Order 1994 (SI 1994 No 2038), as amended by SI 1994 No 2248.

Appendix 7

National Curriculum changes from September 1995 following the Government's acceptance of the Dearing recommendations

The changes to the National Curriculum in response to the recommendations of the School Curriculum and Assessment Authority, made in the light of the review conducted under the chairmanship of Sir Ron Dearing and accepted in full by the Government, were published two months earlier than had been expected, on 10 November 1994, just as this book was going to press. Fortunately, it has been possible to outline the principal changes in this Appendix. New National Curriculum subject documents have been sent to schools in proof form by the DFE. It is expected that the final versions will be published by HMSO in January 1995, and that the necessary Statutory Instruments will be issued to give them legal force. As noted in Chapter 8 (in Part 6(e)), the changes will be implemented from September 1995 in the case of Key Stages 1–3, and from September 1996 in the case of Key Stage 4.

According to the DFE Press Release (277/94) on the changes, the Secretary of State, Mrs Shepherd, promises that the new National Curriculum 'should take us into the next century without further major change'. She claims that the revision of the National Curriculum 'will continue to raise standards by removing overload, stripping out unnecessary bureaucracy and giving more freedom for teachers to exercise professional judgement'.

As noted in Chapter 8 (in Part 6(a)), the Dearing Report recommended that 20 per cent of curriculum time at Key Stages 1–3, and 40 per cent of time in Key Stage 4, should be available for use at the discretion of the school. This would result from the general slimming down of the compulsory curriculum, mostly outside the core subjects. This has been accepted by the Secretary of State and the desired flexibility will be introduced.

The other principal changes are:

- Reduction in the ten-level scale for assessment to eight levels, but with a single description for attainment targets in each subject, to provide an incentive for, and to indicate, outstanding and exceptional performance.

- Around 1,000 individual learning targets are to be cut to 200 broad descriptions of the standards expected of pupils of different ages.
- Confirmation that teacher assessment and national test results are complementary and will be given equal weight in public reporting of results.
- There will be greater rigour in English, especially at the primary-school stages, where there will be more emphasis on grammar, spelling and punctuation. According to Mrs Shepherd, there will be 'proper attention to correct English across the curriculum for the first time' and a greater emphasis on 'the need for pupils to be taught written and spoken standard English' and on 'high-quality literature' (with changes to the lists of authors whose work is to be studied or used).
- Mathematics will place more emphasis on arithmetic, particularly in the primary years. The use of calculators by five to seven year-olds will be restricted 'to the more complex calculations'.
- The subject content of History, which has proved contentious throughout the development of the National Curriculum and remains so (see *The Times*, 11 November 1994, p 7), will also change. There will be 'more emphasis on pupils' ability to recall and deploy knowledge, facts and understanding' and a strong emphasis on British history in Key Stages 1–3.
- At Key Stage 4, pupils will be required, as part of physical education, to participate in competitive team or individual games. Competitive team games will be compulsory at Key Stage 3. There will also be competitive team or individual games at Key Stage 2.

Index